THE BRIDGE TO A GLOBAL MIDDLE CLASS:

Development, Trade and International Finance

The Milken Institute Series On Financial Innovation And Economic Growth

Series Editors

James R. Barth
Auburn University
Senior Fellow at the Milken Institute
Glenn Yago
Director of Capital Studies at the
Milken Institute
Other books in the series:

Barth, James R., Brumbaugh Jr., R. Dan and Yago, Glenn:
> *Restructuring Regulation and Financial Institutions*

Evans, David S.:
> *Microsoft, Antitrust and the New Economy: Selected Essays*

Trimbath, Susanne:
> *Mergers and Efficiency: Changes Across Time*

THE BRIDGE TO A GLOBAL MIDDLE CLASS:
Development, Trade and International Finance

edited by

Walter Russell Mead
and
Sherle R. Schwenninger

Milken Institute
Santa Monica, California

A Council on Foreign Relations Book
New York

KLUWER ACADEMIC PUBLISHERS
Boston / Dordrecht / London

Distributors for North, Central and South America:
Kluwer Academic Publishers
101 Philip Drive
Assinippi Park
Norwell, Massachusetts 02061 USA
Telephone (781) 871-6600
Fax (781) 681-9045
E-Mail <kluwer@wkap.com>

Distributors for all other countries:
Kluwer Academic Publishers Group
Distribution Centre
Post Office Box 322
3300 AH Dordrecht, THE NETHERLANDS
Telephone 31 78 6392 392
Fax 31 78 6546 474
E-Mail <services@wkap.nl>

 Electronic Services <http://www.wkap.nl>

Library of Congress Cataloging-in-Publication Data
The Bridge to a Global Middle Class: Development, Trade and International
    Finance; edited by Walter Russell Mead and Sherle R. Schwenninger
    ISBN 1-4020-7329-1

Permission for books published in Europe: permissions@wkap.nl
Permissions for books published in the United States of America: permissions@wkap.com

Printed on acid-free paper.
Printed in the United States of America

The Milken Institute has chosen the material published in this book series for its quality and seriousness of purpose. But the opinions expressed in the books do not necessarily reflect the views of the Institute or its staff.

TABLE OF CONTENTS

NOTE FROM THE SERIES EDITORS

James Barth and Glenn Yago, Series Editors

MILKEN INSTITUTE SERIES ON FINANCIAL INNOVATION AND ECONOMIC GROWTH

The world has witnessed more financial crises in the past twenty years than at any comparable time in its history. More than two-thirds of countries in all parts of the world and at all stages of economic development have experienced a financial crisis. The costs of these crises, moreover, have been disportionately high and thus especially burdensome for developing countries. This disturbing development has led to calls for reform in financial systems around the globe to prevent such crises in the future.

The studies presented in this book are the product of a working group of diverse researchers and practitioners in finance and economics grappling with issues of increasingly more frequent and costly financial crises in the wake of the 1997-1998 rolling financial instability that started in Thailand and Indonesia, traversed to Russia and eventually Argentina, with many stops in-between. Punctuating the period in which this work was written and edited were the attacks on the World Trade Organization meetings in Seattle and other anti-global protests, and finally, the terrorist attacks on the World Trade Center in 2001. Though widely disparate events, this collection focuses our attention upon the all too often ignored dimension of how to finance the future. This is especially keen for a majority of countries struggling to overcome centuries of income, wealth and educational polarization and enter a period of growth. Capital access denied is all too often democracy and freedom deferred accompanied by political instability that hobbles global development.

Walter Russell Mead and Sherle Schwenninger provide a frequently underemphasized but nonetheless important approach to financial reform. They seek to focus the attention of any reform effort on the need to promote the development of a large and prosperous middle-class in emerging market economies. This approach to reform is consistent with the view of Aristotle, who long ago affirmed the virtues of the middle-class in an ideal society, remarking that "where the middle class is large, there are least likely to be factions and dissension." Many calls for reform, however, have failed to emphasize the value of the middle class in this regard. Indeed, as Mead and Schwenninger point out, despite numerous blueprints for reform, none recognize the importance of encouraging emerging economies to promote what every developed economy benefits from: a middle class that acts as a moderating influence on governments' bad policies and a supporting influence on governments' good policies.

It is the need to establish a source of legitimacy for reform in emerging market economies that underlines the importance of a middle-class oriented financial architecture. At present, capital flows into emerging markets remain volatile and relatively short term. In some countries, flows have turned negative in recent years. In most emerging markets, capital flows have yet to be restored to pre-Asian crisis (1997) levels. Small and medium businesses, moreover, are denied access to the vast pool of capital that the savings of developed countries represent. This situation persists because the much-needed changes to economic policy and to the governance of firms in these economies still lack sufficient popular support. The authors convincingly argue that for market-oriented reforms to succeed and produce lasting stability, they must hold out the prospect that all citizens will directly benefit from them. Reforms, for example, must be designed to allow ordinary people access to home ownership through the availability of affordable long-term financing or for private entrepreneurs to enter long protected, government directed business markets. Expanding economic participation in home and business ownership is key to the expansion of consumption and production in these economies. Not only will a program of middle-class oriented development create a constituency that will support reform, but it will be the best guarantor of global stability. Fortunately, much of the world, indeed most emerging market economies, is ready for middle-class oriented policies. Mead and Schwenninger provide evidence for this favorable climate by noting that 52 countries with a combined population of some 1.5 billion have already achieved levels of GDP comparable to those at which the U.S. and other countries first enacted middle-class oriented policies.

The key to the development of a large middle-class is the access of ordinary people to affordable, long term credit enabling them to realize the hopes and dreams in their business, professional, and home lives. This, in turn, requires low and stable interest rates and an overall stable macroeconomic environment. The main barriers to achieving these goals are the lack of stable, hard currencies and credible central banks, the existence of illiquid and poorly or inappropriately regulated capital markets, and the lack of well-functioning and adequately capitalized regional and international financial institutions. The importance of many of these factors for successful reform is not unappreciated by others also calling for meaningful change in financial systems.

What tends to be neglected in the debate on financial reform, however, is the authors' emphasis on the need for regional institutions. Much of the work on a new financial architecture has stressed the importance of national or international initiatives. The roles of the Bretton-Woods institutions and of private- and public-sector entities at the national level have been considered in depth. Yet, perhaps for historical or political reasons, much less attention has been paid to the potential value of regional institutions. Mead and Schwenninger use the appealing homily of Goldilocks and the Three Bears to emphasize the importance of regional financial institutions. The international level is too distant and too unaccountable, while the national level is too open to political manipulation and short-term public opinion. The regional level, however, is just right. Regional institutions and markets would be neither too distant and lacking in legitimacy nor too open to short-term pressures and lacking in credibility.

The two regional institutions central to the blueprint for a middle-class oriented financial architecture are regional central banks and regional currencies. Recognizing that the currencies of developing countries often lack the credibility of their more developed country counterparts, the authors urge the creation of currency regions either through what has come to be known as currency substitution (or more popularly, dollarization) or the creation of new currencies (or indeed the creation of new "synthetic" currencies pegged to a trade-weighted basket of hard currencies in a manner not unlike the ECU). The adoption of such hard currencies will go far to lower the interest rates entrepreneurs and other borrowers in developing countries must pay as well as lengthen the average time horizon of investments made in such countries.

Properly capitalized regional central banks similar in structure and function to the European Central Bank (ECB) would be established to conduct monetary policy on behalf of the region as a whole. Additionally, such regional central banks would be granted stewardship of member countries' foreign reserves and engage in the prudential regulation of the regions' capital markets. Unlike national central banks – where the national government is generally the sole shareholder – these regional central banks would be responsible to a diverse pool of shareholders including the Bretton-Woods organizations, member and non-member central banks, member and non-member country based banks, and other institutional and individual investors.

Accession to membership of these regional central banks would follow a similar, but less onerous, path than that for accession to the Euro. Budget deficits would be reduced (although not as ambitiously as in the Stability and Growth Pact of the EU), reforms would be made to legal systems and the central banks would oversee the comprehensive restructuring of member states' regulatory systems along a single, common line. Once in place, the regional central banks would be responsible for building middle-class oriented financial systems.

In summary, the authors provide a novel approach to financial reform so urgently needed to eliminate the wide gap that separates the have-nots from the haves among the roughly 200 countries in the world. The promise they offer with their proposal of middle-class oriented policies is "enhanced social stability and reduced conflict even as economies shift to more market-based rather than influence-based methods of credit allocation." This presents a compelling, achievable and urgent goal at this historical crossroad.

This report seeks to focus policy attention around measures to encourage the evolution of an international financial architecture that supports middle-class-oriented development in emerging economies. With this objective in mind, this report presents a series of ideas and policy recommendations that would enhance the effectiveness, security, and flexibility of the international financial system and greatly strengthen the system's ability to meet long-term credit needs in emerging countries. This discussion affords useful insights into international financial architecture, representing an important stimulus for new directions in both U.S. and international economic policy.

LIST OF CONTRIBUTORS
(In alphabetical order)

ROBERT A. BLECKER is Professor of Economics at American University and a Research Associate of the Economic Policy Institute (EPI), both in Washington, D.C. His most recent book is *Taming Global Finance: A Better Architecture for Growth and Equity*. His previous books include *Beyond the Twin Deficits; U.S. Trade Policy and Global Growth* (edited); and *Fundamentals of U.S. Foreign Trade Policy* (co-authored). His articles have appeared in numerous scholarly volumes and journals, including the *Cambridge Journal of Economics, Economical, International Review of Applied Economics, Journal of Post Keynesian Economics, Structural Change and Economic Dynamics*, and *Weltwirtschaftliches Archive*. His current research is focused on international trade policy and global financial reform. Professor Blecker received his B.A. in economics from Yale University and his M.A. and Ph.D. in economics from Stanford University.

AMY L. CHUA is Professor of Law at Duke University and a Visiting Professor of Law at Stanford University (Spring 2000). In Fall 1999, she was Visiting Professor of Law at Columbia University. She was executive editor of the *Harvard Law Review*, law clerk to Chief Judge Patricia Wald of the U.S. Court of Appeals for the D.C. Circuit from 1987–88, and an associate with Cleary, Gottlieb, Steen & Hamilton from 1988–94. She worked on numerous international transactions in Asia and Latin America, including the privatization of Teléfonos de México. She joined the Duke faculty in 1994. In 1995 and 1996, she was consultant to American Bar Association, Central and East European Law Initiative. She was awarded an International Affairs Fellowship from the Council on Foreign Relations in 1996, and served from 1998–99 through affiliation with the World Bank. She received the Duke Law School Excellence in Teaching Award in 1998. Currently, Chua is a member of the Executive Committee and Executive Council of the American Society of International Law. She received her A.B. from Harvard College in 1984, and her J.D. from Harvard Law School in 1987.

JANE D'ARISTA is director of programs at the Financial Markets Center. Previously, she taught in the graduate program in International Banking Law Studies at Boston University School of Law and served as chief finance economist for the Subcommittee on Telecommunications and Finance of the House Energy and Commerce Committee. Before that, she served for five years as an international analyst at the Congressional Budget Office and for 12 years as a staff member of the House Banking Committee. Her publications include *The Evolution of U.S. Finance*, two-volume set published in the Columbia Seminar Series by M.E. Sharpe in 1994.

ROBERT H. DUGGER is Managing Director of Tudor Investment Corporation, a global funds management company participating in all major securities, equities, and commodities markets on both short-term and long-term bases. He was previously director for policy and chief economist at the American Bankers Association, chief economist of the U.S. Senate Banking Committee, and senior staff member of the Financial Institutions Subcommittee of the House Banking Committee. He has also held various positions with the U.S. Federal Reserve Board. Dr. Dugger is a lecturer in International Finance at Georgetown University, a member of the board of directors of Generations United, and founder of the African Capital Markets Committee. He received his BA from Davidson College and his Ph.D. from the University of North Carolina at Chapel Hill.

JOHN EATWELL was educated at Cambridge and Harvard. He has taught economics at Cambridge since 1970, and became President of Queens College, Cambridge in 1997. From 1980 to 1996 he was also a Professor in the Graduate Faculty of the New School for Social Research, New York. He has been a Visiting Professor at Columbia University, New York, the University of Massachusetts, Amherst, and the University of Amsterdam. He is co-founder and chairman of the Institute for Public Policy Research, and sits on the board of the Securities and Futures Authority, Britain's securities markets regulator. From 1985 to 1992 John Eatwell served as economic adviser to Neil Kinnock, the leader of the British Labour Party. In 1992, he entered the House of Lords, and from 1993 to 1997 was Principal Opposition Spokesman on Treasury and Economic Affairs.

BARRY EICHENGREEN is the George C. Pardee and Helen N. Pardee Professor of Economics and Professor of Political Science at the University of California, Berkeley, where he has taught since 1987. He is also research associate of the National Bureau of Economic Research (Cambridge, Massachusetts) and research fellow of the Centre for Economic Policy Research (London, England). In 1997-98 he was senior policy advisor at the International Monetary Fund. He is a fellow of the American Academy of Arts and Sciences (class of 1997) and a member of the ABellagio Group@ of academics and high-level economic officials. Professor Eichengreen has published widely on the history and current operation of the international monetary and financial system. His books include *Toward a New International Financial Architecture* (Washington, D.C.: Institute for International Economics, 1999), *Globalizing Capital: A History of the International Monetary System* (Princeton, N.J.: Princeton University Press, 1997), and *European Monetary Unification* (Cambridge, Mass.: MIT Press, 1997).

JAMES K. GALBRAITH is Professor at the Lyndon B. Johnson School of Public Affairs and at the department of government, University of Texas at Austin, where he teaches economics and a variety of other subjects. He is also a senior scholar with the Jerome Levy Economics Institute and director of the University of Texas Inequality Project. Galbraith holds degrees from Harvard and Yale (Ph.D. in Economics, 1981). He studied economics as a Marshall Scholar at King's College, Cambridge in 1974–75, and then served on the staff of the U.S. Congress, eventually as executive director of the Joint Economic Committee in 1981–82. He was a guest scholar at the Brookings Institution in 1985. Galbraith is national chairman of Economists Allied for Arms Reduction (ECAAR), an international association of professional economists concerned with peace and security issues. From 1994–97 he served as

Chief Technical Advisor to the State Planning Commission of the People's Republic of China on a project on macroeconomic reform.

NINA L. KHRUSHCHEVA is director of communications and special projects at the East West Institute and Senior Fellow of the World Policy Institute at the New School University in New York. She is also senior editor of *Project Syndicate: Association of Newspapers Around the World*, which operates from Columbia University. After receiving her Ph.D. in comparative literature from Princeton University in 1997, she had a two-year appointment as a research fellow at the School of Historical Studies of the Institute for Advanced Study in Princeton.

FLORENCIO LOPEZ-DE-SILANES is Associate Professor of Public Policy at the John F Kennedy School of Government at Harvard University. His research combines the areas of corporate governance, financial economics, and industrial organization, and applies them to the analysis of privatization and legal reform. He has studied the North American Free Trade Agreement and its impacts on industrial integration. He has been an economic adviser to several governments. Currently he advises the Russian, Peruvian, Egyptian, and Mexican governments. He is a senior economic adviser to the Ministry of Industry and Trade in Mexico, and a consultant to the assistant minister for expenditures (Ministry of Finance). He is also an economic adviser to the National Banking and Stock Market Commission of Mexico, and an advisor to the Privatization Office in Moscow. His main publications fall in the areas of privatization, deregulation, legal reform, finance, and trade and industrial policy. He received Harvard's Wells Prize for Best Dissertation in Economics (1995), and won the First Place National Award of Law and Economics of the National Association of Law and Economics in Mexico (1996). He graduated from the Instituto Tecnologico Autónomo de Mexico, and holds master's and Ph.D. degrees in economics from Harvard University.

JIAQING LU is a senior consultant at the Applied Economics Consulting Group, Inc., an Austin, Texas-based consulting firm. He received his Ph.D. in Public Policy from the L.B.J. School of Public Affairs, University of Texas, Austin, in December 1999. His research covered various topics in international economic and financial policy, including financial and currency crisis, income inequality, country risk, and global capital flow.

ROBERT C. MCNALLY is, Vice President with Tudor Investment Corporation, a global funds management company, where he is responsible for monetary and fiscal policy analysis and strategy. Previously, Mr. McNally was an oil market consultant with Energy Security Analysis. He served as a Peace Corps Volunteer in Senegal, West Africa, and helped found the African Capital Markets Committee. Mr. McNally received his M.A. in International Relations from the Johns Hopkins University School of Advanced International Studies, and a B.S. in Political Science and International Relations from the American University.

WALTER RUSSELL MEAD is a Senior Fellow for U.S. Foreign Policy at the Council on Foreign Relations is a political economist engaged in the study of the evolving global economy and its implications for American society and foreign policy. He is the project director for the Working Group on Development, Trade & International Finance, as well as the project director of the Study Group on the History of U.S. Foreign Policy. Mr. Mead is co-director of the Council on Foreign Relations' Independent Task Force on U.S.-Cuba Relations and directs the Council's program on globalization. He is a Senior Contributing Editor at *Worth* magazine, a contributing editor on the opinion section of the *Los Angeles Times,* and he frequently contributes articles to other leading newspapers and magazines. He is the author of *Mortal Splendor: The American Empire in Transition* and his Century Foundation book on the history of U.S. foreign policy will be published in the summer of 2001 by Alfred A. Knopf, Inc.

RICHARD MEDLEY, Chairman of Medley Global Advisors, held positions in academia, on Wall Street and on Capitol Hill before founding the firm in 1995. He was a managing director and the chief political advisor at Soros Fund Management, and also served as the associate director of the Yale University Center for International Finance from 1995–1998. In the early 1980s, Dr. Medley was the chief economist for the U.S. House of Representatives Committee on Banking, Finance, and Urban Affairs, and chief economist for the U.S. Senate Democratic Leadership. He has taught at the Yale University School of Management and is a featured speaker and panelist at numerous international conferences. Dr. Medley has a B.A. from Ohio State University, and Ph.D., M. Phil., and M.A., degrees in political science with an economic focus from Yale University.

HILTON L. ROOT is a Senior Fellow and formerly head of Global Studies at the Milken Institute, where his research focuses on the global economy. With expertise in Asia, Southeast Asia and South Asia, in particular, Root has extensively studied developing countries and the relationship between their economies and political systems. Root came to the Institute from the Hoover Institution, where he was a senior research fellow and director of the Initiative on Economic Growth and Democracy. He was also an associate professor in the public policy and international policy studies programs at Stanford University. From 1994 to 1997 he served as Chief Advisor on Governance at the Asian Development Bank, and his responsibilities focused heavily on South Asia. Dr. Root's work is widely published. A frequent contributor to the *Asian Wall Street Journal, International Herald Tribune* and the *Los Angeles Times,* he is the author of six books and numerous articles. He received his Ph.D. in economics and history from the University of Michigan in 1983.

SHERLE R. SCHWENNINGER is a consultant to the Project on Development, Trade, and International Finance at the Council on Foreign Relations, and a senior fellow at the World Policy Institute at the New School University. He was the founding editor of the *World Policy Journal* (1983–91) and director of the World Policy Institute from 1992 to 1996. He earlier served as director of policy studies at the Institute as well as director of its transnational academic program. A founding board member of the New America Foundation, he currently serves as the Foundation's Treasurer and as an advisor to its Fellowship Program, and is working on a project on the environmental dimensions of international finance. He writes and speaks frequently on U.S. foreign policy and international economic issues and on questions of U.S.-European relations.

LANCE TAYLOR is Arnhold Professor of International Cooperation and Development and Director of the Center for Economic Policy Analysis at the New School for Social Research. Professor Taylor received a bachelor's degree with honors in mathematics from the California Institute of Technology in 1962 and a PhD in economics from Harvard University in 1968. He then became a professor in the economics departments at Harvard and the Massachusetts Institute of Technology, as well as being a visiting professor at the University of Minnesota, the Universidade da Brasilia, Delhi University, and the Stockholm School of Economics. He moved to the New School in 1993. Professor Taylor has published widely in the areas of macroeconomics, development economics, and economic theory. He has been a visiting scholar or policy advisor in over 25 countries including Chile, Brazil, Mexico, Nicaragua, Cuba, Russia, Egypt, Tanzania, Zimbabwe, South Africa, Pakistan, India, and Thailand.

MEREDITH WOO-CUMINGS teaches political science at Northwestern University. She has authored and edited four books, including *Race to the Swift: State and Finance in Korean Industrialization, Past as Prelude: History in the Making of the New World Order, Capital Ungoverned,* and *The Developmental State.* She has also served on President Clinton's Commission on U.S.-Pacific Trade and Investment Policy.

GLENN YAGO is Director of Capital Studies at the Milken Institute. He specializes in financial innovations, financial institutions and capital markets. His work includes extensive analysis of public policy and its relationship to high-yield markets, initial public offerings, industrial and transportation concerns, and public and private sector employment. Before coming to the Institute, Yago was a Professor of Economics at the City University of New York Graduate Center and the State University of New York at Stony Brook, where he was also director of the Economic Research Bureau. He directed the Center for Capital Studies as well, which he founded in 1992 to develop insight into the process of capital access and ownership change. He received his Ph.D. from the University of Wisconsin, Madison in 1980.

ACKNOWLEDGMENTS

The Project on Development, Trade, and International Finance was made possible by the generous support of the Ford Foundation. The project was directed by Walter Russell Mead, Senior Fellow for U.S. Foreign Policy at the Council, with the close assistance of Sherle R. Schwenninger, the Senior Program Coordinator for the project.

The Project staff benefited from the participation and wise counsel of a Working Group made up of leading economic policy experts as well as representatives from Wall Street, the international financial institutions, organized labor, and a range of public interest groups. The Project staff would in particular like to acknowledge those participants who prepared papers for the Working Group's consideration: Robert A. Blecker, Amy Chua, Robert Dugger, Robert McNally, Richard Medley, John Eatwell, Lance Taylor, Barry Eichengreen, James K. Galbraith, Jiaquing Lu, Nina Khrushcheva, Florencio Lopez-de-Silanes, Gerard McDonald, Hilton L. Root, Meredith Woo-Cummings, Michael Vaney, Jane D'Arista, and Glenn Yago. David Kellogg, Patricia Dorff, Leah Scholer, Benjamin Skinner, Laurence Reszetar, and Maria Bustria provided valuable research, editing, and production assistance. The series of papers written by members of the Working Group are available online at www.cfr.org.

The Project staff would like to acknowledge the help and assistance of the New America Foundation, which co-sponsored on June 14, 2000, a Washington, D.C. policy conference to air the recommendations contained in this report and which has cooperated with the project on an examination of the environmental dimensions of international financial architecture. The staff would also like to thank the following organizations for hosting review sessions to consider an earlier version of the report: the Economic Policy Institute, Friends of the Earth, the Office of Development Studies at the United Nations Development Programme, the 3/23 Group, the New America Foundation, and the Latin American Studies Program at the Council on Foreign Relations. Finally, the Project staff would like to thank the Friedrich Ebert Stiftung, who helped inform our study by sponsoring a conference titled "Debt Relief — A New Push for Development?," held in New York on April 30, 1999.

The Milken Institute gratefully acknowledges the efforts and assistance of Sallylynn James in the design and production of this book.

A Financial Architecture for Middle-Class-Oriented Development

A Report of the Project on Development,
Trade and International Finance

Walter Russell Mead
and
Sherle R. Schwenninger

COUNCIL ON FOREIGN RELATIONS
NEW YORK

EXECUTIVE SUMMARY

I. The Case For Middle-Class-Oriented Development
International financial architecture works best when it serves
social goals that command widespread support and legitimacy. Without neglecting the more conventional goal of allowing the greatest possible global flow of capital with the least risk of financial
crisis, for both economic and political reasons, the primary goal
of international financial reform ought to be to promote middle-
class-oriented development around the world.

1. **Middle-class-oriented development is the key to global prosperity and stability.** Extending the system of mass affluence found
   in the advanced industrial economies into the developing world
   as rapidly as possible is the key to global political stability and
   economic growth. It is also the key to building the kind of support that is needed in both developed and developing countries
   for sustaining the necessary reforms for stabilizing and strengthening the international financial system.

2. **Much of the world is now ready for middle-class-oriented
   development.** Thanks to the economic growth of the last generation, a substantial number of economies are ready for the transition to middle-class-oriented development. When considered
   on the basis of purchasing-power parity, fifty-two countries with
   a total population of 1.5 billion have reached levels of per capita GDP similar to those at which the United States inaugurated
   middle-class-oriented development policies. Other large
   economies, such as India and China, have already created substantial middle classes.

3. **Middle-class-oriented development enhances poverty alleviation.** Middle-class-oriented development does not mean taking resources from the poorest to concentrate on assisting

those who already enjoy better living conditions. Rather, middle-class-oriented development seeks to expand the middle class by facilitating the rise of the working poor, thus increasing employment opportunities for both high- and low-skill workers. The reforms envisioned by the report would enhance the ability of the World Bank and other agencies to concentrate on poverty alleviation and would enhance the efficacy of their activities.

4. **Access to reasonably priced, long-term credit is the single most important element in the formation of a mass middle class.** Small business, municipal and other public investment in infrastructure, home ownership (either in single-family homes or apartments), post-secondary education, and other necessities of middle-class life depend upon access to credit. The thirty-year, self-amortizing mortgage is the "canary in the coal mine": if these mortgages are widely available, then credit markets are working for ordinary citizens who aspire to become middle class.

5. **Middle-class-oriented development requires increased long-term capital flows to developing countries.** To facilitate middle-class-oriented development, international financial architecture should promote more long-term capital flows from the capital-rich G-3 advanced industrialized countries to capital-hungry emerging economies. In addition, it should expand democratic access to capital within developing countries for such purposes as home ownership, education, and the start-up and expansion of small and medium-sized business.

II. Obstacles to Middle-Class-Oriented Development
The current international financial architecture poorly serves the middle-class-oriented development needs of emerging economies in three ways.

1. **The lack of stable currencies not only makes developing economies more crisis prone but also distorts their development.** Currency risk is the single greatest deterrent to long-term capital flows to emerging economies, and one of the principal barriers to the development of deeper and more efficient cap-

ital markets upon which middle-class-oriented growth depends. The high cost of capital and short-term structure of the financial markets in most developing countries preclude a whole range of investments that would otherwise be profitable. They also distort development by favoring big companies over smaller firms, foreign firms over domestic ones, and foreign exchange-earners over companies that produce for the domestic markets.

2. **Shallow and badly regulated capital markets in emerging economies tend to deny credit to small businesses and ordinary citizens.** As a result of poorly developed equity and secondary debt markets, most emerging economies are overly dependent upon the banking sector. In many emerging economies banks are not only crisis prone but also highly inefficient at allocating capital, especially to ordinary citizens and small businesses. Most emerging economies lack the legal infrastructure and regulatory machinery upon which deeper and more sophisticated capital markets depend

3. **Poorly capitalized national and international financial institutions lack the resources and legitimacy needed to promote real capital market reform and to stem crises in emerging economies.** In many emerging markets, national institutions are too small, too close, and in many cases too politically influenced to exercise effective regulation and supervision of middle-class-oriented capital markets. The International Monetary Fund, however, is too big, too distant, and lacks both the mandate and resources to exercise effective oversight or to promote reform in most emerging economies.

III. Middle-Class-Oriented Reforms

Middle-class-oriented development requires institutional changes that substantially reduce risk for both domestic and international investors. Without attempting to prescribe in detail for each of the world's very different regions, we offer five recommendations as one example of a coherent strategy for promoting the conditions and institutions necessary for effective market-based, middle-class-oriented development.

Recommendation 1: Create well-capitalized and well-managed regional central banks to serve as the frontline institutions for middle-class-oriented development. The creation of regional central banks (similar to the European Central Bank) would enable emerging economies to pool reserves, consolidate monetary policy, and undertake effective capital-market regulation and development. A diversified shareholder base is the key to well-capitalized and well-managed central banks. The report, therefore, calls for the private sector as well as member and nonmember central banks and governments to become shareholders in a regional central bank (RCB).

Recommendation 2: Regional central banks should create or adopt hard regional currencies. To reduce interest rates and lower the cost of capital, regional central banks should create a stable currency that commands investor confidence. There is no one sure path to a stable currency, and each region will need to chart its own course. The report examines two options: dollarization and the creation of regional super-currencies (artificial currencies based on a basket or combination of currencies).

Recommendation 3: Establish binding covenants for good governance and good policies. In order to develop the deep and efficient capital markets necessary to provide greater democratic access to reasonably priced credit, regional central banks—along with other elements of a regional financial architecture—would need to use their size and influence to facilitate the legal, fiscal, and regulatory reforms needed for the development of such markets. The report envisions an accession process to the RCB similar but less onerous than that to the European Union. The RCB accession process would include three agreements: a fiscal stability pact; an agreement covering legal infrastructure and regulatory standards; and a third agreement relating to the RCB's regulatory authority.

Recommendation 4: Reduce the debt burden. To reduce excessive debt burdens, the report outlines a two-part process of debt reduction and restructuring. First, as part of the capitalization of the regional central bank, both official and private sector creditors would convert government debt into RCB equity. Second, for member countries adhering to the fiscal stability pact, regional central banks would help underwrite and place long- and short-term debt in international markets.

Recommendation 5. Create deep and liquid capital markets. The report calls for the RCBs to: 1) create a long-term mortgage and small-business credit market by chartering and spinning off regional Fannie Mae-like institutions; 2) expand equity and debt markets by chartering investment banks aimed at underwriting corporate debt and initial public offerings and by chartering and supervising for-profit pension management companies linked to compulsory savings programs; and 3) build a popular financial sector serving the needs of small- and medium-sized businesses by chartering and supervising popular financial institutions for mini-lending (loans up to $25,000) for ordinary working people.

INTERNATIONAL FINANCIAL ARCHITECTURE: THE CASE FOR MIDDLE-CLASS-ORIENTED DEVELOPMENT

International financial architecture works best when it is seen in three dimensions. The first dimension relates to the economic principles that guide the construction and operation of any international financial system. In an age of global financial integration, most of these principles are not particularly controversial: transparency, openness, rule of law, uniform accounting standards, the need for prudential regulation, the importance of minimizing moral hazard, and the desirability for some form of lender of last resort to inject liquidity into the system at times of crisis. Indeed, these principles and measures are the subject of many of the reforms now being put forward by governments, public-policy think tanks, and international financial institutions. Some ideas, such as the appropriate exchange rate regime for developing countries, the desirability of bailing in the private sector, and whether short-term capital controls can be used effectively, are still subject to dispute, but even in these cases there is less difference now than before the Asian financial crisis.

The second dimension of international financial architecture concerns the social goals that the financial system must serve in order to command widespread support and legitimacy. Financial architecture is not neutral: it tends to favor some groups over others; some forms of development and not others. Previous innovations in international financial architecture were designed with some specific social goals in mind. The Bretton Woods system, for example, was adopted with the dual purpose of helping the war-devastated European economies to recover and of assisting the newly independent economies of the Third World to develop in the face of a dollar shortage. Indeed, the formal name of the World Bank—the International Bank for Reconstruction and Development—still commemorates that dual purpose.

The third dimension concerns the specific economic context in which the international financial system must operate. At any given historical period, there will be certain demographic and technological trends that cannot easily be altered by policy but nonetheless can have a dramatic effect on policy outcomes. Shifting demographic patterns, for example, can significantly alter savings and investment rates and thus trade and investment flows: as a population reaches retirement age it consumes more and saves less, and what it consumes also changes.[1] If these basic trends are not accommodated in the design of the international financial architecture, they can produce undesirable economic outcomes.

The challenge of this project has been to reconcile these three dimensions of international financial architecture to show how an international financial system based on sound economic principles can evolve over the coming decades to accommodate shifting development and trade patterns in a way that results in substantially improved living standards for most people in developing as well as developed countries.

Since the 1997–98 crisis, the economic debate has largely focused on the first dimension of international financial architecture—with only passing reference to the second and third dimensions. Understandably, the principal reform goals have focused on crisis prevention and containment, and only secondarily has the debate concerned itself with the question of what kind of investment, trade, and development should international financial architecture promote. At the same time, a parallel debate and discussion within civil society circles has above all highlighted second-dimension social objectives, but without a disciplined examination of how these goals—less austerity and more poverty alleviation—can be achieved.

The result has been an unhappy consensus that policymakers face a choice between sound economic policies whose social ben-

---

[1] For further discussion, see Robert Dugger, Robert McNally, and Richard Medley, "The American Stock Market as a Financial Risk," a paper from the Project on Development, Trade, and International Finance, Council on Foreign Relations, New York, 2000.

efits will only be apparent in the middle to long term, or sound social policies that very rapidly produce poor economic outcomes. The perception that sound economic policies inevitably involve many years of pain leads many politicians in democratic societies to postpone reforms, or to carry them out in a half-hearted manner. This can and often does lead to a kind of policy swamp: politicians make enough reforms to make the public unhappy, but either cannot or will not reform aggressively enough to move the economy onto a sustainable, long-term growth path. In these conditions, economies can—and do—flounder for years or even for decades, partly reformed, always reforming, but somehow still stuck in the mud.

Our project has tried to find ways for emerging economies to avoid this policy swamp. More specifically, it has sought to see whether a three-dimensional approach to international architecture can find a road around, or build a bridge over, this unhappy morass. Our principal conclusion after a year of study and consultation with leading economic thinkers as well as representatives from Wall Street, organized labor, and a wide range of public interest groups is positive: certain changes in the international financial architecture can significantly enhance the prospects that emerging economies will be able to build an enduring consensus for reforms that will lead to solid and sustainable growth.

The key to such reform, we believe, is to give additional prominence to a goal that, while widely acknowledged as vital for both the political and economic development of the global system, has rarely been the direct and immediate object of international financial architectural reform. That goal is the creation of a mass middle class in emerging economies.

We believe that it is possible to develop an international financial architecture that would advance middle-class-oriented development without neglecting the more conventional goal of allowing the greatest possible global flows of capital with the least feasible risk of financial crises. An international financial architecture for middle-class-oriented development would facilitate rapid growth in emerging economies in ways that benefit the broad mass of the population and that greatly expand the middle classes of those societies.

While the specific elements of a middle-class-oriented development strategy would differ from country to country—reflecting the level of development, the existing economic structure, and specific cultural values of each country—middle-class-oriented strategies have certain key elements in common. As Nancy Birdsall, former director of policy research at the World Bank, has pointed out, the middle class in today's advanced Western economies has been built on a tripod of employment (rising wages), education (expanding access to formal education), and property (increased ownership of home, small business, and other property).[2]

Underpinning this tripod has been a credit system that supports both the investment and the consumption of households and families. In nearly all middle-class societies, widespread home ownership, often facilitated by various credit subsidies, has figured significantly into middle-class-oriented development. So has widely available credit (again, often subsidized) for such common goods and services as education, automobiles, and household durables. Another building block of middle-class societies has been a vibrant small business sector, which depends upon a credit system that allows individuals to start up new enterprises and that permits already existing enterprises to gain access to financing for expansion.

Beyond this, middle-class societies generally have benefited from a public-financed infrastructure that provides most if not all citizens with electric power, potable water, and transportation. They have also benefited from a nearly universal secondary education system that is free, and post-secondary education that is widely available. Finally, nearly all middle class societies have developed social safety nets and social insurance programs that help middle class working families survive temporary periods of unemployment or such lifetime catastrophic events as long-term disability. They have also developed a combination of public and private pension

---

[2] Nancy Birdsall, "Building a Market-Friendly Middle Class," remarks Before Annual World Bank Conference on Development Economics, April 18, 2000.

programs that assure a dignified and decent retirement to a substantial majority of the working population.

Economists have no agreed-upon definition of the middle class, or any standard measurement by which to gauge the size of the global middle class in developing countries. While virtually every prosperous society is middle-class-oriented, not all middle-class-oriented societies have been affluent by contemporary standards. The United States was a middle-class-oriented society in 1947, when per capita GDP stood at $10,373 in 1996 dollars.[3]

By this standard, a significant number of developing countries either have reached or are about to reach levels of productivity that would support a middle-class standard of living. On a per capita, purchasing-power-parity basis, Argentina, Chile, and South Korea are significantly more affluent than the United States was in 1947. Twenty-seven countries counted as "upper middle income" developing countries by the World Bank, with a combined population of 588 million, have a mean per capita income (on a purchasing power parity basis) equivalent to $7,830, almost 80 percent of the U.S. levels of 1947.[4] These countries, including such diverse places as Mexico, South Africa, and Malaysia, are productive enough to support a modest middle-class society. So are large emerging economies, like Brazil and India, which have lower per capital income but because of their size and technological sophistication have developed sizeable middle classes.

Countries, however, do not need to achieve middle-class levels of productivity before initiating middle-class-oriented development policies. The United States adopted middle-class-oriented development strategies during the Great Depression, when per capita incomes were as low as $4,804—comparable to levels seen in many lower middle income countries today. All told, fifty-two developing countries with a total estimated population of 1.5 billion have reached a level of development roughly comparable to that reached

---

[3]U.S. Bureau of the Census, Population Estimates Program, Population Division and U.S. Department of Commerce: Bureau of Economic Analysis.

[4]The World Bank, *Entering the 21st Century: World Development Report 1999/2000* (New York: Oxford University Press, 2000), p.231.

by the United States when it moved decisively toward middle-class-oriented policies.[5] With proper policies, most if not all of these countries—including all of the major Latin American economies as well as such East Asian countries as Thailand and the Philippines and, taken as a whole, the southern African region of South Africa, Botswana, Zimbabwe, and Lesotho—should have the economic resources to implement the basic features of middle-class-oriented development policies.

In other less-developed countries, middle-class-oriented development policies, particularly those aimed at expanding access to reasonably priced credit, can play a significant role in growth and poverty alleviation—or can help alleviate poverty in such moderately prosperous emerging economies as Mexico and Brazil. Indeed, a focus on expanding the middle class in emerging economies does not mean neglecting the poor. "Microlending," one of the most promising development innovations of recent years, is essentially an adaptation of middle-class-oriented policy to conditions of great poverty. By giving ordinary people access to credit to start a business—one of the most important middle-class-oriented development policies—microlending allows individuals and families to escape poverty and take control of their own lives. The expansion of microlending and the development of "mini-lending" programs (of somewhat larger loans for larger, but still small and community-based enterprises) can play a significant role in national and regional development strategies.

Other classic middle-class policies, such as making home mortgages available, can create opportunity and reduce poverty in poor developing countries. The housing policies that built Levittowns in postwar America, or that put Singapore's once-impoverished working people in owner-occupied apartments, can also serve poorer populations with lower expectations about housing. Given an appropriate credit system that allows affordable long-term loans to working households, working families in developing countries can take the money spent on rent and purchase a home

---

[5]Ibid., p. 231.

over twenty to thirty years. In this way, relatively poor working families can become vested with real capital ownership, which absent such a credit system they could never otherwise afford.

It is not only housing that depends on an effective, appropriate credit system. High interest rates and short maturities are financially crippling for entities seeking to meet the infrastructure needs of emerging economies, be they private utilities, local and regional public authorities, or international development banks. Safe drinking water, electric power, reliable transportation systems, sanitary waste disposal, schools, and other basic necessities of middle-class life are, whether administered by governments or provided by private companies, generally financed by access to long-term credit markets. Without such access, few advanced countries today could provide adequate facilities.

Employment also suffers in the absence of credit. The "missing" housing and infrastructure that cannot be built due to poorly functioning credit markets is matched by missing job opportunities: jobs designing, building, operating, and maintaining the housing and infrastructure that cannot be built. Any serious approach to the labor market problems of emerging economies must look at ways of substantially increasing formal sector opportunities for unskilled and semiskilled workers. Credit systems capable of enabling the construction of the housing and infrastructure needed by a rising middle class will also create the employment opportunities that bring new workers and families into the formal sector and into the rising new class of creditworthy households.

The key missing goal of the international financial reform, in our view, then, is the development of a financial system that allows working people and emerging middle classes access to long-term credit for such purposes of home ownership, education, and the start-up and expansion of small businesses. As the experience of the western democracies in the latter half of the twentieth century demonstrates, the development of a middle-class-oriented financial system is the single most important social prerequisite for the development and consolidation of middle-class living standards for the majority of the population.

Thanks to the growth of international financial markets and the industrial revolution that is taking place in much of the developing world, the creation of a mass class of small business and homeowners and consumers is now, as suggested above, a viable option for many emerging economies. Yet, to date, international capital-market integration has not served the broader middle-class-oriented development needs of emerging economies very well. In fact, the aspiring middle classes in many emerging economies have suffered disproportionately from this decade's financial crises. In East Asia, the urban working and middle classes were particularly hard hit by the 1997-98 crisis, as declining employment and wages hurt middle-income salaried workers, and high interest rates devastated small and medium-sized businesses.

The propensity of the international financial system to crisis, however, is not the only problem. Access to capital for many investments associated with a middle-class economy is limited by a combination of undeveloped domestic capital markets, the perceived risk on the part of international investors, and the volatility and short-term bias of foreign exchange markets. But, as we show in this report, changes in the international financial architecture can reduce if not eliminate many of these constraints and obstacles as well as mitigate the risk of repeated crises.

In our view, the goal of middle-class-oriented development incorporates and reconciles all three dimensions of international financial architecture better than any other alternative development model. To begin with, middle-class-oriented development underscores the need for the kind of economic principles and neo-liberal reforms being advanced in official policy circles. Middle-class-oriented development depends upon the development of deeper, more efficient long-term capital markets in emerging economies. Thus, reforms to create greater transparency, more uniform accounting standards, better bankruptcy and property laws, and more prudent bank regulation are all critical to the success of middle-class-oriented development, as are sound macroeconomic policies and a liberal trade and investment regime. At the same time, middle-class-oriented development supplies what has up to now been the missing ingredient for many of these reforms—namely, a popular basis of support. From the beginning, a policy aimed at putting ordinary people in homes of their own would be politically popular, making it easier for emerging economy politicians to build broader coalitions for sustainable reform.

Creating democratic long-term capital markets in developing countries for such popular purposes as home ownership and small business development is thus both good politics and good economics. And this combination makes for a sound and durable financial system as well. There are, in fact, a number of reasons financial systems are more stable when they serve the long-term credit needs of an emerging middle class. Consider, for example, how making thirty-year mortgages widely available would strengthen the domestic financial systems of emerging markets. Any system involving securitization of mortgages would involve the imposition of serious regulatory controls—to ensure that all mortgages conformed to underwriting guidelines. Such controls are now absent in most emerging economies. It would also involve a fair and orderly bankruptcy system, which again is absent in most developing countries.

More generally, banking systems resting on numerous loans to individual homeowners and enjoying access to strong secondary debt markets are inherently more stable than systems resting on a handful of loans to large borrowers. The United States, for example, has what is widely considered to be the most flexible and best-developed capital market in the world. Yet mortgages remain the cornerstone of this market. Mortgage lending accounted for 30.2 percent of all borrowing in the United States in the third quarter of 1999—by far the largest single component of the credit market.[6] In fact, 25.8 percent of all debt in the United States, excluding open-market paper and Treasury securities, is mortgage debt.[7] The existence of this large, stable pool of finance—with a diversified

---

[6]Board of Governors of the *Federal Reserve System, Federal Reserve Statistical Release: Flow of Funds Accounts of the United States: Flows and Outstandings First Quarter 2000* (Washington, D.C.: Board of Governors of the Federal Reserve System, 2000), p. 11.

[7]Ibid., p. 8.

risk basis, much of it insured—was absolutely critical to the development of U.S. capital markets. Only the large and liquid market in U.S. Treasury obligations has played a greater role in the development of the American capital market. Financial instruments involving securitization were initially developed for the mortgage market, and the experience in this relatively tame market gave firms and investors the experience and the confidence needed to venture into other forms of capital market innovation.

As to the second dimension of international financial architecture, middle-class-oriented development, by its very nature, serves a number of widely recognized social goals: the vesting of ordinary people in property ownership, the alleviation of poverty, the creation of a vast array of both skilled and entry-level jobs, and the reduction of trade tensions. Thus, it is more likely to command political support in both developing and developed countries than is the current emphasis on export-oriented growth. Moreover, it would serve a much larger world policy purpose. Just as Bretton Woods was critical to building a stable democratic peace in Europe and East Asia following World War II, an international financial architecture that supports middle-class-oriented development in populous emerging economies would help create a more stable world by facilitating the growth of a large and sustainable middle class in these countries.

Not without reason, U.S. foreign-policy experts see the growth of a strong middle class in developing countries as the basis for sustainable progress toward stable democratic government—and for a peaceful world. Globalization has promoted rapid change in many emerging economies, but it has not yet delivered a sustainable middle class. Such a disparity is a prescription for greater instability. Most emerging economies have disproportionately large populations under the age of twenty-one. In order to avoid disruptive change, they will need to produce a far larger number of jobs as well as greatly expand their infrastructure of schools, roads, and sewage systems. Only a program aimed at expanding home ownership and public infrastructure to complement export-oriented manufacturing and services has a chance of meeting this daunting challenge.

The development consequences of this kind of middle-class-oriented program should be obvious: expanded job growth, improved infrastructure, and less export dependency, to name just a few. The surge in home-building alone would provide major economic stimulus in developing countries, creating new jobs and opportunities for everyone from day laborers to construction companies to refrigerator factories and shingle-makers. The social and political consequences also bear noting: the creation of an independent middle class of homeowners, the promotion of small and medium-sized business, and the development of new growth zones outside major metropolitan centers. The spread of home ownership in the developed world has been critical to the development of stable middle-class societies, giving hundreds of millions of people increased security and dignity. Indeed, the creation of a homeowner class is one of the surest methods known to help a society achieve long-term political stability. Homeowners have a stake in the system, a piece of property that is very real and important to them. They are thus resistant to crackpot utopian schemes and intolerant of reckless government policies that raise interest rates or otherwise threaten security. Indeed, as one study shows, middle-class voters tend to eschew extremes on both sides of the political spectrum.[8]

Particularly in emerging economies where both democratic institutions and market-oriented economic institutions are relatively new, the importance of mass property ownership for good governance is hard to exaggerate. It is not only the U.S. example, where independent small farmers were the basis of the emerging American democracy, that underscores the link between mass ownership of property and mass support of market economies in a democratic context. The land reforms of the French Revolution created a basis for France's development of democratic and market-friendly institutions in the nineteenth century; similarly, land reform in postwar Japan played a significant role in that country's democratic development. The survival of small farmers helped Poland

---

[8]See Peter Mateju, "Winners and Losers in the Post Communist Transformation," *Innovation*, vol. 9, no. 3 (1996).

make one of the most successful transitions from socialism to a democratic market system in Europe; many observers see the key to South Africa's future in the resolution of currently unanswered housing and land questions. Many reformers in China view the development of a housing market characterized by individual ownership as critical to the further development of both political and economic reforms.

Under contemporary conditions, agriculture can provide only a diminishing minority of the population with a livelihood and a property ownership stake. Thus, in today's modernizing economies it is home ownership rather than agricultural land ownership that becomes the form of property most important for the consolidation of pro-market policies in a democratic social order. Most advanced Organization for Economic Cooperation and Development (OECD) economies have recognized this by devoting significant resources and energy to increasing the rate of owner-occupied housing. As noted earlier, many emerging economies have surpassed the levels of productivity and per capita income that western Europe, the United States, and Japan had at the time the latter societies made the housing question a central element of national economic policy. Developing countries thus have the physical resources to give greater priority to home ownership. What they lack are the credit markets and policies that can make home (or apartment) ownership possible for a majority of their working families.

Finally, as to the third dimension of international financial architecture, middle-class-oriented development offers a much-needed alternative to conventional, manufacturing based export-oriented development. As world economic conditions continue to change, export-oriented development has approached the limits of its success. Indeed, future world economic growth will depend upon tapping pent-up internal demand in emerging economies and that means enlarging the middle classes in those economies.

Export-led development worked remarkably well when, in the early 1980s, there was just a handful of mostly small countries—Japan and the four Asian tigers, Taiwan, Hong Kong, Singapore, and South Korea—that followed the strategy. But by the early 1990s the export output of these countries had begun to outstrip world demand, which was still largely provided by consumers in the United States and Europe.

As more economies joined the export pack, competition tightened. Late emerging, export-oriented countries, like the Philippines, no longer compete against factories in high-wage economies like the United States and Germany but with even lower wage counterparts in Bangladesh, China, and Sri Lanka. The result has been the buildup of excess capacity in many basic manufacturing industries—from textiles to steel to electronics. And with so much excess capacity, the terms of trade for those manufactured goods has declined, as has the return on investment.

Unfortunately, for export-oriented emerging countries everything points to a continuing deterioration in the returns on investment and terms of trade for many manufactured goods. The parallel to an earlier transition from agriculture is instructive. When the manufacturing economy first developed in the nineteenth century, mechanization, transportation, and preservation technologies were opening new areas of the globe to the production of food and fibers. But the increases in agricultural productivity combined with vast expansion of land under cultivation led to a permanent fall in the price of agricultural commodities compared with other goods. Farm employment plummeted along with commodity prices; only well-capitalized and mechanized farms—along with those protected by tariffs and subsidies—were able to survive.

Something similar seems destined to happen in manufacturing. With the industrial revolution expanding into thickly populated districts of the developing world, manufacturing may face the sort of chronic over-capacity problems that agriculture has endured for most of the last century.

Indeed, this trend is already evident in the declining terms of trade for lower wage manufacturing goods, and for a number of reasons it is likely to grow worse in the coming years. One reason is that the demand for manufactured goods will presumably increase more slowly than demand as a whole in the developed economies, which up to now have served as the main markets for the goods of export-led economies. Growth in demand for services has long outpaced growth in demand for manufactured goods in the advanced industrial democracies, and the demographic trends suggest that, if anything, the shift toward consumption of services will accelerate. As populations age, they spend more on medical care and less on stereos and sports cars. Slow population growth, or absolute population decline in countries like Italy and Japan, will also trim the demand for such goods as housing materials and home furnishings. Even where manufacturing demand remains strong—for computer components, for example— ferocious competition will squeeze returns.

While it is unlikely that the course of manufacturing in the next century will exactly repeat the history of agriculture in the last, problems of overcapacity, commoditization, narrow margins, and declining terms of trade are likely to dog the steps of economies that cannot find additional engines of growth to supplement the manufacture of consumer and even capital goods in the years and decades to come.

In short, without a shift in policy away from South-North oriented, manufacturing-based, export-led growth, more and more developing countries will be chasing diminishing export opportunities in the developed world. To suggest that developing countries must move away from dependence on manufacturing exports is not to suggest that they should abandon the export business— or that Western protectionism should be met with indifference. The export of manufactured goods will remain a major factor for many countries, and the availability of cheap manufactured goods from emerging economies will continue to play a significant role in facilitating the transformation to post-industrial economies in the advanced world. (By the same token, while it is no longer realistic to count on agriculture as one's long-term prime source of foreign exchange, many developing countries would benefit substantially from an end to the unconscionable restrictions on agricultural trade.)

With demand for manufactured goods in the North growing more slowly than in the future, domestic demand and regional demand (or more broadly South-South trade) will have to expand to replace demand growth in the North as the major engine of future expansion for manufacturing. And, for better or worse, emerging market consumers do have a lot of catching up to do. China, for example, has barely one-half the television sets per capita as Germany. In the United States, there are forty personal computers per one hundred people; in Brazil, there are fewer than three.[9] The same pattern emerges when it comes to necessities. Effectively, 100 percent of U.S. households enjoy access to safe water. In many developing countries however, only one-fifth of households do.[10] In Germany, there are ten hospital beds for every one hundred people; in Indonesia there is less than one.[11]

Many developing countries face a situation similar to that of the advanced industrial economies in the middle of the twentieth century. Having built the means of mass production, they must now find ways to stimulate and finance domestic mass consumption to substitute for export demand. Such a shift from export-oriented growth will almost certainly require a reduction in savings rates in a significant number of emerging economies. Private and, in some cases, government consumption must rise as a percentage of GDP. And that will require big changes in spending patterns. In France, private consumption represented 79 percent of GDP in 1998; in the United States the figure was 83 percent. By comparison, private consumption in China was just 59 percent of GDP; in Malaysia, 56 percent; and in Singapore, 50 percent[12] Developing countries must be able to consume more while exporting a smaller percentage of their final output to the North.

Growth in demand for manufactured consumer goods in emerging economies is only part of the answer. Emerging economies will also need to participate in the most dynamic sectors of the new technology-based service economy. This implies that even as emerging economies increase the share of private consumption in

---

[9] *Statistical Abstract of United States,* The National Data Book, 119th edition, 1999, p.846.

[10] *World Bank Social Indicators of Development: 1996,* pp. 157 and 360.

[11] *World Bank Social Indicators of Development: 1996,* pp. 127 and 159.

[12] *IMF International Financial Statistics Yearbook, 1999.* All figures referenced are from 1998.

GDP, they must also find ways of funding the considerable educational, technological, and infrastructure investments necessary for success in the industries of the future.

This new development agenda for developing countries has profound implications for international financial architecture. In order to both consume and invest more, emerging economies will need to import capital in order to run sustained external deficits. And in the face of such long-term current account deficits, the international financial system must be able to promote substantial long-term capital flows from the G-3 advanced industrialized countries to emerging economies.

Such an architecture, if properly designed, would help solve another major problem of the world economy: namely, the growing demographic-related imbalance between the savings and investment needs of an increasingly capital-rich group of advanced countries and a growing number of capital-hungry emerging economies.[13] In Europe and Japan, and to a somewhat lesser extent in the United States, aging baby boomers, worried about adequate provision for their retirement over the next two decades, are beginning to produce a pool of savings and capital much larger than can be profitably invested in the G-3 economies themselves. By contrast, many emerging economies have burgeoning young populations, many with a large proportion under the age of twenty-one. These countries need more capital to educate and to create jobs and housing for these expanding populations. While some of these societies, especially those in Asia, have relatively high savings rates, they cannot both increase consumption and expand investment within the constraints of the current system.

An international financial architecture for the early 21st century must come to grips with this problem by facilitating long-term capital flows from the G-3 countries to the emerging economies. Thus, not only must systemic changes be made in the current system of global governance to help re-channel international

---

[13]Wendy Dobson and Gary Hufbauer, assisted by Hyun Koo Cho, "World Capital Markets: Challenge to the G-10," paper published by the Institute for International Economics, Washington, D.C., July 2000.

capital flows, but far-reaching reforms must be enacted in the financial systems of emerging economies in order to efficiently use those capital flows. Such a reform effort would entail a positive-sum bargain between aging savers in the developed world, who need profitable returns to prepare for retirement and maintain current consumption levels, on the one hand, and businesses and consumers in developing countries, who need access to more capital to build more efficient businesses to satisfy rising consumer needs, on the other.

OBSTACLES TO MIDDLE-CLASS-ORIENTED DEVELOPMENT

As attractive as it is as a development model for most emerging economies, middle-class-oriented development cannot succeed without changes in the international financial architecture that substantially reduce risk for both international and domestic investors. The current international financial system simply contains too many risks for there to be a substantial increase in long-term capital flows to emerging economies on a sustainable basis.

There are three features of the current international financial architecture that in particular pose obstacles to middle-class-oriented development: the lack of stable currencies, which not only makes developing economies crisis prone but also distorts their development; shallow and badly regulated capital markets, which tend to deny credit to small businesses and to ordinary citizens; and poorly capitalized national and international financial institutions, which lack the resources and legitimacy needed to promote real capital market reform and stem crises in emerging economies.

1. Lack of Stable Currencies

One of the most serious obstacles to middle-class-oriented development lies in the currency instability that afflicts nearly all developing economies. Currency risk may in fact be the single largest deterrent to long-term capital flows. Moreover, it may be one of the principal barriers to the development of deeper and more efficient domestic capital markets, upon which in turn middle-class-oriented growth depends.

Many emerging economies, of course, lack a stable currency because of a history of inflation and economic mismanagement, which has undermined investor confidence in the currency. Currency devaluations have been a frequent occurrence throughout Latin America, for example, and investors are naturally reluctant to hold assets denominated in a depreciating currency—especially for the long term. To do so in the short term, they often demand large risk premiums that effectively price homeowners and small and medium-sized businesses out of formal credit markets. As a general rule, currency risk steepens yield curves, shortens maturities, and denies all but a relative handful of well- capitalized and or well-connected firms and individuals full access to the international economy.

This problem is not limited, however, to developing countries with bad policies. Virtually all emerging economies have what are called soft currencies in that there is little foreign demand for assets denominated in the local currency and no liquid long-term markets denominated in that currency. Even residents of emerging economies, if they have a choice, often hold significant financial assets denominated in dollars or another hard currency. In other words, a currency is soft when it cannot be used to borrow abroad, or even domestically to borrow long term.

By that definition, only the most advanced OECD economies with long histories of monetary stability—the United States, Britain, the Euro-zone economies, Australia, Canada, Japan, and Switzerland—have hard currencies. Nearly all other countries are presumed to have significant currency risk, which is reflected in the sizeable spreads at which they must borrow in international markets. In an age of open capital markets, the lack of stable currency is not just a question of policy, but also a function of the size of the market for any particular currency. International investors are reluctant to hold for the long term financial assets denominated in currencies with small and illiquid foreign exchange markets— in part, because they cannot properly hedge. This only adds to the short-term bias that troubles the financial markets of soft currency economies.

Because of this short-term bias, economies with soft currencies face risks and distortions in their economies that most advanced economies are able to avoid. To begin with, economies with soft currencies are prone to financial crisis. Financial institutions and firms in soft currency economies face what Pedro Pou, president of the Central Bank of Argentina, has called the "devil's choice": they must choose between borrowing short-term in their own currency domestically, thus creating a maturity mismatch, or they can borrow longer term in dollars and be stuck with a currency mismatch.[14] As a practical matter, many emerging-market financial institutions end up with both currency and maturity mismatches.

In the 1997–98 Asian crisis it was just such maturity and currency mismatches that helped trigger the financial crisis that engulfed most emerging-market economies, beginning with Thailand. Asian banks borrowed short term in foreign-currency debt and lent long term in domestic currency. At the time, that seemed to be a rational business move. By borrowing short term from cheaper foreign markets, Asian banks and companies could substantially reduce their borrowing costs. But in so doing, they accumulated short-term foreign currency liabilities that were not backed up by foreign currency assets or covered by short-term foreign currency income streams. Thus, they set themselves up for devastating losses when investor sentiment turned sour and the currency depreciated, leaving them with foreign currency debts they could no longer service.

The fact that the borrowed funds were used for local speculative purposes or were invested in industries facing excess capacity obviously contributed to the crisis. But even more prudent borrowers from soft currency economies can end up with currency and maturity mismatches. By their very nature, many high-yield projects in developing countries, such as building a factory or a new highway, have only a long-term payoff, or do not have foreign exchange earnings. At the same time, much of the lending to developing countries will continue to be concentrated in short-term maturities.

As long as emerging economies face the devil's choice of either borrowing short-term or borrowing in dollars, it will be difficult for them to avoid ending up with weak and risky balance sheets. Any country with a sizable stock of foreign currency debt is vulnerable to exchange-rate movements, which can have very large

---

[14]Quoted in Eduardo Fernández-Arias and Ricardo Hausmann, "Is FDI A Safer Form of Financing?" Paper prepared for the Annual Meeting of the Board of Governors, Inter-American Development Bank and Inter-American Investment Corporation, March 26, 2000.

balance sheet effects. When a country's currency depreciates, its foreign currency liabilities increase and its assets depreciate accordingly. A large enough depreciation can literally wipe out the capital of an emerging economy company or bank overnight.

This balance sheet effect of currency depreciation makes even well-managed emerging economies vulnerable to exogenous-related shifts in international capital flows. As a number of studies have shown, international capital flows to developing countries increase or decrease for reasons often unrelated to the investment needs or investment climate of a particular emerging economy. In the 1990s, changes in net capital flows were closely correlated with U.S. interest rates, with lower rates heralding an increase in international capital flows to emerging economies such as occurred in 1995–96 and with higher rates precipitating an outflow such as occurred in 1997.[15] Faced with falling interest rates in more mature markets, or what is known as yield famine, many large institutional investors have in this decade sought to increase their return by seeking out higher rates of interest in emerging economy debt, a practice that is likely to continue in spite of recent crises.

Because of the relative size difference between the financial markets of the most advanced industrialized countries and those of emerging economies, even marginal shifts in funds by international players can overwhelm the capacity of small economies and banking systems. As economist Stephen Roach has pointed out, the industrial world has enormous pools of savings and financial capital. By contrast, the developing world has very small capital markets. The combined equity market capitalization of the United States, Europe, and Japan, for example, is close to $30 trillion, compared with less than $1.5 trillion for the leading equity markets of the developing world. As Roach notes, a mere 1 percent allocation out of the United States would mean a movement of

---

[15]See Eduardo Fernández-Arias, "The New Wave of Capital Inflows: Sea Change or Just Another Tide?", Paper prepared for the Annual Meeting of the Board of Governors, Inter-American Development Bank ad Inter-American Investment Corporation, March 26, 2000.

$150 billion.[16] Even that modest shift would overwhelm many of the emerging debt and equity markets, leading to asset bubbles and serious instability.

Market Capitalization
(in millions of U.S. $)

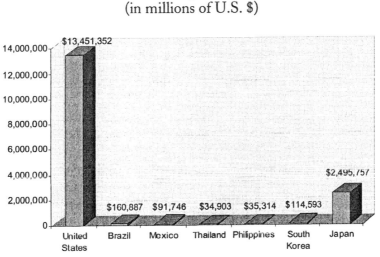

Source: Emerging Stock Markets Fact Book 1999

Such large inflows and outflows relative to the size of most emerging economies leave countries without an optimal exchange rate choice. If they let the currency float, inflows cause the currency to appreciate and the economy to lose competitiveness, widening trade and current account deficits, and leading eventually to a crisis of confidence. On the other hand, if countries peg their currencies, they risk their economy overheating from increases in the money supply. Moreover, as we saw in the Asian crisis, nominal pegs can be an invitation to speculation as well as to over-borrowing. The combination of stable nominal exchange rates along with interest rates differentials between international and domestic rates creates a one-way bet for speculators seeking to benefit from

---

[16]Stephen Roach, "The Frothy Market Scene Looks Ripe for the Next Big Crisis," International Herald Tribune, Opinion Section, April 6, 2000, p. 10.

international arbitrage. This combination also provides a strong incentive for domestic firms and banks to reduce their cost of finance by borrowing abroad. Everything works fine at first but over time the economy becomes extremely vulnerable to capital flight. When capital flows reverse themselves, as they often do when interest-rate spreads disappear or when the peg looks vulnerable, the currency collapses and domestic banks and companies are left with an unsustainable level of short-term debt.

The small size of emerging economies relative to international capital flows also prevents investors from being able to take normal prudential measures, thus making them more skittish at the first sign of trouble. Small, illiquid foreign-exchange markets for soft currencies, for example, make it difficult or too expensive for investors to properly hedge or to employ modern portfolio and risk-management systems. If they do hedge, it is often in a one-way direction that contributes to the eventual collapse of the currency. On the other hand, the central banks of emerging economies find that the small size of their foreign exchange reserves relative to capital flows makes it difficult for them to defend the currency. As we saw during the Asian financial crisis, while many Asian countries had more than enough reserves to cover imports, they did not have enough to both service short-term debt and defend the currency from speculative attack.

There are, of course, a number of ways that developing economies can protect themselves from the vicissitudes of international capital flows. They can adopt Chilean-style, short-term capital controls on inflows in order to stem inflows. But many countries are reluctant to do so for fear of discouraging much-needed foreign capital.

The fact that soft currencies are crisis prone is only part of the problem. An equally serious problem for middle-class-oriented development is how soft currencies distort an economy's financial system and consequently its development. In fact, it is very difficult for countries with soft currencies to develop the efficient, flexible, and democratically accessible capital and credit markets upon which middle-class-oriented development depends.

The basic problem is that soft currencies breed an investment climate of short termism that effectively rules out a credit market for such important middle class purposes as home ownership or small business start-up and expansion. In emerging economies, yield curves are extremely steep, and maturities extend in many cases no further than three years (except perhaps for politically favored enterprises from a state-directed bank). For investors, especially international investors, there is no rate of interest that would compensate them for the risk of investing in a soft currency for, say, five years, let alone ten or thirty years.

As a result, interest rates and the cost of capital in most emerging economies are prohibitively high. Even the cost of capital for governments is very high due to the uncertainty over the future exchange rate. Since the Asian financial crisis, spreads on sovereign emerging market debt have averaged more than 900 basis points.[7] Such a high cost of capital increases the cost of government-funded infrastructure and public investment as well as the cost of debt service. It imposes enormous costs and liabilities on all levels of government, making many social and infrastructure investments prohibitively expensive. By forcing countries to borrow short, it also exposes them to the risk of repeated financial crises when they must roll over large amounts of debt under adverse credit market conditions.

Consider what infrastructure in the United States would look like if state and municipal governments were not able to borrow at low interest rates. School bond issues, highways, sewer systems—all would become more expensive. Taxes would have to increase, and services would have to decline.

Capital is even more expensive for the private sector in emerging economies, if it is available at all. Even when world interest rates are low, domestic interest rates in emerging economies can be prohibitively high. In 1996, for example, real interest rates for domestic companies ran as high as 25.3 percent in Brazil; 10.5 percent in Thailand, and 11.7 percent in the Philippines—in comparison

---

[7] J.P. Morgan Emerging Market Bond Index.

to approximately 5 percent in the United States.[18] This high cost of capital reduces investment. It penalizes the private sector and stunts its development. The result is slower growth, fewer jobs, and more poverty.

The combined impact of high interest rates and short-term loans not only deters investment in general, but it is especially damaging to certain kinds of economic activities. In fact, the high cost of capital precludes a whole range of investments that would otherwise be profitable in the United States and other developed countries. Small businesses and ordinary citizens are unable to borrow at reasonable rates. That leaves small business to rely either on their families or on loan sharks and the informal credit market. Even small and medium-sized businesses find capital markets largely closed. Small entrepreneurs and common citizens wanting to buy houses and other durables are trapped by the high interest rates and short maturities characteristic of economies with soft currencies.

There are no lack of entrepreneurs and enterprising businessmen and women in emerging economies. What they lack is access to financial capital. The cost of capital for business start-ups in Brazil, Mexico, and other emerging economies, if it exists at all, is outrageously expensive. As noted earlier, the real rate of interest charged on a business loan in Brazil, for example—if you can find a commercial bank willing to make such a loan—generally exceeds 25 percent. Even the most brilliantly conceived business plan would be hard pressed to justify paying 25 percent to get the funds needed to service such loans.

This climate of short-termism and high interest rates seriously distorts the development pattern of many emerging markets. For one thing, it tends to favor big companies over small companies and families. In fact, as illustrated by the chart below, large firms tend to dominate the credit markets of most developing economies. This climate also privileges foreign-exchange earning exporters over companies that produce for the domestic market.

---

[18]IMF International Financial Statistics, vol. 53, no. 3 (March 2000).

Additionally, it favors foreign firms with access to the international credit markets over local companies that must borrow in the local currency at much higher rates.

Credit to Largest 20 Firms As A Percentage of Total Credit

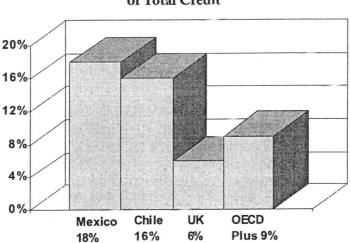

Source: Florencio Lopez-de-Silanes, Investor Protection in Mexico: An Agenda for the Reform of Capital Markets.

As noted earlier, loans in U.S. dollars generally carry much lower interest rates and much longer maturities than do loans in soft currencies. Only the largest, best-positioned firms with foreign exchange earnings have access to international credit markets or to dollar-denominated loans. In many cases, even domestic banks are reluctant to loan in dollars to companies if they do not have foreign exchange earnings. Such discrimination in favor of the large export-oriented sector is understandable, given that lending in dollars to enterprises or individuals whose earnings or assets are denominated in local currency is too risky for banks and would expose them to the kind of crisis-creating currency and maturity mismatches noted earlier.

But however understandable, this discrimination smacks of a form of financial apartheid, which effectively eliminates most households and small business from credit markets. While the wealthy have access to hard currency and reasonably priced credit, the rest of the economy is stuck with the local soft currency and denied access to the credit markets. It is now widely understood that the poor are the chief victims of inflation, and fortunately a number of countries have taken strong action against this long-time scourge. But it is even more true that the poor and the middle class are the victims of short-term, undeveloped capital markets, and much less has been done to address these serious problems.

Prohibitively High Borrowing Rates
for Domestic Companies

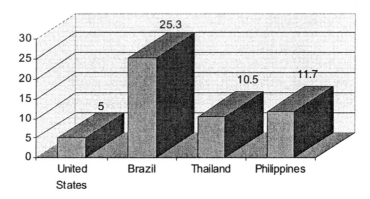

Source: The Economist, SELIC rate & Financial Times

2. Shallow and Badly Regulated Capital Markets
Given their short-term bias, it is not surprising that soft-currency economies have shallow and underdeveloped capital markets. Nearly all emerging economies lack the financial institutions and instruments that one normally associates with middle-class societies. Consider, for example, the range of business and home credit institutions that created the U.S. housing market: among others, cheap and tax-privileged thirty-year self-amortizing mortgages; down payment programs so that veterans and low-income families could purchase homes; and the Fannie Mae system that bundles conforming mortgages into securities for large investors. Or take the variety of government-backed loan programs that have

given small businesses and farmers access to reasonably priced credit.[19] All these are absent in many emerging economies.

Also missing is the system of municipal and utility finance, which has funded much of America's schools, roads, and other public improvements. Because most emerging economies lack capital markets or financial instruments for these purposes, a critical sector of middle-class-oriented development is stunted. Education, public works, and housing are all non-tradable goods and thus a primary sector for domestic-driven growth. They are also principal generators of both skilled and entry-level employment, and thus one key to the growth of an aspiring middle class.

In addition to lacking these home- and consumer-credit institutions, most emerging economies have poorly developed equity and bond markets as well as secondary debt markets. The lack of secondary debt markets—for the securitization of home mortgages, for example—makes it very difficult for primary lenders to diversify adequately their risk, and thus makes the financial systems more vulnerable than those of more advanced economies.

With the help of the World Bank's International Finance Corporation, many emerging markets have in recent years introduced exchanges for the listing and trading of equity and debt securities. But because of their small size, these exchanges tend to be plagued by insider trading and lack of liquidity, and dominated by a few large companies. Disputes over minority shareholder rights are common, as are complaints about share dilution and other asset-stripping practices of majority controlling shareholders.

As a result of poorly developed equity and secondary debt markets, most emerging economies are still overly dependent on the banking sector, both domestically and internationally. This poses two kinds of problems: First, it tends to increase the risk of financial crises. Banks are pro-cyclical institutions: they lend more when times are good and cut back when things go bad. And their own fortunes tend to track those of the business cycle. As a

---

[19]For further discussion, see Jane D'Arista, "Building the Financial Infrastructure for Middle-Class Emerging Economies," a paper from the Project on Development, Trade, and International Finance, Council on Foreign Relations, New York, 2000.

result, banking crises tend to be a more or less permanent feature of the business cycle. Banks are highly leveraged organizations—they have a slender wedge of their own equity capital supporting a large volume of business. As the business cycle advances, they attract more deposits, their equity bases expand, their lending capacity is upgraded, and they make more loans. But no matter how prudent individual bankers may be, many of those loans will be made at inappropriate spreads at the point of the business cycle in which they are approved.

As suggested earlier, banks in developing countries are particularly crisis prone because they must borrow short term, often in foreign currency markets, and lend to projects that have longer term returns in local currency. This leads to both currency and maturity mismatches, which makes the financial system vulnerable to currency depreciations. Moreover, banks in emerging economies are often structurally weak institutions simply by virtue of the high interest rates their loans carry, which substantially increase the risk of lending. They are also weak structurally because they are not able to diversify their risk among a large number of small borrowers and or through secondary debt markets, and because they suffer from a high degree of noncompliance and nonpayment, a reflection in part of poor bankruptcy laws and in part of bad regulation.

The second problem with the over-reliance on the banking system is that in many emerging economies banks are highly inefficient at allocating capital. Banks in some countries are subject to political influence, corruption, and cronyism. Special interest groups can easily capture banks, and have their loans distributed like prizes to a favored few. To be sure, banks can be effective instruments of state-directed industrial development in cases where there is a very conscientious bureaucracy to oversee them, and they are essential for funding small and medium-size businesses. But in practice, this tends to be the exception, not the rule. More often, they misallocate resources to nonproductive, politically protected enterprises and businesses.

Indeed, because many banks are state-related, they often serve as instruments for expropriating wealth from small working and middle class savers to finance politically protected state-directed

enterprises. Even when they are successful at promoting industrial development, they can easily become captive of large conglomerates
that over time become inefficient, as is the case of the banks in South
Korea.

One of the main problems, then, with the present international
financial architecture is that it contains strong biases toward debt
finance, especially intermediation by banks, and does not adequately
support equity finance and direct investment. The need to redirect capital flows toward equity financing was supposedly one of
the main lessons of the Latin American debt crisis of the 1980s.
Yet, despite this consensus, bank lending and borrowing played
a pivotal role in the financial crises of the 1990s. As economist
Kenneth Rogoff has pointed out, if international capital flows to
developing countries took the form of equity investment, there would
be an automatic device for risk sharing. Currency depreciations
could still lead to sharp drops in local stock markets, but there would
be fewer liquidity effects and less risk of a full-blown financial
crisis.[20]

Soft currencies, of course, are not the only reason for shallow,
short-term capital markets. Indeed, most emerging markets lack
the legal infrastructure and regulatory machinery upon which
deeper and more sophisticated capital markets depend. The problems are well known, and do not require elaborate treatment here
except to note what every investor with experience in emerging
market finance knows.[21] Although conditions vary in emerging
economies, too often vague or ambiguous property laws with
weak protections of minority shareholders and lax accounting
principles deter equity investment. Poor bankruptcy laws, biased
enforcement of existing laws, and poorly developed commercial
codes deter bank and other lending. And inefficient and politically influenced judicial systems make enforcement of legal instruments haphazard at best and impractical at worst.

---

[20]Kenneth Rogoff, "International Institutions for Reducing Global Financial Instability," *Journal of Economic Perspectives*, vol. 13 (Fall 1999).

[21]For further discussion, see Glenn Yago, "Private Capital Flows, Emerging Economies,
and International Financial Architecture," a paper from the Project on Development, Trade,
and International Finance, Council on Foreign Relations, New York, 2000.

The absence of an adequate bankruptcy law and court system can have especially deleterious effects on the financial system. It makes legal coercion less credible, exacerbating the willingness-to-pay problem. It also increases the costs of crises because it precludes concerted action to deal with bad debts and to restructure a bank's or company's liabilities.

The shortcomings of many developing countries' legal infrastructure is the focus of many of the proposed neo-liberal reforms taken up by the International Monetary Fund (IMF) and the Financial Stability Forum. These proposals call for greater transparency, for new bankruptcy and commercial codes, and new accounting standards. They also call for more prudent regulation. At question is not whether these reforms are necessary. They are. Rather, the question is why the international community has been so unsuccessful in getting developing countries to move more quickly on these basic reforms-a question to which we will return shortly.

Deep and efficient markets of the kind required for middle-class-oriented development depend upon an effective system of regulation and supervision, in addition to a proper legal infrastructure. But historically, such systems emerge only slowly as both elite and popular opinion learn from repeated experience that the inconveniences and costs of regulation and supervision are far less than the inconveniences resulting from their absence. Regulation in emerging markets is often suspect because it is subject to undue political influence and pressure from economic interests close to the government. This is particularly true in emerging economies like Indonesia and Mexico, where one party or group has dominated the institutions of government for a long period of time. But it also a problem in advanced emerging economies like South Korea, where there has been a long-standing interlocking relationship between the nation's banks, the largest *chaebols*, and the government bureaucracy. Even when political influence and corruption is absent, regulation and supervision may be inadequate because local administrators lack appropriate training or experience, or are so preoccupied with crisis management that they do not have the time or resources to exercise effective regulatory power.

In the aftermath of the Asian financial crisis, the IMF and the World Bank have been forced to devote more time and attention to questions of bank regulation and supervision. Accordingly, they have made their assistance contingent not just on certain macroeconomic targets but also on implementing certain microeconomic changes, including the adoption of appropriate supervisory and regulatory standards. Necessary though these efforts may be, it is unrealistic to expect the IMF to be able to fulfill or even substantially augment national regulation. The IMF, like most global institutions, is too distant and lacks both the mandate and resources to exercise effective oversight. Even when IMF officials have the time or detailed knowledge required for effective supervision, they lack the legitimacy and authority they need to operate national banking systems. Indeed, many of the reforms the IMF has proposed are considered suspect in the countries concerned because the IMF is perceived to be carrying out the agenda of its major shareholders. In particular, one such shareholder is the U.S. Treasury, which is sometimes suspected of being motivated more by the interests of U.S. banks and financial institutions than by the well-being of the country concerned.

The Asian financial crisis exposed a major regulatory gap in the global financial system. Regulating financial markets is increasingly beyond the capacity of many national governments—and certainly beyond the existing capacity of many governments in developing countries. Yet the IMF and Bank for International Settlements (BIS) do not have the mandate or resources to provide the kind of extensive oversight required. At best, a system of divided sovereignty is emerging; at worst, no one is really in control.

3. Inappropriate International Governance

This brings us to the final problem with the international financial architecture: namely, that national and international institutions as now structured are not able to provide effective governance for the development of integrated financial markets. Nor are they able to advance the reforms necessary for the development of financial markets for middle-class-oriented development. Part of the problem stems from the fact that both national and international institutions lack the resources needed for managing international financial integration.

At the national level, central banks often suffer from inadequate reserves, which make their currencies easy targets for speculative attack. By comparison to central banks in the most advanced OECD countries, most emerging-market central banks are poorly capitalized and not sufficiently independent from political influence to command credibility in the world's financial markets. What is worse, in today's world of open capital markets, it is very difficult for the national banks of developing countries, even the largest, to serve as effective lenders of last resort—to provide liquidity at a moment of crisis. Because emerging-market banking crises and currency crises are now often related, national central banks would need reserves large enough to be able to both defend the currency and to inject liquidity into the banking system. As a practical matter, that is virtually impossible for most emerging economies. Indeed, soft-currency economies have found that their ability to exercise an independent monetary policy has been negated by the vulnerability of their currency to speculative attack. As a result, when a banking crisis develops, emerging economies find that they cannot lower interest rates or pump money into the system. Instead, they must raise interest rates in an effort to restore confidence and to stem capital outflows. Raising interest rates, however, exacerbates the debt-servicing burdens of the nation's debtors, and produces an economic downturn.

The lack of an appropriate scale of resources at the national level is of course the reason why most emerging economies have been forced to turn to the IMF, not only to deal with persistent current account problems but to handle capital account crises such as those experienced by many countries during the 1997–98 crisis. Yet the IMF has not been prepared to handle the magnitude of the crises it has faced in recent years. In a world of extreme exchange-rate volatility and interlocked financial markets that are prey to herd behavior, what is needed is what economics columnist Martin Wolf calls, "a lender of last resort with deep pockets." As Wolf points out, a true lender of last resort would stand ready to provide liquidity in support of any country deemed structurally sound that was running out of reserves or suffering a currency crisis.[22] But because the IMF's capital base has not expanded to keep pace with the growth of international capital flows, it cannot perform this role with any assurance. IMF bailouts are simply too small in relation to the sums that can rush into and out of countries without controls.

IMF's Capitalization Relative to the Growth of World GDP

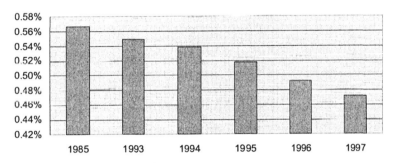

Source: IMF Annual Reports & CIA Handbook of International Economic Statistics

With its eleventh quota increase in 1997, the IMF has lendable resources of roughly $287 billion.[23] As a percentage of world capital flows, this amounts to a fraction of the resources the IMF had upon its initiation in 1946. Because it has limited resources at its disposal, the IMF has few tools except high interest rates and austerity to deal with an economy suffering from a liquidity crisis. Only by shrinking domestic demand can it restore a country's external account to the black in order to generate a needed current account surplus and to replenish foreign exchange reserves. As numerous commentators have pointed out, there are good reasons why the IMF is so rarely, if ever, successful in restoring confidence in a country hit by a foreign exchange crisis. While the IMF has in recent

---

[22]Martin Wolf, "Contagion and Capital Flows," *Financial Times*, October 6, 1998, p. 12.

[23]International Monetary Fund, 1999 *Annual Report.*

years put together sizable credit packages for crisis-stricken countries, it cannot freely lend to them at the time of greatest need. Rather, it disperses its funds only after countries have met a series of extensive conditions. And because these conditions are complex, it is not possible for private creditors and investors to know whether or when the funds will actually be available and thus whether a county will have enough foreign exchange reserves to meet its obligations and to defend itself against further speculative attacks.

In the wake of the Asian financial crisis, the IMF has taken some steps to improve its capability to act like a lender of last resort—or at least one with shallow pockets. In December 1997, it set up a special window—the Supplemental Reserve Facility—to deal specifically with capital account problems, a facility that was used to put together the Korean, Russian, and Brazilian rescue packages.

It has also moved toward the establishment of a contagion contingent fund for pre-approved countries, which would improve the IMF's ability to act quickly. Through this fund, the IMF would offer a new emergency line of credit, for which countries would have to prequalify by meeting certain macroeconomic and regulatory standards. The existence of this line of credit, it is hoped, would help stave off speculative attacks and runs on a country's reserves. But so far most large emerging economies have been wary about signing up for the fund for fear that would send the wrong signals to the market.

These are useful innovations and improvements, but in order to make a difference they will require further substantial increases in IMF resources. Given the tarnished credibility and diminished popularity of the IMF in many G-7 countries, especially the United States, such additional support is unrealistic. Even if such support were to become available, there is another question about the IMF's ability to act like a true lender of last resort, and that has to do with moral hazard. It is true that the growth of the global system demands an institution that provides liquidity in times of crisis, much like the Federal Reserve does in the United States. However, in order to avoid the risk of moral hazard, this institution also needs to have the ability to supervise its members, to detect problems, and to force remedial actions. As it is, the IMF's conditionality powers, although seen as unnecessarily intrusive by some critics, are no substitute for effective supervision and regulation.

With each new crisis, the IMF and World Bank have taken on more tasks and charges, from financial-sector reform to poverty alleviation. To add yet one more function without rethinking others would only add to a serious case of institutional over-stretch. Even as it is, the IMF and World Bank cannot cope with the variety of demands that the world has placed upon them. As the Meltzer Commission has warned, there is a danger in that by attempting to become "universal" institutions covering all problems in all countries, they are unable to focus effectively and thus undermine their own ability to effectuate real reform in the world economy.[24]

Indeed, it is doubtful that the IMF can serve as the principal institution for promoting needed financial reforms in many emerging economies. For one thing, it lacks political legitimacy in emerging economies. Fairly or unfairly, the IMF is seen as unduly influenced by its largest Western shareholders, especially the United States. The whole purpose of independence in central banking is to remove political influence from the supervision of the financial system. Yet despite the high professional standards of their staffs, decision-makers at the IMF and, to a lesser extent, the World Bank are widely regarded as dominated by U.S. politicians. This gives us the worst-case form of international governance: the Bretton Woods institutions are controlled by politicians who are not responsible to the citizens of the countries most affected by their actions. The recent disgraceful row over the leadership of the IMF only underscores the degree to which the current system is political and not responsible or accountable to the billions of people who live in the countries where the IMF plays its major role.

Moreover, the IMF's performance in the 1997–98 crisis has created a legacy of bitterness in Asia, which threatens its ability to

---

[24]Report of the International Financial Institution Advisory Commission, Washington, DC, 2000.

function effectively as a promoter of reforms in that critical region. Throughout many countries in Asia, there is a palpable desire to resist what is seen as the undue influence of the IMF, undermining the efficacy of IMF attempts to lead reform.

If the IMF lacks the moral leverage it needs to stimulate reform, it also lacks any substantial carrots by which to encourage reform in most emerging economies. In this sense, the IMF's underfunded capital base undercuts its leverage to effect real reforms in many emerging economies. Many of the reforms it proposes are either extremely painful to the population as a whole or threatening to the current power elite. Faced with the loss of power and popularity and without any hope of immediate economic results, many governments choose to put off many necessary reforms, doing just enough to win IMF funding. And despite the populist nature of some of the reforms the IMF champions, there is virtually no popular support for IMF reforms in most of the countries it serves, a legacy of its reputation for being a closed institution committed to austerity-oriented policies.

This helps to explain, then, why the international community has been so unsuccessful in promoting needed reforms in emerging economies. In short, profound popular and elite suspicion of existing international institutions and the lack of a stable currency conspire to make difficult and painful reforms even more difficult and painful. Well-meaning IMF officials can tell emerging economies that good policies create good results, but for many developing country leaders the evidence gets obscured by frequent international financial crises for which they bear little responsibility. Under current conditions, the connection between good policies and good outcomes is weak: in too many cases it takes a long time for good policies to bear fruit in better economic conditions. During that long time period there are too many possibilities for exogenous shocks that can derail economies even as they try to reform—or that can test the political will of countries when reforms become unpopular.

In short, good policies may not be enough in the short term to produce better economic results—although better economic results are needed to facilitate deeper reforms. The relationship between reform and sound money is of course controversial. But on balance it seems that many emerging economies will be doomed to start-and-stop reform if efforts are not made to correct that part of international financial architecture that denies emerging economies sound currencies and supportive international institutions.

TOWARD A NEW INTERNATIONAL
FINANCIAL ARCHITECTURE

Problems as deep and as pervasive as these will of course not be remedied easily or quickly. Nor can they be solved by good policies alone. Indeed, one of the central questions is how to create a system that facilitates what is often a painful and contentious process of reform in many emerging economies. The architecture of the international financial system does matter in this regard, and it especially matters if the goal is middle-class-oriented development.

As the previous discussion made clear, middle-class-oriented development depends upon institutional changes that substantially reduce risk for both domestic and international investors. It is not enough to focus on policies that, by making the financial systems more open and transparent, enable investors to better evaluate the risks. Nor is it enough to try to slow down capital flows, as other popular proposals would do. Reducing capital flows to developing countries or raising the cost of capital to borrowers in those countries are precisely the wrong steps to encourage.

Institutional changes, it is clear, do not occur overnight. But as we have seen with recent institutional innovations—the creation of the European Monetary Union, the coming into being of the European Bank for Reconstruction and Development (EBRD), and the establishment of the World Trade Organization (WTO)—they can evolve out of existing institutional arrangements or as a result of enlightened response to new circumstances and new needs in a remarkably short period of time.

Our analysis has led us to the conclusion that the creation of a new layer of regional institutions—led where appropriate by regional central banks—within a global system of international finance and governance holds the key to overcoming many if not all the obstacles to middle-class-oriented development. The regional central banks and other regional arrangements we propose would become the frontline institutions of the international financial architecture in their regions. They would accomplish what national and global institutions are currently unable to accomplish. In particular, they would do the following:

- Solve the soft currency problem by adopting an external hard currency or by creating regional super-currencies;

- Overcome the lack of resources by taking advantage of economies of scale on a regional basis, by pooling capital from member governments, and by bailing in G-3 central banks, international financial institutions, and the private sector in a proactive way;

- Promote good governance and good policies by offering emerging economies regionally organized systems of financial market development and services;

- Provide mechanisms for the restructuring of existing debt, as well as debt relief for highly indebted countries willing to pursue good policies; and

- Facilitate capital-market development by offering regionally organized market institutions and instruments, and by putting in place the legal infrastructure necessary for deep and efficient capital markets.

This emphasis on regional central banks is not to suggest that existing international institutions do not have a critical role to play in the proposed international financial architecture. By any standards, the IMF and the World Bank are among the more successful and well managed of the great international institutions. Much of the criticism that these institutions receive should be directed less at their policies or intentions than at an international economic status quo that has been unable to liberate billions of human beings from lives of extreme poverty. Any program of effective reform will require the continuing help and support of the Bretton Woods organizations. Yet the fact remains that the current international financial architecture does not and cannot provide all the support that the emerging world economy needs.

Today's international financial architecture essentially rests on two pillars: national governments and international institutions. A well functioning international financial architecture, in our view, needs three equally strong pillars—national, regional, and global. In today's financial architecture, the regional pillar, to the extent it exists at all, is by far the weakest yet the one potentially best suited for a broad range of policy matters.

For all the talk of globalization, much of the economic integration of the past decade has been regional rather than truly global. America's two largest trade partners are Canada and Mexico; the greatest proportion of European Union (EU) trade is among its member countries. Even intra-regional trade in East Asia has increased dramatically in the past decade, despite its continued dependence on the American market, as has inter-regional trade among the Mercosur countries of Latin America. The popularity of area-wide trade initiatives, such as the European single market, Asian-Pacific Economic Cooperation (APEC), the North American Free Trade Agreement (NAFTA), and Mercosur, is reflective of this underlying trend.

Moreover, despite the many common problems developing economies face, differences among regions—Latin America, Southeast Asia, Sub-Saharan Africa, Eastern Europe, and Central Asia—are quite large and have considerable influence on policy. These regions have different histories of development, different patterns of industrialization, different savings and investment patterns, different experiences with international capital flows, and different systems of law and corporate governance. Accordingly, they face different challenges, have different strengths, and need different policy mixes and even different institutional cultures. In fact, as was evident during the Asian financial crisis, there is a danger in trying to treat one region with the prescriptions designed for another—as many believe happened when the IMF dusted off prescriptions for Latin American-style current account and sovereign debt problems and applied them to the Asian capital account and corporate debt problems in the 1997–98 crisis.

To be sure, globalization in general, and international financial integration, in particular, require the development of certain common global standards. As international financial integration increases, higher and higher degrees of regulatory and policy conformity among participating countries are needed. Just as increased trade liberalization has forced countries to conform their practices to WTO norms, continuing integration of capital markets will force countries to adopt common standards and practices in the management of their financial systems. But, in our view, regional institutions involving first a process of regional harmonization and then increased coordination among different regional bodies offer a better and more reliable path to this kind of convergence than does the current system of national organizations and weak international institutions.

Indeed, the regional level offers unique advantages from the standpoint of financial governance. Think of Goldilocks. The global level is too high and too distant; the national level is too close to the ground, and too subject to political interests and control. By contrast, regional institutions are "about right": close enough to member states and their peoples in culture and orientation to have more legitimacy than global institutions. Yet they are also more independent than national governments in that the presence of different states and interests in the governance structure of regional institutions makes it harder for national elites to capture them in ways that undermine their credibility or effectiveness.

Regional institutions thus offer us a means not only to close the regulatory gap that is left by global institutions that are too distant and national institutions that are too close, but also to promote the kinds of reforms needed for the development of deeper and more efficient capital markets. It is not likely that global organizations like the IMF will either have the legitimacy or be granted the authority to effectively mandate these essential reforms.

At the same time, experience teaches that the state and political structures of many emerging economies make effective and transparent policing of the credit sector virtually impossible at the national level. This reflects not just the recent experience of developing countries but the historical experience of advanced industrial economies as well. Despite repeated financial market panics

and crashes, the United States did not establish the Federal
Reserve System until 1913; a credible national system of small-saver
deposit insurance took another generation to appear. The United States is hardly unique in this respect; the financial histories
of Britain, France, and most other advanced economies show
recurring patterns of regulatory failure—and the advanced industrial democracies cannot yet claim to have invented foolproof
methods of regulating their capital and financial markets. Left to
their own devices, emerging economies may take a similarly long
time to voluntarily and consistently embrace the often painful disciplines associated with the sound management of a financial
system.

No set of institutional changes can guarantee good outcomes
without good policy and wise judgment. Nonetheless, there are
good structural reasons why a regional institution, widely regarded as legitimate and accountable, offers a more benign climate for
the growth of the kind of governance the world economy will need.
For one thing, deeper regional economic integration gives each prospective member of a regional institution a greater stake in ensuring
that its neighbors pursue good policies. Formal regional institutions would give each state the means to force good policies on
its neighbors or to place checks on politically motivated credit abuses by neighboring states.

Second, because of the greater legitimacy this economic proximity accords them, regional organizations, we believe, are more
likely to command the resources needed to promote reforms and
good governance. By pooling their resources—their foreign-
exchange reserves and their regulatory expertise—and by taking
advantage of economies of scale on a regional level, regional organizations can overcome the lack-of-resource problem that now afflicts
both national governments and international institutions. Better
capitalized than either the IMF or the World Bank in proportion
to their responsibilities, they would be more likely to be able to
offer their members greater inducements for carrying out reforms
than can these currently underfunded international institutions.
Moreover, as many EU members have discovered, from union comes
strength. Countries too small to protect their economies on a nation-

al basis from international crises, or to make their voices heard in international bodies, can gain more autonomy and authority as parts of strong regional organizations than they can acting on their own.

Finally, building up the regional pillar would also help strengthen the global pillar by allowing existing international institutions, like the IMF and the World Bank, to become more focused and thus more effective. If regional institutions become the frontline institutions of international financial architecture, particularly as it pertains to emerging economies, then the IMF and BIS can focus more upon the tasks of global surveillance and oversight and less on trying to micromanage the economies of developing countries. The IMF could also take on a major new role in coordinating policy and regulatory standards among regional bodies and devote more resources and attention to the potentially explosive problems arising out of the imbalances and failures of policy coordination among the G-3 economies.

Similarly, the World Bank would be able to focus more on poverty alleviation, human capital development, and technical assistance. Indeed, the significant expansion of the World Bank's ability to support anti-poverty initiatives under an effective regional architecture is one of the strongest arguments for moving in this direction.

Owing to geopolitical rivalries or historical animosities or differences in size or level of development among countries in a particular region, regional institutions are not the answer in all parts of the world. But regional integration is advancing in many areas, and there are a number of regions and sub-regions where strengthened regional architecture and policy seems both immediately feasible and desirable. In Latin America, one area is constituted by Mexico, Central America, and the Caribbean; the Mercosur economies plus Chile constitute another. In Asia, the Association of Southeast Asian Nations (ASEAN) perhaps with the addition of South Korea would be the basis of another set of regional institutions; already ASEAN represents the most sustained and far-reaching regional initiative in international politics other than the European Union. In Africa, southern Africa has had some positive experience in regional cooperation, and this success could serve as the basis for stepped-up regional efforts. There have also been previous efforts at regional economic cooperation in both west and east Africa, although the current political turmoil in both areas suggests that real regional cooperation and integration lies some distance off.

Other potential arenas for stronger regional action would include the "outlying" candidates for EU membership, who face a decade or more before joining the European Union; the Euro-Med economies of Northern Africa and the Near East; as well as those members of the CIS for whom EU membership is, at best, a remote prospect.

China and India (possibly including willing neighbors like Bangladesh and Sri Lanka) are so large that they can and should be seen as regions on their own. In these cases, there may be no realistic alternative to an essentially nationally based approach to financial architecture. Yet because of their size, both China and India would profit by adopting on a national basis some of the strategies and institutional reforms we are suggesting that other countries pursue as part of regional coalitions. To a significant extent, many of the recently announced Chinese banking reforms, including measures to support securitization of mortgages and other debt instruments, anticipate many of the recommendations we make below.[25]

In areas where regional cooperation is currently unlikely or inappropriate due either to political or economic factors, the international financial institutions would continue to act as the "frontline" institutions. But even in these cases, the IMF and World Bank would be well advised to seek to build regional cooperation and thus to lay the foundation for regional institutions to function in these areas in the future.

The priorities for regional agreements and architecture will differ among the various regions identified above. Furthermore, the roles of existing regional institutions will vary. In some cases,

---

[25]For further discussion, see James Galbraith and Jiaquing Lu, "Sustainable Development and the Open-Door Policy in China," a paper from the Project on Development, Trade, and International Finance, Council on Foreign Relations, New York, 2000.

such as in Asia and Latin America, the region's development banks—Inter-American Development Bank and the Asian Development Bank—could play a key role in establishing new institutions, or may themselves develop into much stronger and more influential organizations. Other regional organizations, such as regional stock exchanges, would also play a role in a growing and deepening process of integration and cooperation. Such regional alliances, unlike the European Union, would probably not aim at political integration; rather, the goal would be effective economic cooperation within a framework of independent sovereign states.

The path toward a stronger network of regional agreements and institutions will be a long and winding one—and no two regions will follow the same path or move at the same pace. The following recommendations are intended as guide posts to shape policy discussions and suggest priorities rather than as detailed proposals for immediate action. Much wider research, consultation, and investigation are needed before we can present detailed recommendations tailor-made for any, much less all, of the regions and sub-regions where some or all of our recommendations may apply.

Recommendation 1: Create well-capitalized and well-managed regional central banks to serve as the frontline institutions of an international financial architecture for middle-class-oriented development.

In light of the many advantages that regional institutions would have for international financial governance, our first recommendation is to create, wherever feasible, regional central banks. Such banks would serve as the frontline institutions of a new international financial architecture for middle-class-oriented development within a global system of international finance and governance. Regional central banks would perform for their members many of the functions associated with large advanced-economy central banks—managing a common currency and monetary policy, chartering and supervising member banks and branches, studying and reporting on financial and economic developments within the region, and acting as a lender of last resort for regional financial institutions. In addition, regional central banks would facilitate capital-market development by offering regionally organized market institutions and instruments and by putting in place the legal infrastructure for capital-market development.

Regional central banks would be open to membership to all governments and their central banks in a particular region that were willing to abide by covenants of good governance and good policies. The process of accession to a regional central bank would include three agreements: a fiscal stability pact, which would set limits on the size, duration, and composition of fiscal deficits and overall debt levels; an agreement covering legal infrastructure and regulatory standards; and an agreement relating to the regional central bank's regulatory authority.

To be both credible and flexible, regional central banks would need to be well-capitalized and well-managed, and in the case of most regions this would mean extending its shareholding structure beyond member governments and central banks. More specifically, it would require bailing in the private sector as well as both member and nonmember governments, member and nonmember central banks, and the international financial institutions. Discussions about international financial architecture since the 1997–98 crisis have repeatedly examined the question of "bailing in" the private sector—ensuring that private lenders and investors bear their share of the risks and costs associated with international investment. Much of the debate has focused on proposals for incorporating so-called collective-action clauses in sovereign bond contracts, which would make it easier to gain support among bondholders for debt rescheduling and restructuring, a measure that some fear would slow down capital flows to and raise the cost of capital for emerging economies.

Here our focus is on bailing in the private sector as well as member and nonmember central banks in a way that reduces interest rates for borrowers in emerging economies. We propose bailing in these other actors by making them shareholders in regional central banks and giving them a say in their management. Indeed, the key to well-capitalized and well-managed regional central banks is to have a diversified shareholder base. As the accompanying chart illustrates, regional central banks could have up to six classes of shareholders. From the public sector, the shareholders would include member states; member central banks; nonmember central banks, like the Fed, the Bank of Japan, and the European Central Bank; and international financial institutions such as the regional development banks, the IMF, and the World Bank. Private sector shareholders would include member banks and financial institutions, and individual and institutional investors.

Regional Central Bank Capitalization: Shareholder Structure

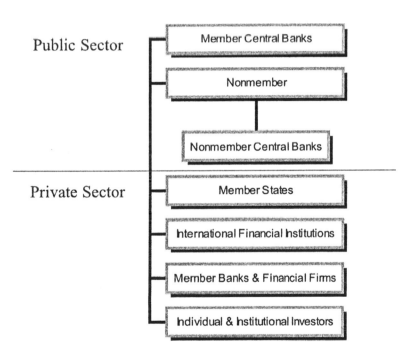

This diversified shareholding base would serve two purposes. First, it would help ensure good governance. Each class of shareholder—public and private, regionally based and international—would want to control and limit the perceived excesses and abuses of the other shareholders. This would create a healthy system of internal checks and balances, ensuring a more effective and transparent overall governance.

Second, a diversified shareholder base would significantly increase each central bank's capital and the reserves it has at its disposal. The principal shareholders of the regional central bank would be the member governments and their central banks, which would exchange their current hard currency reserves for a special class of RCB stock. In addition, the IMF might then allow these countries to deposit their newly acquired RCB stock to count against their IMF quotas as well; this "double counting" of reserves would not weaken the system but would increase the resources available to all countries and especially developing countries. The issuance of stock to member governments and central banks would provide the RCB with funds to buy up existing national currencies at an agreed-upon exchange rate and therefore would enable member countries to convert to a dollar or regional super-currency basis.

The pooling of existing member government reserves would create major economies of scale. ASEAN countries plus South Korea currently have foreign-exchange reserves totaling about $300 billion.[26] The Mercosur countries have reserves of about $80 billion—not substantial by Asian standards but still greater than the reserves Brazil had at the time of the Russian devaluation or that the IMF could muster in response to the crisis. By pooling resources in one regional central bank, member governments can defend one currency they all share more effectively than they can five or ten different currencies individually. One pool of $300 billion is much more powerful than ten little pools of $30 billion, especially when it comes to defending a currency or acting as a lender of last resort.

In most cases, the reserves of member governments would not by themselves meet all the needs of the new banks. Additional capital and reserves will be required. For that reason, the great central banks—namely, the Fed, the Bank of Japan, the European Central Bank, and perhaps such nonmember banks as the Bank

---

[26]IMF International Financial Statistics, vol. 53, no. 3 (March 2000).

of China—should be encouraged to take up significant equity positions in the regional central banks. These nonmember central banks would do so by exchanging currency and reserves in dollars, euros, or yen for RCB stock, thereby further adding to the regional central bank's reserves. (By capitalizing the value of swap agreements or other arrangements, the available reserves of the regional central banks could be greatly expanded beyond their nominal reserves.) Cross share holding among regional central banks would provide additional levels of insurance and stability by diversifying risk across many regions and economies.

The nonmember central banks would have several incentives for making these investments. Holding stock would permit them to participate in the management of the new banks, helping them avoid a regional regulatory failure that might affect their own financial health. It would also enable them to influence the evolution of financial systems of large emerging markets, thereby also producing potential benefits for their own financial firms and institutions.

From the standpoint of nonmember governments, the investment approach resolves some painful problems. Investments are not foreign-aid giveaways. Profitable investments that stabilize financial markets in developing economies are more beneficial than many types of conventional foreign aid, and they are much less politically difficult to get through legislatures. Such investments would also greatly reduce the need for emergency bailouts—while substantially increasing the funds available for financial emergencies.

Existing international financial organizations would also participate in the ownership and governance of the Banks. They would thus constitute another source of capital for the new institutions. In some cases, the existing development banks might evolve into regional central banks. The international financial institutions, including the IMF and the World Bank, would in any case play vital roles in providing policy advice, working to identify best practices, and otherwise contributing to the establishment of credible, solid institutions.

Finally, there would be the capitalization provided by private sector investors. At first glance, bailing in the private sector in this fashion may seem unorthodox. But in fact it is nothing new.

Many of the great central banks—including the Banks of England, France and the United States—began their lives as private institutions or with significant private equity. Indeed, private equity increased the reserves and credibility of these organizations, and allowed them to evolve into strong public institutions.

Central banks are profitable organizations and could attract significant flows of private capital. The Fed last year reported profits greater than the combined profits of the top four Fortune 500 companies.[27] The Bank of France was more profitable than any private company in the world. The Bank of Japan had a 1999 profit of $14.1 billion; the Bundesbank was a relative laggard, with profits of just $8 billion.[28] Assuming that the profitability of a regional central bank would resemble that of other central banks, a regional central bank for Latin America would see profits of more than $10 billion per year. And assuming it would have a price/earnings ratio similar to GE, a world-class financial services company, it would command a market capitalization well in excess of $500 billion. The limit to private-sector capitalization of regional central banks would not be their profitability, but rather a policy argument. For reasons relating to maintaining public control over these institutions, it would be desirable to limit the private sector's stake in any regional central bank to 49.9 percent of the equity. But even then private-sector investment would substantially increase the reserves and credibility of these institutions, and movements in their stock prices would provide the bank managers, as well as investors and the citizens of member countries with transparent performance measurements to consider when evaluating the bank's effectiveness.

In sum, by bailing in the private sector, regional central banks could command substantially greater resources than do the central banks of even the largest emerging economies. Regional central banks with hundreds of billions of dollars in equity and with many hundreds of billions more in reserves and swap and "rediscount" agreements to draw on would be powerful institutions.

---

[27] www.federalreserve.gov/boarddocs/press/general, January 6, 2000.
[28] www.boj.or.jp/en and www.bundesbank.de.

They could operate currency board arrangements without the artificial limits on monetary policy endured by, say, Argentina. They could also make provisions for lender-of-last-resort functions that are both more credible and less disruptive than the arrangements that now exist in most developing countries.

Recommendation 2: Create or adopt hard regional currencies.

One of the chief aims of international financial architecture reform should be to reduce long-term currency risk in emerging economies as part of a broader program of building more democratic capital markets. For that reason, our next recommendation is that regional central banks should create or adopt hard regional currencies as a way of overcoming the problems caused by the current system of soft national currencies.

By hard currency, we do not mean a currency with an overvalued exchange rate. Rather, we mean a currency so respected that regardless of a temporary exchange-rate fluctuation, lenders and investors are willing to make long-term commitments in that currency. Hard currency economies like the United States, the European Union, Switzerland, and Japan enjoy a singular advantage: foreign investors are willing to hold assets denominated in dollars, euros, Swiss francs, and yen for the long term, facilitating investment and avoiding the destabilizing currency and maturity mismatches mentioned earlier. The U.S. government can borrow on international markets in its own currency. Now with the euro so can most European governments, including Ireland, Spain, and Portugal, which only a decade ago were considered high-risk, low-investment-grade economies.

Currency questions are difficult. There are no perfect regimes, no one-size-fits-all solutions. Every alternative entails disadvantages and drawbacks. In seeking to establish a regional hard currency, then, regional central banks will need to pursue the path best suited to their region's development, trade, and investment needs. Over time, all regional central banks are likely to seek the goal of hard currencies with flexible exchange rates. However, each region will find its own path to the goal.

One short- to medium-term option for some regions would be to "dollarize"—to adopt a foreign hard currency as their own national currency. Under the dollarization option, a country would actually replace the banknotes in its own currency with banknotes from the hard currency country. Under today's conditions, that could mean not only the dollar but also the euro and yen. Given that no solution is perfect, for small countries with a history of inflation and currency devaluations, dollarization may be the fastest and perhaps only way to establish a hard currency. It may also make sense for countries and regions whose trade and investment flows are closely tied to one major reserve currency. For Mexico, Central America, and the Caribbean, for example, the dollar might well be the most logical currency for a regional bank to adopt. Similarly, a North African or East European regional central bank might find it makes sense to adopt the euro.

Other countries, however, face a more complex situation. In much of East Asia, trade and investment flows are divided between the dollar and the yen, and to a lesser extent the euro. The Mercosur countries of Latin America are oriented to both the euro and the dollar, as are southern and much of eastern Africa.

For these "mixed" regions, there is another option that would make more sense: namely, that regional central banks create "super-currencies." Regional super-currencies would be based either on a basket of the core currencies or on a simple parity rule—i.e., the regional currency would always be equal either to one dollar or one euro, whichever was lowest. These regional super-currencies—all them the yendo, the eurdo, and the euryendo—would replace national currencies among the member states of the regional central banks.

In choosing between dollarization and regional super currencies, regional central banks must look beyond the simple question of trade and investment flows. The two currency alternatives work very differently. Dollarization delivers the fastest results, and in the short term provides, where feasible, a quick and effective answer to the currency problem. Some of the common drawbacks associated with dollarization, such as the loss of seigniorage, can be eliminated or at least minimized through arrangements between the regional central banks and nonmember institutions like the Fed, the Bank of Japan, and the ECB.[29]

Moreover, the arguments that countries that dollarize would sacrifice monetary autonomy and lose the flexibility to use exchange rates to soften competitiveness losses are often exaggerated. In much of the world, these disadvantages are more apparent than real. As Ricardo Hausmann, chief economist of the Inter-American Development Bank, has pointed out in a comparative study of Latin American exchange-rate regimes, those countries operating under more flexible exchange-rate regimes, which were presumed to enjoy monetary autonomy, found themselves unable to use that autonomy when they needed it.[30] As noted earlier, the interest rates of emerging economies tend to track U.S. interest rates. But contrary to what one might expect, the correlation between U.S interest rate increases and those of Latin American countries was somewhat higher under flexible than under fixed rates. Such an outcome suggests that—at least in the case of Latin America—flexible rates may actually provide less monetary autonomy than is conventionally assumed.

Yet, as currency board economies like Hong Kong and Argentina have discovered, the shift to hard currency regimes can create problems and can impose competitiveness-related costs on the economy. Some of the competitiveness-related costs would be avoided under a regional central bank scenario, because most if not all of a country's major trading partners would be adopting the same exchange-rate policies. But while the problems associated with dollarization should not be overstated, neither should they be made light of. In fact, over time, the straitjacket of dollarization will grow tighter than is good for a growing economy. The seigniorage problems and the problem of monetary dependence on a foreign central bank become more severe as a growing economy needs an ever larger money supply.

---

[29]U.S. Senator Connie Mack (R-Fla.) has introduced a bill under whose terms the United States would rebate seigniorage to dollarizing economies.

[30]Ricardo Hausmann, Michael Gavin, Carmen Pages-Serra, Ernesto Stein, "Financial Turmoil and the Choice of the Exchange Rate Regime," Working Paper 400, Inter-American Development Bank, Washington, D.C., 1999.

With regional super currencies, however, the calendar works differently. Regional currencies must earn the trust of skittish markets; and, for that reason, interest rates in regional super-currency economies many fall more slowly than those in dollarizing economies. Meanwhile, in order to win the trust of markets, regional central banks would need to pursue more rigid exchange-rate policies to build confidence. As a practical matter, that means many of the regional central banks—whether they dollarize or create new regional super-currencies—may need to follow currency board rules. They will also need to be transparent in their operations and subject themselves to outside auditors in order to reassure skittish investors.

Over time, however, the inherent advantages of regional super-currencies would manifest themselves. Assuming prudent, solid currency management by the regional central bank, markets will learn to trust the new currency and interest rates will fall. Seigniorage problems would not exist. Because the profits of seigniorage would fall to the regional central bank, they could be used to increase the confidence and strength of the regional institutions or could be returned to governments to reduce indebtedness. Finally, regional super-currencies would allow the regional central bank some flexibility in maintaining the region's trade competitiveness with countries outside the region. As mentioned earlier, the yendo, for example, could track the lower of the dollar and the yen, thereby helping to insure countries within the region against currency-related trade shocks, such as those that hit the Southeast Asian economies prior to the Asian financial crisis.

Whatever policies they start with, the ultimate goal of regional central banks would be to enjoy the same monetary independence and policy flexibility that the Fed, the Bank of Japan, and the European Central Bank now have. This flexibility will become possible as the currencies gain credibility—as investors became comfortable in holding these currencies long term, and as long-term markets and foreign exchange markets denominated in these currencies develop.

Almost certainly, different regions would find different paths—and take different amounts of time—to reach the final goal of a hard currency that enjoys a significant degree of flexibility. In some cases, dollarization may be a necessary first step in this process: sending a powerful message both to markets and to the citizens of the member countries that a new era has dawned and that the old ways are gone. But once the new institutions and practices have established themselves, the dollarizing central bank might choose to introduce its own currency, under a currency board system, in parallel circulation with the external hard currency. Over time, the public could be encouraged to shift from the dollar (or euro or yen) into the regional currency, and by measured, slow, and prudent steps the regional central bank could move toward true monetary freedom.

For a country to give up its currency and monetary independence—whether by dollarizing or by joining a regional super-currency—is of course a radical step. But in a world of open capital markets and international financial integration, the advantages of having a hard currency clearly outweigh the short-term problems associated with dollarization or the adoption of a regional super-currency. Indeed, a hard currency is a prerequisite not only for reducing a major source of risk for foreign investors and thus for increasing long-term capital flows but also for developing the kind of deeper, more efficient capital markets needed for middle-class-oriented development. It is no coincidence that the only developing country with a thirty-year fixed-rate mortgage market is Panama, a dollarized economy.[31]

As a general rule, hard currency economies have a more stable and predictable business and investment environment and are less subject to the periodic financial crises that afflict soft currency economies. Achieving a hard currency would eliminate currency and maturity mismatches and thus one major source of crisis for many emerging economies. It would also lower the cost of capital and would permit companies as well as governments to borrow long term both domestically and internationally. Consider the beneficial effects the adoption of the euro has had even for heavily indebted countries like Italy. Bond yields, historically the

---

[31]Juan Luis Moreno-Villalaz, Minister of Economy and Finance for Panama. Information taken from his congressional testimony statement on June 22, 2000.

highest of any major euro-zone country, fell from nearly 14 percent in 1995 to below U.S. levels by late 1997. The Italian government can now borrow ten-year money at less than 6 percent, dramatically reducing its debt-service burden and freeing up money for other public investment purposes.[32]

Again the experience of Panama, a dollarized economy in Latin America, is instructive. Real interest rates in Panama have been relatively low and steady in comparison to other Latin American economies. Panama's sovereign spreads have been consistently lower than those of other Latin American countries. According to the JP Morgan Emerging Market Index, the average stripped spread on Panamanian bonds for a period from July 1996 to April 1999 was 405 basis points, with a brief spike to about 700 basis points in late August 1998 at the time of the Russian devaluation. Other major Latin American countries—Brazil, Mexico, Peru, and Venezuela—all saw higher average spreads in the period and higher peaks in 1998. Even Argentina, which enjoys lower interest rates as a result of its currency board arrangement, had a much higher average spread: more than 700 basis points. Only Costa Rica had lower spreads than Panama.[33]

Average Real Interest Rates Under Alternative Exchange Regimes In Latin America

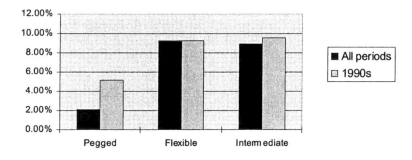

Source: Inter-American Development Bank

---

[32]J.P. Morgan Emerging Market Bond Index.
[33]See Zeljko Bogetic, "Official or Full Dollarization: Current Experiences and Issues," unpublished paper, June 1999, available from the author at the International Monetary Fund.

But perhaps, most importantly for middle-class-oriented development, the adoption of a hard currency would facilitate the deepening of domestic capital markets, including the development of a corporate bond market and a market for long-term mortgages. It would expand the access of ordinary citizens and small and medium-sized businesses to a whole range of financial services that are now available only to wealthy individuals and large companies, thus effectively ending the financial apartheid that exists in soft currency economies. Finally, by making it possible for utilities and other entities to borrow long term, adoption of a hard currency would greatly facilitate environmentally sound long-term investments. Energy efficient and/or renewable investments are often more capital intensive to build and only pay off over the longer term. Thus, soft currency countries are often forced to forego environmentally beneficial alternatives. With a hard currency, however, governments, utilities, and other agencies would be able to borrow long term and at lower rates, thus enabling them to take longer term environmentally related savings into account in their investment decisions.

Recommendation 3: Establish binding covenants for good governance and good policies.

Creating a hard currency system built around regional central banks in which investors can have confidence is a major step in the direction of a new international financial architecture. Critical as this is, it is only one step toward a middle-class-friendly international financial system. In order to develop the deep and efficient capital markets necessary to provide greater democratic access to reasonably priced credit, regional central banks—along with other elements of a regional financial architecture—would need to use their size and influence to facilitate the legal, fiscal, and regulatory reforms needed for the development of such markets.

Prospective membership in a well-capitalized, well-managed regional central banking and financial system would carry with it enormous benefits and advantages for member countries in the region: restructuring of existing debt; reduction of future borrowing costs; currency stability and greater access to the international capital markets; provision of a reliable lender of last resort; participation in liquid and efficient regional capital markets; increased technical assistance and financial help in the form of credit guarantees. Conversely, exclusion from such a system would entail serious economic costs for any country in the region. The benefits offered by regional central banks create incentives, including increased popular support, for elites to undertake meaningful legal and fiscal reform. The prospect of owning one's own home or starting one's own business ensures a popular constituency for reform now missing from IMF-led reform efforts.

For these reasons, a regional financial system would have significant leverage over prospective members, and it could use such leverage to promote real reforms. The positive inducements for reform that a regional central bank would be able to offer would make the reform process more like that entailed in the EU accession process than like the current system of IMF conditionality. The European Union requires that all prospective members participate in a lengthy accession process whereby they bring their economies, regulatory standards, and legal systems into conformity with EU standards. The EU accession process has thirty-one chapters of conditions and standards that prospective EU members must "close" before they are admitted to membership. In addition, those countries wanting to join the European Monetary Union must meet additional macroeconomic and debt-related standards. The EU process has been remarkably successful in transforming countries like Portugal, Spain, and Greece into law-based market democracies. Even the prospect of EU membership has spurred reforms in countries like Bulgaria, Slovakia, and Romania that many observers just a few years ago thought were impossible.

A similar but less extensive and onerous accession process should be established for membership in regional central banks and related regional financial institutions. As noted earlier, this EU-like process would create covenants of good governance and good policies for member governments. It would also establish an appropriate regulatory and supervisory framework for financial institutions operating under the regional central bank. It would do so by requiring adherence to the three agreements identified earlier as necessary for RCB membership: a fiscal stability pact; an agreement covering legal infrastructure and regulatory standards; and a third agreement relating to the RCB's regulatory authority.

Fiscal Stability Pact. Countries wanting to join a regional central bank would have to accept a fiscal stability pact, setting limits on the size, duration, and composition of fiscal deficits and on overall debt levels. Larger deficits would under certain circumstances be allowed for public investment purposes and during periods of economic downturns. Such limits would apply not merely to central government debts, but to all debt by all governmental and official bodies. The stability pact would include procedures for monitoring adherence to the pact and would provide for regular independent audits of the member governments.

Agreement on Legal Infrastructure and Regulatory Standards. Member governments would agree to establish and enforce common codes relating to a broad range of issues ranging from commercial codes, bankruptcy laws, judicial procedures, accounting standards, bank operations, shareholder rights, and other legal instruments deemed necessary to the creation of smoothly functioning capital markets. In addition, they would undertake to adopt common regional standards and regulatory codes for brokerages, insurance firms, investment banks, and other financial institutions.

Regulatory Charter. Member governments would also agree to a regulatory charter that would give the regional central bank regulatory powers over banks and most nonbank financial institutions. As part of this charter, member governments would require all banks, both foreign and domestic, as well as certain nonbank financial institutions operating in their territory, to receive RCB charters and accept RCB supervision. The regional central banks would have authority to conduct independent audits of all member banks and of all member states, including any provincial, regional, and municipal bodies involved in issuing debt. And in cooperation with the BIS and other international organizations, the regional central banks would ensure the transparent, honest, and efficient management of a regional system of bank regulation, including a deposit insurance program that primarily protects small retail deposits.

Recommendation 4: Create mechanisms for debt relief and restructuring and make markets in long-term member country debt.

The economic prospects of many developing countries are seriously constrained by excessive debt levels acquired over several decades of economic mismanagement and repeated currency crises. Several Latin American economies—for example, Bolivia, Ecuador, Panama, and Uruguay—have an international debt equal to more than 50 percent of GDP.[34] This debt overhang imposes an enormous debt-servicing burden on many developing countries, and greatly restricts their economic freedom and their ability to meet reasonable budget targets. Other countries face high levels of debt related to the costs of recent financial crises.

Becoming part of a regional hard currency zone would help countries reduce their debt-service burdens and their future borrowing costs. But some counties have debt levels that are inconsistent with the fundamental principles of the fiscal stability pact discussed in the last section. Rather than exclude these countries for past sins, it would be better to use accession to the regional central banks to reduce and restructure existing debt.

Countries agreeing to the fiscal stability pact would be eligible for a two-part process of debt reduction and restructuring. First, as part of the capitalization of the regional central bank, we would propose that both official and private sector creditors convert excess government debt into RCB equity and debt. In this way, all member governments would be able to clear unsustainable and crippling levels of debt off the balance sheet.

Second, for member countries that adhere to the stability pact, the regional central bank would assist these members with the underwriting and placement of long and short-term debt in international markets. Either directly or in cooperation with the private sector, it would also underwrite, insure, and securitize municipal, provincial, and central government debt as a way of lengthening the maturity structure on outstanding government debt. It would do so in consultation with national treasury authorities and at times in coop-

---

[34]United Nations: Economic Commission For Latin America and the Caribbean, *Economic Survey of Latin America and the Caribbean 1998–1999*, Santiago, Chile, 1999.

eration with regional development banks and the World Bank. By lengthening the maturity of existing debt and by reducing interest rates on all official debt, this process will make member governments less susceptible to future financial crises and thus less likely to put strains on the regional central bank's lender of last resort facilities.

Together these steps would drastically reduce the debt servicing costs of most emerging economy governments and open the doors to attractive new financing. As a result, member governments would find that they have more fiscal flexibility than before, even while observing fiscal stability pact limits.

One of the goals of the regional central banks in this debt restructuring process would be to create a long-term market for debt denominated in the new regional super-currency. At the beginning, this will require a clear RCB policy aimed at flattening the yield curve and extending debt maturities. Investors naturally will be cautious initially about making significant investments in long-term debt markets with only short-term track records, little liquidity, and considerable volatility. But at the outset, the regional central banks, in cooperation with the international financial institutions, can play a major role in creating and sustaining market confidence.

Market conditions for such an exercise may be favorable in the near-to-medium term, as the supply of investment grade, sovereign debt declines. The improved fiscal prospects of the European Union and the United States mean that the supply of long-term, high-grade government paper is likely to further decline over the next decade. Already the softening of long-term rates in gilts and U.S. Treasury bonds show the effect that a "bond famine" can have on interest rates. Thus, there may be a window of opportunity in the coming years for new institutions to develop new markets in new types of high-grade, long-term debt.

There are a number of steps the regional central banks, in cooperation with the international financial institutions, can pursue to take advantage of this window of opportunity. First, the regional central banks should issue investment grade paper of their own at a variety of maturities. Their substantial reserves would support a number of large debt issues. In order to help establish confidence in these instruments, the IMF and World Bank, the regional development banks, and nonmember central banks should make the political decision to hold some portion of their reserves in this RCB paper and to use RCB paper as a normal part of their operations.

Second, the World Bank should assist the process of creating a market in new super-currency denominated debt by providing guarantees on long-term issues. By insuring this paper, the World Bank can help make it attractive to entities like pension funds in advanced countries, which would be able to hold high grade, long term paper at attractive rates. Though insured, yields would still be sensitive to international and regional developments. Thus, as the various measures outlined in this report come into effect, it is likely that spreads between regional and G-3 long term paper would decline steadily, offering very significant rewards to those investors hardy enough to come in at the beginning. This payoff in itself would go far to bringing more participants into these markets.

There are other steps that can and should be taken to draw private participants into long- term regional debt markets. Favorable tax treatment on certain classes of long-term obligations would be a politically less sensitive and economically more effective form of development assistance than many traditional forms of aid. Governments in advanced countries could make commitments to place some of their current pension reserves in high-grade paper. This move would increase the yields that advanced countries receive on their pension trusts, and assure private investors that the market for regional paper would remain liquid far into the future.

Finally, the regional central bank in collaboration with interested member governments should explore ways of directing the savings of the region toward long-term investments in high-grade regional paper. Compulsory savings programs and state and private pension programs could be encouraged where they exist, and established where they do not, and authorized if not required to invest a given percentage of their assets in certain classes of securities. Once again, this would help reassure external investors of the security and stability of demand for these debt instruments.

At the same time, by using their retirement savings to fund such instruments as mortgage-backed securities and infrastructure bonds, the populations of these countries would in effect be borrowing money from themselves to build houses and improve their living conditions.

Recommendation 5: Create the financial markets and infrastructure for deep and liquid capital markets on a regional basis.

One of the main arguments of this report is that the availability of long-term home mortgages and financing for small and medium-size businesses is the key to both financial market development and middle-class-oriented development. Creation of mortgage-backed securities and other credit institutions for small and medium-sized businesses would lower borrowing costs for working people while empowering the banking system. The regional-based financial architecture outlined above affords an opportunity to develop these kinds of financial markets and instruments. But there will need to be a concerted effort to build a new infrastructure in member RCB countries in order to take advantage of this opportunity. This effort will require cooperation with the IMF, the World Bank, regional development banks, member and non-member governments, the private sector, and civil society.

Many of the financial institutions and markets envisioned here would need to be organized on a regional basis to take advantage of economies of scale and to ensure necessary liquidity and diversification of risk. Others, such as the popular financial institutions, would take on a more local or national character. But even in these cases, regional central banks would need to provide regional oversight and encourage securitization on a regional basis.

The primary tasks for regional central banks to build a middle-class-oriented financial markets in emerging economies include the following:

1) Create a long-term mortgage and small-business credit market by chartering and spinning off regional Fannie Mae–like

institutions for the insuring, bundling, securitization, and sale of mortgages and other debt;

2) Expand and deepen equity and debt markets by chartering and supervising investment banks aimed at underwriting corporate debt and initial public offerings, as well as by chartering and supervising for-profit pension management companies linked to compulsory savings programs;

3) Build a popular financial sector serving the needs of small and medium-sized businesses by chartering and supervising retail banks aimed at expanding credit to small and medium-sized enterprises, and by chartering and supervising popular financial institutions for mini-lending (loans up to $25,000) for ordinary working people.

Long-Term Mortgage Market. The development of a secondary debt market is essential for the expansion of reasonably priced credit for home ownership, small-business start-up expansion, and public infrastructure improvement. Once agreements on regional financial governance are in place, the regional central banks should have as a priority the chartering and launching of national and regional institutions, similar in some ways to U.S. institutions like Fannie Mae and Freddie Mac, that would securitize different types of securities: mortgage backed, small business loan backed, and infrastructure loans. These institutions, operating under close supervision and regulation, would bundle conforming loans into securities to be sold on regional and international capital markets.

As soon as would be feasible, these institutions would be privatized as for-profit publicly traded companies. Like the regional central banks themselves, they would be able to attract a substantial private shareholder base. As of the end of the second quarter 2000, Fannie Mae and Freddie Mac, the two largest such organizations in the United States, had a combined market capitalization of more than $80 billion.[35] Some of this equity would be distributed to existing shareholders in the RCBs; the rest

---

[35] Wall Street Journal, June 30, 2000, p. A10.

would be sold to the public. Member governments and central banks could retain their equity in these organizations or sell it to private investors, using the proceeds to increase or redeem RCB stock, or to further reduce debt.

Regional Equity and Debt Markets. The formation and effective regulation of nonbank capital markets would be another important objective of the regional financial architecture. As indicated earlier, most emerging economies are overly dependent on the banking sector and need to develop better regulated equity and debt markets. With the help of the World Bank's International Finance Corporation, the regional central banks could advance this goal in a number of ways. First, they could charter and supervise investment banks aimed at underwriting corporate debt and initial public offerings. Second, they could help create regional exchanges for the trading of equity and debt securities. Taking advantages of economies of scale, regionally organized exchanges would be better able to offer investors the liquidity and volume many larger investors need. Third, they could charter and supervise for-profit companies to manage pension funds linked to compulsory or state-assisted savings programs. These companies would become major investors in regional securities, and with certain limits, pension funds collected under compulsory savings programs could be invested in securities that promote socially desirable development, such as water treatment, mortgage lending, and small business loans.

Popular Financial Sector. The regional central banks would have a mandate to ensure the development of a healthy retail banking sector, whose mission is to provide banking and credit services to small borrowers. To this end, they would develop a system of bank charters for small retail institutions, with limits placed on the size of deposits they can accept and loans they can extend to a single borrower. Such loans might also be limited as to purpose. If regulated closely and supervised properly, these institutions can and should be capitalized on liberal terms with credits from the World Bank and regional development banks for the purpose of assisting such small organizations to meet capital adequacy standards. In addition, the regional central bank should charter nonbank financial institutions to fund small and medium-sized business, with mandates ranging from mini-lending (loans up to $25,000) to operations in support of medium-sized businesses with revenues in the range of $50 million. The regional central bank and its branches would take care to ensure that applications for charters for these institutions would be issued to groups representing a variety of local and civic interests. Once experience shows that such ventures are profitable, the regional central bank would be able to issue debt for purposes of investment in these institutions without compromising its credit rating.

Regional central banks, development banks, national governments, international aid agencies, and the nongovernmental organization (NGO) sectors will all have a role to play in developing more efficient democratic capital markets in emerging economies. By working to train and assist ordinary people to harness the full power of the modern credit system, they would help them to take control of their own lives and shape the destinies of their families and communities. In this and other ways, a reformed international financial architecture could stimulate a vast and unpredictable range of human progress and development, and give hundreds of millions if not billions of people new hope for a new century.

CONCLUSION: THE POLITICS OF INTERNATIONAL FINANCIAL ARCHITECTURE

If we have discussed financial architecture in three dimensions, the reason is at least partly because international financial architecture must ultimately function in the fourth dimension: the dimension of politics. Without a sufficient basis of political support in advanced and developing countries alike, no proposals for economic reforms, however well intended or conceived, can succeed in the real world.

The political challenges to international financial architecture are tough and getting tougher. In many important countries, both developed and developing, public support for current international economic policy and reform efforts is disturbingly low, yet the challenges facing the international economy suggest that more, not less, political commitment will be required in coming years.

Any consideration of the fourth dimension must begin with the United States, the country that remains the most important single actor in the field of international financial and economic policy. The end of the Cold War initiated profound changes in the politics of American foreign policy whose full effects are only beginning to be seen. Politically, the end of the Cold War has substantially reduced the willingness of the American people to make sacrifices of any kind for the sake of foreign policy objectives. Across the board, we see declining support for foreign aid, for international cooperation that is perceived to place limits on American unilateral action, or for trade agreements perceived as benefiting other countries at the expense of American workers.

Institutionally, since the end of the Cold War, executive authority in foreign policy has tended to diminish, while the authority of Congress has increased. In wartime or even Cold Wartime conditions, Congress tends to defer to presidential authority; in peacetime, Congress historically is far more assertive. Trade policy and international financial policy were once considered part of a broader Cold War strategy of wielding the Free World together into a coherent, prosperous, and stable anticommunist alliance. With this consideration removed, Congress feels much more free to question and counter executive proposals and policy.

At the grass-roots level, growing opposition to the current direction of international economic policy is found among trade unionists, environmental activists, churches, right wing populists, and some human rights activists. While originating in opposition to trade agreements and policies perceived as flawed, this opposition now focuses increasingly on the institutions and practices of international financial institutions such as the World Bank and the IMF. Thanks in large part to the power of the Internet, this opposition is increasingly international and coordinated, and may pose a significant long-term threat to the sustainability of current policy.

Taken together, these conditions and forces have substantially reduced the ability of the U.S. government to pursue a vigorous and consistent foreign policy. These effects are not limited to international financial policy. Rather, the failure of agreements like the Kyoto Protocol to gain congressional support, the defeat of the Comprehensive Test Ban Treaty, the loss of fast-track negotiating authority, and the long, slow, and apparently inexorable decline of foreign aid all point to decreased executive effectiveness in foreign policy generally, as well as in foreign economic and financial policy specifically.

For somewhat different reasons, both Japan and the EU nations also face serious obstacles in summoning the will and the resources for strong and effective action. Japan, while increasingly interested in supporting the development of regional institutions in Asia, is hampered by its own growing debt, recent poor economic performance, and the prospect of massive and costly measures ahead as its number of pensioners skyrockets while its active labor force shrinks. Additionally, Japan faces constraints on its ability to act independently; it prefers to act in association with the United States and it remains unwilling to transform the yen into a true international currency.

Preoccupied with the consequences first of monetary union and later by the institutional reforms and economic consequences of enlargement, the European Union also has relatively little political energy to spare for questions of global financial policy and reform. Moreover, key elements of the current international reform agenda are distasteful to broad and influential sectors of EU opinion. Concerned about both the "Anglo-Saxon model of capitalism" and the "Washington consensus," both public and elite opinion in much of the European Union have serious questions about the viability or the desirability of the current international architecture and agenda. This doubt is reinforced by a growing desire on the part of some important EU institutions and member states to reduce what some see as excessive U.S. influence in the international order. Concretely, that has expressed itself as dismay over the degree to which the United States used the international financial institutions to bail out Mexico at the time of the 1994–95 crisis. Political conflicts and tensions between the United States and the European Union have already been exacerbated by growing trade conflicts, as well as by divisions over military and security issues (for example, U.S. interest in a national missile defense program). Such a situation is likely to weaken the ability of the international financial system to mobilize either the financial resources or the political commitments necessary for pursuing a vigorous policy of reform.

The internal problems and lack of consensus among the world's leading economies are particularly troubling when considered against the degree to which the current reform agenda has run up against strong and resourceful opposition in the developing world. Western observers often underestimate the political obstacles that financial system reform faces in the developing world. The allocation of credit, for example, by government agencies or informal channels to favored borrowers has become in many countries one of the key pillars of state authority and national unity. In countries like Malaysia, where maintaining a balance among ethnic and religious groups is critical to national unity, any reforms that threaten the state's ability to use credit allocation as a political tool threaten, potentially, the most vital interests of the state. Even where the ethnic tensions of a Malaysia are absent, credit allocation in many countries remains one of the chief means by which political elites cement power and maintain national harmony.[36]

Given this consideration, it is not surprising that most developing countries have moved slowly, reluctantly, and only very short distances when it comes to reform of their credit and finance systems. The link between politics and credit allocation is simply too strong for the forces arrayed against it to make much progress. Reform often is casual, spotty, and "para o Inglês ver," in the old Brazilian expression: "for the Englishman to see." Sheer financial necessity is likely to drive a continuing reform process in many countries, but the likelihood is that many will end up back in the "policy swamp" we described at the beginning of this paper, where necessity has forced the start of a reform process, but the political will and ability to carry the process through to a successful conclusion is lacking. Unless conditions change, for the foreseeable future many countries are likely to suffer the consequences of failed or incomplete reform processes, and the international system itself will suffer an increased risk of shocks, contagion, and disturbance as volatile international markets subject weak and poorly regulated financial systems in emerging economies to great stress.

The recommendations we make are intended, among other things, to improve the political context of the international financial system. Reinforcing the regional pillar of the international system and shifting toward middle-class-oriented development strategies can substantially strengthen the political support for necessary economic reforms and policies in developed and developing countries alike.

In the United States, moving toward market-based, middle-class-oriented development policies can attract support from a range of political positions and forces. From a trade-union perspective, encouraging middle-class development around such initiatives as mortgage banking and securitization represents a much desired shift

---

[36]For further discussion, see Hilton L. Root, "Korea's Comeback: The Government's Predicament," paper from the Project on Development, Trade, and International Finance, Council on Foreign Relations, New York, 2000.

of policy away from encouraging export growth in emerging economies. Labor leaders can convincingly and explain to their members that the new U.S. policy is aimed at reducing export dependency in the developing world and also at increasing demand for U.S.-made products in foreign markets. Increasing employment in developing countries based on growth in domestic demand will tend to raise wages in developing countries while reducing the importance of anti-union laws and policies. Environmentalists will find that these policies offer significantly greater scope for environment-friendly projects—yet business will find that these reforms increase opportunities for profitable activities around the world.

For the European Union, the policies we propose address some of the social model concerns that many Europeans have with the current direction of international economic policy. They also give European institutions, especially the ECB, an expanded global role. Our proposals also hold out the possibility of increased U.S. and Japanese commitments to the financial health of some of the peripheral European and Mediterranean economies (Morocco, Algeria, Egypt, Turkey, Ukraine, Belarus, Russia, the Caucasian states, Romania, and Bulgaria) whose well-being matters to the key EU members.

Similarly for Japan, the ability to pursue a program of regional cooperation and monetary stabilization in East Asia with the active blessing and support of the United States could help solve major foreign policy and economic problems.

In developing countries as well, the financial architecture proposals in this paper have the potential to win broad support from many sectors of society. Middle-class development programs will prove broadly popular among those newly able to purchase homes, to build businesses, to benefit from newly possible infrastructure programs, and to invest their money in a solid and sound financial system using a currency that can serve as a lasting store of value. These recommendations would end the association of reform with austerity and recession and make reform, potentially, a populist rallying cry. Nationalist and anti-colonial feeling would welcome the rise of regional institutions as an improvement—even if only an incremental one—over the current system in which the

IMF appears to serve as the de facto policy-making body of some developing country governments. For elites, the dangers of losing control over the credit allocation process would be offset to a large degree by the much greater availability of credit. Middle-class-oriented policies offer the prospect of enhanced social stability and reduced conflict even as economies shift to more market-based rather than influence-based methods of credit allocation.

APPENDIX: MAKING DOLLARIZATION WORK

As noted in the text above, dollarization, or the adoption of an external hard currency by a country or group of countries, has both advantages and drawbacks. The chief advantages—that dollarization may be the fastest way both to capture the public imagination for a new policy and to reduce interest rates for domestic borrowers in a dollarizing economy—are most important in the initial phases of a shift to a hard currency policy. Later, the disadvantages of dollarization over other hard currency strategies—particularly, the loss of seigniorage and the lack of monetary autonomy—begin to take a larger toll.

It is, however, possible to offset some of these disadvantages with the right policy mix and some assistance from the "home country" of the chosen hard currency. That assistance is most likely to be forthcoming when the dollarizing countries are close to the home nation or, in the case of the euro, the home region.

As an example, dollarization under certain circumstances could become a viable, long-term option for Mexico and the Caribbean if the United States and, to a lesser degree, Canada, were willing to support some policies that would ensure a steady flow of U.S. dollars into the Mexican and Caribbean economies. These policies would involve a substantial, long-term commitment but could well result in a successful long-term shift of Mexico, Central America, and the Caribbean to a dollar economy.

The first program would involve massive infrastructure investment. In the Mexican case, a tripartite "NAFTA Commission" made up of representatives from each of the NAFTA governments, would let contracts and, with government backing, guarantee bond issues for a series of infrastructure projects: highways and roads, water treatment plants and sewage facilities, electricity generating stations, among others. These projects would cumulatively be large enough to provide a significant boost to the Mexican economy during the early years of dollarization, while dollarization would reduce the interest cost of the projects and extend the maturity of the loans.

It is easier to win political support for loan guarantees than for direct aid programs, and there are several additional steps that could be taken to gain the necessary political support for such an infrastructure initiative. Thus, for example, the projects funded under this initiative would have to meet environmental tests, and contractors participating in these programs would have to observe basic labor rights. Additionally, a proportion of the equipment and materials used by the projects would be purchased in the United States and Canada.

Second, simultaneously with such an infrastructure initiative, the United States, Canada, Mexico, and other countries in the region would embark on a "regional retirement program"—a series of measures aimed at facilitating and promoting the voluntary relocation of retired U.S. and Canadian citizens into the region. Agreements covering tax, property, and estate matters would be part of this package; so, crucially, would be agreements by the U.S. authorities to reimburse qualified health-care facilities abroad for the treatment of U.S. citizens covered by Medicare and other public insurance programs.

With seventy million U.S. residents expected to reach sixty-five years of age during the next thirty years, and with many retired households unable to afford the standard of living they desire in the United States, a substantial number of retirees will seek warmer weather and lower prices in Mexico and the Caribbean. These retirees and the insurance programs that cover their health needs would, ultimately, pump hundreds of billions of dollars into the regional economies.

The combination of an infrastructure program in the early years, with a regional retirement program whose full effects would only gradually be felt, would assure a constantly growing stream of dollars into the regional economies and substantially reduce any problems that dollar shortages or the loss of seigniorage would create for the economic development prospects of the region.

In the case of the euro, candidates for "euro-ization" would be countries that could ultimately be expected to join the European

Union. The removal of the currency risk for investors, together with the prospect of ultimate EU membership, would help bring in enough foreign exchange to maintain liquidity in these economies during the run-up to membership. Infrastructure programs and other forms of assistance from the European Union would also help; so too would euro-denominated remittances from citizens admitted as temporary workers.

Without this kind of policy support, however, it is likely that dollarization could only serve as a transitional economic regime for emerging economies; over the long term, more durable, less constrained answers to the currency question would have to be found.

Private Capital
Flows, Emerging
Economies, and
International
Financial
Architecture

A Paper from the Project on Development,
Trade and International Finance

Glenn Yago

A Council on Foreign Relations Paper

Private Capital Flows, Emerging Economies, and International Financial Architecture[1]

INTRODUCTION

Firms and development strategies based on a rear-view mirror view will leave companies, projects, and entrepreneurs scrambling for capital access. The control of capital in the developed world continues to shift away from private and state-owned institutions and toward public markets. Small and medium-sized firms with the best prospects for innovation and income/wealth generation need to be liberated from their dependence upon bank-based financial systems. They must also have the ability to turn to market-based systems with access to institutional capital providers at home and abroad.[2]

---

[1]This paper was presented to a meeting of the Council on Foreign Relations Working Group on Trade, Development, and International Finance, New York, New York, June 10, 1999. It represents ongoing work underway at the Milken Institute with my colleagues Lalita Ramesh, James Barth, and R. Dan Brumbaugh.
[2]The credit channel magnifies monetary/financial shocks disproportionately on the basis of firm size. During the Korean crisis, spreads (which capture credit channel effects) were disproportionately larger for small and medium-sized enterprises, which had no access to close substitutes for bank credit. This echoes classic credit crunch problems in the U. S. markets as well which gave rise to financial innovations and new capital market developments in the 1970s and 1980s. See Ilker Domac and Giovanni Ferri, "The Real Impact of Financial Shocks: Evidence from Korea," World Bank Working Paper (Washington, D.C., World Bank, October 1998).

Discussion of financial architecture cannot be separated from the problems of concentration of political power, industrial control, and financial capital. Growth and equity in the economy is limited by entrepreneurs' dependence upon commercial banks that are state-owned or directed, and thus historically removed from shareholder and creditor accountability. If politically connected holding companies can shift most of their liabilities to a few subsidiaries and then give those units to the government for liquidation through restructuring authorities, new investment will not occur. As the *Wall Street Journal* recently reported, hints of recovery promoted by financial assistance packages may well have stalled efforts at financial reform and corporate restructuring.[3] In Thailand, where thousands of companies stopped paying their debt in 1997, restructuring is at a standstill. In Malaysia, corporate debtors have been insulated with a government-directed credit committee. In South Korea, *chaebols* have expanded their debt and state-linked companies and family conglomerates have resisted change throughout the crisis countries.

Table 1 and Figure 1 recite the rescue packages in East Asia, Russia, and Brazil. This suggests that existing financial-aid strategies

Table 1. Rescue Packages in East Asia, Russia, and Brazil: 1997–98 (Billions of U.S. dollars.)

Country	IMF	Multilateral	World Bank	Bilateral	Total	Total as a Percent of 1997 GDP	Total as a Percent of 1997 Bank Assets
Indonesia	11.2	10.0	5.5	26.1	42.3	19.7	43.8
Korea	20.9	14.0	10.0	23.3	58.2	13.2	16.3
Thailand	4.0	2.7	1.5	10.5	17.2	10.9	7.0
Russia	11.2	1.5	1.5	9.9	22.6	5.1	17.2
Brazil	18.0	9.0	4.5	14.5	41.0	5.2	7.7

[3]"Bankers Worry that Signs of Asian Recovery will Forestall Crucial Corporate Restructurings," *Wall Street Journal,* April 28, 1999. In a study of 106 bankruptcies of 4,569 publicly traded East Asian firms, Stijn Claessens, Simeon Djankov, and Leora Klapper found that the likelihood of bankruptcy filing is lower for firms with ownership links to banks and families, controlling for leverage and Tobin's Q. See "Resolution of Corporate Distress: Evidence from East Asia's Financial Crisis," World Bank Working Paper (Washington, D.C.: World Bank, May 1999).

Figure 1. Increasing Financial Assistance From the IMF: 1980–98

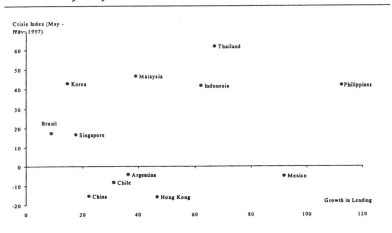

have effectively recapitalized not only existing banking institutions, but also a considerable proportion of the respective countries' economies. The growth and expansion of bank credit supported by this assistance appears to have exacerbated these crises.

Figure 2 correlates the growth in lending with a crisis index (the sum for each country of the depreciation rate minus the percentage change in international reserves). The countries with the

Figure 2. Bank Credit Boom: 1990–96

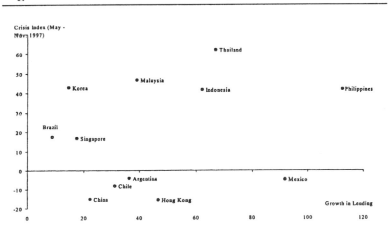

highest rates of bank-credit growth had the highest crisis index ratings as well. Similar to banking and financial institution crises in developed countries, the combination of real estate overexposure and restrictive regulation appears to have contributed to these ongoing crises (see Table 2 and Table 3). The dominance of banks and underdevelopment of secondary debt and equity markets along with the minimal role of privately owned or directed debt and equity capital sources (see Figures 3 and 4) is suggestive of the fundamental structural problems in financial reform and capital access for more entrepreneurial growth.

Policy failures in crisis countries converted national savings into nonperforming loans. The fact that savings can be invested inefficiently and retard growth is at the core of the financial architecture debate. As Rene Stulz has recently argued, differences in the organization of financial activities affects business formation and the efficiency of investment in existing firms. A growing body of empirical research supports this conclusion.[4]

Table 2. Commercial Property Price Declines, Bank Real Estate Exposure, Bank Restructuring Cost and Bank Ownership

Country	Percentage Commercial Property Price Decline	Bank Real Estate Exposure (%)	Cost of Bank Restructuring (Percent of GDP)	Limitation on Foreign Ownership of Domestic Bank	Percentage of Commercial Bank Total Assets	
Japan	68.3	NA	20	No	7	0
Thailand	48.3	30–40	30	Yes	19	7
Indonesia	35.0	25–30	19	Yes	7	43
Hong Kong	28.4	40–55	NA	No	67	0
Korea	23.0	15–25	30	Yes	6	0
Malaysia	14.0	30–40	20	Yes	21	10
Singapore	11.0	30–40	NA	Yes	44	0
Philippines	8.0	15–20	NA	Yes	14	20

Source: Bank for International Settlements, World Bank, [U.S.] Office of the Comptroller of the Currency, U.S. Treasury Department, and Bertrand Renaud

[4]For a review of this empirical literature, see Rene Stulz, "Financial Structure, Corporate Finance, and Economic Growth," Annual Bank Conference on Development Economics (Washington, D.C.: World Bank, June 1999).

Table 3. Real Estate Investment, Development, and Management as Allowable Activities of Commercial Banks and Bank Problems in Selected Countries: 1997

Income Group	Subgroup	Yes	No
Low Income		Armenia*, Gambia*, Moldova*	Albania*, Ghana*, Madagascar*, Mozambique*, Pakistan*, Rwanda*, Tanzania**, Zimbabwe*
Middle Income	Lower	Russia**, Peru*, Suriname, Belarus*, Korea*, Papua New Guinea*, Philippines**, Thailand**	Belize, Bolivia*, Fiji*, Guatemala, Guyana*, Jordan**, Latvia**, Morocco, Namibia, Tonga
Middle Income	Upper	Czech Republic*, Estonia**, Hungary*, Isle of Man, Poland*, Saudi Arabia, Seychelles, Slovakia*, South Africa**	Bahrain, Barbados, Botswana*, Brazil*, Chile**, Lebanon**, Malaysia**, Malta, Mexico**, Oman, Turkey**, Venezuela**

(cont.)

Table 3. (continued)

High Income	OECD Countries	Austria Canada* Denmark* Finland** France* Germany* Iceland*	Luxembourg Netherlands New Zealand* Norway** Switzerland United Kingdom	Australia* Belgium Greece* Ireland* Italy*	Japan* Portugal Spain** Sweden** United States*
	Non-OECD Countries	Aruba Cayman Islands Guernsey[1]	Hong Kong[1] Netherlands Antilles	Cyprus Gibraltar[1] Kuwait**	Liechtenstein Qatar Slovenia*

Note: Countries with a * denotes a significant banking problem and a ** denotes a banking crisis during the 1980 to 1998 period. A "crisis" refers to runs or other substantial portfolio shifts, collapses of financial firms, or massive government intervention. A "significant problem" refers to extensive unsoundness short of a crisis.

How can we move beyond obfuscatory language and the growing policy backlash against globalization and global capital markets and disentangle the policies that could restore world economic growth and keep it alive?

Figure 3. Commercial Bank Total Assets Relative to Equity Market Capitalization and Bonds Outstanding for Selected Countries: 1997

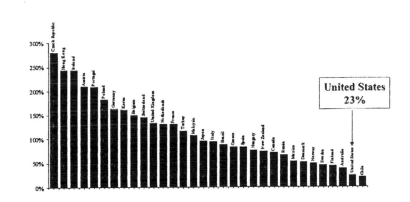

Figure 4. Relationship between GNP per capita and Percentage of Private Ownership of Commercial Bank Assets for Selected Countries: 1997

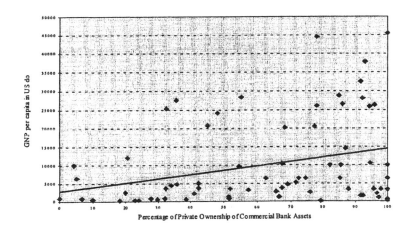

CONTAGION AS METAPHOR

Contagion hysteria has infected most intelligent discussions about global financial policies since the Asian crisis struck in the summer of 1997. But is fear of "contagion" a sociological, psychological, and political phenomenon, or is it an economic one? Careful economic analysis emerging from the crisis confirms the interdependence of national economies, but does not confirm some kind of pathological and irrational "contagion." Common structural problems in those economies most exposed to crisis persist.[5] "The contagion" characterization of the global financial crisis basically pathologizes and institutionalizes bad economic policies and financial practices.[6] For example, contagion language paints Argentina and Chile with the brush of Brazil. Michael Bordo and

---

[5]Aaron Tornell, *Common Fundamentals in the Tequila and Asian Crises*, Working Paper (Cambridge, Mass.: Harvard University and National Bureau of Economic Research, July 1998); James R. Barth, R. Dan Brumbaugh, Lalita Ramesh, and Glenn Yago, "The Role of Governments and Markets in International Banking Crises: The Case of East Asia," in George Kaufman, ed., *Research in Financial Services: Private and Public Policy*, vol. 10 (New York: JAI Press, Inc., 1998), pp. 177–233.

[6]"Contagion" was indeed the most overused word to describe the global crisis both in the press and including the recently released *Economic Report of the President*, February 1999. Carmen Reinhart and Graciela Kaminsky define contagion as a situation where a crisis elsewhere increases the probability of a crisis at home even when the fundamentals are accounted for. Possible transmission channels of "contagion"—international bank lending, cross-market hedging, and bilateral and third-party trade in propagating crisis—are found to be indistinguishable from trade-linked effects; see "On Crisis, Contagion and Confusion," Working Paper (University of Maryland at College Park, 1999). Robert Rigobon examined the correlation between Mexican and Argentinean stock markets and finds no evidence of such contagion in any recent crisis when account is taken of endogenicity, unobservable variables, and changes in the variance of stock market returns. In fact, there is little to distinguish this recent financial crisis from earlier ones; see "On the Measurement of Contagion," presentation at Conference on Globalization, Capital Markets Crises, and Economic Reform (Cartagena, Colombia, January 1999). Sergio Schmukler and Graciela Kaminsky examine financial cycles in twenty-eight countries during the last two decades, looking at duration of upturns and downturns, amplitude, and spillover effects across countries and regions. They find that financial cycles have not become more unstable in the 1990s and that they replicate experience with Latin America in the 1980s; see "On Booms and Crashes: Are Financial Cycles Changing," Working Paper (Washington, D.C.: George Washington University, 1999).

Anna Schwartz lead us to a more differentiated conclusion about the propagation effects of structural crises:

> Pure contagion would occur only in circumstances in which other emerging countries were free of the problems facing the first emerging country. We know of no evidence of pure contagion. Transmission is another story. Shocks to one country will spill over to other countries through trade and the capital accounts. When investors withdraw their capital from countries with the same problems as were present in the first such country, this is a demonstration effect, not contagion.[7]

When used in analyzing financial crises, contagion language employs a sometimes lethal metaphor of fear to supplant empirical analysis. As cultural critic Susan Sontag long ago observed, using illness as a metaphor can have damaging consequences for those afflicted.[8] This is as true in clinical situations in economics and finance as in medicine. The contagion metaphor has stigmatizing effects through the myths it creates; damaging the prospects of recovery both in diagnosing the problems and resolving them. Fear and loathing about globalization becomes common when such rhetoric dominates debates.[9]

International economic integration has always been a politically contentious topic. A spate of new books and conferences from Davos to Delhi have provided caricatures of the capital market operations and financial-institution complexity that drive expanded participation in the global economy.[10] But most empirical evidence

---

[7]Michael D. Bordo and Anna J. Schwartz, "Under What Circumstances, Past and Present, Have International Rescues of Countries in Financial Distress Been Successful?" Working Paper no. 6824 (Cambridge, Mass.: National Bureau of Economic Research, December 1998), pp. 44–45.

[8]Susan Sontag, *Illness as Metaphor* (New York: Farrar, Straus & Giroux, 1990).

[9]See *New York Times* series on Global Contagion, February 15–18, 1999, and its editorial "Global Markets Lethal Magic," February 21, 1999.

[10]Timothy Goringe, *Fair Shares: Ethics and the Global Economy* (London and New York: Thames & Hudson, May 1999); Dani Rodrik, *The New Global Economy and Developing Countries: Making Openness Work* (Washington, D.C.: Overseas Development Council, November 1998); Harry Shutt, *The Trouble with Capitalism: An Enquiry into the Causes of Global Economic Failure* (New York: St. Martin's Press, Inc., August 1998).

suggests that continued crises reflect the persistence of corporatist and socialist statist economies, not entrepreneurially driven market economics.

Nevertheless, the policy backlash against globalization permeates most discussions about the global financial crisis. Reaction to the Anglo-American model of financial liberalization is widespread. The vice finance minister of Japan, Eisuke Sakakibara, put it this way:

> The Asian financial crisis occurred not because Asia had a problem. The problem is the global capitalism that allows funds to move all over the world based on a profit-oriented motive.[11]

Or take the position articulated by Karel van Wolferen:

> The project of a globalized economic order ruled by unregulated markets is utopian, as much as the notion of the withering away of the state was in Communist imagery.[12]

Or former Mexican President Carlos Salinas de Gortari:

> Insisting that North American neoliberalism is the only way turns people into enemies of the market because they see the markets as enemies of the people.[13]

Lionel Jospin (prime minister of the Republic of France), Gerhard Schroeder (chancellor of the Federal Republic of Germany), Oskar Lafontaine (finance minister of the Federal Republic of Germany), and other European Union political leaders continue to hammer away at the need for new international regulation and state-mediated responses as opposed to market responses.[14]

Compare this blame-mongering by politicians to the recently released essay by the currently embattled former deputy Malaysian prime minister, Anwar Ibrahim, who introduces his per-

---

[11]Eisuke Sakakibara, "Mahathir is Right," *New Perspectives Quarterly* (Winter 1999), p. 10.

[12]Karel van Wolferen, "The Global Conceptual Crisis," *New Perspectives Quarterly*, vol. 16/1 (Winter 1999), p. 17.

[13]Carlos Salinas de Gortari and Roberto Mangabeira Unger, "From North Atlantic Neoliberalism to Market Pluralism," *Challenge*, vol. 41/6 (February-March 1999).

[14]Oskar Lafontaine and Christa Mueller, *Keine Angst vor der Globalisierung* [*Don't Fear Globalization*] (Frankfurt: Dietz Verlag, 1998).

spective by noting that ". . .it is not normal to conduct economic discourse from behind prison walls." He writes:

> Do we not take the individual and collective responsibility for our problems, just as we have taken credit for our successes in the last decade?. .Asian nations would do well to put their houses in order first. The international financial system does indeed need a new architecture, but structural reforms must begin at home. . . The Asian renaissance should encompass not only political transparency and better corporate governance, but also reforms to society and culture, and respect for human rights, the environment and the independence of the judiciary. Without this commitment to these values, debate on resolving the Asian crisis may well turn out to be mere lip service.[15]

Taking Anwar's lead, we should deconstruct the debate about global financial architecture. We must understand both its context and component parts. In this paper, we focus upon the emerging globalization backlash in policy that could limit future capital and job formation in both emerging and developed economies. Discussions of global financial architecture, when decomposed, represent a new technocratic language that obscures discussion of the structural problems. At the recent Davos conference of the World Economic Forum, for example, there was a great deal of discussion about protectionism, prospective government controls over capital flows, exchange rate differentials, and mergers and acquisitions.[16]

Remarkably absent was a discussion of how new job, income, and wealth creation are to occur in Europe and in the transition and emerging economies, particularly during the process of business consolidation, restructuring, and transition to the new economy. These topics lead to the fundamental question of alternative regulatory proposals to achieve those goals.

---

[15] http://members.tripod.com/~Anwar_Ibrahim/main.htm

[16] Lawrence Minard, "What They Didn't Talk About in Davos," *Forbes Global* (February 22, 1999), p. 2.

The following questions need to be discussed as we evaluate discussions of global financial architecture.

- How much globalization is there?

- Does globalization exacerbate inequality?

- How significant are the benefits of globalization?

- Are global governance structures adequate to deal with globalization?

- Are financial integration and globalization to blame for crises and volatility, or do they simply reflect structural problems in corporate governance and unevolved financial institutions and capital markets?

- Does global capital market integration require the loss of national macroeconomic policy autonomy?

- Can the International Monetary Fund and World Bank—designed for a world of fixed exchange rates and limited capital mobility—promote stability in a radically changed world, or do their practices destabilize markets further?

Globalization and Deglobalization: Back to the Future?
Today's globalization is a resumption of trends that preceded World War I. Indeed, many of the present debates about globalization echo debates of that period. In examining globalization before World War I, a sobering picture emerges. The economy of the late nineteenth century was one of rapid globalization: capital and labor flowed and commodity trade boomed as transport costs dropped. The convergence of incomes, prices, and wages that occurred from 1850–1914, due to open trade and mass immigration, came to a halt between 1914–50 as deglobalization and autarky emerged as dominant economic and political forms.

An important lesson from the implosion of past globalization is that growing nation-state and intra-state inequality created a backlash against globalization. Significant distributional events caused a drift toward more restrictive policies—in trade, migration, and capital flows. The deglobalization implosion after 1914 was not independent of economic events. The retreat from open immigration policies was driven by a defense of the deteriorating relative position of the working poor. The retreat from free trade that culminated in rabid protectionism after World War I was manifested in protection of domestic agriculture from negative price shocks associated with globalization and trade-induced deterioration in the relative economic position of classes within Europe and the United States.[17]

---

[17]As Jeffrey Williamson writes, "(Prior to World War I) the evolution of well-functioning global markets in goods and labor eventually brought a convergence between nations. This factor price convergence planted, however, seeds for its own destruction since it created rising inequality in labor-scarce economies and falling inequality in labor-abundant economies. The voices of powerful interest groups who were hit hard by these globalization events were heard, however, and these were in particular the ordinary worker in labor scarce economics and the landlord in the labor abundant economies. These interest groups generated a political backlash against immigration and trade, and this backlash, which had been building up for decades, was brought to a head by event around World War I." See *Journal of Economic Perspectives*, vol. 12/4 (Fall 1998), p. 61.

THE INTEGRATION OF GLOBAL
CAPITAL MARKETS

Today globalization, particularly of capital markets, is both exaggerated and can be reversed as it has been in the past.

The two driving forces of globalization are technology and liberalization. The natural barriers of time and space that separate national markets are collapsing at record speed as communications, information, and transportation technologies have transformed and integrated national economies.

In examining product, labor, and capital markets, the degree of integration can be overstated. Though the ratio of trade to output in product markets has increased sharply in most countries since World War II, it is not substantially higher in Western European countries than it was in 1914, and in Japan it is relatively less. Price convergence across countries is still elusive, and other indicators of product market integration still lag. Financial markets are also not fully integrated. Until recently, the index of capital controls was declining and net private capital flows by banks, foreign direct investment, and portfolio investment were increasing.[18] The strict test of capital market integration—real (inflation-adjusted) interest rates—should converge; but real interest rates differ substantially. Only 10 percent of domestic investment in emerging economies has been financed from abroad. Foreign direct

---

[18]Survey evidence on the use of capital controls to attain objectives of monetary control are largely pessimistic; see Michael P. Dooley, "A survey of Literature on Controls over International Capital Transactions," IMF Staff Papers 43 (Washington, D.C.: International Monetary Fund, December 1996), pp. 639–87). Reports on panel studies of the incidence of capital controls for twenty industrial countries during the years 1950–89, and for sixty-one industrial and developing countries from 1966–89 find that the probability of capital controls lowers the likelihood of more flexible exchange-rate regimes and greater central bank independence; see Vittorio Grilli and Gian Maria Milesi-Ferretti, "Economic Effects and Structural Determinants of Capital Controls," IMF Staff Papers 42 (Washington D.C.: International Monetary Fund, September 1995), pp. 517–51. Using liquid asset reserve requirements as opposed to capital controls might be a more effective strategy of reducing credit risk.

investment relative to domestic GDP is much smaller now than during the period before World War I. The net outflow of capital (i.e., the current account surplus) for most developed countries is actually lower than before World War I. Today the average level of current account balances has not quite attained the magnitude common before World War I. Labor markets are considerably less integrated than at the turn of the century, despite integration of product and capital markets.

In short, gross capital flows may be very large. But net flows are actually smaller than those observed during the period of the gold standard. Trade flows are not significantly higher than they were prior to 1914, if measured against GDP, but are higher if measured against industrial production. While international investment flows commonly topped 3 percent of GDP before 1914, they slumped to less than half that level in the 1930s and only began to move upward after 1970.

Current Trends in Financial Integration

Foreign direct investment is the largest source of net capital flows to developing countries. The largest share of such investment is by multinational corporations in their overseas operations under their own control. It is the only area that has shown some stability. Net flows in portfolio equity, bond, and commercial bank loans grew substantially during the 1990s but face severe declines, as shown in Figure 5.

The fundamental global financial crisis is this: The turmoil at the end of the 1990s has created very wide spreads and curtailed market access. Net private capital flows to leading emerging market economies have fallen to $160 billion compared to $240 billion in 1998, which was after a peak of $310 billion in 1996. Portfolio equity, bonds, and bank lending all reflect similar declines. (See Table 4). The context of this crisis, after ten years of explosive growth in international financial transactions, needs to be recalled: a tenfold increase in global foreign exchange markets, a fivefold increase in foreign direct investment, and a tenfold increase in cross-border bond and equities transactions.

Figure 5. Regional Net Capital Flows

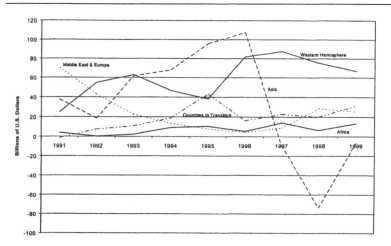

Source: Milken Institute; World Economic Outlook October 1997 & October 1998

Table 4. Emerging Market Economies' External Finance (billions of U.S. dollars)

	1995	1996	1997	1998f	1999f
Current account balance	⁻95	⁻95.4	⁻76.2	⁻44.8	⁻27.1
External financing net	267.8	311.1	282.4	200.4	184.6
Private flows, net	228.1	307.6	241.7	158.2	158.3
Equity investment	106.7	128.2	144.9	116.7	119.9
Direct equity	82.2	94.9	119.7	105.9	101.8
Portfolio equity	24.5	33.4	25.2	10.7	18.1
Private creditors	121.4	179.3	96.8	41.5	38.3
Commercial banks	103.1	113.3	22.2	⁻0.7	11.9
Non-bank private creditors	18.3	66	74.6	42.2	26.4
Official flows, net	39.7	3.5	40.7	42.2	26.3
International financial institutions	20.4	7.2	28.3	32.2	14.1
Bilateral creditors	19.3	⁻3.7	12.4	10	12.2
Resident lending/other, net*	⁻77.7	⁻128.6	⁻161.3	⁻115.9	⁻95.7
Reserves excl. gold (⁻ = increase)	⁻95	⁻87.1	⁻44.8	⁻39.7	⁻61.8

e = estimate f = forecast
* Including resident net lending, monetary gold, and errors and omissions
Source: Institute of International Finance, Inc.

Regulatory frameworks in developed countries have until recently created and exacerbated this problem. Present bank regulation evaluates asset riskiness individually by using risk-based capital standards. As Credit Suisse First Boston Global Credit Strategist David Goldman has pointed out, "modern portfolio theory offers a different view, namely that portfolio risk is not additive: the riskiness of a portfolio is an entirely different thing from the sum of the risks of the individual assets. In effect the present risk-based capital standards sum the risk of individual assets. Diversified portfolios, however, may have a far lower level of risk than the average riskiness of their elements." Portfolio-based risk measures currently contemplated by the Bank for International Settlements would lower the cost of capital to borrowers and raise the return to equity for financial institutions.

Regulatory restrictions of various kinds[19] discourage mainstream financial institutions such as banks, life insurance companies, and pension funds from participating in the market for riskier credits in emerging countries. Most of the world's population lives in emerging markets. Such countries must sell risky assets to obtain capital. Newer market entrants in the developed world are also riskier. Accordingly, given these restrictions, the unregulated segment has taken a disproportionately large role in such markets.

The problem with emerging markets during 1998 stemmed from the fact that virtually all capital flows to emerging capital markets came from hedge funds buying emerging-market securities:

> The regulatory system in effect matched up borrowers with volatile returns to lenders with volatile sources of capital and produced a near catastrophe. The problem with hedge funds and the unregulated market was the interaction between well-informed specialists and uninformed investors in the markets. As margin calls forced hedge fund specialists to liquidate part of their holdings, the price downturn was amplified. To the extent that emerging markets and

---

[19]James Barth, R. Dan Brumbaugh, and Glenn Yago, eds., *Restructuring Financial Regulation* (Santa Monica, Calif.: Milken Institute, Forthcoming).

their participants were liquidity-constrained, emerging-market security and bond prices were slow to recover. High interest rates combined with the slow recovery to adversely affect demand, output, and employment.[20]

In response securitization is only part of the answer. Changing the regulatory structure in the industrial world is just as important.

The application of portfolio risk analysis in place of risk-based capital standards in financial institution regulation could well increase capital access and decrease imprudent uses of leverage. However, the incentives for expanding net credit exposure by regulated institutions may not be implemented as fast as the disincentives for hedge-fund lending, which could further exacerbate liquidity shortages in the global financial markets.

Global Financial Architecture and the Evolution of International Capital Mobility

There is an underlying tension between markets and governments that explains the long stretch of high capital mobility prior to World War I, its subsequent breakdown, and then the slow rebuilding of the postwar world financial system. This tension involves the way in which openness to the world capital market constrains government power through the choice of the exchange rate mechanism.

Before 1914, currency prices were pegged in terms of gold, which maintained a fixed rate of exchange. The Great Depression discredited gold-standard orthodoxy. Financial products and markets were banned or otherwise more closely regulated. The Bretton Woods conference set up a fixed, but adjustable, exchange-rate parity system in the belief that floating exchange rates would exhibit instability that would damage international trade. Accordingly, after 1973, industrial countries moved to a floating dollar-rate regime.[21]

---

[20]David P. Goldman, "Risk-Based Capital Standards and the Future of Banking," (Credit Suisse First Boston, September 30, 1998), p. 4; see also Glenn Yago, Lalita Ramesh, and Noah Hochman, *Hedge Funds and Systemic Risk Demystified* (Santa Monica, Calif.: Milken Institute, December 1998).

[21]Maurice Obstfeld, "The Global Capital Market: Benefactor or Menace?" *Journal of Economic Perspectives*, vol. 12/4 (Fall 1998), pp. 9–30.

Debates over financial architecture are part of that ongoing discourse as markets discipline governments and meet resistance. Each country's financial system is an important intangible asset that can help to facilitate both its own and others' economic growth. Given the enormous disparity in national wealth between rich and poor countries, developed countries offer an important source of development funds for countries unable to finance their future solely with internal savings. In order for an efficient and innovative global financial system to evolve, borrower countries' financial systems need some fundamental compatibility with those of lender countries. Any discussion of global financial architecture must deal directly with the form developing financial systems take.

Financial systems are intangible assets that promote economic growth by facilitating the transfer of funds from savers (savers or lenders) to borrowers (spenders or investors). This relationship is depicted in Figure 6. The benefits provided to individuals by financial systems involve risk sharing, liquidity, and information. Savers can hold many different types of assets and thus diversify risk. Likewise, investors can fund projects in large numbers of different ways.

Figure 6. Designing Financial Systems

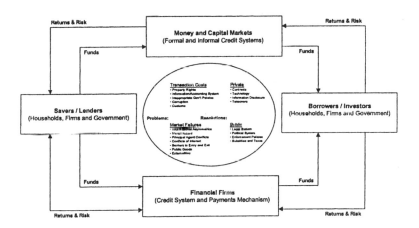

However, there are a host of economic obstacles to matching savers and investors. These obstacles include transaction costs, market failures, firm size, available information, sources of capital, property rights and information, regulation, negative externalities, bank runs, moral hazard, agency problems, barriers to entry, and exit by investors, to name a few.

DECONSTRUCTING GLOBAL FINANCIAL ARCHITECTURE PROPOSALS

The Major Proposals (see Table 5)

Since the spring of 1997, when the East-Asian financial crisis began to develop, a proliferating number of proposals for a "new financial architecture" have come forward to reduce the turbulence in world financial markets.

Table 5 presents a representative listing of the major types of reform proposals that have evolved. Although there are a seemingly ever expanding number of reform proposals, as the table shows, several trends have emerged among prominent economists and government officials.[22]

These proposals can be roughly classified as those that advocate:

• major new government institutions;

• changes in government regulatory practices;

• a mix of policy changes and market-based reforms; and

• market-based reforms alone.

For those who want to rely on either increased or improved government or trans-national agency intervention in financial markets, there are three major strands of proposals. Many have proposed some form of international lender of last resort or global central bank. Others have argued for perfecting in some way how the IMF presently works. Still others have proposed currency boards.

---

[22]George Soros' model suggests a new international agency that would insure investors against debt defaults. Countries would pay a fee when floating loans in order to underwrite the cost of insurance. Each country's debts would be limited to a ceiling set by the IMF. Loans in excess of the ceiling would not be insured. And the IMF would not aid countries having difficulty servicing uninsured loans. See George Soros, *The Crisis of Global Capitalism* (New York: Public Affairs Press, 1998).

Table 5: Global Financial Architectural Proposals

A. Major New Government Institutions

Author	Affiliation	Proposal	Source
Gordon Brown	Chancellor of the Exchequer, U.K.	New permanent Standing Committee for global financial regulation involving the IMF, the World Bank, the Basel Committee, and other regulatory groups.	"Reforming the International Monetary Fund: ...And Impose New Codes of Conduct," Wall Street Journal, October 6, 1998
Sebastian Edwards	UCLA	Replace the IMF with three specialized institutions: Global Information Agency, Contingent Global Financial Facility, and Global Restructuring Agency.	"Abolish the IMF," Financial Times, November 13, 1998
Stanley Fischer	International Monetary Fund	International lender of last resort to serve as crisis manager and crisis lender, not necessarily global central bank.	"Frequency of Global Crises Highlights Need to Consider International Lender of Last Resort," IMF Survey, January 11, 1999
Jeffrey Garten	Yale University	Independent global central bank that could inject liquidity to spur growth and oversee operations of troubled financial institutions; should not be able to override the decisions of the Federal Reserve.	"Needed: A Fed for the World," New York Times, September 23, 1998
Henry Kaufman	President, Henry Kaufman & Co.	Board of Overseers of international financial markets that would develop global financial standards, and also supervise and evaluate institutions under its purview.	"Preventing the Next Global Financial Crisis," Washington Post, January 28, 1998

A. Major New Government Institutions (continued)

Author	Affiliation	Proposal	Source
Steven Radelet & Jeffrey D. Sachs	Harvard University	• International regulator of bankruptcy laws, deposit insurance, lender of last resort. • Floating exchange rate. • Reform IMF conditionality.	"What have we learned, so far, from the Asian Financial Crisis?" mimeo, Harvard Institute for International Development, January 4, 1997. Available at: www.hiid.harvard.edu
George Soros	Chairman, Soros Fund Management	• International central bank; lender of last resort to select group of countries. • Restrictions on short-term capital flows. • Mandatory insurance (similar to deposit insurance), issued by an international credit insurance corporation to maintain creditor confidence.	George Soros, "The Crisis of Global Capitalism," Wall Street Journal, September 15, 1998

B. Changes In Government Regulatory Practices

Author	Affiliation	Proposal	Source
C. Fred Bergsten	Institute for International Economics	G-7 governments should adopt target zones for exchange rates to contain destabilizing swings in the dollar-yen/dollar-euro exchange rates.	"How to Target Exchange Rates," Financial Times, November 20 1998
Charles Calomiris	Columbia University	• Banks should police themselves by financing a small proportion of their assets by selling subordinated debt to other institutions. Yield on this debt should not be allowed to rise beyond a point. Since these debt holders only have downside risk, they would be rigorous monitors of bank behavior. • Recasts the IMF as a provider of liquidity, only to countries that fulfill a strict set of conditions. All IMF lending would be short-term; if a country did not make timely payments it would not be eligible for IMF money for five years.	"Blueprints for a New Global Financial Architecture," October 7, 1998. Available at: www.house.gov/jec/imf/blueprnt.htm
Michel Camdessus	International Monetary Fund	• Make IMF surveillance more effective and enhance transparency. • Strengthen financial and banking systems as well as their supervision. • Establish more effective procedures to involve the private sector in preventing and resolving debt crises. • Continue to liberalize international capital flows.	"The IMF and its Programs in Asia," Remarks at the Council on Foreign Relations, New York, February 6, 1998

B. Changes In Government Regulatory Practices (continued)

Author	Affiliation	Proposal	Source
Barry Eichengreen	University of California, Berkeley	• New international standards for bank regulation, bankruptcy laws, auditing, corporate governance. • Taxation of all short-term capital inflows into emerging markets. • Promotion of orderly debt restructurings through majority voting, burden-sharing, and collective representation of creditors to avoid lawsuits and obstruction of settlements. • Flexible exchange rates. • Capital controls for emerging markets. • Independent central bank. • Perhaps an independent national fiscal council. • Measures that enhance transparency.	Toward a New International Financial "Architecture: a Practical Post-Asia Agenda," Institute for International Economics, February 1999 "Capital Mobility: Ties Need Not Bind," Milken Institute Review, First Quarter, 1999
Alan Greenspan	Chairman, Federal Reserve Board	Restricting controls to short-term capital inflows—as often recommended—is not a solution. 21st-century financial regulation must increasingly rely on counterparty surveillance to achieve safety and soundness. There is no credible way most government financial regulation can be anything other than oversight of process.	Remarks at the Annual Meeting of the Securities Industry Association, Boca Raton, Florida, November 5, 1998

B. Changes In Government Regulatory Practices (continued)

Author	Affiliation	Proposal	Source
Group of Thirty		Among the recommendations are: • Create a standing industry committee to promulgate and review global principles for managing risk. • Agree upon how auditors should approach audits of financial statements and other information for portraying risk. • Supervisors should agree upon a lead coordinator for all global financial institutions. • National legislatures should provide a reliable legal framework for international transactions.	"Global Institutions, National Supervision and Systemic Risk," A Study Group Report, Group of Thirty, 1997
Paul Krugman	MIT	• Limit capital flows to emerging-market countries that are unsuitable for currency unions, free floating exchange rates. • Reregulate capital markets to some extent. • For some countries, low inflation might be a preferred alternative to price stability.	"Depression Economics Returns," Foreign Affairs, January/February, 1999

C. Mix of Policy Changes and Market-Based Reforms

Author	Affiliation	Proposal	Source
APEC Business Advisory Council		• The IMF should take into account social implications of its programs. • Enhance domestic capital-market infrastructure. • Countries should undertake legal, regulatory, and accounting reforms to facilitate financial reorganization. • Develop domestic capital markets through the development of liquid bond and asset-backed securities markets. • Countries should consider mechanisms for restructuring corporate debt through debt-equity swaps. • Remove restrictions on and encourage the use of securitization structures of trade receivables for trade finance.	"Letter from the APEC Business Advisory Council to the Economic Leaders," The 1998 APEC Report to the Economic Leaders
Robert Barro	Harvard University	• Capital controls, while not ideal, are preferable to the IMF's customary fix of intervention with high interest rates. The best policy would entail a fixed exchange rate without capital controls, with the central bank intervening, but not sterilizing. • A currency board is worth considering in more countries.	"Malaysia could do worse than this economic plan," Business Week, November 2, 1998
Basel Committee on Banking Supervision	Bank for International Settlements	• Emphasizes complementary interaction of prudential supervision and market discipline. • Reinforce the efforts of supervisors by rewarding banks that manage risk effectively and penalizing banks whose risk management is inept or imprudent.	"Enhancing Bank Transparency," September 22, 1998, Publication of the Board for International Settlements

(cont.)

C. Mix of Policy Changes and Market-Based Reforms (continued)

Author	Affiliation	Proposal	Source
G-7		• Countries adopt and apply codes of conduct founded on minimum standards and best practice. • Countries must comply with an internationally agreed code of conduct on monetary and fiscal policy. • Countries must comply with an international standard of best practice for transparency and disclosure by financial institutions and their regulators.	HM Treasury News Release, October 30, 1998. Available at: www.hm_treasury.gov.uk/pub/html/press98/p179_html
Robert Rubin	U.S. Treasury Department	• Countries should provide better information through improved disclosure and transparency. • Countries building strong national sectors should create mechanisms so that the private sector more fully bears the consequences of its credit and investment decisions. • Need to provide for international surveillance of countries' financial regulatory and supervisory systems.	Office of Public Affairs, U.S. Treasury Department, April 14, 1998
Joseph Stiglitz	World Bank	• Greater transparency and more information about capital flows. • Countries should try to influence the pattern and composition of capital flows.	Address to the Chicago Council on Foreign Relations, Chicago, February 27, 1998
Paul Volcker	Former Chairman, Federal Reserve Board	Emerging economies should seek financial safety and currency stability in diversity (foreign ownership in financial sector) and size (regional currency arrangements). Emerging markets should link up with leading regional currency.	"Global Finance," Economist, January 30, 1999

D. Market-Based Reforms

Author	Affiliation	Proposal	Source
James Barth, R. Dan Brumbaugh, Lalita Ramesh, & Glenn Yago	Milken Institute	• Eliminate state-owned banks. • Allow foreign bank entry. • Permit the freer flow of international capital. • Promote allocation of credit by market forces. • Discourage inappropriate bailouts for creditors.	"The Role of Governments and Markets in International Banking Crises: The Case of East Asia," Research in Financial Services: Private and Public Policy, JAI Press Inc., 1998
Michael Bordo & Anna Schwartz	National Bureau of Economic Research	• Floating exchange rates. • In a world of deep capital markets, few good reasons why private markets cannot perform as the role of lender of last resort instead of the IMF.	"Under What Circumstances, Past and Present, Have International Rescues of Countries in Financial Distress Been Successful?" NBER, Working Paper no. 6824
Rudiger Dornbusch	MIT	Establishment of a currency board.	"After Asia: New Directions for the International Financial System," July 1998 Available at: http://www.mit.edu/~rudi/papers.html
Steve Hanke	Johns Hopkins University	Developing countries should unify their currencies with stronger ones via fixed exchange rates supported by currency board monetary institutions.	Cato Institute's 16th Annual Monetary Conference, mimeo, October 22, 1998
Randall Kroszner	University of Chicago	• Public regulation should not crowd out private regulation. • A unified international regulator is likely to slow innovations and growth of international financial markets. • Public regulations should be subject to a rough cost-benefit analysis to assess feasibility.	"The Role of Private Regulation in Maintaining Global Financial Stability," 16 Annual Monetary Conference, Cato Institute, October 22, 1998

(cont.)

D. Market-Based Reforms (continued)

Author	Affiliation	Proposal	Source
Robert Litan	Brookings Institution	• Countries should pass simple bankruptcy legislation. No need for new international bankruptcy agency. Debt problems are internal and plague firms, not governments.	"Bankruptcy Bailout Could Fix Asia's Woes," Newsday, March 4, 1998 "Asian Problems and the IMF," testimony
Allan Meltzer	Carnegie Mellon University	The BIS (as a central bank for all central banks) can perhaps replace the IMF.	prepared for the Joint Economic Committee, U. S. Congress, February 24, 1998
George Schultz, William Simon, and Walter Wriston	Former U.S. Secretary of State; Former U.S. Secretary of Treasury; Former Chairman of Citicorp	Contend that the IMF is "ineffective, unnecessary, and obsolete." Bailouts insulate financiers and politicians from consequences of unwise economic and financial practices.	"Who Needs the IMF?" Wall Street Journal, February 3, 1998

There have also been specific policy proposals that do not necessarily require new or improved government or trans-national agencies but would nonetheless rely on some additional government intervention. These include establishing regional currencies, new forms of bank supervision, and limitations on international capital flows, as well as on monetary and fiscal policies.

In contrast to these types of proposals, many proposals would rely on less intervention on the part of governments or trans national agencies. Three senior public and private figures have called for the outright abolishment of the IMF.[23] Others have endorsed more limited policy changes. These include greater transparency of information and also development of mechanisms that would require the private sector to bear more fully the consequences of their private decisions. A particular form of the latter proposal would, for example, require banks to issue subordinated debt, relying on the debt holders to monitor and limit excessive risk-taking.

How to Evaluate the Global Financial Architecture Proposals
Whether or which global financial architecture proposals make sense must depend on how well they address the causes and exacerbating factors that seem to be involved in contemporary global financial difficulties. Contemporary international financial difficulties have demonstrated remarkably similar patterns of development from Mexico in 1994 to East Asia in 1997–98 to Brazil in 1998–99.

In the crises affecting these countries, the final stage of the crises has been when the countries attempt, successfully or not, to use foreign reserves to defend the value of their currencies. This stage is really the result of preceding events. Those events have tended to be excessive lending and investment in projects that failed, with subsequent severe consequences to the real economy of the affected country. The perception of an imminent decline in the real economy has tended to precipitate the final stage of the crises.

Two extremely important but often overlooked characteristics have affected contemporary crises. First, state-owned banks have

---

[23]George Schultz, William Simon, and Walter Wriston, "Who Needs the IMF?" *Wall Street Journal*, February 3, 1998.

been involved with the excessively risky lending and investment, often to state-owned or influenced enterprises. Second, the financial sectors of the stricken countries have lacked breadth and depth, with relatively smaller and less-well-developed non-bank sectors. Thus, direct and indirect government influence is greater in bank-dominated in financial markets.

Global financial architecture proposals should be evaluated on how well they address these key events in contemporary financial difficulties.

How Do the Proposals Stack Up?

Clearly, proposals that call for an international lender of last resort or a central bank essentially would deal with the final stage of a crisis when currencies need to be defended with foreign reserves. They would not deal directly with the process that created the crisis. Assuming that an international lender of last resort would work as intended, it raises a moral hazard problem that already exists with IMF interventions. Would the prospect of even more effective interventions (by an international lender of last resort instead of the IMF) tend to exacerbate the underlying causes of the crisis, such as excessively risky or imprudent lending and investment?

This, of course, is a major criticism of the IMF and why some have argued that the IMF should revise the conditions upon which it will lend to countries experiencing difficulties. IMF conditionality should have dampened the likelihood of further crises. But this does not appear to have been the case. As a result, marginal changes in IMF policies cannot be expected to bear great fruit. In the long run, the moral hazard incentives of a complete bailout cause a rise in the probability of financial runs.

Similarly, currency boards have proved effective in some, but may not be feasible in all cases. The conditions necessary for currency boards to work could rule them out in some countries because under this arrangement, foreign exchange reserves would have to be high enough to fully cover domestic notes and coins as well as deposit liabilities.

The remaining proposals that rely on new forms of intervention are limited because of the problem of state-owned banks in financial systems that are bank dominated. New forms of regulation and the imposition of subordinated debt requirements, for example, will not address the effects of state-owned or influenced banks often lending or investing in state-owned or influenced enterprises.

Likewise, restrictions on foreign capital flows also do not address the problems caused by state-owned banks. Inappropriate short-term foreign lending, moreover, has often been encouraged in countries that have subsequently suffered, and may well have been exacerbated by the moral hazard problem created by the IMF. Again, there appears to be a dubious rationale for a proposed resolution with a relatively modest promised contribution.

What About the More Market-Based Approaches?

The primary rationale for proposals that would eliminate the IMF is based in the moral hazard problem caused by predictable IMF lending. The worry is that predictable IMF lending leads to excessive risk-taking by entities—both governments and private parties—who are "bailed out" by subsequent IMF loans. Ongoing rounds of excessive risk-taking in turn lead to future, and perhaps escalating, crises. On balance, those who would eliminate the IMF think that increased market discipline would lead to fewer and less severe crises.

To some extent all of the remaining major proposals are designed to increase market discipline. They include increasing subordinated debt for banks, increasing foreign ownership in the financial structure, maintaining floating exchange rates, establishing more efficient bankruptcy systems, increasing disclosure and transparency, and making certain that private parties bear the consequences of their credit and investment decisions.

Private lender of last resort methods are just beginning to be explored. The Central Bank of Argentina, for example, has set up contingent repurchase arrangements with a group of New York banks that would provide $17 billion if Argentine banks faced an emergency, such as a run on deposits. Between liquid reserves and repurchase agreements, around 40 percent of the deposit base is protected. Variations on capital controls such as those explored by Chile are more capital-market sensitive. Specifically, Chile's plan uses short-term exit taxes, which are more promising than the customary fixed-entry fees in reducing the probability of crises relative to fixed-entry fees.[24]

While there are clearly pluses and minuses to each of the more market-based proposals, these are the kinds of proposals that will survive and provide a basis for efficient, and hence more stable, capital markets in the future. Still underestimated, however, is the extent to which state-owned banks in bank-dominated financial systems remain a major source of instability in financial markets.

Corporate Capital Structures and Macro Financial Architecture
A key to the future of efficient financial markets is:

* to eliminate direct state involvement in financial markets, and

* to increase the depth and breadth of financial markets.

The overwhelming emphasis of most global financial architectural proposals is upon macro-policy reform, which, while necessary, is not nearly enough to revitalize these countries and prepare them for entry into the global financial system. Micro-reform is fundamental to:

* reform of legal, regulatory, and accounting systems;

* reform of banking systems and banks;

* create secondary debt markets; and

* restructure corporate balance sheets.

Sovereign and corporate capital structure both matter and are interrelated. Explanations of the global financial crisis have largely focused on macroeconomic factors leading to crisis. Recent research on the

---

[24]Ilan Goldfajn and Rodrigo Valdés, *Liquidity Crises and the International Financial Architecture* Working Paper (Santiago: Central Bank of Chile, 1999).

micro-areas has highlighted the paradox that, in a time of increasing capital mobility, corporations did not adhere to global standards of creating shareholder value. Corporate financial analysis shows unsustainable investment in fixed assets financed by excessive borrowing, which resulted in poor profitability, as well as declining returns on equity and returns on capital employed. Poor capital structures, and the inability to manage them, led to heightened financial distress.

As suggested by Figures 7 & 8, financially distressed regions have exhibited over-dependence on the banking sector and under-reliance on capital markets in both absolute and relative terms.

This suggests the need for a more open, balanced, and competitive financial system, in which capital is allocated in a more transparent fashion. In addition to rehabilitation of the banking system, development of domestic capital markets will be required. Attendant benefits in terms of transparency, risk assessment and pricing, and dispersion of risk among participants would have an important effect upon corporate accountability and performance. These problems of financial concentration are exacerbated by corporate capital concentration as well. Despite the increase in foreign participation, the context has been one of limited floats and

Figure 7. Structure of Financial Markets: Latin America

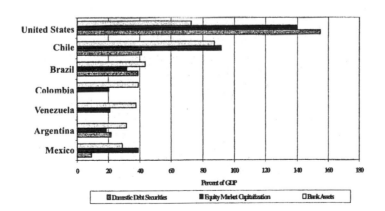

Figure 8. Structure of Financial Markets: Asia

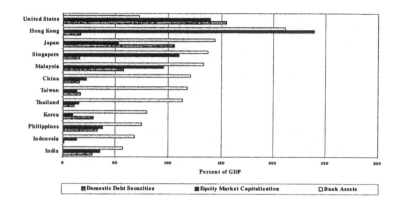

large, closely held positions of shares. Large portfolio equity inflows in an illiquid market have had a disproportionate impact on valuations unhinged from performance fundamentals.[25]

Inflexibility in corporate capital structures, resulting from the absence of local capital markets and the capacity to manage corporate balance sheets, also has reflected and amplified the macro crisis. Because East Asian corporations used outside equity sparingly, leverage was high and short-term borrowing became increasingly important.[26] The aforementioned concentration of ownership was enhanced by pyramid structures, as well as diminished economic and institutional development. In short, increasing ownership and control concentration hurt market performance. As predicted by economic theory, the interests of small shareholders are damaged by concentration when corporations are affiliated with business groups or when there is uncontested control by a single large shareholder, or when there are large cross-holdings.[27] The weaknesses of the legal system and the lack of an independent judiciary

---

[25]Michael Pomerleano, *The East Asia Crisis and Corporate Finances: The Untold Micro Story,* Policy Research Working Paper no. 1990 (Washington, D.C.: World Bank, 1998).

[26]Stijn Claessens, Simeon Djankov, and Larry Lang, *Corporate Growth, Financing, and Risks before the Crisis,* Working Paper no. 2017 (Washington, D.C.: World Bank, 1998).

[27]Stijn Claessens, Dimeon Djankov, Larry Lang, and Joseph Fan, *Ultimate Ownership and Performance of East Asian Corporations,* Working Paper (Washington, D.C.: World Bank, February 1999).

are influenced by these prevailing ownership structures and the resulting corruption and lack of transparency. The absence of institutional and transaction trust in market arrangements acts as a drag upon growth.

The linkages between capital and job formation to income growth and wealth creation are becoming more apparent in economic research.[28] The linkage between degrees of financial regulation and economic growth has been demonstrated.[29] Growing securities markets in the private sector positively affect the labor market through the supply side. Market capitalization and valuations combine two things that make assets a desirable investment: the current rate of profit and the price that investors will pay for those profits. When the market is highly valued, assets are worth more than they cost, so additional fixed investment makes sense. Resultingly, a shift toward higher investment increases employment at any given level of aggregate demand. As Edmund Phelps has recently shown, highly valued markets indicate that profits from investment have increased and/or that the market value of those profits has increased, resulting in higher employment.[30]

---

[28]Glenn Yago, *The Jobs/Capital Mismatch: Financial Regulatory Chokeholds on Economic Growth* (Santa Monica, Calif.: Milken Institute, November 1999).

[29]James Barth, Gerard Caprio, and Ross Levine, *Financial Regulation and Economic Performance*, Policy Brief (Santa Monica, Calif.: Milken Institute, March 1999).

[30]Edmund Phelps, "Behind the Structural Boom: The Role of Asset Valuations," *American Economic Association Papers and Proceedings* (May 1999). Economic evidence confirms that global financial integration leads to more active, liquid, and efficient domestic financial markets. The increased depth and breadth of those markets encourages faster growth and more rapidly rising living standards. World Bank, *Private Capital Flows to Developing Countries: The Road to Financial Integration* (New York: Oxford University Press, 1997)

Countries that have structured their capital markets to receive relatively large portfolio capital inflows have seen disproportionate growth in transaction volume, liquidity, market capitalization, and growth in bank loans to the private sector. The ratio of liquid financial assets to GNP will have a strong correlation with subsequent economic growth in the years ahead. This development accompanies foreign direct investment findings as well. Domestic firms learn from foreign investment enterprises evidencing positive spillovers from foreign direct investment. The overall effect is positive for countries with the educated labor force to take advantage of investment spillovers in export growth and additionally triggered domestic investment. Eduaardo Borenzstein, Jose de Gregario and Jon-Wha Lee, *How Does Foreign Direct Investment Affect Economic Growth*, Working Paper no. 5057 (Cambridge, Mass.: National Bureau of Economic Research, 1995); Barry Eichengreen, *Globalizing Capital: A History of the International Monetary System*, (Princeton, N.J.: Princeton University Press, 1998)

Building the Financial Infrastructure for Middle Class Emerging Economies

A Paper from the Project on Development, Trade and International Finance

Jane D'Arista

A Council on Foreign Relations Paper

Building the Financial Infrastructure for Middle Class Emerging Economies

INTRODUCTION

The export-led growth model for emerging economies is driven by their need to service external debt and build foreign exchange reserves. It has foundered in the aftermath of financial crises characterized by collapsing currency and asset values, widespread bankruptcies in real and financial sectors, rising unemployment, and negative growth rates.[1] In many developing countries, a higher volume of exports is needed to earn the same income that previously sufficed to meet external obligations. As a result, profits and wages have fallen, lowering earlier gains in per capita income and threatening past improvements in income distribution, education, and life expectancy.

The sustainability of the export-led growth model is also threatened by dramatic increases in the current account deficits, external debt, and domestic debt ratios of the major global importer/consumer.[2] As U.S. ability to maintain its role becomes less certain, fewer countries appear to be willing or able to absorb more imports or to accept current account deficits. Continued slow growth in Japan, the second-largest national economy in the

---

[1]Blecker, Robert A, "The Diminishing Returns to Export-Led Growth," Discussion Paper (New York: Council on Foreign Relations, October 1999).

[2]Blecker, Robert A, "The Ticking Debt Bomb: Why the U.S. International Financial Position is Not Sustainable," Briefing Paper (Washington, D.C.: Economic Policy Institute, June 1999).

global system, would hamper its ability to assume some of the burden carried by the United States, even if its own adherence to an export-led growth model were not in itself a major inhibiting factor. Continued restructuring, high levels of unemployment, and constrained monetary and fiscal policies within the European Community also do not suggest robust increases in demand for imports of goods and services in the near future.

Diminishing returns to the export-led growth strategies that emerging economies have followed (and have been encouraged to follow) during the last two decades will require the development of new strategies to promote growth. Both developing and developed countries will need to reintroduce domestic demand-driven growth as a policy objective. However, emerging economies will require more than a shift in the direction of macroeconomic policy to stimulate demand. Also required will be the development of domestic capital markets and financial systems like those in industrialized countries, which are capable of mobilizing and channeling domestic savings to expand internal economic activity. That, in turn, will require changes in global capital markets and financial infrastructure to support and encourage reinstatement of a role for domestic demand-driven growth in the global economy and particularly in emerging economies.

The choice of an economic paradigm necessarily has important social and political consequences. Export-led growth strategies have tended to increase income gaps across and within countries as wage levels succumbed to the pressure to maintain competitiveness. Domestic demand-driven growth strategies have greater potential to reinstate conditions for rising wages and reduced income disparities. If that potential were realized, the resulting expansion of middle classes in emerging economies like those that have characterized North American and European societies would strengthen the viability of democratic institutions and build more stable societies. Perhaps the very least that can be expected of societies in which per capita income is rising and a majority of the population holds a rising share of total income is that they provide opportunities for escape from poverty unmatched by societies with other income distribution patterns. Building such societies in emerging economies may be the only means to redress the immense waste of human resources caused by widespread poverty in today's global economy.

This paper explores ways in which the institutional and regulatory structures of financial markets can be shaped to contribute to the goal of expanding shared prosperity in emerging markets. It opens with descriptions of various strategies used by industrialized countries to achieve economic and social goals by using monetary tools and public financial institutions to allocate credit to preferred sectors. The following section discusses the shift in financial flows from banks to securities markets in industrialized countries and in many emerging economies. Given the increased use of pension funds as a primary channel for collecting and allocating savings flows in both developed and developing countries, the paper focuses on ways in which these pools of private savings can be structured to (1) broaden and deepen capital and financial markets, and (2) support demand-driven growth policies and promote equality in income distribution. It proposes a more balanced division between government and private institutions in (1) making decisions involving the allocation of credit; (2) using expanding ownership of financial assets as the means to promote wider participation in overseeing and assessing the performance of the financial sector; (3) exercising corporate governance; and (4) shaping macro-economic policy decisions.

The final section of the paper outlines the changes needed in the international monetary and financial architecture to permit the shift from export-led growth to growth strategies that rely on the expansion of domestic demand. It concludes that public sector support for major changes in both international and national financial structures will be required to ensure a resumption of balanced growth in the global economy.

BUILDING ON PAST STRUCTURES AND PROGRAMS

Monetary and financial policies and tools were widely used to promote economic and social objectives by industrialized countries in the post-World War II period and had been used by the United States during the 1930s. In some countries, direct government expenditures supplied loans and grants. Others used the financial system to allocate funds to preferred sectors and lower the interest rates paid by those sectors for credit. Although the various strategies chosen were also used to increase financing for exports, the primary objective in many industrialized countries was to favor borrowing sectors such as housing, agriculture, small and medium sized businesses, and underdeveloped regions. The objective was also to increase the total supply of savings and promote balanced economic growth. In all cases these strategies constituted systems that exercised "a substantial degree of public control without public ownership."[3]

Countries used various types of controls to achieve the different objectives. Direct controls specified the kinds of assets institutions could hold to ensure that institutions would channel credit to a preferred sector. One example would be federally chartered U.S. savings and loan institutions, created by legislation enacted in 1934. Indirect controls provided credit incentives by using strategies that altered the relative rates of return on investments in favored sectors by lowering their cost of borrowing. Techniques used to implement indirect controls included asset reserve requirements, government borrowing in capital markets for relending to favored sectors, and government savings institutions (such as postal savings banks) designed to compete with private institutions in capturing savings flows for onlending to preferred sectors.

While the various techniques used tended to have features that accommodated both the government's economic or social priority and the characteristics of the national financial system, they have common elements that permit them to be adapted to the needs of other countries. In general, the following descriptions of national experiences with particular strategies show how effective these

---

[3]U.S. House of Representatives, *Foreign Experience with Monetary Policies to Promote Economic and Social Priority Programs*, Staff Report of the Committee on Banking and Currency (Washington, D.C.: U.S. Government Printing Office, 1972).

strategies can be in promoting the goals of shared prosperity and domestic demand-driven economic growth.

The U.S. Reconstruction Finance Corporation

The Reconstruction Finance Corporation (RFC) was organized and began operations in February 1932, one month after the enactment of the legislation authorizing its establishment. It was patterned on the War Finance Corporation, created during World War I, which provided a precedent for government assistance to private enterprise. Its initial capital was $500 million, but it had unlimited authority to borrow from the U.S. Treasury. It was also permitted to retain earnings for expansion of its activities, and it remained outside the congressional appropriation process throughout its active life (1932–54). At the time of its liquidation in 1957, it had disbursed $40 billion in loans and purchases of stocks and other obligations, and had made commitments for many billions more in guarantees for loans made by private financial institutions.[4]

The original legislative directive to the RFC was to extend aid to agriculture, industry, and commerce by making direct loans to banks, trust companies, and other financial institutions. Subsequent emergency legislation (1935) authorized the RFC to make direct loans to solvent businesses unable to obtain credit from other sources and to recapitalize the financial system by buying the stock of banks, insurance companies, agricultural credit corporations, and national mortgage associations. A further extension of its powers (1938) authorized the RFC to purchase the securities and obligations of any business enterprise and thus to provide both capital and credit when it could not be obtained from other sources.

During its first two years of operation, the majority of the RFC's loans were to banks and trust companies ($3.3 billion out of $3.9 billion), with preference given to small state banks. While these efforts and the creation of the deposit insurance program in 1933 helped stabilize the banking system, they were not sufficient to reignite

---

[4] The discussion of the RFC is based on a study written by the present author and inserted in the *Congressional Record* by U.S. Rep. Wright Patman (D.–Texas), Chairman of the House Banking and Currency Committee, on August 4, 1969.

an expansion of lending. Part of the problem was that the traditional maturity of commercial bank lending was one year or less. Most small businesses needed more secure lines of credit and easier repayment schedules. Thus, in 1935 the RFC itself became the major lender to small business, and 70 percent of its loans had a maturity of five years or more. The RFC set a precedent that effected a permanent extension in the terms of business lending. As its loans to businesses declined during the war years, commercial banks began to issue term loans.

Another substantial component of RFC lending was to agricultural agencies, most of which were part of the public agricultural credit system that had been established in earlier periods of distress for this sector. Credit programs exercised by these agencies (Federal and joint-stock land banks, regional and other agricultural credit corporations) were augmented by loans from the RFC rather than by direct lending. But the particular contribution of the RFC was to make loans to finance the sale of U.S. agricultural surpluses abroad.

Mortgage lending also became a major component of RFC financing. Its original directive was to make loans to private mortgage loan companies. However, in 1935, it was also authorized to subscribe to the capital stock of those companies. In addition, it created its own mortgage lending subsidiary, the RFC Mortgage Corporation. In 1938, it capitalized a second subsidiary, the Federal National Mortgage Association, which was transferred to the Housing and Home Finance Agency in 1950 and remains in existence as a government sponsored enterprise today. The mortgage lending program focused on residential mortgages but also financed nineteen large housing projects and made loans for income-producing properties. The RFC disbursed over $1.7 billion through its two subsidiaries during the life of the program, $1.3 billion of which was disbursed by FNMA as financing for 414,499 mortgages during the twelve years that it was an RFC subsidiary.

Other RFC programs provided financing for public works, including the purchase of bonds from the Metropolitan Water District of Southern California, and making loans for the San Francisco–Oakland Bay Bridge, the Pennsylvania Turnpike Commission, for drainage and irrigation, and numerous other projects. It also capitalized and made loans to the newly established U.S. Export-Import Bank , made disaster and relief loans, refinanced the debts of public school facilities and, in 1934, paid the salaries of teachers in the Chicago school system.

In the 1940s, the RFC was the critical agency in financing conversion to the war effort. Through eight new subsidiaries, it financed plant conversion and construction; acquired, constructed and operated its own war plant facilities; made subsidy payments to stockpile strategic and critical materials; administered the war-damage insurance program; and engaged in many other activities in conjunction with other government agencies. More than 80 percent of the RFC's activities during this period were unrelated to its normal lending operations, and about half ($20 billion) of its total loans were disbursed during the war. At the end of the war, it shifted into a new role in financing reconversion. Almost half of its total business loans were disbursed after June 1948, and lending to businesses peaked in 1949. Lending for residential mortgages reached its highest level in 1949–50, and the RFC provided additional assistance to veterans by making a market in Veterans Administration-insured loans.

Like any other financial institution, the RFC sustained losses. Overall, however, it was a profitable institution with earnings substantial enough to pay dividends to the Treasury on its capital stock. It was able to assist the Treasury in 1941, when the public debt was approaching the limit, by directly issuing its own securities and using the funds to buy the stock of the Federal home loan banks to provide the government with additional funds. Congressional support for the RFC's activities diminished after the war, however, and the degree of discretion and flexibility that had been the hallmark of its lending programs was curtailed on the grounds that it should no longer be permitted to compete with private sources of credit. It was argued that the Corporation's countercyclical role was no longer justified in the inflationary environment of the postwar period. The winding down of its activities began as early as 1947 and continued until its final closing in 1957. Still, many of its programs survived in other forms. The most notable continuations are small business lending, shifted to the newly created U.S. Small Business Administration, and the FNMA.

Credit allocation techniques in other industrialized countries [5]
Sweden's credit allocation program from 1950–70 focused on providing steady credit flows to housing. It used asset reserve requirements to achieve the objective of constructing "a countercyclical shield against finance problems" for this sector.[6] One measure of the program's success was as follows: during periods when tight monetary policy lowered the flow of funds to the industrial sector, financing for housing did not dry up, but continued to increase.

When a government uses asset reserve requirements to achieve policy objectives, it decides what share of total credit flows should go to a preferred sector. Then it requires all financial institutions to hold that percentage of their total portfolio in assets that finance that sector. If an institution does not hold the total percentage of assets required, the remainder must be entered on the balance sheet as reserves. The choice is to make an interest-earning loan to the preferred sector or an interest-free loan to the government. The authors of the 1972 House Banking Committee report that describes these techniques note that asset reserve requirements are "simple and straightforward," do not require an elaborate regulatory framework and, unlike the U.S. savings and loan structure used to promote housing in this period, do not discriminate between small and large savers.[7]

In a small country like Sweden, asset reserve requirements can be implemented on a voluntary basis by using moral suasion and negotiating the targeted shares with different financial sectors. There were many mortgage lenders in Sweden during this period: mortgage banks, housing credit societies, savings banks,

---

[5]This section is based on a study prepared for the U.S. House of Representatives Banking and Currency Committee under the direction of Professor Lester C. Thurow, Assistant Professor Robert Engle, Laura D'Andrea, Raymond Hartman, and Charles Pigott of the Massachusetts Institute of Technology. Entitled *Foreign Experience with Monetary Policies to Promote Economic and Social Priority Programs*, it was published as a Committee Print in May 1972

[6]U.S. House of Representatives, ibid., 1972.

[7]U.S. House of Representatives, ibid, 1972.

the Post Office Bank and commercial banks. The major lenders issued bonds to obtain funding, and their liabilities could be purchased and held by other financial institutions (insurance companies, for example) to satisfy their reserve requirements.

Italy is a postwar example of a country that used government borrowing and relending to achieve economic and social objectives. This is an allocative technique that, in general, shifts the costs of supporting preferred sectors onto taxpayers rather than savers. In the Italian model, the central bank did not play the major role in the program, as did the Swedish central bank. As the program implies, however, fiscal and monetary policy were closely related, and the Bank of Italy had considerable influence in formulating the credit policies that welded the two policy tools together.

The policies themselves were implemented through special credit institutions that intermediated between private sources of funds and private borrowers, using public funds to provide credit incentives. Special credit institutions collected funds from securities markets. The buyers of the securities were private investors and commercial banks. About half of the funding came from banks that used savings held in deposits to provide long-term credit by rolling over their investments. The Bank of Italy supported this maturity transformation by issuing the securities of the special credit institutions and allowing them to be pledged by banks as collateral for four-month renewable advances.

Like several U.S. programs in the post-World War II period—housing loans to veterans, loans to small and minority businesses and to students, for example—the Italian program achieved its objectives by directly subsidizing interest payments to lower the cost of borrowing to favored sectors. Most of the subsidies were for industry, but primarily to small and medium sized industries, and for the industrialization of Italy's southern region, known as the Mezzogiorno. In the 1950s, the Mezzogiorno had remained an underdeveloped country within the borders of a country that had become heavily industrialized. Per capita income was 47 percent of that in the North. Most of the essential infrastructure for industrialization and social progress was missing: adequate roads, telephone lines, electrical generating plants, irrigation systems, etc.

The first goal of the program was to modernize and increase productivity in agriculture, the region's dominant sector. Establishing new industrial facilities was emphasized in the 1960s. Overall, the program's lending priorities reflected the belief that growth in output was the best way to alleviate high levels of unemployment in this very poor region.

Because of its emphasis on the South, the primary objective of Italy's economic program was developmental. In addition to the Cassa per il Mezzogiorno, the government's "Credit Mobiliare" group included institutions that specialized in industrial credit and credit to public works projects; others that specialized in real estate and agricultural credits; and still others that operated as special departments in the commercial banks. The range of eligible types of credit included loans to artisans, to depressed and mountainous regions in north central Italy, for disasters and natural calamities, and for hotels and tourism.

From 1960 to 1970, the Italian program succeeded in raising the flow of credit to the South and other depressed regions. Since then there have been major transformations and growth in these areas. There are still disparities in the South's proportionate share in total output and income relative to the North and Central regions, but the progress that has been made attests to the success of this nation's efforts to take responsibility for development within its own borders.

Japan's system of credit allocation is often referred to as the unique model for Asia. It could be argued, however, that what was unique about it was the way it adapted the U.S. RFC structure to both accommodate and reform the existing Japanese financial system. Rather than having the government borrow to finance support for lending by private financial institutions, the Japanese program channeled private savings through government owned or controlled financial institutions. Then it lent them to private financial institutions for onlending to the industrial sector. A critical objective of this strategy was to distribute credit across the entire industrial sector to promote the emergence of more promising industries. That constituted an important financial reform that weakened the *zaibatsu* system in which financial institutions were committed to lend within a conglomerate structure. But the overall goal of the strategy was to maximize economic growth. That objective was the overriding "social" priority of the government throughout the postwar period. Thus, investment in housing, for example, was significantly lower than in other G-7 countries. However, the rate of economic growth was substantially higher.

Personal savings were the primary source of loanable funds in the Japanese economy, and a large share of savings was held in postal savings accounts. These funds were not loaned out by postal savings institutions, but rather channeled directly to the Treasury and reloaned to other financial intermediaries that specialized in specific sectors. These specialized public institutions would then reloan their funds to private financial intermediaries. In turn, the intermediaries would loan the funds as directed to private companies in the form of short-term notes that usually were rolled over automatically and were assumed to be long-term commitments.

This financing strategy had important consequences for the structure of the Japanese financial system and the relationship between private companies and the government. Because the volume of lending was so large, companies were deeply in debt to the government. Equity and bond markets were little used and high debt levels constrained companies' ability to retain earnings for investment. While seemingly long-term, the maturity structure of loans allowed the government to shift funds from stagnant to high-growth sectors. Such a shift occurred in the 1970s when the government recognized the extent of global overcapacity in the shipbuilding industry and downsized the Japanese sector. But the short-term structure of the lending allowed it to implement that decision gradually and with minimal disruption to the private financial sector.

The strategies that made the Japanese lending system so successful resulted in the government taking a primary role in credit decisions. As Japanese companies and banks moved abroad and gained access to alternative sources of credit in external markets, the system was weakened and, in the view of many, became counterproductive. The loss of direct government control was not replaced by a system of effective indirect controls such as those that had been provided by monetary policy and financial regulation in other industrialized countries. The explosion of credit that led to the stock market and real estate bubbles in the 1980s could not have happened under the earlier lending system. But it would appear that such consequences are inevitable as liberalization dismantles old paradigms without providing adequate policy and regulatory infrastructure for the new systems that are to take their place.

BUILDING ON EXISTING STRUCTURES AND TRENDS

One of the more profound changes that has occurred in financial markets during the last two decades is the rise in securities markets as increasingly important channels for both domestic and international private investment flows. In many industrialized countries, a growing share of private savings are placed in pension plans and other institutional pools that invest those funds directly in securities rather than placing them in the hands of intermediaries such as depository institutions. In Canadian, German, Japanese, U.K. and U. S. financial markets, assets of institutional investors more than doubled as a percentage of GDP from 1980 through 1995.[8] In the United States, the share of total financial sector assets held by institutional investors rose from 32 percent in 1978 to 54 percent in 1998. At the same time, the share of depository institutions fell from 57 percent to 27 percent .[9]

Similar trends are occurring in emerging economies. The number of countries characterized as emerging markets by the World Bank's International Finance Corporation (IFC) and that have established stock markets rose from 31 in 1985 to 48 in 1994, while the number of listed domestic companies rose from 8,916 to 19,397. Mar-

---

[8]Bank for International Settlements, *68th Annual Report* (Basel: BIS, June 1998), and International Monetary Fund, *International Capital Markets: Developments, Prospects, and Policy Issues* (Washington, D.C.: International Monetary Fund, 1995).

[9]U.S. Board of Governors of the Federal Reserve System, *Flow of Funds Accounts of the United States* (Federal Reserve Statistical Release Z.1, September 15, 1999, www.bog.frb.fed.us/releases/).

ket capitalization jumped from $171 billion to $1.929 trillion over the same period, and climbed from 3.8 to 14.6 as a percentage of developed markets' capitalization.[10]

Another major development in emerging economies is the establishment of mandatory pension systems, many of which have been privatized. Chile was the first Latin American country to privatize its pension system, but other countries in the region have followed suit. Peru (1993), Argentina (1994), Colombia (1994), Uruguay (1995), Bolivia (1997), Mexico (1997), and El Salvador (1998) have implemented pension reforms. In 1997, Hungary, Poland, and Kazakhstan enacted legislation mandating the creation of private pension plans.[11] While some countries have shifted to a wholly privatized system, others that are implementing or considering reform have adopted the "three pillar approach" promoted by the World Bank and also used by Switzerland. This approach retains a government-funded first pillar to alleviate poverty in old age, establishes a second pillar to manage workers' mandatory contributions to provide retirement income, and advocates a third pillar that encourages additional, voluntary contributions to savings for retirement.

In several Latin American countries, the second pillar is privatized as in the Chilean model. Other countries retain a government role in collecting funds from employers but privatize their management. Others, like Malaysia, require mandatory contributions to a funded system but retain centralized national control.[12] Most countries that have followed World Bank guidelines in inaugurating a second, privatized pillar have created individual retirement accounts. Other basic components of reform include diversifica-

---

[10]International Finance Corporation, *Investment Funds in Emerging Markets* (Washington, D.C.: World Bank, 1996).

[11]P.S. Srinivas and Juan Yermo, *Do Investment Regulations Compromise Pension Fund Performance? Evidence from Latin America* (Washington, D.C.: World Bank, 1999).

[12]Salvador Valdés-Prieto, "Cargos por administración en los sistemas de pensiones de Chile, los Estados Unidos, Malasia y Zambia" (English summary), *Cuadernos de Economía* vol. 31, no. 93 (August 1994).

tion over multiple asset classes and prefunding to ensure that there will be adequate assets to pay benefits.[13]

Meanwhile, many emerging economies have also been active in developing public and private domestic mutual funds or investment trusts. The IFC has invested in domestic funds in Thailand, Sri Lanka, India, Pakistan, and Kenya. It has also advised the government of Zimbabwe in establishing a regulatory framework for a domestic mutual fund industry. But the main thrust of the IFC's program has been the establishment of international emerging market equity funds to channel foreign capital into the domestic markets of developing countries. Both the number of international funds (953 at year-end 1994, up from seventeen in 1985) and the value of assets under management ($106 billion in 1994) dwarf the size of domestic funds. Nevertheless, the IFC data show that international equity funds and other holdings by foreign investors amounted to only $200 billion or 10 percent of total emerging market capitalization at year-end 1994. In a 1996 report, the IFC asserted that, while stock markets in emerging economies were primarily places where local companies raised equity from local investors, foreign funds had played "a disproportionately large role in improving the functioning of emerging markets."[14]

The IFC also credits Chile's 1981 shift from a public to a private pension system for playing a sizable role in increasing the savings rate and developing the country's equity market. It argues that lifting restrictions on investment assets was critical to its success. Like all other public pension funds, Chile's government-managed fund had asset restrictions that limited its investments to government paper and bank deposits. Under the new private pension system, investments in equities were permitted. The growing pool of assets encouraged more companies to issue stock. Issuers were listed to increase the share of funds raised in equity markets. By 1995, the pool of savings in pension funds had reached 46 percent of GDP, prompting the IFC to remark that this "deep pool of domestic cap-

---

[13]Srinivas and Yermo, *Do Investment Regulations Compromise Pension Fund Performance?*
[14]International Finance Corporation, *Investment Funds in Emerging Markets* (Washington, D.C.: World Bank, 1996).

ital helped the country weather the fallout from the Mexican peso crisis almost unscathed. ..."[15] It fails to mention the contribution of capital controls, which others believe played an equally important role.

In the aftermath of the massive financial crises that have affected emerging economies since 1994, the number of developing economies that have established stock markets has risen to 67 at year-end 1998. However, aggregate market capitalization—which had peaked at $2.3 trillion in 1995—fell back to the level of 1994 in dollar terms.[16] Nevertheless, pools of assets valued in local currencies in both public and private prefunded pension plans, mutual funds, and unit trusts have continued to grow. They provide the infrastructure for a new form of import substitution that has the potential to raise the value of domestically held financial assets as a percentage of GDP. The levels implied would add stability to national markets and reduce dependence on foreign investment flows to finance development.

Pension Funds in Emerging Economies: Benefits and Problems
Despite the number of institutions and the diversity of their functions, the financial systems of many emerging economies are viewed as weak and inefficient. Whether controlled by government or private owners, regulation is inadequate and institutions are undercapitalized. Banking systems in particular are easily controlled by political interests or private oligarchs, and their loans distributed like prizes to a favored few. While one analysis of financial developments in sub-Saharan Africa concludes that stock markets have been more difficult for self-serving governments to control than banking systems, markets can be dominated by the foreign sector as well as by high income domestic residents.[17] In such systems, lack of access leads to indifference rather than outrage.

---

[15]International Finance Corporation, ibid.

[16]"Schools Brief. Stocks in Trade," *The Economist*, (November 13, 1999).

[17]Leonce Ndikumana, "Financial Development and Economic Growth in Sub-Saharan Africa: Lessons and Research Agenda," paper prepared for the Gwendolen Carter Symposium on African Development in the 21st Century at Smith College, September 24–26, 1999.

Those excluded from opportunities to borrow in the formal sector accept what they can afford to borrow from the informal sector. Neither the favored few nor the excluded seem to notice the extent to which lack of access to capital and credit for the majority of its citizens stunts a country's economic growth and development.

Prefunded pension fund systems have the potential to counter these tendencies by mandating the ownership of financial assets. The creation of individual accounts in countries that have reformed unfunded pay-as-you-go systems could, over time, significantly raise the level of interest of participants in the soundness of financial institutions and the overall performance of the economy. Moreover, as the pools of assets grow, ownership of companies becomes more widely dispersed, gradually but effectively eroding the control of various oligarchical structures in many emerging economies.

In some countries these benefits are already beginning to occur. In others, they are constrained by restrictions on the allocation of pension fund assets. Investment limits are the norm for public pension funds across the globe. Privatization has opened the way for investments in equities. However, even in reformed systems, some observers consider limits on holdings of stocks as a percentage of fund assets and of outstanding shares of individual companies to be "draconian" regulations that limit returns.[18] While acknowledging the lack of managerial experience, the fragility of markets, and the concern for soundness needed to build confidence in newly established systems, these critics argue for adopting the "prudent person rule" prevalent in private investment systems in many (but not all) industrialized countries.

The prudent person rule emphasizes diversification as opposed to restrictions on asset allocation. Its overall objective is to achieve the highest rate of return within the boundaries of acceptable risk. Adoption of this model by emerging economies is urged to counter the herd behavior characteristic of pension funds in Latin America, for example, as well as large concentrations of assets held

---

[18]Srinivas and Yermo, *Do Investment Regulations Compromise Pension Fund Performance?*

in funds that constrain liquidity. It is argued that restraints on investments in foreign assets in particular should be lifted to achieve diversity and improve returns.[19]

But looking to this model as it is played out in industrialized countries offers little hope that it would encourage diversity or restrain herd behavior. Pension funds and other institutional investors in the major industrialized economies tend to concentrate holdings in shares and bonds. They rely heavily on rating agencies in making investment decisions, and increasingly look to foreign stock and bond markets for additional opportunities to diversify portfolios, moving in herd-like fashion from one national market to another in search of the highest returns. Moreover, they have been accused of imposing short-term horizons on the corporate sector because the goal of maximizing shareholder value has been measured on the basis of quarterly or annual returns and has led to higher levels of portfolio turnover.

On the other hand, the "three pillar" model that emerged from the World Bank's 1994 report on old age pension programs worldwide has itself been criticized. Teresa Ghilarducci argues that it overlooks the importance of the first "pillar": social insurance. Noting the rising share of social security payments in the total incomes of U.S. middle-class retirees in the 1990s compared to the 1980s, she argues that the failure of U.S. private plans to pay adequate retirement income indicates that a mixed system is desirable only if it is based on universal social insurance. This is important even in the "mandatory" systems that have been adopted by emerging economies because they do not cover workers who are outside firms in the formal sector. Moreover, the mandatory deductions in wages are so high (13 percent in Chile, 13.5 percent in Mexico) that they may encourage low-income workers to opt out of the formal sector, thereby losing benefits.[20]

Ghilarducci also questions the assumption that high rates of return will continue to justify the shift from pay-as-you-go

---

[19]Srinivas and Yermo, ibid.

[20]Teresa Ghilarducci, "Pension Policies to Maintain Workers' Access to Retirement," in Ray Marshall, ed., *Back to Shared Prosperity* (Armonk, N.Y.: M. E. Sharpe, 1999)

public sector systems to privatized plans in emerging economies. In her view, "[t]he high return to privatizing only works in an elaborate system in which populations with different age distributions are buying and selling each other's investments." Thus, plans in emerging economies with young populations would need to be allowed to buy foreign assets to support sales of assets by aging populations in industrialized countries.

But even that strategy might have adverse consequences. In the United States, for example, buying and selling of stocks has not been motivated by intergenerational differences such as the need to support income levels of retirees. Even as middle-class workers poured retirement savings contributions into mutual funds and the foreign sector bought more shares of U.S. stocks, wealthier U.S. individuals sold more than $2 trillion of direct holdings of corporate equities from 1994 through the second quarter of 1999.[21] These sales from what might be called the U.S. version of the "third pillar" contributed to a sharp decline in the personal savings rate in recent years. They also provided funding for increased consumption and helped widen disparities in income between the top wealth-holders and all other income groups.

Like many critics of the failure of private pension systems to incorporate strategies to increase employment and income, Ghilarducci notes that using pension monies for job creation would be as important to workers as current stock market gains, which primarily benefit employers.[22] But creating jobs and raising incomes will become even more important as markets for exports contract and increased domestic demand becomes the alternative path to growth. Most of the pension reform programs have not yet addressed these issues. For example, Chile's 1997 reform focused on liberalizing restrictions on instruments. It enlarged the number of companies in whose stocks pension funds could invest from 30 to 200 out of a total of 300 listed companies, and it

---

[21]U.S. Board of Governors of the Federal Reserve System, *Flow of Funds Accounts of the United States.*

[22]Investing in affordable housing is another area that would seem to be particularly important to unskilled workers, because it would improve their quality of life.

authorized investments in project financings, securitized bonds, and venture capital funds. But it did not introduce specific policy objectives to promote economic and social programs.[23]

Mexico's reformed pension fund law has gone further than Chile's in expanding the range of investment instruments for pension contributions. But it also incorporates a mission statement that centers investment strategy on development and macroeconomic policy, by requiring investments in securities that encourage national productive activity, create infrastructure, and generate employment, housing development and regional development.[24] While limited progress has been made toward achieving these goals, it is the Mexican model that has the potential to support a transition to domestic demand-driven growth, transform the financial systems of emerging economies, and support the development of broad-based prosperity.

STRUCTURING PENSION FUNDS IN EMERGING ECONOMIES FOR GROWTH AND DEVELOPMENT

Past models for development have tended to focus primarily on the role of public international financial institutions and national governments in mobilizing funds for investment in sectors that are underdeveloped or that have underutilized potential for growth. The array of domestic development institutions in emerging economies ranging from Brazil to Zimbabwe provides evidence of how widely used this model has been. In many countries these institutions have operated in tandem with nationalized banking systems and provided structures for credit allocation to agricultural, small business, and other borrowers. In many cases, their inability to realize growth objectives in the sectors they served was due to the failure to ensure the necessary degree of impartiality in making credit decisions.

---

[23]Srinivas and Yermo, *Do Investment Regulations Compromise Pension Fund Performance?*
[24]Srinivas and Yermo, ibid.

But another equally serious problem was providing a source of funding for those institutions. In countries with nationalized banking systems, government backing meant that banks did not need to be well capitalized. Moreover, loans were funded by deposits. But specialized institutions required longer-term funding and were usually supported directly by the government or by sales of government-guaranteed paper. As discussed above, government paper and bank deposits tended to constitute the majority of instruments available for public pension funds and for private investment. The lack of options for investment and the low retirement income associated with public pension plans tended to encourage capital flight among middle- and high-income households. Thus, lower-income workers bore the burden of financing the government and its financial institutions, and governments were induced to borrow abroad to maintain growth.

Capitalizing the Financial Sector
As the Mexican pension reform law's statement of objectives suggests, one of the more important goals of pension reform in emerging economies should be to provide sufficient capital to financial institutions. Like the U.S. Reconstruction Finance Corporation in the 1930s, pension funds should be authorized to purchase the capital stock of banks, insurance companies, mortgage banks, agricultural cooperatives, lenders to small business, local credit cooperatives, regional development agencies, venture capital funds, and various other institutions that comprise national financial systems. Capitalizing these institutions would help create the financial structure needed to mobilize savings and distribute investments efficiently and productively across all segments of these economies.

The growth of a larger and more varied financial sector will, in turn, increase the menu of financial assets in which pension funds can invest, thus expanding opportunities for portfolio diversification and enhancing market liquidity. Recent reforms that have privatized banking systems using the universal bank model have not been sufficient to meet this need. Institutions are undercapitalized and, so far, have failed to introduce needed innovations. Using pension funds to capitalize the financial sector will be critical in countries where financial crises and bank failures have wiped out the capital base of much of the domestic system, opening the gate for increased foreign entry. But using retirement savings to provide capital to financial institutions must be accompanied by appropriate safeguards in the form of adequate regulation, effective governance, and financial guarantees as discussed below.

Bond markets are a segment of emerging economies' financial systems that have not yet recovered from the recent crises.[25] These markets could particularly benefit from domestic pension fund investment. Like life insurers, pension funds can hold long-term debt obligations more comfortably than banks. Thus, they can ensure the repayment schedules necessary to fund corporations' long-term capital investments and provide ongoing funding for domestic development institutions. Bond markets are essential if domestic funding is to grow relative to international sources as a share of total financing for public works projects and for creating infrastructure. Overall, augmenting domestic sources of long-term debt will be critical to the process of shifting to domestic demand-driven growth. The process will reduce dependence on external debt and reliance on export-led growth and will increase national ownership of both real and financial sector assets.

Deeper bond markets are also essential for the development of securitization to increase the supply of mortgage credit to middle-income households, as well as to back publicly supported affordable housing for lower-income families. Increasing and improving the housing stock is essential to the process of raising living standards. Constructing and renovating housing are activities that generate and maintain employment at both skilled and entry levels. Like public works and infrastructure, housing is a non-tradable good and thus a primary sector for leading the transition to domestic demand-driven growth.

Securitization is a technique that shifts the risk of holding long-term mortgages from depository institutions to institutional investors. Widely used in the United States, it has expanded the

---

[25]Jonathan Fuerbringer, "The Wounds Haven't Healed in Emerging-Markets Debt," *The New York Times* (November 28, 1999).

volume and lowered the cost of housing finance. The process of securitization involves the pooling of mortgages by originators and the sale of shares in the pool to outside investors. Freed from the necessity to hold mortgages in a portfolio backed by a limited amount of capital, mortgage originators can use their special skills to perform the function of originating and servicing mortgages in an expanding market. As the technique implies, securitization requires a large institutional investor sector—pension funds, mutual funds, and insurance companies—and contributes to the soundness of their portfolios by increasing the variety of investment instruments. As was the case in the United States, however, securitization is unlikely to be developed without government support. For example, in order to support the growth of securitized mortgage pools, governments will need to develop institutions that will play the role of market makers.

Private placements are another potential avenue for pension fund investment in emerging economies. These are a form of credit that is negotiated directly between lenders and borrowers, often with the assistance of a financial institution in locating and advising the two parties. In the United States, insurance companies have played an active role as lenders in the market for private placements. The borrowers have tended to be smaller and innovative enterprises without standing in bond markets. Unlike bond issues, private placements can be tailored to the particular needs of the borrower. A single placement may include short-, medium-, and long-term tranches that will better meet the needs for growth than credits in a single maturity range. Private placements are particularly useful for developing economies, enabling them to provide funding for established private companies. Such placements can also offer funding for public development institutions that subsidize private credits to small borrowers. Otherwise, the private financial institutions granting the credits would have to pass along the higher cost of servicing many such small loans.

Investing in domestic *venture capital funds*, as Chilean pension funds are now allowed to do, is illustrative of a unique role that pension funds can assume with less risk (in an admittedly risky field) than other investors simply because the number of participants is so large and the risk can be spread more widely. The IFC has encouraged the activities of foreign venture capital funds and is promoting local funds and joint ventures using foreign management. Because venture capital investments tend to be very small, they can fund businesses that are too small for direct pension fund investments, IFC officials point out. They benefit the economy by contributing to innovation and to business and job creation. They are an instrument of ownership that does not require a well-developed and liquid stock market for transactions. However, they can help develop the new companies that will augment equity markets by providing the source for initial public offerings

Like private placements, venture capital funds' commitments of patient capital require oversight. But that, in turn, provides opportunities to offer technical assistance in such areas as planning, marketing, and reporting that microlenders and other small institutions cannot provide.[26] True, the potential for disproportionately large gains relative to outlays, which can cushion losses in the overall portfolio, does not make venture capital funds risk free. However, it does justify the inclusion of a limited amount of investment in these funds in well-diversified pension pools.

Encouraging Participation in Investment Decisions and Corporate Governance

It is widely recognized that pension funds are becoming the new owners of businesses in the United States.[27] Peter Drucker has described this development as "pension fund socialism" in view of the fact that ownership of a rising share of the means of production is concentrated in the hands of institutional investors.[28] Many legal and economic analysts agree, however, that the problem with this form of ownership is the lack of legal clarity in determining which participants control choices and exercise the responsibili-

---

[26]International Finance Corporation, *Investment Funds in Emerging Markets.*

[27]U.S. House of Representatives, Hearing before the House Education and Labor Subcommittee on Labor-Management Relations, February 9, 1989 (Washington, DC: Government Printing Office, 1989).

[28]Peter F. Drucker, *The Pension Fund Revolution* (New Brunswick, NJ: Transaction, 1996).

ties of ownership: sponsors (employers), beneficiaries (employees and retirees), or fund managers?

In defined-benefit plans, the commitment of the employer to a contractual retirement income for the employee puts the risk of performance on the employer. Defined-benefit plans are governed by the Employee Income Retirement Security Act (ERISA), which authorizes the employer to act as a fiduciary (or to appoint fiduciaries) and to make investment decisions that will ensure sufficient income to meet future contractual obligations. In state and local government defined-benefit plans, the sponsor/employer is the political jurisdiction, and fiduciaries are appointed by elected officials.

Many public and private defined-benefit plans employ outside managers to make investment decisions. The larger plans use multiple managers with different managerial skills (or styles) and concentrations. Although fiduciaries of state and local government plans have assumed a major role in corporate governance during the last two decades, it is often the money managers in the private pension fund industry that exercise this major responsibility of ownership. Critics argue that numerous conflicts of interest arise from allowing outside pension fund managers to choose investments and exercise a dominant role in corporate governance. For example, a management firm's decisions about purchases or sales of the stock of a particular corporation may be influenced by its role in managing the corporation's pension assets. It may decide not to sell the stock and risk losing a customer.

Another criticism is that money managers tend to emphasize short-term gains in order to win or retain customers. In designing strategies for managing defined-benefit plans, for example, fund managers are aware that higher earnings in one quarter or over a year lower contributions in the next and, therefore, increase corporate profits. Meanwhile, the beneficiaries may be disadvantaged over the long-term. The emphasis on short-term gains in stock prices often leads many companies to adopt management strategies that will produce those gains. However, such strategies shortchange investment programs that have longer-term payouts—e.g., expanding plant and equipment, upgrading technology, or increasing funding for research and development—but are nevertheless necessary for future growth.[29]

Defined-benefit plans remain a very large segment of the U.S. pension fund industry, although the number of defined-contribution plans is now greater. Under defined-contribution plans, the employer agrees to contribute a contractual amount based on wage levels. The employee also contributes an agreed-upon basic contribution that can be augmented at his/her discretion. Under some plans, the employer pools individual accounts and selects managers for the pool, which usually limits discretion as to the range of investments. Under other plans, the employee receives and makes contributions to an individual account that can be self-managed or invested in a mutual fund or annuity managed by professionals. In either case, the risk of performance and the size of future retirement income are not the responsibility of the employer.

Defined-contribution plans do offer beneficiaries more portability, i.e., the ability to move an account from one employer to another in case of a job change. They also offer beneficiaries some choice as to the amount to be contributed by the employee. However, the beneficiaries' role in making investment decisions and exercising corporate governance is still highly restricted. If their contributions are pooled either by the employer or if they have invested individual accounts in mutual funds or purchased annuities, the beneficiaries remain passive investors without active rights of choice. Corporate governance remains passive either because it is exercised by fund managers chosen by the employer or because the beneficiaries' individual holdings in mutual funds or direct investments are too small to be effective in influencing corporate management decisions.

In short, there is no channel for participation in the rights and obligations of ownership in pension plans in the United States, except in state and local government plans, union funds, and funds administered by the Teachers Insurance and Annuity Association (TIAA). Both union funds and TIAA funds are multi-employ-

---

[29]Jane D'Arista, *The Evolution of U.S. Finance, Volume II* (Armonk, N.Y.: M. E. Sharpe, 1994).

er funds. Union funds are jointly controlled by employee and employer trustees, while TIAA funds are controlled by board members elected by beneficiaries. The governing structures of these two types of plans, as well as the type of control exercised by publicly appointed fiduciaries of state and local funds, offer the only U.S. models for the democratization of the immense private U.S. pension plan system. At issue in the debate on U.S. pension reform is one of the fundamental elements in a private market-based system. As articulated by Ghilarducci: "Workers own and bear the risk of failure if pension funds collapse. The first principle of property rights is that risk-bearers are property owners and have the right to some control."[30]

Many privatized pension systems in emerging economies face the same issues and concerns. Given that many emerging-economy pension systems involve mandatory contributions from wages, the importance of participation is underscored by the need to build confidence in the newer systems. Also, narrow elites in either public or private sectors must be prevented from capturing control over the allocation of assets for their own benefit. There is real danger that oligarchical control could dissipate the advantages of wider ownership of financial assets, particularly in Latin America where—except for a few countries, including Mexico— the government does not collect contributions. In those countries, private fund managers collect and invest contributions without public participation.[31] In Chile private management has thus far resulted in uniquely high fees and charges compared to international standards.[32] Yet this may be the least of the conflicts of interest that could emerge without direct oversight by those whose savings are at risk.

Reforms of existing and proposed private pension plans in emerging economies must address the issue of participation in ways

---

[30]Ghilarducci, "Pension Policies to Maintain Workers' Access to Retirement."

[31]Srinivas and Yermo, *Do Investment Regulations Compromise Pension Fund Performance?*

[32]Valdés-Prieto, "Cargos por administración en los sistemas de pensiones de Chile, los Estados Unidos, Malasia y Zambia."

that acknowledge the tension inherent in the mandatory nature of a privatized structure. Oversight could be provided by committees of legislative bodies; by local, regional, and/or national boards made up of representatives elected by beneficiaries; by union funds; or by all of the above. Active public debate concerning investment policies and governance issues should be encouraged in meetings of these and other groups of beneficiaries and their representatives or advocates.

In many emerging economies where private pension plans are already in place, they pose a particular challenge for the future of those economies. Analysts already foresee that shifts to fully funded systems will give rise to a large pension fund sector, as has been the case in the United States.[33] Thus, pension funds have the potential to become a powerful and comprehensive source of funding for economic policies that emphasize domestic demand-driven growth and shared prosperity. Alternatively, they may fall under the control of elites who will use them as they have used other financial institutions (such as banks) to cement political and economic control. As one analyst of financial development and economic growth has noted: "Concentration of financial resources is nothing but a consequence of concentration of political power. One cannot address the former issue without addressing the latter because they are intimately intertwined."[34] The hope in this case is that the roles will be reversed: that the concentration of financial resources in the hands of many wage earners will result in the diffusion of economic and political power across entire populations of emerging economies.

Protecting the Value of Contributions to Private Pension Plans
Emerging economies that have established private pension plans funded by mandatory deductions from wages are necessarily concerned with soundness and performance. Both are critical for building confidence in the new systems and avoiding fraud. Latin

---

[33]Valdés-Prieto, ibid.
[34]Ndikumana, "Financial Development and Economic Growth in Sub-Saharan Africa: Lessons and Research Agenda."

American countries rely on prudential regulations, such as fiduciary standards, accounting and auditing standards, insider trading rules, investor protection rules, and requirements for disclosure. Prudential regulations also require diversification and minimum risk-rating of assets. They also impose limits on self-investment and limit market power by restricting concentrations in share ownership. In addition, Colombia, Mexico, and Uruguay offer a rate-of-return or benefit guarantee of second-pillar pensions, at least in the initial years. In all Latin American countries with privatized systems, the highest priority is the safety of retirement assets.[35]

In the United States, by contrast, there has been little discussion of the safety of private pension fund assets even in the context of heated debates on privatizing social security. Those debates also tended to overlook the enormous amount of assets already held by private pension plans at year-end 1998 ($4.3 trillion) or their size in relation to the assets of depository institutions backed by deposit insurance ($5.1 trillion).[36] While it can be assumed that state and local government pension plans (another $2.8 trillion at year-end 1998) are backed by the taxing authority of the political jurisdictions that sponsor them, the only private plans that have public backing are defined-benefit plans ($2.1 billion). These plans are guaranteed by the Pension Benefit Guaranty Corporation (PBGC), which assumes responsibility for underfunded plans of companies that go bankrupt, thus ensuring that contractual benefits will be paid to retirees. Like other financial guarantees within the U.S. system, the PBGC relies for funding on premiums paid by covered participants—i.e., all companies that offer defined-benefit plans. The PBGC also has authority to borrow from the U.S. Treasury. However, private defined-contribution plans—the type of plans that were to be established in place of social security accounts— have no public or private backing to cover losses. With $2.2 trillion in assets at year-end 1998, they are the fastest growing segment

---

[35]Srinivas and Yermo, *Do Investment Regulations Compromise Pension Fund Performance?*
[36]U.S. Board of Governors of the Federal Reserve System, *Flow of Funds Accounts of the United States.*

of the U.S. pension fund industry and the weakest in terms of customer protection.

As pension fund systems continue to grow in both developed and developing economies, the issue of protecting the contributions and earnings of beneficiaries will become more important. A minimum annual real rate of return guarantee of 2 percent such as that offered by the government of Uruguay may be an appropriate means of providing protection for savings deducted from wages.[37] But unless the guarantee itself is prefunded, a serious market contraction would put considerable strain on governments coping with lost tax revenues and other calls on resources, such as unemployment insurance.

An alternative method of providing financial guarantees to pension fund beneficiaries would be to have the contributors themselves pay premiums into a prefunded insurance pool that would invest in government securities. Premiums would be deducted periodically from earnings on assets in individual accounts. The fact that such accounts already exist in many countries, and that accounting and reporting procedures are already in place, would make deducting premiums from earnings a routine matter. Given the growth in the size of the pension fund sector in countries with established prefunded systems, the pool of government securities backing the system would itself grow to substantial size over time. Even an annual deduction of 10 percent from *earnings*—not contributions—would eventually provide a sizable cushion to protect beneficiaries from losses.

In tandem with the growth in the insurance pool, the guarantee fund could adjust the level and coverage of benefits. For example, all contributions might be covered up to a certain amount in the years immediately following the introduction of the insurance scheme. Thereafter, the amount of covered contributions could be raised and coverage could be extended to include a portion of accumulated earnings with additional adjustments at five-year inter-

---

[37]Srinivas and Yermo, *Do Investment Regulations Compromise Pension Fund Performance?*

vals. In any event, the first priority should be coverage of the value of an individual's contribution up to the limit imposed by the aggregate value of the insurance pool. Setting a limit on coverage would introduce a redistributive element to privatized plans that does not currently exist. This would seem a particularly appropriate place to introduce it, because higher income individuals and households can bear the risk of loss on mandated savings above the level needed to ensure adequate retirement income more easily than can middle- and lower-income wage earners.

REFORMING THE INTERNATIONAL MONETARY AND FINANCIAL ARCHITECTURE TO PROMOTE DOMESTIC DEMAND-DRIVEN GROWTH IN EMERGING ECONOMIES

During the 1970s, middle-income developing countries were the primary recipients of recycled surpluses from the Organization of Petroleum Exporting Countries. They bought oil from OPEC countries, capital goods from industrialized countries, and borrowed heavily to support the import-led growth strategy of that period. But the burden of servicing rising levels of external debt denominated in dollars and other strong currencies eventually became insupportable. Oil prices rose again at the end of the decade and existing loans had to be rolled over with higher interest rates and shorter maturities. The most burdensome element was that the foreign exchange needed to service debt had to be earned, and the only way to earn it was to export goods to industrialized countries with strong currencies.

The debt crisis in 1982 made clear that the heavily indebted middle-income countries—most of which were in Latin America— would have to export their way out of debt. Foreign lending dried up. Private and public international financial institutions focused on expanding export capacity as a sign that a country was regaining creditworthiness. The International Monetary Fund (IMF) instituted conditions for multilateral credits that suppressed demand in these countries. Thus, imports would fall and export surpluses would result in external adjustment. The export-led growth strategy emerged in tandem with immense resource transfers. Over the years from 1983 through 1989, negative net outflows from Latin America amounted to -$116 billion as heavily indebted countries used all foreign exchange earned from exports to service external debt.[38]

Given the debt overhang, rising exports could not spur growth in the heavily indebted countries in the 1980s. But the export-led growth strategy also failed to inhibit the growth of external debt. The total external debt of developing countries continued to grow, rising from about $1 trillion at the beginning of the 1990s to $2 trillion in 1999. True, the decline in debt as a share of exports of goods and services from 186.2 percent to 160.9 percent between 1991 and 1998 attests to the success of the strategy in raising the volume and value of exports. However, the ratio of debt service payments to exports rose from 22.4 percent to 24.0 percent during the same period. For developing countries in the Western Hemisphere, however, debt service as a percentage of exports rose from 39.3 percent to 45.7 percent.[39]

A central element in any future strategy for growth in the global economy must involve efforts both to reduce developing countries' dependence on external debt and to lower the level of external debt denominated in foreign currencies. This does not mean that these countries will not need foreign private capital and/or bilateral and multilateral flows, nor does it mean such funds should be prohibited. But inflows must be rechanneled in ways that minimize the burden of debt service. In addition, the system of using one or a few strong currencies as vehicle currencies in international trade and investment and as reserve assets must be changed. The following three proposals suggest a framework through which old and new institutional arrangements could be used to lower debt levels, provide new channels for capital inflows,

---

[38]International Monetary Fund, *International Capital Markets: Developments, Prospects, and Policy Issues, 1995*.

[39]International Monetary Fund, *International Capital Markets* (Washington, D.C.: International Monetary Fund, September 1999).

and alleviate the barriers to growth in demand imposed by servicing foreign currency-denominated debt.[40]

Issuing a New Allocation of SDRs

A 1987 IMF staff report affirmed that allocations for Special Drawing Rights (SDRs) could serve as "a 'safety net' to cope with an international financial emergency of limited, though uncertain, duration." In the absence of a true lender of last resort, SDRs represent the single instrument in place at the global level to address the problem. Moreover, new SDR allocations provide a uniquely benign alternative to bailout loans, which compound the underlying inequities inherent in a global system organized around foreign currency-denominated debt.

Given the unprecedented amount of IMF resources already committed to crisis-ridden member countries, new sources of funding are urgently needed. In theory, the IMF could obtain these funds by borrowing in private markets. But member country taxpayers would remain the guarantor of IMF obligations. And the IMF would simply perpetuate the worst features of its current crisis-response operations if it reloaned privately raised funds to impacted countries. Debt owed to the IMF is no different than debt owed to the private sector in terms of the pressure it puts on countries to export their way out of massive loan obligations.

By issuing a new allocation of SDRs, the IMF could accomplish three objectives. First, it could provide badly needed debt relief. Second, it would permit countries to shift from an export-led growth paradigm toward fostering deeper, stronger internal markets. Third, it could foster conditions for a resumption of growth in developing countries and in the global economy.

Ideally, new allocations should be directed only to highly indebted poor countries (HIPCs) and to those nations that have been hit hardest by the effects of financial crises. But changing the IMF's Articles of Agreement to direct allocations to particular countries would be contentious and time consuming. On the other hand,

---

[40]A lengthier version of these three proposals was published in November 1999 by the Financial Markets Center.

a general allocation based on quotas—a system that would distribute almost half the newly issued SDRs to G-7 countries—could be done quickly, if agreed to by 85 percent of the IMF Board.[41]

In any event, allocations for debt relief should supplement the so-called "equity" allocations (adopted in April 1997 but not yet ratified) for countries that had not become members of the IMF in 1981when the last SDR allocations were made. Allocations to HIPCs should be sufficiently large to enable them to pay off public and private external debt. Allocations to other countries should be used to repay public debt and a needed portion of private debt. In the case of Russia, allocations should cover all debt incurred by the former Union of Soviet Socialist Republics. In repaying private debt, SDR recipients would exchange the drawing rights with central banks of strong-currency countries for foreign exchange, which would then be used to pay off private lenders.

In addition, recipient countries should retain a portion of the new drawing rights as reserves to back a resumption of domestic bank lending. Adding reserves to their central banks' balance sheets would increase the countries' liquidity, enable monetary expansion and thereby allow domestic banks to lend at reasonable rates of interest. The current reliance on high interest rates to attract foreign capital and raise currency values suppresses growth in crisis-battered countries. Borrowers can't earn enough to repay their loans, undercapitalized banking systems drain public resources, and credit crunches deter—rather than spur—new infusions of capital by foreign and domestic investors.

Moreover, unless newly allocated SDRs are also employed as domestic financial reserves, the export-led growth paradigm inevitably will continue. Absent an injection of liquidity in domestic markets, hard-hit countries must struggle to earn the reserves needed to rebuild financial systems capable of funding job creation and income growth in the domestic economy. Currently, these coun-

---

[41]David Lipton of the Carnegie Endowment for International Peace has suggested that a large general allocation be used to create a pool of funds to defend the international financial system in time of dire threat. Lipton's proposal constitutes a sensible use of SDRs allocated to countries that do not need debt relief or access to international liquidity.

tries must either increase the volume of exports or borrow from external sources to augment domestic liquidity.

Creating a Public International Investment Fund for Emerging Markets

The second proposal puts forward a plan for establishing a public international investment fund for emerging markets. Structured as a closed-end mutual fund, this investment vehicle would address the problems that have emerged with the extraordinary growth in cross-border securities investment transactions in the 1990s. The proposal advocates a role for the public sector in managing those problems. Thus, private portfolio investment, which became the dominant channel for flows into emerging markets from 1990-94, can promote steady, sustainable growth rather than the boom and bust cycles that so far have been its primary contribution.

This proposed closed-end investment fund for emerging markets builds on existing activities of the World Bank's International Finance Corporation (IFC), whose mandate is to promote private-sector investment in developing countries. Private foreign portfolio investment in emerging markets has been actively promoted by the IFC since 1984, when the first country fund was structured in Korea. The IFC's objective in promoting portfolio investment was " to integrate domestic and international capital markets."[42] Initially, country funds were structured as closed-end funds but quickly shifted to open-ended mutual funds as the IFC concluded that exit possibilities encouraged more entry. Its Global Index Fund, formed in January 1994 to target pension funds in industrialized countries, adopted a semi-open structure that allowed issuances and redemptions on the last day of the month rather than continuously. As noted above, the number of country funds investing in emerging markets had exceeded 1,000 by 1994, with assets totaling $100 billion.[43]

---

[42]International Finance Corporation, *Investment Funds in Emerging Markets*.
[43]International Finance Corporation, ibid.

As the IFC realized, the phenomenal growth of institutional investors' assets in G-7 countries suggests that foreign portfolio capital is an ideal channel for financing long-term economic expansion in emerging economies. To achieve this beneficial result, however, these economies need portfolio investment inflows that are sizable, stable, and supportive of the policy objectives of both their governments and domestic enterprises. Chile has been fairly successful in using capital controls to achieve some of these results by requiring foreign investors to hold securities for at least a year. Also, Chilean companies must maintain reserve requirements on direct borrowing abroad. Korea, too, imposed limits on foreign borrowing by domestic companies for many years before its recent liberalization. Such controls are very useful but cannot accomplish the dual task of injecting long-term private capital into developing countries while deterring the destructive fluctuations in asset prices and exchange rates associated with procyclical surges in foreign portfolio flows.

One innovation that might be equal to this task is to return to the closed-end fund structure for foreign investment in emerging market securities, but have the manager be a public international agency. The new fund could issue its own liabilities to private investors and buy stocks and bonds of private enterprises and public agencies in a wide spectrum of developing countries. Both the number of countries and the size of the investment pool would be large enough to ensure diversification. The fund's investment objectives would focus on the long-term economic performance of enterprises and countries rather than short-term financial returns. Selecting securities in consultation with host governments and representatives of pension fund beneficiaries would help the fund meet those objectives.

Unlike open-end mutual funds that must buy back an unlimited number of shares whenever investors demand it, closed-end investment pools issue a limited number of shares that trade on a stock exchange or in over-the-counter markets. This key structural difference makes the holdings in closed-end portfolios much less vulnerable to the waves of buying and redemptions that sometimes characterize open-end funds. Thus a closed-end fund would provide emerging markets a measure of protection by allowing the prices of shares in the fund to fluctuate without triggering destabilizing purchases and sales of the underlying investments.

To further balance the goals of market stability and economic dynamism, the closed-end fund should possess a solid capital cushion. Between 10 and 20 percent of the value of shares sold to investors should be used to purchase and hold government securities of major industrial countries in amounts roughly proportional to the closed-end fund shares owned by residents of those countries. These holdings would provide investors a partial guaranteed return, denominated in their own currencies, while the government securities would explicitly guarantee the value of the fund's capital. This dual guarantee would moderate investors' concerns about potential risk.

Creating one or more closed-end funds on this model would reduce the need for capital controls, especially in countries that choose to accept foreign portfolio investment solely through this vehicle. The closed-end fund would have several additional benefits as well. It would help pension plans in developing and developed countries diversify their portfolios while minimizing country risk and transactions costs. And it would help institutional investors in developing countries share the cost of information and collectively combat the lack of disclosure by domestic issuers in those markets.

These arrangements need not reinvent the wheel. Just as the structural mechanisms and potential assets of an emerging-economies closed-end fund already exist in the marketplace, so the capacity for managing such a fund falls well within the reach of an existing public institution: the World Bank and its IFC subsidiary. Indeed, this management function follows in the line of the IFC's current activities and is thus consistent with the Bank's mandate to facilitate private investment in developing countries. Moreover, the Bank's experience in issuing its own liabilities in global capital markets would expedite the startup of a closed-end fund.

Creating an International Clearing System

The third proposal articulates an alternative to the privatized, dollar-based international monetary system that is a root cause of global instability and market failure. This proposal would create an international transactions and payments system managed by a public international agency in which cross-border monetary exchanges can be made in each country's own currency. This critical feature would help governments and central banks conduct effective economic policies at a national level. Equally important, it would allow all countries—not just a privileged few—to service external debt with wealth generated in their domestic markets. Thus it would help end the unsustainable paradigm of export-led growth governing the global economy.

A major objective of the proposal is to end the devastating declines in currency values that raise the value of external debt, wipe out foreign exchange reserves and bankrupt whole sectors of emerging economies virtually overnight. Despite repetitions of these events across the globe, establishment debate over monetary matters remains narrow, generally contenting itself with rehashing the relative merits of fixed versus floating exchange rate regimes. The Clinton Administration did propose that the IMF provide these countries' central banks more reserves to preclude traders' bets against their national currencies. But experience clearly shows that such injections only reassure investors if coupled with policies that constrain domestic growth. When growth falters, the resources invariably wind up as profits for speculators. Modest, well-intentioned adjustments to the prevailing international monetary arrangements are not capable of restoring financial stability or facilitating sustainable economic activity. A new system of currency relations is needed.

To succeed, this new system must possess three essential attributes. First, it must enable national governments and central banks to reclaim from financial markets their sovereign capacities to conduct appropriate national economic policies. Second, it must promote the ability of governments and central banks to employ effective countercyclical policies at a national level. And third, it must support a symmetrical relationship between the creation of real wealth and the servicing of financial liabilities, regardless of the country of origin or currency of the creditor.

An international clearing agency (ICA) functioning as a clearinghouse and a repository for international reserves should be the keystone for this new system of monetary relations. Although its creation would demand significant collaboration among nations, such an institution would not be a supranational central bank. It would not issue a single global currency. Indeed, it would not issue currency at all. That would remain the prerogative of national central banks. But, by providing a multinational structure for clearing payments, it would enable countries to engage in international trade and financial transactions in their own currencies.

The proposed international clearing agency would hold debt securities of its member nations as assets and their international reserves as liabilities. Those assets and liabilities would allow the ICA to clear payments between countries. Exchange rates would be readjusted within a set range and over a set period of time in response to changes in levels of reserves held by the ICA. These periodic adjustments would reflect the valid role of market forces in shaping exchange rates through trade and investment flows. But speculators would no longer dominate the process.

The ICA's asset and liability structure also would allow it to conduct open market operations on an international basis, much as the Federal Reserve and other central banks do at the national level. By conducting these operations, the ICA would help smooth changes in international reserves caused by imbalances in trade or investment flows. For example, if a nation were experiencing excessive capital inflows, the ICA could help the national central bank absorb liquidity by selling its own holdings of that country's government securities to residents in the national market. In the case of a country experiencing excessive capital outflows, the ICA could assist the national central bank in supplying liquidity by buying government securities from residents in the national market and augmenting that country's supply of international reserves.

Thus, its ability to create liquidity would allow the ICA to act as a global lender of last resort—a role that neither the IMF nor any other existing institution is structured to play effectively. In this capacity, the ICA could also help countries counter the effects of political shocks, commodity price gyrations, and natural disasters on international payments.

Membership in the ICA would be open to national central banks of all participating countries and branches of the clearinghouse would conduct operations in every major financial center in order to implement its critical role in international payments. The institution would fund its operations with earnings from the government securities on its balance sheet. Like the U.S. Federal Reserve System, the ICA would remit to the issuers of those securities (e.g., the U.S. Treasury in the case of the United States) any annual earnings that exceeded expenses.

Like national central banks, the ICA should be equipped with a highly skilled transactional, policy, and legal staff. To guard against becoming a clubhouse for creditors or unrepresentative elites, the new ICA must level the central bank playing field upward. It must hew to tough disclosure and reporting standards, and its mandate must focus on the interests of people and their institutions of self-government. ICA eligibility standards should require member central banks to demonstrate genuine accountability to citizens in their own countries.

Population as well as economic output would determine participating nations' governing power within the ICA. For example, the executive committee in charge of the ICA's operations and policy should be appointed on a rotating basis, with the requirement that its members represent countries that, in the aggregate, constitute more than half the world's population and more than half its total output. To ensure diverse inputs into policy deliberations, the ICA's staff and advisory bodies would represent a variety of regions, occupations, and sectors, and include constituencies that are frequently overlooked in the formulation of national policy.

While the ICA's independent directors would be the coequals of national central bank officials, their obligations and perspective must be mega-economic in scope. In seeking to influence the course of national economic policy, the ICA would operate primarily through persuasion and negotiation rather than resorting to unilateral exercise of its financial leverage in the open market. However, with a super-majority or consensus of member countries, the ICA would have the ability to redirect national policy in the long-term economic interest of all.

This aspect of the ICA's operations may seem radical, even with an unprecedented degree of transparency and accountability built in. In fact, it is far less radical and far more respectful of national sovereignty than financial markets' existing capacity to override national policy goals and undermine democratic institutions. Moreover, numerous precedents exist for international efforts to reshape economic policy in one country in the interest of global stability and widely shared prosperity. Among the most visible and recent precedents are attempts by the other six members of the G-7 to redirect the course Japan's macroeconomic policy.

Restoring the public sector to its historic role as facilitator and guardian of the international payments system would have deep and lasting benefits. A stable regime of currency relations is key to reversing incentives in the current global economic system for lower wages and the export of goods and capital on ruinous terms.

CONCLUSION

Key elements in the financial infrastructure for emerging economies are participation and ownership. The discussion of widening ownership of both financial systems and real sectors through investments in pension funds implies that a larger and more effective private sector would take a broader than usual role in economic decision-making. Moreover, ownership that returns a share of profits to holders of financial assets is an important consideration in countries where religious beliefs prohibit interest payments. Such an ownership structure is also important in countries whose economies are built around the development of natural resources, because it answers concerns about the right to share in the national patrimony. Overall, ownership promotes interest and involvement to counter the apathy and even hopelessness that characterize attitudes toward economic life in many countries.

There is no guarantee that wider ownership of financial assets and of the enterprises and institutions that issue them will result in more active participation in economic life. Participation will need to be encouraged by both governments and civil society. But the potential for involvement may be greater in countries that have established mandatory private pension plans than in those that have not. In any event, interest and involvement are critical in providing the oversight to ensure that governments, financial institutions, and businesses act in the broader public interest.

Finally, in addition to arguing for adoption of national and global structures and policies that will encourage domestic demand-driven growth in emerging economies, this paper also argues for the reinstatement of a strong role for national governments in determining national economic policies. Few of the reforms needed to promote a new paradigm for growth or to ensure that gains will be broadly shared will be implemented without that role. Even in countries where privatized pension systems have been established, it is the mandatory contributions that make these systems effective. And the mandatory requirement can only be put in place and enforced by government.

Capital Flows and the International Financial Architecture

A Paper from the Project on Development,
Trade and International Finance

John Eatwell and Lance Taylor

A Council on Foreign Relations Paper

Capital Flows and the International Financial Architecture

John Eatwell and Lance Taylor

The Asian crisis of 1997 precipitated a worldwide reappraisal of the performance of international financial arrangements. This debate has been labeled "Reform of the International Financial Architecture." Almost all serious commentators have now abandoned the presumption, widely held before 1997, that financial liberalization is invariably beneficial. But there is as yet no consensus either about the appropriate analysis of the impact of financial liberalization, or about what should be done. This paper addresses both questions.

Our analysis is based on a research project, sponsored by the Ford Foundation, that began in mid-1997. For that project, we gathered together a number of colleagues to evaluate the effects of liberalization on the performance of real economies throughout the world. Our synthesis of their insights was contained in a coauthored report entitled *International Capital Markets and the Future of Economic Policy*, presented to the Ford Foundation in August. Further elaboration led to our forthcoming book, *Global Finance at Risk: The Case for International Regulation*.

Both the report and the book concentrate on the effects of liberalization. Our evaluation covers both long-term trend performance and explores the recurrent financial crises that have, during the past 30 years, periodically disrupted both developed and developing economies. While international liberalization has brought some benefits, those benefits have been tarnished by considerable costs. The costs could have been substantially mitigated if a key lesson had been drawn from the development of domestic financial markets: liberal markets are only efficient if they are efficiently regulated. The task of financial regulation is to manage the risks that follow in the wake of liberalization. Without regulation, the risks and associated costs can become unbearable. We propose the establishment of a World Financial Authority (WFA), to function in world financial markets as national regulators do in domestic markets. A natural place to build the WFA is on the foundations for global financial surveillance and regulation that have already been laid by the Bank for International Settlements, in Basel.

Ideas similar to ours have come from prominent sources. In the United States, for example, the February 1999 *Economic Report of the President* argued that "Financial liberalization and innovation have rendered national boundaries irrelevant. If regulation was necessary within national boundaries, then it is now (at least) equally necessary in the international market." In the United Kingdom in late September 1998, one of us (Eatwell) received a telephone call from a *Financial Times* reporter asking him to comment on a speech that British Prime Minister Tony Blair had given the day before. The speech had covered aspects of international financial reform, and, declared the journalist, "we know you wrote it." Eatwell protested he had done no such thing. His protests were cut short by the journalist: "The Prime Minister's press officer is telling us that you did." In fact, Eatwell had not written Blair's speech. But he had sent Blair's office a copy of our Ford Foundation report, and parts of the speech were based on some of our proposals.

Despite the similarities between our analysis and arguments emanating from the White House and Downing Street, our specific recommendation for the creation of a WFA has been dismissed by some (including a few people generally sympathetic to our analysis) as "utopian" and "lacking political feasibility."

To us, these criticisms seem misconceived.

First, even if the WFA as a specific institution is not created, it is still important to identify the *WFA function*, i.e., the tasks that need to be done by somebody. In this respect the WFA is a template for our analysis of markets and of policies to enhance the efficiency of international finance. In the book we stress that financial markets are not automatically self-regulating, and we illustrate the point in four key areas:

- There has been a breakdown of national regulatory capacities as liberalization has spread worldwide during the past four decades. Consequences have included high and variable real interest rates, volatility of asset prices, poor national economic performances, and the contagious spread of market instabilities worldwide.

- Such developments create the possibility for massive upheavals even in the large and integrated financial markets of the industrialized economies. Past examples are presented and potential risks to the American economy are pointed out.

- The recent wave of currency crises in developing and transition economies has clearly been associated with rapid capital market liberalization and the absence both internationally and at the country level of appropriate regulatory procedures to deal with the financial flows that were unleashed.

- There is a complete absence of "fundamentals" in the determination of exchange rates; changes in rates are driven exclusively by shifting speculative "conventions" in the markets. Exchange rate volatility exacerbates all the deficiencies of unregulated markets.

In all four areas, intelligent international regulation is essential to help markets perform more effectively, and to reduce the danger of massive market failures. A major component of the WFA function is the provision of the surveillance, enforcement, and policy development that lie at the heart of efficient regulation.

Second, if the experience of policy changes in international finance over the past few years has taught us anything, it is that what is utopian one day is the conventional wisdom the next. Financial innovation happens at breakneck speed. That includes institutional and political innovation. In the nine months following the Russian default on August 17, 1998, an event that sent shock-waves around the financial world, the G-7 took the initiative to establish the Financial Stability Forum (FSF), a nascent international regulatory institution. Whether the FSF develops to perform the WFA function only time will tell. After the Brazilian crisis of early 1999 waned, a period of relative calm in financial markets slowed the pace of institutional reform. Further storms will quicken the pace again. There are no absolute standards of what is and is not politically feasible. What does matter is the balance of powers and interests, and the fear of the consequences of doing nothing. In the face of another severe crisis a WFA may well become politically feasible, and if that should happen it is important to think through in advance how it would actually work.

In the discussion to follow, we begin with a capsule history of world capital markets, to establish a common ground. We then review our analysis of the four points mentioned above, and close with a presentation of the functions and operations of a WFA.

LIBERAL CAPITAL MARKETS IN HISTORY

Since around 1870, there have been three periods during which cross-border movements of financial capital were substantially unregulated: first, under the "high" gold standard before World War I; second, the gold exchange standard between the two world wars; and, third, the new liberal financial order existing today. Was global macroeconomic stability assured during the two gold-standard episodes? In the first it was, after a fashion. In the second it most clearly was not.

The high gold standard was the linchpin of the late Victorian world economic order. Under its rules, most countries fixed their currencies in terms of gold (thus maintaining fixed exchange rates among themselves), held gold reserves to settle their international accounts, and often used gold coins as well. Between 1870 and the outbreak of World War I, international macro adjustment pivoted on the Bank of England, often acting in cooperation with other central banks. Capital flows stabilized the system, because they tended to move out of Britain when it was at the bottom of its business cycle and the London interest rate was low. When import demand fell in Britain, the low rate stimulated real investment in borrower countries of European settlement and the colonies. In time, the British economy would recover or the Bank of England would raise the discount rate to counter reserve losses. Capital would move back toward London and high rates would force raw-materials exporters to sell off stocks on unfavorable terms, improving the British terms of trade and trade balance as well. The system operated counter-cyclically, stimulating demand outside Britain when local demand was low, and reducing demand outside Britain when local demand was high.

This overall stability did *not* rule out national crises. When their capital inflows dried up, capital-importing countries often could not raise exports sufficiently to avoid suspending debt payments or abandoning gold parity. The U.S. crashes of 1893 and 1907 are cases in point. But such local financial volcanoes erupted without threatening the system as a whole. Even repeated crises in Britain itself failed to topple the gold standard, primarily because of the financial support of the Banque de France, the investment of the Indian surplus in London (to the detriment of the Indian economy), and South African gold production. Nonetheless, by the outbreak of the First World War, the gold standard was becoming unsustainable as more countries established central banks, complete with gold reserves that were no longer susceptible to the free-flowing influence of London interest rates.

The adjustment mechanisms central to the operation of the gold standard resulted in the *real* interest rate (that is, the nominal rate minus the rate of inflation) being very high. Between 1870 and 1890, average long-term real rates in the major industrial countries were around 4%. From 1950 to 1970, the so-called "Golden Age" of rapid economic growth worldwide—and a time when capital markets were highly regulated—real interest rates were about 2%. They fell to near zero in the inflationary 1970s. From 1981–93, when the international financial market was once again deregulated, the average real rate in major industrial countries was at the historic high of 5.1%. Free international capital markets appear to go hand-in-hand with high real interest rates, that is, high returns to rentiers. Some of the reasons why are taken up below.

Under the gold standard as it functioned between the two world wars (the gold-exchange standard) stability properties were very different. The United States had become the biggest international lender, meaning that its national saving (the "source" of funds directed toward financial markets) exceeded its domestic investment (the major domestic "use" of funds after they filter through the financial system). Because the excess of sources over uses had nowhere else to go, it had to take the form of international lending. Moreover, the U.S. aggregate savings supply rose substantially during a business cycle upswing, so that at the peak both its exports of financial capital and its import demand were high. In contrast to Britain under the high gold standard, capital movements out of and trade flows into the U.S. economy both moved *with* the trade cycle. They thereby tended to stimulate economies elsewhere, with further positive feedback effects on the United States: both upswings and downswings were strongly amplified.

During the inter-war years international cooperation was weak, in contrast to the earlier period when the Bank of England could always rely on help from counterpart institutions on the Continent. One crucial example was the wave of banking crises that spread across Europe in 1931. Following bank failures in Austria, Germany encountered difficulties in midyear, throwing the Reichsbank into dire need of external credit. France had ample gold reserves (built up through annual trade surpluses, a partial result of the franc's having been pegged at a weak level when it re-entered the gold standard). But it attached so many political strings to the credits it offered that the Germans would not accept: money with strings is not liquid. A Continent-wide crisis and the spread of the Great Depression worldwide followed in turn.

This collapse was deepened by "currency" or "locational" imbalances in balance sheets of the financial systems in many of the affected countries. In Germany (and elsewhere), a large share of domestic bank deposits were held by foreign investors and banks. At the same time, the German banks' assets were largely domestic. Rising fears of devaluation would lead almost automatically to deposit withdrawals, possibly igniting bank runs and subsequent crises. Sixty-six years later and half the world away, these same factors exacerbated the Asian crisis of 1997 and spilled over into Russia the following year.

In the United States, the major creditor country, the financial system was fragile for a different reason. Many of its clients had borrowed heavily to undertake financial investments. In the jargon, they were highly "leveraged" or "geared." In principle, such a position cannot be maintained when the value of the collateral assets an investor holds falls below the level of his or her debt. In practice, he or she often fails when current income flows (including capital gains) fall short of current interest obligations. After the 1929 Crash, the first condition applied. "Margin calls" on the loans many investors had taken out to buy shares when prices were rising bankrupted many credit-worthy borrowers when share prices fell. This process of "debt-deflation" (Yale economist Irving Fisher's term from 1933) was another contributing factor to the Great Depression. A similar process was clearly visible in Asia in 1997–98.

One effect of the competitive devaluation and beggar-my-neighbor policies of the 1930s was to encourage wartime economists (led by John Maynard Keynes from the United Kingdom and Harry Dexter White from the United States) to design a system with fixed exchange rates that did *not* rely on anachronistic national gold hordes. At the famous Bretton Woods, New Hampshire, conference in 1944 they replaced the liberal international financial markets of the gold standard with strict controls on capital movements. These controls were a fundamental characteristic of the new Bretton Woods system. Insofar as its institutional structure reflected the Keynesian theoretical concerns of the time, Bretton Woods may be interpreted as a set of rules under which national authorities might, if they wished, pursue full employment policies, free of some of the anxieties that accompany open capital markets. Exchange-rate stability was central to this system.

The success of the Bretton Woods design must be a key factor in the evaluation of the impact of the subsequent, post-1971, liberalization. Growth and employment rates during the 25 years of the system's effective operation from the end of World War II until about 1970 were at historic highs in most countries. Productivity growth was also at an historic high, not only in countries that were "catching up" but also in the technological leaders. It *was* a Golden Age. How the Bretton Woods system broke down after 25 years of extraordinary economic success is a well-known story. For present purposes, the objective is not the resurrection of Bretton Woods—that is economically and politically impossible. Rather, the post–World War II system provides a point of reference. From there, we can study the impact of the reduction in barriers to international capital movements that got underway as the system started to fail.

THE BREAKDOWN OF FINANCIAL REGULATION

The present wave of capital-market liberalization began with the opening of Eurocurrency markets in the 1950s. But it was with the breakdown of Bretton Woods and the consequent privatization of foreign-exchange risk that the explosion of foreign-exchange markets began, followed by the creation of global bond markets in the 1980s, and global equity markets in the early 1990s.

The international financial flood of the past 25 years rose from the tiny spring begun by Eurodollar (later Eurocurrency) markets in the 1950s. A Eurodollar deposit is just a deposit denominated in dollars in a bank outside the political jurisdiction of the United States. As the name implies, offshore banking operations were originally limited to Europe (with London as the major trading point), but they soon could be carried out worldwide. Net Eurocurrency deposit liabilities amounted to around $10 billion in the mid-1960s and grew to $500 billion by 1980. By the mid-1980s in the industrial countries, bank deposits in currencies other than each nation's own currency amounted to around one-quarter of the total.

A major contributing factor to growth in Eurocurrency markets was the American "interest equalization tax" of 1964–73, which raised costs for banks to lend offshore from their domestic branches. The resulting higher external rates led dollar depositors such as foreign corporations to switch their funds from onshore U.S. institutions to Eurobanks. A second massive Eurodeposit inflow came in 1973-74, with the onset of "recycling" of OPEC trade surpluses after the first oil shock. The developing country debt boom followed in turn, as rich countries' banks used OPEC's deposits to back massive loans to middle income economies in Latin America and elsewhere. The subsequent crash after the Mexican default of August 1982 led to a "lost decade" of growth in most of the developing world (with Asian economies as the major exceptions until 1997, for reasons discussed below).

Eurocurrency transactions rapidly taught market players that they could shift their deposits, loans, and investments from one currency to another in response to actual or anticipated changes in interest and exchange rates. These moves were early warnings of a pervasive regulatory problem that dominates the world economy today: *any nation's financial controls appear to be made for the sole purpose of being evaded.* Even the ability of central banks to regulate the supply of money and credit was undermined by commercial banks' borrowing and lending offshore. By the early 1980s, national authorities had been forced to scrap long-established interest rate ceilings, lending limits, portfolio restrictions, reserve and liquidity requirements, and other regulatory paraphernalia. These instruments acted on the supply side of financial markets by limiting the ability of private sector players to seek capital gains, hedge risk, or undertake arbitrage. They all could be circumvented by the new freedom to pursue offshore transactions. All finally had to be abandoned.

Dropping their supply-side regulatory tools meant that central banks could now operate only on the demand side of the money market, buying and selling securities to influence short-term interest rates. The result has been higher and more volatile real rates. The 1995 Annual Bulletin of the Bank for International Settlements (BIS) commented, "... interest rates generally have to become higher and more variable" as they are managed to influence demands for financial assets. The new interest-rate regime became the norm in every major economy. The result was a powerful inducement for even greater cross-border surges of portfolio investment. As under the inter–world war gold standard, central banks in the advanced economies lost much of their power to pursue counter-cyclical monetary policies. And as under the nineteenth-century gold standard, high interest rates seemed to settle in for good.

ACTUAL AND POTENTIAL PROBLEMS IN INDUSTRIALIZED ECONOMIES

Capital-market decontrol is the background for three issues that have dominated the recent experiences of almost all the major industrial countries: *first*, the slowdown in growth to about two-thirds of the growth rate attained in the 1950s and 1960s; *second*, a common fall in the share of GDP devoted to investment; and *third*, a rise in unemployment (only in the United States is the unemployment rate at levels comparable to the 1960s, an important exception that will be considered in detail below).

This commonality of experience throughout the major industrial countries is striking. It suggests that the causes of low growth and higher unemployment during the past twenty-five years are to be found in factors that affect *all* countries in a broadly similar manner, rather than in the individual circumstances of each country.

Four candidates for the role of a common source are: *first*, the impact of the oil crises of the 1970s; *second*, the end of the post-World War reconstruction boom in which Europe and Japan were "catching up" with the United States; *third*, the structural changes in world trading relationships associated with the increasing mobility of capital and the rapid growth of third world manufactured exports, particularly from China and the Pacific Rim; *fourth*, changes in the international financial environment since 1973.

As we argue in *Global Finance at Risk: The Case for International Regulation*, the first three explanations are far weaker than the last. With regard to the oil shocks of the 1970s, for example, the obvious comparisons are with other big relative price movements in the postwar world economy. During the Korean war era, the rich countries got through a large increase in all raw material prices without notable deceleration of growth. And oil and other commodity prices collapsed in 1986 without stimulating a new round of high performance (although, as the major consumer of energy, the U.S. economy benefited from the price reductions, in comparison to its rivals).

Productivity growth rates in the G-7 countries have tended to converge in those industries, such as manufacturing, that are exposed to international competition. This convergence has coincided with a general reduction in the overall pace of productivity growth. "Catching up" explains part of this process, but not all. It does not explain the common, general reduction in productivity growth observed worldwide.

Recently there has clearly been a rise in competition from the newly industrializing countries, particularly those on the Pacific Rim, which has jeopardized growth in the major industrial countries. In 1968 just 1% of G-7 domestic demand for manufactures was satisfied by imports from the Third World. By 1980 developing countries' market share had risen to 2%; by 1988 to 3.1%; and by 1998 to 6%.

The complication is that the phenomenon of low-wage competition from newly industrializing countries is not new to the developed world. The experience of the past 20 years was not dissimilar to the competition that the northern European countries experienced from southern Europe in the late 1950s; e.g., the growth of Italy's share of world manufactured trade from less than 2% to over 6% in twenty years. However, greater import penetration did *not* result in slow growth or unemployment in northern Europe. On the contrary, throughout the period in which competition was most intense northern Europe suffered from a labor shortage, with about 10% of the labor force in West Germany and France being immigrants. High overall growth enabled the North to absorb Southern Europe's export and emigration surge.

The new international financial order is the fourth "common factor" influencing the economic performance of all countries. Is there a credible story to be told that links financial market liberalization to the deteriorating economic performance of the major industrial countries? Such a story surely must involve deflation-

ary pressures on both public and private sectors by the sheer scale
of international capital flows, and the actual and potential volatility of those flows.

There are at least three ways in which liberalized financial
markets can cause deterioration in overall economic performance.
First, as Keynes profoundly observed in 1936 in *The General Theory of Employment, Interest, and Money,* finance operates along the
lines of a "beauty contest" popular in down-market English Sun-
day newspapers in the 1930s. The contestants' goal was *not* to pick
the prettiest face from the array of young women's photos that appeared
in the paper; rather, it was to pick the face voted prettiest by all
the players that day. The game, therefore, was to guess the players' average opinion about what average opinion regarding the prettiest face would be, and so on to "higher degrees" of conjecture.

Keynes argued that financial markets in essence operate along
beauty-contest lines. Few thoughtful players or observers disagree. A crucial implication is that such a market is likely to be
dominated by "conventions" about its behavior, just as conventional
standards about beauty would have directed the contestants'
choices in the 1930s. Financial conventions can be stable for
extended periods of time. But they also can be highly *unstable* and
prone to occasional severe loss of liquidity when all opinion tends
to shift in the same direction. This will increase the cost of capital and sometimes lead to severe capital shortages. Both are factors that will tend to discourage investment and reduce levels of
activity in the medium term.

Second, the operation of the beauty contest means that movements of asset prices and rates of return do *not* obey the normal
or log-normal statistical distributions typical of many physical phenomena. Rather, their distributions have "fat tails," with changes
concentrated at the extremes—at times, market conditions can jump
dramatically. Because the beauty contest is intrinsically historical,
the behavior of asset markets ultimately eludes standard statistical tracking procedures.

Third, the operation of the beauty contest in a liberal environment may produce systematic changes in the behavior of both pub-

lic and private sectors as conventions settle in. Even if these changes succeed in reducing instability for a time, they may achieve this position at the cost of medium-term worsening in overall economic performance.

THE PERFORMANCE OF THE PRIVATE SECTOR

The pattern of volatility in financial markets means that they generate economic inefficiencies, because volatility creates financial risk. Even if the facilities exist for hedging that risk, the cost of hedging must be added to the cost of any financial commitment. More generally, volatility may well result in decisions being made on the basis of false information, and may induce a general reluctance to take any step that will increase exposure to unpredictable fluctuations in exchange rates or interest rates. A simple premise might be: the greater the volatility, the greater the reluctance to undertake any exposure to fluctuating variables. The greatest danger of all in open capital markets is, of course, posed by a general loss of liquidity. The potential costs of liberalization are also raised by the possibilities for contagion created by the newly integrated markets.

Analyses of financial instability typically focus on short-term volatility; e.g., monthly or even daily price movements. Such indicators have risen since the end of Bretton Woods system. On average, the monthly volatility of G-7 exchange rates has tripled, with the largest increases being experienced by Japan, the United Kingdom, and the United States. There was no tendency for volatility to decrease in the 1980s and early 1990s, but equally, after the sharp increase between the 1960s and early 1980s, there has been no tendency for volatility to increase further despite the fact that currency trading has grown enormously.

Similar increases in volatility are evident in bond yields although they too generally eased a little during the 1990s, while international bond trading has increased sharply. There has also been increased volatility of short-term interest rates.

There is limited evidence of a significant impact of short-term financial volatility on the real economy. However, studies of the U.S. economy in the 1980s did reveal that for manufacturing industries the move to flexible exchange rates was accompanied by significant and widespread increases in uncertainty about real wages, the real price of materials inputs, and real output prices. This greater uncertainty about real output prices seemed to have a negative impact on the investment rate and productivity growth. The key distinction seems to be whether exchange rates are fixed or fluctuating. Major damage can come from large exchange-rate movements over the medium term.

Capital-market liberalization was accompanied in the 1970s and 1980s by huge swings in exchange rates, with no obvious relationship to the needs of production. For example, the appreciation of the sterling's effective exchange rate by more than 20% between 1978 and 1981 was accompanied by a doubling of the United Kingdom's inflation rate. The stronger real exchange rate resulted in a rapid deterioration in the balance of trade in manufactured goods and a 20% fall in domestic manufacturing output, declines from which British manufacturing has never fully recovered. Similarly the 40% swings in the U.S. effective exchange rate in the 1980s were associated with the growth of the U.S. current account deficit to more than $160 billion in 1987 (with a counterpart deterioration in the federal budget deficit). In the first half of 1999 the dollar strengthened as the U.S. trade balance deteriorated and U.S. jobs were lost.

As well as exchange rate instability, the 1980s and 1990s also experienced both an increase in the volatility of interest rates on bonds and a general increase in the real level of the long-term bond rate. Clear evidence links the volatility and high rates of return demanded in deregulated capital markets to bond default and corporate failure. Volatility makes the cost of capital uncertain and limits a firm's ability to borrow, and small firms in particular can be hard hit by the impact of high interest rates on the cost of loans. But the greatest impact comes via corporate cash flow. Retained profits are the key determinant of corporate investment. High and volatile interest rates reduce cash flow and make it less predictable, and hence undermine investment plans. High and volatile rates can lead to a significant deterioration in corporate performance, especially for companies with high debt-equity ratios. In the United States, both corporate bond default and outright failure rates were low in the Bretton Woods era and rose sharply in the 1980s. The key explanatory factors were the real interest rate and the corporate debt-equity ratio.

THE PERFORMANCE OF THE PUBLIC SECTOR

It is widely believed that the power of liberal financial markets places a "healthy" discipline on the public sector, encouraging the pursuit of "market friendly," anti-inflationary policies, which should support investment and growth. For example, it was argued in *The Economist* magazine in October 1995 that:

> ..... a government's loss of powers is reason to cheer, not fear: all that is being lost is the power to pursue damaging policies and practice economic deception by letting inflation rip.

That governments have lost power is undeniable. Open financial markets place government's financial policy at the mercy of market confidence. A general loss of confidence will result in weakening exchange rates, falling bond prices, and higher interest rates.

The tendency for financial markets to move erratically is an important qualification of the alleged "healthy" discipline they are believed to impose. The International Monetary Fund (IMF) has, for example, argued that "the discipline exercised by capital markets over policy is neither infallible nor is it applied smoothly and consistently. The rise and fall and rise again of the dollar in the last two decades, the rise and fall of world bond markets in 1993 and 1994, and the Mexican peso crisis at the end of 1994 are all examples of highly erratic 'discipline'." The BIS recently concluded that operations of liberal markets often result in significant medium-term price "misalignments," and that "Such misalignments have great potential costs in terms of a misallocation of resources.

They also heighten the risk of abrupt and disorderly corrections and hence of broader financial instability."

Such a "disorderly correction" in 1995 forced the United States and the IMF into the unaccustomed role of lender of last resort to the Mexican money markets and compelled Mexico to increase its already crippling burden of foreign debt. As the BIS commented at the time, the crisis was precipitated by financial factors despite the fact that "external deficits in Mexico have this time coincided with both microeconomic and macroeconomic 'fundamentals' that were healthy by any standards." The Mexican economy, far from staying "healthy," became distinctly "unhealthy," with severe social consequences.

GOVERNMENTS IN SEARCH OF CREDIBILITY

Liberalization of financial markets has clearly reduced the power of governments to manipulate the economy. If exchange rates are fixed, governments face (in the jargon) a "trilemma" or "impossibility problem": the impossibility of sustaining fixed exchange rates, free capital movements and an independent monetary policy. With flexible exchange rates, control over short-term rates is recovered, to some degree, but long-term rates are still subject to the judgments and whims of the international bond traders. Moreover, control over short rates is only recovered if, like the U.S. Federal Reserve Bank, the authorities are apparently unconcerned about movements in the exchange rate—a rare luxury, and perhaps a costly one.

If the financial markets are simply enforcing the logic of real economic efficiency and strengthening the self-adjusting powers of competitive markets, then the "disciplining" of governments would be benign. But if markets are following the rules of a beauty contest and imposing self-fulfilling prejudices on the workings of the real economy, then the outcome may be very damaging.

Faced with the overwhelming scale of potential capital flows, governments must today, as never before, attempt to maintain market "credibility." Credibility has become the keystone of policymaking in the nineties. A credible government is a government that pursues a "market-friendly" policy; that is, a policy that follows what the markets believe to be "sound" and "efficient." Particularly favored are measures designed to meet a "prudent" predetermined monetary target or impose nominal anchors on monetary policy, as well as balance the budget (preferably by cutting public expenditure rather than raising taxes). Governments that fail to pursue "sound" and "prudent" policies are forced to pay a premium in higher interest rates. Severe loss of credibility will lead to a financial crisis. The determination of what is credible, and how governments lose credibility, is a product of the market players' beliefs about what other market practitioners are thinking.

The costs of losing credibility can reverberate over many years, and reacquiring credibility can be very costly in real terms. So if governments are risk averse, the demands of credibility will impose broadly deflationary macroeconomic strategies. In the 1960s, the managed international financial framework permitted expansionary, full employment policies that were contagious both domestically, encouraging private investment, and internationally, underwriting the growth of world trade. In the 1980s, the deregulated financial framework has encouraged policies that elevate financial stability above growth and employment. This has ratcheted up real interest rates, which have in turn reduced domestic investment, reduced the growth of world trade and slowed the rate of growth of effective demand.

Markets are just as likely to settle into a low-growth, high unemployment equilibrium as into any other. The behavior of financial markets may well be an important factor driving the economy toward such an equilibrium. The markets are neither omniscient nor benign. When their influence is combined with the persistent search for government "credibility," defined in terms of "sound money" and "prudent" deflationary policies, then the low-level position is a likely outcome.

This is in sharp contrast with the 1950s and 1960s, when public-sector objectives were expressed in terms of target levels of growth and employment (usually the target was *full* employment), rather than financial and monetary targets, today's "macroeconomic discipline." It is clearly true that *lack* of macroeconomic discipline is no way to secure sustainable growth. Burgeoning fiscal deficits and high and rising inflation will undermine any growth strategy. But what is most striking about the superior economic performance of the 1960s, when objectives were customarily defined in terms of growth and employment, is that fiscal balances typically displayed lower deficits than has been the case since liberalization. Indeed, fiscal surpluses were not uncommon. The reason for this outcome was, of course, the interdependence between public sector balances and private sector activity. High levels of investment by the private sector, encouraged by a public sector commitment to growth and employment, in turn resulted in healthy tax revenues.

There is thus a clear story linking financial market liberalization to the deterioration in overall economic performance in the major industrial countries. High and volatile interest rates, together with other uncertainties, have reduced the potential return on investment, and cut into the cash flow that finances investment. Public sector policymakers, seeking safety in a volatile financial world, set their objectives in terms of financial stability, and hope that the some stimulus may be forthcoming from the private sector.

THE POSITION OF THE UNITED STATES

The apparent exception to these generalizations is the United States. Because of the international role of the dollar, only in the United States can government policymakers safely take expansionary fiscal and monetary stances (as the Reagan experience amply demonstrated), although by the mid-1990s the push for a "balanced budget" showed that they were beginning to have their doubts. Corporate managers can plan investment programs without nagging international worries, though volatile bond rates cause concern. The contribution of business capital formation to demand growth in the 1990s was less vigorous than in previous upswings. The American household sector was the main source of demand expansion during the latter part of the decade. Consumption-led output growth and falling unemployment were backed by internal financial expansion and external borrowing on a scale that no other economy could dream of.

However, even in the United States, growing financial imbalances may be storing up future problems with the markets. The external position bears a strong family resemblance to those in East Asia in 1997 and Brazil in 1999 as analyzed below. There is a risk of destabilizing capital movements as in Asia. The current account is vulnerable to an interest rate shock as in Brazil. Internally, the household sector's portfolio is increasingly shaky. Stock-stock and stock-flow disequilibria between financial portfolios and the real side of the economy are by no means confined to the developing world.

Analogous to foreign lending by the United Kingdom and United States under the high gold standard and gold exchange standard, respectively, the key driving force in the world economy today is the American current account deficit. The United States has been able to run large deficits for many years because global financial markets have been open and increasingly dominant institutional investors in all countries initiated a large and sustained flow of foreign capital into the United States. But the persistent American deficit has produced a peculiarly unbalanced structure of financial stocks and flows, which may well threaten the future stability of the global economy.

At the world level, there are three main financial actors—the United States, the fifteen countries in the European Union (EU) functioning as a rather tightly coordinated group, and Japan. At the core of the EU is Euroland, with eleven members that now share a single currency, the euro. China and the other historically rapidly growing economies in East Asia play supporting roles, with the rest of the world (ROW) picking up the slack. Table 1 summarizes their current account performances during the 1990s.

The first point to note is that international payments data do not add up as they should. As shown in the last line the world seems to run a substantial current account deficit with itself—an impossibility because the sum of all nations' current accounts should be

Table 1.

	1990	1991	1992	1993	1994	1995	1996	1997	1998
USA	-92	-6	-56	-91	-134	-129	-148	-166	-211
Japan	45	68	112	132	131	110	66	95	125
EU-15	-31	-80	-81	9	23	52	91	126	125
E. Asia	5	-2	3	6	-3	-22	-31	0	52
China	12	13	6	-12	7	2	7	23	12
ROW	-196	-249	-228	-200	-177	-137	-148	-150	-205
World Total	-257	-256	-244	-156	-153	-124	-163	-72	-102

Source: OECD (Figures for 1998 are estimates from the OECD Economic Outlook No. 64, December 1998

zero. After all, one country's exports are another country's imports. The error is comparable in magnitude to the flows of the major players. So the scales, though probably not the directions, of the forces about to be discussed are imprecise.

The two surplus players in the late 1990s were the EU-15 and Japan. Europe ran a current account deficit earlier in the decade, but then switched to a surplus partly as a consequence of the contractionary macro policy packages most countries adopted as part of the run-up to the introduction of the euro on January 1, 1999. Aside from 1991–92 when the Bush-era recession, prior depreciation, and payments for mercenary services rendered during the Persian Gulf War generated a transient surplus, the estimates in the table suggest that the United States has run the major deficit. An American current account gap in the $200–$300 billion range injects effective demand to the tune of about 1% of world GDP into the global macro system. This is not a trivial amount. The world economy can be very sensitive to "one percent" shocks. That was about the size of the 1973 oil price shock.

There are four key international financial flows:

The United States has a structural deficit, financed by borrowing from abroad. It has used the resulting capital inflows to support steady if unspectacular GDP growth beginning in the early 1990s, based on stable although not low real interest rates. Calling the decade's results a "boom" is an exaggeration. All around the world, trend output growth during recent decades has been around two-thirds as fast as in the 1960s.

Japan has been stagnant since its "bubble" economy burst around 1990, and it runs a secular surplus. As a consequence of the collapse of the bubble, the country's internal credit supply has been limited, leading to slow growth, a weakening yen through 1997, and a strong current account surplus with corresponding capital outflows. In recent years, Europe's growth has been slow and its foreign surplus large. Since the middle of the decade, the sum of the European and Japanese surpluses has exceeded the American deficit.

The ROW is the main sink for surpluses originating elsewhere. China/East Asia ran deficits in 1995–96 and then switched to a surplus position after the Asian crisis, as the countries of the region attempted to export their way out of depression. The region's famous bilateral current account surplus with the United States consistently exceeded its overall surplus. The difference is the deficit that the East Asian economies ran with the EU and with Japan. In effect, they were absorbing some of the excess saving in the EU and Japan and recycling it toward American shores. After all, the U.S. external deficit *had* to be financed from somewhere.

How do the national economies supporting these flows interact? In terms of its output dynamics, the U.S. current account deficit is pro-cyclical. When world activity is low, the U.S. deficit—and hence U.S. borrowing—rises, pumping demand into the rest of the world. Similarly, when world activity is high the U.S. deficit falls, limiting the injection of demand into the rest of the world. America's net borrowing therefore varies against the cycle, meaning that its incoming financial flows have behaved in a globally stabilizing fashion (as did Britain's outgoing flows of loans when it was the pivot of the system under the gold standard of the nineteenth century).

THE AMERICAN PREDICAMENT

For a nation that borrows, however, capital movements are not a matter of its own volition. A better way to describe the current role of the United States is to say that its creditors—Japan directly and the EU at one remove—have agreed to lend pro-cyclically to finance the American injection of global effective demand. The inflows have built up a huge stock of debt. At the end of 1997, gross U.S. external "liabilities" (in a broad sense, including foreign holdings of corporate equity) were about $4.8 trillion. According to Federal Reserve data, a rough breakdown was government debt, $1.5 trillion; corporate debt, $0.5 trillion; corporate equity, $0.9 trillion; financial sector, $0.7 trillion; and "miscellaneous" (mostly obligations of business and finance), $1.2 trillion. These sums could lie at the root of at least three potential imbalances among stocks and flows of assets and liabilities, and output and trade flows from the real side of the economy:

First, the consolidated government sector's foreign debt was 27% of its total obligations of $5.5 trillion. But less than 50% of the $1.5 trillion it owed externally was owed to foreign governments. Most corporate debt was held privately. Foreign governments' holdings of U.S. debt are at least subject to international negotiation. The same cannot be said of the U.S. debt and equity held by the private sector in the rest of the world. A jump downward of just 6% of total foreign holdings of American liabilities (as of 1997) would equal the projected current account deficit in 1999. Just as in East Asia before 1997, there is the potential for huge, rapidly destabilizing capital outflows. The federal government's T-bills, in particular, could be sold off very rapidly.

A *second* potential source of trouble would be an interest rate increase. If the short-term rate went from its current 5% to 10%, for example, American payments to foreigners on government and corporate debt of $2 trillion would go up by $100 billion. To pay these bills the projected 1999 foreign borrowing would need to be increased by one-third. In this sense, the external position of the United States resembles Brazil's in 1998.

A *third* source of concern is who is actually to do America's borrowing in the future. The main component of *net* U.S. external liabilities (including equity) of $1.3 trillion is government debt, built up during the long period of fiscal deficits from 1980 until 1997. Future external borrowing can only take the form of new liabilities issued by the government and/or the three main private subsectors: finance, corporate business, and non-corporate business and households. The consolidated government sector has been in fiscal surplus since 1997, thus reducing both its domestic and foreign liabilities. The corporate sector largely finances its capital formation with retained earnings and over the medium term keeps its annual increments of financial assets and liabilities in rough balance (within a range of $200 billion or so). At most, its contribution to the growth in the stock of liabilities available to the rest of the world will be well less than the current account deficit. Similar statements apply to the financial sector's and "miscellaneous" claims, for which foreign assets and liabilities are broadly offsetting. By a process of elimination, households emerge as the *only* major sector in a position to borrow from the rest of the world in the future. But in 1999 households were beginning to demonstrate financial distress just as they were supposed to begin a foreign borrowing spree that would be the fundamental corollary of a reasonable rate of growth in the United States.

So a household stock-flow imbalance threatens. Household debt is approaching $6 trillion (roughly 70% in the form of mortgages, 25% consumer credit, and the balance miscellaneous). At the end of 1997, the ratio of household debt to personal disposable income was 0.98, up from 0.89 in 1993.

Given the structure of global trade and payments, the United States will have to borrow $200–$300 billion externally every year for the foreseeable future. The government sector seems intent on running an annual budgetary surplus in the $100–$200 billion range. If they follow their traditional borrowing patterns over the cycle, the business and finance sectors will soon start saving more than they invest. It is the spending of households that must offset all these savings. If household income is (optimistically) assumed to grow steadily at 2.5% per year, then the household debt/income ratio would rise to about 1.12 by the end of 2002. It is impossible to say how households and their creditors would respond to new borrowing of such magnitude, especially if a fall in the stock market (which must happen some time) results in a serious plunge in personal sector wealth ($33.6 trillion at the end of 1997, up from $19.6 trillion ten years before).

To illustrate the potential American debt trap(s), it makes sense to take a look at how the external position is likely to evolve if business continues as usual. At the end of 1997, the breakdown of U.S. *net* foreign assets by type of instrument was monetary, $0.1 trillion; credit market, –$1.7; equity, $0.1 trillion; and miscellaneous, $0.2 trillion. Historically the United States has received a strong positive return on its equity and similar holdings, with profits on net direct foreign investment (DFI) exceeding interest on America's net debt. However, that surplus vanished in 1997, when portfolio and DFI income were –$82 billion and $68 billion respectively.

Forward projections under fairly conservative assumptions about the trade deficit, volumes of DFI, and investment income flows, suggest that net foreign liabilities may rise from $1.3 trillion at the end of 1997 to $2.5 trillion at the end of 2002 *if current levels of macroeconomic activity and hence foreign borrowing are sustained.* Which of the major economic sectors—business, government, or households—will directly or indirectly run up this new foreign debt per year is a key policy question. For the reasons already discussed, households may not be able to shoulder the burden. If they do not and deep recession is to be avoided, the federal budget will have to move into substantial deficit. This is not a question of "fine-tuning." It is a question of whether the government will be capable of moving to counter a potentially very deep recession when the private sector's borrowing spree runs out. The popular prejudice against government deficits suggest that it will not.

EXTERNAL DANGERS?

The most recent runs on the dollar took place in the 1970s and 1980s. The former helped provoke the Volcker interest rate shock, a significant recession worldwide, the developing country debt crisis, and other major adjustments. Doubts about the dollar in the mid-1980s were instrumental in triggering the 1987 stock market crash. A decade is a long span of time in terms of such events; after all, the Bretton Woods system lasted for only about twenty-five years. What scenarios may unfold if the United States in particular and the world system more generally get into trouble once again?

So far, the United States has managed to borrow in a globally stabilizing fashion and faces only potential disequilibria involving its international stocks and flows. There are risks, however, on both fronts. With regard to borrowing, the real decisions will be made in Europe and Japan. The latter has been under international pressure for years to restructure its economy so that aggregate demand can be driven by domestic spending as opposed to exports. Through early 1999, very little had been achieved and the Japanese current account surplus continued to be recycled via Wall Street. This situation may very well continue despite an uptick in Japan's growth rate in early 1999.

Europe, on the other hand, may grow more rapidly now that the Maastricht process has ended and the euro has been born. In that event, higher activity levels and interest rates in the EU would draw in imports and capital flows. U.S. borrowing could begin to be squeezed as the European trade surplus declines. It is also possible that the introduction of the euro, the only currency with a potential status in international trade and finance similar to that of the dollar, will create a potentially unstable currency duopoly. It is argued below that international arrangements might be put into place to limit fluctuations among the dollar, euro, and yen.

On the other hand, suppose the limits are not enacted, and speculative pressure mounts against the dollar. A sell-off of the dollar would produce sharp falls in U.S. bond prices, and hence a rise in interest rates. Would higher interest rates stop the rot, would they be "credible"? The potential disequilibria—portfolio shifts away from the United States, bigger interest obligations on its debt, and growing financial stress on the household sector—could begin to feed on one another, and on the views of the markets. At that point, with an expectational run on the dollar fuelled and not stanched by higher interest rates, dollar devaluation, austerity, and the other usual policy moves, all hopes for global macro stability could disappear. A massive international rescue campaign would certainly be required, with worldwide implications impossible to foretell.

A medium-term policy mix for the United States, then, will require an expansion in government spending to offset the solvency problems that the private sector (especially the household sector) will soon confront. Monetary expansion will not do the trick, given that *some* domestic sector has to borrow to offset the current account deficit. But still more is required. The dollar is perhaps not so "overvalued" as it was in the mid-1980s, but a real exchange rate correction could help reduce the external deficit and slow the debt accumulation process just described. Talk of depreciation in the 20%–30% range was in the air in the first part of 1999.

DEVELOPING AND TRANSITION ECONOMIES

Are there common factors that underlie the tidal waves of volatility, contagion, and crisis that have hit developing countries beginning with the Mexican events of 1994–95? Contrary to widely held perceptions, the crises were *not* caused by an alert private sector pouncing upon the public sector's foolishness, whether in pursuing overly expansionary fiscal and monetary policies, or setting up moral hazards. They are better described as private sectors (both domestic and foreign) acting to make high short-term profits when policy and history provided the preconditions and the public sector acquiesced. Mutual feedback between the financial sector and the real side of the economy then led to crises. By global standards, the financial flows involved were not large: $10–$20 billion of capital flows annually (less than 10% of the inflow the United States routinely absorbs) for a few years are more than enough to destabilize a middle-income economy. The outcomes have been visible worldwide.

To see how they occurred, one can think in terms of a stylized model in which initially the exchange rate is "credibly" fixed; i.e., the central bank consistently enters the market to support a chosen value of the current spot rate e. It is easy to sketch how an unstable dynamic process can unfold. The cycle begins in local financial markets, which set up incentives that generate capital inflows. They spill over to the macroeconomy via the financial system and the balance of payments as the upswing gains momentum. At the peak, before a (more or less rapid) downswing, the economy-wide consequences can be overwhelming.

To trace through an example, suppose that a spread on interest rates (e.g., on Mexican government peso-denominated bonds with a high nominal rate but carrying an implicit exchange risk) or asset prices (e.g., capital gains from booming Bangkok real estate) opens. A few local players take positions in the relevant assets, borrowing abroad to do so. Their exposure is risky but *small*. It may well go unnoticed by regulators; indeed for the system as a whole the risk is negligible.

Destabilizing market competition enters in a second stage. The pioneering institutions are exploiting a spread of (say) 10%, while others are earning (say) 5% on traditional placements. Even if the risks are recognized, it is difficult for other players not to jump in. A trader or loan officer holding 5% paper will reason that the probability of losing his or her job is close to 100% *now* if he or she does not take the high risk/high return position. Such potentially explosive behavior is standard market practice. In one description from an interview study, "...the speculative excesses of the international investors in the Asian financial crisis were not an exception,... but instead the result of normal business practices and thus to a certain degree inevitable."

After some months or years of this process, the balance sheet of the local financial system will be risky overall. It will feature "short" (indebted) positions in foreign claims and "long" positions in local assets. There may also be problems with maturity structures of claims, especially if local players borrow from abroad short-term. Nervous foreign lenders may then contrast a country's total external payment obligations over the next year (say) with its international reserves. Such comparisons proved disastrous for Mexico in 1995 and several Asian countries in 1997.

But the real problem lies with the currency or locational mismatch of the balance sheet, which for developing countries has emerged as a convention/fundamental that can lead to exchange rate crises. Potential losses from the long position are finite: at most, they amount to what the assets cost in the first place. But losses from short-selling foreign exchange are in principle unbounded. Who knows how high the local currency-to-dollar exchange rate may have to climb?

In a typical macroeconomic paradox, individual players' risks have been shifted to the aggregate. Any policy move that threatens the overall position—for example, cutting interest rates or pricking the real estate bubble—could cause a collapse of the currency and local asset prices. The authorities will use reserves and/or regulations to prevent a crash, consciously ratifying the private sector's market decisions. Unfortunately, macroeconomic factors will ultimately force their hand.

For example, suppose that the initial capital inflows have boosted domestic output growth. The current account deficit will widen, leading at some point to a fall in reserves as capital inflows level off and total interest payments on outstanding obligations rise. Higher interest rates will be needed to equilibrate portfolios and attract foreign capital. There will be adverse repercussions for both the private and public sectors. Business saving will fall or turn negative as illiquidity and insolvency spread, threatening a systemic crisis. Bankruptcies of banks and firms may further contribute to reducing the credibility of the exchange rate. If the government has debt outstanding, escalating interest payment obligations as rates shoot up can provoke a fiscal crisis—witness events in Russia and Brazil in the late 1990s.

A downturn becomes inevitable, because ultimately no local interest rate will be high enough to induce more external lending in support of what is recognized as a short foreign exchange position at the economy-wide level. Shrewd players will unwind their positions before the downswing begins (as Mexican nationals were said to have done before the December 1994 devaluation). They can even retain positive earnings over the cycle by getting out while the currency weakens visibly. But others—which typically includes the macroeconomic policy team—are likely to go under.

Case studies presented in *Global Finance at Risk* show that the scenario just sketched broadly describes developing country currency crises beginning with those in Latin America's Southern Cone in the early 1980s and running through Russia's and Brazil's in 1998–99. The common factors in all these events included liberalized capital markets and (more or less) fixed exchange rates. But as we now discuss, flexible exchange rates in and of themselves are unable to guarantee market stability.

EXCHANGE RATES

The key issue in a floating rate regime the exchange rate has no anchor; it only floats against its expected future values. In a fixed rate system, if the peg is out of line with expectations, then there is a danger of external attack. However, in both cases, the root cause of instability is an unregulated capital market. To see why, we have to look at how exchange rates are supposed to be determined in the standard models of open economy macroeconomics, broadly following a more formal discussion in Lance Taylor's 1999 study.[1] The bottom line is that the exchange rate has no "fundamentals." At best, its behavior is subject to the conventions of the market's beauty contest.

The so-called Salter-Swan model is the standard for the trade account. It suggests that a low ratio internally of traded to nontraded goods price indexes (for example, the ratio of indexes of producers' and consumers' prices) will be accompanied by a trade deficit that could be corrected by devaluation. The logic is impeccable, but the problem is that in the world today the volume of annual currency trading is around 80 times as large as the yearly value of foreign trade and long-term investment. The trade account makes up such a tiny fraction of total external transactions that it cannot possibly play a central role in determining the exchange rate. Either the exchange rate is fixed by the authorities, or it is deter

[1]Lance Taylor, "Neither the Portfolio Balance nor the Mundell-Fleming Model Can Determine the Exchange Rate—Each Has One Fewer Independent Eqution than People Usually Think," New York: Center for Economic Policy Analysis. New School for Social Research. 1999.

mined in currency markets. With the rate determined one way or the other, domestic prices and output flows adjust so that markets for non-traded goods clear. The current account of the balance of payments comes out as a consequence.

Similar observations apply to another relative price war-horse, purchasing power parity (or PPP). The basic idea is that the dollar should buy as much of a traded good in a foreign country as at home. If P and P^* are the home and foreign price indexes respectively, then the spot exchange rate e should satisfy the relationship $e = P/P^*$. If P exceeds eP^*, then the home country should be inundated with goods from its foreign providers until P is forced down or e up to restore market balance. Purchasing power parity is a "fundamental" that is conventionally supposed to hold. In the "overvalued" $P > eP^*$ case, violation of PPP should be associated with a widening trade deficit, so that two well-known fundamental indicators reinforce one another. However, such concordance is not observed in practice. By most price comparisons the United States is "undervalued." In one familiar example, price quotations in the local currency for many consumer goods in the United Kingdom and United States are just about the same, although in exchange markets it costs about $1.60 to buy one pound. At the same time the chronic U.S. trade deficit signals that the dollar is too strong.

If the exchange rate is determined in asset markets, then which ones? We must distinguish between forward and current transactions. Formulated in the 1920s by Keynes, "uncovered interest rate parity" (UIP) is an arbitrage condition that supposedly describes forward markets. In the short run, it is represented by the equation

$$(1) \quad e = e/(i - i^*)$$

in which e is the current spot rate (home currency to foreign currency), i and i^* are the home and foreign interest rates, and e is the expected change in the rate. For a foreign investor, a positive value of e portends a capital loss if he or she moves into the home currency. Hence i has to exceed i^* to compensate.

"Testing" the validity of UIP has been a playground for econometricians for the past few decades. They have endless fun trying to formulate and quantify expectations. The general conclusion seems to be that UIP does not hold in the data. But that does not mean that expectations are irrelevant. Rather, expected future values of the exchange rate provide the only point of reference against which it can be measured. Moreover, as discussed above, wide spreads between foreign and domestic asset returns were key factors underlying payments crises in developing countries. The problem is that they provided no clear guidance as to when and how the fixed exchange rate regimes in question would get into trouble.

For current (or temporary equilibrium) asset market relationships among i, i^*, and , e the portfolio balance model is the standard. It is usually set up with four financial assets: money and bonds in the home and foreign countries. Three market clearing conditions are traditionally assumed to be independent and thereby able to determine the three variables. An economic truism known as Walras's Law then is supposed to assure that the fourth market clears as well. That is, in any economic system, if one market is out of balance with (say) its supply exceeding demand at the current prices, then in some other market demand must exceed supply. So in an economy with N markets, if $N-1$ are clearing, then the Nth must also clear. This is Walras's Law in a nutshell.

The problem with the standard analysis of portfolio balances is that it fails to take into account the balance sheets of its asset-holders, which add another restriction to the system. When its complete wealth accounting is respected, the model has just two independent equilibrium conditions, say for bonds in the two countries.

To trace through the details with a *given* spot rate, suppose that the central bank creates money (deposits it in bondholders' accounts) to buy home bonds in an open market operation. The bond price will rise and in a standard market response the home interest rate will fall. Home portfolios will shift toward home money and ROW bonds until the home money market clears. So now both of home's asset markets are in balance.

Foreign portfolios will also shift toward ROW bonds. The combined new demands from home and the ROW will drive up the latter's bond price or reduce its interest rate until the foreign bond market clears. But by Walras's Law applied to the foreign economy, then its money market has to clear as well. All four financial markets rebalance *without* any need for the exchange rate to change—it is irrelevant to the adjustment process.

The same sort of incompleteness carries over to the Mundell-Fleming (or IS/LM/BP) model, which is the open economy macro standard. The results just quoted extend to Mundell-Fleming. Its balance of payments or BP equation is not independent.

To see why, suppose that the home country is running up external arrears by not meeting contracted payment obligations on outstanding debt. Its capital account surplus will be less than its deficit on current account. There are two possible forms of repercussion on home's flow asset market balances and flows of funds. One is that some other flow of funds relationship will not balance. The other is that if home's domestic flows of funds equalities hold, then some flow market balance for a financial asset must fail to clear.

Consider the second case. The obvious counterpart to a non-clearing balance of payments is the domestic bond market. The run-up in external arrears would be reflected into a flow excess supply of home bonds, because foreigners would not be picking up enough domestic securities to provide home the wherewithal to meet its external obligations. Under such circumstances, a spot devaluation of appropriate magnitude could be expected to reduce the cost of home bonds to foreigners, erase the excess supply, and remove the disequilibrium. The balance of payments would clear.

The rub is that if home's other financial markets are clearing then this sort of adjustment *cannot* happen. We know from the analysis of the portfolio balance model that if the home money market clears then so will the market for bonds. And with both money and bond markets in balance, there is simply no room in the accounting for an open balance of payments gap.

The other possibility is that the non-clearing balance of payments is reflected into another flow of funds relationship. For example, one can imagine and even observe (as in recent developing country experiences) situations in which the home country is running up external arrears at the same time as the domestic business sector is borrowing in anticipation of investment projects that aren't working out. An exchange rate realignment might even reverse such simultaneous buildups of external and internal bad debt. But at the macroeconomic level such situations are unusual, because the banking sector at home is *not* usually in the business of providing non-performing loans to corporations. In harmonious times, the balance of payments emerges automatically from output and asset market equilibria. There is *no* need for the exchange rate (or any other variable) to adjust to ensure that external balance is satisfied.

In sum, neither the traded/non-traded goods price ratio, nor PPP, nor UIP, nor portfolio balance, nor a balance of payments disequilibrium serves to determine the exchange rate. The same conclusions apply to the fiscal deficit in "twin deficit" analyses and "overly expansionary" policy in the trilemma involving a fixed rate, liberalized capital markets, and a country's fiscal and monetary stance.

So where does the spot rate come from, if there are no fundamentals? From the Sherlock Holmes procedure of eliminating all possibilities until only one remains, the answer has to be that the spot rate is determined in forward markets, as it varies against expected future values of itself and other asset prices. In the real world, forward markets are intrinsically unpredictable and subject to a mix of rational and irrational behaviors.

There is no real difference between the market's "conventions" about future values of the exchange rate, and the rate's "fundamentals." There are no clear causal channels between the factors listed in the preceding paragraphs and the spot rate. Yet if market players come to believe that a floating rate will depreciate because some fundamental is "wrong," then they will revise expectations accordingly and force the rate to move. One is reminded of a famous passage from *The General Theory*: "Speculators may do no harm as bubbles on a steady stream of enterprise. But the position is serious when enterprise becomes the bubble on a whirlpool of speculation.

When the capital development of a country becomes a by-product of the activities of a casino, the job is likely to be ill-done."

Liberalization of international capital markets and speculation in exchange rates have extended the reach of the casino from mere countries to the entire world. The past three decades show that destabilization and the hindrance of "capital development" are of enormous policy concern. In short, the job has been ill-done.

DEALING WITH THE PROBLEMS AT HAND

The best way to summarize the foregoing arguments is simply to observe that in the early 1970s the international financial system collapsed under the strains imposed on the fixed exchange rates that were a vital component of the Bretton Woods arrangements. That collapse, and the privatization of risk it precipitated, led in turn to the dismantling of barriers to the movement of capital in domestic and international markets. Floating exchange rates were incompatible with capital controls—they had to go. With rates floating and controls dismantled, it was vital for the successful operation of the world economy that investors should be able to spread their risks by diversifying the contents of their portfolios among different assets, currencies, and contingent contracts, and that they should be able to change the composition of those portfolios at will.

So was born the modern open financial system, a system of massive, highly liquid flows, and of complex hedging instruments, of widespread speculation, and extensive arbitrage. The scale of financial flows today dwarfs both the real economy and the financial resources of international agencies and of nation states.

Financial flows are propelled by the shifting patterns of convention. Prices in financial markets are determined by what average opinion believes average opinion believes those prices should be. In the attempt to ascertain average opinion participants in the marketplace rely on convention, otherwise known as the fundamentals. This can be a fragile foundation. The result is volatility, and, given the worldwide interconnection of financial markets, contagion.

In recent years the volatility and contagion associated with the new international financial order have produced major financial crises in both developed and developing countries. Many, though not all, of these crises have taken the form of currency crises. Most have resulted in sharp reductions in levels of output and employment, with growth being retarded for years. These reductions have been particularly severe in developing countries.

But the new international financial order has not only been characterized by recurring crises. It has also been associated with declines in the rate of growth and the rate of investment throughout the world. These declines may well be attributable to changed behavior in both the private and public sectors in the face of volatility and contagion. The private sector has become more risk averse, attempting to maintain high levels of liquidity and reluctant to commit resources to longer term real investments. The public sector has redefined the objectives of economic policy in terms of monetary and financial stability, rather than, as was the case previously, in terms of employment and growth.

Regulation can be macroeconomic in the form of capital controls and other direct interventions, or microeconomic in the form of prudential regulation of banks, securities firms, insurance companies, and of financial markets in general. The new international financial order embodies a significant reduction in the degree of regulation of financial markets. That reduction derives both from the conscious removal of controls that was a necessary part of the privatization of foreign exchange risk, and from the very process of internationalization itself. Liberalization has created a seamless financial world, with its regulators confined within what are increasingly irrelevant national boundaries. But at the same time, from the very beginnings of the drive toward liberalization in the early 1970s, measures have been taken to attempt to recover some of the regulatory control that has been lost. A fundamental locus of this effort has been in the "Banking Committees" based at the Bank for International Settlements (BIS), in Basel.

As the negative aspects of liberalization became more pronounced, so did the attempt to recover some of the regulatory power that had been deployed by national economies in the era of Bretton Woods. Within countries, following the Asian crisis, there has been a growing acceptance of the proposition that capital controls, especially controls over short-term capital inflows, might be an efficient policy response in certain circumstances. Between developed countries there has been a move toward more concerted regulatory coordination exemplified by the establishment of the Financial Stability Forum (FSF).

The coordination of the regulation of international financial markets via the Basle committees has from its beginning been consensual and informal. Increasing governmental anxiety, evident in G-7 communiqués, has now, in the shape of the FSF, reached a point at which the informal procedures have been placed on a more formal basis. At the same time, however, governments are attempting to maintain the flexibility of the consensual approach. The history of national economies suggests that this tentative extension of the role of the authorities will in due course become more closely coordinated. The FSF or successor agencies may one day acquire decision-making powers. Despite the obvious difficulties in the exercise of supranational authority, the regulator will need to operate over the same terrain as the markets. The public domain will attempt to insert itself into the operations of the international market economy, to ensure that the market economy survives.

A number of proposals are on the table, aimed at assuring these ends. We take up three in rapid succession: exchange-rate bands, capital controls, and the role of the international regulator.

BANDS

The mixed records of both fixed and floating exchange rates reviewed above reflect a fundamental problem. In a world in which stocks of international debt are so large, and potential capital flows so overwhelming, something needs to be done to lessen the foreign exchange risk that is undermining confidence and reducing growth and employment. In a completely liberal financial world, a return to fixed exchange rates is just not possible. Fixed rates need to be buttressed by exchange controls. What might be feasible would be to raise market confidence by establishing broad bands in the 5%-10% range above and below agreed midpoint bilateral exchange rates of the major currencies (the dollar, euro, and yen). Rates would be subject to "dirty floats" within the bands, but the authorities would make clear to the markets their official intention to maintain the limits by joint interventions.

Management of markets would be unavoidable because (to repeat) exchange rates have no clear and direct linkages to fundamentals such as trade and fiscal deficits, or relative price levels. They are the outcome of a beauty contest. The linkages that do exist are in the minds of market players, subject to the moving expectations and possibilities for rapid jumps in conventions that are the hallmark of the financial beauty game. The management of the bands would therefore be a management of conventions, with all the potentially fragility that that implies. To move rates up and down within their permitted ranges, policy coordination (including coordination among central banks jealous of their "independence") would be required. To steer them away from the bounds, international collaboration would be essential.

A system of bands would require close monitoring of markets, but it could yield considerable benefits. Private capital flows would be stabilized because the authorities would have explicitly stated their degree of tolerance of fluctuations. The entire history of liberal capital markets clearly indicates that a lack of government guidance encourages contagion when a currency is subject to speculative attack. Third-party countries would gain because they could peg their currencies to one of the big three without running the risk of major misalignment such as occurred in East Asia in the 1990s.

If the public sector were to readopt some of the foreign exchange risk that was privatized in 1973, then the authorities would need to create a system to manage that risk. In the absence of capital controls this would require a commitment to defend the limits of the bands by supporting to an indefinite degree any currency that comes under speculation. This in turn would require international collaboration in the conduct of monetary policy. The absorption of risk by the public sector would also encourage the private sector to take excessive currency risks. So the bands would need to be complemented by a regulatory regime that would diminish the moral hazard implicit in the public sector guarantee. The interrelationship of greater exchange rate stability and regulatory control will be considered further in the context of the responsibilities of a World Financial Authority.

CAPITAL CONTROLS

The fixed exchange rate regime of the Bretton Woods era was buttressed by capital controls. It is difficult to imagine such extraordinary stability without them. In the new international financial order controls have a somewhat different role. They are for the management of risk. The volatility and contagion associated with uncontrolled markets is highly inefficient. Capital controls are simply part of the regulatory framework for the management of risk at both macroeconomic and microeconomic levels. This is why so much attention has been focused of late on the control of capital *inflows*, rather than the traditional concern with outflows.

It is important to recognize that there is a significant difference between limiting short-term capital flows into a country on the one hand, and closing markets to foreign goods on the other. In the latter case a country may attempt to acquire a beggar-my-neighbor advantage. The same argument does not apply in the case of limitations on short-term inflows of capital.

The demand for the across-the-board abolition of capital and exchange controls has been pursued insistently by the United States and a few other developed countries in recent years in a number of forums, including the OECD, WTO, and IMF. What they urge on others is contrary to their own history of successful economic development experience, which in fact featured long periods of capital controls and only gradual liberalization of capital accounts. The experiences of developing countries schematized above clearly show that abrupt or premature liberalization of the capital account is inappropriate for developing and transition economies, a fact that is now generally recognized. Strong domestic financial systems, regulation, and supervision are essential elements to guarantee successful liberalization. However, even with strong performances in these areas, it has proved difficult for developing and transition economies to adapt to the volatile international flows that have followed liberalization of their capital accounts. Boom-bust cycles are frequently associated with portfolio and short-term capital flows. The composition and not just the magnitude of flows plays an essential role in generating external vulnerability.

Under these conditions, developing and transition economies should retain the right to impose disincentives or controls on inflows (particularly in times of capital surges), as well as on outflows during severe crises. A flexible approach in this regard is certainly superior to mandatory capital account convertibility. Best practices in these areas may include reserve requirements on short-term inflows, various taxes on capital inflows intended to discourage them, appropriate put and call provisions in borrowing agreements, and minimum stay or liquidity requirements for investment banks and mutual funds that wish to invest in a country. These measures will tend to increase the cost of capital to the developing country. But that is exactly what is in the interest of economic efficiency. The higher cost of capital is a measure of the externality of risk being internalized.

Controlling measures taken by developing countries could also include complementary prudential regulations on domestic financial institutions. Such regulations could include higher reserve or liquidity requirements on short-term deposits into the financial system that are managed in anti-cyclical fashion, and upper limits on the prices of assets used as collateral during periods of economic expansion. Mechanisms to guarantee a healthy maturity structure for both external and domestic public-sector indebtedness are crucial complementary tools. Such instruments should be regarded as permanent, rather than temporary devices, as long as international financial markets remain volatile and domestic economic structures are weak. Parallel reforms should be oriented toward developing long-term segments of domestic capital markets.

MANAGING GLOBAL FINANCIAL RISK

The new international financial order requires effective regulation. The macroeconomic regulation deployed in the management of exchange rates and capital flows must be supplemented by microeconomic regulation of the behavior of banks, securities houses, insurance companies, highly leveraged institutions such as hedge funds, and other financial firms. Regulation will never be able to protect firms and markets against abnormal risk. Even the best risk management practices will be overwhelmed. But effective regulation can make a significant contribution to the management of normal systemic risk. By building confidence in the maintenance of market stability in normal times, it will make abnormality all the more rare.

The key to the effective management of systemic risk is that the regulatory authorities should operate across the same domain as the institutions that they regulating, whether that domain is defined in terms of products or currencies or legal jurisdictions. That is why the development of the new international financial order poses such a difficult challenge to the financial authorities of nation-states. Supranational jurisdiction is a very uncomfortable idea. Yet if liberal markets are to survive the challenge must be met in one way or another.

In the attempt to meet that challenge, the development of international regulation has gone through two phases since the early 1970s. First came cooperation andthen coordination. During the next few years, the process may enter a third phase of control. In the cooperation phase, national authorities exchanged information and established the division of responsibilities in regulation of international markets. In the coordination phase, they have sought to establish common standards and procedures. In the control phase, an international authority would acquire, via treaty, responsibilities for policymaking, surveillance and enforcement.

The Financial Stability Forum (FSF, recently established by the G-7) is a bold step forward in the international structure of regulatory authorities. But the very boldness of the structure exposes the limitations of the consensual approach as currently conceived. Any international authority will need to work with and through national regulators. It is the relationship between the national regulator and the international organization that determines whether the organization does indeed exercise authority over the domain of the international market. Up until now committees of central bankers and other regulators, meeting since 1975 at the BIS, in Basel, have steadily increased their harmonizing role, moving from cooperation to coordination. Their powers have not been extended to control mediated by treaty or through similar statutory powers. Indeed, their informality is one of their strengths. Informal structures do facilitate speedy decision-making and prompt action. But experience suggests that the development of international financial markets has now reached a such level of sophistication and fragility that informal cooperation has reached the limits of its effectiveness. The FSF does not (at present) possess surveillance or enforcement powers. More importantly, it does not possess the power to make and enforce policy. Without this latter power, the ability of the FSF to adapt its principles and codes to rapid change in the marketplace is severely limited. It lacks the power to act, to impose its authority in the management of systemic risk. The FSF is probably as far as the coordination phase can go.

A WORLD FINANCIAL AUTHORITY

The concept of a World Financial Authority (WFA) provides a template for examining the scale of the challenge posed by the control phase. Whether a supranational organization would actually take the institutional form of a WFA does not matter very much. Rather, consideration of the economic advantages of a WFA, as well as the economic and legal challenges it would face, would clarify the problems that must be solved by any institution or set of institutions that can successfully and efficiently regulate the new international financial order.

If the WFA is indeed to be a regulator operating over the same domain as do the markets that it regulates, then it will need to perform the same tasks as are performed today by efficient national regulators, namely information, authorization, surveillance, guidance, enforcement, and policy. Most of these functions would in reality be performed by national authorities acting in conjunction with and as agents for the WFA. The importance of the WFA is in the harmonization of standards and procedures, and in developing the global scope and relevance of decision-making.

The primary task of the World Financial Authority is the management of systemic risk, and hence the enhancement of the stability and efficiency of international financial markets. A WFA could also play an important role in the battle against international financial crime and money laundering. However, the consideration below is devoted to the management of risk. This requires policies at both the macroeconomic level, where much market risk is created, and the microeconomic level, where market risk and counter-party risk reinforce one another to the detriment of the real economy.

MACROECONOMIC REGULATION AND RISK MANAGEMENT

The management of the market risk created by swings in exchange rates, in interest rates, and other macro variables requires international cooperation. Many of the goals of an efficient international financial policy can be achieved by effective coordination of the activities of national monetary authorities. The problem is that the means of achieving that coordination are, at the moment, very limited. The WFA should be a forum within which the rules of international financial cooperation are developed and implemented. The key to success is mutual support.

Perhaps the most important area of macroeconomic regulation for the WFA would be the management of the restrictions imposed on capital markets by national authorities. Nation states, after appropriate consultations with the WFA, should be empowered to impose restrictions on external capital movements as they see fit. Effective controls, particularly on short-term capital inflows, may well be necessary not only to manage systemic risk efficiently, but also to sustain free trade in goods and services, because trade controls may well be imposed in the wake of financial crises. If microeconomic regulation of firms is to be effective then it may need to be supplemented with quantitative or tax-based obstacles to cross-border flows of funds. While there should be a presumption in favor of national policies, the form, scale, and duration of such restrictions (which may, if necessary, be deemed permanent) should be determined in consultations with the WFA. Those consultations, and the monitoring that accompanies them, would ensure that the management of risk does not develop into the stifling of enterprise.

Secondly, a macroeconomic "vision" within WFA policymaking would provide an important complement to microeconomic regulation. This macro "vision," fundamental to the management of market risk, is currently not prominent in the work of the BIS committees. For example, the current BIS risk weighting of capital adequacy requirements for banks *encourages* short-term flows to developing countries. Loans of less than a year's maturity are weighted at 20%, while maturities in excess of a year are weighted at 100%. The differential is entirely understandable in terms of microeconomic risk to the banks in lending countries, but tends to increase macroeconomic risk in recipient countries by providing an incentive for banks to concentrate their lending to developing countries in the short term. In a meeting in June 1999, the G-7 heads of state recognized this problem and promised to address it, but their response would have been less tardy had an effective WFA-like regulator been in existence.

A macroeconomic vision may also provide a safeguard against the imposition of excessively pro-cyclical microeconomic regulation. Most capital adequacy requirements induce strongly pro-cyclical behavior. Most risk management techniques do too, with the added downside that they promote contagion as negative risk assessment spreads throughout financial markets. The difficulties facing the regulator are obvious: to enforce pro-cyclical behavior in the interests of the management of counter-party risk, or to relax risk management standards in the face of adverse macroeconomic developments. One goal of developing a new financial framework is to reduce these dilemmas by limiting imbalances in which national financial systems have long internal and short external net positions or blatant stock-flow disequilibrium positions.

MICROECONOMIC REGULATION AND RISK MANAGEMENT

It will be the responsibility of the WFA to provide the lead in the creation, operation, and continuous modernization of a comprehensive regulatory framework for all financial services. There is a great need for a comprehensive view, encouraging the design of efficient risk management techniques for *all* major institutions and operations. This includes banks, mutual funds, highly leveraged institutions (e.g., hedge funds), and insurance and pension funds, as well as all onshore and offshore and on-balance sheet and off-balance sheet operations (recognizing how difficult the identification of some of these operations may be). Traditional notions of capital adequacy monitoring are inadequate in today's capital markets. Capital is no substitute for effective management. Risk management should be central to regulatory activity, internalizing, as much as possible, risk externalities.

By establishing harmonious standards of regulation throughout international financial markets the WFA will spread and establish best practice, limit regulatory arbitrage, and hence limit market distortions.

Thorough microeconomic regulation will help stabilize macro-markets. This is particularly true of foreign exchange markets. The micro regulation that limits the foreign exchange exposure of domestic institutions (by regulating both borrowers and lenders) will enhance the stability of the foreign exchange markets by increasing confidence in the ability of the economy to weather foreign exchange shocks. This will substantially ease the task of managing exchange rates among the key currencies as discussed above.

THE WAY FORWARD

The above description of the WFA is a description of what needs to be done to sustain an efficient liberal international economy. There remains the question of what kind of entity should perform these tasks and to whom it should be responsible.

It is clear that there is no appetite today (especially in Washington) for the creation of a new international bureaucracy. Fortunately, the infrastructure for the WFA already exists in the form of the BIS committees. These institutions have the experience to do the job, and enjoy the confidence of governments and of the financial community. The Financial Stability Forum (FSF), while it brings together all G-7 and international institutions with an interest in regulatory matters, derives its current character from its BIS origins. This is simply a recognition of the success of the BIS committees within their remit.

An alternative to developing the BIS committees into a WFA, would be to place the WFA function within the IMF. Given that the IMF is an international organization, accountable in principle to its membership, rather than a cozy central bankers' club, this option has some attractions. Moreover, the IMF already has statutory responsibility for surveillance of international economies, and it has the power and responsibility of an international lender. To locate the WFA function within the IMF would be to combine the international roles of a quasi-central bank and a quasi-regulator. In these circumstances the grant of regulatory pre-conditionality would be a natural extension of the IMF's lending responsibilities.

However, a number of arguments suggest that locating the WFA function within the IMF would be less successful than developing the BIS system. *First*, it is clearly the BIS committees that have the expertise and experience to develop international regulation. It is a system that works. *Second*, it is increasingly recognized that there is a strong case for separating the roles of the regulator and the lender of last resort, even though they must collaborate in the management of systemic risk. The task of dealing with normal risk over the entire financial services industry is quite different from dealing with a liquidity crisis generated by abnormal risk. *Third*, the IMF's expertise is in dealing with the current fiscal and trade balances, not with the capital account. Confusion between the needs of an insolvent economy and the needs of an illiquid capital market was clearly an element in the IMF's mishandling of the Asian crisis. *Fourth*, an important part of the role of the WFA will be in developing and enforcing regulatory standards in prosperous developed economies. This is familiar territory for the BIS committees. It is unfamiliar territory for the IMF. If the WFA function were located in the IMF there would be an understandable tendency to see regulatory problems as an issue relating to borrowing countries. They are not. They are as much a problem of the prosperous lenders as the poorer borrowers. *Fifth*, the BIS committees command the confidence of the financial services industry and of governments. In financial regulation that is a priceless resource.

There is, however, an important problem in extending the role of the BIS and the BIS committees. Their success has been based on informality and consensus. It will be difficult to extend that effective process to fulfill the WFA function. The G-7 countries acknowledged as much in the communiqué establishing the FSF, in which they declared their intention of widening the membership of the FSF to include developing economies. A powerful WFA will certainly attract more scrutiny.

The key problem will be to balance accountability and political legitimacy with the effective informality of the BIS club. An effective regulator needs to be flexible, to be able to act quickly, and to maintain a close relationship with the industry (though regulators will never be loved). This is difficult to attain if the regulator is itself closely confined within a tight code of legal practice. It is also difficult to maintain transparency and accountability while working with confidential information, offering guidance, and reacting decisively on knowledge gleaned in some of the darker recesses of the industry. The solution must surely be to build on the achievements of the BIS committees, widen their authority and their remit, widen their role, and widen their membership. The club will undoubtedly become less club-like. But if the achievements of the past twenty years are anything to go by, the operating procedures that have been successful in the past will be adapted to the new, proactive WFA function. This is a major reason for building the WFA function on the secure foundations of the BIS and the BIS committees.

Coordination has been taken to what is probably its limit in the formation of the Financial Stability Forum. In the next few years, probably spurred by another financial crisis, international financial regulation will enter the third phase of control. The WFA functions will be performed by someone, somewhere.

But it is important to get on record that developed countries need the WFA almost as much as do developing countries. Of course the shocks to developing countries are more severe, but the long-term impact of volatility and contagion on developed countries has been no less costly. Moreover, the rising scale of exposures in highly leveraged markets is ratcheting up systemic risk throughout international financial markets, developed and developing alike.

The institutional framework of the WFA, and the role it would perform in the international economy, derive both from analysis and from historical experience. Historical experience has confirmed the necessity of regulation and of the lender of last resort in domestic markets. The same sorts of measures are now required internationally. Indeed, these measures are required if a broadly liberal world order is to survive.

BIBLIOGRAPHY

Eatwell, John, and Lance Taylor. *International Capital Markets and the Future of Economic Policy*. New York: Center for Economic Policy Analysis, New School for Social Research, 1998. Available on the website www.newschool.edu/cepa.

Eatwell, John, and Lance Taylor. *Global Finance at Risk: The Case for International Regulation*. New York: The New Press, 2000.

Keynes, John Maynard. *The General Theory of Employment, Interest, and Money*. London: Macmillan, 1936.

Taylor, Lance. "Neither the Portfolio Balance nor the Mundell-Fleming Model Can Determine the Exchange Rate—Each Has One Fewer Independent Equation than People Usually Think." New York: Center for Economic Policy Analysis, New School for Social Research, 1999.

Solving the Currency Conundrum

A Paper from the Project on Development,
Trade and International Finance

Barry Eichengreen

A Council on Foreign Relations Paper

Solving the Currency Conundrum[1]

INTRODUCTION

In recent months the debate over strengthening the international financial architecture has taken an unexpected turn. For more than a year that debate revolved around the causes of financial crises, the International Monetary Fund's response, and the need to involve the private sector in crisis resolution. Little was said about the exchange-rate problem.

Now one cannot open a financial newspaper without encountering yet another article on how to "fix" the exchange rate system. What has changed? Well, Brazil changed once the *real's* peg blew up in the face of the government and the IMF, providing one more illustration that fragile currency pegs are central to the problem of financial instability in emerging markets. Argentina changed as the government began exploring the possibility of replacing the *peso* with the dollar as a way of banishing exchange-rate instability once and for all. The relationship between the world's leading currencies changed with the advent of the euro. To paraphrase Henry Kissinger, central bankers now know whom to call when they need to telephone Europe. Moreover, for the first time there exists a rival capable of challenging the dollar's finan-

[1]Prepared for a meeting of the Council on Foreign Relations Study Group on Economic and Financial Development on January 21, 2000. Additional support for this research was provided by the Ford Foundation through the Berkeley Project on New International Financial Architecture. This paper is circulated as an occasional paper for the convenience of Working Group participants and other Council members. A revised, edited, and updated version is forthcoming in an edition of the publication *Economic Notes*.

cial hegemony. Asia changed as green shoots of recovery sprout-
ed and the crisis countries used their respite to ponder a common
basket peg as a way of containing exchange-rate instability in the
region. And maybe, just maybe, Japan changed, as the Ministry
of Finance (if not necessarily also the Bank of Japan) accepted the
need for a more expansionary monetary policy, which could mean
a significantly weaker yen-dollar rate and heightened trade tensions vis-à-vis the United States.

For all these reasons, the question of what to do about the exchange
rate has moved to center stage. Recent events have also highlighted
the absence of a consensus answer. For Brazil it is a more flexible
exchange rate backed by inflation targeting. For Argentina it is an
immutably fixed currency peg leading to dollarization. For Europe
it is a regional central bank and a regional monetary union. For
the United States, Japan, and the euro area it is floating between
their respective currencies.

This paper reviews the debate over the exchange-rate system
and the choice of regime for countries in different economic,
financial, and political circumstances. It would be presumptuous
to claim that the paper will bring to a close a debate that has riven
the official and academic communities for the better part of a century. But it will at least attempt to provide a framework for thinking about the issues that should help readers and policymakers make
up their own minds.

GOING TO EXTREMES

If there is anything approaching a consensus on the exchange-rate problem, it is that high capital mobility has rendered problematic the operation of intermediate arrangements between the extremes of floating and rigidly fixed rates.[2] The premise underlying this conclusion is that rising capital mobility has undermined the viability of those intermediate regimes. The presence of large and liquid international capital markets makes it infinitely more difficult for the authorities to support a shaky currency peg, because the resources of the markets far outstrip the reserves of even the best-armed central banks and governments. Effective defense of the exchange rate requires raising interest rates and restricting domestic credit, something that will have significant costs unless

---

[2] The locus classicus of this argument is Andrew Crockett, "Monetary Implications of Increased International Capital Flows," in Federal Reserve Bank of Kansas City, *Changing Capital Markets: Implications for Policy* (Kansas City, Mo.: Federal Reserve Bank of Kansas City, 1994), pp.331–64, and Barry Eichengreen, *International Monetary Arrangements for the 21st Century* (Washington, D.C.: The Brookings Institution, 1994). It is fair to say that this consensus is now embraced by scholars at both ends of the economics profession's ideological spectrum. From one end come hard-core free-market economists who argue that only markets, not bureaucrats, can be counted on to get it right. They believe the two *market* solutions to the currency conundrum are a floating exchange rate free of official intervention and an immutably fixed exchange rate in which the government again puts exchange-rate policy on autopilot. In their view, intermediate arrange ments (pegged but adjustable rates, target zones, crawling bands) in which the government uses its discretion to manage the rate also introduce damaging noise into the market mechanism. From the other end come economists less confident in the efficiency of markets, who worry that intermediate arrangements are fragile, conducive to crises, and prone to problems of multiple equilibria. A free float may not be the only viable float, in this view, but the authorities should at all costs avoid framing their interventions with reference to an explicit exchange-rate target, which offers speculators an irresistible one-way bet that is ultimately paid for by society as a whole.

the economy is strong.[3] If the markets detect a chink in the country's armor—be it high unemployment, a heavy load of short-term debt, or a weak banking system—that could render the authorities reluctant to raise interest rates in order to defend the currency, the markets will pounce, exposing the authorities' weakness. For most governments, the choice between raising interest rates and further aggravating domestic economic difficulties on the one hand, and not raising rates and allowing the currency to collapse on the other, is no choice at all; collapse is almost always the result.

What is new and different about the current environment is the growth of international financial markets and transactions. Table 1 shows that net inflows of portfolio capital (the kind of financial capital flows that make exchange-rate management particularly difficult) rose between the mid-1970s and mid-1990s, in absolute-value terms, by a factor of 10 in the industrial countries and a factor of 20 in emerging markets.

This growth of capital flows reflects the relaxation of statutory barriers to inward and outward financial transactions by industrial and developing countries alike, which itself reflects the operation of deeper forces. Most important have been moves toward domestic financial liberalization. As long as domestic financial markets and institutions were tightly regulated, restraining international flows was straightforward. Tight limitations on the business in which financial intermediaries could engage, together with strict oversight, limited the scope for evasion. But

---

[3]In technical terms, the availability of reserves allows the authorities to undertake sterilized intervention, in which they attempt to support the exchange rate by selling foreign exchange without at the same time altering the domestic money supply. But when speculative sales of the currency are large relative to reserves, this strategy will not remain feasible for long. A credible defense of the exchange rate will then require the authorities to buy the domestic currency that market participants sell, reducing the supply of domestic credit, raising interest rates, and tightening the screws on weak banks and corporates. For a definitive analysis of sterilized intervention, see Kathryn Dominguez and Jeffrey A. Frankel, *Does Foreign Exchange Intervention Work?* (Washington, D.C.: Institute for International Economics, 1993). The authors suggest sterilized intervention can be effective in the short run as a way of signaling the authorities' intentions, but only if it is backed up subsequently by unsterilized intervention (changes in the money supply).

Table 1. Portfolio and Direct Investment Flows, 1973–96
(in billions of U.S. dollars, annual averages)

	Gross outflows					Gross inflows					Net inflows				
	1973–78	1979–82	1983–88	1989–92	1993–96	1973–78	1979–82	1983–88	1989–92	1993–96	1973–78	1979–82	1983–88	1989–92	1993–96
Industrial Countries															
Direct															
Investment	28.6	46.9	88.2	201.3	259.6	17.9	36.6	69.3	141.9	173.0	−10.7	−10.3	−18.9	−59.4	−86.6
Portfolio															
Investment	11.8	35	126.5	274.6	436.4	24.4	51	139.1	343.0	549.9	12.2	15.9	12.8	68.4	113.5
Developing Countries															
Direct															
Investment	0.4	1.1	2.3	10.4	19.2	5	14.6	51.2	37.8	106.4	4.6	13.5	13.2	27.3	87.2
Portfolio															
Investment	5.5	17.8	−5.1	10.3	19.2	1.3	3.1	53.9	27.5	95.9	−4.2	−14.7	9.1	17.2	76.7

Source: Barry Eichengreen and Michael Mussa, with Giovanni Dell-Ariccia, Enrica Detragiache, Gian Maria Milesi-Ferretti, and Andrew Tweedie, "Capital Account Liberalization: Theoretical and Practical Aspects," Occasional Paper no. 173 (Washington, D.C.: International Monetary Fund, August 1998).

when domestic financial repression was abandoned, it became harder to halt flows at the border. Banks could more easily channel international financial transactions through affiliates and subsidiaries, and they could disguise and repackage such transactions as derivative securities. Effective controls had to become increasingly draconian and distortionary, and therefore less attractive to policymakers and their constituents. There is a logic, in other words, for why domestic and international financial liberalization have gone hand in hand.

Reinforcing this trend is the development of information and communication technologies. Computerized trading, the Internet and inexpensive telecommunications technology have made it increasingly difficult for governments to segment national capital markets. Ensuring that capital controls are effective thus means clamping down on a wide range of economic activities and civil liberties. This is something that few governments are willing to contemplate in the age of democratization.

But the fundamental implication of democratization is that few governments can credibly attach priority to defending a currency peg above all other goals of policy. The prototypical dilemma is that of a government just willing to bear the pain of high interest rates and other policies of austerity in return for enhancing its reputation for following policies of exchange-rate and price stability, whose benefits accrue later. But if the markets attack the currency, forcing the government to raise interest rates to defend it, the game may no longer be worth the candle. The costs of austerity now—in the form of higher unemployment, more financial and commercial failures, and a weaker economy generally—have risen relative to the benefits accruing down the road. Thus, the authorities may prefer to let the currency peg collapse. And the markets, knowing that the authorities attach importance to other aspects of economic performance in addition to exchange-rate stability, have an obvious incentive to force the issue.[4] Prior to democra-

---

[4]This is a simple illustration of how problems of multiple equilibria can arise in foreign-exchange markets. Note that if the markets attack, then the currency peg collapses. But if the markets do not attack, the peg can persist indefinitely. Thus, there are two equilibria, one in which the peg collapses and one in which it does not.

tization, governments enjoyed insulation from pressure to use their policy instruments to minimize unemployment and foster economic growth. They could credibly assign priority to the maintenance of exchange-rate stability over and above all other economic goals. In our modern world this is no longer the case.

Thus, the changes making for greater exchange-rate flexibility are not just financial and technological but also political. They render currency pegs increasingly fragile, given that they rob governments of the capacity to defend them and at the same time give the markets more ammunition with which to attack them.

Maintaining an exchange rate peg or band in the face of open capital markets is especially difficult for developing and emerging-market economies. Developing countries are often dependent on exports of a few primary commodities, rendering them especially vulnerable to terms-of-trade shocks. Their financial systems are small relative to world markets and even to the assets of a handful of hedge funds and investment banks. Their delicate banking systems are incapable of withstanding sharp hikes in interest rates. Their political systems are ill designed to deliver a broad-based, stable consensus in favor of exchange-rate stabilization over and above all other economic and social goals.

Moreover, while the devaluation of a previously-pegged currency may enhance international competitiveness and even stimulate economic growth in industrial countries (or so the cases of the United Kingdom and Italy in 1992–93 suggest[5]), the Mexican and Asian crises suggest that currency devaluation in developing countries can be strongly contractionary. Because developing countries borrow in foreign currency, depreciation increases the burden of debt service and worsens the financial condition of domestic banks and firms. Because those banks and firms don't hedge their foreign exposures, they get smashed when the currency band collapses.

The previous statement begs two questions: why don't banks and firms hedge if doing so is in their interest, and why don't the

---

[5]Robert Gordon, "The Aftermath of the 1992 ERM Breakup: Was there a Macroeconomic Free Lunch?" NBER Working Paper no. 6964 (Cambridge, Mass.: National Bureau of Economic Research, February 1999).

authorities abandon the peg before it collapses? Taking the second question first, there is always an incentive to leave the exit problem for another day. If the government has built its entire operating strategy for monetary policy around the maintenance of the band, abandoning it can be a sharp shock to confidence. To keep the exchange rate within its band, the authorities have to reiterate that this is their intention. Exiting means going back on this promise. If monetary credibility is anchored by the peg, then credibility is inevitably lost when the peg is abandoned. It is not possible (in the presence of open capital markets, anyway) to pre-announce that the peg will be abandoned tomorrow, or currency traders will start betting against it today.

This is why so few banks and firms hedge their exposures when the authorities operate a currency band or peg. For that arrangement to be credible, the authorities have to commit to preventing the exchange rate from moving beyond certain limits. They have to assert their willingness and ability to do so, or the exchange rate will not behave as desired. To defend the peg, the government is inevitably forced to insist that there is absolutely no prospect that it will change. How many chief financial officers will then be rewarded for purchasing costly exchange-rate insurance before the fact? A pegged rate thus provides an irresistible incentive for the private sector to accumulate unhedged foreign debts. And unhedged foreign debts imply a crisis if the band or peg collapses.

Indonesia illustrates the consequences.[6] For some time prior to the outbreak of the Asian crisis, the country had been operating a crawling band allowing for fluctuations of plus-or-minus 4 percent against a basket of currencies. As is typical for many emerging economies, it had relatively high interest rates, which attracted funds from international investors. These large capital inflows worked

---

[6]I choose this example because John Williamson cites it as an example of the benefits of having a crawling band in his article "Crawling Bands or Monitoring Bands: How to Manage Exchange Rates in a World of Capital Mobility," *International Finance*, vol. 1 (1998), pp.59–80.. For an account by an informed insider running parallel to mine, see Miranda Goeltom, "Remarks," in Federal Reserve Bank of Boston, *Rethinking the International Monetary System*, Proceedings of a Conference Held in Chatham, Mass., June 7–9, 1999 (Boston: Federal Reserve Bank of Boston, Forthcoming).

to push the rupiah toward the strong end of its band. Because the authorities were committed to limiting exchange-rate fluctuations (and because the strength of the currency lent credibility to that commitment), domestic banks and (especially) corporations accumulated large unhedged foreign exposures.

When Thailand devalued the baht, capital flows reversed direction. On August 13, 1997, the exchange rate went from the strong edge of the band (which had been widened to 6 percent) to the weak edge of the band in one day. This 12 percent depreciation was a sharp shock to Indonesian corporations with unhedged exposures, and their solvency was cast into doubt. Now openly questioning the stability of the economy, investors scrambled out of the rupiah. Further interest-rate increases to defend it were out of the question, given the financial distress of the corporate sector and banking system. Instead, the authorities abandoned the band, allowing the exchange rate to drop further. Given the damage already done to the economy, it dropped like a stone, falling by as much as 10 percent a day. This is a stylized version of recent Indonesian history, to be sure, but it makes an essential point about the fragility of currency bands and the high costs of their collapse.

Figure 1 summarizes the consequences. It shows that in developing countries, where these financial, technological, and political changes have been particularly pronounced, the removal of exchange restrictions has been dramatic. Capital-account liberalization has been accompanied by the decline of pegged exchange rates in favor of greater flexibility. At the same time, some countries—most recently in Western Europe but also West-Central Africa and other outposts including Argentina, Estonia, Bulgaria, and Hong Kong—have moved in the other direction. They are seeking to eliminate the exchange-rate problem by eliminating the exchange rate, either by installing a currency board or going one step further and dollarizing the economy.[7]

---

[7]Note that for present purposes I use dollarization as shorthand for the adoption of a foreign currency, whether the latter is the dollar, the euro, or another unit.

Figure 1. Capital Controls and Exchange-Rate Regimes

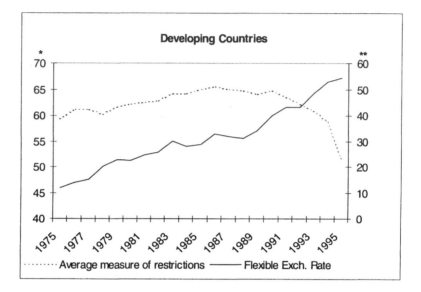

Source: International Monetary Fund, "Annual Report on Exchange Arrangements and Exchange Restrictions," 1997
* Percent of total number of developing countries
** Cross-country average of an index which includes restrictions on capital account transactions, multiple exchange rates, and surrender of export proceeds. The index ranges from zero when no restriction is present to 100 when all restrictions are present.

THE BACKLASH

Fairness forces one to admit that the theory of the disappearing middle is not unanimously embraced. The skepticism has both theoretical and empirical strands. On the empirical front, Jeffrey Frankel observes that reports of the missing middle are greatly exaggerated.[8] Of the 185 countries for which the IMF classifies the exchange-rate regime by degree of flexibility, forty-seven were categorized at last count as independently floating and forty-five as having rigid pegs (such as currency boards or monetary unions, including the franc zone in Africa). That left ninety-three still operating some kind of intermediate regime. Paul Masson constructs transition matrices for exchange-rate regimes for the past two and one-half decades, and upon examining their properties finds little support for the hypothesis of disappearing middle.[9] Guillermo Calvo and Carmen Reinhart note that official IMF categorizations of member countries' exchange-rate regimes tend to overstate the actual flexibility of their rates, so that the conclusions of these previous authors are, if anything, rather conservative.[10] In a tract written in reaction against the theory of the shrinking middle, John Williamson observes that countries like Chile, Colombia, and Israel have long succeeded in operating crawling pegs, crawling bands, and other hybrid systems.[11]

---

[8]Jeffrey A. Frankel, "No Single Currency Regime is right for All Countries or All Times," Graham Lecture, Princeton University, May 6, 1999.

[9]Paul Masson, "Exchange Rate Regime Transitions," unpublished manuscript (Washington, D.C.: The Brookings Institution and Georgetown University, 2000).

[10]Guillermo Calvo and Carmen Reinhart, "Capital Flow Reversals, the Exchange Rate Debate, and Dollarization," unpublished manuscript (University of Maryland at College Park, 1999).

[11]John Williamson, *The Crawling Band as an Exchange Rate Regime: Lessons from Chile, Colombia, and Israel* (Washington, D.C.: Institute for International Economics, 1996). In fact, as I describe below, both Chile and Colombia abandoned their crawling-band regimes in 1999.

Other evidence is not so obviously consistent with these claims. For one thing, the process of evacuating the unstable middle is still underway. The trend is clear in Figure 1, not to mention from recent events in countries like Brazil and Ecuador. In addition, many countries that continue to inhabit the middle are able to do so because they continue to restrict capital inflows and outflows. There is nothing in the thesis of the disappearing middle that denies the ability of countries to occupy this space so long as they continue to restrict capital movements. However, there are reasons to believe that effective control of capital flows will become more difficult as market development proceeds. These pressures are evident in the tendency for countries operating crawling bands to widen the range of permissible fluctuations. And the point is directly applicable to Williamson's three counter cases. Chile widened its band from plus-or-minus 0.5 percent in 1984–85 to plus-or-minus 2.0 percent in 1985–87, plus-or-minus 3 percent in 1988–89, plus-or-minus 5 percent in 1989–91, plus-or-minus 10 percent in 1992–97, and plus-or-minus 12.5 percent since February 1997. Finally, in September 1999, a year after eliminating its last remaining taxes on capital inflows, Chile dropped the peso's fluctuation band entirely. Colombia widened its band from 14 percent in early 1994 through mid 1999 to 20 percent in the third quarter of 1999, before abandoning it entirely, also in September 1999. Israel widened its band from plus-or-minus 0 in 1986-88 to plus-or-minus 3 percent in 1989–90, plus-or-minus 5 percent in 1990–95, plus-or-minus 7 percent in 1995–97, and to plus-or-minus 29 percent since June 1997.[12] Other examples could be cited. They all illustrate the growing difficulty of reconciling domestic priorities with narrow exchange-rate bands. Aside from quibbles over the accuracy of IMF categorizations of exchange-rate arrangements

---

[12]This only a brief summary description of the complex arrangements operated by these countries. For more information, see Barry Eichengreen and Paul Masson, with Hugh Bredenkamp, Barry Johnston, Javier Hamann, Esteban Jadresic, and Inci Otker, "Exit Strategies: Policy Options for Countries Seeking Greater Exchange Rate Flexibility," Occasional Paper no. 168 (Washington, D.C.: International Monetary Fund, August 1998), Appendix 3.

and transition probabilities derived from historical data, the evidence is overwhelming.

At the theoretical level, the question is why the sufficient conditions for the smooth operation of floating rates and rigid pegs are not also the prerequisites for the smooth operation of intermediate regimes. For a floating exchange rate to be well-behaved—that is, to display limited volatility and provide a framework conducive to economic growth—fiscal policy must be strengthened, debt management and prudential regulation must be upgraded, and a coherent and credible monetary policy operating rule must be installed. In the absence of these prerequisites, the floating rate is likely to fluctuate erratically and perform to no one's satisfaction.

Similarly, for a currency board or dollarization to be conducive to stability and growth, it must be accompanied by a stronger fiscal policy. Financial policy must be upgraded, and a coherent and credible monetary policy rule must be adopted (this time by pegging to or adopting the currency of a country that itself follows a sound and stable monetary policy). Otherwise the rigid peg will only bequeath high unemployment and high inflation, undermining public support and therefore the credibility of the monetary rule, while heightening the risk of debt and banking crises.

I elaborate on the importance of these prerequisites for a well-functioning float and a politically sustainable currency board in subsequent sections of the paper. The question here is why these same prerequisites cannot also support a crawling peg, a narrow band, or a target zone. To pose the question in traditional fashion, why can an intermediate regime not be maintained indefinitely as long as fiscal, financial, and monetary policies are consistent with the exchange-rate target and vice versa? Countries that have failed to successfully operate adjustable or crawling pegs and succumbed to crisis, in this view, have done so because their monetary and fiscal policies have been too expansionary. In other words, their policies have been incompatible with the currency peg. They have failed because lax debt management and imprudent supervision have rendered their financial systems too fragile to survive the requisite level of interest rates. It is not true that countries attempting to operate intermediate regimes but succumbing to crisis have done so because the model has lacked viability. Rather, the proper diagnosis is that implementation has been inadequate.

From this perspective, the key difference between the polar extremes and intermediate regimes would appear to be the following: If the country commits to either abandoning or hardening the currency peg, there will be strong incentives for policymakers and market participants to make their affairs conform to the new regime. Consider, for example, the behavior of the banking system. If the exchange rate floats, banks will have an object lesson, on a daily basis, of the need to hedge their foreign currency exposures. If the exchange rate is pegged once and for all, they will be well aware of the need to raise capital standards to compensate for the much more limited lender-of-last-resort capacity of the monetary authorities. They may not adapt immediately, as explained in the next section, but there will be strong incentives for adaptation to get under way.

Under an intermediate regime, in contrast, the incentives to adapt are less. Neither markets nor policymakers have an irresistible incentive to adjust to the imperatives of the currently prevailing rate. Banks will have limited incentives to raise their capital standards or risk-management practices, because they think that any exchange-rate-related limits on the capacity of the authorities to act as lenders of last resort are only temporary. Debt managers will not shun short-term debt because they will be aware that the authorities retain the capacity to adjust the exchange rate and monetary policy so as to backstop the market. Fiscal policymakers will have mixed incentives to eliminate excessive deficits, because they will have reason to suspect that the revocation of the inflation tax is only temporary. For all these reasons, adaptation will be limited. In turn, that will make it correspondingly harder for the authorities to defend the exchange rate when it comes under attack.

Thus, the failure of markets and policies to conform to the imperatives of a temporary peg—where the temporariness of the level of the exchange rate is the essential definition of an intermediate regime—is more than a manifestation of suboptimal policy. Indeed, it is an integral feature of this sort of hybrid system.

WHICH ALTERNATIVE?

For which of the extremes—floating or a hard peg—should countries opt? This question being nothing more than the long-standing debate over the merits of fixed versus floating rates, it cannot be definitively resolved here. Still, it is useful to review the terrain.

The choice is typically framed as a tradeoff between credibility and flexibility. Floating rates maximize the flexibility with which the authorities can use monetary policy for stabilization policies. They leave the central bank free to intervene as a lender of last resort to financial markets. The value of these merits is disputed. Some dispute the stabilizing value of exchange-rate changes when shocks are real rather than monetary and when the country's external obligations are denominated in foreign currency. They similarly question the capacity of the central bank to act as an effective lender of last resort when domestic banks and firms incur foreign-currency denominated debts.[13]

The less the benefits of monetary policy flexibility, the greater the appeal of the additional credibility imparted by the currency board/dollarization option. With monetary policy now dictated by the United States, it immediately acquires all the credibility U.S. Federal Reserve Chairman Alan Greenspan has accumulated over the last fifteen years. The commitment to the currency peg is enshrined in the adoption of a constitutional amendment (or by requiring a super-majority vote in the parliament) mandating

---

[13]For two discussions that question the value of monetary autonomy under most circumstances, see Ricardo Hausmann, M. Gavin, C. Pages-Serra, and E. Stein, "Financial Turmoil and the Choice of Exchange Rate Regime," unpublished manuscript (Washington, D.C.: Inter-American Development Bank, 1999), and Willem Buiter, "Optimum Currency Areas: Why Does the Exchange Rate Regime Matter? With an Application to UK Membership in EMU," unpublished manuscript (Bank of England and Cambridge University, 1999)

that the central bank or the government defend the rate.[14] These barriers to exit, by buttressing credibility, will minimize the kind of speculative pressures described in the previous section. By ensuring greater exchange rate stability, they should in turn enhance the economy's access to foreign capital.[15]

---

[14]In the currency board case, the government or the central bank is required to maintain a fixed rate of exchange between the domestic currency and a specific foreign counterpart. This commitment is operationalized by permitting the monetary authorities to issue additional currency notes only upon acquiring a matching amount of foreign exchange (and to mechanically remove domestic currency from circulation when reserves are lost). Dollarization goes one step further by removing the domestic currency from circulation and redenominating domestic assets and liabilities in dollars; even more than a currency board, it raises the bar to the restoration of domestic monetary autonomy. Turning the domestic currency into mulch creates additional barriers to exit from the dollar link. Devaluation is even more difficult for a dollarized economy like Panama than for a currency-board country like Argentina. In Argentina, the only technical requirement is for the central bank to buy financial assets using pesos from its vaults. In Panama, the authorities would have to inject the domestic currency into circulation, force the banks to redenominate their deposits, and force employers to pay their workers in that currency. Knowing that these additional difficulties would have to be overcome, the markets are less likely to challenge the monetary regime. Even if investors remain skeptical of the government's financial intentions, they no longer have an instrument with which to act upon their doubts—that is, there is no domestic currency to sell. Investors can sell government bonds if they fear that the authorities may ultimately be unable to service their debts, but that debt run or even the fact of default can no more affect the relative price of cash in Panama and cash in the United States than Orange County's default in the mid-1990s could affect the exchange rate between California and the other forty-nine states.

[15]The operation of this factor is evident in the strikingly low correlation of savings and investment in particular regions of larger countries (within which a single currency circulates), compared to the much higher correlations for countries as a whole. In their article "Domestic Saving and Intra-National Capital Flows," Tamim Bayoumi and Andrew Rose provide evidence of this for the regions of the United Kingdom; see *European Economic Review*, vol. 37 (1993), pp.1197-1202. Bayoumi does the same for the regions of Canada in *Financial Integration and Economic Activity* (Manchester: Manchester University Press, 1997). The correlation is conspicuous by its absence in Puerto Rico, a dollarized economy that has succeeded in importing more capital than the rest of Latin America and the Caribbean and in adjusting more smoothly to external shocks; see James C. Ingram, *Regional Payments Mechanisms: The Case of Puerto Rico* (Chapel Hill: University of North Carolina Press, 1962), and Barry Eichengreen, "One Money for Europe? Lessons from the U.S. Currency and Customs Union," in *Economic Policy*, vol. 10 (1990), pp.118-187. (Skeptics of dollarization would counter that interest rate convergence between Puerto Rico and the U.S. mainland reflects not just the absence of currency risk but also the fact that Puerto Rico is subject to the U.S. legal system.) Another example is Panama which, having eliminated exchange risk by dollarizing and locking in low inflation, is the only Latin American country that has succeeded in developing a thirty-year mortgage market. To be sure, it is not clear how to interpret this fact. A problem with attributing it to

These benefits do not come for free.[16] In the case of dollarization, the immediate cost is seigniorage forgone. A currency-board country holds U.S. treasury bills or equivalent foreign assets to back the domestic currency and earns interest on the backing. In Argentina this amounts to some $750 million a year, assuming an interest rate of 5 percent on the $15 billion of U.S. treasury bills that back the $15 billion of pesos in circulation.[17] For a government already under budgetary strain, this is a significant cost.

The other cost, which is incurred with both dollarization and a currency board, is the loss of monetary policy flexibility. To repeat, there is no consensus regarding the value of this sacrifice. But even if one believes that there are significant costs associated with the sacrifice of monetary autonomy, against which credibility gains must be weighed, those costs will be less if the economy adapts quickly to the absence of the monetary instrument. Given that there is now essentially no prospect of a change in the exchange rate or of a domestically controlled monetary policy, there will be additional incentive to adapt to the newly inflexible monetary conditions. Labor markets will adapt to the absence

---

dollarization is that the growth of Panama's financial sector and the development of an active thirty-year mortgage market post-dated dollarization by sixty years. The growth of the Panamanian banking sector only began following the adoption of Law No. 18 of 1959, which enhanced secrecy and opened the way for numbered bank accounts. Cabinet Decree No. 238 of 1970 then reorganized the country's banking system, adding flexibility in bank licensing and further refining secrecy provisions to lure foreign banks to Panama. This made Panama attractive as an offshore banking center (and some would say as a center for money laundering). Through this mechanism as much as dollarization, Panama was able to grow a banking system with the resources to support a thirty-year mortgage market.

[16] If they did, we would observe everyone dollarizing.

[17] It can be argued that a treaty with the United States in which the United States would give Argentina a fraction of that $750 million as a grant could render both countries better off. Say the transfer was $600 million per annum. (The example and the arithmetic are from Guillermo Calvo's "Argentina's Dollarization Project: A Primer," unpublished manuscript, (University of Maryland, at College Park, 1999). The United States would then save $150 million a year. The Argentine government could turn around and use that $600 million as collateral for a commercial credit line with foreign banks, something it already does to a limited extent. But having eliminated residual currency risk, it would be charged a lower commitment fee and more attractive interest rates and be able to obtain more credit. It would have more resources with which to intervene, if necessary, on behalf of distressed financial institutions.

of the exchange rate as an instrument of adjustment, as unions acknowledge the need for additional labor-market flexibility, wage flexibility in particular. Banks will adapt to the more limited
lender-of-last-resort capacity of the authorities, raising their capital standards and strengthening their risk-management practices. Fiscal policymakers will adapt to the disappearance of the
inflation tax by strengthening their fiscal self-discipline and eliminating excessive deficits. Financial managers, recognizing the
absence of a domestic central bank to backstop short-term markets, will rely less on easily accessible short-term debt. Together,
these adaptations will make it easier to live with the absence of
exchange-rate flexibility.

If one believes that such adaptations will occur quickly, then
the currency board/dollarization option becomes more attractive, both because structural reform makes it easier to live with the
absence of monetary-policy flexibility, and because reform is
desirable in its own right. Unfortunately, theory does tell us how
quickly the requisite reforms are likely to take place. Consider, for
example, labor-market reform. While there are assumptions under
which labor-market reform will accelerate as a result of dollarization,
there are also models in which dollarization will slow it down. In
particular, insofar as labor-market reform no longer promises
lower inflation in a dollarized economy, the incentive for labor-
market reform is correspondingly less.[18] Similar ambiguities arise
in models of hard exchange rate-constraints and fiscal consolidation.[19]

---

[18]Lars Calmfors obtains this result in a Barro-Gordon model of optimal monetary policy; see "Unemployment, Labour-Market Reform, and Monetary Policy," unpublished
manuscript, Institute for International Economic Studies (Stockholm: Stockholm University, 1998). He extends the Barro-Gordon framework to include in the government's
loss function not just inflation and unemployment but also the amount of (costly) labor
market reform, where equilibrium unemployment is declining in the level of reform. In
the standard one-shot game, there is an optimal amount of labor-market reform whose
costs are just matched by the benefits in terms of the reduction in equilibrium unemployment (and hence expected unemployment) plus the benefits of the reduction in inflation (because lower equilibrium unemployment reduces inflationary bias). With
dollarization, labor-market reform no longer results in a lower average rate of inflation.
Hence, labor-market reform following dollarization is less, not more.

[19]Aaron Tornell and Andrés Velasco, "Fiscal Discipline and the Choice of Exchange
Rate Regime," in *European Economic Review*, vol. 39 (1995), pp.759–70.

If exit from the currency peg is still an option, then there is absolutely no presumption that adoption of the peg will speed fiscal consolidation. Although dollarizing (which, for present purposes, I take as analogous to eliminating all possibility of exit) will encourage fiscal consolidation by eliminating the inflation tax, it will not at the same time eliminate all possibility of debt default. So long as default remains an option, it is not clear at a theoretical level that progress toward fiscal consolidation will accelerate significantly.

What of the evidence?[20] Observers of Argentine convertibility will be skeptical that a hard exchange-rate constraint guarantees rapid labor market reform. Reform there has been, but it has been halting and partial. The same conclusion flows from the experience of Europe, where monetary union implies a similar reduction in monetary policy flexibility for the individual member states. Taking the Organization for Economic Cooperation and Development's quantitative measures of the extent of labor-market reform, it does not appear that countries that have been in the European Exchange Rate Mechanism (ERM) the longest, or those that have been among the founding members of Europe's monetary union, have made the most progress in reforming labor markets.[21]

What about the argument that the adoption of a hard currency peg will lead banks to strengthen their risk-management practices? In Europe, there is little evidence that investors, bank managers, and regulators responded to the impending reduction in lender-of-last-resort services by raising capital standards and limiting risk-taking. European banks were in the vanguard of lending to East Asia during the period that culminated in that region's financial

---

[20]Dollarized economies tend to be special: historically, they have been very small and have had a highly unusual economic structure. Inferences of general applicability regarding the speed and extent of reform are hard to draw from their exceptional circumstances. This is why in what follows I focus on "near dollarizers," that is to say, countries that have adopted currency boards, such as Argentina, and those that have formed monetary unions, as in Europe.

[21]I present the evidence in "When to Dollarize?" unpublished manuscript, University of California, Berkeley, 1999.

crisis. Their exposure to the crisis countries was considerably greater than that of U.S. banks, despite prospects of a more limited safety net. The best way to understand this is as gambling for return in the effort to survive in an increasingly brutal competitive environment. If dollarization leads to an intensification of competition in the financial sector and forces some scaling back of the financial safety net, then Europe's experience suggests it may lead to less risk-taking—rather than more—in the short run.

What about pressure for fiscal consolidation? There is some evidence that removing the inflation tax from the hands of Europe's more inflation-prone governments intensified the pressure for consolidation. Budget deficits in the euro area fell from 4.8 percent of GDP in 1996 to 2.1 percent in 1998 and are projected to fall further. But Europe's experience also provides indirect support for the point that monetary union and dollarization do not rule out the possibility of default. The fear that fiscal profligacy could precipitate debt-servicing difficulties explains why the Maastricht Treaty features an extensive set of procedures designed to avert excessive debts and deficits along with penalties for countries failing to comply. Given the deep political links tying together the members of Europe's monetary union, there is reason to think that a debt crisis will be met with an inflationary debt bailout of the crisis country by the European Central Bank. The Maastricht Treaty and the Stability Pact negotiated subsequently are designed to limit this danger.

In summary, neither theory nor evidence suggests that eliminating all scope for an independent monetary policy will dramatically accelerate the pace of labor-market reform, financial-sector reform, and fiscal reform. Dollarizing will not automatically deliver the complementary reforms needed in order for the new regime to operate painlessly; those reforms will be completed only with the passage of time. Some countries with histories of erratic policy (one thinks of Argentina) may still opt for a currency board or dollarization on the grounds that the benefits associated with the additional credibility will outweigh the losses from the reduced flexibility. Others with particularly strong ties to a large partner (one thinks of Mexico) or extensive dependence on foreign capital (one thinks of Panama) may opt for a currency board or dol-larization in order to solidify these links. Some countries with an especially pressing need for structural and policy reform (one thinks of Ecuador) may still opt for a currency board or dollar-ization on the grounds that, even if this new regime provides no guarantee of quick progress, it nevertheless ratchets up the pres-sure. But for the foreseeable future, at least, the majority of emerg-ing markets are likely to continue to prefer the other alternative, namely, greater exchange-rate flexibility.[22]

---

[22]Dollarization will progress more rapidly if the United States supports it. So far, the attitude of the U.S. Treasury has been, shall we say, ambivalent. Its worry is that plac-ing the monetary fate of the entire Western Hemisphere in the hands of a small num-ber of U.S. citizens working in the Northwest quadrant of Washington, D.C., will create strains on the Federal Reserve System. Dollarization by Panama is one thing, but dollarization by Argentina, Mexico, and Brazil would be another. The larger the num-ber of individuals outside U.S. borders for whom the Fed makes monetary policy, the more intense the pressure will be for it to tailor its decisions to conditions beyond those pre-vailing in the fifty states. And the larger the number of such individuals, the greater the danger of a political backlash if the Open Market Committee neglects the impact of its policies south of the border. The Fed could be placed in the position of the Bundesbank in the 1980s and early 1990s, when the German central bank effectively set monetary con-ditions for the entire set of countries participating in the European Monetary System but was criticized for neglecting the impact of its decisions on its European partners.

MONETARY UNION

A scenario in which all of Latin America goes over to the dollar is far-fetched. More plausible is that some countries, say Argentina, will dollarize while others, say Brazil, will not. This raises the specter of trade and exchange-rate tensions within Mercosur, the Southern Cone's free-trade area composed of Argentina, Brazil, Paraguay, and Uruguay. The links between the first two countries are substantial: Brazil absorbs more than 30 per cent of Argentina's sales abroad. Thus, Brazil's depreciation of the *real* in early 1999 dealt a heavy blow to Argentina. Argentine producers demanded protection from cheap imports from Brazil, while exporters demanded compensation for their loss of competitiveness. Mercosur came under threat. If Argentina dollarizes while Brazil continues to float, this volatility could become an everyday event. It is not clear that the free-trade agreement would survive the resulting tensions.

For those who see regional free trade agreements in Latin America's Southern Cone and elsewhere as the wave of the future, the recent currency tensions provide obvious motivation for regional monetary unification. In fact, the idea of a single currency for Mercosur has been under discussion for some time. Argentine President Carlos Menem raised the idea in December 1997 and again at a regional summit in June 1998. Argentina's former finance minister Domingo Cavallo mooted the idea in the spring of 1999.

Does monetary unification make sense as a corollary of regional commercial and economic integration? Europe's experience—and the Western Hemisphere's own-suggests that whether Mercosur needs a common currency depends on what kind of regional market its architects are building.[23] In a free-trade area like NAFTA (the North American Free Trade Agreement, link-

---

[23]I elaborate this argument in my paper "Does Mercosur Need a Single Currency?" NBER Working Paper no. 6821 (Cambridge, Mass.: National Bureau of Economic Research, 1998), on which the remainder of this paragraph draws.

ing the United States, Canada, and Mexico), integration is essentially limited to the removal of barriers at the border, thus producing a limited rise in cross-border trade. This trade, in turn, can be sustained in the presence of exchange rates that fluctuate against one another. A free trade area like Mercosur can survive exchange-rate fluctuations because, while Brazil absorbs 30 percent of Argentine exports, exports account for only 8 percent of Argentina's GNP. Integration in the Southern Cone is limited to trade integration; it has not yet extended far beyond the border. Deeper integration, encompassing the harmonization of domestic regulations of all kinds, a la the European Union, implies more open domestic markets, more rapid growth of international transactions, and more intense cross-border competition. Thus, exchange-rate changes are likely to prove more disruptive. If South American policymakers are prepared to stop at the customs-union stage, then limited exchange-rate fluctuations should be tolerable. But if they intend to push ahead to deeper integration, then they, like their European predecessors, will want to contemplate monetary integration.

Brazil would be the four-hundred-pound gorilla of any South American monetary union. For Argentina, however, trading monetary stability for the uncertainties of monetary cohabitation with Brazil is unattractive. This has led Cavallo to suggest that the single Mercosur currency should be anchored to a fixed currency basket with positive weights on the dollar, euro, and perhaps the yen.[24] A common peg would deliver many the benefits of monetary unification by eliminating exchange-rate fluctuations within the economic and commercial zone. At the same time, relying on a basket rather than a single currency would better accommodate the diverse trading patterns of countries in the region.[25] A common basket peg would relieve countries of rigid dependence on the Federal Reserve, while the peg's currency-board structure would ensure monetary discipline. Such an arrangement would lack

---

[24]Hugh Bronstein, "Argentina's Cavallo Calls for a Mercosur Currency," Reuters, April 26, 1999, 6:42 pm Eastern Daylight Time.

[25]John Williamson has made similar arguments in advocating the adoption of a common basket peg by the countries of East Asia; see "The Case for a Common Basket Peg for East Asian countries," unpublished manuscript (Washington, D.C.: Institute for International Economics 1999).

the transparency of a single-currency peg, however, which would lessen its credibility. In any case, this proposal assumes that Brazil is prepared to put in place the economic and financial prerequisites for the adoption of a currency board, something that it has been unwilling to do to date.

This leaves the option of regional monetary union. Monetary unification is a theoretically impeccable solution to the financial instabilities and economic and commercial strains created by distinct national currencies. And the European Union has shown that what works in theory can also work in practice. Unfortunately, a monetary union limited to the Mercosur countries with a single currency that floats, a la the euro, against the U.S. dollar is unlikely to be attractive to South America. While the countries of the Southern Cone trade with one another and are likely to do so increasingly over time, especially if they eliminate the volatility of the exchange rates between them, they continue to import capital from the rich countries, mainly the United States. Even if a Mercosur currency is attractive on trade-related grounds, it is unlikely to be attractive on financial grounds. For a monetary union to be attractive to the Latins, it would have to include the United States.

Here enters another lesson of European experience: that monetary unification is likely to be feasible only as part of a larger political bargain. Monetary unification is a concession for the large, strong-currency country that dominates financial conditions throughout the region absent the creation of a single currency; it would want to obtain something in return, which implies an ability on the part of the partners to make binding political commitments. Thus, the German government sacrificed monetary autonomy and accepted a greater degree of uncertainty about inflation by agreeing to European monetary unification. In return, it got a commitment from its partners to pursue political integration, in which context Germany hopes to obtain a greater foreign policy role in the context of an EU foreign policy.[26] This commitment to political as well as economic and monetary integration allowed

---

[26]This is my favored interpretation of the political economy of EMU, as developed in Barry Eichengreen and Fabio Ghironi, "European Monetary Unification: The Challenges Ahead," in Francisco Torres, ed., *Monetary Reform in Europe* (Lisbon: Catholic

Europe to build truly transnational institutions like a European Central Bank to formulate the common monetary policy, as well as a European Parliament to hold it accountable, however imperfectly. As part of this larger political bargain, the euro does far more than insulate the eleven members of Europe's monetary union from intra-European exchange-rate fluctuations. One can imagine that it will provide monetary and exchange-rate stability over an even wider zone as the holdouts join and as the countries to the east, already regarded as integral members of the European polity, become members first of the EU and then of its monetary union.

This interpretation of Europe's recent monetary history underscores why this path will be difficult to trod in the Americas and East Asia, two popular candidates for monetary unification. NAFTA is not seen in Canada, Mexico and United States as a platform for political integration. There is little desire in either Canada or Mexico to become the fifty-first and fifty-second U.S. states. And there would be strong resistance in the United States to giving votes on the Federal Reserve Board to a sovereign Argentina, Mexico, or Canada. Absent deeper political links, this would be seen as an unacceptable compromise of U.S. economic and monetary sovereignty. The same is true in Asia: given the history of tensions between Japan and Korea and between Japan and China, it is hard to conceive of them moving toward significantly deeper political integration any time soon. To be sure, circumstances can change; Europe emerged from World War II riven by equally deep divisions. But the fact that it took Europe fifty years of effort to complete the transition—and this in the context of an integrationist tradition stretching back over centuries—suggests that such a transition takes many years even under favorable circumstances. Europe is sui generis; its approach is unlikely to provide a solution to Asia and the Americas' currency conundrum any time soon.

University Press, 1996), pp.83–120. The case of political unions that disintegrated, leading shortly to the disintegration of existing monetary unions (the Austro-Hungarian Empire after World War I, Czechoslovakia after the Cold War), are equally revealing.

ACHIEVING GREATER FLEXIBILITY
IN EMERGING MARKETS

Saying that most emerging markets should adopt policies of greater exchange-rate flexibility is easy; creating a framework and incentives that make it attractive is harder. As emphasized above, where the currency peg has been the cornerstone of the government's entire economic-policy strategy, abandoning it will come as a sharp shock to confidence. If investors already harbor doubts about the government's commitment to the pursuit of sound and stable policies, jettisoning the peg will be seen as the equivalent of an obese man announcing that he has stopped going to Weight Watchers. The markets will fear that the government is about to revert to its bad old ways of monetary and fiscal excess. Capital will flee, undermining economic and financial stability. Fearing the consequences, the authorities have an obvious incentive to postpone the transition to greater exchange-rate flexibility to another day.

Emerging markets therefore need to create a framework within which the transition to greater flexibility can occur smoothly, while the IMF needs to provide incentives for them to lay the requisite institutional foundations sooner rather than later. Specifically:

- Governments should initiate the transition to greater flexibility when global market conditions are favorable and not wait until sentiment begins to turn. Historically, emerging markets have been reluctant to move to greater flexibility when foreign capital is freely available; instead, they have held onto their currency pegs in order to maximize their access to cheap foreign finance. In fact, when the markets are flush is best the time to undertake the transition. During good times, investors have a favorable view of emerging markets, and the country is not being forced to abandon its peg under duress, which means the shock to confidence will be least. The fact that the exchange rate will begin its more flexible life by appreciating should reassure investors in domestic-currency-denominated assets that greater flexibility does not necessarily imply capital losses. Moreover, greater exchange rate flexibility is helpful for moderating the domestic credit booms and asset market bubbles that tend to cause small open economies to overheat when large amounts of capital are flowing in.

- Investors will be reassured that abandoning the currency peg does not mean that the government has lost all monetary and fiscal discipline if the authorities substitute an alternative monetary-policy operating strategy. The classic substitutes are monetary targeting and inflation targeting. Targeting the money stock is unlikely to be credible and effective in emerging markets, which are undergoing rapid structural change that in turn disturbs the relationship between the monetary aggregates and inflation rates.[27] Inflation targeting, in which the authorities specify a target for inflation and explain how they plan to alter their policies if they miss it, is a more feasible and credible alternative.

- Domestic corporations can better cope with exchange-rate flexibility when there exist currency forward and futures markets on which to hedge their exposures. Financial liberalization and deepening, including opening the financial sector to entry by international banks, is therefore important for fostering the growth of an interbank market in foreign currency forward contracts. Similarly, the adoption of transparent and effective securities-market regulations can encourage the growth of exchange-traded futures products.

- Even if greater flexibility is in the social interest, it may not be in politicians' interest, because they are not certain of being in office in the future when the returns on their investment are

---

[27] In other words, because the money-stock target may not produce a reasonable inflation outcome, the authorities will have an incentive to modify that target ex post, so it will not be credible ex ante.

reaped. This creates a role for the IMF to tip the balance by signaling that it will not help to prop up shaky currency pegs and that it stands ready to assist countries that adopt policies of greater flexibility.

The recommendation that emerging markets abandoning their currency pegs should consider inflation targeting is especially controversial. Inflation targeting has been attempted by only a relatively small number of advanced-industrial countries like Canada, the United Kingdom, Sweden, and New Zealand. Moreover, the economic and political conditions that have supported its operation there are unlikely to be present in many emerging markets. In emerging markets, the pace of structural change introduces additional uncertainty into the link between the authorities' policy instruments and the inflation rate they are seeking to target. It is harder for them to articulate a model of those linkages, which means it is more difficult to convince the markets that a certain monetary stance today implies a certain inflation rate tomorrow. Perhaps most importantly, the authorities cannot credibly commit to targeting low inflation when the government budget deficit is out of control. This problem of "fiscal dominance" implies that the pressure for the central bank to help finance (monetize) government budget deficits will prove irresistible. Knowing this, inflation targeting will not be credible. Investors will not be reassured, and neither capital flows nor the exchange rate will be well behaved.

These are valid objections, but it is worth asking (as always), "What are the alternatives?" While emerging markets may find it difficult to make inflation targeting work, there is good reason to think that they will find alternatives like monetary targeting more difficult still. The only thing that is worse than an imperfect monetary-policy operating strategy is no strategy at all. And while excessive fiscal deficits are a problem for inflation targeting, they are an equally serious problem for any alternative monetary-policy strategy that the authorities might contemplate. Fiscal dominance is a critique of excessive deficits, not a critique of inflation targeting.

Brazil's recent experience lends credence to these arguments. Brazil offers the first case in which an IMF program embraced inflation targeting as the framework for post-devaluation monetary policy. Although questions about the budget remained, the exchange rate stabilized and interest rates came down faster than the consensus forecast once the central bank adopted this operating strategy. This gives reason to hope that what has worked for Brazil might also work in other emerging markets.

The IMF's principal shareholders, led by the United States, have signaled that Fund resources will no longer be used to prop up shaky currency pegs.[28] If this commitment is credible, it will create strong incentives for emerging markets—no longer able to count on IMF support—to adopt policies of greater flexibility. But simply saying that the IMF will no longer prop up shaky currency pegs will not make it so. Once a currency is attacked, worries that its collapse will inflict a recession on the crisis country and fears that its distress might spread contagiously to other emerging markets may still impel the IMF to intervene, its reluctance to do so notwithstanding. And knowing that the Fund is likely to give in, the emerging markets in question will have no incentive to embrace greater currency flexibility as a precaution.

Lending credibility to this new IMF commitment not to prop up shaky currency pegs requires institutional innovations to minimize the recessionary impact of devaluations, as well as to limit the incidence and effects of contagion. The policy community's new emphasis on transparency and data dissemination is designed to address the contagion problem by making it easier for investors to distinguish weak and strong economies. As for recessions, devaluations are especially recessionary in emerging markets, because, as noted above, they inflate the cost of servicing short-term foreign-currency-denominated debts, potentially to unsustainable levels. The recessionary impact of devaluation can thus

---

[28]This was the theme of then–U.S. Treasury secretary Robert Rubin's speech on April 21, 1999, in which he laid out the U.S. agenda for reforming the international financial architecture. See Robert Rubin, "Remarks on Reform of the International Financial Architecture to the School of Advanced International Studies," *Treasury News* (April 21, 1999), RR-3093.

be minimized if countries limit their banks' and corporations' accumulation of short-term foreign-currency debts. The holding-period taxes used by Chile in the 1990s to lengthen the maturity structure of the external debt are the obvious means to this end.[29]

In addition, a credible commitment by the IMF not to run to the rescue of a country that would otherwise find it impossible to keep current on its obligations presupposes the existence of other mechanisms for dealing with problem debts. It is easy to *say* that the Fund should no longer bail out governments and their creditors, but it is hard not to *do* so as long as there do not exist other way of addressing financial problems when they arise. The shortcoming of existing arrangements is that they make debt restructuring excessively difficult. Because many international bonds include provisions requiring the unanimous consent of bondholders to the terms of a restructuring agreement, there is an incentive for "vultures" to buy up the outstanding debt and hold the process hostage by threatening legal action. Unlike syndicated bank loans, most such bonds lack sharing clauses designed to discourage recourse to lawsuits by requiring individual creditors to share with other bondholders any amounts recovered from the borrower.

---

[29]The Chilean authorities discovered, inter alia, that limits on bank borrowing abroad simply encouraged the mining companies to borrow for the banks and on-lend the proceeds. There is an enormous debate over the effectiveness of these taxes. Some critics complain that evasion remains a problem. Others observe the lack of evidence that Chile's taxes limited the overall level of foreign borrowing. The second objection can be dismissed on the grounds that the goal was never to limit the overall level of foreign borrowing but to alter its maturity structure, and on the maturity front the evidence is compelling. For the definitive analysis, see Leonardo Hernández and Klaus Schmidt-Hebel, "Capital Controls in Chile: Effective? Efficient? Endurable?" unpublished manuscript (Santiago: Central Bank of Chile, 1999). More generally, Calvo and Reinhart, in "Capital Flow Reversals, the Exchange Rate Debate, and Dollarization," find the following: in a fifteen-country panel, including Chile, the presence of capital controls is significantly associated with a lower share of portfolio plus short-term capital flows as a percentage of total flows. That they do not find the same when they look at portfolio flows alone suggests that the impact on short-term flows is doing most of the work. As for the first objection, it is important to recall that such a measure, to effectively lengthen the maturity structure of the debt, need not be evasion free. The last word on this subject should go to Chile's finance minister, who has asked (I paraphrase), "If these capital-import taxes are so easily evaded, then why do we have so many non-interest-bearing foreign deposits at the central bank?"

Those who believe that countries may have to take occasional recourse to suspensions and subsequent restructurings argue that these provisions in bond covenants should be modified. Majority voting and sharing clauses would discourage maverick investors from resorting to lawsuits and other ways of obstructing settlements beneficial to the debtor and the creditor community alike. Collective-representation clauses, which specify who represents the bondholders and make provision for a bondholders committee or meeting, would allow orderly decisions to be reached. This was suggested in 1996 by the G-10 and echoed by the G-22 and G-7 in a series of subsequent reports and declarations. In February 2000 the G-7 placed the issue on its work program for reforming the international financial system.

If implementing this change is such a good idea, then why have the markets not done so already? The obvious answer is adverse selection. It is intrinsic to capital markets that lenders know less than borrowers about the latter's willingness and ability to pay. For the same reason that only patients who anticipate succumbing to a fatal disease buy expensive life insurance, only countries that anticipate with high probability having to restructure their debts may wish to issue securities with these provisions. Left to its own devices, neither market may function. The danger is that adverse selection would render the market in these modified bonds illiquid and thereby impair the ability of emerging economies to borrow.

The G-10's 1996 report, where the idea of collective action clauses was first mooted, said little about this dilemma. While acknowledging the first-mover problem and suggesting that official support for contractual innovation should be provided "as appropriate," it failed to specify concrete steps to be taken by the authorities. The G-22 subsequently recommended that unnamed governments, presumably those of the United States and United Kingdom, should "examine" the use of such clauses in their own sovereign bond issues. The G-7 recommended that its members should "consider" them. Then–U.S. Treasury Secretary Robert Rubin, in a speech designed to set the tone for the Interim Committee's April 1999 meeting, reiterated that the international community should "encourage" their broader use.[30] But the official community needs to do more than examine, consider, and encourage. Given the adverse selection problem, progress is unlikely without the introduction of legislation and regulations in the creditor countries. And without progress on this front, the international community will lack credibility when it insists that it will not automatically run to the rescue of crisis-stricken countries.

---

[30]See Rubin, "Remarks on Reform of the International Financial Architecture to the School of Advanced International Studies."

G-3 TARGET ZONES

Authors such as Bergsten and Henning, as well as Volcker, suggest that the advanced industrial countries have options not always available to their developing brethren.[31] The banking and political systems of advanced industrial countries, are stronger, and their economies more diversified. They possess the currency forward and futures markets (interbank markets in the first case, exchange-based markets in the second) needed for financial and nonfinancial firms to hedge their exposures and protect themselves from exchange-rate volatility. Investors seeking to act as stabilizing speculators can take positions in such markets. Moreover, a durable system of target zones for the dollar, the euro, and the yen with fluctuation bands of, say, plus or minus 15 percent would help to avoid the misalignments between major currencies that make life so difficult for developing countries.

"Durable" is the key word here. For target zones for the dollar, yen, and euro to solve problems and not create them, they must be credible and defensible. Unless the markets believe that the authorities are committed to their maintenance, they will speculate against them. This is problematic. Few observers would believe that Alan Greenspan, U.S. Treasury Secretary Lawrence Summers, and the U.S. Congress to which they are accountable would be prepared to sacrifice domestic objectives such as full employment and the control of inflation in order to defend an exchange-rate target zone. Can we really imagine Alan Greenspan, seeing the dollar strengthen and inflation heating up as a result of fast U.S. economic growth, *reducing* interest rates to keep the dollar in its band at the cost of additional inflation? Or some future Alan Greenspan,

---

[31]See C. Fred Bergsten and Randall Henning, *Global Economic Leadership and the Group of Seven* (Washington, D.C.: Institute for International Economics, 1996), and Paul A. Volcker, "The Quest for Exchange Rate Stability: Realistic or Quixotic?" speech given at the Senate House (London University, November 29, 1995).

seeing the dollar weaken and the economy slow, *raising* interest rates to keep the dollar from falling despite rising unemployment?

Target-zone supporters would respond that if the credibility of the commitment to defend the band can be established, this tradeoff between domestic and international objectives will disappear. It will still be possible, they argue, for the authorities to direct monetary and fiscal policies at inflation and unemployment without driving the exchange rate beyond the edge of its band. This free lunch is the so-called "honeymoon effect" that arises when the commitment to defend the target zone is credible.[32] It derives from the fact that, *assuming* sufficient credibility, speculation will be stabilizing—that is, it will tend to drive the exchange rate back toward the center of its band, or at least prevent it from diverging further as the limit of permissible fluctuations is reached.

The argument goes as follows. Say that, absent the target zone, an increase in the money supply designed to stimulate growth and reduce unemployment would also weaken the exchange rate. But if the markets believe that the authorities are committed to preventing the exchange rate from continuing to weaken beyond a certain point, which they will do by reducing the money supply down the road, investors will buy the currency now in anticipation of its subsequent recovery. Such action will limit the currency's current weakness. It is this credibility—the belief that the authorities will hold the exchange rate at a certain level—that creates an expectation of future policy adjustments that keeps the exchange rate from falling out of its band. The expectation that the central bank will lean against the wind to prevent the exchange rate from drifting outside its band in the future works to stabilize it in the present. The fact that the current exchange rate depends not just on the current money supply but on the entire expected future time path of money supplies relaxes the tradeoff between the exchange rate and other policy targets today. In technical

---

[32]Paul Krugman and Marcus Miller, "Why Have a Target Zone?" *Carnegie-Rochester Conference Series on Public Policy* (December 1993), pp.279–314.

terms, the elasticity of exchange rate with respect to the current money supply is less than in the absence of the target-zone commitment.

Economists view free lunches with suspicion. In the present context, Clarida provides a catalogue of reasons for questioning whether the honeymoon effect will obtain.[33]

- Even in the presence of the honeymoon effect (indeed, in order for the target-zone honeymoon to obtain), the central bank must attach priority to supporting the exchange rate and disregard all other goals of policy when the edge of the band is reached.[34] The tradeoff between competing objectives may be attenuated when the level of the exchange rate is a nonissue, but it reemerges with a vengeance as pressure on the rate intensifies.

- If central banks instead follow Williamson by adopting "soft buffers" and allowing the currency to drop out of its band when pressures build, then the honeymoon effect will weaken or disappear, and the tradeoff between internal and external objectives will reemerge earlier.[35]

- If centtral banks never let the exchange rate bump against the edge of its band, instead adjusting the location of the band to prevent the accumulation of speculative pressure, then the honeymoon effect will again be attenuated. Indeed, as the markets come to anticipate this behavior, the target-zone honeymoon may give way to a "separation" or "divorce" effect. If the markets expect the authorities to adjust the band downward when

---

[33]Richard H. Clarida, "G3 Exchange Rate Relationships: A Recap of the Record and a Review of Proposals for Change," unpublished manuscript (New York: Columbia University, 1999).

[34]As Clarida puts it, "when an exchange rate weakens to the edge of a target zone band, the objective function of the central bank must collapse to a lexicographic ordering in which price stability and the exchange rate receive no weight. It is not sufficient for the central bank to place some, or even a lot of, weight on stabilizing the exchange rate. Rather, when the exchange rate is at the edge of the band, the central bank must place *all* the weight on the exchange rate."

[35]John Williamson, "Exchange-Rate Management," *Economic Journal*, vol. 103 (1993), pp. 188–97.

the exchange rate moves downward, then the elasticity of the exchange rate with respect to the money supply may rise rather than falling as it nears the edge of the band. Target zones with adjustable bands then create the possibility of "vicious spirals."

• When the dollar reaches the bottom of its band against the euro, the euro reaches the top of its band against the dollar. There is then the need for an assignment of responsibilities between the Fed and the European Central Bank for keeping the rate within its band. If the country with the weak currency has sole responsibility, then exchange-rate tensions will always be resolved by reductions in money supplies, which will be deflationary. It is not plausible that the markets will believe that the authorities are really prepared to countenance the indefinite pursuit of deflationary policies. If the country with the strong currency has sole responsibility, on the other hand, then exchange-rate tensions will always be resolved by increases in money supplies, which will be inflationary. The markets will similarly disbelieve that the authorities are really prepared to tolerate the resulting inflationary bias. A credible target zone therefore requires a commitment for joint intervention by both countries whose bilateral rate the system is designed to stabilize. They will have to agree on what share of the intervention burden each of the two countries will shoulder. Thus, a credible system requires not just modest adaptations in domestic policies but systematic policy coordination between the partners. This sacrifice of autonomy is not something that central bankers are prepared to give lightly and therefore not something that the markets would be prepared to assume.

These are fundamental criticisms. They constitute serious grounds for questioning the feasibility of G-3 target zones.

HOW THE INTERNATIONAL MONETARY SYSTEM WILL LOOK IN TWENTY YEARS

How then will the international monetary system look in 2020? My analysis rules out radical changes like a single world currency and three regional monetary unions centered on the dollar, the euro, and the yen. It rules out pegged-but-adjustable exchange rates, crawling bands, target zones, and other intermediate arrangements in which governments try to have their cake and eat it too. But neither is a floating exchange rate likely to be attractive for small economies that are highly exposed to international trade and financial flows.

The three principal regions of the world economy—Europe, Asia and the Americas—are likely to square this circle in different ways. In Europe, where integration is a political as well as an economic and financial project, the euro and its associated institutions should provide the basis for an ever larger zone of monetary stability. Greece wants to join. The countries of Eastern Europe want to join. Turkey wants to join. Others could follow suit.

In the Americas, in contrast, the United States will not accede to the formation of an EU-style monetary union anytime soon. Dollarization may be the solution for countries like Argentina, Costa Rica, and El Salvador, which have strong financial links to the United States and little wish to run an autonomous monetary policy. Other countries may adopt currency boards as a halfway house while they contemplate this final step. Meanwhile, larger, more diversified economies like Canada and Brazil may make a strategic decision to live with the costs (and, one hopes, benefits) of a floating rate.

Asia's dilemma is the particularly difficult. Its trade and financial flows are regionally diversified: neither the dollar nor the yen is an attractive currency-board anchor for most of the smaller countries of the region. Basket-backed boards are conceivable, but they lack transparency and therefore credibility. Moreover, countries would have to agree on the composition of the basket in order for it to minimize intra-region currency fluctuations. This requires a degree of political comity that does not exist. Moreover, basket-backed boards with positive weights on the dollar, the yen, and conceivably the euro do not offer the promise of a subsequent transition to monetary union. That is to say, it is not clear whether such a country would logically proceed to monetary unification with the United States, Europe, or Japan. Hence, while Europe is likely to solve the currency conundrum through monetary unification and the Americas through dollarization, the plausible outcome in Asia, given the obstacles to the alternatives, is continued floating. One must hope that the countries of the region succeed in putting in place the institutional and political prerequisites necessary to effectively manage their managed float.

This vision of the international monetary architecture in the year 2020 suggests that the currency conundrum will not be solved by some grand design adopted at a new Bretton Woods Conference. Rather, it will be solved in an evolutionary fashion, with arrangements evolving in different ways in different parts of the world. Looking even further down the road, it is possible to envisage more radical outcomes. But that is something for future generations to write papers about.

The Diminishing Returns to Export-Led Growth

A Paper from the Project on Development,
Trade and International Finance

Robert A. Blecker

A Council on Foreign Relations Paper

The Diminishing Returns to Export-Led Growth

1. PROLOGUE: THE SUDDEN COLLAPSE OF THE EXPORT-LED ECONOMIES

In the 1970s and 1980s, there was a tremendous sea-change in development policy thinking, among both academic economists and policymakers. The inward-oriented, import-substitution strategy of the 1950s and 1960s became discredited and was replaced by an outward-oriented, export-promotion strategy. Although there was resistance, both intellectual and political, to this shift, by the early 1990s the battle was essentially over, and the export-promotion approach had won. This victory was aided in part by pressures from the U.S. government and the Bretton Woods institutions (the World Bank and the International Monetary Fund) in the aftermath of the 1980s debt crisis. However, it was also based on the apparently superior outcomes of the leading export-oriented economies in terms of both growth and equity objectives.

By the 1990s, the debate had shifted. Rather than focusing on whether an outward-oriented approach was superior, discussion now centered on why it was superior and what kinds of policies best promoted export-led growth. With regard to why export promotion was so vital, discussion focused on the relative importance of factors such as encouraging efficiency in resource allocation, stimulating learning effects and technological dynamism, and relaxing balance-of-payments constraints. With regard to policies, debate centered around whether export promotion was best achieved by laissez-faire policies that "let markets work" and "got prices right," or by government intervention that directed resources to strategic industries and altered price signals accordingly.[1]

In all of this discussion, the countries that were held up to the world (by every side in each debate) as the shining exemplars of successful, export-led, outward-oriented growth were the so-called "Four Tigers" (South Korea, Taiwan, Singapore, and Hong Kong), and the next wave of newly industrializing countries (NICs) in southeast Asia (such as Thailand, Malaysia, Indonesia, and China). Accordingly, it came as a major shock when many of these nations fell victim to a widespread financial crisis that sparked a sharp economic downturn in 1997–98. Although some non-Asian countries such as Russia and Brazil were caught in the shock waves after the Asian crisis, the core mystery is why a region whose development process had been widely viewed as highly successful, if not miraculous, was at the epicenter of such a gargantuan economic earthquake.[2] Was Asia merely the victim of some contingent (and potentially correctable) circumstances, such as mismanaged exchange-rate pegs or prematurely liberalized financial markets? Or did the financial crisis reveal some deeper, underlying flaws in the Asian development model—and if so, what are

---

[1]See, for example, Alice Amsden, *Asia's Next Giant: South Korea and Late Industrialization* (Oxford: Oxford University Press, 1989); Anne O. Krueger, *Liberalization Attempts and Consequences* (Cambridge, MA: Ballinger, 1978); Sanjaya Lall and Georg Kell, "Industrial Development in Developing Countries and the Role of Government Interventions," *Banca Nazionale del Lavoro Quarterly Review* (September), excerpted in Gerald M. Meier, ed., *Leading Issues in Economic Development*, 6th ed. (New York: Oxford University Press, 1995); Demetris Papageorgiu et al., eds., *Liberalizing Foreign Trade* (Cambridge, MA: Blackwell, 1991); Stephen C. Smith, *Industrial Policy in Developing Countries: Reconsidering the Real Sources of Export-Led Growth* (Washington, D.C.: Economic Policy Institute, 1991); Robert Wade, *Governing the Market: Economic Theory and the Role of Government in East Asian Industrialization* (Princeton: Princeton University Press, 1990); World Bank; *Development Report* 1987 and 1991 (New York: Oxford University Press), and World Bank, *The East Asian Miracle: Economic Growth and Public Policy* (Oxford: Oxford University Press, 1993).

[2]Russia and Brazil both had large public-sector deficits and debts, which distinguished them from the Asian countries, most of which had small budget deficits (or surpluses) and mostly private debts. They also have a much greater reliance on primary commodity exports, compared with most of the Asian crisis countries.

those deeper flaws, how can they be fixed, and what are the implications for development strategies in other regions?

There is no question that contingent factors played a dominant role in terms of the timing, location, and severity of the crisis.[3] The constellation of recently liberalized financial markets, overvalued exchange rates, speculative bubbles in asset markets, and large amounts of short-term, foreign-currency–denominated debt is a common factor in most of the crisis situations both in Asia and elsewhere in the 1990s—including Mexico in 1994, Russia in 1998, and Brazil in 1999, as well as Thailand, Korea, and other Asian coun-

---

[3]Alternative analyses have focused either on macroeconomic policies that allowed exchange rates to become overvalued or the inherently destabilizing effects of liberalized capital markets and speculative financial flows. Those who blame pegged but adjustable exchange rates tend to advocate either rigidly fixed or perfectly flexible rates, though there is no consensus on which way to go. For a variety of views, see Steve H. Hanke, "How to Establish Monetary Stability in Asia," *Cato Journal* 17, no. 3 (Winter 1998), pp. 295–301; Steve H. Hanke, Lars Jonung, and Kurt Schuler, *Russian Currency and Finance: A Currency Board Approach to Reform* (London: Routledge, 1993); Jeffrey D. Sachs, "Brazil Fever: First, Do No Harm," *Milken Institute Review* (Second Quarter, 1999), pp. 16–25; Barry Eichengreen, *Toward a New International Financial Architecture: A Practical Post-Asia Agenda* (Washington, D.C.: Institute for International Economics, 1999); Ricardo Hausmann et al., "Financial Turmoil and the Choice of Exchange Rate Regime," photocopy, (Washington, D.C.: Inter-American Development Bank, March 1999); and Jeffrey A. Frankel, "The International Financial Architecture: Exchange Rate Regimes and Financial Integration," Brookings Policy Brief, no. 51 (June 1999). Those who blame destabilizing effects of capital market liberalization tend to call for reimposing capital controls and foreign exchange restrictions, or for creating a new global regulatory authority or an international lender of last resort. For example, see Robert A. Blecker, *Taming Global Finance: A Better Architecture for Growth and Equity* (Washington, D.C.: Economic Policy Institute, 1999); Jane D'Arista and Tom Schlesinger, "Reforming the Privatized International Monetary System" (Philomont, Va.: Financial Market Center, 1998); John Eatwell and Lance Taylor, *Global Finance at Risk: The Case for International Regulation* (New York: New Press, 2000); Henry Kaufman, "Preventing the Next Global Financial Crisis," *Washington Post*, January 28, 1998; Paul R. Krugman, "Saving Asia: It's Time to Get Radical," *Fortune*, September 7, 1998; Robert Wade, "The Asian Debt-and-Development Crisis of 1997? Causes and Consequences," *World Development* (August 1998), and "From 'Miracle' to 'Cronyism': Explaining the Great Asian Slump," *Cambridge Journal of Economics*, 22, no. 6 (November 1998), pp. 693–706; Robert Wade and Frank Veneroso, "The Asian Crisis: The High Debt Model vs. the Wall Street-Treasury-IMF Complex," *New Left Review* 228 (March/April 1998).

tries in 1997–98.[4] Moreover, it is now generally recognized that speculative attacks on pegged exchange rates helped to provoke the rash of currency collapses, and that self-fulfilling panics worsened the ensuing economic downturns and contagion effects. Finally, although this is more controversial, many observers blame the International Monetary Fund (IMF) and the U.S. Treasury for inept handling of the crisis, including misguided efforts to support indefensible exchange-rate pegs and inappropriate policy recommendations that worsened both financial panics and real recessions.[5]

Nevertheless, debate still rages over what were the most important underlying factors that created a vulnerability of these apparently successful economies to such a financial (and real) crash. The official view, promoted by the U.S. government, other G-7 governments, and the IMF, blames inadequate financial supervision

---

[4]See, for example, Guillermo A. Calvo, Morris Goldstein, and Eduard Hochreiter, eds., *Private Capital Flows to Emerging Markets After the Mexican Crisis* (Washington, D.C.: Institute for International Economics, 1996); Jenny Corbett and David Vines, "The Asian Crisis: Competing Explanations," Center for Economic Policy Analysis, Working Paper Series III, no. 7 (New York: New School for Social Research, July 1998); Jason Furman and Joseph E. Stiglitz, "Economic Crises: Evidence and Insights from East Asia," *Brookings Papers on Economic Activity* 1998, no. 2, pp. 1–135; Graciela L. Kaminsky, Saul Lizondo, and Carmen M. Reinhart, "Leading Indicators of Currency Crises," *IMF Working Paper* no. WP/97/79 (Washington, D.C.: International Monetary Fund, July 1997); Graciela L. Kaminsky and Carmen M. Reinhart, "The Twin Crises: The Causes of Banking and Balance-of-Payments Problems," *American Economic Review*, vol. 89, no. 3 (June 1999), pp. 473–500; Paul R. Krugman, *The Return of Depression Economics* (New York: Norton, 1999); Brian K. MacLean, Paul Bowles, and Osvaldo Croci, "Understanding the Asian Crisis and Its Implications for Regional Economic Integration," in Alan M. Rugman and Gavin Boyd, eds., *Deepening Integration in the Pacific Economies* (Northampton, Mass.: Edward Elgar, 1999); Steven Radelet and Jeffrey D. Sachs, "The East Asian Financial Crisis: Diagnosis, Remedies, Prospects," *Brookings Papers on Economic Activity* 1998, no. 1, pp. 1–90; Jeffrey D. Sachs, Aaron Tornell, and Andrés Velasco, "Financial Crises in Emerging Markets: The Lessons from 1995," *Brookings Papers on Economic Activity* 1996, no. 1, pp. 147–215, and "The Mexican Peso Crisis: Sudden Death or Crisis Foretold?" *Journal of International Economics* 41, nos. 3/4 (November 1996), pp. 265–83; Ajit Singh, " 'Asian Capitalism' and the Financial Crisis," Center for Economic Policy Analysis, Working Paper Series III, no. 10 (New York: New School for Social Research, August 1998); Joseph E. Stiglitz, "The Global Financial Crisis: Perspectives and Policies" (Rochester, N.Y.: McKenzie Lecture, April 1999); Lance Taylor, "Capital Market Crises: Liberalisation, Fixed Exchange Rates and Market-Driven Destabilisation," *Cambridge Journal of Economics*, 22, no. 6 (November 1998), pp. 663–76; Robert Wade, ibid., 1998.

[5]See Blecker, ibid.; Martin Feldstein, "Refocusing the IMF," *Foreign Affairs* 77, no. 2 (1998), pp. 20–33; Steven Radelet and Sachs, ibid.; Taylor, ibid.; Wade and Veneroso, ibid.

and a lack of transparency within the crisis countries. According to this view, the crisis revealed a fundamental flaw in the Asian financial system, namely the so-called "crony capitalist" relationships between corporations, banks, and governments, which allegedly created too much "moral hazard" through explicit or implicit loan guarantees. This view supports the official proposals for a "new financial architecture," which emphasize improved transparency and surveillance—essentially, making over the financial systems of the Asian economies in the Western image (and, not coincidentally, opening them up to foreign ownership in the process).

It is true that close connections between private lenders, corporate borrowers, and government agencies (or officials) contributed to the buildup of bad loan portfolios in many of the Asian countries. However, it is not clear that most lenders really counted on being bailed out if their loans failed—rather, the possibility of borrowers being unable to services their debts was simply discounted. The problem of overlending appears to have been due more to investors' myopia and willful ignorance of risk than to moral hazard.[6] Moreover, these same domestic financial systems worked well for the previous three decades, when the Asian economies achieved their record-breaking growth, during which time those financial systems successfully channeled national savings into productive investments in strategic sectors.[7]

In fact, it was the *removal* of government controls over capital inflows and investment finance in countries like Korea and Thailand in the 1990s—not the prior existence of such controls—that allowed lending to reach excessive proportions and permitted unsustainable levels of short-term, foreign currency borrowing to occur in the mid-1990s.[8] The removal of those controls was

[6]On this point see Marcus Noland, Li-Gang Liu, Sherman Robinson, and Zhi Wang, *Global Economic Effects of the Asian Currency Devaluations* (Washington, D.C.: Institute for International Economics, 1998); Radelet and Sachs, ibid.; Taylor, ibid.

[7]See Amsden, ibid.; Robert Wade, ibid., 1990; and Ajit Singh, "Savings, Investment, and the Corporation in the East Asian Miracle," *Journal of Development Studies* 34, no. 6 (August 1998), pp. 112–37.

[8]This argument is made by Ha-Joon Chang, "Korea: The Misunderstood Crisis," *World Development*, vol. 26, no. 8 (1998), pp. 1555–61; and Singh, " 'Asian Capitalism' and the Financial Crisis."

pushed and promoted by the U.S. government and the IMF in the early 1990s, without regard for the lack of adequate transparency and prudential regulation that were later blamed for causing the crisis. Also, the fact that several major Asian countries that never liberalized external capital flows (notably China, Taiwan, and India) escaped the financial meltdown of 1997–98 lends credence to the argument that financial market liberalization was a direct cause of the crisis—especially since these countries are not necessarily lacking in "crony" relationships between borrowers, lenders, and governments. At most, one could claim that the nature of the Asian financial systems created a vulnerability to overlending when those systems were opened up to liberalized capital inflows.

Nevertheless, it will be argued here that there is *another* fundamental flaw in the development strategy of the Asian countries and in the efforts of other developing countries to emulate the Asian model. This flaw is the "fallacy of composition" of so many countries simultaneously relying on export-led growth policies and the resulting overinvestment that has created an overhang of excess capacity in key export industries. While these policies did not directly cause the financial crisis, the competition of an increasing number of developing nations for a limited range of export markets in similar products was a source of underlying vulnerability to a crisis. In fact, the location and timing of some of the recent financial crises can be associated with situations of disappointing growth in countries that were counting on export booms to propel their development.

The increasing openness to imports and reliance on export growth in a large number of competing countries helps to account for the fact that countries with overvalued currencies were so vulnerable to speculative attacks and financial collapses. And the fact that all of the countries that are attempting to recover from financial crises are simultaneously trying to promote similar exports via depreciated currencies is an important reason why this recovery has been so slow and uncertain—and why even some countries that escaped the financial crisis of 1997–98 without suffering currency collapses of their own nevertheless saw their growth rates reduced.

The rest of this paper is organized as follows. First is a more precise statement of the hypothesis about the constraints on export-led growth and discussion of some important qualifications to the argument. This is followed by a brief literature survey, including studies of exports and growth, models of balance-of-payments-constrained growth, analyses of the Asian development model and financial crisis, and previous studies of the "fallacy of composition" and of excess capacity in developing countries. Following the literature survey is a discussion of some preliminary empirical evidence that establishes the plausibility of diminishing returns to export-led growth becoming a problem in the 1990s. The final section offers a tentative discussion of the policy implications of the analysis, with emphasis on what it implies for the redesign of both domestic development policies and the international financial "architecture."

THE HYPOTHESIS: STATEMENT AND QUALIFICATIONS

The basic flaw in the export-led growth strategy is that, under a given set of global demand conditions, the market for developing country exports of manufactures is limited by the capacity (and willingness) of the industrialized nations to absorb the corresponding imports. The market for imports of labor-intensive manufactures and other NIC exports can only grow so fast, and as a result the export-led strategy can work only for a limited number of countries at a time. If this market is growing at, say, 7 percent per year, then not all of the NICs can have their exports increase at rates of 10 percent or 15 percent per year—although a few can, *provided that the market shares of other exporters or domestic producers are falling at the same time.* If all try to grow faster than is possible in the aggregate, the result can only be an overhang of excess industrial capacity and/or falling prices. And if some countries' export performance is disappointing, they will suffer economic stagnation and become more prone to a currency collapse or financial crisis—especially if they attempt to paper over their growth slowdowns with international borrowing that creates a fragile financial position and makes the currency overvalued.

Of course, total exports of manufactures from the developing countries can grow faster than domestic demand in the industrialized countries, provided that the former countries as a group increase their productive capacity and lower their average costs, thus permitting them to take away market share from domestic producers in the latter. In this respect, the ability of all developing country exporters to increase their total market share abroad is limited by two factors: first, by protectionist policies, either previously existing protection or responses to import surges; and second, by the eventual disappearance of domestic import-competing producers (or the survival of only a few "niche" producers), which then constrains total import growth to the growth rate of the domestic market in the industrialized countries.

To the extent that the total market share of developing country exporters cannot be increased further (e.g., because they are concentrated in product lines where there is no domestic production left in the industrialized countries, or remaining domestic producers in the latter countries have solid market niches or enduring protection), then each new entrant can achieve above-average rates of export growth only if it displaces some other exporting countries, whose export growth will inevitably falter as a result. A key variable in this process is the exchange rate: countries with low, competitive rates will succeed, while those with high, overvalued rates will lose out. But no amount of competitive devaluations can allow *all* of these countries to succeed in the same game of export-led growth at the same time with the same products.[9]

The current wave of export-led growth was initiated by Japan in the 1960s and 1970s, with its tremendous success in tradition-

---

[9]One way out is to try to follow the Japanese and Korean model by upgrading the quality of exports, so as to avoid competition at the low end of the product scale with other low-wage exporters. But then, those markets too can become saturated and their prices can fall, and not all countries are prepared to go that route. See the discussion of Korkut Erturk, "Worldwide Intersectoral Balance, Overcapacity and the East Asian Crisis," photocopy (New York: New School for Social Research, and Salt Lake City: University of Utah, 1999), below.

al "smokestack" industries such as textiles, automobiles, and steel. By the late 1970s and early 1980s, when Japan was moving up the industrial ladder into more technologically advanced products, the Four Tigers stepped up their exports of labor-intensive products, thus initiating what became known as the "flying geese formation." At that time, the Four Tigers were the only major developing country exporters of labor-intensive manufactures, and they grew rapidly by achieving rising shares of the U.S. consumer market in particular. Then, in the late 1980s and 1990s, one country after another tried to emulate the East Asian Tigers: Thailand, Mexico, China, Malaysia, Indonesia, and various other countries in Latin America and the Caribbean, South and Southeast Asia, Eastern Europe, and the Middle East.

As the market for developing country exports of manufactures became more crowded with new entrants, signs of intensified competition among these countries for export opportunities began to emerge in the 1990s. In particular, the success of the export-promoting nations became extremely sensitive to exchange-rate changes, both domestic and foreign. First Japan and then other East Asian nations (e.g., Korea) whose currencies had appreciated relative to others began to suffer slower export growth and reduced market share abroad, with negative repercussions for their own domestic growth. In this process, not only changes in the countries' own exchange rates, but "cross-effects" of other countries' exchange rate changes began to have significant effects. For example, the Chinese and Mexican devaluations of 1994 boosted those countries' export growth, but put pressure on other countries some of which (notably Thailand and Korea) suffered currency collapses only a few years later.

There are a number of important qualifications to this hypothesis, in regard to both the Asian development model in particular and export-led growth in general. Regarding the Asian model, an obvious caveat is that the Asian nations are diverse, and do not all exactly fit what Singh aptly calls the "ideal type" of the Asian model.[10] For example, three of the original Four Tigers (all except

---

[10]Singh, " 'Asian Capitalism' and the Financial Crisis."

Hong Kong) had significant government direction of their industrial development strategies and restrictions on foreign direct investment, as does China today, while some other Southeast Asian economies have had less policy intervention of this type. Also, rapid export growth was a necessary, but not a sufficient, explanation for the "miraculous" growth of the East Asian economies in the 1980s and early 1990s. Other policies were also key to East Asia's success, including the financial arrangements that have since been derided as forms of "crony capitalism." Also important were various types of restrictions on imports and direct foreign investment, not to mention a variety of domestic policies usually touted as indicating "strong fundamentals" (including agricultural reforms, small budget deficits, low inflation rates, and high educational achievement).

The Asian model also included high private saving and investment rates, and has been referred to as a case of "investment-led growth" rather than export-led.[11] However, the high investment rates were linked to export promotion efforts and appear to have fostered excess capacity in key export sectors. More importantly, the high saving rates beg the question of what forces kept the Keynesian "paradox of thrift" from emerging. Our argument is that the combination of rapid export growth and high investment demand focused on export activities provided the aggregate demand stimulus that enabled these countries to sustain such high saving rates. As a result, when a country with such a high saving rate loses competitiveness in export markets (e.g., because its own currency appreciates or other countries' currencies depreciate) and its export growth and investment demand fall off, the country is left with no source of demand stimulus as long as domestic consumer spending continues to be repressed.

---

[11] See William H. Branson, "Trade and Structural Interdependence Between the United States and the Newly Industrializing Countries," in Colin I. Bradford, Jr., and William H. Branson, eds., *Trade and Structural Change in Pacific Asia* (Chicago: University of Chicago Press, 1987). The importance of high investment rates in the East Asian experience has also been emphasized by Paul Krugman, "The Myth of Asia's Miracle," *Foreign Affairs*, 73 (1994), pp. 62–78.

Another qualification is that not all of Asia's export growth has been targeted to the industrialized countries. East Asia especially has had significant growth of intraregional trade, which partly ameliorates the risks of relying on exports to the United States and Europe. Ironically, however, this did not help, and in fact contributed to regional contagion effects when the entire region became depressed in 1997–98. However, Japan has remained more closed to such intraregional trade in manufactures than most of its less-developed neighbors, implying that they have had to rely mainly on exports to each other and to the United States.[12] There have also been other efforts at "South-South" regional integration, notably Mercosur [Southern Cone Common Market] in South America. But again, an important lesson from the recent financial crisis is that such trade agreements do not work well, and can even spread regional contagion effects, when macroeconomic and financial weaknesses are not addressed.[13]

There are also important qualifications to the general idea of constraints on export-led growth. Most importantly, the constraints in terms of the growth of global markets for manufactured imports are not fixed and given. These constraints can be relaxed if the industrialized countries stimulate their domestic economies more and open up their import markets more to developing nations' exports. This point applies especially to Japan, which is notoriously closed to manufactured imports[14] and has been stuck in a chronic growth depression for most of the 1990s. However,

---

[12] For supporting data and analysis, see Yilmaz Akyüz, Ha-Joon Chang, and Richard Kozul-Wright, "New Perspectives on East Asian Development," *Journal of Development Studies* 34, no. 6 (August 1998), pp. 4–36.

[13] This problem was foreseen by Robert A. Blecker and William E. Spriggs, "Beyond NAFTA: Employment, Growth, and Income Distribution Effects of a Western Hemisphere Free Trade Area," in *Trade Liberalization in the Western Hemisphere* (Washington, D.C.: Inter-American Development Bank and U.N. Economic Commission on Latin America and the Caribbean, 1995).

[14] See Robert Z. Lawrence, "Imports in Japan: Closed Markets or Minds?" *Brookings Papers on Economic Activity* 1987, no. 2, pp. 517–54; and "Efficient or Exclusionist? The Import Behavior of Japanese Corporate Groups," *Brookings Papers on Economic Activity* 1991, no. 1, pp. 311–41.

the same point applies to Europe—which has thus far mainly opened itself up to more intraregional trade rather than more trade with outside regions,[15] and which has maintained slow growth and high unemployment in the 1990s for a combination of macroeconomic and structural reasons that are hotly debated. In this author's view, the restrictive macroeconomic policies adopted under the Maastricht plan for monetary union are the primary cause of high European unemployment, rather than the alleged structural problems in European labor markets (rigid real wages, lack of "flexibility"). However, whatever one's view on this issue, it is clear that European economies are unnaturally depressed and are not providing growing markets for developing country exports of manufactures.

Even the United States, while more open to developing country exports of manufactures than most other industrialized countries, maintains a number of limitations on imports of these goods such as the application of the "fair trade" or "contingent protection" laws (anti-dumping, countervailing duty, etc.) that effectively inhibit imports in certain sectors such as steel. Still, the United States is hardly alone in this respect. In spite of these restrictions, U.S. imports of manufactured products from developing countries have grown more rapidly than similar imports into any other major industrialized country, and they have contributed significantly to the growing U.S. trade deficit. As of 1998, 56 percent of the U.S. merchandise trade deficit was accounted for by Mexico plus the Asian developing nations, with 23 percent accounted for by China alone.[16] By 1999–2000, the United States was able to maintain large and growing trade deficits only as a result of the willingness of foreigners to lend this country more than $300 billion annually, while Europe and Japan were running large trade sur-

---

[15]See A. Kleinknecht and J. ter Wengel, "The Myth of Economic Globalisation," *Cambridge Journal of Economics*, vol. 22, no. 5 (September 1998), pp. 637–47.

[16]See Table 1 in Robert A. Blecker, "The Causes of the U.S. Trade Deficit," Statement to the U.S. Trade Deficit Review Commission (Washington, D.C., August 1999), based on data from the U.S. Department of Commerce, Bureau of Economic Analysis.

pluses. However, the resulting increase in the U.S. net international debt position and vulnerability of the dollar to depreciation pressures suggests that this pattern of global imbalances is not sustainable in the long run.[17]

This comparison of Japan, Europe, and the United States suggests that the industrialized nations of the "North" cannot be treated as a uniform bloc with regard to either macroeconomic or commercial policies. As Table 1 shows, only the United States has a significantly higher ratio of trade to GDP today than it did in the pre-World War I epoch, while (by this measure) the major European countries' openness to trade has barely returned to its pre-1914 level and Japan's overall openness is still notably lower than it was at that time. Although the individual European countries appear more open to trade than either the United States or Japan, most of their trade is with each other, and the external trade of the

Table 1. Exports and Imports of Goods as Percentages of GDP (in current prices), Selected Countries and Years

	1913	*1950*	*1973*	*1994*
United States	11.2	6.9	10.8	17.8
Japan	30.1	16.4	18.2	14.6
United Kingdom	47.2	37.1	37.6	41.8
France	30.0	21.4	29.2	34.2
Germany	36.1	20.1	35.3	39.3
European Union (EU-12)[a]	NA	NA	14.8[b]	17.2[c]

Source: See A. Kleinknecht and J. ter Wengel, "The Myth of Economic Globalisation," *Cambridge Journal of Economics*, vol. 22, no. 5 (1998), Tables 1 and 4, pp. 638, 641, and author's calculations.

[a]Outside-EU exports and imports only.
[b]The figure shown is the sum of outside-EU exports and imports for 1970.
[c]The figure shown is the sum of outside-EU exports and imports for 1995.

[17]For analyses of the sustainability of the U.S. external deficit and foreign debt, see Robert A. Blecker, "International Capital Mobility, Macroeconomic Imbalances, and the Risk of Global Contraction," Center for Economic Policy Analysis, Working Paper Series III, no. 5 (New York: New School for Social Research, 1998) and "The Ticking Debt Bomb: Why the U.S. International Financial Position Is Not Sustainable," Briefing Paper (Washington, D.C.: Economic Policy Institute, June 1999); and Catherine L. Mann, *Is the U.S. Trade Deficit Sustainable?* (Washington, D.C.: Institute for International Economics, 1999).

European Union countries as a group is about the same order of magnitude as that of the United States (and higher than Japan's).

In recent years, and in spite of the occasional bouts of contingent protection referred to above, the United States has served as the "consumer of last resort" for exporters from all continents and regions due to a combination of relatively open markets, robust economic growth, and booming consumer demand (the latter of which is in turn attributable partly to the stock market boom and partly to growing consumer debt). Much of the tension in the international trading system today results from the disproportionate share of global manufactured exports that is absorbed in the U.S. market, which widens the U.S. trade deficit and causes political resentments in the United States, while also restricting export growth in the developing countries.

To be fair, Western Europe has been engaged in a process of continental integration, in which the Northern and Central European countries are increasingly absorbing manufactured imports from relatively low-wage countries in the European periphery (e.g., Ireland, Spain, Portugal, and Eastern Europe)—and suffering some of the same industrial dislocations and employment losses as the United States as a result. Still, Europe's absorption in its own internal integration and slow growth combined with Japan's general closure and malaise put the main burden of absorbing developing country exports of manufactures squarely on the United States. Greater macroeconomic stimulus policies together with increased market openness and structural reforms in Europe and Japan could help to relieve these pressures on the United States while increasing export opportunities for developing countries.

Finally, it is important to recognize that, in principle, simultaneous export expansion can potentially provide increased reciprocal demand for all nations' exports. This is the vision of a prosperous, open international economy promoted by classical liberal economic thinkers since the time of Adam Smith. If this vision holds true, the constraints on export-led growth can become very elastic or even nonbinding. However, for such simultaneous export growth to be successful in expanding the global market for all countries' exports in reality, it is vital that the countries that are promoting their exports are also opening their own markets to imports and maintaining high domestic demand at the same time. In this way, simultaneous export expansion with roughly balanced trade can occur. What is not feasible is for all countries to attempt to achieve trade surpluses by promoting their exports while simultaneously restricting their imports in mercantilist fashion. Because all countries cannot have trade surpluses at the same time,[18] the widespread pursuit of this type of neomercantilist policy only tightens the global constraints on export-led growth—because not enough countries are willing to absorb the corresponding imports— and thus fosters intensified conflict over foreign market share.

In short, the classical liberal vision of a world in which export-led growth solves the demand problem through reciprocal and balanced market expansion is not flawed as a vision, but rather as a characterization of the real world in which we live. The challenge for policy today is whether and how that vision could be achieved in the future, and what nations should do in the present while that vision is not fulfilled in practice. We shall return to this policy dilemma in the concluding section, but first we take a detour through a review of studies of exports and growth followed by a discussion of some preliminary evidence on growing conflict over shares of the U.S. import market.

LITERATURE SURVEY: STUDIES OF EXPORTS, GROWTH, AND THE FALLACY OF COMPOSITION

The notion of a fallacy of composition in the widespread promotion of the export-led growth strategy among developing countries is commonly discussed in popular accounts of globalization, such as William Greider's *One World, Ready or Not: The Manic Logic of Global Capitalism*, published in 1997. However, there has been remarkably little attention to this issue in the academic

---

[18]This point was stressed by Joan Robinson, *Contributions to Modern Economics* (New York: Academic Press, 1978) and Amit Bhaduri, *Macroeconomics: The Dynamics of Commodity Production* (Armonk, N.Y.: M. E. Sharpe, 1986).

literature on trade and development. This section will briefly review some of the relevant literature, starting with studies of exports and growth that have largely ignored the issue and then move on to those exceptional studies that have taken the problem seriously.

Studies of Exports and Growth

A useful place to start is with the large literature that has found positive effects of export growth or economic openness on overall economic growth and development.[19] These studies generally find a positive association of export growth (or export shares or some other measure of trade openness) with aggregate (or per capita) income growth, which is robust across a wide array of modeling specifications and measurement techniques. In addition, some studies have focused on testing for the direction of causality between export growth and output growth, generally finding that exports have significant causal effects on output.[20]

It is important to distinguish what these types of studies prove and what they don't prove, or don't even consider. Even if the results of these studies are accepted at face value, they simply show that the countries that actually had faster export growth (or were otherwise more open to trade) succeeded in growing faster than the other countries, subject to certain qualifications (e.g., other variables that are controlled for in the analyses). What these studies do *not* show, however, is that the countries with slower export growth could have increased their export growth without, to some extent,

---

[19]See, for example, Bela Balassa, "Exports and Economic Growth: Further Evidence," *Journal of Development Economics* 5 (June 1978), pp. 181–89, and "Exports, Policy Choices, and Economic Growth in Developing Countries after the 1973 Oil Shock," *Journal of Development Economics*, vol. 18 (May–June 1985), pp. 23–35; Michael Michaely, "Exports and Growth: An Empirical Investigation," *Journal of Development Economics* 4 (March 1977), pp. 49–53; Demetris Papageorgiu et. al., *Liberalizing Foreign Trade*, and Jeffrey D. Sachs and Andrew Warner, "Economic Reform and the Process of Global Integration," *Brookings Papers on Economic Activity* 1995, no. 1, pp. 1–118.

[20]See, for example, Peter Chow, "Causality between Export Growth and Industrial Development: Empirical Evidence from the NICs," *Journal of Development Economics* 26 (June 1987), pp. 55–63; Ali Darrat, "Are Exports an Engine of Growth? Another Look at the Evidence," *Applied Economics* 19 (February 1987), pp. 277–83; and Jeffrey A. Frankel and David Romer, "Does Trade Cause Growth?" *American Economic Review*, vol. 89, no 3 (June 1999), pp. 379–99.

diminishing the export growth of the more successful exporting countries, during the same time periods. In other words, these studies assume that each country's export growth is independent of the others; they do not consider (or test for) whether there may be an "adding-up constraint" on total export growth by less-developed-country producers of manufactures.

Furthermore, the results of these studies should not be accepted uncritically. A number of careful studies have found decidedly more mixed results about the robustness of the export-growth or openness-growth relationship, and they undercut (or at least qualify) the general euphoria about export-led growth strategies in most of the economics profession. For example, McCarthy, Taylor, and Talati find that high-performing economies are *less* open to trade than low-performing economies,[21] for a sample of developing countries in the 1964–82 period. They also find that high-performing economies do not generally have higher shares of exports in GDP, although they are somewhat more specialized in manufactures than the low-performing countries.

Sprout and Weaver divide developing nations into groups based on country size and type of specialization.[22] They find that the positive export-growth relationship is strongest for small, nonprimary-product exporters, weaker for large less-developed countries, and weakest (and statistically insignificant) for small, primary-product exporters. This study also finds a positive effect of trading partners' growth (an exogenous variable) on export growth in the small, nonprimary-product exporters, although the effect was not statistically significant. These results suggest that it is not open-

---

[21] See F. Desmond McCarthy, Lance Taylor, and Cyrus Talati, "Trade Patterns in Developing Countries, 1964–82," *Journal of Development Economics*, vol. 27 (1987), pp. 5–39. High and low performance were defined via the following method. The authors ran a regression of the average growth rate for each country for the whole sample period (1964–82) on the level of GNP per capita achieved in 1982; countries that lay above the (positively sloped) regression line were categorized as "high performers," while those lying below the line were designated as "low performers." All of the East Asian countries included in the study (Korea, Indonesia, Malaysia, Philippines) were counted as high performers by this criterion.

[22] Ronald V. A. Sprout and James H. Weaver, "Exports and Economic Growth in a Simultaneous Equations Model," *Journal of Developing Areas*, vol. 27 (April 1993), pp. 289–306.

ness or exports in general that promote growth, but rather a specialization in manufactures, and that the growth of the manufacturing exporting countries (at least the smaller ones) may have been constrained to some extent by the growth rates of their trading partners.

Sachs and Warner are distinguished by their focus on the trade policy regime, rather than on export growth rates or export shares of GDP.[23] They define countries as having a "closed" trading regime if they have *any one* of the following five characteristics: nontariff barriers covering 40 percent or more of trade; average tariff rates of 40 percent or more; a large black market exchange-rate premium (20 percent or more); a socialist economic system; or a state monopoly on major exports. Countries are defined as "open" if they have *none* of these five features. Based on this classification, Sachs and Warner find strong evidence that open countries tend to grow faster than closed countries and that "open [developing] economies display a strong tendency toward economic convergence" in per capita income with the industrialized countries while closed economies do not. However, this definition of openness falls far short of perfectly free trade, and does not exclude significant industrial policies, moderate import restrictions, or export-promoting interventions. Sachs and Warner also do not consider to what extent the successes of the relatively more "open" countries could be duplicated by other countries without running into global demand constraints.

A similar point applies to the literature on balance-of-payments-constrained (BPC) growth in the post-Keynesian tradition.[24] The simplest BPC growth model assumes that countries have to balance their trade in the long run and also assumes that relative price effects are weak (i.e., exchange-rate adjustments are not effective

---

[23]Sachs and Warner, "Economic Reform and the Process of Global Integration," p. 41.

[24]The BPC growth model was originally applied to the industrialized countries by A. P. Thirwall, "The Balance of Payments Constraint as an Explanation of International Growth Rate Differences," *Banca Nazionale del Lavoro Quarterly Review*, no. 128 (March 1979), pp. 45–53, and later extended to developing countries by, among others, A. P. Thirwall and M. Nureldin Hussain, "The Balance of Payments Constraint, Capital Flows and Growth Rate Differences Between Developing Countries," *Oxford Economic Papers*, vol. 34, no. 3 (1982), pp. 498–510.

for balancing trade). Then a country's growth rate is constrained by the ratio of the growth rate of its exports to the income elasticity of its demand for imports.[25] The simple version of the model yields remarkably close predictions of actual, long-run average growth rates of GDP for the industrialized countries, while extensions of the model incorporating net capital inflows fit the data for the developing countries.[26]

The novelty of this approach—aside from its stark parsimony of explanation and neglect of "natural" supply-side factors (such as population growth) usually assumed to determine growth rates—lies in its emphasis on the *negative* effects of excessive openness to imports (as reflected in a high income elasticity of import demand) on output growth, as well as the positive effects of rapid export growth. This emphasis accords with the view that the East Asian countries' success can be attributed to a *limited* form of openness, in which exports were promoted but imports were selectively restricted.[27] Moreover, the BPC approach suggests a

---

[25]This simple formulation can be modified to take account of various complexities, such as capital flows, mark-up pricing behavior, or labor-market dynamics. See Juan Carlos Moreno-Brid, "On Capital Flows and the Balance-of-Payments-Constrained Growth Model," *Journal of Post Keynesian Economics*, vol. 21, no. 2 (Winter 1998–99), pp. 283–98; Robert A. Blecker, "International Competition, Relative Wages, and the Balance-of-Payments Constraint," *Journal of Post Keynesian Economics*, vol. 20, no 4 (Summer 1998), pp. 495–526; and Maurizio Pugno, "The Stability of Thirlwall's Model of Economic Growth and the Balance-of-Payments Constraint," *Journal of Post Keynesian Economics*, vol. 20, no. 4 (Summer 1998), pp. 559–81.

[26]See the evidence summarized by John S. L. McCombie and A. P. Thirlwall, *Economic Growth and the Balance-of-Payments Constraint* (New York: St. Martin's Press, 1994) and John S. L. McCombie, "Empirics of Balance-of-Payments-Constrained Growth," *Journal of Post Keynesian Economics*, vol. 19, no. 3 (Spring 1997), pp. 345–75. However, José Alonso and Carlos Garcimartín, "A New Approach to the Balance-of-Payments Constraint: Some Empirical Evidence," *Journal of Post Keynesian Economics*, vol. 21, no. 2 (Winter 1998–99), pp. 259–82, criticize the econometric methodology of earlier empirical tests of the BPC growth model that were based on correlating actual and predicted growth rates. They argue for an alternative approach that tests for whether balance-of-payments deficits tend to be eliminated by relative price adjustments (the neoclassical view) or income adjustments (the post-Keynesian view). Their results strongly support the latter view.

[27]For example, Sachs and Warner's data show that Taiwan had quotas on 38 percent of its imports, barely below the 40 percent threshold for being considered "closed" (Table 7, p. 32). Their definition does not even include other types of nontariff barriers or government interventions, such as subsidies.

reason why exports are so critical in the growth process: namely that they relieve the balance-of-payments constraint imposed by the high import requirements of rapid growth (e.g., to pay for imported capital goods and debt service).

But the BPC growth model suffers from the same problem as the development literature on exports and growth, discussed earlier: export growth rates of individual countries are taken as independent of each other, when in fact they are related insofar as total world exports must add up to equal total world imports, and the growth of the latter is not unlimited. Moreover, the standard BPC growth model considers only the relative prices of home goods compared with one composite foreign good, and ignores differences between prices of imported and exported goods as well as cross-price effects of competition with "third countries" in export markets.[28]

The Asian Model and the Financial Crisis

Most studies of the Asian development model acknowledge the important role of international trade in facilitating the region's growth, but they differ in how they account for the region's stunning export success.[29] Generally, rapid growth of export markets is taken for granted in this literature, and the main issue is whether the policies that enabled these countries to take advantage of expanding export markets should be regarded as free-market or interventionist. Ajit Singh summarizes the East Asian approach to trade policy as follows:

> the East Asian governments have sought not "close" but what might be called "strategic" integration with the world economy; i.e.,

---

[28]Some ideas for correcting these deficiencies and using a modified BPC model to test for global demand constraints on export-led growth are discussed in Robert A. Blecker, "The Fallacy of Composition and the Limits of Export-led Growth," paper presented at the Meeting on the World Financial Authority, July 1999, organized by the Center for Economic Analysis of the New School for Social Research, New York City.

[29]See Yilmaz Akyüz et. al., "New Perspectives on East Asian Development," and Ajit Singh, "'Asian Capitalism' and the Financial Crisis," for useful surveys of the main previous studies as well as new critical perspectives.

they have integrated up to the point where it has been useful for them to do so. Thus during their high-growth, developmental phases, Japan (between 1950–1973) and Korea (1970s and 1980s) integrated with the world economy in relation to exports but not imports; with respect to science and technology but not finance and multinational investment.[30]

Most of the literature on export-led growth in Asia is curiously silent on the possibility of global demand constraints. When this issue is raised, it is usually quickly dismissed:

> Regarding the danger of a 'fallacy of composition' in manufactured exports, while there is some evidence that this could become a constraint on industrial development in the South, particularly if slow growth persists in the advanced industrial countries, the potential scope for developing countries to enter Northern markets for textiles, clothing and other such goods is considerable .... Moreover, the very success of the East Asian economies means not only that they are facing pressures to vacate these markets and shift to higher value-added exports, but also that their own markets for low-skill manufactures are expanding, providing new export opportunities for the next generation of industrialising countries.[31]

In a 1994 article in *Foreign Affairs*, Paul Krugman claimed that the Asian economies were destined to slow down their phenomenal growth rates.[32] Specifically, he claimed that the Asian economies (including Japan) grew through almost Soviet-style "capital deepening": investing in a large amount of capital per worker, and thus raising labor productivity substantially, but without much overall improvement in efficiency in the sense of "total factor productivity." Krugman's interpretation of the productivity numbers has been challenged,[33] but the biggest problem is his basic conceptual framework, which assumes that one can distin-

---

[30]Singh, ibid., p. 8.

[31]Akyüz ibid., p. 30.

[32]Paul R. Krugman, "The Myth of Asia's Miracle."

[33]For example, by Steven Radelet and Jeffrey D. Sachs, "Asia's Reemergence," *Foreign Affairs*, vol. 76, no. 6 (1997), pp. 44–59, cited by Jenny Corbett and David Vines, "The Asian Crisis: Competing Explanations."

guish the "quantity" of capital from the technology embedded in that capital. Krugman's claim is simply that a large increase in the quantity of physical capital relative to other factors (including human capital, which was also accumulated rapidly in East Asia) would inevitably lead to diminishing marginal productivity and hence a reduction in the rate of return to capital. Problems of export markets—or the fact that so much of the capital was invested in similar export activities in competing countries—play no role in Krugman's analysis.[34] The policies that were used to boost "rents" or oligopolistic profits in East Asia in order to finance investment are also ignored in the debate between Krugman and his critics, which is based on a methodology that assumes that economic profits are zero and that returns to capital are determined by marginal productivity.

Although the notion of limits to export-led growth has thus attracted little attention within the literature on the pre-1997 Asian miracle, there are greater hints about it in studies of the 1990s financial crises. One of the most robust findings in empirical studies of financial crises is the importance of real exchange rate overvaluation in explaining the outbreak of speculative attacks or contagion effects.[35] While any exchange-rate overvaluation may call for an eventual adjustment, the question is why overvaluation has proved to be so utterly disastrous in recent years. Part of the answer lies in the logic of speculative behavior in liberalized financial markets: once a currency is perceived as overvalued and is expected to have to depreciate in the future, the expectation of a depreciation becomes a self-fulfilling prophecy as soon as investors start to act on this expectation and begin to sell the cur-

---

[34]Krugman has since backed away from claims that his diminishing marginal productivity of capital story explains the Asian crisis of 1997, because the latter occurred too rapidly to have been caused by a gradual falling tendency of the returns to capital.

[35]See Graciela L. Kaminsky and Carmen M. Reinhart, "The Twin Crises: The Causes of Banking and Balance-of-Payments Problems"; Steven Radelet and Jeffrey D. Sachs, "Asia's Reemergence"; Jeffrey D. Sachs, Aaron Tornell, and Andrès Velasco, "Financial Crises in Emerging Markets: The Lessons from 1995"; and Aaron Tornell, "Common Fundamentals in the Tequila and Asian Crises," photocopy (Cambridge, Mass.: Harvard University and National Bureau of Economic Research, 1998).

rency short. This effect is then exacerbated if the country has large amounts of short-term, foreign-currency-denominated debt and creditors become worried about default risk. But there is another aspect to the problem, namely that in countries that have relied heavily on the stimulus of export growth, and especially in those that have also opened themselves significantly to imports (e.g., Mexico), the risks of currency overvaluation for the real economy are heightened. In such a policy environment, the negative consequences of currency overvaluation for the balance of payments are much more quickly realized, and the need for a corrective devaluation is much more rapidly perceived.[36]

The current debate over alternative exchange rate policies for developing nations also highlights, albeit implicitly, the importance of export markets in countries promoting exports of manufactures to the industrialized countries. There is a new "conventional wisdom" that claims countries must choose between rigidly fixed exchange rates and perfectly free-floating systems. Intermediate regimes such as crawling pegs have suddenly fallen out of vogue and are now regarded as untenable (a view that assumes, among other things, that reinstating capital controls is not an option). Leaving the merits of this new orthodoxy aside for the moment,[37] it is interesting to consider the political economy of which countries have opted for floating rates versus fixed rates.

---

[36]Another finding in the crisis literature is that a currency crisis is often preceded by a prior slowdown in output growth (see Kaminsky and Reinhart, "The Twin Crises: The Causes of Banking and Balance-of-Payments Problems"). In export-oriented economies, such a slowdown in output growth can be a product of an overvalued currency, or—what authors in this literature have missed—of a currency devaluation by a competitor nation, which has taken export market share away from the country in question. For example, Corbett and Vines ("The Asian Crisis: Competing Explanations," pp. 15–16) point out that, by conventional measures of real effective exchange rates, some Asian countries (such as Korea and Taiwan) did not have a substantial real appreciation prior to the 1997 crisis. However, Corbett and Vines do not consider whether real depreciations in *other* countries (such as China or Mexico) may have contributed to the slower export growth they identify in all the Asian crisis nations.

[37]For skeptical views of this new orthodoxy on exchange rates, see Jeffrey A. Frankel, "The International Financial Architecture: Exchange Rate Regimes and Financial Integration," and John Williamson, "Filling the Void: Viable Intermediate Exchange Rate Regimes for East Asia," photocopy (Washington, D.C.: Institute for International Economics, February 2000).

Argentina has opted for a strong form of a fixed exchange rate with a currency board, and is now seriously considering legal dollarization, in spite of the drag that this policy has placed on the country's balance of payments and growth. In contrast, Mexico has ended up keeping the flexible exchange rate regime that it originally adopted out of dire necessity at the end of 1994. This contrast might seem anomalous, because by conventional criteria Mexico is far more integrated with the United States than Argentina, and hence seems the more likely candidate for a dollar-based monetary union. Clearly, the desire to achieve "credibility" in financial markets and to avoid the reemergence of high inflation or large interest rate spreads is a key consideration for Argentina. However, Argentina does not have to worry as much about maintaining its bilateral competitiveness vis-à-vis the United States. Only 8.6 percent of its exports go to the United States, compared with 82.0 percent of Mexico's exports[38]—and Mexico's exports are much more concentrated in manufactured goods that compete with Asian exports.[39] Hence, the flexible exchange rate has become a crucial ingredient in Mexico's export-led recovery from the 1994–95 crisis, as well as in its relatively mild contagion effects from the Asian and Brazilian crises. The Mexican peso has depreciated further in nominal terms since 1995, thus keeping the real exchange rate from appreciating too much in spite of Mexico's higher inflation relative to the United States. (However, renewed capital inflows are once again threatening to push the Mexican peso too high in the early 2000s). At present, the Mexican authorities are content with how their (managed) floating exchange rate protects

---

[38]These data are for 1997 and were calculated by the author from the World Trade Analyzer database produced by Statistics Canada and licensed to this author at the Economic Policy Institute.

[39]According to a report from the Inter-American Development Bank, 53.1 percent of Mexico's total exports fall into the category of "exports exposed to Asian competition in [the] OECD market; only 5.4 percent of Argentina's total exports fall into this category". See *Integration and Trade in the Americas, Special Report, The International Financial Crisis: Implications for Latin American and Caribbean Trade and Integration,* Periodic Note (Washington, D.C.: Inter-American Development Bank, February 1999), Table 13, p. 26.

their external competitiveness, and they show no interest in dollarization or even less drastic forms of fixed exchange rates.[40]

Perhaps the most explicit consideration of the limits to export-led growth in the crisis literature has come in regard to the trade dimension of "contagion effects." For example, Radelet and Sachs acknowledge that pressures from surging Chinese and Mexican exports after 1994 contributed to slowing the growth of exports from other Asian countries in subsequent years, although they argue the effect was quantitatively "moderate."[41] Along the same lines, the Inter-American Development Bank highlights the "potential displacement of LAC [Latin American and Caribbean] exports in third markets such as those of the OECD [Organization for Economic Cooperation and Development], or the LAC regional market itself, where they compete with East Asian products which have become more price competitive."[42]

A related point is the oft-stated importance of China's decision *not* to devalue its currency following the financial crisis in the rest of East Asia. When China's neighbors' currencies were collapsing in 1997–98, it was widely feared that China would respond by devaluing its currency, thus possibly instigating a destabilizing cycle of competitive devaluations. Yet this did not happen. One

---

[40]Guillermo Ortiz, governor of the Banco de México [Central Bank of Mexico], "Dollarization: Fad or Future for Latin America," remarks at IMF Economic Forum (Washington, D.C.: International Monetary Fund, June 24, 1999).

[41]Steven Radelet and Jeffrey D. Sachs, "Asia's Reemergence."

[42]Inter-American Development Bank, *Integration and Trade in the Americas*, p. 19. The report points out that six key Asian currencies (those of Indonesia, Singapore, Korea, Malaysia, Philippines, and Thailand) fell by between 13 percent and 70 percent vis-à-vis the currencies of nine major Latin American exporters (Argentina, Brazil, Chile, Colombia, Costa Rica, Dominican Republic, Mexico, Peru, and Venezuela) between mid-1997 and mid-1998. Of course, the significance of this loss of price competitiveness for Latin American countries varies widely depending on the degree to which they export products that compete with Asian exports. In general, South American countries tend to export more primary products that do not compete with Asian exports, while Mexico and several Central American and Caribbean nations export more manufactures that compete with Asian exports. According to the IDB report (Table 13, p. 26), the following countries have at least 30 percent of their total exports in sectors exposed to competition from the Asian countries in OECD markets: Costa Rica (32.6%), Dominican Republic (58.9%), El Salvador (33.6%), Haiti (63.3%), Honduras (46.7%), Mexico (53.1%), and Panama (38.3%).

reason was that the rest of Asia's export growth was initially disappointing after the currencies depreciated (a result generally
attributed to the tightening of financial constraints on Asian
firms as a result of high interest rates and large debt burdens). Another reason was that the Chinese authorities made a conscious decision not to destabilize the region. Nevertheless, as of early 2000
China's efforts at preventing a growth slowdown without a devaluation appear to be faltering, and it is still feared that China will
devalue in the next few years. How a future Chinese devaluation
would actually affect other developing country exporters remains
to be seen. However, the perceived threat of dire consequences of
a Chinese devaluation for other newly industrializing countries implicitly recognizes that the significance of competition among these
countries for market share in the industrialized countries constitutes a limiting factor on export-led growth.

The Fallacy of Composition and Excess Capacity

Previous studies that explicitly test for the existence of a fallacy of composition in the export-led growth strategy are remarkably scarce. One notable (and prescient) exception is William Cline's
1982 study of whether the East Asian growth model could be generalized.[43] While supporting an outward orientation of development efforts, Cline noted that "it may reasonably be asked whether
the recent emphasis on export-oriented growth has sufficiently taken
account of the constraints on international market demand."[44] In
this regard, Cline focused on one dimension of those constraints:
the potential threat of increased protectionism in the industrialized countries if imports of manufactured commodities exceeded a critical threshold as a share of total domestic consumption
of those commodities. Cline's original conclusion is worth quot-
ing at length:

---

[43]William R. Cline, "Can the East Asian Import Model of Development be Generalized?" *World Development*, vol. 10, no. 2 (1982), pp. 81–90.

[44]Ibid., reprinted in William R. Cline, *Exports of Manufactures from Developing Countries* (Washington, D.C.: Brookings Institution, 1984), p. 198.

...generalization of the East Asian model of export-led development across all developing countries would result in untenable market penetration into industrial countries. Generalization of the G-4 [Gang of Four, or Four Tigers] export strategy would require developing-country exports of manufactures to rise sevenfold, implying a surge in their share of industrial country manufactured imports from about one-sixth to about three-fifths. If a developing-country import-penetration ratio of 15 percent is used as a threshold beyond which protective responses would be expected, fully four-fifths of the industrial country markets for manufactured exports from developing countries would be vulnerable to probable protective action in the face of the flood of such exports caused by a general adoption of the East Asian export model.[45]

In his 1984 study, *Exports of Manufactures from Developing Countries*, Cline tempered his results by considering more moderate growth rates of other developing-country exports of manufactures to the industrialized countries than the rates that are implied by imitating the Four Tigers. He concluded that

> there is a speed limit on the expansion of manufactured exports that developing countries would do well to observe if they wish to avoid a protectionist reaction. In the aggregate, developing countries can probably expand their manufactured exports at real rates of 10 to 15 percent annually without provoking a strong protectionist response ..., but expansion at rates of 30 percent or higher would be much more likely to provoke problems of market absorption and protection.... [46]

Cline concludes that moderate manufactured export growth in the 10–15 percent per year range would suffice for achieving high growth rates in most developing countries. However, he does not consider whether (even in the absence of increased protection) the industrialized countries' total market for such exports would be likely to grow at that rate or what would happen if some

---

[45]Cline, "Can the East Asian Export Model of Development be Generalized?", reprinted in Cline, *Exports of Manufactures from Developing Countries*, p. 213.
[46]Cline, *Exports of Manufactures from Developing Countries*, pp. 129–30.

developing countries tried to exceed the "speed limit" at the expense of others.[47]

A few other papers have considered the possibility of "immiserizing growth" resulting from the creation of excess capacity in export-oriented manufacturing industries in developing countries. Raphael Kaplinsky argues that this has occurred in the export-processing zones of countries like the Dominican Republic, which export labor-intensive commodity products such as apparel.[48] Kaplinsky argues that the countries exporting these goods have engaged in a process of competitive devaluation that has succeeded mainly in reducing their terms of trade and depressing the real wages of the workers who get jobs in these sectors. He defines this as "immiserizing employment growth, that is employment growth which is contingent upon wages falling in international purchasing power."[49] Kaplinsky also applies a similar argument to the explanation of the Asian financial crisis:

> ...most of the East Asian economies locked themselves into a growth trajectory in which specialization in factor and product markets associated with low barriers to entry led to high rates of competition. This has led to falling terms of trade and persistent currency realignments, placing long-term pressures on real exchange rates.... the wider significance of the East Asian crisis is that competitive devaluations will be repeated there and elsewhere whenever out-

---

[47]In future research on this topic, it will be useful to compare the actual growth of developing country exports of manufactures since the early 1980s with Cline's alternative projections.

[48]Raphael Kaplinsky, "Export Processing Zones in the Dominican Republic: Transforming Manufactures into Commodities," *World Development*, vol. 21, no. 11 (November 1993), pp. 1851–65. In a similar vein, Robert E. Scott argues that the slower growth of textile and apparel exports from Central America and the Caribbean in the late 1990s was caused by a surge in competitive exports from the East Asian countries following their currency depreciations in 1997–98, rather than by a lack of parity with Mexico's access to the U.S. market under NAFTA. See Robert E. Scott, "Rebuilding the Caribbean: A Better Foundation for Sustainable Growth, "Briefing Paper (Washington, D.C.: Economic Policy Institute, 1999).

[49]Kaplinsky, ibid., p. 1861.

ward-oriented growth strategies cluster in competitive activities.[50]

Korkut Erturk argues that overinvestment occurred in East Asia's export sectors in the 1990s, as the former "flying geese formation" broke apart. In the flying geese model, the more advanced countries (i.e., first Japan, followed by Korea and Taiwan) move on to more capital-intensive and technologically sophisticated products as newer low-wage competitors enter the market for more labor-intensive, standardized types of manufactures. Erturk argues that too many countries began to enter the more advanced product categories at once in the 1990s, thus creating excess capacity and fostering falling prices.[51]

EMPIRICAL PLAUSIBILITY: A PRELIMINARY LOOK AT EXPORT GROWTH TRENDS

This section discusses some simple, aggregated measures of developing country exports into the U.S. market, which are shown in Table 2. These data are for total exports, not just manufactures, and do not include other OECD export markets besides the United States. The point of presenting these admittedly limited data[52] is simply to illustrate the plausibility of the hypotheses proposed here in terms of competition over market shares in the United States. (As discussed earlier, the United States has been the largest and most open market for developing-country exports

---

[50]Raphael Kaplinsky, "'If you want to get somewhere else, you must run at least twice as fast as that!': The Roots of the East Asian Crisis," *Competition & Change*, vol. 4 (1999), pp. 1–30; this extract from pp. 2–3.

[51]Korkut Erturk, "Worldwide Intersectoral Balance, Overcapacity and the East Asian Crisis." Erturk also claims that the flying geese pattern was successfully maintained by greater "regional coordination" prior to the liberalization of capital inflows and domestic investment in the 1990s, but he does not specify how such coordination was achieved at that time.

[52]Future work by the present author on this topic will include more comprehensive and detailed data analysis. For a prospectus, see Robert A. Blecker, "The Fallacy of Composition and the Limits of Export-led Growth."

of manufactures). Also, the developing countries selected for this table are mostly countries with a high proportion of manufactured exports.

The data in Table 2 were collected for 1979 (1980 for some countries), 1989, 1994, and 1997. The first two years are intended to bracket the decade of the 1980s, while eliminating business-cycle effects in the U.S. economy by choosing starting and ending years that were both cyclical peaks (because recessions broke out in 1980 and 1990). The years 1994 and 1997 correspond to the outbreaks of the

Table 2. U.S. Merchandise Imports, by Country of Origin, Selected Countries and Years, 1979–1997

(Average annual growth rates of nominal values and shares of total U.S. imports)

	Average Annual Percentage Changes			Shares (percentages of total imports**)			
	1979–89	1989–94	1994–97	1979	1989	1994	1997
European Union	10.0	7.2	9.8	15.6	17.9	18.1	18.3
Japan	13.5	5.0	0.7	12.4	19.6	17.8	13.9
Canada	8.6	7.8	9.3	18.5	18.8	19.6	19.5
Mexico	11.9	13.0	20.1	4.2	5.7	7.5	9.9
Argentina*	5.9	7.7	6.1	0.3	0.3	0.3	0.3
Brazil*	9.8	1.6	1.6	1.5	1.9	1.4	1.1
Chile*	12.7	6.3	8.7	0.2	0.3	0.3	0.3
Korea	17.2	−0.2	5.7	1.9	4.1	2.9	2.6
Taiwan	15.7	0.9	6.9	2.8	5.3	4.0	3.7
Hong Kong	9.2	0.0	2.0	1.9	2.0	1.5	1.2
Singapore	19.8	11.4	9.3	0.7	1.9	2.3	2.3
China	35.0	26.4	17.3	0.3	2.5	5.8	7.1
Indonesia*	−2.8	9.3	8.0	2.2	0.9	1.0	0.9
Malaysia*	8.6	21.2	5.9	0.9	1.0	1.8	1.7
Philippines*	7.4	9.7	20.0	0.7	0.7	0.8	1.0
Thailand*	20.0	16.1	6.8	0.4	1.0	1.4	1.3
Total Imports**	8.5	7.0	9.5	8.3	8.8	9.6	10.8
Memo: Nominal GDP	7.8	5.0	5.3				

Notes: Based on underlying data in current U.S. dollars.
*Data for these countries begin in 1980.
**The shares shown for total imports are total imports as a share of GDP.

Sources: U.S. Department of Commerce, Bureau of Economic Analysis, U.S. International Transactions and National Income and Product Accounts, *Survey of Current Business* (various issues); Statistics Canada, *World Trade Analyzer Suite*; and author's calculations.

Mexican and Thai currency crises, respectively. As may be seen, total U.S. imports (in current dollars) grew at average annual rates of 8.5 percent in 1979–89, at 7.0 percent in 1989–94, and 9.5 percent in 1994–97. Countries whose growth rates of exports exceeded these rates were gaining market share in the United States, while those whose growth rates were lower were losing market share.

The data for the 1980s show rapid growth of U.S. imports from all of the leading developing country exporters of manufactures at that time, including the Four Tigers (with average annual growth rates of 17.2 percent for Korea, 15.7 percent for Taiwan, 9.2 percent for Hong Kong, and 19.8 percent for Singapore). China and Thailand also have spectacular growth rates in the 1980s (35.0 percent and 20.0 percent, respectively), although China began from a very low base. Japanese exports to the United States continued to boom throughout the 1980s, growing at a 13.5 percent annual rate on top of previous rapid growth in the 1970s. Mexico's exports to the U.S. grew at a respectable 11.9 percent clip in the 1980s, during which (after the debt crisis and oil bust) Mexico reduced its import restrictions, opened up more to direct foreign investment, and devalued its currency. As a result of this above-average growth of their exports to the United States, all of these countries increased their shares of the overall U.S. import market between 1979 and 1989 at the expense of other countries.[53]

The 1990s were then marked by a series of notable shifts in relative growth rates and market shares. First, Japanese export growth fell off, to a 5.0 percent annual growth rate in 1989–94 and a mere 0.7 percent growth rate in 1994–97; as a result, Japan's share of the U.S. import market plummeted from 19.6 percent in 1989 to 13.9 percent in 1997. Not coincidentally, this sharp drop-off in Japanese export performance followed a major appreciation of the yen in the late 1980s. The drop-off also coincided with the slow-

---

[53]The data for 1979–89 in Table 2 are affected by the fall in oil prices over that time period—a problem that can be solved in future research by using data for trade in manufactures or by correcting for price changes. Nevertheless, the fact that oil prices were falling makes Mexico's overall export growth in the 1980s all the more spectacular, because at the beginning of the decade Mexico was exporting large amounts of oil at high prices.

down in Japanese economic growth and the country's slide into chronically depressed conditions. Today, we hear many complaints of Japanese consumers' unwillingness to spend—but in the 1980s the same frugal consumer behavior was praised for the high saving rates it produced. In the 1980s, Japan didn't need consumer spending because its exports were growing so rapidly; today, with export growth stagnant, the lack of consumer spending is holding the entire Japanese economy down. Thus, the "liquidity trap" is not the only old Keynesian idea being vindicated in Japan, as the country also appears to be suffering from a notable "paradox of thrift."[54,55]

---

[54]A liquidity trap occurs when a country's interest rates are driven to near-zero levels so that they cannot be reduced any further to stimulate the economy. For the application of this concept to recent economic problems in Japan, see Paul Krugman, "It's Baack! Japan's S???p and the Return of the Liquidity Trap," *Brookings Papers or Economic Activity 1998*, no. 2, pp. 137–205." The paradox of thrift refers to the fact that a higher saving rate requires a reduction of consumer demand that can depress an economy's performance.

[55]For an alternative explanation of Japan's problems, see Ronald I. McKinnon, "Wading in the Yen Trap: The Origins of Japan's Deflation Lie Not in the Domestic Economy, But in the Movements of the Yen," *Economist* (July 24, 1999), based on an earlier book by McKinnon and Kenichi Ohno, *Dollar and Yen: Resolving Economic Conflict between the United States and Japan* (Cambridge, Mass.: MIT Press, 1997). McKinnon blames most of Japan's troubles on the perpetual expectation of future (long-term) yen appreciation, which he in turn attributes to pressures from the United States to resolve the Japanese-U.S. trade imbalance. According to McKinnon, the expected appreciation of the yen creates several problems. These include (1) the liquidity trap (because Japan's interest rates have to be lower than U.S. interest rates in order to maintain uncovered interest parity, but the former cannot be pushed below zero); (2) a deflationary psychology that inhibits investors' and consumers' spending; and (3) a rise in the "speculative demand for money." This argument makes some sense, although it does not explain why *short-term* interest rates are so low in Japan (surely short-term exchange rate expectations are not always in the direction of yen appreciation). But McKinnon's preferred solution—for the two governments to announce that the current yen/dollar exchange rate is acceptable in order to eliminate expectations of it to fall, and suspending U.S. protectionist responses to Japanese trade surpluses—would not solve the problems of the Japanese economy. The expectation that the currency of the country with the world's largest trade surplus needs to appreciate is not created by U.S. government policy, but by a rational view of international investors about the long-run unsustainability of the present pattern of international trade imbalances.

The only way for Japan to reduce its trade surplus without a substantial further appreciation of the yen is through a massive stimulus of *domestic* demand, along with whatever structural reforms are needed to spur Japanese households to consume more. By presuming that Japan will need to export its way out of its doldrums, McKinnon's solution would only perpetuate the export orientation of the Japanese economy that has been at the root of its recent problems.

All of the Four Tigers' export growth rates slowed down in the 1990s compared with the 1980s, although less dramatically in the case of Singapore than for the other three countries. The exports of Korea, Taiwan, and Hong Kong to the United States were completely stagnant between 1989 and 1994. Exports from the first two of these countries recovered somewhat in 1994–97, but only to growth rates in the 5–7 percent range. This was far below their performance in the 1980s, and below the average annual 9.5 percent growth in total U.S. imports during the strong economic recovery of the 1994–97 period. On the whole, three of the Four Tigers lost market share in the United States during the 1990s.

Countries with high export growth rates and rising U.S. market shares throughout the 1990s were led by China and Mexico.[56] However, there are also notable differences in some countries' export performance before and after the 1994 "Tequila Crisis" in Mexico. Mexico's exports to the United States grew at a 13.0 percent annual rate in 1989–94, as the country moved from unilateral trade liberalization toward membership in the North American Free Trade Agreement (NAFTA). Nevertheless, Mexico had a rising current account deficit throughout those years because, with liberalized trade and an overvalued peso, imports rose even faster than exports.[57] After NAFTA went into effect and the peso was devalued in 1994, Mexican export growth shot up to an astounding 20.1 percent annual rate in 1994–97 (and, unlike in China in the 1980s, this was from an already high base). Such a high rate of growth of Mexican exports could not have been achieved without the peso devaluation, which gave Mexico a far greater competitive boost than NAFTA alone. Meanwhile, China's exports

---

[56]The apparent slowdown in China's export growth over the time periods shown is misleading, because the country's exports started from a very low base, and the absolute growth of Chinese exports continues to be spectacular (resulting in steadily rising market shares) despite falling percentage growth rates.

[57]Robert A. Blecker, "NAFTA, the Peso Crisis, and the Contradiction of the Mexican Economic Growth Strategy," Center for Economic Policy Analysis, Working Paper Series I, no. 3 (New York: New School for Social Research, July 1996), and J. A. Kregel, "East Asia is Not Mexico: The Difference between Balance of Payments Crises and Debt Deflations," Jerome Levy Economics Institute of Bard College, Working Paper no. 235 (Annandale-on-Hudson, N.Y.: Bard College, May 1998).

continued to grow at a very rapid 17.3 percent annual rate in 1994–97. Though down from the astronomical growth rates recorded earlier, it was still about double the average growth rate for U.S. imports, thus resulting in a further increase in China's market share.

What is especially interesting about 1994–97 is whose exports were not growing as fast as before, namely Thailand's. Thailand was expected to be one of the next "Tigers,"[58] but in fact its export growth slowed down from a healthy 16.1 percent annual rate in 1989–94 to a mere 6.8 percent annual rate in 1994–97. This was below the average growth rate of U.S. imports of 9.5 percent at that time. One reason usually cited for Thailand's disappointing export performance and rising current account deficit in 1994–97 is the effective appreciation of the baht, which occurred because the baht was pegged to the U.S. dollar and the dollar was rising relative to the European and Japanese currencies. But this factor cannot explain why Thailand's exports to *the United States* stagnated. To explain this, we need to look at the surging exports of *other* countries that exported similar products and whose market shares were rising as a result of devalued currencies, such as China and Mexico. Also, the baht appreciated at that time relative to other developing countries' currencies that were not pegged to the dollar alone.

The only other Asian developing country that shows the same pattern as Thailand (i.e., with a major slowdown in exports to the United States between 1989–94 and 1994–97) is Malaysia, whose export growth fell from 21.2 percent per year to 5.9 percent per year between those two periods. The other Asian crisis countries—Korea, Indonesia, and the Philippines—all had steady or rising export growth rates to the United States during those times. But only in the case of the Philippines was the export growth truly rapid in 1994–97. In Korea it was still comparatively low at a mere 5.7 percent per

---

[58]For example, see Stephen C. Smith, *Industrial Policy in Developing Countries.*

year, while in Indonesia it was 8.0 percent per year, which was still lower than average U.S. import growth at the time.

The point here is not that slowing export growth caused all the financial crises, which it did not—although it seems to have been a major contributing factor in the case of Thailand, where it contributed to severe balance-of-payments problems that undermined confidence in the government's pegged exchange-rate policy. The point, rather, is to confirm that the "fallacy of composition" began to hit home in the 1990s, when a large number of countries had begun to compete with the original "Four Tigers," and surging exports and rising market shares for some countries meant sluggish exports and falling market shares for others. Exactly how those other countries were affected varied, depending on a host of contingent factors. As discussed earlier, those that maintained capital controls, had relatively small international debts (especially of the short-term, foreign-currency variety), and did not try to keep their currencies pegged at unsustainable levels did relatively better. Those who liberalized their capital markets, relied on short-term international borrowing, and kept their exchange rates pegged did the worst. But all of the countries whose export growth faltered also saw their domestic economic growth tumble, even those countries (such as Taiwan) that averted a purely financial crisis.[59]

POLICY IMPLICATIONS: WHICH WAY OUT OF THE DILEMMA?

This paper has argued that the widespread adoption of a development strategy that relies primarily on high rates of growth of manufactured exports, especially exports targeted mainly on the U.S. consumer market, was bound to cause problems of growing excess capacity, intensified competitive pressures, and disappointing growth performance. At the same time, there is much that

---

[59]See the data in the International Monetary Fund's *World Economic Outlook* (Washington, D.C.: International Monetary Fund, April 1999).

could be done to expand global export markets and allow all countries to provide more reciprocal demand for each other's products. Growth has been sluggish in Japan and much of Western Europe for many years, resulting in weak demand for developing-country exports and forcing the United States to serve as the "consumer of last resort." A significant economic recovery in Europe and Japan, which in turn would require macroeconomic stimulus policies as well as possible structural reforms, is vital for relieving the constraints imposed on the developing countries by present global market conditions, as well as for other reasons (e.g., to reduce global trading imbalances and to alleviate tensions in the global trading system). Moreover, to the extent that some industrialized countries have not opened their economies fully to developing country exports of manufactures (Japan especially comes to mind), there is much that could be done via trade agreements (both bilateral and multilateral) and structural reforms to increase market opportunities specifically for those exports. Regional trade arrangements such as Mercosur and APEC (Asia Pacific Economic Cooperation) could also be strengthened, although this will require resolving the financial and macroeconomic problems of those regions in order to make further South-South regional integration an attractive alternative.

Thus, it is possible to imagine an optimistic scenario of economic recovery and market opening in Europe and Japan, along with continued robust growth in the United States and expanding intra-regional trade among the developing countries. But the likelihood of such an optimistic scenario occurring in reality cannot be taken for granted. The problems of high European unemployment and sluggish Japanese growth are long-standing and, whatever their causes, are not likely to be resolved soon. The opposite scenario of global deflation and depression, while looking distinctly less likely at the time of this writing (early 2000) than it did at the peak of the Asian crisis two years earlier, still cannot be ruled out—especially if the bubbles in U.S. asset markets burst and the U.S. economy goes into a recession. The most likely scenario is probably that the global economy will continue to muddle along with very uneven growth, sputtering recoveries, more unbal-anced trade, and recurring financial crises.

Moreover, the prospects for further global trade liberalization seem quite limited at present. In part, this is due to a political impasse over the direction that future trade negotiations should take, including the debate over whether they should incorporate labor rights, environmental standards, and other social concerns. But more fundamentally, the impasse results from the fact that the remaining trade barriers in the most closed countries in the world (e.g., Japan and China) are not mostly or exclusively formal trade barriers, such as tariffs and quotas, that can easily be negotiated downward. The closed character of these countries' markets results from intrinsic characteristics of their domestic political-economic systems, such as their unique corporate structures, financial arrangements, and close government-business relationships that inhibit entry of foreign firms or products except on terms favorable to local industrial development. The record of efforts to negotiate over these types of "structural impediments" is not very encouraging, to say the least. Even when agreements are reached on paper (and that is difficult in itself), they are often not enforced in practice. As the IMF is discovering in its efforts to promote financial transparency, long-standing domestic institutions and deeply ingrained practices are not easily changed. This point applies as much to industrial policies, corporate-financial linkages, and pro-saving biases as it does to banking regulation or fiscal policy.

From this more pessimistic point of view, the constraints on export-led growth are not likely to be relaxed in the near future. If this pessimism proves to be accurate, then continued efforts to rely on export-led growth will only result in more of the same problems: recurrent balance of payments problems, unstable currencies, competitive devaluations, and conflictive trade relations. In this situation, the only way forward for the Asian countries (and for developing countries in other regions as well) is to pursue more internally oriented development. This means less reliance on export markets especially in the United States, and more acceptance of the need for rising domestic wages in order to create a mass consumer market. In part, such a goal could be promoted by pro-

viding greater labor rights and upgrading labor standards (as contemplated in some approaches to trade negotiations), so that
workers would be able to win wages more commensurate with their
productivity and thus raise their living standards.[60] Furthermore,
in East Asia, all the high-saving countries (including Japan) need
to move away from the excessive saving rates they have achieved
and start spending more on consumption. Countries with such high
saving rates can avoid economic slowdowns only by relying on rapidly growing export markets and high rates of export-oriented
investment; when these falter, the high saving rates turn from a
blessing into a curse as the Keynesian paradox of thrift takes over
and the lack of domestic consumer demand leads to depressed economic conditions.

While a shift toward a domestic orientation of development
efforts will require significant internal changes and reforms, it does
not necessarily require all developing countries to make themselves
over in the Western image of liberalized markets and deregulated competition. Ironically, the prospects for recovery of the Asian
crisis economies may be enhanced by their retaining, rather than
eliminating, some of the government direction and financial linkages that have served them well in their export drives in the past,
provided that these can be reoriented toward preparing them for
a new direction in their economic development. Indeed, one of the
advantages of a domestic reorientation of development efforts is
that it permits the maintenance of many different economic
development models, while preventing differences in national
economic systems from fostering international tensions and imbalances as much as they do in an export-led development regime.
The bottom line is that the current emphasis on export-led
growth in developing countries is not a viable basis on which all
countries can grow together under present structural conditions
and macroeconomic policies.

---

[60]For an argument along these lines, see Thomas I. Palley, "The Economic Case for
International Labor Standards: Theory and Some Evidence," Economic Policy Paper no.
E036, Public Policy Department (Washington, D.C.: AFL-CIO, 1999)

The American Stock Market as a Financial Risk

A Paper from the Project on Development, Trade and International Finance

Robert H. Dugger, Robert C McNally, and Richard Medley

A Council on Foreign Relations Paper

The American Stock Market as a Financial Risk:

A Discussion of Historic and Demographic Risks[1]

Robert H. Dugger, Robert C. McNally, and Richard Medley

INTRODUCTION

From the standpoint of crisis anticipation, standard macroeconomic forecasting and risk management methods share three weaknesses. First, standard methods embody very little of our experience and understanding of the information and liquidity-driven herding and contagion behavior that characterize crises. Second, the models are distinctly country-centric. A disaster outside an economy that benefits domestic markets will often result in econometrically estimated parameters that suggest the benefits are the consequence of domestic policies and events. Accordingly, crisis probabilities in the tails of outcome distributions may be much higher than estimated. Third, standard methods are not well suited to assessing macroeconomic trends when large economic restructuring changes are under way. If one part of an economy consists of shrinking "old economy" sectors that are no longer competitive and represent, say, two-thirds of GDP, macro models will overestimate the effectiveness

[1] The authors are grateful for extensive comments and guidance from working group members, and others, and the assistance of Joel Prakken and Chris Varvares of Macroeconomic Advisors. The views and findings presented in this paper, however, are solely those of the authors.

of traditional monetary and fiscal policy measures. Japan is undergoing such a restructuring. Not surprisingly, *ex ante* estimates of fiscal and monetary policy effectiveness repeatedly turn out to be overestimates.

Effective macroeconomic and risk management models are critical. A record low proportion of U.S. private wealth is held in the form of deposits that are both liquid and have a known fixed value, and a record high proportion of assets are invested in volatile securities and defined-contribution (rather than defined-benefit) retirement plans. The consequences of a large negative surprise have never been greater.

Sources of Risk

We see the U.S. economy and stock market as exposed to two sources of real sector risk: (1) Diminishing returns for Asian and European import-substitution and export-led growth strategies, and for the mechanics of U.S. current and capital account flows. (2) The aging of industrialized-economy populations and the significant undersaving of households and the underfunded[2] condition of public retirement support programs. These are generally thought of as very long-term processes that could have no immediate effect on markets. In our judgment, this perception is likely to be wrong. In fact, we believe they are affecting markets now.

The first risk source encompasses the production-consumption and investment-savings relationships that sustained the United States and its allies throughout the Cold War decades. They are also reflected in U.S. current and capital account flows. These relationships have been undergoing historic change in the past decade. In this paper, we refer to this group of economic and geopolitical events as the "post–Cold War transition."

The second risk source includes imbalances resulting from the undersaved condition of American households and the underfunded condition of national retirement and healthcare commitments. Birth and growth rates in industrialized countries have been

---

[2] In this context, "underfunded" means that program assets and liabilities are unmatched in an actuarial accounting sense, not that policymakers have failed to appropriate adequate revenues to fund the programs.

declining without comparable reductions in pension and health-care benefits, which means that all the major industrialized countries face generational accounting imbalances. This is a very important kind of financial leveraging. American households will almost certainly have to increase savings rates to assure secure retirements. In this paper, we refer to this effort of households to meet their retirement wealth needs as "generational deleveraging."

Both risks are linked in a critically important way. U.S. Treasury Secretary Lawrence H. Summers referenced the linkage in the opening paragraphs of his speech on global financial reform just before the September 1999 International Monetary Fund/World Bank meetings.

> Supporting successful economic development in the developing world has always been—and will remain—an overriding global moral imperative. But it takes on increasing economic significance for the industrial countries today, when retirement rates in these nations are rising, rates of labor force growth are decreasing, and the investment of retirement savings is a key concern. All of the world's population growth over the next twenty-five years, and most of its growth in productivity, will take place in the developing world.[3]

As productivity rises in the developing world, so do returns on capital that could exacerbate necessary U.S. current and capital account adjustments. However, the large pools of more productive young people in the developing world could ease the equally necessary adjustments of generational imbalances in the developed world.

Asian Downturns, Herding, and Contagion
The historical foundations of the Asian crises are now widely recognized. Barry Eichengreen explored them with particular scrutiny and concluded, "… Asia's crisis can only be understood in terms of a conjuncture of long-standing historical forces and short-term financial policies." Eichengreen observed specifically:

> Ultimately, the explanation for the crisis lies in the region's history and economic development trajectory, which relied on bank-cen-

---

[3]Lawrence H. Summers, "Priorities for a 21st Century Global Financial System," Remarks at Yale University, New Haven, Connecticut, September 22, 1999.

tered financial systems, the use of the banks as instruments of industrial policy, and close connections between banks and politicians,
all of which were designed to sustain high rates of investment and
rapid economic growth.[4]

This paper is motivated by a concern that Eichengreen's conclusions and observations about key Asian financial systems may also
be true in important ways about the U.S. financial system. In the
U.S. case, however, <u>the central relationship would not be between
banks and businesses via bank credit, but between the U.S. stock
market and undersaved households</u>.

There are many ways to talk about stock market risk. U.S. Federal Reserve Chairman Alan Greenspan identified two aspects of
asset pricing risk: adverse event probability distributions, and
balance sheet instabilities. Regarding event distributions, he
observed:

> Probability distributions estimated largely, or exclusively, over
> cycles that do not include periods of panic will underestimate the
> likelihood of extreme price movements because they fail to cap-
> ture a secondary peak at the extreme negative tail that reflects the
> probability of occurrence of a panic. Furthermore, joint distribu-
> tions estimated over periods that do not include panics will under-
> estimate correlations between asset returns during panics. Under
> these circumstances, fear and disengagement on the part of
> investors holding net long positions often lead to simultaneous declines
> in the values of private obligations, as investors no longer realis-
> tically differentiate among degrees of risk and liquidity, and to increas-
> es in the values of riskless government securities. Consequently,
> the benefits of portfolio diversification will tend to be overestimated
> when the rare panic periods are not taken into account.[5]

And, regarding balance sheet effects:

> As the value of assets and liabilities have risen relative to income,
> we have been confronted with the potential for our economies to
> exhibit larger and perhaps more abrupt responses to changes in fac-

---

[4]Barry Eichengreen, *Toward a New International Financial Architecture, A Practical Post-Asia Agenda* (Washington, D.C.: Institute for International Economics, 1999), p. 162.

[5]Alan Greenspan, "Measuring financial risk in the Twenty-First Century," at conference sponsored by the Office of the Comptroller of the Currency, Washington, D.C., October 14, 1999, p. 2.

tors affecting the balance sheets of households and businesses. As a result our analytic tools are going to have to increasingly focus on changes in asset values and resulting balance sheet variations if we are to understand these important economic forces. Central bankers, in particular, are going to have to be able to ascertain how changes in the balance sheets of economic actors influence real economic activity and, hence, affect appropriate macroeconomic policies.[6]

Financial risk from our perspective arises from negative surprises that move from the real to the financial sector. Over time the foundation for financial problems are laid when financial sector and asset price conditions diverge from the underlying real sector economic and political conditions. At some point, asset prices realign with the real sector. The realignment is a crisis if the asset price adjustment significantly increases unemployment, reduces growth, or destabilizes political processes. Generally, this occurs when some informational or liquidity shock surprises the financial sector and triggers a sudden and large price adjustment.

Such adjustments are asymmetric in the sense that the prices decline much more rapidly than they rise. In such cases, gray-haired market participants like to observe that , "Prices fall three times faster than they rise." The price movements are nonlinear in that as they occur they seem to take on a life of their own, triggering within-market "herding"[7] and cross-market "contagion" [8] that are mutually amplifying.[9]

---

[6]Alan Greenspan, "New challenges for monetary policy," Symposium sponsored by the Federal Reserve Bank of Kansas City, Jackson Hole, Wyoming, August 27, 1999.

[7] Christopher Avery and Peter Zemsky, "Multidimensional Uncertainty and Herd Behavior in Financial Markets," *American Economic Review* 88, no. 4 (September 1998), pp. 724–47.

[8]Laura Kodres and Matthew Pritsker, "A Rational Expectations Model of Financial Contagion," FEDS Working Paper 1998-48, U.S. Board of Governors of the Federal Reserve System, 1998.

[9]The author's view that herding and contagion in declining markets are mutually amplifying is not a specific conclusion of either Avery-Zemsky (AV) or Kodres-Pritsker (KP). AV focuses on multidimensional uncertainty within a market and concludes that trader perceptions of deterioration in information quality can lead to significant, short-run mispricing. KP focuses on contagion through cross-market hedging of shared macroeconomic risks and concludes that the pattern and severity of contagion depends on markets' sensitivities to shared risks and information asymmetry.

Assessing whether the U.S. stock market poses a financial risk requires identification of the significant potential divergences between financial asset prices and real sector conditions. We must also note why financial markets may be underpricing the divergence. To do this, we first discuss two long-term real sector trends that may not be fully reflected in current or projected U.S. financial market conditions. We then look at a carefully modeled macroeconomic forecast of the U.S. economy that assumes a 30 percent stock market decline, and we note its rather benign longer-term effects under standard economic response assumptions. Focusing specifically on its projected personal savings rate, we outline how there may be a real/financial sector divergence. The scale of the divergence could cause an asset price adjustment of significant proportions.

TRADE, DEVELOPMENT, AND THE POST–COLD WAR TRANSITION

Many stock market skeptics point to U.S. current and capital account flows and conclude that current U.S. stock market valuations are not sustainable. The restructuring recoveries under way in Europe and in all the Asian countries (possibly including Japan) are said to mean that the amounts of capital inflows previously directed toward the United States can be maintained only if U.S. interest rates go up. Higher rates, they argue, will cause the broad stock market to fall.

The rebuttal to this argument generally consists of the observation that if U.S. growth is reduced by economic growth in the rest of the world, more capital will be allocated within the U.S. stock market to sectors that serve this growth and less to U.S. consumption. Proponents of this view argue that consumption-related stocks will decline, while capital goods and other development-related stocks will rise. They conclude that such an outcome may be hard on the owners of shares in Internet companies that are basically consumer marketing schemes, but that this is hardly a reason to be concerned about a general equity-market collapse.

However, this rebuttal may not be correct if U.S. current and capital account imbalances are part of a larger historic process that is significantly adverse to U.S. consumption and is not reflected in standard macroeconomic forecasts or current financial asset prices. This would be the case if the Asian crises of the 1990s and the U.S. current and capital account imbalances were understood to be linked consequences of the end of the Cold War geopolitical strategic consensus. From this perspective, the Asian downturns may foreshadow a U.S. consumption contraction. Indeed, it may not be possible for Asian restructuring downturns to occur without a U.S. restructuring occurring also.

As we noted earlier, Eichengreen, among others, has stressed the historical foundations of Asia's downturns. The likelihood that the development of the U.S. economy and financial system was not also influenced by similar historical priorities is hard to dismiss. In the U.S. case, the central risk relationship is likely to be asset market buoyancy and undersaved households.

In the following section we lay out an interpretation of the economic events of the 1990s in which current U.S. conditions are seen as components of a longer post–Cold War restructuring process. Because standard risk management and macroeconomic models do not treat the Asian downturns and other economic restructuring crises as linked within a longer-term process, parameter estimates may not adequately reflect true risk levels.

Import and Export Strategies for Growth
There is general agreement that import-substitution and later export-led growth strategies were key ingredients of the recovery and economic development plans of World War II–scarred Japan and Germany, as well as other Western-ally countries surrounding the former Union of Soviet Socialist Republics and China. This is particularly clear in Asia from the 1950s into the early 1990s. Japan, followed by the Asian Tigers and the Newly Industrializing Countries in "flying geese formation," successively pursued national plans to substitute domestic production of basic goods for

imports and then moved up the production chain to maximize growth through exports to the developed world.

There is also general agreement that the United States served initially as a capital provider and then as the linchpin importer/consumer-of-last-resort to support these recovery and development strategies. In the 1950s, the United States met the early capital needs of its Cold War allies through grants, development loans, and defense arrangements. At the same time, the de-emphasis of saving and encouragement of consumption, even to the point of providing tax deductions for consumer credit interest expenses, supported the evolving export-led growth strategies of U.S. allies. The high-production, high-savings strategies of the recovering and developing countries were matched by a high-consumption, low-savings strategy in the United States.[10]

The cooperative mirroring of economic and geopolitical needs is reflected in the table below. In the early decades of the Cold War the United States and U.S.-backed international financial institutions were net suppliers of capital to Iron Curtain allies to finance recovery and import-substitution development strategies. As these countries stabilized and shifted to export-led growth strategies, U.S. trade deficits appeared and then deepened, and U.S. dependence on allied capital inflows became established.

---

[10]Following World War II the United States plunged into a recession severe enough to trigger fears of a renewal of the Great Depression. Washington responded with a Keynesian spending program that included the GI Bill, boosting consumption and restoring the economy to positive growth.

Capital and Trade Flows from the United States to "Iron Curtain" Allies[11]
(% of Allied GDP and U.S.$ millions)

Five-year Periods, yearly average

Allies	46–49	50–54	55–59	60–64	65–69	70–74	75–79	80–84	85–89	90–94	95–98
Capital Flows											
European*	1,118	960	439	506	142	−468	−1,299	−4,725	−6,388	−1,260	−32,647
Asian**	613	757	955	1,430	951	673	−94	−5,747	−28,951	−21,054	−64,502
Trade Flows											
European		654	611	856	−427	−1,706	−2,349	−5,263	−19,500	−15,741	−30,024
Asian		598	899	638	−92	−4,073	−13,063	−33,833	−83,898	−69,298	−70,226

Five-year Periods, average flows/average GDP

Allies	50–54	55–59	60–64	65–69	70–74	75–79	80–84	85–89	90–94	95–98
Capital flows as % of GDP										
European*	1.9%	0.5%	0.4%	0.1%	−0.1%	−0.1%	−0.4%	−0.4%	−0.04%	−0.9%
Asian**	3.5%	2.7%	1.8%	0.6%	0.2%	−0.01%	−0.4%	−1.1%	−0.5%	−1.2%
Trade Flows as % of GDP										
European	1.3%	0.7%	0.6%	−0.2%	−0.4%	−0.3%	−0.4%	−1.1%	−0.5%	−0.5%
Asian	2.8%	2.6%	0.8%	−0.6%	−1.1%	−1.5%	−2.5%	−3.2%	−1.6%	−1.3%

* Germany, Austria, Italy

** South Korea, Japan, Taiwan, Hong Kong

[11] The underlying data and sources for this table are extensive and available as an excel spreadsheet upon request. The authors are indebted to and deeply appreciate the unstinting efforts of Mr. Dong Zhang for gathering the data and preparing this table under the auspices of a Tudor Graduate Internship.

There is also general agreement that this system of export-to-the-United States and United States-buy-from-its-allies started to break down in the 1990s. Robert Blecker thoroughly describes the diminishing marginal returns to export-led growth and pinpoints the zeroing out of the strategy as occurring some time in the mid-1990s.[12] In our judgment, Blecker rightly criticizes as incomplete the U.S. and other G-7 explanations that the Asian downturns of the mid-1990s were mainly the result of "crony capitalism," inadequate financial supervision, and a lack of transparency. Of course, the downturns were partly due to these factors, but the important question is how "Asian miracle workers" became "crony capitalists" in a matter of three or four years. Something is missing in the conventional analysis.

Blecker suggests the missing item is a "fallacy of composition" effect of so many countries attempting the same strategy. Marginal returns decline and perhaps even become negative, thus undermining financing structures. We agree and see Blecker's composition-fallacy as part of a larger historic process. For us, what Blecker says about the Asian export strategies is also a statement about the U.S. consumption strategy.

We are not surprised to look back and see that the United States pursued increasingly consumption-maximizing and savings-minimizing strategies throughout the Cold War decades. Our understanding of political science leads us to conclude that national security is the highest domestic political priority. For example, the United States pursued a high-production, high-savings strategy to win World War II, essentially focusing on out-producing its enemies. In contrast, the United States's Cold War–era high-consumption, low-savings strategy won because it essentially out-consumed China and the Union of Soviet Socialist Republics. The United States was able to support its allies in a recovery, development, and growth process that exhausted the Union of Soviet Socialist

---

[12]Robert Blecker, "The Diminishing Returns to Export-Led Growth," paper presented to the Working Group on Development, Trade, and International Finance (New York: Council of Foreign Relations, October 7, 1999) and published as a part of a series by the CFR Project of the same name.

Republics and forced China to change its policies on inward investment.

The post–Cold War (PCW) hypothesis implies that the matching consumption-led and export-led strategies pursued by the United States and its Cold War allies was optimal for addressing the priority of winning the Cold War, but not for a non-war environment. The magnitude of the Asian adjustments since the end of the Cold War suggests that Asian economic, financial, and political frameworks were not optimal for a post-war environment. Apparently, as soon as the Western capital markets and democracies were not required to prop up those frameworks, they ceased doing so and "Asian miracles" became "crony capitalism".

During the Cold War years, the United States would not have let the yen strengthen as it did in the mid-1990s, to the point that it nearly wrecked the Japanese economy. Nor would it have been as unconcerned in the Cold War years as it was in the mid-1990s that economic conditions were destroying political leadership of the LDP, Japan's long-time dominant party. In the 1990s, the leading Western democracies became willing to allow the "invisible hand" of markets to take over from the "guiding hand" of allied-government Cold War strategy. After the fall of the Berlin Wall, it became acceptable for markets to determine the fate of Asian and European export-led economies.

Old and New Economies

A central idea of the PCW transition is the distinction between "old" and "new" economics. Few analysts disagree that the problems in the East-Asian economies seem to be most serious in the heavy industry, small manufacturing, agriculture, construction, and retailing sectors. These sectors were the foundations of import-substitution and export-led growth strategies during the Cold War decades, and they comprised two-thirds or more of GDP. They were heavily subsidized, trade protected, and regulated. Such sectors are what we meant when a decade ago we referred to "Japan Inc." Now, these sectors are what we mean when we refer to "old Japan." In all the Asian countries the shrinkage (even collapse in some instances) of the "old" sectors threatened the private and public institutions that financed them and the political systems that organized them.

Moreover, no one disagrees that "new" sectors such as communications, information technology, professional services of all kinds, biomedical research, and high-end design and manufacturing are growing strongly in all the Asian countries. Because these sectors represent only about one-third of GDP, however, their rapid growth is not enough to offset the negative GDP effect of the "old" contracting sectors.

Is there an "old" versus "new" issue in the U.S. economy? On this point there would be very heated disagreement. Most economists and analysts believe the U.S. economy is very "new" in every respect. The prevailing view is that the banking system has been reformed, old industries have been restructured, and the bulk of GDP is represented by "new" information and service oriented businesses.

The risk to the U.S. stock market is that this view is not correct, and that what is "old" about the U.S. economy is its consumption orientation. Estimates vary but there is general agreement that almost 70 percent of GDP consists of consumption. If the PCW hypothesis is correct, we need to consider the United States's ongoing priority on consumption as being a mirror of the Asian import-substitution and export-led growth strategies.

Implications for Europe and Asia

If the PCW transition risk is plausible, it should have some applicability to Germany and Italy, two key European Cold War countries, as well as to Japan and other Asian ally countries. Important similarities should surface between Japan, guarding the eastern front of Communist Eurasia, and German and Italy, guarding the Western front.

One similarity is evident in the nature and scale of their old-age care promises. An important element of the recovery and development strategies of key U.S. Cold War allies was the assurance to workers that their retirement needs would be well-covered. The result is an imbalance between the tax burdens on younger and older generations to pay for the benefits. The PCW hypothesis suggests that the Japanese, German, and Italian imbalances should be larger than those of other industrialized countries. Laurence Kotlikoff and Willi Leibfritz provide the following estimates of these imbalances.[13]

Generational Imbalance in Real Terms
Relative to U.S. GDP
(Per Capita, 1995 U.S. dollars)

Japan	$300.9 thousand
Germany	$203.9 thousand
Italy	$197.1 thousand
France	$101.7 thousand
United States	$ 45.3 thousand
Canada	$ 3.4 thousand

The Japanese, German, and Italian imbalances are notably higher. Though fragmentary, the data suggest that the farther a country is from a former Communist border the lower its imbalance is likely to be.

From the European Central Bank we get affirming data from another perspective.[14] In very rough terms, "old" sectors of advanced countries are primarily industrial and government-related, and they are financed by banking systems rather than securities markets. Thus, the larger the share of industrial production, government, and bank deposits in the economy, the "older" or less restructured it is likely to be. From the January 1999 ECB monthly bulletin:

Industrial sector as a percentage of GDP

U.S.	26%
Euro 11	31%
Japan	39%

---

[13]Laurence Kotlikoff and Willi Leibfritz, "An International Comparison of Generational Accounting," in Alan Auerbach, Laurence Kotlikoff, and Willi Leibfritz, eds., *Generational Accounting Around the World* (Chicago: University of Chicago Press, 1999), pp.73–103.

[14]European Central Bank, "The Euro Area at the Start of Stage Three," in European Central Bank *Monthly Bulletin* (January 1999), pp. 11–13.

Government as a percentage of GDP
U.S.	36%
Euro 11	47%
Japan	33%

Bank deposits as a percentage of GDP
U.S.	55%
Euro 11	84%
Japan	99%

Service sectors are also generally thought of as "new" economically, dynamic and capable of creating many new jobs. On this measure too, the Euro 11 lies between the United States and Japan.

Size of service sector in economy as a percentage of GDP
US	72%
Euro 11	67%
Japan	59%

The PCW hypothesis says the financial crises of the past ten years are linked and form a pattern of post–Cold War economic and political restructuring. The collapses of the Asian Tigers, the Japanese recession, and slow European growth all reflect the rapid shrinkage of economic sectors that were important to Cold War strategies. Economic sectors essential to maintaining full employment and the banks that financed those sectors in Japan and Asia all saw growth plunge and losses mount. By implication, key import-substitution and export-led growth sectors in Germany and Italy, as well as the banks that financed them, may face contraction and increasing difficulties.

Implications for Japan
The PCW hypothesis emphasizes analysis of a country's economic sectors in addition to its more familiar macroeconomic trends. Such an analysis offers a fuller understanding of Japan's mounting debt problem. Examined through a sectoral lens, a "debt trap" rather than "liquidity trap" seems to be a more accurate and useful description of what is plaguing Japan's economy.

The Japanese government's long-held hope for generating an economic recovery is that it will be able to "pass the baton" to the private sector via a self-sustaining economic recovery produced by "new Japan." However, despite the largest peacetime injection of fiscal stimulus in postwar history, the economy nominally has contracted eight of the last ten quarters. Moreover, most "new Japan" enterprise ventures have yet to make any real money (i.e., operating profits), and "old Japan" industrial bankruptcies are running at a rate of nearly 3% of GDP.[15]

Modeling the economy as two sectors, old and new Japan, highlights the workings of the PCW hypothesis and the nature Japan's problem. From data on nonperforming bank and prefectural government debt, we know which sectors are contributing to the debt problem. Nonperforming loans and bankruptcies are concentrated in the agriculture, manufacturing, construction, and retailing-related sectors. These sectors, and all their related households, businesses, and government activities, were the foundation blocks of Japan's Cold War–era import-substitution and export-led growth strategies. U.S. compliance and participation built them up to massive levels to assure success in the competition with the Union of Soviet Socialist Republics and the People's Republic of China. The commitment level made geopolitical sense before 1990, but not afterward.

From the 1950s into the early 1990s, Japan's laws, financial institutions, and economic practices were focused on building the agriculture, construction, retailing, and manufacturing sectors into an economic powerhouse we used to call "Japan Inc." Loans and credits from commercial banks, the postal savings system, fiscal investment and loan systems, and the central and prefectural governments financed these sectors. This is the credit architecture that fell into nonperforming status in the early-1990s and by 1998 brought down the banking system. Credits extended by prefectural governments are now crippling local governments. To keep

---

[15]David Asher and Robert Dugger, "When Will Japan's Financial Mount Fuji Blow Its Top?" (Cambridge, Mass.: MIT Press, forthcoming).

the mountain of debt from toppling, the central government has had to guarantee banking system and local government solvency, as well as shoulder the burden alone of further borrowing.

The debt mountain continues to grow rapidly for two reasons: first, interest on the existing debt can be paid only by borrowing more; and second, the "Japan Inc." economic sectors constitute the bulk of Japan's GDP and are shrinking. Of the two reasons, the second is the more important and the least understood. The "Japan Inc.," now "old Japan", economic sectors are dragging down Japanese GDP. "New Japan" is growing rapidly, but its GDP share is too small for its growth to offset the shrinkage of old Japan. Old Japan's shrinkage is desirable and necessary from an economic restructuring standpoint, but it has a powerfully adverse effect on Japan's debt mountain. The shrinkage drags down national GDP and forces the government to borrow and spend enough to offset the negative effect.

The tables below illustrate the interaction of old and new Japan, including an "interim Japan" consisting of the small portion of GDP represented by sectors that are not adding to GDP and are in the process of actively restructuring.[16] We estimate that old Japan constituted about 80 percent of GDP in the mid-1990s and has been shrinking 3 to 4 percent per year. The contraction in 1998 following the Asian downturns was particularly violent. So violent in fact that the fiscal stimulus needed to stabilize the economy in 1999 was almost enough to cause old Japan to grow. In 2001 and beyond we assume old Japan's contribution to GDP is negative, but less so each year.

We estimate new Japan constituted about 20 percent of GDP in 1996, and project its growth rate will increase steadily from 7 percent in 1996 to 15 percent in 2001 and decline thereafter.

---

[16]Several commentators on an earlier draft of this paper pointed out the existence and function of this third component of GDP. It consists of businesses, households, and government entities that are in transition from dependence on noncompetitive export-led growth strategies to non-Cold War–era domestic growth strategies. A Bank of Japan commentator estimated Interim Japan now accounts for about 10 percent of GDP.

Old Japan, New Japan Sector Effect on GDP
(Trillions of Yen and % of GDP)

	1996	1997	1998	1999	2000	2001	2002	2003	2004	2005
Nominal GDP	503.8	505	494.5	493	500	505	510.1	515.2	520.3	525.5
Old-Jpn GDP Share	80%	73%	67%	67%	63%	60%	58%	56%	54%	53%
Old-Jpn Growth Rate		-1%	-5.0%	-1.0%	-5.0%	-4.5%	-4.0%	-3.5%	-3.0%	-2.5%
Int-Japan GDP Share	1.0%	0.5%	10.8%	9.8%	11.0%	9.9%	8.8%	6.9%	6.0%	4.9%
Int-Japan Growth Rt	0.0%	0.0%	0.0%	0.0%	0.0%	0.0%	0.0%	0.0%	0.0%	0.0%
New-Jpn GDP Share	19%	20%	22%	24%	26%	30%	33%	37%	40%	42%
New-Jpn Growth Rate	7.0%	7.5%	8.0%	9.0%	15.0%	12.0%	12.0%	7.0%	6.0%	

Fiscal Stimulus Needed to Offset Old/New Japan Effect (Trillions of Yen)

	1996	1997	1998	1999	2000	2001	2002	2003	2004	2005
Nominal Target GDP	503.8	505	494.5	493	500	500	500	500	500	500
Old+New GDP	498.8	502.6	441.0	444.9	445.2	454.8	465.1	479.8	489.3	499.0
Needed Fiscal Stim		2.4	53.5	48.1	54.8	50.2	45.0	35.4	31.0	25.5

Total Public Sector Borrowing (Fiscal Stimulus plus Interest Expense)

	1997	1998	1999	2000	2001	2002	2003	2004	2005
Needed Fisc Stimulus	2.4	53.5	48.1	54.8	50.2	45.0	35.4	31.0	25.9
Interest on Existing Debt @ 4%	18.4	19.2	22.1	24.5	27.2	31.4	36.3	42.0	50.8
Total Borrowing Need	20.8	72.8	70.1	79.3	77.4	76.3	86.7	87.0	95.7
Total Pub Sector Debt		551.4	613.0	679.6	757.0	833.3	920.0	1007.0	1102.7
Total Public Sector Debt/GDP		124%	136%	151%	167%	184%	201%	221%	

Public Pension Assets and Deficits

	1996	1997	1998	1999	2000	2001	2002	2003	2004	2005
Pub Pension Assets	85	95	76	51	30	17	3	-12	-26	-45
Pub Pension Deficits								15	14	19

In this projection, to keep GDP at roughly 500 trillion yen, total central and local government deficit spending has to remain between 40 and 50 trillion yen through 2002. The emergence of pension deficits in 2003 and beyond keep the total public sector borrowing needs above 70 trillion yen through 2005.

As shown in the projection, the sum of Japan's central and local government bonds and borrowings will approach 140% of GDP in 2000, and be over 220% in 2005. This debt growth is the sum of borrowing to cover the interest expense on existing debt, borrowing to finance spending to offset the "new-old Japan" negative GDP effect, and more borrowing to pay the interest on new rounds of borrowing.

A worrisome aspect of Japan's debt situation is the fact that it is worsening at a time when global growth, led by a record-setting U.S. economy, is generally strong. The U.S. role is critical. Just as it did during the Cold War years, the United States for the past decade has served as the importer-consumer of last resort. This role stabilized the global economy following the Mexican, Asian, and Russian crises, and has enabled many nations to preserve democratic stability and initiate needed reforms.

For the United States, the role of global growth engine has driven its trade and current account deficits to record levels. Moreover, it has triggered a steady round of U.S. Federal Reserve rate increases to prevent inflation and led to G-7 fears of an unsustainable situation, as well as calls for the United States to increase savings. If the Federal Reserve is successful and G-7's (including the U.S. Treasury's) calls for increased savings are heeded, the U.S. economy must slow and import growth rates must decline. For Japan, and Asia generally, a slowing of U.S. imports is serious risk.

Asia's dependence on U.S. imports has risen sharply since the mid-1990s. South Korea's exports to the United States accounted for 21 percent of its total 1999 exports, up from 16 percent in 1996. Of the large Asian nations, China (including Hong Kong and Taiwan) is the most dependent on the U.S. economy. Exports to the United States in 1999 totaled almost 27 percent of all Chinese exports, up from 17 percent in 1996.[7] A downturn in US imports from Asia would depress the entire Asian trade matrix in which Japan is the key participant.

Japan is heavily dependent on trade growth. Data for March 2000 indicate Japan's trade surplus expanded 23 percent year-on-year in dollar terms. In volume terms, real exports climbed by 5.9 percent compared with the final three months of 1999—an annual rate of 25 percent. Imports rose by only 0.1%. The difference is giving Japan's GDP a significant boost. The bilateral trade surplus with the United States is 40 percent higher than the same period a year ago and implies that Japan's trade imbalance with the United States has reached a record $66 billion during the past twelve months. With U.S. nominal GDP growth running at almost 9 percent and real growth over 6 percent, these trade deficit numbers should not be surprising.

Japanese exports are the key support element of Japan's debt structure. Export related companies are the principal income earners and taxpayers. A meaningful reduction in Japanese exports would have multiplier effects that would ripple through the already heavily stressed economy and seriously aggravate the debt problem.

If U. S. Federal Reserve and Treasury efforts are successful in slowing the U.S. economy and increasing household savings rates, the trade deficit will decline. If it is merely reduced back to its 1999 level, the reduction could be as much as 30 percent. From a U.S. perspective such a reduction would be regarded as moderate and salutary. From an Asian perspective, the 30 percent reduction could be difficult to accommodate. Directly and indirectly, Japanese GDP growth could be depressed a full percentage point.

Implications for the United States
The PCW hypothesis has two implications for the United States and its stock market.

---

[7]Morgan Stanley Dean Witter, "Fatal Attraction: Asia's Rising Export Dependence on the U.S.," *Global Insights* (April 19, 2000).

First, if the allies' Cold War export/consumption paradigm was optimal for winning, it was so because it raised and kept the real incomes of developing-country allies higher than they would have been otherwise. That is, the strategy succeeded in keeping voter allegiances in those countries from migrating to the promises of Communism by providing and promising as much or more well-being.

For the United States the cost of this strategy has been a very large and steadily growing current account imbalance and an unavoidable adjustment of that imbalance. Putting the discussion in currency terms, the U.S. current/capital account adjustment will ultimately involve a fall in the dollar relative to other major world currencies—the euro and the yen. The dollar's decline may surprise policymakers and market participants for the same reason they were surprised by the speed and depth of the Asian downturns: they did not give adequate consideration to the contractionary power of long-standing trends when they reverse. Governments and markets were equally surprised by the speed of the Asian upturns. They did not anticipate how rapidly capital flows to countries when restructuring is clearly under way.

The U.S. current and capital account adjustment process seems to depend on two things. First is the degree to which actual restructuring deviates from baseline market expectations. Second is the extent to which foreign demand, especially emerging market demand, for U.S. good and services increases and offsets the decline in domestic U.S. demand that must accompany an increase in U.S. savings rates. We can be optimistic about the second, if the first does not prove to be destabilizing.

The strength of the U.S. economy and its vulnerability are evident in the data below.

U.S. Projected Change in Net Savings ($ Billions)[18]

Savings	1999	2000	2001	2002
Houschold	158	87	16	−56
Gross Business Savings	1205	1259	1316	1376
Government Savings	120	161	193	246
Gross National Savings	1483	1507	1525	1566
Gross Private Domestic Investment	1622	1755	1900	2057
Shortfall (Inflows from Abroad)	−139	−248	−375	−491

---

[18]Bureau of Economic Analysis and Congressional Budget Office.

A major reason so much capital flows into U.S. markets appears to be a perception that the United States is the most attractive place in the world to do business. This is America's principle strength. The United States is said to have a positive culture, as well as the legal and accounting resources needed to support business activity. It is reported that it takes about two weeks to start a limited partnership LLC business in the United States. It takes about two months in Japan, and about twenty months in Europe. In the United States there are 250 million people and 350 thousand CPAs. In Japan there are 120 million people and 12 thousand CPAs.

America's principle vulnerability, however, is its increasing dependence on inflows of foreign capital. In and of itself, dependence is not a problem. Global growth occurs on a foundation of increasing interdependence.

The question is whether the US dependence is stable. The fact that capital's continued attraction to U.S. markets depends on its trading-partners remaining competitively backward suggests that it is not—or, at least, that there is a significant risk that it is not. U.S. trading partners are doing everything possible to restructure and catch up. Will they do it quickly, that is, in the next year or so? Certainly not. But with the U.S. example at hand and the opportunity to avoid U.S. mistakes, they eventually can and almost certainly will.

At the same time U.S. household spending continues to outstrip income, with the difference made up by either borrowing or spending capital gains. Households are liquidating or selling more financial assets than they are buying. Spending growth has accelerated in the past two years while income growth remained stable. The rise in spending that has been fueled by capital gains in stocks and home ownership has hidden a gradually increasing interest burden. While consumers rate their present situation as very good, their interest burden as a percentage of their total spending is now at an all-time high.

To understand the U.S. current account adjustment path, it is essential to keep in mind that usually the worse a country's conditions are, the higher its potential marginal return on investment is. That is, the worse a country's conditions, the more attractive it is to investors once true restructuring reforms are initiated. When real restructuring reforms get under way, "potential" becomes "expected," and currency markets begin to do what they are supposed to do—allocate capital to its highest expected marginal rate of return.[19]

Two rules flow from this:

(1) When restructuring initiatives are not under way or are very slow, capital flows to the country with the lowest amount of needed restructuring—it generally has lower taxes, is more productive, and is growing faster.

(2) When restructuring efforts are actively under way, capital flows to the country whose restructuring needs are the greatest—its expected marginal rate of return is higher.

A recent example of the first rule is the United States vis-à-vis Europe. Examples of the second are Japan vis-à-vis Europe, and emerging market countries like Brazil vis-à-vis both Europe and the United States.

Just as capital markets repriced the Asian economic and political frameworks, they will also reprice the U.S. consumption commitment. In our judgment, that repricing actually began several years ago but has been masked by the effects of the Asia-to-U.S. wealth transfer and the Europe-to-U.S. capital inflows.

For the U.S. stock market this means that stocks of companies that provide and finance consumer goods and services are at greatest risk. In general, if there is a broad PCW downward restructuring adjustment of U.S. consumption that roughly approximates the adjustments that are under way in the economies of U.S. Cold War allies, all companies and countries that depend on continued high levels of U.S. consumption are at significant risk.

Moral Hazard and the PCW Transition
Government moral hazard risk-taking almost always reflects the efforts of the government to preserve the "old" or to minimize the

---

[19]Robert H. Dugger, "U.S. Trade and Current Account Deficits and the Market Adjustment Path: America's Consumption Orientation is What is 'Old' about the U.S. Economy," statement before the U.S. Trade Deficit Review Commission, March 13, 2000.

pain of restructuring and downsizing. This was true in U.S. efforts to avoid dealing with problems in the Savings & Loan sector. It is true now in the Japanese government's efforts to keep noncompetitive intermediate-sized businesses open and their employees "employed" via government guaranteed loans through the banking system. If there is any point on which the wide range of "new architecture" findings and recommendations agree, it is that the Asian down-turns involved significant moral hazard risk-taking and that such risk-taking should be avoided.

Were U.S. government efforts to sustain strong U.S. con-sumption in the latter years of the 1990s a form of moral hazard risk-taking? The question is an open one. Michael Prell, U.S. Fed-eral Reserve Board research director, raised the issue early in 1999 soon after it was evident that the 75 basis points of rate reductions the preceding autumn had succeeded in restoring U.S. stock mar-ket buoyancy.

> ... So let me cite Notion Number Ten, which is that the Fed has learned how eradicate the business cycle and how to ensure eter-nal bull markets in stocks and bonds. I hope that I shall not be viewed as disloyal if I express a little skepticism that my bosses really have achieved quite that degree of insight and power.
>
> But, given that one hears something akin to that thought being expressed by people with some frequency these days, might one not ask, in all seriousness, whether a new sort of moral hazard hasn't been introduced into the macroeconomic scene. Might people—business managers, consumers, investors—be taking risks that they would not have taken were it not for an exaggerated con-fidence in the ability of the Fed to cushion the economy and financial markets against any and all shocks? If so, there conceiv-ably could be a greater potential instability in the system than is readily apparent at this time. Of course, in expressing that concern, I may simply be showing the propensity people who have been around central banks for a long time have for looking for something to worry about when the times are good.[20]

---

[20]Michael J. Prell, "Economic Outlook," remarks at the Charlotte Economics Club, Charlotte, North Carolina, January 14, 1999.

Moral hazard risk-taking is a complex subject, however, just about all that can be said about it has been said by Morris Goldstein and Barry Eichengreen, despite their significantly different policy perspectives.[21]

Eichengreen focused particularly on the historical sources of moral hazard and observed that:

Asia's crisis can only be understood in term of a conjuncture of long-standing historical forces and short-term financial policies. Ultimately, the explanation for the crisis lies in the region's history and economic development trajectory, which relied on bank-centered financial systems, the use of the banks as instruments of industrial policy, and close connections between banks and politicians, all of which were designed to sustain high rates of investment and rapid economic growth. This was not a formula that could work forever: by the second half of the 1990s it had been in place for several decades and was showing growing signs of strain. At another level, the explanation lies in financial errors committed in the mid-1990s. Growth may have been slowing, but the day of reckoning was delayed by the selective liberalization of capital accounts to facilitate short-term financial flows, aided and abetted by the low level of interest rates in the major money centers and by the migration of U.S. and European investment banks to middle-income Asia. These developments on the borrowing and lending sides enabled the newly industrializing countries to borrow their way out of their difficulties for a time. In the end, however, this only set them up for a harder fall.[22]

Eichengreen concludes that his interpretation of the Asian crisis has five important implications. First, large current-account deficits are not benign. Second, how the current account is financed is critically important: dependence on foreign funding is risky. Third, financial institutions are a special source of vulnerability—the

---

[21]See, for example: Barry Eichengreen, *Toward a New International Financial Architecture, A Practical Post-Asia Agenda* (Washington, D.C.: Institute for International Economics, 1999); and *Safeguarding Prosperity in Global Financial System, the Future International Architecture, Report of an Independent Task Force Sponsored by the Council on Foreign Relations,* Carla A. Hills and Peter G. Peterson, Co-Chairs, Morris Goldstein, Project Director (Washington, D.C.: Institute for International Economics, 1999).

[22]Eichengreen, ibid., p. 162.

belief that the government stands ready to run to the rescue is a source of moral hazard that encourages inflows of more foreign capital. Fourth, developing countries should press for greater exchange-rate flexibility. And fifth, it will not always be possible to prevent or predict financial crises.[23]

These five implications were intended to illuminate developing-country conditions. However, if the PCW transition hypothesis is true, all but the fourth of Eichengreen's implications have important meaning for the United States. In the U.S. case, the large current account deficit is financed by foreign capital inflows. The fact that most of these inflows are into marketable debt and equity securities makes them potentially very short term in nature.

No one should be confused and think that U.S. debt and equity markets are not like "banks" or financial institutions more generally; i.e., that somehow "markets" have powers that mere banks do not have. As LTCM demonstrated starkly, markets have implicit capital ratios, and when capital positions are reduced by losses, financial and economic contractions result. The real probability such a contraction could occur may be higher than perceived if last autumn's Federal Reserve rate cuts, intended to stabilize markets, introduced a significant moral hazard risk.

Eichengreen's fifth implication—that crises are hard to predict—certainly applies to the United States also. As we will see when we review a macroeconomic simulation of the effects of a significant stock market decline, prediction may be made more difficult if the historical context of the model is not carefully considered.

HOUSEHOLD BALANCE SHEETS AND GENERATIONAL DELEVERAGING

To win the Cold War, American households and government were encouraged to spend and did. It is not surprising, therefore, that as the Cold War decelerated in the 1980s, a shift in U.S. political philosophy from consumption and spending to savings got under-

---

[23]Eichengreen, ibid., p. 167.

way. Steadily through the 1980s, caps on household savings-deposit interest rates were removed, the tax deductibility of consumer interest expenses was eliminated, and a variety of tax-incentive savings programs were established. Balanced-budget efforts to change government spending and saving priorities saw fruition in the early 1990s. By the late 1990s, the U.S. government in current terms was adding significantly to national savings.

While these shifts have been real, they may not adequately address the financial risks both households and the public sectors faces due to aging. Although precisely calculating retirement savings is nearly impossible, survey and poll data point to a large variance in perceptions between how well-prepared households are for a comfortable retirement and how well-prepared they need to be. Also, household perceptions of retirement comfort may be undermined by well-documented and widespread doubts about the U.S. Social Security system's ability to pay current benefits, especially if accumulated private savings would suddenly be perceived as inadequate.

Perceived household savings adequacy is critically important to knowing whether the U.S. stock market represents a financial risk to the economy. A decline in the stock market is important only for what economic, political, and social events it triggers. If households are well-prepared for retirement, that is, their net worth is growing and their benefits can reasonably be expected to provide sufficient assets for a secure retirement, then we can be reasonably confident that a stock market downturn will not trigger a sharp and destabilizing increase in personal savings rates. If they are not, that risk exists.

There is broad, though certainly not complete, agreement that most households, especially among the dominant pre-retirement Baby Boomer generation, are not financially well prepared for retirement and will at some point need to reduce consumption and increase savings. An analysis by Catherine P. Montalto that mined the recently updated household financial data from the U.S. Federal Reserve's Survey of Consumer Finances concluded that only 44 percent of households with a currently employed householder will accumulate retirement savings that will be adequate to maintain the pre-retirement level of living throughout their retirement years.[24] The authoritative 1999 Retirement Confidence Survey by the Employee Benefit Research Institute (EBRI) concluded that less than 10 percent of current workers are doing a very good job preparing for retirement, though 70 percent believe they are saving adequately.[25] Of the 70 percent of workers polled in the survey who believe they are saving adequately for retirement, the median amount of accumulated financial assets is only $29,000, which EBRI called "unimpressive."[26]

Moreover, these data and surveys indicate current working households entertain unrealistic expectations about how long they will work; how much they will depend on Social Security benefits for retirement income; and how high their pension benefits will be.

Private Savings Adequacy

Determining accurately whether Boomer households need to increase their savings rates to assure a secure retirement is fraught with the need to make many assumptions on a variety of variables, without the benefit of comprehensive, timely household financial data. There is a lively debate over whether Baby Boomers are saving adequately. In 1997, Douglas Bernheim of Stanford University estimated that the Baby Boom generation was saving only 38 percent of what it will need to save for retirement.[27]

At the other end of the spectrum, optimists like William Gale dispute Bernheim's methodology and results. As noted in a June 1999 AARP study, [28] "Gale estimates that close to half of boomers

---

[24]Catherine P. Montalto, *Retirement Savings of American Households: Asset levels and Adequacy*, report to the Consumer Federation of America and DirectAdvice.com, April 26, 2000.

[25]Employee Benefit Research Institute (EBRI). *Retirement Confidence Survey and RCS Minority—1999 Results and Tools.* http://www.ebri.org/rcs/1999/1999_results.htm

[26]EBRI, http://www.ebri.org/rcs/1999/1999_results.htm

[27]Douglas Bernheim, Merrill Lynch Baby Boomer Retirement Index(SM), 1997

[28]J W. Gale, "Are Americans Saving Enough for Retirement?" A Century Foundation Report, The Twentieth Century Fund Foundation (1998) and "Will the Baby Boom Be Ready for Retirement?" The Brookings Review, Summer 1997, pp. 5–9, cited in John Gist, Wu Ke Bin, and Charles Ford, "Do Baby Boomers Save and, If So, What For?" Paper no. 9906, (Washington, D.C.: AARP, June 1999), pp. 6-7. http://research.aarp.org/econ/9906_do_boomers.pdf

are saving adequately for retirement, even if no home equity is counted. He estimates that nearly two-thirds are saving adequately if half of home equity is included, and over 70 percent are if all housing equity is counted."

The AARP study authors go on to succinctly describe the high degree of uncertainty inherent in any estimate of savings adequacy:

> Arriving at a reliable assessment of saving adequacy is difficult because it depends on som many other factors: the standard or benchmark of adequacy, the inclusion of annuitized Social Security and pension wealth in measured saving, possible inheritances, age of departure from the labor force, and special needs and obligations (children, dependent parents, debts, medical needs, etc.)[29]

Median estimates from the June 1999 AARP study show that older Boomer couples without a private pension would have to save between 8 and 22 percent of their income to retire comfortably, depending on replacement rates, longevity, and rates of return. Younger Boomer couples would have to save between 6 and 15 percent of their income.[30] Using their data, as shown in the table below, a plausible best-case estimate is that the savings need was a little more than the net worth of older Boomer couples. In the median worst case, the savings need was more than three times their net worth.

Baby Boom Household Balance Sheet Conditions

<u>1994 Median Net Worth, less home equity, of</u>

Older Boomers	$25,000
Younger Boomers	$11,000
Total Boomers	$17,807

<u>Amount and Percentages of Wages that Must Be Saved to Reach Retirement Target</u>

Older Boomer Couple	per year	over 15 years
Median with DB Pension*	$2,411	$28,932
Median without DB Pension	$6,549	$78,588

---

[29]Gist, Wu, and Ford, ibid.p. 7
[30]Gist, Wu, and Ford, ibid., Tables 2 an 11.

<u>Savings Need of Older Boomers as Percentage of Net Worth</u>
With DB Pension   116%
Without DB Pension   314%
*DB = Defined-Benefit

EBRI data indicate that current workers say private savings will be the most important source of retirement income. On the other hand, current retirees list Social Security as the most important source of their retirement income. Presumably current retirees are better informed about retirement realities than current workers are, and it is only a matter of time that workers will have to adjust their expectations.

How Will I Pay for Retirement?

Most important sources of retirement income (expected sources for workers and actual sources for retirees.)[31]

	Workers	Retirees
Personal Savings	49%	18%
Employer-funded Plans	20	30
Social Security	12	39
Employment	11	3
Sale of home or business	5	2
Other government programs	1	4
Support from children/family	<1	<1

If current workers are biased toward overestimating their retirement well-being, the risk is that a sharp stock market decline could trigger a sharp correction in their expectations. The top two numbers for workers in the table above could shift suddenly in the direction of the same numbers for retirees. A shift to an increase perceived reliance on private pensions and Social Security take place would run in to evidence of common overestimating of pension benefits and well-documented and widespread doubts about Social Security's ability to pay current benefits.

---

[31]EBRI, http://www.ebri.org/rcs/1999/1999_results.htm

Private Pension Adequacy

The U.S. Commission on Pension Policy found in evidence of a substantial "expectations gap" between what retirees think they are going to get and what they actually get.[32] Before retirement, households seem to consistently overestimate their benefits. A large decline in consumption immediately after retirement has troubled economists for many years and now appears to be the result of benefits overestimation.[33] In a 1994 survey, 40 percent of the respondents said their retirement income was less than they expected. Less than 10 percent said pension income exceeded their pre-retirement expectations.[34]

An overestimation of benefits should not be surprising. Relatively few workers actually do the calculations needed to determine retirement incomes. Even though the portion of workers who have tried to determine how much they need to save by the time they retire has increased steadily since 1996, only half of all current workers have actually tried to do this calculation (49 percent in 1999, compared with 32 percent in 1996).[35]

Social Security

Without treading on the sensitive political question of Social Security reform, we note that, under current official projections, Social Security payroll taxes will no longer cover benefits after 2015, requiring either an increase in the public debt, tax hikes, or spending reductions to pay current benefit levels beyond then. Since each of these options would entail significant political opposition, experts assume and the public believes current benefits may have to be reduced beforehand.

Perhaps this fact explains why surveys continuously show most workers expect little or no income from Social Security when they

---

[32]James Banks, Richard Blundell, and Sarah Tanner, "Is There a Retirement-Savings Puzzle?" *American Economic Review*, vol. 88, no. 4 (September 1998), p. 785.

[33]Banks, et. al., pp. 769–88.

[34]Andrew Dilnot, Richard Disney, Paul Johnson, and Edward Whitehouse, "Pensions Policy in the U.K." (London: Institute for Fiscal Studies, 1994).

[35]EBRI, http://www.ebri.org/rcs/1999/1999_results.htm

retire. A March 2000 poll[36] conducted for the Montalto study found that, when asked how much retirement income workers expected to receive from Social Security, 39 percent responded "none." Of those who did expect to receive Social Security benefits, eight out of ten expected them to provide less than half of Social Security benefits. An AARP poll found that only 6 percent of Boomers are very confident Social Security will still be available when they retire; 64 percent were "not too confident" or "not at all confident." A CBS poll found that 55 percent of the public doubted that Social Security will have the money to provide the benefits they expect for retirement.[37] An NBC New/*Wall Street Journal* poll found only 28 percent believe Social Security will be paying current benefit levels when they retire.[38]

This variance in perceptions will become very important if workers have reason to doubt their private savings adequacy.

Later Retirement

It is commonly assumed that the growing burden of societal aging will require workers to postpone retirement. Many people think they will be able to work until they are 65, but the facts indicate otherwise. EBRI's survey points to another form of "retirement illusion": overestimating when retirement will occur. Nearly half of today's workers expect to retire at age 65 or later, and 5 percent expect they will never retire. In contrast to these expectations, however, most retirees report actual retirement ages younger than age 65. Moreover, for many retirees, the earlier retirement age was not by design—more than four out of ten (43 percent) of today's retirees say they retired earlier than planned.[39] If current workers follow the pattern set by today's retirees, many are also likely to retire earlier than planned and many will do so for negative rea-

---

[36]Caravan Opinion Research, March 2000, Question R10, p. 37; http://www.consumerfed.org/opinion.pdf.

[37]CBS News Poll. May 11, 1999. N=578 adults nationwide, including 408 who are currently employed.

[38]NBC News/*Wall Street Journal* Poll conducted by the polling organizations of Peter Hart (D) and Robert Teeter (R). Latest: March 47, 1999. N=2,012 adults nationwide.

[39]EBRI, http://www.ebri.org/rcs/1999/1999_results.htm

sons. Forty percent of today's retirees who left the work force earlier than expected say they did so because of health problems or disability.

Conclusion

Though forming precise estimates and forecasts of savings and pension adequacy is enormously complicated, the weight of survey data points to a need for households to start saving more. Yet the gap between working households' expectations and likely reality concerning retirement remains wide, as we can see below.

Consume much less now to save for later? Boomers are already finding it hard to save for retirement. Using a scale of one to five, an AARP poll[40] concluded that 47 percent found it hard to save given other needs, while 31 percent did not. The rest were in the middle.

Cut back on consumption in retirement? Only 35 percent expect they will have to scale back their lifestyle during retirement. Only 23 percent think they will have to struggle to make ends meet.

Work well into their seventies or eighties? The survey found that the median age at which Boomers say they want to retire and not work for pay is 59. But they expect to retire and not work for pay at all at 64 years, either for financial reasons or to get Social Security benefits.

Given this contrast of attitudes and the size of the Boomer's saving need, the likelihood is that they will be spooked into changing their saving behavior if they are presented with unpleasant new information about their current and prospective net worth. Data over the past 10 years show that, on the margin, the public is growing more concerned about retirement savings adequacy. The Federal Reserve's Survey of Consumer Finances show households have increasingly cited retirement as their reason for saving. And EBRI's survey found that households that do their retirement calculations have saved a median $66,000, compared to the median $14,000 saved by households that have not.

---

[40]American Association of Retired Persons, "Baby Boomers Envision Their Retirement: An AARP Segmentation Analysis," (Washington, D.C.: American Association of Retired Persons, February 1999); http://research.aarp.org/econ/boomer_seg.html.

Regardless of how the stock market performs, it is becoming increasingly clear that most households have borrowed from the future to finance current consumption, and as a consequence, their current net worth, expected earnings, and private and public pensions are not sufficient to meet their retirement income requirements. While undertaking this borrowing, households may hold overly optimistic expectations of how their retirement will be financed. They are "generationally leveraged," and their leveraging has buoyed the global economy. But should the gap between optimistic expectations and a looming reality close, households will try to deleverage. Triggered perhaps by a stock market decline, household deleveraging could slow growth worldwide. The weaker the stock market, the stronger the deleveraging incentive will be.[41]

Moreover, the two phenomena—a very weak stock market and consumption cutbacks—are likely to be mutually amplifying. Our review of history suggests two potentially useful historical analogues of the scale of household perception shift that may be possible. The more recent is the response of household buying patterns to rising gasoline prices in the mid-1970s. The other is the response of household saving rates to the sudden entry of the United States into World War II, when household savings jumped from 5 to 25 percent in one year.

MACROECONOMIC FORECASTS INCLUDING A MAJOR MARKET DECLINE

Asking the question how is the American stock market a financial risk is roughly equivalent to asking why the benign results from large-scale macroeconomic model simulations of a large stock market downturn might not be accurate. To initiate this inquiry, we compare a carefully modeled current forecast of the U.S. econo-

---

41 The Federal Reserve will publish its exhaustive 1998 Survey of Consumer Finance and provide a new national benchmark for evaluating household financial strength. The last survey was done in 1995. Information currently available from other, more limited sources, suggests strongly that the new survey is going to document that U.S. households are more leveraged and dependent on stock market strength than ever.

my with a simulation of the economy assuming a large downturn. The forecast we use as a baseline for comparison is Macroeconomic Advisors current U.S. forecast, which incidentally includes a 12% stock market decline. The simulation includes a 30% market downturn and was prepared by Macroeconomic Advisors specifically for this paper to show how the U.S. economy would likely respond to the downturn under standard assumptions.[42] A 30 percent decline was specified because it is roughly the amount by which many analysts said the U.S. stock market was overvalued in mid-1999.[43]

The simulation indicates that following a sharp stock market decline, appropriate monetary policy adjustments are made, fis-

---

[42]Macroeconomic Advisors, 231 South Bemiston Ave., Suite 900, Saint Louis, Missouri.

[43]See for example: Douglas R. Cliggot, "Be Careful, The Gulf Between the S&P 500 and 'Fair Value' Is Big; We Think the Risk/Return Profile of the Market Is Poor," in *U.S. Equity Portfolio Strategy* (New York: J.P. Morgan Securities Inc., June 28, 1999). Cliggott concluded:

> From 1986 through 1994 fair value increased at a strong 13.5 percent average annual rate. One part was 8.5 percent average annual EPS growth. Another 2 percent per year came from declining bond yields, and the last 3 percent per year came from a drop in the average EY/BY ratio from 0.95 to 0.71—effectively, the measured risk premium dropped by about 25 percent. During the nine-year stretch, the S&P 500 rose 9 percent per year, so it underperformed fair value by 450 bps per year.
>
> But then things changed. From 1994 through 1998 the rate of appreciation of fair value accelerated by 450 bps, to an 18.0 percent average annual rate. EPS growth contributed 6 percent per year. The big drop in bond yields accounted for a huge 10.5 percent per year, and further decline in the average EY/BY ratio to 0.67 added 1.5 percent per year. And in these four years, the S&P 500 averaged a 28 percent gain each year, or 1,000 bps faster than fair value. ... Market values have doubled in a span of four years a couple times in the past four-and-a half decades, but each time we reverted back below the mean (7 percent per year gain) pretty quickly.
>
> What next? The sharp decline in fair value in 1999 has been driven by the back-up in bond yields. Everything else equal, a move from a 5 percent 30-year yield to a 6 percent yield reduces fair value on the S&P 500 by just about 200 index points. So one way to bring fair value and current market levels closer in line would be a big bond rally. Maybe ... but we doubt it. We think a bond yield in the 6.0–6.5 percent range makes sense if CPI inflation is in the 2.0–2.5 percent range. So in the near term (12–18 months) most of the lifting probably needs to be done by earnings. We expect S&P 500 EPS to rise a cumulative 28 percent over the course of 1999 and 2000. If we match that with a 6 percent bond yield, we get an S&P 500 fair value level of 1219 at year-end 2000. Hmmm ... let's hope we are wrong about bonds.[43]

cal stabilizers in existing law work, the United States endures a period of reduced growth, and then stabilizes onto a path of continued strong, stable growth. See the Appendix for the detailed forecast and simulation results. The model specifically does not include consideration of asymmetric, nonlinear saving and spending responses by households.

The simulation results are benign mainly because the personal savings rate increases only from −1.4 percent to +2.6 percent in 1999 and from −2.3 percent to +3.2 percent in 2000.[44] The new levels are only about half the levels observed at the beginning of the 1990s. See the reported savings rate line in the graph below. (The graph also shows what Macroeconomic Advisors (MA) estimates the savings rate would have been if the stock market had risen in line with nominal economic growth during the 1990s.)

MA conducted the simulation again in April 2000 and obtained quite similar results. Specifically, MA reported that they simulated the their model for a different beginning of Third Quarter 2000 equity corrections after making the following adjustments:

1. Switched on the reaction function and forced the effective funds rate (RFFEFF) to the values in MA's latest base forecast (BASE003, dated April 3, 2000). This resets the adjustment factors on the reaction function.

2. Froze household equity net worth (NMAQ$) for beginning of First and Second Quarters 2000, since these are already historical values.

3. Updated First Quarter 2000 spending figures to reflect incoming data as of April 14, 2000. These boost GDP growth in First Quarter 2000 to 6.1 percent

For each of three alternatives, MA assumed a large decline in household equity net worth during the second calendar quarter of 2000 (i.e., beginning of Third Quarter 2000). Subsequent to Third Quarter 2000, the adjustment factor on household equity

---

[44]The savings rate data, of course, are those reported before the GDP revisions of late October 1999. The revisions affect the levels of reported savings rates, but are not expected to affect the relative movement of the rates over time.

net worth was re-leveled to its new Third Quarter 2000 value. This produced a gradual and slight rebound in equity net worth in 2001. The results would not have been much different had MA just held household equity net worth constant following the correction. Three corrections were simulated: 12.7 percent (this corresponds to the decline in the Wilshire 5000 between March 31, 2000 and April 14, 2000), 20 percent, and 30 percent.

Results: 12.7 percent. With the 12.7 percent correction, the funds rate stops rising at 6.75 percent, as GDP growth is about 0.2 percentage point lower in the middle of the short-term forecast. Inflation is also about 0.1 percentage point lower.

20 percent: The funds rate briefly hits 6.5 percent, but quickly declines to 6.25 percent, and perhaps even down to 6 percent. Growth is more than 0.5 percentage point lower during the middle of the short-term forecast. Inflation is about 0.2 to 0.3 percentage point lower.

30 percent: The funds rate never heads much above 6 percent, and by next year declines sharply to near 5 percent. GDP growth falls to about 1.5 percent before rebounding to above 2.5 percent. GDP-price inflation falls gradually and continuously to around 1.8 percent, or by about 0.6 percentage point below the base forecast by the end of 2001.

Caveats: These results do not take into account severe financial disruptions, either domestic or overseas, so they do not represent what the Fed's reaction might be if there was a repeat of September 1998. Because there are no disruptive foreign financial spillovers, the paths of net exports in the alternative correction simulations are certainly higher than they would be if foreign spillovers were to significantly hurt foreign growth or lead to a significant rebound in the trade-weighted value of the dollar. These considerations suggest that a large equity correction could lead to even lower interest-rate paths than these simulations suggest, at least in the near term.

Confidence in the simulated savings-rate response depends significantly on plausibility of the model itself. There are four reasons to doubt the model's results.

Wealth Effect & Saving Rate

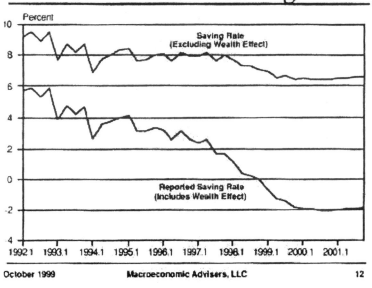

First, the model is shaped by the experience of the past thirty years in which US savings was in a secular decline. Any upturn in savings is dampened by the models' expectation that the trend of the preceding thirty years will continue.

Second, to take population aging into consideration, the model managers do an offline calculation that further dampens any upturn in savings. They calculate population aging and put the result in a formula that assumes a steady increase in the marginal propensity to consume as people age.

Third, the model disregards "Peter Lynch" rationality. Peter Lynch, a US household investment icon, says in television advertisements that average Americans need to have about $300,000 in financial assets by the time they are 65 years old in order to assure a secure retirement. An investor is said to be "Peter Lynch" rational if they have a "target pile of dough" (TPOD) they are trying to reach.

"Peter Lynch" rationality says that if an American investor is pushed off his TPOD path, he will increase his saving rate, and the older he is, the more he will do so—exactly the opposite of what the model designed to assume.[45]

This is critically important. If American baby boomers sharply slow their consumption in an effort through saving to get back onto a life-cycle wealth accumulation path, the economy will slow and the stock market will fall further. The additional stock market downturn will necessitate a larger savings increase, resulting potentially in a self-reinforcing GDP downturn that would be relatively immune to Fed rate cuts.

The seriousness of this threat is evident in a number of recently released reports. As noted earlier, the Consumer Federation of America analysis of the Federal Reserve's Survey of Consumer Finances shows that 56% of American working households are undersaved now.[46] The authoritative 1999 Retirement Confidence Survey by the Employee Benefit Research Institute concludes that less than 10 percent of current workers are doing a very good job preparing for retirement, though 70 percent believe they are saving adequately.[47] Of the 70 percent of workers polled in the survey who believe they are saving adequately for retirement, the median amount of accumulated financial assets is only $29,000, which EBRI called "unimpressive." Moreover, these data and surveys indicate current working households entertain unrealistic expectations about how long they will work; how much they will depend on Social Security benefits for retirement income; and how high their pension benefits will be.

The fourth deficiency in the model projections is there is no consideration of the effects outside the US of a sharp downturn in US consumption. The model managers acknowledge this limitation but fail to note that by not including risks of this sort, the model behaves as if the risks do not exist. A forthcoming MIT

---

[45]Macroeconomic Advisers is studying ways now to estimate the effects of different savings responses and how to model them.

[46]Catherine P. Montalto. *Retirement Savings of American Households: Asset levels and Adequacy*. Report to the Consumer Federation of America and DirectAdvice.com. April 26,2000.

[47]Employee Benefit Research Institute (EBRI). *Retirement Confidence Survey and RCS Minority – 1999Results and Tools*. http://www.ebri.org/rcs/1999/1999_results.htm.

Press publication argues that the stability of Japan's massive public debt, for example, is dependent on the US continuing to increase its rates of consumption.[48] It is very unlikely that that a meaningful decline in US consumption could occur without triggering significant problems elsewhere in the world.

CONCLUDING COMMENTS

For Japan and Europe, the post–Cold War transition will involve higher real marginal propensities to consume, lower savings rates, significant contractions of older trade-protected and subsidized sectors, and a general scaling-back of the welfare state pension, healthcare, and unemployment benefit promises of the 1950s and 1960s. For the United States the transition will mean higher savings and lower real consumption propensities, and some scaling back of pension and healthcare promises. The immensely positive productivity effects of the structural changes associated with the transition justify it being also called a "new paradigm." While the transition is for the most part historical in its orientation, it fully includes the consequences of current and capital account adjustments arising from stronger growth around the world.

Generational deleveraging, however, makes the post–Cold War transition much more difficult. Japan's electorate, for example, is aging rapidly and saving desperately in an effort to assure adequate living standards and health during the many years to come. In this circumstance, it is almost certainly impossible for Japan to generate consumption levels and growth rates high enough to resolve its breathtaking fiscal imbalances. The scale of the challenge is mirrored by the fact that to finance its pension commitments, Japan would have to increase its consumption tax from 5 percent to a politically and economically inconceivable 17 percent.

The aging of the electorates of Europe and the United States is still sufficiently far in the future that it is feasible to adjust pen-

---

[48] *When Will Japan's Financial Mount Fuji Blow its Top?* David Asher and Robert Dugger, MIT Press, May 22, 2000.

sion and healthcare commitments enough to prevent fiscal conditions from deteriorating into a crisis, as has occurred in Japan. To do this, European and U.S. voters have to save more for their own retirements and accept rollbacks in pension and healthcare commitments that will involve a combination of longer working lives and reduced benefits.

The political obstacles are daunting. In the mid-1990s, when the Hashimoto government attempted to stabilize Japan's fiscal situation and cut-off wasteful subsidies to older, noncompetitive economic sectors, he and his government were thrown out of office, and the succeeding Obuchi government implemented a new round of deficit spending. More recently, in Germany, the relatively modest fiscal reforms proposed by the Schroeder government have triggered an astonishing decline in voter support. In the United States, Social Security and Medicare reforms languish on the desks of policymakers despite employment, growth, and budget surplus conditions that are so favorable as to be almost unimaginable just a few years ago.

The effects of a significant U.S. market downturn would be global and geopolitical. Several decades of U.S. current account deficits financed by capital account inflows have made foreigners significant holders of U.S. financial assets. World equity-market movements are also highly correlated: a significant U.S. decline would be associated with equity-market declines in the rest of the world.

Some of the declines would be less and some greater depending on the country's relationship to the United States. These relationships need to be carefully studied for their geopolitical implications. National and global security issues may be at stake to a greater degree than is generally realized. Countries that are significant exporters of consumer goods to the United States, such as China, are likely to be hurt most by a U.S. stock-market downturn.

BIBLIOGRAPHY

American Association of Retired Persons. "Baby Boomers Envision Their Retirement: An AARP Segmentation Analysis." Washington, D.C.: American Association of Retired Persons,February 1999. http://www.research.aarp.org/econ/boomer_seg.html

Abelson, Alan. "Up and Down Wall Street: Next Time Around." *Barrons*. October 10, 1999. http://interactive.wsj.com/articles /SB939423317146465946.htm

Avery, Christopher, and Peter Zemsky. "Multidimensional Uncertainty and Herd Behavior in Financial Markets." *American Economic Review*, vol. 88, no 4 (September 1998), pp. 724–47.

Asher, David, and Robert Dugger, *When Will Japan's Financial Mount Fuji Blow Its Top?* MIT Press. May, 2000.

Banks, James, Richard Blundell, and Sarah Tanner. "Is there a Retirement-Savings Puzzle?" *American Economic Review* vol. 88, no. 4 (September 1998), pp. 769–88.

Blecker, Robert. "The Diminishing Returns to Export-Led Growth." Paper presented to the Working Group on Development, Trade, and International Finance. New York: Council on Foreign Relations, October 7, 1999. Also published in the series by the Project on Development, Trade, and International Finance.

Caravan Opinion Research, March 2000, Question R10 [concerning expected Social Security benefits], p. 37; http://www.consumerfed.org/opinion.pdf.

CBS News Poll. May 11, 1999. *Confidence in Social Security Availability for Your Retirement.*

Cliggott, Douglas R. "Be Careful, The Gulf Between the S&P 500 and 'Fair Value' Is Big; We Think the Risk/Return Profile of the Market Is Poor." *U.S. Equity Portfolio Strategy* New York: J.P. Morgan Securities Inc., June 28, 1999.

Dilnot, Andrew, Richard Disney, Paul Johnson, and Edward Whitehouse. "Pensions Policy in the UK." London: Institute for Fiscal Studies, 1994.

Dugger, Robert H. "U.S. Trade and Current Account Deficits and the Market Adjustment Path: America's Consumption Orientation is What is 'Old' about the U.S. Economy." Statement before the U.S. Trade Deficit Review Commission. March 13, 2000.

Eichengreen, Barry. *Toward a New International Financial Architecture, A Practical Post-Asia Agenda.* Institute for International Economics, 1999.

European Central Bank. "The Euro Area at the Start of Stage Three." *Monthly Bulletin* (January 1999), pp. 11–13.

Employee Benefit Research Institute. *Retirement Confidence Survey and RCS Minority—1999 Results and Tools* http://www.ebri.org/rcs/1999/1999_results.htm

Gist, John, Ke Bin Wu, and Charles Ford. "Do Baby Boomers Save and, If So, What For?" Paper no. 9906. Washington, D.C.: American Association of Retired Persons, June 1999.

Greenspan, Alan. "Measuring Financial Risk in the Twenty-First Century." At Conference sponsored by the Office of the Comptroller of the Currency, Washington, D.C. October 14, 1999.

Greenspan, Alan. "New Challenges for Monetary Policy." Symposium sponsored by the Federal Reserve Bank of Kansas City. Jackson Hole, Wyoming. August 27, 1999.

Group of Ten. "The Macroeconomic and Financial Implications of Aging Populations." April 1998.

Hills, Carla,Peter Peterson, and Morris Goldstein. *Safeguarding Prosperity in Global Financial System, the Future International Architecture*. Report of an Independent Task Force Sponsored by the Council on Foreign Relations. Washington, D.C.: Institute for International Economics, 1999.

Kodres, Laura and Matthew Pritsker. "A Rational Expectations Model of Financial Contagion." FEDS Working Paper 1998-48. The Federal Reserve Board, 1998.

Kotlikoff, Laurence and Willi Leibfritz. "An International Comparison of Generational Accounting." In Auerbach, Alan; Laurence Kotlikoff, and Willi Leibfritz, eds., *Generational Accounting Around the World*. Chicago: University of Chicago Press, 1999.

Merrill Lynch Baby Boomer Retirement Index (SM), Douglas Bernheim, 1997.

Montalto, Catherine P. *Retirement Savings of American Households: Asset levels and Adequacy*. Report to the Consumer Federation of America and DirectAdvice.com. April 26, 2000.

Morgan Stanley Dean Witter. "Fatal Attraction: Asia's Rising Export Dependence on the U.S." April 19, 2000.

NBC News/*Wall Street Journal* Poll. *How Much Money Do You Expect to Receive from Social Security for Retirement*. Conducted by the polling organizations of Peter Hart (D) and Robert Teeter (R). Latest: March 4–7, 1999.

Prell, Michael J. "Economic Outlook." Remarks at the Charlotte Economics Club, Charlotte, North Carolina. January 14, 1999.

Summers, Lawrence H. "Priorities for a 21st Century Global Financial System." Remarks at Yale University, New Haven, Connecticut. September 22, 1999.

APPENDIX

Macroeconomic Advisors, LLC
Forecast and Simulation Results

Macroeconomic Advisors' Forecast
Assumes a 30 percent Decline in Equity Wealth

YEAR ON YEAR % CHANGE

	1998	1999	2000	2001	2002	2003	2004	2005	2006	2007	2008
Real GDP & Components											
Gross domestic product*	4.3	2.6	1.7	3.8	4.3	3.7	3.6	3.2	2.2	2.1	2.8
Composition of real GDP growth											
Final sales	4.4	2.5	1.9	3.5	3.9	3.5	3.5	3.1	2.3	2.2	2.7
Change in inventories	−0.3	0.1	−0.3	0.2	0.2	0.0	0.0	0.0	−0.1	−0.1	0.1
Personal consumption expenditures*	5.3	3.9	1.7	1.8	2.0	1.8	2.2	2.3	2.0	2.2	2.6
Fixed investment*	12.1	5.3	1.5	10.1	11.6	7.7	6.8	5.9	3.4	1.9	3.0
Inventory investment (bil chained (92) $)	57.4	32.3	31.1	34.0	55.6	63.7	60.5	60.8	53.1	40.5	41.2

(cont.)

Macroeconomic Advisors, LLC
Forecast and Simulation Results

Macroeconomic Advisors' Forecast
Assumes a 30 percent Decline in Equity Wealth (*cont.*)

Net exports (bil chained (92) $)	−238.2	−346.3	−364.7	−320.2	−264.6	−183.1	−99.0	−44.5	−15.0	3.6	23.7
Exports*	1.1	3.9	7.3	9.6	9.4	8.4	7.3	5.8	4.2	4.0	5.1
Imports*	9.7	13.0	3.8	3.8	3.6	1.5	1.9	3.0	2.8	3.0	3.7
Government consumption & gi*	1.6	1.4	1.7	1.2	1.2	1.6	1.8	1.8	1.8	1.9	2.0

(* Percentage change at annual rate)

Baseline - No Decline in Equity Wealth
Major Economic Indicators

YEAR ON YEAR % CHANGE

	1998	1999	2000	2001	2002	2003	2004	2005	2006	2007	2008
Real GDP & Components											
Gross domestic product*	4.3	3.4	2.8	1.8	2.1	3.0	4.3	3.8	2.5	2.0	2.5
Composition of real GDP growth											
Final sales	4.4	3.2	2.7	1.9	2.1	2.9	3.9	3.6	2.6	2.1	2.4
Change in inventories	−0.3	0.0	0.0	−0.1	0.0	0.1	0.2	0.1	−0.2	−0.2	0.0
Personal consumption expenditures*	5.3	5.1	3.3	1.6	1.4	1.7	2.5	2.2	1.5	1.5	1.8
Fixed investment*	12.1	7.0	3.6	2.7	3.6	4.7	8.2	7.8	4.5	2.7	3.6
Inventory investment (bil chained (92) $)	57.4	31.2	46.8	38.8	30.0	34.3	50.3	67.2	60.7	43.9	38.3
Net exports (bil chained (92) $)	−238.2	−350.8	−421.0	−412.4	−378.9	−313.4	−237.2	−159.9	−82.8	−20.9	22.9
Exports*	1.1	4.0	6.5	7.2	7.0	7.7	8.7	8.0	5.9	4.7	4.8
Imports*	9.7	14.4	7.1	3.6	2.5	1.5	2.6	2.4	1.3	1.5	2.5
Government consumption & gi*	1.6	1.4	1.6	0.9	1.1	1.7	1.8	1.6	1.6	1.7	1.9

(cont.)

Real Activity

	1623	1643	1382	1238	1345	1484	1644	1701	1619	1548	1548
Private housing starts (thous. Units)	1623	1643	1382	1238	1345	1484	1644	1701	1619	1548	1548
Light vehicle sales (mil. units)	15.6	16.7	16.0	15.1	14.6	-4.9	16.0	16.8	16.6	16.1	16.3
Light truck sales	7.3	8.0	7.6	7.2	6.9	7.1	7.6	7.9	7.9	7.6	7.7
Auto sales	8.2	8.7	8.4	8.0	7.7	7.8	8.4	8.8	8.7	8.5	8.6
Industrial production*	1.9	3.2	1.5	-0.2	0.1	2.1	4.2	2.8	0.4	-0.4	0.4
Capacity utilization (mfg, %)	80.8	79.8	80.1	78.6	76.7	76.0	77.7	80.4	81.3	80.4	79.6
Nonfarm payroll employment (mil.)	125.8	128.6	130.5	131.7	132.1	132.7	134.6	137.4	139.3	140.0	140.6
Unemployment rate (civilian, %)	4.5	4.2	4.3	4.9	5.8	6.4	6.1	5.1	4.8	5.2	5.6

Prices, Productivity, & Costs

	1623	1643	1382	1238	1345	1484	1644	1701	1619	1548	1548
GDP price index*	0.9	1.5	2.2	2.4	1.8	1.4	1.5	2.2	2.5	2.2	1.9
CPI (all urban)*	1.5	2.6	2.8	3.0	2.7	2.6	2.6	3.2	3.4	3.0	2.6
PPI (finished goods)*	-0.4	2.8	1.2	1.7	1.0	0.5	0.7	1.5	1.8	1.6	1.2
Compensation per hour*	4.1	4.6	4.5	4.5	4.1	3.6	3.7	4.1	4.3	4.2	3.9
Output per hour*	2.6	2.0	2.0	2.1	2.5	2.8	2.7	2.0	1.8	2.1	2.3
Unit labor cost*	1.5	2.5	2.5	2.4	1.5	0.8	0.9	2.1	2.5	2.1	1.6
Exchange rate (G-10 index)	98.8	99.8	95.7	95.0	93.2	87.6	83.1	81.6	82.1	82.5	81.9
Price of imported oil ($/barrel)	12.1	17.0	21.6	20.2	20.7	21.1	21.5	21.9	22.4	22.3	23.3

Selected Interest Rates

Federal funds rate	5.35	4.99	6.20	6.73	6.16	4.95	4.31	4.91	5.68	5.79	5.33
30-year Treasury bond yield	5.58	5.83	6.30	6.82	6.72	6.42	6.07	6.03	6.13	6.18	6.17
Aaa corporate bond yield	6.53	7.00	7.56	8.12	7.99	7.61	7.21	7.20	7.34	7.41	7.37

Incomes & Related Measures

Corporate profits w/iva & cccadj*	0.1	5.1	‾3.0	‾3.7	0.8	7.5	12.3	7.8	3.1	3.9	7.2
Real personal disposable income*	3.5	3.0	2.9	1.9	1.6	1.9	2.9	2.8	2.1	2.0	2.2
Personal saving rate (%)	0.5	‾1.4	‾2.3	‾2.2	‾1.9	‾1.7	‾1.4	‾0.9	‾0.3	0.2	0.5
HH net worth, equities (4-qtr % ch.)	0.4	35.3	0.0	0.0	0.0	0.0	0.0	0.0	0.0	0.0	0.0

Baseline - No Decline in Equity Wealth
Personal Income & Its Disposition

ANNUAL LEVELS

	1998	1999	2000	2001	2002	2003	2004	2005	2006	2007	2008
Personal income	7126.1	7491.6	7907.0	8308.6	8663.1	9024.5	9467.2	10010.6	10559.1	11067.3	11567.3
Wage & salary disbursements	4149.9	4418.4	4674.1	4897.4	5087.5	5287.5	5549.4	5881.5	6202.9	6477.6	6753.0
Other labor income	407.0	422.3	451.5	483.7	513.7	545.5	584.7	632.7	680.9	725.4	761.8
Proprietors' income with											
Iva & ccadj	577.2	608.7	641.1	667.6	695.1	735.0	789.5	841.2	880.2	914.7	957.2
Farm	28.8	18.1	17.4	18.3	18.9	20.2	22.3	24.5	25.9	26.9	28.1
Nonfarm	548.5	590.5	623.7	649.3	676.2	714.3	767.2	816.7	854.2	887.8	929.1
Rental income of persons with											
Iva & ccadj	162.6	170.4	177.9	185.9	194.3	203.1	212.2	221.7	231.7	242.1	253.0
Personal dividend income	263.1	274.6	291.6	299.9	298.6	305.2	328.7	359.0	379.4	392.6	411.3
Personal interest income	764.8	782.3	824.4	873.7	919.3	931.1	927.8	942.4	976.1	1011.1	1034.7
Transfers payments to persons	1149.0	1186.1	1239.3	1307.0	1382.4	1462.5	1543.6	1629.5	1732.0	1850.6	1964.3
Federal transfers to persons	803.4	826.3	859.6	903.6	953.8	1007.1	1059.6	1113.9	1181.3	1262.1	1335.1
Social Security benefits	369.6	379.5	391.5	404.7	419.9	435.0	450.9	466.9	487.1	511.7	522.9
Medicare	217.0	223.9	237.5	256.3	276.9	300.1	325.2	355.0	389.9	429.0	472.6
Unemployment insurance	19.5	19.4	20.5	24.0	29.5	33.6	33.1	29.1	28.3	31.6	35.3
Other	197.4	203.5	210.2	218.6	227.5	238.5	250.4	262.9	276.1	289.9	304.3

State & local transfers to persons	317.4	330.3	348.9	371.2	394.9	420.2	447.3	477.2	510.6	546.6	585.4
Medicaid	174.1	181.1	192.8	207.2	222.8	239.5	257.5	277.9	301.3	326.9	354.7
Other	143.3	149.2	156.1	163.9	172.1	180.8	189.8	199.3	209.2	219.7	230.7
Business transfers to persons	28.2	29.4	30.8	32.2	33.6	35.1	36.7	38.4	40.1	41.9	43.8
Less: Personal contributions for social insurance	347.4	371.2	392.9	411.6	427.7	445.3	468.7	497.4	524.1	546.8	568.1
Less: Personal tax & nontax payments	1098.3	1171.0	1241.9	1302.6	1353.3	1406.4	1476.5	1565.2	1650.6	1724.0	1798.4
Equals: Personal disposable income	6027.9	6320.5	6665.2	7006.1	7309.8	7618.1	7990.7	8445.4	8908.5	9343.3	9768.9
Less: Personal Outlays	6000.3	6407.3	6815.5	7157.0	7447.2	7748.0	8101.9	8522.4	8936.4	9325.6	9719.1
Personal consumption expend.	5807.9	6201.5	6598.3	6930.1	7210.0	7500.2	7842.9	8251.7	8653.6	9030.1	9410.2
Interest paid by persons	172.4	184.7	195.0	203.8	213.0	222.6	232.6	243.0	254.0	265.4	277.4
Personal transfer paymts. to ROW	19.9	21.1	22.1	23.1	24.2	25.3	26.4	27.6	28.8	30.1	31.5
Equals: Personal saving	27.6	-86.8	-150.4	-151.0	-137.4	-129.9	-111.2	-77.0	-27.9	17.7	49.8

(cont.)

Addenda:

Real disposable personal income	5348.5	5526.4	5690.4	585-5.7	5916.4	6016.9	6172.0	6350.5	6499.8	6626.6	6763.5
Personal saving rate (%)	0.5	−1.4	−2.3	−2.2	−1.9	−1.7	−1.4	−0.9	−0.3	0.2	0.5
Household Net Worth–Total	35.1	38.9	40.2	40.9	41.5	42.0	42.5	43.1	44.0	44.9	45.8
Household Net worth–Equities	12316	14936	15602	15602	15602	15602	15602	15602	15602	15602	15602

Copyright © 1999 Macroeconomic Advisers, LLC

Difference: Baseline v. 30% Decline
Major Economic Indicators

YEAR OVER YEAR % CHANGE

Real GDP & Components	1998	1999	2000	2001	2002	2003	2004	2005	2006	2007	2008
Gross domestic product*	0.0	-0.8	-1.1	2.0	2.2	0.7	-0.7	-0.6	-0.3	0.1	0.3
Composition of real GDP growth											
Final sales	0.0	0.0	0.0	0.0	0.0	0.0	0.0	0.0	0.0	0.0	0.0
Change in inventories	0.0	-0.8	-0.8	1.5	1.8	0.7	-0.4	-0.5	-0.3	0.0	0.3
Personal consumption expenditures*	0.0	0.1	-0.3	0.4	0.3	-0.1	-0.3	-0.1	0.0	0.1	0.1
Fixed investment*	0.0	-1.1	-1.6	0.2	0.6	0.1	-0.3	0.1	0.4	0.7	0.8
Inventory investment	0.0	-1.7	-2.1	7.5	8.1	2.9	-1.5	-1.9	-1.2	-0.8	-0.7
(bil chained (92) $)	0.0	1.2	-15.7	-4.8	25.5	29.4	10.1	-6.4	-7.6	-3.4	2.9
Net exports (bil chained (92) $)	0.0	4.5	56.3	92.3	114.3	130.4	138.1	115.4	67.8	24.5	0.8
Exports*	0.0	0.0	0.8	2.4	2.5	0.7	-1.3	-2.2	-1.7	-0.7	0.3
Imports*	0.0	-1.5	-3.3	0.2	1.0	0.0	-0.7	0.6	1.4	1.5	1.2
Government consumption & gi*	0.0	0.0	0.1	0.3	0.1	-0.1	0.0	0.2	0.2	0.2	0.1

(cont.)

Real Activity

Private housing starts (thous. units)	0.0	-41.2	-38.9	230.0	276.4	122.8	-83.5	-169.4	-120.0	-10.4	82.2
Light vehicle sales (mil. units)	0.0	-0.2	-1.3	-0.1	0.9	1.0	0.2	-0.2	-0.1	0.4	0.7
Light truck sales	0.0	-0.1	-0.6	-0.1	0.4	0.5	0.1	-0.1	0.0	0.2	0.3
Auto sales	0.0	-0.1	-0.7	-0.1	0.5	0.5	0.1	-0.1	0.0	0.2	0.4
Industrial production*	0.0	-0.9	-2.2	3.0	3.5	1.2	-1.0	-1.0	-0.5	0.1	0.5
Capacity utilization (mfg, %)	0.0	-0.2	-2.4	-1.3	1.7	3.6	3.4	2.5	2.0	1.9	2.2
Nonfarm payroll employment (mil.)	0.0	-0.1	-1.6	-2.0	-0.1	1.5	1.5	0.6	0.1	-0.2	0.0
Unemployment rate (civilian, %)	0.0	0.1	1.0	1.2	-0.1	-1.1	-1.0	-0.4	0.0	0.3	0.3

Prices, Productivity, & Costs

GDP price index*	0.0	0.0	-0.6	-1.2	-0.5	0.2	0.2	-0.2	-0.3	-0.4	-0.3
CPI (all urban)*	0.0	0.0	-0.4	-0.9	-0.3	0.3	0.0	-0.5	-0.6	-0.5	-0.3
PPI (finished goods)*	0.0	0.0	-0.8	-1.4	-0.6	0.2	0.2	-0.1	-0.3	-0.4	-0.3
Compensation per hour*	0.0	0.0	-0.6	-1.0	-0.3	0.3	0.4	0.2	0.1	0.0	-0.1
Output per hour*	0.0	-0.5	0.6	1.3	0.4	-0.1	0.1	0.3	0.2	0.3	0.2
Unit labor cost*	0.0	0.5	-1.2	-2.2	-0.7	0.4	0.3	0.0	-0.2	-0.3	-0.3
Exchange rate (G-10 index)	0.0	-0.1	-3.2	-7.9	-8.9	-6.9	-3.9	-1.2	0.1	-0.2	-1.0
Price of imported oil ($/barrel)	0.0	0.0	0.0	0.0	0.0	0.0	0.0	0.0	0.0	0.0	0.0

Selected Interest Rates

Federal funds rate	0.0	-0.2	-1.9	-3.1	-2.7	-1.2	-0.2	-0.1	-0.4	-0.9	-1.2
30-year Treasury bond yield	0.0	0.0	-0.7	-1.5	-1.6	-1.4	-1.1	-0.7	-0.5	-0.5	-0.6
Aaa corporate bond yield	0.0	0.0	-0.9	-1.7	-1.9	-1.6	-1.1	-0.8	-0.5	-0.5	-0.7

Incomes & Related Measures

Corporate profits w/iva & cccadj*	0.0	-3.9	0.7	13.0	7.7	-2.3	-6.7	-5.3	-4.1	-2.1	0.0
Real personal disposable income*	0.0	-0.3	-1.3	0.8	1.2	0.4	-0.2	0.1	0.3	0.4	0.4
Personal saving rate (%)	0.0	0.2	0.9	1.2	1.9	2.3	2.5	2.6	2.5	2.3	2.0
HH net worth, equities (4-qtr% ch.)	0.0	-40.6	0.0	0.0	0.0	0.0	0.0	0.0	0.0	0.0	0.0

Differences: Baseline v. 30% Decline
Personal Income & Its Disposition

ANNUAL LEVELS

	1998	1999	2000	2001	2002	2003	2004	2005	2006	2007	2008
Personal income	0.0	-6.6	-114.4	-179.6	-125.3	-45.8	-32.9	-72.8	-110.1	-134.8	-138.1
Wage & salary disbursements	0.0	-4.6	-83.4	-127.3	-71.9	-5.4	0.6	-32.8	-61.4	-79.8	-81.7
Other labor income	0.0	-0.4	-8.1	-12.5	-7.2	-0.5	0.1	-3.5	-6.7	-8.9	-9.2
Proprietors' income with	0.0	0.0	0.0	0.0	0.0	0.0	0.0	0.0	0.0	0.0	0.0
Iva & ccadj	0.0	-0.4	4.1	24.3	42.9	44.4	26.8	6.3	-2.4	0.8	9.4
Farm	0.0	0.0	0.3	1.4	2.7	3.1	2.4	1.3	0.6	0.6	1.1
Nonfarm	0.0	-0.4	3.8	22.9	40.2	41.3	24.5	5.0	-3.0	0.2	8.3
Rental income of persons with	0.0	0.0	0.0	0.0	0.0	0.0	0.0	0.0	0.0	0.0	0.0
Iva & ccadj	0.0	0.0	0.0	0.0	0.0	0.0	0.0	0.0	0.0	0.0	0.0
Personal dividend income	0.0	-0.5	-9.7	1.3	28.9	43.1	38.6	27.1	15.4	6.0	1.9
Personal interest income	0.0	-1.4	-27.8	-76.3	-111.1	-107.8	-81.3	-58.2	-43.4	-37.2	-39.2
Transfers payments to persons	0.0	0.3	4.3	2.3	-9.1	-16.4	-15.3	-13.4	-16.2	-21.3	-24.4
Federal transfers to persons	0.0	0.3	4.3	2.3	-9.1	-16.4	-15.3	-13.4	-16.2	-21.3	-24.4
Social Security benefits	0.0	0.0	0.0	-0.7	-4.2	-6.4	-5.8	-5.2	-7.4	-10.7	-10.9
Medicare	0.0	0.0	-0.4	-2.4	-4.0	-4.1	-3.9	-5.4	-8.2	-11.4	-14.4
Unemployment insurance	0.0	0.3	4.6	5.3	-0.8	-5.3	-5.6	-2.8	-0.6	0.8	0.9
Other	0.0	0.0	0.0	0.0	0.0	0.0	0.0	0.0	0.0	0.0	0.0

State & local transfers										
to persons	0.0	0.0	0.0	0.0	0.0	0.0	0.0	0.0	0.0	0.0
Medicaid	0.0	0.0	0.0	0.0	0.0	0.0	0.0	0.0	0.0	0.0
Other	0.0	0.0	0.0	0.0	0.0	0.0	0.0	0.0	0.0	0.0
Business transfers to persons	0.0	0.0	0.0	0.0	0.0	0.0	0.0	0.0	0.0	0.0
Less: Personal contributions	0.0	0.0	0.0	0.0	0.0	0.0	0.0	0.0	0.0	0.0
for social insurance	0.0	−0.4	−6.2	−8.1	−2.3	3.2	2.4	−1.6	−4.5	−5.6	−5.1
Less: Personal tax & nontax payments	0.0	−1.3	−22.6	−33.1	−17.4	0.5	1.8	−7.6	−15.6	−20.6	−21.1
Equals: Personal disposable income	0.0	−5.4	−91.8	−146.5	−107.9	−46.2	−34.7	−65.2	−94.5	−114.3	−117.0
Less: Personal Outlays	0.0	−17.0	−153.2	−233.6	−245.2	−220.5	−234.3	−280.5	−314.9	−325.2	−306.8
Personal consumption expend.	0.0	−17.0	−153.2	−233.6	−245.2	−220.5	−234.3	−280.5	−314.9	−325.2	−306.8
Interest paid by persons	0.0	0.0	0.0	0.0	0.0	0.0	0.0	0.0	0.0	0.0	0.0
Personal transfer paymts. to ROW	0.0	0.0	0.0	0.0	0.0	0.0	0.0	0.0	0.0	0.0	0.0
Equals: Personal saving	0.0	11.7	61.4	87.1	137.3	174.3	199.7	215.3	220.3	211.0	189.7

Addenda:											
Real disposable personal income	0.0	0.0	0.0	0.0	0.0	0.0	0.0	0.0	0.0	0.0	0.0
Personal saving rate (%)	0.0	-4.7	-69.4	-70.5	-3.7	43.3	43.5	43.9	63.0	90.5	121.4
Household Net Worth–Total	0.0	0.2	0.9	1.2	1.9	2.3	2.5	2.6	2.5	2.3	2.0
Household Net worth–Equities	0.0	-1.2	-4.7	-5.0	-5.1	-5.0	-4.7	-4.6	-4.5	-4.4	-4.3
	0.0	-1170.2	-4680.7	-4680.7	-4680.7	-4580.7	-4680.7	-4680.7	-4680.7	-4680.7	-4680.7

Reforming and Deepening Mexico's Financial Markets

A Paper from the Project on Development, Trade and International Finance

Florencio Lopez-de-Silanes

A Council on Foreign Relations Paper

Reforming and Deepening Mexico's Financial Markets[1]

by Florencio Lopez-de-Silanes

INTRODUCTION

Throughout the world the role of the state is being redefined to accommodate the needs of a market economy. Institution-building is becoming widely accepted as the principal means of fulfilling this role. As in other emerging markets, the policy process in Mexico has gone beyond macroeconomic stability, and in the next decade will be critically focused on institution-building. This includes development of financial institutions such as banks and stock exchanges, development of the legal infrastructure supporting business, and creation of regulatory mechanisms compatible with best world practice.

In this paper, I focus on a central aspect of long-term growth: the development of capital markets so that firms can gain access to the external funding needed to undertake investments. The establishment of self-sustainable capital markets has gained particular importance in Mexico as the rate of integration into the global economy has speeded up. Without self-sustainable capital markets, local firms will find it hard to survive, because they will not be able to secure the funding needed to reach the appropriate scale for international competition.

In this paper, I compare Mexico with the rest of the world and present the empirical evidence on the relevance of legal institutions to large capital markets. Specifically, I am interested in why there are large differences in the size,

[1]Please send comments to Prof. Florencio Lopez-de-Silanes (f_lopezdesilanes@harvard.edu or Littauer Room #110, John F. Kennedy School of Government, Harvard University, Cambridge, MA 02138.)

breadth, and valuation of capital markets. Why, for example, are equity markets so much larger in South Africa than in Mexico or Peru? Why do many companies go public in India and Hong Kong every year, while only a handful of firms go public in Mexico or Turkey? Why do countries like New Zealand have large credit markets with hundreds of firms issuing public bonds while Mexico and the Philippines do not?

In a simple Modigliani-Miller framework the size of capital markets is determined only by the cash flows that accrue to investors.[2] Therefore, the size of capital markets should be roughly proportional to Gross National Product (GNP). To explain the large discrepancies in the size of financial markets across countries with similar GNP, we need to recognize that securities are more than the cash flows they represent, because they entitle investors to exercise certain rights. Shares not only entitle investors to dividend payments, but also to exercise control over management through the voting process. Similarly, debt not only entitles creditors to receive interest payments, but also to regain their collateral in the event the firm goes bankrupt. The separation between ownership and control can have a large effect on the size of capital markets once we depart from the Modigliani and Miller assumptions and allow for the existence of agency costs. To take an extreme view, outside equity would have no value if shareholders did not have control rights to force managers to pay out dividends. In the same vein, creditors would be unwilling to lend money at any interest rate if their control rights did not allow them to punish debtors who default on their financial obligations. Both financiers and management would benefit from the elimination of the agency conflict if they could write a complete contract that specified what

---

[2]Franco Modigliani and Merton Miller, "The Cost of Capital, Corporation Finance, and the Theory of Investment," *American Economic Review* 48 (June 1958), pp. 261–97.

managers should do with the funds and how they would give funds back to investors under all potential circumstances. Of course, a complete contract cannot be implemented in practice, making it necessary for management to have a level of discretion.[3] Management discretion, although a cost-effective way of dealing with the separation of ownership and control, can unfortunately be used to expropriate financing through outright theft, transfer-pricing, or asset-stripping.

A legal approach based on the agency model could, in principle, explain why some countries have much larger capital markets than others, because legal protection for investors differs enormously from country to country. For example, shareholder rights in Mexico differ greatly from the shareholder rights in the United States; furthermore, the shareholder's recourse to redress is likely to be significantly weaker. The legal approach predicts larger capital markets in countries where agency costs are reined in by the law and the institutions support their enforcement.[4]

I summarize the cross-country evidence on the influence of institutions on capital market development and propose an agenda for reforming Mexico's financial markets.

---

[3]Sanford Grossman and Oliver Hart, "The Costs and Benefits of Ownership: A Theory of Vertical and Lateral Integration," *Journal of Political Economy* 94 (1986), pp. 175–202.

[4]The study "Law and Finance," by Rafael La Porta, Florencio Lopez-de-Silanes, Andrei Shleifer, and Robert W. Vishny, in *Journal of Political Economy,* Volume 106, Number 6, (December 1998), pp. 1113–1155, systematically assess the rights of investors as well as the quality of their enforcement for forty-nine countries. The previous article, as well as two other articles by the same authors cited in this footnote, relate legal institutions to the size and breadth of external capital markets as well as to corporate ownership concentration around the world. See "Legal Determinants of External Finance," Journal of Finance LII (July 1997), pp. 1131–50, and "Corporate Ownership Around the World," Journal of Finance, Vol. LIV, (April 1999), pp. 471-517.

The paper is divided into four sections after the introduction. The first section ("Legal Protection for Investors") describes the differences in legal protection for shareholders and creditors in Mexico and a cross-section of forty-eight other countries. Because investor rights are not only determined by laws, the following section ("Enforcement of Laws") compares the quality of the legal enforcement and accounting standards across nations. The ultimate question is whether countries with poor investor protections actually do suffer. If laws and their enforcement matter, then countries that offer entrepreneurs better terms of external finance would have both higher-valued and broader capital markets. The theory also predicts that countries offering entrepreneurs better terms should have widely held corporations. "Consequences of Investor Protection" reviews the evidence on the consequences of poor investor protection for Mexico. This section also compares external finance and ownership concentration across countries as a function of the origin of their laws, the quality of legal investor protections, and the quality of law enforcement. The evidence shows that countries with weaker investor protection suffer greater exchange-rate depreciation and stock market declines when hit by a shock. Through its effects on capital markets, investor protection also influences the real economy.

The section on "Reforms for Deepening Mexico's Financial Markets" attempts to answer several questions: What is the evidence on capital-markets reform and its success? Can changes in specific laws significantly affect institutions? Is it particularly effective to change corporation laws, securities regulations, or bankruptcy law? Do these measures need to take account of the efficiency of the judicial system? After answering these questions, the section proposes an agenda of reforms to develop and strengthen Mexico's stock and credit markets.

The final section, entitled "Conclusions and Policy Implications," discusses the policy implications of the results. Capital markets are a key ingredient for sustainable development. Therefore, the reform of financial-markets regulations should be included among the key areas to foster the integration of Mexico into the North American Free Trade Agreement (NAFTA). As the evidence from the European Community shows, successful economic integration of lower per-capita-income countries like Spain, Portugal, or Greece needs to be tied to mechanisms that foster institutional development. It is only through the development of efficient institutions that these countries can secure the basis for sustainable long-run development.

LEGAL PROTECTION FOR INVESTORS

The December 1998 study by La Porta, Lopez-de-Silanes, Shleifer, and Vishny assembled a data set covering legal rules pertaining to the rights of investors, and to the quality of enforcement of these rules, for forty-nine countries with publicly-traded companies. Laws tend not to be written from scratch, but rather to be transplanted–voluntarily or coincidentally–from a few legal families or traditions. In general, *commercial* laws come from two broad traditions: common law and civil law. Most English-speaking countries belong to the common-law tradition based on the British Company Act. The rest of the world belongs to the civil-law tradition, derivative of Roman law, which has three main families: French, based on the Napoleonic Code of 1804; German, based on Bismarck's Code of 1896; and Scandinavian, which legal scholars describe as less derivative of Roman law but "distinct" from the other two civil families.

The common-law family includes former British colonies, such as the United States and Canada, and other nations such as Thailand and Israel which modeled their initial corporation laws on the laws of England. There are eighteen common-law countries in the sample. The French legal family includes France, Spain, Portugal, and their colonies. There are twenty-one French legal origin countries in our sample, including Mexico and eight other countries in Latin America. The German tradition has had less influence, and we have only six countries in this family: Austria, Germany, Japan, South Korea, Switzerland, and Taiwan. Finally, the Scandinavian family includes the four Nordic countries of Denmark, Finland, Norway, and Sweden.

There are numerous differences among company and bankruptcy laws in different countries. We focus on those basic rules that scholars believe to be essential to corporate governance.[5] Furthermore, it is beneficial to restrict our attention to those basic rules that are pro-investor.

Shareholder Rights

Shareholders have residual rights over the cash flows of the firm. The right to vote is the shareholders' main source of power. This right to vote in the general meeting to elect directors and make major corporate decisions guarantees shareholders that management will channel the firm's cash flows to shareholders through the payment of dividends rather than divert the funds to pay themselves higher compensation, undertake poor acquisitions or take other measures not in the interest of shareholders. Therefore, voting rights and the rights that support voting mechanisms are the defining features of equity.

---

[5]See Paul Vishny, Guide to International Commerce Law (New York: McGraw-Hill, 1994); Michelle White, "The Costs of Corporate Bankruptcy: the U.S.-European Comparison," manuscript (Ann Arbor: University of Michigan, Department of Economics, 1993); and, Multinational Commercial Insolvency (Chicago, IL: American Bar Association, 1989 and 1993). Also see observers such as Institutional Shareholder Services, Inc., Proxy Voting Guidelines for several countries (Washington, DC: ISS Global Proxy Services, 1994) and Investor Responsibility Research Center, Proxy Voting Guide (Washington, D.C.: Global Shareholder Service, Investor Responsibility Research Center, 1994).

Appendix A provides a detailed description of all the variables used in this paper, and Table 1 presents the evidence on shareholder rights for the cross-section of forty-nine countries. A useful way to begin the discussion of shareholder rights is to assume the role of an investor in a U.S. firm and then become an investor in a Mexican corporation. This also illustrates the differences between a legal systems based on English common law and on French civil law.

The first column of Table 1 shows that not all U.S. shareholders have the right to vote. That is probably a bad thing, because when votes are tightly linked to capital contributions, it is more difficult to control a company by having just a small fraction of the equity. Yet, as it turns out, one-share-one-vote rules are uncommon everywhere—including Mexico and Canada.

The next six columns of Table 1 provide different measures of how strongly the law governing corporations protects minority shareholders against oppression by managers or dominant shareholders. These rights are thus labeled as "anti-director" rights. The first four anti-director rights measure how easy it is for an investor to exercise any voting rights that she may have. Shareholders in the United States will receive proxy statements two weeks in advance of the shareholders' meeting with detailed information on the items to be discussed at the meeting. They do not need to show up in person at the meeting—they can mail their proxy vote instead. The shares of investors who have indicated that they will participate in the shareholders' meeting will not be blocked in the days prior to the meeting, because the freedom to trade shares before shareholders' meetings is an important right for people who may want to form alliances to challenge management proposals. Directors are not necessarily chosen one at a time through a majority vote, and thus shareholders are entitled to have proportional representation or cumulative voting for directors. Our hypothetical investor has the right to call an extraordinary shareholders meeting (ESM) to consider a resolution if he owns 10 percent of the share capital.

The next right listed in Table 1 measures the protection of minority shareholders against a particular type of expropriation: issuing shares at favorable prices to, for example, associates of the controlling shareholders. Out of the six rights in this table, this is the only one that shareholders in U.S. corporations do not have. The law does not guarantee shareholders a preemptive right to buy new issues of stock in their holdings. Finally, U.S. investors who feel they have been hurt by the decisions of the majority can seek redress through the courts. When the court believes that oppression has indeed taken place, it may order that the oppressed members' shares be bought out at a fair price or that the firm remedy the matters at issue. More generally, best-practice countries such as the United States provide legal mechanisms for the protection of oppressed minorities. To give just another example, a dissenting investor in Chile has the right to request–at the meeting–that the firm buy back his shares at the market price prevailing before the meeting.

In Mexico, as in the United States, not all shares are endowed with the same right to vote. However, unlike in the United States, investors in Mexico are not usually sent detailed information about the agenda when they are notified of forthcoming shareholders' meetings. Only by going to the meeting will they know what is discussed. In fact, attending the meeting–or designating someone to do so in their place–is the only way in which they can vote; proxy by mail is not allowed. Furthermore, announcing that they intend to vote their shares will cause them to be blocked, making it impossible for them to trade the shares in the days surrounding the meeting. At the meeting, shareholders vote on the slate of directors proposed by management and are not allowed proportional representation on the board. Investors in Mexican firms must have at least 33 percent of share capital to have a resolution considered by the ESM. Fortunately, investors in Mexico do have a preemptive right that prevents dilution. Regrettably, this is the only right (of those that we collect) that shareholders in Mexico have, because they do not have any legal recourse against the decisions of the majority. To summarize, Table 1 paints a very bleak picture of shareholder rights in Mexico.

A convenient way of summarizing shareholder rights is to aggregate anti-director rights into an index, adding 1 if the corporation law protects minority shareholders, and a zero otherwise. For the case of the percentage of share capital needed to call an ESM, we give a 1 to those countries where this percentage is at or below the world median of 10 percent. When we add up these six anti-director rights scores, the United States and Canada have a score of 5 while Mexico's score is only 1.

A corroboration of the findings in this table can be exemplified by the opinions of various institutions that advise institutional investors around the world. As Table 2 illustrates, associations such as Investor Responsibility Research Center and Institutional Shareholders Services argue that corporate practices of Mexican firms are not best-practice. (See Table 2 for some examples.)

The comparison between Mexico and the United States illustrates the broad findings of Table 1: Shareholder protection in common-law countries is significantly better than in French civil-law countries. While the incidence of one-share-one-vote rules, cumulative voting for directors, and preemptive rights are not statistically different across English and French legal systems, the remaining four measures show marked differences. Common-law countries more frequently allow shareholders to exercise their vote by mail than French-origin countries (39 percent vs. 5 percent). No common-law country blocks shares before shareholders' meetings, while 57 percent of French civil-law countries do. On average, 9 percent of the share capital is sufficient to call an ESM in common-law countries, whereas 15 percent of share capital is required in French civil-law nations. Finally, 94 percent of common-law countries have an oppressed minority mechanism in place, while only 29 percent of French-origin countries do. The differences between English- and French-origin countries are captured in the anti-director's index, which has an average of 4.00 for common-law countries and only 2.33 for French civil-law nations (t-statistic of 4.73).

German civil-law countries share the French-origin lack of protection of shareholder rights. Although German-origin countries have a significantly higher incidence of oppressed minority mechanisms, they block shares more often than French countries do. The average anti-director scores for the German and French families are the same (2.33). Finally, Scandinavian-origin countries, although inferior to common-law countries in shareholder protection, are the best within the civil-law tradition. The average Scandinavian anti-director rights score is 3. In short, relative to the rest of the world, common-law countries have the package of laws most protective of shareholders.

Creditor Rights

In principle one would like to measure the ability of creditors to use the law to force companies to meet their credit commitments. In practice, creditor rights are difficult to assess for two main reasons. First, most countries have in place both reorganization and liquidation procedures that are used with varying frequency and may confer different levels of protection to creditors. For example, a country may be very protective of creditors if it offers strong rights in liquidation and weak protection in reorganization, provided that the reorganization procedure is seldom used. Second, creditors, unlike shareholders, do not have a homogeneous claim against the firm–i.e., they differ in the priority of their claim. As a result, it is possible that measures that favor some creditors (e.g., unsecured creditors) may hurt others (e.g., secured creditors).

To undertake a cross-country analysis of creditor rights, Table 3 scores creditor rights in both reorganization and liquidation, and adds up the scores to create a creditor-rights index, in part because almost all countries rely to some extent on both procedures. In assessing creditor rights below, the table also takes the perspective of senior secured creditors, in part for concreteness, and in part because much of the debt in the world has that character. Once again, to illustrate differences between English common-law countries and French civil-law countries, we describe the data by comparing the rights of an investor who has given credit to a firm incorporated in the United Kingdom, considered best-practice in terms of creditor rights in the world, versus the rights of an investor who has given credit to a firm incorporated in Mexico.

Suppose that a debtor to whom the creditor has lent money files a petition for reorganization in London. The court will then notify the creditor, who will have two weeks to oppose reorganization. A secured creditor who chooses to oppose a reorganization petition has the right to appoint a so-called *trustee* to decide what will happen to the firm. The important thing is that the debtor does not have the right to unilaterally file for reorganization. Even if the borrower's petition for reorganization is accepted, there is not an "automatic stay" that prevents a secured creditor from gaining access to her collateral. In addition, secured creditors who choose not to withdraw their collateral are paid first in the event that reorganization fails and liquidation ensues. Finally, the bargaining position of creditors is strengthened by the fact that pending the resolution of the bankruptcy procedure, the old management team will not continue to run the firm.

Rather, a trustee appointed by the creditors would be in charge of the firm's day-to-day operations.

Now suppose that a debtor to whom the creditor has lent money files a petition for reorganization in Mexico City.[6] Creditors have no say in whether the firm's reorganization petition is accepted or declined. But if the petition is accepted, secured creditors cannot pull their collateral out of the firm; rather, an "automatic stay" is triggered by the acceptance of the reorganization petition. Secured creditors have additional worries, because if liquidation takes place, they are not paid first. Rather the state and the firm's employees take priority. The creditors' predicament is aggravated by the fact that the debtor not only writes the reorganization proposal, but continues to run the firm pending the resolution of the bankruptcy procedure, which will likely take several years.

As with shareholders, one way to summarize the difference in creditor rights across countries is to create an index that adds 1 when the pro-investor right is granted by law, and zero otherwise. This index is shown in the last column of Table 3 and takes a value of 4 for the United Kingdom and zero for Mexico. Again, as with shareholder rights, the picture for creditor rights in Mexico is substantially bleaker than in the United Kingdom.

Although the Mexico-U.K. comparison is extreme, common-law countries in general offer creditors stronger legal protections against managers. Table 3 shows that all four measures of creditor rights are weaker for countries of French legal origin by an amount that is statistically significant. 72 percent of common-law countries place

---

[6]The rights coded in this document are those of the Mexican Bankruptcy and Reorganization Law that was in effect until May 2000. In that month, the Mexican Congress approved a new law that will change some creditor rights. For our purposes, which is to measure the effect of laws on the development of Mexico's debt markets, it is correct to codify the law in effect for the last thirty years, because the rights in that law are the ones generating the outcomes.

restrictions on managers seeking court protection from
creditors, compared to only 42 percent of French civil-law
nations. The incidence of having no automatic stay on
assets is 72 percent in common-law countries versus only 26
percent in French civil-law nations. Relatively fewer
countries of French legal origin (65 percent) assure that
secured creditors are paid first than countries of English
legal origin (89 percent). Finally, only 26 percent of French
civil-law countries remove managers in reorganization,
compared with 78 percent of countries of the common-law
family. In brief, the average aggregate creditor rights score
is 3.11 for English origin and a mere 1.58 for French origin.

As Table 3 shows, the United States and Canada do
not score particularly high in terms of creditor rights. This
is one of the main reasons why various groups have
repeatedly demanded a reform of current bankruptcy laws:
it is thought that Chapter 11 (reorganization) provides too
many advantages to debtors and fails to protect creditors. As
we will see below, the problem of poor creditor protection
in terms of legal rights in the United States and Canada
might be alleviated with good judicial enforcement, which
is not the case for Mexico.

German legal origin countries are relatively more pro-
creditor than French civil-law countries, averaging an
aggregate score of 2.33. The differences between German-
and French-origin countries are particularly significant in
liquidation measures: 67 percent of German civil-law
countries have no automatic stay and always pay secured
creditors first. Finally, countries of Scandinavian origin
always pay secured creditors first, but always allow
management to stay pending reorganization. In three out of
four cases they impose an automatic stay on assets and
place restrictions on reorganization. As a result, the
aggregate creditor-rights index for countries of Scandinavian
legal origin has a value of 2.00–a difference that is not

statistically significant from the 1.58 value for countries of French legal origin.

To summarize the results thus far, bankruptcy laws differ a great deal across countries. In particular, they differ because they come from different legal families. Relatively speaking, common-law countries protect creditors the most, and French civil-law countries—Mexico in particular—protect them the least. German and Scandinavian civil-law countries are in the middle. The one exception is the strong protections that German civil-law countries afford secured creditors.

ENFORCEMENT OF LAWS

Legal rules are only one element of investor protection; the enforcement of these rules may be equally or even more important. If good laws are not enforced, they cannot be effective. Likewise, investors may enjoy high levels of protection despite bad laws if an efficient judiciary system can redress expropriations by management. In this way, strong legal enforcement may serve as a substitute for weak rules.

Table 4 presents several categories for the quality of enforcement of laws in different countries. These measures are collected by private credit-risk agencies for the use of foreign investors interested in doing business in the respective countries. (The agencies include Business International Corporation and Political Risk Services). Table 4 shows three measures: efficiency of the judicial system, rule of law, and corruption. The first two of these proxies pertain to law enforcement, while the last one captures the government's general attitude toward business. In addition to these measures, the table also shows data on the quality of accounting standards of publicly-traded firms in different countries. Accounting is central to corporate governance, as it may be difficult to assess management performance without reliable accounting standards. More broadly, cash flows may be very difficult to verify in countries with poor accounting standards, consequently, the menu of financial contracts available to investors may be substantially narrower in such countries. The index of accounting standards in Table 4 is provided by the Center for International Financial Analysis and Research based on examination of company reports of firms in each country. It is available for forty-one of the forty-nine countries in the sample.

Compared with the English-origin average, as well as with Canada and the United States, Mexico has very weak legal institutions and accounting standards. Mexico's scores for all enforcement variables are below the world's average. In fact, Mexico ranks between the thirtieth and fortieth in the world, from top to bottom, for these measures. Mexico shares poor enforcement with the rest of the French legal family which has the weakest quality of legal enforcement and accounting standards. Note that rule of law is the only measure where differences in means between common law and French legal origin are not statistically significant. Scandinavian countries have the strongest enforcement mechanisms, with German civil-law and common-law countries close behind. Common-law countries, although behind Scandinavian nations, are still ahead of the French civil-law countries.

These results do not support the conclusion that the quality of law enforcement substitutes or compensates for the quality of laws. An investor in Mexico–and more generally in a French civil-law country–is poorly protected by both the laws and the system that enforces them. On average, the converse is true for an investor in a common-law country. Poor enforcement and accounting standards aggravate, rather than cure, the difficulties faced by investors in French civil-law countries. The weak scores obtained by Mexico in shareholder and creditor rights may actually understate the severity of the corporate governance problem in Mexican corporations.

CONSEQUENCES OF INVESTOR PROTECTION

There are at least two reasons why legal institutions may have no effect on the pattern of external financing of firms. First, laws may not be necessary to support external financing if, for example, companies keep their promises not because they are forced to but because they want to build a good reputation to facilitate their access to capital markets.[7] Their reputations unravel if the gains from cheating ever exceed the value of keeping external financing open, because investors, once they employ inductive reasoning, would never extend financing to such a firm to begin with.

Second, poor laws and their enforcement may have no real consequences if firms can easily opt out of the laws of their legal jurisdictions. Easterbrook and Fischel question whether legal rules are binding in most instances, because entrepreneurs can offer better investor rights, when it is optimal to do so, through corporate charters that effectively serve as contracts between entrepreneurs and investors.[8] In practice, however, opting out may be costly both for firms that need to write non-standard contracts and for investors who need to study them. In addition, courts may be unwilling or unable to enforce non-standard contracts, further limiting the scope for opting out.

Alternatively, if legal institutions matter, ownership concentration should be higher in countries with poor

---

[7]Douglas Diamond, "Reputation Acquisition in Debt Markets," *Journal of Political Economy* 97 (1989), pp. 828–62, and "Debt Maturity Structure and Liquidity Risk," *Quarterly Journal of Economics* 106 (1991), pp. 1027–54; see also Armando Gomes, "The Dynamics of Stock Prices, Manager Ownership, and Private Benefits of Control," manuscript (Harvard University, 1996).

[8]Frank Easterbrook and Daniel Fischel, "The Economic Structure of Corporate Law" (Cambridge, Mass.: Harvard University Press, 1991).

investor protection than in countries with strong
protections for investors for at least two reasons: First,
agency problems may call for large-scale shareholders to
monitor managers and thus prevent or minimize
expropriation. Second, minority shareholders may be
unwilling to pay high prices for securities in countries with
weak legal protection. At the same time, entrepreneurs will
be more reluctant to offer shares at discounted prices, thus
resulting in higher ownership concentration as well as
smaller and narrower markets for external equity.[9] Similarly,
bad creditor rights may have analogous price and quantity
effects on debt markets. In other words, if laws do not
protect the rights of creditors, debt markets may be small
because creditors may demand high interest rates.
Moreover, firms may be reluctant to borrow from arm's-
length sources in such conditions.

Ultimately, the question of whether legal institutions
matter is fundamentally empirical: If opting out were cheap
and simple, the patterns of ownership and external finance
of firms would not be affected by differences in legal
institutions across countries. Accordingly, in this section,
we examine two types of evidence regarding the influence
of legal institutions on external finance: ownership
concentration, and the size and breadth of capital markets.
Table 5 summarizes the results.

---

[9]Ownership concentration per se may be efficient, because the
existence of large-scale shareholders monitoring management reduces
the agency problem between management and shareholders; see
Michael Jensen and William Meckling, "Theory of the Firm: Managerial
Behavior, Agency Costs, and Ownership Structure," Journal of Financial
Economics 3 (October 1976), pp. 305–60; and Andrei Shleifer and
Robert W. Vishny, "Large Shareholders and Corporate Control,"
Journal of Political Economy 94 (June 1986), pp. 461–88. But large-
scale concentration comes at a cost, because it creates another agency
problem: the expropriation of minority shareholders' stakes by large-
scale shareholders. An additional cost of heavily concentrated
ownership is that the core investors are not diversified.

Ownership Concentration

The first striking result of Table 5 is that in the world as a whole, dispersed ownership is a myth: In a typical top–ten firm in the world, 45 percent of the common shares are held by the three largest shareholders.[10] The second result is that those countries with weaker investor protections have larger share ownership concentration. In particular, countries of the French legal family have an average ownership concentration of 55 percent. Statistically this number is significantly higher than the mean for the rest of the world and for the mean for each of the other three legal families individually.

Like the rest of the French origin, Mexico has highly concentrated ownership. With the exception of Chile, which has strong shareholder rights, all Latin American countries in the sample have higher ownership concentration than the world mean. After Greece and Colombia (68 percent), Mexico has the third-largest ownership concentration level in the world (67 percent). In sum, these data indicate that Mexico has unusually high ownership concentration, possibly as an adaptation to weak legal protection.

The Size and Breadth of Capital Markets

Several interesting patterns emerge from looking at our categories for external equity finance in Table 5.[11] First,

---

[10]To measure ownership concentration, a 1998 study assembled data for the ten largest publicly traded, non-financial private domestic firms in each of forty-five countries. For each country the study measures ownership concentration as the median percentage owned by the three largest shareholders in each of these ten firms; see La Porta, Lopez-de-Silanes, and Vishny, December 1998.

[11] This paper uses the three measures of equity finance developed in Rafael La Porta, Florencio Lopez-de-Silanes, Andrei Shleifer, and Robert W. Vishny, "Legal Determinants of External Finance," *Journal of Finance* 52 (July 1997), pp. 1131–50. The first measure is the 1994

access to external equity financing is most limited in countries such as Mexico and the rest of the French civil-law countries. Specifically, the ratio of external capital to GNP is roughly half the world mean and one-third of that in the United States. Meanwhile the ratio of domestic firms to total population is between 10 and 15 times lower than the world mean and the U.S. number. Finally, the ratio of Initial Public Offerings (IPOs) to population is roughly thirty to fifty times lower than the equivalent number for the world mean and for the United States. In contrast, all three equity measures indicate that, on average, access to external equity is easiest in common-law countries: The ratio of outsider-held stock market to GNP is 60 percent, vs. 40 percent for the world mean; the number of listed firms per 1 million people is 35, vs. 21.6 for the world mean; and the number of IPOs per million people is 2.2, vs. 1.02

---

ratio of external equity finance to GNP in each country. To compute a rough proxy of external equity finance, they multiply the total market value of common stock of all publicly traded firms by the average fraction of the equity not held by the largest three investors (i.e., the complement of the ownership variable just described). They scale the total market value of common stock by the fraction of equity held by minority shareholders to avoid overestimating the availability of external financing. For example, when 90 percent of a firm's equity is held by insiders, looking at the market capitalization of the whole firm gives a tenfold overestimate of how much it has actually raised externally. The procedure followed may still overestimate the level of external financing, because the ownership concentration figures are based on the largest firms and because they ignore cross-holdings. Still, this procedure is conceptually better than looking at the ratio of market capitalization to GNP. The remaining two measures of external equity finance capture market breadth. The first is the number of domestic firms listed in the stock exchange of each country relative to its population. The second is the number of initial public offerings of shares in each country between mid-1995 and mid-1996, also relative to the population. They look at both the stock and flow of new companies obtaining equity financing, because the development of financial markets has accelerated greatly in the last decade, and hence the IPO data provides a more recent picture of external equity financing.

for the world mean. Finally, equity markets in countries of Scandinavian origin are smaller but broader than in countries of German origin. To summarize, external equity markets line up rather well with shareholder rights and legal institutions: They are smallest in French civil-law countries and largest in common-law countries.

The last column in Table 5 shows the aggregate debt measure.[12] The ratio of total debt to GNP is 45 percent for French civil-law countries, 57 percent for Scandinavian countries, 68 percent for common-law countries, and 97 percent for German countries. Mexico, with a ratio of total debt to GNP of only 47 percent, is at an approximately average level within the French civil-law family. Low creditor rights line up with small markets when we compare countries with French, Scandinavian, and English legal systems.[13]

The differences among countries described in this section are supported by regression results on all of these outcome variables, which include the indices of investor protection, legal enforcement, and control for country characteristics.

---

[12]As in LaPorta, Lopez-de-Silanes, Shleifer, and Vishny, July 1997, this paper measures the availability of debt financing in each country as the ratio of the sum of private-sector bank debt and corporate bonds outstanding to GNP. The choice of debt variable is partly determined by data availability, because the analogue of the stock market data used to measure external equity financing does not exist for debt markets. However, the fact that the debt measure includes not only corporations but the whole private sector may actually be an advantage, because in many countries entrepreneurs raise money on their personal accounts to finance their firms (for example, by mortgaging their properties).

[13] A possible explanation of the German-origin anomaly is that firms in both Germany and Japan have large liquid assets and, therefore, the debt measure overstates their true liabilities; see Raghuram Rajan and Luigi Zingales, "What do we Know about Capital Structure: some Evidence from International Data," *Journal of Finance 50* (December 1995), pp. 142–160.

The Depth of Collapses

Although the evidence reviewed above suggests that expropriation of investors is endemic, it does not imply that there is a zero cost of stealing. Furthermore, expropriation may be of particular importance as a cause of prolonged and deep collapses.

One of the implications of the previous section is that weaker legal institutions lead to fewer projects being financed. Weak legal institutions can also contribute to economic crises. Weak protection of investor rights does not make shocks more likely, but it does enlarge the negative effect shocks have on the overall economy. For this reason, institutions matter for a particular aspect of volatility after collapses. Reasonable corporate finance arrangements in a weak legal environment can lead to a bimodal distribution of outcomes; i.e., either the economy does well or it collapses.

Investor protection may have effects on macroeconomic outcomes. If expropriation by controlling investors increases when the expected rate of return on investment falls, then an adverse shock to investor confidence will lead to increased theft, to lower capital inflow, and greater attempted capital outflow from a country. These, in turn, will translate into lower stock prices and a depreciated exchange rate.

This hypothesis is examined in Johnson et al., who analyze the depreciation of currencies and the decline of the stock markets in twenty-five countries, including Mexico, during the Asian crisis of 1997—98.[14] Their results show that investor protection indices and especially the measures of the quality of law enforcement are powerful

---

[14] Simon Johnson, Peter Boone, Alasdair Breach, and Eric Friedman, "Corporate Governance in the Asian Financial Crisis," *Journal of Financial Economics*, 2000, forthcoming.

predictors of the extent of market declines during the crisis. In fact, these variables explain the cross-section of declines much better than the macroeconomic variables that have been the focus of the policy debate. Again, the empirical evidence bears out the implications of the theory.

Real Consequences

A large literature links financial development to economic growth. King and Levine initiate the modern incarnation of this literature by showing that countries with better developed capital markets grow faster in the future.[15] Subsequent work extends these findings.16[16] Some of these papers show that the association between external finance and growth holds even at the industry level. Others show that an exogenous component of financial market development, obtained by using legal origin as an instrument, predicts economic growth.

Through its effect on financial markets, investor protection influences the real economy. There is a large amount of literature that ties financial development to economic development. Financial development can accelerate economic growth in three ways. First, by raising opportunities, financial development can enhance savings.

---

[15]R. King and R. Levine, "Finance and growth: Schumpeter might be right," Quarterly Journal of Economics, vol 108, no 3 (August 1993), pp. 717–738.

[16] A. Demirguc-Kunt and V . Maksimovic, "Law, finance, and firm growth," *Journal of Finance*, vol 53, no 6 (December 1998), pp. 210–2139; R. Levine and S. Zervos, "Stock markets, banks and economic growth," American Economic Review, vol 88, no 3, (June 1998), pp. 537-558; R. Rajan and L. Zingales, "Financial dependence and growth," *American Economic Review*, vol 88, no 3 (June 1998), pp. 559-586; Ross Levine, "Law, Finance, and Economic Growth," *Journal of Financial Intermediation*, vol 8, no 2 (April 1999); and W. Carlin and C. Mayer, Finance, investment and growth. Unpublished working (London: University College, 1999).

Second, it can channel these savings into real investment and thereby foster capital accumulation. Third, to the extent that the financiers exercise some control over the investment decisions of the entrepreneurs, financial development improves the efficiency of resource allocation, as capital flows toward the more productive uses. All three channels can in principle have important effects on development.

Along this line of thought, Beck, Levine, and Loayza find that banking sector development exerts a large impact on total factor productivity growth, and a less obvious impact on private savings and capital accumulation.17[17] Moreover, this influence continues to hold when an exogenous component of banking sector development, obtained using the origin of the legal system as an instrument, is taken as a predictor. Wurgler finds that financially developed countries allocate investment across industries more in line with industry-related growth opportunities than do the financially undeveloped countries.[18] This research suggests that the improvement in resource allocation is an important consequence of financial development, and that through this channel, investor protection can benefit the growth of productivity and output.

---

[17]T. Beck, R. Levine, and N. Loayza, "Finance and the Sources of Growth," *Journal of Financial Economics,* vol 58 (October 2000), forthcoming.

[18]J. Wurgler, "Financial markets and the allocation of capital," *Journal of Financial Economics*, vol 58 (October 2000), forthcoming.

REFORMS FOR DEEPENING MEXICO'S FINANCIAL MARKETS

The previous sections have two broad implications. First, they show that the most developed financial markets are protected by regulations and laws. However, they do not tell us what the best form of regulation is, which may well include self-regulation as well as government regulation. Still, totally unregulated financial markets do not work well, presumably because they allow corporate insiders to expropriate too much from outside investors. One dramatic illustration of this phenomenon is the fact that the most sought-after place for listing by publicly held companies around the world happens to be New York–a heavily regulated exchange when it comes to disclosure and protection of minority shareholders–rather than Mexico City.

Second, improving the functioning of financial markets through the protection of outside investors has real benefits both in terms of overall economic growth and for the allocation of resources across sectors. The analysis in the previous pages suggests that the objective of corporate governance reform in most countries should be to protect outside investor rights, including both shareholder and creditor rights. As the empirical research shows, the benefits of such reform would be to expand a country's financial markets, to facilitate external financing of new firms, to move away from concentrated ownership, and to improve the efficiency of investment allocation. What can be done to achieve this goal, and what are the obstacles? This analysis raises a number of questions for reform. How can a policymaker try to improve markets? What reforms are good? We address these questions in the concluding section, but first pause and examine an alternative approach to the study of corporate governance.

Possibilities of Legal Reform

In the last decade, the reform of corporate governance has preoccupied policymakers all over the world, from Western to Eastern Europe, Latin America and Asia. The proposals of how to improve governance have covered a broad range of areas. The Cadbury Committee focuses on the reform of the boards of directors. The European Corporate Governance Network stresses improved disclosure as a useful reform strategy. In the aftermath of the emerging-markets crisis, several Latin American and Asian countries are reforming regulations covering bankruptcy, disclosure, and several other aspects of governance, yet there the progress has been rather tentative as well.

To organize this discussion, it is useful to follow Coffee in drawing a distinction between legal and functional convergence.1[19] Legal convergence refers to the changes in the rules and in enforcement mechanisms toward some desirable standard. To achieve legal convergence to effective investor protection, most countries require extensive legal, regulatory, and judicial reform. Alternatively, functional convergence refers to more decentralized, market-based changes, which do not require legal reform per se, but still bring more firms and assets under the umbrella of effective legal protection of investors. I discuss these two alternative paths of reform in turn.

Coffee argues that there is an important movement towards "functional convergence," through which firms around the world are adopting U.S.-type mechanisms to protect investors. There is certainly a move towards issuing American Depositary Receipts (ADRs), and these seem to improve access to external capital markets. An ADR is equivalent to listing a foreign company's securities on an exchange that protects shareholders, mainly through stricter

---

[19]J. Coffee, "The future as history: the prospects for global convergence in corporate governance and its implications," Northwestern Law Review, vol 93, pp. 631–707.

disclosure requirements. This, in fact, is done by many companies when they list they shares as ADRs in New York. Such a listing in New York (or London), supported in part by the threat of delisting, raises the level of shareholder protection.

Lins, Strickland, and Zenner2[20] show that the sensitivity of investment to cash flow falls when an ADR is issued by a company from a country with a weak legal system and a less-developed capital market (as defined by La Porta, Lopez-de-Silanes, Shleifer, and Vishny[21]). Reece and Weisbach22[22] show that companies in civil law countries are more likely to list ADRs on an organized exchange in the United States, thus committing themselves to greater disclosure. In particular, Mexico is the country with the highest percentage of locally listed firms that have ADRs in the United States. Close to 38 percent of all Mexican firms listed on the Mexican Stock exchange have some listing in the United States stock markets. This evidence supports the view that in countries with weak investor protection, firms try to find ways to access external capital markets.

A related mechanism of opting into a more protective legal regime is an acquisition by a company already operating in such a regime. When a U.S. company acquires a Mexican company, the possibilities for legal expropriation of investors diminish. In a friendly acquisition, the

---

[20]Karl Lins, Deon Strickland and Marc Zenner, Do non-US firms Issue equity on US Stock Exchanges to Relax Capital Constraints? Mimeograph, University of North Carolina at Chapel Hill, January 2000

[21]La Porta, Lopez-de-Silanes, Shleifer, and Vishny, July 1997.

[22]Michael S. Weisbach, and WIlliam A. Reese, Protection of Minority shareholder interests, cross-listings in the United States, and Subsequent Equity Offerings, Mimeograph, University of Illinois Department of Finance.

controlling shareholders of the Mexican company can be compensated for the benefits they lose, making it more likely that they will go along. Such acquisitions enhance efficiency, because the wasteful expropriation is replaced by publicly shared profits and dividends. Some of the acquisitions in the NAFTA region, as well as in the European Community in the last few years, reflect this particular phenomenon.

In summary, the mechanisms of functional convergence, particularly those taking the form of opting into the more protective legal regimes, are moving assets to the countries which give investors a stronger claim to them. This movement should facilitate the development of external finance in many countries. However, such "opting in" cannot fully replace bona fide legal reform. International contracts can get around some of the deficiencies of domestic investor protection, but they cannot solve them, as shown in the previous sections. The majority of Mexican firms cannot reach the scale necessary to access U.S. markets and are therefore left with the local financial markets as their only potential source of finance.

Most companies in Mexico, particularly the smaller growth companies, are in desperate need of external funds but not ready to list in New York or to be acquired. Furthermore, cross-border acquisitions are politically sensitive. Even for those firms that do have access to ADRs, the listing does not solve the problem completely, because the insiders still have a variety of ways of taking advantage of shareholders open to them (and presumably utilize them, for why would they give up their private benefits in exchange for a mere listing?). Even if the insiders violate the listing rules, the threat is a fine or at worst a delisting from the exchange. Opting in may well be the politically feasible solution to the problems of legal reform, but it is by no means a fully adequate solution.

Another important limitation of functional convergence is in the area of creditor rights. Assets located in particular countries generally remain under the jurisdiction of these countries' laws. Without bankruptcy reform, opt-in mechanisms are unlikely to address the legal problems faced by domestic, and especially foreign, creditors.

For most countries, Mexico included, the improvement of investor protection would require rather radical changes in the legal system. Securities, company, and bankruptcy laws would generally need to be amended, and the regulatory and judicial mechanisms of enforcing shareholder and creditor rights would need to be radically improved. There is no reason to think that the particular list of legal protections of investors is either necessary or sufficient for such reforms. In principle, some mechanisms–such as giving shareholders the right to a quick redress mechanism or a class-action suit against directors–could work powerfully even in an environment where other shareholder rights are missing. On the other hand, the evidence presented in previous sections is clear that the historical origin of the country's legal system plays a key role in shaping investor rights. In turn, the status of investor rights could be considered representative of the law's general stance toward outside investors, and suggests at least tentatively that many more rules will need to be changed simultaneously in countries with poor investor protection.

Effective legal reform in Mexico, as in many other countries, runs into tremendous political obstacles. Perhaps the most important objections come from the controlling shareholders at the top of large corporations. The reason for that is straightforward. From the point of view of the controlling investors, an improvement in the rights of outside investors is first and foremost a reduction in the value of control, as opportunities deteriorate. This is so despite the fact that the total value of these firms increases as a result of legal reform, as expropriation declines and investors finance new projects on more attractive terms.

There is perhaps a further reason why the insiders of major firms oppose corporate governance reform and the expansion of capital markets. Under the status quo, the existing firms can finance their own investment projects through internal cash flows as well as relationships with either captive or closely tied banks. In fact, the lion's share of credit in Mexico goes to the few largest firms: 18 percent of all private claims in the Mexican economy go to the largest 20 private firms listed on the stock exchange. This number is twice as high as the world mean and almost three times as high as in the United States or Canada. As a consequence, the large firms not only get the finance they need, but also the political influence that comes with the access to such finance, as well as security from potential competition that would come when smaller firms could also raise external capital. When new entrepreneurs have good projects, they often have to come to the existing firms for finance. Poor corporate governance delivers the insiders not only secure finance, but also relatively secure politics and markets.

In a country like Mexico, the opposition to reform may also be supplemented by opposition from labor interests. After all, these interests are also receiving some rents from the existing arrangements, for example when managers invest in large plants that are irrelevant and employ large numbers of people. The losers in the existing arrangements are the new entrepreneurs who cannot raise external funds to finance new investment, and the parts of the labor force that do not have access to the privileged jobs.

Consistent with these apparent difficulties of reform in the context of interest group politics, the successful reforms have only occurred when the special interests could be destroyed or appeased. In this respect, corporate governance reform is no different from most other reforms in developing or developed countries.[23]

Although difficult, reform has taken place in several countries, such as the United States in 1933—34, Japan after World War II, Chile in the 1980s, and more recently in Germany, Korea, and Poland. These examples illustrate the possibility of legal reform in the area of investor protection, but also point to the substantial political difficulties. Yet there are some countervailing political interests as well, including foreign (institutional) shareholders and creditors, who have recently begun to insist on having some rights as investors. In some countries, these outside investors are beginning to have influence. Their influence becomes particularly great in the times of financial crisis, such as the emerging world has experienced in 1997—98, when companies and the insiders who run them desperately needed funds. Indeed, Thailand has recently introduced a new bankruptcy law, and Korea has allowed outside investors to successfully sue the directors who act against their interests. It remains to be seen how far these efforts go. Slow and difficult as it is, real legal reform needs to take place in Mexico. But what parameters should that reform follow?

An Agenda of Reforms in Mexico
Who needs protection?

A central question concerning the reform of capital markets is: which investors need protection? Berglof and Von Thadden suggest that although poor protection is likely to deter small investors, small investors are not always likely to play an important role.[24] This might lead us to believe that

---

[23]Albert O. Hirschman, Journeys Toward Progress (New York: The Twentieth Century Fund, 1963).
[24]Eric Berglof and Leopold Von Thadden, The changing corporate governance paradigm: implications for transition and developing countries, unpublished working paper (Stockholm, Sweden: Stockholm Institute of Transition Economics, 1999).

investor protection may not be necessary in countries where small investors are unimportant, such as Mexico. But the effectiveness of large investors (shareholders or creditors) also depends on the degree of legal protection. All non-controlling investors–large or small–need their rights protected.

Poor investor protection also deters strategic investors, "modest-size," and large shareholders. Although large shareholders are able to monitor management actions more closely and thus solve the free-rider problem that affects small investors, the large investors still need legal protection of their voting rights. Some examples from developing countries and transition economies help illustrate this point. In most joint ventures in Mexico and other developing countries, it is common practice for the foreign partner to write a "shareholders' agreement" to protect her rights. Strategic investors need the courts to enforce these agreements; otherwise they are unwilling to share their technological know-how.

Poor investor protection also deters creditors. Creditors need clear bankruptcy procedures and courts that enforce the law in order to be able to repossess collateral. The absence of creditor protection deters the development of the financial sector. For example, the evidence in Levine shows that moving a country from the lowest quartile in terms of creditor protection to the next quartile translates into a 20% rise in financial development, which accelerates long-run growth by almost one percentage point per year.[25] La Porta, Lopez-de-Silanes, Shleifer, and Vishny show that creditor protection leads to large debt markets.[26] Creditors have less power in Mexico and other French civil-law

---

[25]Levine, Ross, "Law, Finance, and Economic Growth," *Journal of Financial Intermediation*, vol 8, no 2 (April 1999).

[26] La Porta, Lopez-de-Silanes, Shleifer, and Vishny, July 1997.

countries because the procedures for turning over control to the banks are not clear. Countries such as Mexico, Greece, or the Philippines have poor creditor protection and poor legal enforcement, and as a result have small and concentrated debt markets.

The implication of the legal approach to corporate governance is that a method of financing develops when financiers are protected by the law and its enforcement. The key issue is that poor protection of investors deters not only very small investors, but also strategic investors, large and modest-size shareholders, and creditors.

What can policymakers do to foster better investor protection? There are capital-markets reforms at work in many countries, and the evidence suggests that some of these efforts have important effects on investor protection and the financing of firms. Some mechanisms adopted in other places might be appropriate for Mexico, though others might not work, given current enforcement environment. Unfortunately, our understanding of the principles of reform of investor protection remains limited. There is no checklist of what needs to be done. However, the available evidence indicates that reforms to foster financial markets in Mexico must meet four tentative principles:

1. Legal reform is slow and complicated; therefore, complementary market-based mechanisms should be adopted, because they can help create the necessary pressures for reforms to take place.

2. Rules do matter. It is not just the stance of the law or the political sentiment that shapes financial markets.

3. The enforcement of legal rules is deeply connected with the rules themselves.

4. Potentially more controversial, government regulation of financial markets may be useful when

court enforcement of private contracts or even of government laws cannot be relied on.

With these principles in mind, there are seven policy recommendations that form the agenda for deepening Mexico's financial markets. I will classify these measures into two groups: (1) mechanisms that allow market forces to create a culture of investor protection; and (2) legal reforms that create rules which reduce the room for discretion.

Market-based Mechanisms

As explained above, legal reform may be slow and complicated. Therefore, market-based mechanisms should be designed to temporarily substitute or complement the reform of laws and regulations. These measures should be a set of public measures that facilitate competition and ratings, making it possible for the firms that adhere to such measures to access capital at lower cost. At the same time, these mechanisms also have the objective of extending/publicizing the concept of better corporate governance practices. The adoption of such measures should constitute a useful first step in Mexico as they will foster the culture of respect for investor protection and set the basis for the coming legal reform.

Committee on Best Corporate Governance Practices

The lack of investor protection also has cultural causes. The Mexican "Committee on Corporate Governance," created in January 2000, is an ideal measure to promote the development of a culture of respect for investor protection among entrepreneurs. Mexico has followed the example of Australia, New Zealand, and England, which established commissions formed by members of the private sector and government to review corporate practices and investor protection. In each of these countries, the committee in charge of the analysis produced a document called "Code of Best Practices," detailing rules of good corporate governance mechanisms and investor protections. These codes are mainly concerned with the organization of the board and special committees, but in the case of Mexico (probably as a result of the current lack of investor protection), the code also details several shareholder protections.

The philosophical principle underlying these codes is that the disclosure of information about corporate governance practices and investor protections by the firm allows the market to perceive the differences among the policies followed by various companies. Information should allow shareholders to distinguish those firms that adhere to investor protections, in turn making the shareholders more willing to give the companies funds. In the end, those firms with better practices should find it easier to access capital and at lower cost, as they provide a more certain environment for the investor.

The adoption of the principles of the Code of Best Practice in Mexico, as in most other countries, is voluntary, but the disclosure by each firm in the stock is compulsory. Starting with fiscal year 2000, all publicly-traded firms on the Mexican Stock Exchange must state in their annual report to the shareholders which rules of the code they follow, and which they do not. They may state why they do not follow the rules they have elected not to follow, and describe any alternate mechanisms they may have for the protection of investors. The experience of other countries shows that adopting the code starts movement toward modernizing investor protection because it is equivalent to an agenda of reforms shareholders could submit to the board or at the shareholders' meeting.

This code is a substantial step forward in the creation of a culture of investor protection, as it allows investors: (1) to distinguish firms that do have effective corporate governance mechanisms in place; and (2) to reward firms that offer better protection with higher valuation multiples or lower costs of capital. Recent developments at TV Azteca, the second-largest television chain in Mexico, illustrate this point. Accused of poor corporate practices, TV Azteca decided to be among the first in Mexico to adopt all the recommendations of the code. In the last ten months, the markets have seen the change and have rewarded the company with much higher multiples: its stock price has nearly tripled. Additionally, TV Azteca has been named by Institutional Shareholders Services, one of the largest U.S. advisors to pension funds, as one of the eight firms in the world that adopted substantial changes in its corporate governance practices in the world in 2000.

Alternative Markets with Higher Standards
The positive effects of Code of Best Practice illustrate the second principle of successful reform mentioned above: rules do matter. Germany's Neuer Markt is an excellent example, as well as an additional policy recommendation. In Mexico and in many European countries, there is a perception that their stock markets do not attract initial public offerings, and that this slows the development of new high-technology firms. There has been considerable debate about how to address this issue, but the main problem is that established firms like the existing rules[27] which allow them to raise capital on favorable terms, in part because they do not have to compete with new firms.

Germany, however, has experimented successfully since 1997 with the Neuer Markt, a sub-exchange of the Frankfurt Stock Exchange created especially for new firms wishing to go public.[28] Corporation law, the securities law,

---

[27]M. Hellwig, On the economics and politics of corporate finance and corporate control, unpublished working paper (Mannheim: University of Mannheim, 1999).

[28] Simon Johnson, Does investor protection matter: Evidence from Germany's Neuer Markt, unpublished working paper (Cambridge, MA: Massachusetts Institute of Technology, 1999).

and other basic laws and regulations applied to the companies listed there are the general German rules. The politics are German as well. However, the Deutsche Bourse has mandated that companies wishing to list on the Neuer Markt must comply with international accounting standards (U.S. GAAP or IAS), which include, in English, more stringent disclosure requirements than those applicable to already listed firms. The major effect of this new market has been to allow new firms easier access to the market: more than two hundred firms have gone public in the past three years, more than during the first fifty years after World War II.

Korea, despite a relatively weak legal system, has recently implemented the German-type approach. Most of the companies choosing to list on this market (KOSDAQ) have clear ownership structures and, at least so far, there have not been significant allegations of expropriation by these firms.

In Mexico, a new listing venue–with U.S.-style rules and greater restrictions on entrepreneurs–may accelerate the pace of initial public offerings. The powerful titans of Mexican industry may accept it because their firms are not affected, pointing to one possible strategy for overcoming political opposition to reform.

Prudential Measures for Institutional Investors

Enhanced disclosure requirements may not be sufficient in countries with weak legal institutions or where investors have very few rights, which prevent them from demanding changes. In such instances, as in Mexico, it may be desirable to restrict institutional investors to investments in companies that meet minimum corporate-governance standards. These standards may be determined in relation to the code of best practices or by independent best-practice commissions.

This recommendation is based on purely prudential reasons as well as on the need to create an incentive for firms to agree on better investor protection. A similar idea has been implemented in Chile, also a civil law country, where a commission detailed a large list of minimum requirements that issuers of securities must meet in order to be the object of investment by institutional investors (Decree. No. 3.500 in Chile).

State-Controlled Enterprises

Finally, among those decentralized measures I recommend that the State improve the corporate governance practices for those firms that still have participation. Despite widespread privatization in Mexico, there are still close to 150 state-controlled enterprises. These firms could set the example for private firms by adopting better investor protections.

Most of the state-run firms in Mexico are large public utilities or in natural resources. External funding is just as important for them, if not more important, than for private firms, because of substantially reduced government expenditures. They need higher levels of investment to meet the demand from the growing private sector. Therefore, it becomes imperative for them to find mechanisms to fund their projects from capital markets. Reform of corporate charters and improved investor protection would also alleviate the government budget constraint. The adoption of the code of best practices outlined above can provide a quick and easy way for these state-controlled firms to substantially transform themselves and secure access to funds at better rates.

Legal Reforms

As the evidence in this paper shows, the law and its enforcement are a good predictor of the development of capital markets. We also see that although the market-based mechanisms outlined above may help foster the growth of external funding, they have limitations. They do not solve all the problems with investor protection as they only reach a small group of firms that are either already in the stock market or that belong to the State. There are also limits to what can be obtained by improved disclosure and voluntary adoption of higher investor protection standards.

Even in the best-case scenario, firms might adopt improved protections with non-standard contracts, but when violations occur, enforcement of the contracts may be harder in weak legal systems. For these reasons, market-based mechanisms should be complemented with legal reforms whose effects can reach all firms and can be more easily enforced as the standard in the country.

The design of successful legal reforms in Mexico needs to take into account the weakness of the legal system. This area illustrates the third principle mentioned above: the enforcement of legal rules is deeply connected with the rules themselves. The strategy for reform is not to create an ideal set of rules and then see how they can be enforced, but rather to enact the rules that can be enforced with the existing enforcement structure.

Securities Regulation
The recommendation here is to try to refocus regulation so that supervision is concentrated on intermediaries, rather than on issuers. This idea is sometimes credited to James Landis, a contributor to the 1933 and 1934 Securities Acts in the United States.[29] Landis reasoned that regulators by themselves could hardly monitor the compliance with disclosure, reporting, and other rules by all listed firms, and the trading practices of all market participants. Rather, the commission would regulate intermediaries, such as the brokers, the accounting firms, the investment advisors, etc.,

---

[29]Thomas K. McCraw, Prophets of Regulation (Cambridge, MA: The Belknap Press of Harvard University, 1984).

who would in turn attempt to assure compliance with regulatory requirements by the issuers and the traders. Moreover, by maintaining substantial power over the intermediaries through its administrative relationships, including the power to issue and revoke licenses, the commission could force them to monitor market participants.

The principle of bringing private intermediaries into the enforcement of securities regulations has since been followed by a number of countries in their regulation of financial markets, including Germany and Poland. In Poland, for example, stringent and toughly enforced regulations concerning intermediaries have stimulated rapid development of securities markets and enabled a large number of new firms to go public.[30] In contrast, during the same period of time in the Czech Republic, a very similar country, the lax–and laxly enforced–regulations have been associated with the stagnation of markets, the delisting of hundreds of privatized companies from the stock exchange, and virtually no new listings. These findings suggest that smarter regulations, particularly in countries with relatively weak legal systems, such as Mexico, can improve the protection of investors, and that this improvement will help firms to obtain external finance.

Corporate Law

The successful regulation of the U.S. securities markets, the Polish financial markets, and the Neuer Markt in Germany share a common element, namely the regulatory insistence on extensive disclosure of financial information by the issuers. But this point illustrates why securities regulations alone, which basically focus on disclosure, may need to be complemented with changes in the corporations law of the country to give shareholders the rights to act on

---

[30] E. Glaeser, S. Johnson, and A. Shleifer, Coase v. the Coasians, unpublished working paper (Cambridge, MA: Harvard University, 2000)

the information they receive. A right to act appears to be a key element of their protection.

As illustrated in previous sections, Mexican Shareholderes' rights are among the worst in the world. In order for improved disclosure standards to have an effect, the current "Ley de Sociedades Anónimas" of the Commercial Code must be revamped. In some instances, this might require refining existing principles to make them more applicable. In other cases, it is necessary to create rights that are easily enforceable. The reform of Mexican corporation law may not need to follow the U.S.-type mechanisms that rely heavily on the judicial system, by means of derivative or class-action suits. Instead, once one recognizes the state of the legal system, the application of more "automatic" principles, such as some of those in Chile, may be a better answer for Mexico. The reform of Mexico's corporate law must include the following shareholder rights:

1. Increase information available prior to the shareholders' meetings and simplify procedures for attending such meetings.

2. Increase the ease of voting and expressing opinions different from those of the managers and controlling shareholders.

3. Create a mechanism to allow qualified minorities to submit proposals to be discussed at shareholders' meetings.

4. Allow proportional representation on the board of directors for minorities with at least 10 percent of the shares.

5. Guarantee non-discriminatory treatment of minorities by allowing a semi-automatic procedure that permits dissenting minorities to be compensated if the controlling shareholders approve

actions that are detrimental to the corporation and in their own favor (as in the case of Chile).

6. Define fiduciary obligations and judicial responsibilities of officers and board members.

7. Regulate conduct in cases of conflicts of interest.

8. Reinforce internal auditing procedures and committees for material transactions.

Bankruptcy Law

The importance of enforcement is also illustrated by the so-far unsuccessful reforms of bankruptcy procedures in East Asian countries. In general, improving bankruptcy procedures is more difficult than improving shareholder rights because different types of creditors, unlike the different non-controlling shareholders, have different objectives. Senior creditors, especially the secured senior creditors, prefer rapid liquidation of bankrupt firms. Junior creditors and shareholders, whose claims are less secure, may prefer more orderly liquidation or even reorganization. These conflicts have pushed most countries to opt for slow, reorganization-focused bankruptcy schemes rather than liquidations.[31]

Another complication is that bankruptcy procedures almost inevitably rely on significant adjudication by the courts. Yet courts in many countries are reluctant to play too active a role in matters as political and complicated as closure or liquidation of companies. In the aftermath of the Asian crisis, several East Asian countries, including Indonesia, Korea, and Thailand, have reformed their bankruptcy laws. Yet few companies have been taken through the bankruptcy process so far, largely because courts are politicized and not ready to adopt the new

---

[31]Hart, Oliver, Different Approaches to Bankruptcy, mimeograph (Cambridge, MA: Harvard University, November 1999)

procedures. They tend to throw out most creditor applications–especially those against powerful borrowers–on technicalities.

For this reason, one may want to emphasize bankruptcy procedures that minimize the involvement of courts. The United Kingdom's bankruptcy procedure puts most of the discretion in the hands of creditors rather than in the courts. Another departure from current practice would introduce market forces into the bankruptcy process by auctioning off bankrupt firms much in the same way that state-owned enterprises are currently privatized.[32]

In May 2000, Mexico adopted a new bankruptcy law addressing some of the main deficiencies of its prior legislation, but it still falls short in key areas. It is essential that the new law and its forthcoming regulations include mechanisms that achieve the following six points:

1. Minimize the transaction costs of the process and the discretionary ability of third parties, such as the judiciary.

2. Facilitate firms' access to credit in order to foster productive investment.

3. Ensure that the assets of the firm are used efficiently, either through reorganization or liquidation.

4. Preserve the absolute priority of creditors

5. Allow creditors holding collateral to repossess their collateral in due course and before other creditors benefit from it.

6. Maximize the payments to all those investors that provided financing to the firm.

---

[32]Oliver Hart, Rafael La Porta, Florencio Lopez-de-Silanes, and John Moore, "A New Bankruptcy Procedure that Uses Multiple Auctions," *European Economic Review* 41 (1997), pp. 461–73.

An efficient bankruptcy procedure is essential to expand credit access and restore the stability of the banking sector. Without essential creditor rights, the future functioning of credit institutions in Mexico is compromised.

CONCLUSIONS AND POLICY IMPLICATIONS

In this paper I have surveyed the laws governing investor protection, the quality of enforcement of these laws, and their effect on the availability of external financing in Mexico as compared to forty-eight other countries. Based on this evidence, the last two sections of the paper have outlined the possibilities for legal reform in Mexico and an agenda for successfully increasing investor protection and thus deepening Mexican financial markets. The analysis suggests five broad conclusions:

First, investors in different legal jurisdictions have very different bundles of rights. Therefore, investor rights are not inherent to securities but rather are determined by laws. In particular, French civil-law countries, including Mexico, protect investors the least, while common-law countries, such as the United States, protect them the most.

Second, law enforcement differs a great deal around the world. Mexico and other French civil-law countries have the worst quality of law enforcement and accounting standards, which are critical for investor protection.

Third, the evidence suggests that large capital markets require countries to protect financiers against expropriation by entrepreneurs and to provide good enforcement mechanisms to exercise such rights. In the absence of a good legal environment, financiers are reluctant to surrender funds in exchange for securities, and hence the scope of capital markets is limited. Specifically, we see evidence that weak legal institutions result in high levels of ownership concentration, low availability of external equity financing, narrow equity markets, and small debt markets. Mexico offers investors a rather unattractive legal environment. Both shareholder and creditor rights, as well as the quality of enforcement, lag behind common-law origin countries. As a result, credit markets are exceedingly small, and stock markets are both small and very narrow.

Fourth, the immediate reaction to the evidence here is to call for wholesale legal reform. However, because improving the efficiency of the judicial system and asserting the rule of law are slow processes, it is important to incorporate those constraints into the policy design. Finally, it is clear that improving corporate governance should be at the top of the policy agenda if Mexico is to embark on a self-sustainable path of long-term development. Institution-building is a critical part of the success of a market economy. The reform of those institutions that allow for a deepening of financial markets is key to ensuring business growth. Therefore, the reform of business laws and financial market regulations in Mexico should be part of the reforms that will allow smoother integration of the economies in the NAFTA region. The example of the European Community's effort to promote institutional development in new entrant countries, such as Spain, Portugal, and Greece, is evidence of the importance of this element in assuring long and prosperous economic relations.

Table 1: Shareholder Rights Around the World

This table classifies countries by the origin of their legal systems. Definitions for each of the variables can be found in Table 1. Panel B reports the test of means for the different legal systems.

Panel A: Shareholder rights (1=investor protection is in the law)

Country	One share One Vote	Proxy by mail allowed	Shares not blocked	Cumulative vote / proportional representation	% capital to call ESM	Preemptive rights	Oppressed minority	Anti-director rights
Australia	0	1	1	0	0.05 d	0	1	4
Canada	0	1	1	1	0.05	0	1	5
Hong Kong	0	1	1	0	0.10	1	1	5
India	0	0	1	1	0.10	1	1	5
Ireland	0	0	1	0	0.10	1	1	4
Israel	0	0	1	0	0.10	0	1	3
Kenya	0	0	1	0	0.10	0	1	3
Malaysia	1	0	1	0	0.10	1	1	4
New Zealand	0	1	1	0	0.05	0	1	4
Nigeria	0	0	1	0	0.10	0	1	3
Pakistan	1	0	1	1	0.10	1	1	5
Singapore	1	0	1	0	0.10	1	1	4
South Africa	0	1	1	0	0.05	1	1	5
Sri Lanka	0	0	1	0	0.10	0	1	3
Thailand	0	0	1	1	0.20 e	0	0	2
UK	0	1	1	0	0.10	1	1	5
US	0	1	1	1	0.10	0	1	5
Zimbabwe	0	0	1	0	0.05	0	1	3
English origin avg.	**0.17**	**0.39**	**1.00**	**0.28**	**0.09**	**0.44**	**0.94**	**3.06**

(continued on next page)

Table 1: Shareholder Rights Around the World (continued)

This table classifies countries by the origin of their legal systems. Definitions for each of the variables can be found in Table 1. Panel B reports the test of means for the different legal systems.

Panel A: *Shareholder rights* (1=investor protection is in the law)

Country	One share One Vote	Proxy by mail allowed	Shares not blocked	Cumulative vote / proportional representation	% capital to call ESM	Preemptive rights	Oppressed minority	Anti-director rights
Argentina	0	0	0	1	0.05	1	1	4
Belgium	0	0	0	0	0.20	0	0	0
Brazil	1	0	1	0	0.05	0	1	3
Chile	1	0	1	1	0.10	1	1	5
Colombia	0	0	1	1	0.25	1	0	3
Ecuador	0	0	1	0	0.25	1	0	2
Egypt	0	0	1	0	0.10	0	0	2
France	0	1	0	0	0.10	1	0	3
Greece	1	0	0	0	0.05	1	0	2
Indonesia	0	0	1	0	0.10	0	0	2
Italy	0	0	0	0	0.20	1	0	1
Jordan	1	0	1	0	0.25	0	0	1
Mexico	0	0	0	0	0.33	1	0	1
Netherlands	0	0	0	0	0.10	1	0	2
Peru	1	0	1	1	0.20	1	0	3
Philippines	0	0	1	1	open	0	1	3
Portugal	0	0	1	0	0.05	1	0	3
Spain	0	0	0	1	0.05	1	1	4
Turkey	0	0	1	0	0.10	0	0	2

Table 1: Shareholder Rights Around the World (continued)

This table classifies countries by the origin of their legal systems. Definitions for each of the variables can be found in Table 1. Panel B reports the test of means for the different legal systems.

Country	One share One Vote	Proxy by mail allowed	Shares not blocked	Cumulative vote / proportional representation	% capital to call ESM	Preemptive rights	Oppressed minority	Anti-director rights
				Panel A: Shareholder rights (1=investor protection is in the law)				
Uruguay	1	0	0	0	0.20	1	1	2
Venezuela	0	0	1	0	0.20	0	0	1
Latin American avg.	**0.44**	**0.00**	**0.67**	**0.44**	**0.18**	**0.78**	**0.44**	**2.67**
Rest of French origin avg.	0.17	0.08	0.50	0.17	0.12	0.50	0.17	2.08
French origin avg.	**0.29**	**0.05**	**0.57**	**0.29**	**0.15**	**0.62**	**0.29**	**2.33**
Austria	0	0	0	0	0.05	1	0	2
Germany	0	0	0	0	0.05	0	0	1
Japan	1	0	1	1	0.03	0	1	4
South Korea	1	0	0	0	0.05	0	1	2
Switzerland	0	0	0	0	0.10	1	0	2
Taiwan	0	0	0	1	0.03	0	1	3
German origin avg.	**0.33**	**0.00**	**0.17**	**0.33**	**0.05**	**0.33**	**0.50**	**2.33**
Denmark	0	0	1	0	0.10	0	0	2
Finland	0	0	1	0	0.10	1	0	3
Norway	0	1	1	0	0.10	1	0	4
Sweden	0	0	1	0	0.10 e	1	0	3
Scandinavian origin avg.	**0.00**	**0.25**	**1.00**	**0.00**	**0.10**	**0.75**	**0.00**	**3.00**
Sample average	**0.22**	**0.18**	**0.71**	**0.27**	**0.11**	**0.53**	**0.53**	**2.65**

(continued on next page)

Table 1: Shareholder Rights Around the World (continued)

This table classifies countries by the origin of their legal systems. Definitions for each of the variables can be found in Table 1. Panel B reports the test of means for the different legal systems.

Panel B: Tests of Means (t-statistics)

Country	One share One Vote	Proxy by mail allowed	Shares not blocked	Cumulative vote / proportional representation	% capital to call ESM	Preemptive rights	Oppressed minority	Anti-director rights
Common vs. civil law	-0.72	3.03[a]	4.97[a]	0.15	1.48	-0.91	5.59[a]	5.00[a]
English vs. French origin	-0.87	2.82[a]	3.87[a]	-0.05	-2.53[b]	-1.08	5.45[a]	4.73[a]
English origin vs. Latin America	-1.57	3.29[a]	2.00[c]	-0.85	-3.56[a]	-1.67	3.44[a]	2.98[a]
French vs. German origin	-0.22	1.00	-1.78[c]	-0.22	2.64[b]	1.23	-0.96	0.00
French vs. Scandinavian origin	2.83[b]	-1.37	-3.87[a]	2.82[b]	2.43[b]	-0.48	2.83	-1.06
Rest of French origin vs. Latin America	-1.39	1.00	-0.74	-1.39	-1.71	-1.29	-1.39	-1.11

a=Significant at 1% level; b= Significant at 5% level ; c=Significant at 10% level; d=as a percentage of votes; e= as a percentage of the number of shares

Table 2: Example of Management Proposals to be Voted on at Annual General Meeting Mexico

PROPOSAL No. 1: Amend statutes

Status: Non-routine
Sponsor: Management
Opposition: None known
Proxy materials contained no information on this agenda item. Most likely it is intended to restate the Company's capital stock in its statutes.

PROPOSAL No. 2: Approve financial statements

Status: Routine
Sponsor: Management
Opposition: None known

PROPOSAL No. 3: Set dividend

Status: Routine
Sponsor: Management
Opposition: None known
Management is asking of shareholders to approve a dividend of 0.08 pesos per share. It is not clear from materials furnished by the company whether this is full dividend or just the fourth-quarter payment.

PROPOSAL No. 4: Authorize share repurchase

Status: Routine
Sponsor: Management
Opposition: None known
Management is asking for shareholders' authorization to repurchase its shares. It gives no reason, time limit, or maximum or minimum amount for this proposal.

PROPOSAL No. 5: Proforma Ratification of board actions, elect directors, and appoint shareholder representative

Status: Routine
Sponsor: Management
Opposition: None known
The proposal wants shareholders to approve any board candidates who might be standing for election or reelection. As is common in Mexico, the Company does not include information identifying the nominees in its proxy statement. If directors are to be elected, their names will be announced at the annual meeting.
Shareholders are asked to approve the fees for the directors, their alternates, and the stockholders examiners. The amounts are not disclosed in the proxy materials.

(continued on next page)

Table 2: Example of Management Proposals to be Voted on at Annual General Meeting Mexico (continued)

PROPOSAL No. 6: Appoint auditors and set their fee

Status: Routine

Sponsor: Management

Opposition: None known

Shareholders are being asked to approve the appointment of "independent" auditors and their fees. Managementhas not published the name of the authors, but will announce both that and the proposed fees at the annual meeting itself.

Table 3: Creditor Rights Around the World

This table classifies countries by the origin of their legal systems. Definitions for each variable can be found in Table 1. Panel B reports tests of means for the different legal systems.

Panel A: Creditor Rights (1 = creditor protection is in the law)

Country	Restrictions for reorganization	No automatic stay on secured assets	Secured creditor paid first	Management does not stay in reorganization	Creditor rights
Australia	0	0	1	0	1
Canada	0	0	1	0	1
Hong Kong	1	1	1	1	3
India	1	1	1	1	3
Ireland	0	0	1	0	1
Israel	1	1	1	1	3
Kenya	1	1	1	1	3
Malaysia	1	1	1	1	3
New Zealand	1	1	0	1	2
Nigeria	1	1	1	1	3
Pakistan	1	1	1	1	3
Singapore	1	1	1	1	4
South Africa	1	0	1	1	2
Sri Lanka	1	1	0	1	2
Thailand	0	1	1	1	3
U.K.	1	1	1	1	3
U.S.	0	0	1	0	1
Zimbabwe	1	1	1	1	3
English origin avg.	0.72	0.72	0.89	0.78	2.44

(continued on next page)

Table 3: Creditor Rights Around the World (continued)
This table classifies countries by the origin of their legal systems. Definitions for each variable can be found in Table 1. Panel B reports tests of means for the different legal systems.

Country	Restrictions for reorganization	No automatic stay on secured assets	Secured creditor paid first	Management does not stay in reorganization	Creditor rights
	Panel A: Creditor Rights (1 = creditor protection is in the law)				
Argentina	0	0	1	0	1
Belgium	0	1	1	0	2
Brazil	1	0	0	0	0
Chile	1	0	1	0	1
Colombia	0	0	0	0	0
Ecuador	1	1	1	1	3
Egypt	1	1	1	1	3
France	0	0	0	0	0
Greece	0	0	0	1	1
Indonesia	1	1	1	1	3
Italy	1	0	1	0	1
Jordan	na	na	na	na	na
Mexico	0	0	0	0	0
Netherlands	1	0	1	0	1
Peru	0	0	0	0	0
Philippines	0	0	0	0	0
Portugal	0	0	1	0	1
Spain	0	1	1	0	2
Turkey	1	0	1	0	1

Table 3 Creditor Rights Around the World (continued)

This table classifies countries by the origin of their legal systems. Definitions for each variable can be found in Table 1. Panel B reports tests of means for the different legal systems.

Country	Restrictions for reorganization	No automatic stay on secured assets	Secured creditor paid first	Management does not stay in reorganization	Creditor rights
			Panel A: Creditor Rights (1 = creditor protection is in the law)		
Uruguay	0	0	1	1	2
Venezuela	na	na	1	na	na
Latin American avg.	0.38	0.13	0.56	0.25	1.25
Rest of French origin avg.	0.45	0.36	0.73	0.27	1.81
French origin avg.	0.42	0.26	0.65	0.26	1.16
Austria	1	1	1	0	2
Germany	1	1	1	0	2
Japan	0	0	1	1	2
South Korea	0	1	1	1	3
Switzerland	0	0	1	0	1
Taiwan	0	1	1	0	2
German origin avg.	0.33	0.67	1.00	0.33	2.00
Denmark	1	1	1	0	2
Finland	0	0	1	0	1
Norway	1	0	1	0	1
Sweden	1	0	1	0	1
Scandinavian origin avg.	0.75	0.25	1.00	0.00	1.25
Sample average	0.55	0.49	0.81	0.45	1.77

(continued on next page)

Table 4: Enforcement of Laws

This table classifies countries by the origin of their legal systems. Definitions for each of the variables can be found in Table 1. Panel B reports the tests of means for the different legal systems.

Country	Efficiency of judicial system	Rule of law	Corruption	Accounting standards	GNP per capita (U.S. $)
			Panel A: Means		
Australia	10.00	10.00	8.52	75	17,500
Canada	9.25	10.00	10.00	74	19,970
Hong Kong	10.00	8.22	8.52	69	18,060
India	8.00	4.17	4.58	57	300
Ireland	8.75	7.80	8.52	na	13,000
Israel	10.00	4.82	8.33	64	13,920
Kenya	5.75	5.42	4.82	na	270
Malaysia	9.00	6.78	7.38	76	3,140
New Zealand	10.00	10.00	10.00	70	12,600
Nigeria	7.25	2.73	3.03	59	300
Pakistan	5.00	3.03	2.98	na	430
Singapore	10.00	8.57	8.22	78	19,850
South Africa	6.00	4.42	8.92	70	2,980
Sri Lanka	7.00	1.90	5.00	na	600
Thailand	3.25	6.25	5.18	64	2,110
U.K.	10.00	8.57	9.10	78	18,060
U.S.	10.00	10.00	8.63	71	24,740
Zimbabwe	7.50	3.68	5.42	na	520
English origin avg.	**8.15**	**6.46**	**7.06**	**69.62**	**9,353**

(continued on next page)

Table 4: Enforcement of Laws (continued)
This table classifies countries by the origin of their legal systems. Definitions for each of the variables can be found in Table 1. Panel B reports the tests of means for the different legal systems.

Country	Efficiency of judicial system	Rule of law	Corruption	Accounting standards	GNP per capita (U.S. $)
Argentina	6.00	5.35	6.02	45	7,220
Belgium	9.50	10.00	8.82	61	21,650
Brazil	5.75	6.32	6.32	54	2,930
Chile	7.25	7.02	5.30	52	3,170
Colombia	7.25	2.08	5.00	50	1,400
Ecuador	6.25	6.67	5.18	na	1,200
Egypt	6.50	4.17	3.87	24	660
France	8.00	8.98	9.05	69	22,490
Greece	7.00	6.18	7.27	55	7,390
Indonesia	2.50	3.98	2.15	na	740
Italy	6.75	8.33	6.13	62	19,840
Jordan	8.66	4.35	5.48	na	1,190
Mexico	6.00	5.35	4.77	60	3,610
Netherlands	10.00	10.00	10.00	64	20,950
Peru	6.75	2.50	4.70	38	1,490
Philippines	4.75	2.73	2.92	65	850
Portugal	5.50	8.68	7.38	36	9,130
Spain	6.25	7.80	7.38	64	13,590
Turkey	4.00	5.18	5.18	51	2,970
Uruguay	6.50	5.00	5.00	31	3,830
Venezuela	6.50	6.37	4.70	40	2,840

Table 4: Enforcement of Laws (continued)

This table classifies countries by the origin of their legal systems. Definitions for each of the variables can be found in Table 1. Panel B reports the tests of means for the different legal systems.

Country	Efficiency of judicial system	Rule of law	Corruption	Accounting standards	GNP per capita (U.S. $)
Argentina	6.00	5.35	6.02	45	7,220
Belgium	9.50	10.00	8.82	61	21,650
Brazil	5.75	6.32	6.32	54	2,930
Chile	7.25	7.02	5.30	52	3,170
Colombia	7.25	2.08	5.00	50	1,400
Ecuador	6.25	6.67	5.18	na	1,200
Egypt	6.50	4.17	3.87	24	660
France	8.00	8.98	9.05	69	22,490
Greece	7.00	6.18	7.27	55	7,390
Indonesia	2.50	3.98	2.15	na	740
Italy	6.75	8.33	6.13	62	19,840
Jordan	8.66	4.35	5.48	na	1,190
Mexico	6.00	5.35	4.77	60	3,610
Netherlands	10.00	10.00	10.00	64	20,950
Peru	6.75	2.50	4.70	38	1,490
Philippines	4.75	2.73	2.92	65	850
Portugal	5.50	8.68	7.38	36	9,130
Spain	6.25	7.80	7.38	64	13,590
Turkey	4.00	5.18	5.18	51	2,970
Uruguay	6.50	5.00	5.00	31	3,830
Venezuela	6.50	6.37	4.70	40	2,840

Table 4: Enforcement of Laws (continued)
This table classifies countries by the origin of their legal systems. Definitions for each of the variables can be found in Table 1. Panel B reports the tests of means for the different legal systems.

Country	Efficiency of judicial system	Rule of law	Corruption	Accounting standards	GNP per capita (U.S. $)
Latin American avg.	**6.47**	**5.18**	**5.22**	**46.25**	**3,077**
Rest of French origin avg.	**6.62**	**6.70**	**6.30**	**55.10**	**10,121**
French origin avg.	**6.56**	**6.05**	**5.84**	**51.17**	**7,102**
Austria	9.50	10.00	8.57	54	23,510
Germany	9.00	9.23	8.93	62	23,560
Japan	10.00	8.98	8.52	65	31,490
South Korea	6.00	5.35	5.30	62	7,660
Switzerland	10.00	10.00	10.00	68	35,760
Taiwan	6.75	8.52	6.85	65	10,425
German origin avg.	**8.54**	**8.68**	**8.03**	**62.67**	**22,067**
Denmark	10.00	10.00	10.00	62	26,730
Finland	10.00	10.00	10.00	77	1,930
Norway	10.00	10.00	10.00	74	25,970
Sweden	10.00	10.00	10.00	83	24,740
Scandinavian origin avg.	**10.00**	**10.00**	**10.00**	**74.00**	**19,843**
Sample average	**7.67**	**6.85**	**6.90**	**60.93**	**10,801**

(continued on next page)

Table 4: Enforcement of Laws (continued)

This table classifies countries by the origin of their legal systems. Definitions for each of the variables can be found in Table 1. Panel I reports the tests of means for the different legal systems.

Country	Efficiency of judicial system	Rule of law	Corruption	Accounting standards	GNP per capita (U.S. $)
Panel B: Tests of means (t-statistics)					
Common vs. civil law	1.27	-0.77	0.39	3.12^a	-0.94
English vs. French origin	2.65^a	0.51	1.79^c	4.66^a	0.85
English origin vs. Latin America	2.37^b	1.25	2.33^c	6.53^a	2.08^b
French vs. German origin	-2.53^a	-2.55^a	-2.49^a	-2.10^b	-3.79^a
French vs. Scandinavian origin	-9.34^a	-20.80^a	-9.77^a	-3.32^a	-4.28^a
Rest of French origin vs. Latin America	0.19	1.52	1.28	1.49	2.27^b

a=Significant at 1% level; b=Significant at 5% level; c=Significant at 10% level.

Table 5: External Finance and Legal Institutions

This table classifies countries by the origin of their legal systems. Definitions for each of the variables can be found in Table 1. Panel B reports tests of means for the different legal systems.

Country	Ownership Concentration	External Cap / GNP	Domestic Firms / Pop	IPOs / Pop	Debt / GNP	GDP growth	Log GNP
			Panel A: Means				
Australia	0.28	0.49	63.55	–	0.76	3.06	12.54
Canada	0.24	0.39	40.86	4.93	0.72	3.36	13.26
Hong Kong	0.54	1.18	88.16	5.16	–	7.57	11.56
India	0.43	0.31	7.79	1.24	0.29	4.34	12.50
Ireland	0.36	0.27	20.00	0.75	0.38	4.25	10.73
Israel	0.55	0.25	127.60	1.80	0.66	4.39	11.19
Kenya	–	–	2.24	–	–	4.79	8.83
Malaysia	0.52	1.48	25.15	2.89	0.84	6.90	11.00
New Zealand	0.51	0.28	69.00	0.66	0.90	1.67	10.69
Nigeria	0.45	0.27	1.68	–	–	3.43	10.36
Pakistan	0.41	0.18	5.88	–	0.27	5.50	10.88
Singapore	0.53	1.18	80.00	5.67	0.60	1.68	11.68
South Africa	0.52	1.45	16.00	0.05	0.93	7.48	10.92
Sri Lanka	0.61	0.11	11.94	0.11	0.25	4.04	9.28
Thailand	0.48	0.56	6.70	0.56	0.93	7.70	11.72
U.K.	0.15	1.00	35.68	2.01	1.13	2.27	13.86
U.S.	0.12	0.58	30.11	3.11	0.81	2.74	15.67
Zimbabwe	0.51	0.18	5.81	–	–	2.17	8.63
English Origin avg.	0.42	0.60	35.45	2.23	0.68	4.30	11.41

(continued on next page)

Table 5: External Finance and Legal Institutions (continued)

This table classifies countries by the origin of their legal systems. Definitions for each of the variables can be found in Table 1. Panel B reports tests of means for the different legal systems.

Country	Ownership Concentration	External Cap / GNP	Domestic Firms / Pop	IPOs / Pop	Debt / GNP	GDP growth	Log GNP
Argentina	0.55	0.07	4.58	0.20	0.19	1.40	12.40
Belgium	0.62	0.17	15.50	0.30	0.38	2.46	12.29
Brazil	0.63	0.18	3.48	0.00	0.39	3.95	13.03
Chile	0.38	0.80	19.92	0.35	0.63	3.35	10.69
Colombia	0.68	0.14	3.13	0.05	0.19	4.38	10.82
Ecuador	–	–	13.18	0.09	–	4.55	9.49
Egypt	0.62	0.08	3.48	–	–	6.13	10.53
France	0.24	0.23	8.05	0.17	0.96	2.54	14.07
Greece	0.68	0.07	21.60	0.30	0.23	2.46	11.25
Indonesia	0.62	0.15	1.15	0.10	0.42	6.38	11.84
Italy	0.60	0.08	3.91	0.31	0.55	2.82	13.94
Jordan	–	–	23.75	–	0.70	1.20	8.49
Mexico	0.67	0.22	2.28	0.03	0.47	3.07	12.69
Netherlands	0.31	0.52	21.13	0.66	1.08	2.55	12.68
Peru	0.57	0.40	9.47	0.13	0.27	2.82	10.92
Philippines	0.51	0.10	2.90	0.27	0.10	0.30	10.44
Portugal	0.59	0.08	19.50	0.50	0.64	3.52	11.41
Spain	0.50	0.17	9.71	0.07	0.75	3.27	13.19
Turkey	0.58	0.18	2.93	0.05	0.15	5.05	12.08
Uruguay	–	–	7.00	0.00	0.26	1.96	9.40
Venezuela	0.49	0.08	4.28	0.00	0.10	2.65	10.99

Table 5: External Finance and Legal Institutions (continued)

This table classifies countries by the origin of their legal systems. Definitions for each of the variables can be found in Table 1. Panel B reports tests of means for the different legal systems.

Country	Ownership Concentration	External Cap / GNP	Domestic Firms / Pop	IPOs / Pop	Debt / GNP	GDP growth	Log GNP
Latin American avg.	**0.57**	**0.23**	**7.49**	**0.10**	**0.29**	**2.84**	**11.11**
Rest of French origin avg.	**0.53**	**0.19**	**11.89**	**0.28**	**0.56**	**3.43**	**11.89**
French Origin avg.	**0.55**	**0.21**	**10.00**	**0.19**	**0.45**	**3.18**	**11.55**
Austria	0.51	0.06	13.87	0.25	0.79	2.74	12.13
Germany	0.50	0.13	5.14	0.08	1.12	2.60	14.46
Japan	0.13	0.62	17.78	0.26	1.22	4.13	15.18
South Korea	0.20	0.44	15.88	0.02	0.74	9.52	12.73
Switzerland	0.48	0.62	33.85	–	–	1.18	12.44
Taiwan	0.14	0.88	14.22	0.00	–	11.56	12.34
German Origin avg.	**0.33**	**0.46**	**16.79**	**0.12**	**0.97**	**5.29**	**13.21**
Denmark	0.40	0.21	50.40	1.80	0.34	2.09	11.84
Finland	0.34	0.25	13.00	0.60	0.75	2.40	11.49
Norway	0.31	0.22	33.00	4.50	0.64	3.43	11.62
Sweden	0.28	0.51	12.66	1.66	0.55	1.79	12.28
Scandinavian Origin avg.	**0.33**	**0.30**	**27.26**	**2.14**	**0.57**	**2.42**	**11.80**
Sample Average	**0.45**	**0.40**	**21.59**	**1.02**	**0.59**	**3.79**	**11.72**

(continued on next page)

Table 5: External Finance and Legal Institutions (continued)

This table classifies countries by the origin of their legal systems. Definitions for each of the variables can be found in Table 1. Panel B reports tests of means for the different legal systems.

Country	Ownership Concentration	External Cap/GNP	Domestic Firms/Pop	IPOs/Pop	Debt/GNP	GDP growth	Log GNP
			Panel B: Tests of Means (t-statistics)				
Common vs. Civil Law	-0.91	3.12[a]	3.16[a]	3.97[a]	1.33	1.23	-1.06
English vs. French Origin	-2.68[a]	3.29[a]	3.16[a]	4.50[a]	2.29[b]	1.97[c]	-0.28
English origin vs. Latin America	-2.34[b]	1.97[c]	2.29[b]	3.21[a]	3.42[a]	1.93[b]	0.46
French vs. German Origin	3.29[a]	-2.38[b]	-1.85	0.78	-3.39[a]	-1.96[c]	-2.48
French vs. Scand. Origin	3.32[a]	-0.91	-3.31[a]	-5.45[a]	0.82	0.97	-0.33
Rest of French origin vs. Latin America	-0.54	-0.35	1.36	2.41[b]	2.20[b]	0.88	1.22

a=Significant at 1% level; b=Significant at 5% level; c=Significant at 10% level.

Appendix A: The Variables

This table describes the variables collected for the forty-nine countries included in our study. The first column gives the name of the variable. The second column describes the variable and gives the range of possible values. The third column provides the sources from which the variable was collected.

Variable	Description	Sources
Origin	Identifies the legal origin of the Company Law or Commercial Code of each country. Equals 1 if the origin is English Common Law; 2 if the origin is the French Commercial Code; and 3 if the origin is the German Commercial Code.	Foreign Law Encyclopedia Commercial Laws of the World
One share – one vote	Equals one if the Company Law or Commercial Code of the country requires that ordinary shares carry one vote per share, and zero otherwise. Equivalently, this variable equals one when the law prohibits the existence of both multiple-voting and nonvoting ordinary shares and does not allow firms to set a maximum number of votes per shareholder irrespective of the number of shares owned. Zero otherwise.	Company Law or Commercial Code
Proxy by mail	Equals one if the Company Law or Commercial Code allows shareholders to mail their proxy vote to the firm. Zero otherwise.	Company Law or Commercial Code
Shares not blocked	Equals one if the Company Law or Commercial Code does not allow firms to require that shareholders deposit their shares prior to a General Shareholders Meeting, thus preventing them from selling those shares for a number of days. Zero otherwise.	Company Law or Commercial Code

(continued on next page)

Cumulative voting or proportional representation	Equals one if the Company Law or Commercial Code allows shareholders to cast all of their votes for one candidate standing for election to the board of directors (cumulative voting) or if the Company Law or Commercial Code allows a mechanism of proportional representation in the board by which minority interests may name a proportional number of directors to the board. Zero otherwise.	Company Law or Commercial Code
Oppressed minorities mechanism	Equals one if the Company Law or Commercial Code grants minority shareholders either a judicial venue to challenge the decisions of management or of the assembly or the right to step out of the company by requiring the company to purchase their shares when they object to certain fundamental changes, such as mergers, assets dispositions, and changes in the articles of incorporation. The variable equals zero otherwise. Minority shareholders are defined as those shareholders who own 10 percent of share capital or less.	Company Law or Commercial Code
Preemptive rights	Equals one when the Company Law or Commercial Code grants shareholders the first opportunity to buy new issues of stock. This right can only be waived by a shareholders' vote. Zero otherwise.	Company Law or Commercial Code
%capital to call an ESM	The minimum percentage of ownership of share capital that entitles a shareholder to call for an Extraordinary Shareholders' Meeting. Ranges from one to 33 percent.	Company Law or Commercial Code

		Company Law or Commercial Code
Anti-director rights	An index aggregating the shareholder rights that we labeled as "anti-director rights." The index is formed by adding 1 when: (1) the country allows shareholders to mail their proxy vote to the firm; (2) shareholders are not required to deposit their shares prior to the General Shareholders' Meeting; (3) cumulative voting or proportional representation of minorities in the board of directors is allowed; (4) an oppressed-minorities mechanism is in place; (5) the minimum percentage of share capital that entitles a shareholder to call for an Extraordinary Shareholders' Meeting is less than or equal to 10 percent (the sample median); or (6) shareholders have preemptive rights that can only be waived by a shareholders' vote. The index ranges from 0 to 6.	Company Law or Commercial Code
Restrictions for going into reorganization.	Equals one if the reorganization procedure imposes restrictions, such as creditors' consent, to file for reorganization. It equals zero if there are no such restrictions.	Bankruptcy and Reorganization Laws
No automatic stay on secured assets	Equals one if the reorganization procedure does not impose an automatic stay on the assets of the firm upon filing the reorganization petition. Automatic stay prevents secured creditors from gaining possession of their security. It equals zero if such restriction does exist in the law.	Bankruptcy and Reorganization Laws
Secured creditors first	Equals one if secured creditors are ranked first in the distribution of the proceeds that result from the disposition of the assets of a bankrupt firm. Equals zero if non-secured creditors, such as the government and workers, are given absolute priority.	Bankruptcy and Reorganization Laws

(continued on next page)

Management does not stay	Equals one when an official appointed by the court, or by the creditors, to be responsible for the operation of the business during reorganization. This variable also equals one if the debtor does not keep the administration of the property pending resolution of the reorganization process. Zero otherwise.	Bankruptcy and Reorganization Laws
Creditor Rights	An index aggregating different creditor rights. The index is formed by adding 1 when: (1) the country imposes restrictions, such as creditors' consent or minimum dividends to file for reorganization; (2) secured creditors are able to gain possession of their security once the reorganization petition has been approved (no automatic stay); (3) secured creditors are ranked first in the distribution of the proceeds that result from the disposition of the assets of a bankrupt firm; and (4) the debtor does not retain the administration of the property pending the resolution of the reorganization. The index ranges from 0 to 4.	Bankruptcy and Reorganization Laws
Efficiency of judicial system	Assessment of the "efficiency and integrity of the legal environment as it affects business, particularly foreign firms" produced by the country-risk rating agency Business International Corporation. It "may be taken to represent investors' assessments of conditions in the country in question". Average between 1980–83. Scale from 0 to 10, with lower scores signifying lower efficiency levels.	Business International Corporation.

Rule of law	Assessment of the law and order tradition in the country produced by the country-risk rating agency International Country Risk (ICR). Average of the months of April and October of the monthly index between 1982 and 1995. Scale from 0 to 10, with lower scores for less tradition for law and order.(We changed the scale from its original range of 0 to 6).	International Country Risk Guide
Corruption	ICR's assessment of the corruption in government. Lower scores indicate "high government officials are likely to demand special payments" and "illegal payments are generally expected throughout lower levels of government" in the form of "bribes connected with import and export licenses, exchange controls, tax assessment, policy protection, or loans". Average of the months of April and October of the monthly index between 1982 and 1995. Scale from 0 to 10, with lower scores for higher levels of corruption. (We changed the scale from its original range of 0 to 6).	International Country Risk Guide
Accounting standards	Index created by examining and rating companies' 1990 annual reports on their inclusion or omission of ninety items. These items fall into seven categories (general information, income statements, balance sheets, funds-flow statement, accounting standards, stock data, and special items). A minimum of three companies in each country were studied. The companies represent a cross-section of various industry groups where industrial companies numbered 70 percent while financial companies represented the remaining 30 percent.	*International Accounting and Auditing Trends,* Center for International Financial Analysis & Research, Inc.

(continued on next page)

Ownership, ten largest private firms	The average percentage of common shares owned by the three largest shareholders in the ten largest nonfinancial, privately owned domestic firms in a given country. A firm is considered privately owned if the State is not a known shareholder in it.	Moodys International, CIFAR,, EXTEL, World Scope, 20-Fs, Price Waterhouse, and various country sources.
External Cap / GNP	The ratio of the stock market capitalization held by minorities to gross national product for 1994. The stock market capitalization held by minorities is computed as the product of the aggregate stock market capitalization and the average percentage of common shares not owned by the top three shareholders in the ten largest nonfinancial, privately owned domestic firms in a given country. A firm is considered privately owned if the State is not a known shareholder in it.	Moodys International, CIFAR,, EXTEL, World Scope, 20-Fs, Price Waterhouse, and various country sources.
Domestic Firms / Pop	Ratio of the number of domestic firms listed in a given country to its population (in millions) in 1994.	Emerging Market Factbook and World Development Report 1996
IPOs / Pop	Ratio of the number of initial public offerings of equity in a given country to its population (in millions) for the period 1995:7–1996:6.	Securities Data Corporation, Asia-Money, LatinFinance, GT Guide to World Equity Markets, and World Development Report 1996.

Debt / GNP	Ratio of the sum of bank debt of the private sector and outstanding nonfinancial bonds to GNP in 1994, or last available.	International Financial Statistics, *World Bond-market Factbook.*
GDP Growth	Average annual percent growth of per capita gross domestic product for the period 1970–93.	*World Development Report 1995.*
Log GNP	Logarithm of the Gross National Product in 1994.	*World Development Report 1996.*

BIBLIOGRAPHY

American Bar Association. Multinational Commercial Insolvency. (Chicago, IL: American Bar Association, 1989 and 1993).

Beck, T., R. Levine, and N. Loayza, "Finance and the sources of growth," *Journal of Financial Economics*, vol 58 (October 2000), forthcoming.

Berglof, E. and L. von Thadden, The changing corporate governance paradigm: implications for transition and developing countries, unpublished working paper. (Stockholm, Sweden: Stockholm Institute of Transition Economics, 1999).

Carlin, W., and C. Mayer, Finance, investment and growth, unpublished working paper. (London: University College, 1999).

Coffee, J., "The future as history: the prospects for global convergence in corporate governance and its implications," Northwestern Law Review, vol 93, (1999), pp. 631-707.

Demirguc-Kunt, A. and V. Maksimovic, "Law, finance and firm growth," *Journal of Finance*, vol 53, no 6 (December 1998), pp. 2107-2139.

Diamond, Douglas. "Reputation Acquisition in Debt Markets." Journal of Political Economy 97 (1989), pp. 828–62.

Diamond, Douglas. "Debt Maturity Structure and Liquidity Risk." Quarterly *Journal of Economics* 106 (1991), pp. 1027–54.

Easterbrook, Frank and Daniel Fischel. The Economic Structure of Corporate Law. Cambridge, Mass.: Harvard University Press, 1991.

Glaeser, E., S. Johnson, and A. Shleifer, Coase v. the Coasians, Gomes, Armando. "The Dynamics of Stock Prices, Manager Ownership, and Private Benefits of Control." Manuscript. Harvard University, 1996.

Grossman, Sanford and Oliver Hart. "The Costs and Benefits of Ownership: A Theory of Vertical and Lateral Integration." *Journal of Political Economy 94* (1986), pp. 175–202.

Hart, Oliver, Different Approaches to Bankruptcy, mimeograph (Cambridge, MA: Harvard University, November 1999).

Hart, Oliver, Rafael La Porta, Florencio Lopez-de-Silanes, and John Moore, "A New Bankruptcy Procedure that Uses Multiple Auctions," European Economic Review 41 (1997), pp. 461-73.

Hellwig, M.., On the economics and politics of corporate finance and corporate control, unpublished working paper (Mannheim: University of Mannheim, 1999).

Hirschman, A., Journeys Toward Progress (New York: The Twentieth Century Fund, 1963).

Institutional Shareholder Services, Inc. Proxy Voting Guidelines for several countries. (Washington, DC: ISS Global Proxy Services, 1994).

Investor Responsibility Research Center. Proxy Voting Guide. Washington, D.C.: Global Shareholder Service, IRRC, 1994.

Jensen, Michael and William Meckling. "Theory of the Firm: Managerial Behavior, Agency Costs, and Ownership Structure." *Journal of Financial Economics 3 (*October 1976), pp. 305–60

Johnson, Simon, Peter Boone, Alasdair Breach, and Eric Friedman, "Corporate Governance in the Asian Financial Crisis," *Journal of Financial Economics,* 2000, forthcoming.

Johnson, Simon, Does investor protection matter? Evidence from Germany's Neuer Markt, unpublished working paper (Cambridge, MA: Massachusetts Institute of Technology, 1999).

King, R., Levine, R. "Finance and growth: Schumpeter might be right," *Journal of Economics,* vol 108, no 3, (August 1993), pp. 717-738.

La Porta, Rafael, Florencio Lopez-de-Silanes, Andrei Shleifer and Robert W. Vishny. "Legal Determinants of External Finance." *Journal of Finance 52* (July 1997), pp. 1131–50.

_____. "Law and Finance." *Journal of Political Economy,* vol 106, no 6 (December 1998), pp. 1113–1155.

_____. "Corporate Ownership Around the World." *Journal of Finance,* vol LIV, no 2 (April 1999), pp. 471-517.

_____. "Agency Problems and Dividend Policies Around the World." Working Paper no. 6594. Cambridge, Mass.: *National Bureau of Economic Research,* June 1998.

Levine, Ross, "Law, Finance, and Economic Growth," *Journal of Financial Intermediation,* vol 8, no 2 (April 1999).

Levine, Ross and S. Zervos, "Stock markets, banks and economic growth," *American Economic Review,* vol 88, no 3 (June 1998), pp, 537-558.

Lins, Karl, Deon Strickland and Marc Zenner, Do non-US firms Issue equity on US Stock Exchanges to Relax Capital Constraints? Mimeograph, University of North Carolina at Chapel Hill, January 2000

McCraw, Thomas K. Prophets of Regulation (Cambridge, MA: The Belknap Press of Harvard University, 1984).

Modigliani, Franco and Merton Miller. "The Cost of Capital, Corporation Finance, and the Theory of Investment." *American Economic Review 48* (June 1958), pp. 261–97.

Rajan, Raghuram and Luigi Zingales. "What Do We Know about Capital Structure: Some Evidence from International Data." *Journal of Finance 50* (December 1995), pp. 1421–60.

Rajan, Raghuram and Luigi Zingales, "Financial dependence and growth," American Economic Review, vol 88, no 3, (June 1998), pp, 559–586.

Reynolds, Thomas and Arturo Flores. Foreign Law: Current Sources of Basic Legislation in Jurisdictions of the World. Littleton, Colo.: Rothman and Co., 1989.

Shleifer, Andrei and Robert W. Vishny. "Large Shareholders and Corporate Control." Journal of Political Economy 94 (June 1986), pp. 461–88.

Vishny, Paul. Guide to International Commerce Law. New York: McGraw-Hill, 1994.

Weisbach, Michael S. and WIlliam A. Reese, Protection of Minority shareholder interests, cross-listings in the United States, and Subsequent Equity Offerings, Mimeograph, University of Illinois Department of Finance.

White, Michelle, "The Costs of Corporate Bankruptcy: the U.S.-European Comparison," manuscript (Ann Arbor: University of Michigan, Department of Economics, 1993).

Wurgler, J., "Financial markets and the allocation of capital, Journal of Financial Economics, vol 58, (October 2000), forthcoming.

Economic Crisis and Corporate Reform in East Asia

A Paper from the Project on Development, Trade and International Finance

Meredith Woo-Cumings

A Council on Foreign Relations Paper

Economic Crisis and Corporate Reform in East Asia

Meredith Woo-Cumings

The Asian financial crisis of 1997–98 involved, among other things, a failure of regulation. Some believe this failure is endemic to global capitalism, and others believe it was profoundly local and idiosyncratic, emanating from regulatory flaws in the affected countries, stretching an arc from Thailand and Indonesia to Korea and Japan. There is also a debate about the nature of the regulation that failed. Some argue that the crisis emanated from a surfeit of nettlesome regulations and endemic industrial policy; while others claim it happened for want of effective regulations and (even) industrial policy. Across the hypotenuse of these disagreements, however, stretches a universal recognition that regulatory infrastructure and institutions do matter and that they must play a major role in the way we think about economic development. After the miracle years in East Asia, "good governance" has become the Spirit of the Age.

I intend to examine one aspect of this trend toward good governance: corporate governance. Reform of corporate governance was at the heart of the comprehensive reform package put together during the Asian crisis by the International Monetary Fund, especially with regard to Korea. The ambition behind the reform package was to alter, once and for all, the way that the Korean big businesses conducted themselves. Thus the IMF, in full cooperation with the newly elected government of Kim Dae Jung, demanded that Korea's big businesses reduce their reliance on debt financing by half—from over 400 percent to 200 percent by the end of 1999—and suggested specific ways it could be done. The

IMF also asked Korea's big businesses to sell off their "non-core" subsidiaries, and to stop diversifying into unrelated fields. Moreover, it demanded that Korea institute a governance system whereby the power of minority shareholders and outside directors would be vastly enhanced.

I will argue that the issue of corporate governance must be understood in time and place, and in historical and political context. Such an approach may mean eschewing common assumptions about regulatory frameworks and reform proposals that make more sense in settings, such as the United States, accustomed to complex legal regulation. In presenting my argument, I will also underscore the enormity of the economic, social, and political problems lurking in the shadow of this innocuous term, corporate governance. To instruct the present and to caution future expectations of reform, I will examine past practices of *corporate governance* in East Asia. Several East Asian countries have now embarked upon reforms, prompted by the exigencies of the 1997–98 financial crisis and the disciplines of the International Monetary Fund. Much American commentary in the past six months blames the Asian crisis on certain generic attributes—"crony capitalism," absence of transparency, moral hazards, and a general failure of the rule of law, all characteristics considered ubiquitous throughout the region. However, I sharply distinguish Northeast Asia from Southeast Asia and find two highly distinctive patterns of corporate governance. The first is a Japan-shaped model that influences Taiwan and the current leadership in China, but is best exemplified by South Korea (hereafter Korea). The second is a Chinese business-practice model whose roots are at least 150 years old. It is market-adaptive and efficient enough to need little reform of corporate practice— or perhaps, from an Anglo-Saxon standpoint, to need so *much* as to make the task impossible.

Other experts can say more than I about the types of reforms that *should* have occurred or that *ought* to be enacted now, in the suddenly distressed East Asian region. I hope to illuminate the nature of corporate governance and discover what past experiences with reform can tell us. Finally, I will explore the possibilities and limits of corporate reform in the current climate of crisis and change:

what *could* have been done in the past and what *can* perhaps be done now, given the very different business experiences of the two regions.

In the midst of financial crisis and IMF reform programs, corporate governance came to be associated with international demands for transparency and accountability (especially with regard to Korea's corporate reforms). Few in the United States would object to these seemingly reasonable general principles. They sound like sweet reason. But what things are *called* can be infinitely more important than what they *are*. To many people in East Asia, the term corporate governance has a neologistic ring to it. In the context of societies that may lack the legal norms and traditions that undergirded the rise of the rational modern corporation, corporate governance is a problematic concept. Let's look briefly at several reasons for this, in order to clear away conceptual underbrush and arrive at a better comprehension of this complex subject.

The traditional discourse of corporate governance was predicated on the long-standing practice in the United States of separating corporate ownership from control. In the context of "modern" enterprise, good governance is really about holding corporate management accountable to the interests of shareholders, or reducing *agency costs* (meaning the costs to shareholders of managerial behavior not consistent with their interests). The methods for achieving this accountability are often formal and legalistic and, according to some, idiosyncratic to Anglo-American traditions. In this sense, corporate governance can be thought of as a separate taxonomic entity from, say, "contractual governance," which is said to characterize the "Nippo-Rhenish" model of business organization. In the latter, good governance is a matter of reducing *transactions costs* by building and investing in stable and long-term commercial relationships among transacting companies.[1]

To avoid equating corporate governance with the ideal type of Anglo-American business practice (which would have limited utility as a template for countries with substantially different legal norms

[1] Peter Gourevitch, "The Macropolitics of Microinstitutional Differences in the Analysis of Comparative Capitalism," in Suzanne Berger and Ronald Dore, eds., *National Diversity and Global Capitalism* (Ithaca, N.Y.: Cornell University Press, 1966).

and traditions), we can seek a broader conceptualization that transcends the regional-specificity of governance models. Carl Kester provides a functional definition in which corporate governance is understood simply as "the entire set of incentives, safeguards, and dispute-resolution processes used to order the activities of various corporate stakeholders, each seeking to improve its welfare through coordinated economic activity with others."[2] In this rendering, both the Anglo-American and Nippo-Rhenish systems of governance are economically rational attempts to resolve problems of coordination and control among corporate stakeholders, and no *a priori* judgment is made about the ultimate superiority of either national configuration. This catholic definition of corporate governance is still, however, predicated on the highly evolved structure of the modern corporation, with a whole panoply of legal or otherwise regularized sets of norms that dictate the behavior of transacting parties.

Furthermore, the debate on corporate governance in the context of global competition has been particularly fickle and prone to reevaluations. In the 1980s and well into the 1990s, for instance, it was fashionable to argue that the Anglo-American style of corporate governance (and various corporate-restructuring movements in particular) reduced investment and forced American managers to think "short-term." In contrast, Japanese corporate managers were thought to enjoy certain freedoms in retaining excess capital (rather than returning it to shareholders) and in determining long-term investment strategies (without oversight of shareholders). Once upon a time, this was viewed as the core of Japan's competitive edge.

Today, this historical verdict has been completely reversed. Michael Jensen argues that in periods of industrial transformation, in the late nineteenth century and in the last two decades, rapid technological and organizational change encourages reduced production costs and increased average productivity of labor. Rapid

---

[2]Carl Kester, "American and Japanese Corporate Governance: Convergence to Best Practice?" in Suzanne Berger and Ronald Dore, ibid.

change results in widespread excess capacity and reduced rates of growth in labor income, causing corporate downsizing and exit. The best example would be the mergers-and-acquisitions wave of the 1980s that ended up sharply reducing capacity (by consolidating some 1,800 U.S. firms into roughly 150). Combined with leveraged takeovers and buyouts, the mergers-and-acquisitions phenomenon represented "healthy adjustments" to overcapacity that burdened many sectors of the U.S. economy. Corporate raiders turned out to be the "ephors," the overseers, of modern capitalism. Likewise, the decline in the Japanese economy was viewed as the result of a "structural" overcapacity, fueled by lax investment criteria employed by Japanese companies and the failure to pay out excess capital in the form of higher dividends or share repurchases.[3]

Such periodic revaluation reflects profound (or at least shifting) uncertainty about what constitutes a good system of corporate governance. We all agree that good corporate governance is important, as are motherhood, the flag, peace, and good will to humanity. But what exactly constitutes truly *good* governance, and how is it obtained? The contemporary discourse on corporate governance, influenced as it is by Western practice and experience, offers little hope of achieving a consensual understanding of the meaning of good governance. This makes institutional emulation on the part of "late" developers that much more difficult—particularly for the economies of East Asia, where the norm is not the "modern" corporation, with a long-standing separation between management and ownership, but the family-owned and controlled firm, which can take the form of the modal Korean conglomerate, the *chaebol*, or the Chinese family enterprise in Southeast Asia.

A reform project of corporate governance first must determine which measures will work. And the essence of making dramatic reform *work* is to ask, "*Cui bono?*" Societies differ in their collective goals and priorities, and in the moral valence they assign them,

---

[3]Michael Jensen, "The Modern Industrial Revolution, Exit, and the Failure of Internal Control Systems," in Donald H. Chew, ed., *Studies in Corporate Finance and Governance Systems: A Comparison of the U.S., Japan, and Europe* (New York: Oxford University Press, 1997); and Donald H. Chew, ibid., "Introduction."

so it is conceivable that improved welfare of stakeholders may not always have priority, for better or worse, over other collective goals. The rise of particular business systems bears some relationship to the collective goals of the society, whether they are popularly mandated or unilaterally imposed from above. The *chaebol* in Korea, like the prewar Japanese *zaibatsu*, is unthinkable without the vast project of nationalist economic mobilization that prevailed over three decades. The aim was to create, through all variety of state subsidies and supports, world-class competitive enterprises. Likewise, the behavior and organization of Chinese enterprises in Southeast Asia are influenced by the highly charged political terrain where they operate, leading to catch-as-catch-can outcomes— that is, ethnic divisions of labor and ethnically demarcated redistributive policies, both perhaps most visible in Malaysia.

In light of the current debate on corporate governance, the only possible answer to the question "who benefits" is that good governance enhances the welfare of corporate stakeholders, regardless of their nationalities, affiliations, goals, and designs. In other words, reform of corporate governance has to be plausible in the context of what *is* (and not simply what ought to be) and resonant with larger social goals that enjoy broad support. It is best to think of corporate governance in an idiosyncratic *national* context—for example, the absence in many countries of effective institutions of property rights and, related to that, the persistence of a traditional, family-owned corporate structure. Some scholars of East Asian business organization eschew the concept of corporate governance altogether, and instead favor a study of different "business systems." Richard Whitley defines the latter as a "distinctive configuration of hierarchy-market relations which become institutionalized as relatively successful ways of organizing economic activities in different institutional environments."[4] A "business system," of course, is a distinctly vague category if we are grappling with the reform of corporate governance. But the merit of Whitley's sociological approach may be to alert us to the true magni-

---

[4]Richard Whitley, *Business Systems in East Asia: Firms, Markets, and Societies* (New York: Sage Publications, 1992), p. 13.

tude of social change that would have to accompany any meaningful reform in corporate governance. Furthermore, it brings us to that sphere where any serious reflection on corporate governance should start: state and society.

NORTHEAST AND SOUTHEAST ASIA
BETWEEN THE STATE AND THE
"SIB-FETTERS" OF THE ECONOMY

Westerners have been remarkably consistent in the way they have discussed the problems they have seen in capitalist enterprise in East Asia during the past century. As early as 1904, Max Weber postulated that the modern rational enterprise was predicated on "the separation of business from the household" and the "rational bookkeeping" that would issue forth from independent firms, thus presaging today's debate about family-controlled firms in East Asia and the lack of transparency in their business accounting.[5] For Weber, the predominance of family-run enterprises and the relative absence of rational accounting were prima facie evidence not merely of bad corporate governance, but also that capitalism in East Asia was not modern, rational, or normal—that is to say (and Weber said it over and over), not Occidental. Weber found it puzzling that the Chinese, who generally seemed to exhibit the appropriate "acquisitive virtuosity" and "deification of wealth" (in the Confucian sense that wealth was the means toward a virtuous and dignified life), failed to achieve the kind of depersonalization of business reflected in the commercial laws of the Italian city-states. The "unceasing and intensive economic ado" of the Chinese did not originate in the legal forms and social foundations of capitalist enterprise, Weber argued, because of a double bind consisting of a premodern political order on the one hand and a particular type of kinship structure ("acquisitive familial community") on the other.[6] This focus on the *state* and the *family* is of particular interest to us here.

---

[5]Max Weber, *The Protestant Ethic and the Spirit of Capitalism* (New York: Charles Scribner's Sons, 1976 [1958]), p. 22.

[6]Max Weber, *The Religion of China* (New York: The Free Press, 1951), pp. 85, 242, 245.

Weber had an extensive lexicon for describing the political order that connived with Confucian and Taoist predilections to deny modernity and rationality to East Asia and that filled the well of ideas and definitions from which many scholars continue to draw. China had what Weber called "political capitalism," or sometimes "bureaucratic capitalism," in the form of "usury connected with office, emergency loans, wholesale trade and industrial *ergasteria,*" or capital connected with extortionist practices in office. This lexicon has been continuously replayed in discussions of capitalism in East Asia. It is used to explain why no capitalism existed in the past and what kind of capitalism can be observed now.[7] Weber also used the terms "booty capitalism," which experts still use to describe the worst excesses of the government and the oligarchy in the Philippines, and "pariah capitalism," which remains a common description of Chinese entrepreneurship in Southeast Asia.[8] In other words, Westerners have thought that East Asia possessed a system of capitalism that is nothing like what Werner Sombart might call "high capitalism," whether in the precapitalist dynasties of a century ago or in the "miracle" economies that seemed to define the meaning of Third World development for a generation.

Cultural tendencies or "mentalities" cannot be conceived apart from the existing political and market opportunities and incentives. Even Weber, who spoke disparagingly of the kinship organization in China as the "sib-fetter" of the economy, understood that the communal, or sib economic organization "protected the individual against the dangers of proletarization and capitalist subjection." The patriarchal sib was, for him, an expression of "the abolition of feudal estates" as well as "the extensiveness of patrimonial bureaucratic organization."[9] Just as Marx thought religion was both

---

[7] Weber, ibid., p. 242. For a representative example of the current usage of "bureaucratic capitalism," see Maurice Meisner, *The Deng Xiaoping Era: An Inquiry into the Fate of Chinese Socialism, 1978–1994* (New York: Hill & Wang, 1996), ch. 11.

[8] "Booty capitalism" is a variant of "adventure capitalism," referring to a system where rulers raid the population for treasures. Paul Hutchcroft uses the term to describe the predatory behavior of the oligarchy in the Philippines, especially in the Marcos years. See Paul D. Hutchcroft, "Patrimonial State, Predatory Oligarchy: The Politics of Private Commercial Banking in the Philippines," Ph.D. diss., Yale University, 1993.

[9] Weber, *The Religion of China*, pp. 96–97.

the "sigh" and the opium of the oppressed, Weber maintained that the Chinese sib-based economic organization seemed to work both to protect against the incipient capitalism of late imperial China and to prevent the rise of a culture of universalistic trust. That is, in the absence of or amid the rise of a contract-based system of business trust, one's own family was still the best bet. Given the tenuous political exigencies of the Chinese diaspora and the prevalence of particularistic trust in East Asia, it is not surprising that this tried-and-true system of Chinese enterprise persists to this day, especially since the organization of Chinese business enterprises appears ideally suited for small businesses. But it is also not difficult to imagine that large, globally competitive Chinese firms will eventually look and behave more like Western-style enterprises. Indeed, they already do in places like Hong Kong and Singapore; for big firms, sib-based "familism" may now be yielding diminishing returns as a form of corporate organization.

The main point is that the Western discourse on East Asian capitalism tends to miss two key points. First, East Asian business has developed in a cocoon of particular historic practice. What appears irrational from an ideal or typical Western standpoint may be an effective local adaptation in the interest of wealth accumulation. Second, development has been so incredibly rapid that practices that might have been expected to die out have persisted because everything seemed to work. For nearly fifty years, East Asian capitalism developed at a phenomenal speed, in many cases in a single generation; therefore, rapid growth was not so much the solvent of outdated practice as its preservative.

Today, that era seems forgotten, and the term "crony capitalism" is often used to refer indiscriminately to the economic systems of East Asia. But no single category can encompass all of East Asian capitalism. Even in the worst periods of authoritarianism in Korea and Japan, the "cronyism" of Northeast Asia never approached that of Southeast Asia.[10] The relationship between the

---

10One might argue that even Southeast Asia, with the exception of Indonesia, never came close to the original context of "cronyism." According to Kunio Yoshihara, the term "crony capitalism" was coined in the Philippines during martial law, to denote those who benefited greatly from close relations with Ferdinand Marcos. Because the power of

state and the big corporations was forged through industrial policy, which was simultaneously disciplinarian *and* munificent with
regard to big business. But in Southeast Asia, the relationship between
the state and big business was forged through an ethnic division
of labor in managing politics and economy, in the context of ethnic apartheid between political and economic powers. Indonesia
under President Suharto was always the worst case, a classic
"cronyism" of sultan-like dictatorship and political monopoly. It
was a kind of capitalism in one family, with Suharto and his rel-
atives and children constituting by far the biggest conglomerate.
The truly entrepreneurial element in Indonesia, the ethnic Chinese business class, was always at risk of being prostrated before
the rifle butt or the ethnic pogrom (or both, as in the 1965 blood-
letting). A state like this is interested in economic development
only to the extent that it receives its payoffs. Otherwise it is not
at all interested in development, in part because the ethnically alien
group is synonymous with entrepreneurial business. This does not
mean that the state was absent in the development effort. On the
contrary, it played an important role in expanding markets, foreign capital inflows, new technologies, and the growth of an
urban, educated middle class—in short, everything that the 1993
World Bank report, *The East Asian Miracle,* argued that it did. Suharto worked with and protected the ethnic Chinese, as long as their
payoffs continued. But it is also true that there were occasional serious efforts in Southeast Asia to break the "economic stronghold
of the overseas Chinese" by excluding them altogether from certain lines of business, especially in Malaysia.[11] The main point is
that, in Southeast Asia, the widely discussed lack of transparency and accountability in corporate governance grows out of
a very different state-society interaction. It is the result of the

---

Marcos was so absolute, the length of his rule so long, and the benefits accruing from
associating with him so enormous, Yoshihara thinks that the terms ought to be used with
utmost specificity. See Yoshihara, *The Rise of Ersatz Capitalism in South-East Asia* (Singapore: Oxford University Press, 1988).

[11]Jamie Mackie, "Changing Patterns of Chinese Big Business in Southeast Asia," in
Ruth McVey, ed., *Southeast Asian Capitalists.* (Ithaca, N.Y.: Cornell Southeast Asian Program, 1992), pp. 162, 165.

elaborate ethnic give-and-take of Malaysia or of the protection/racketeering that prevails in Indonesia.

Westerners are not alone in finding it difficult to fathom the worst excesses of "crony capitalism" in Southeast Asia. From the vantage point of Northeast Asian political economy, it can also appear quite baffling. The Japanese economist Kunio Yoshihara, for example, argues in an influential book that capitalism in Southeast Asia is "ersatz" because it is developed by foreign and overseas Chinese capital and is not, therefore, wholly dedicated to building a sound, national, manufacturing base. It is also ersatz, he claims, because it is "technology-less" and consequently "dependent" on the multinationals. Finally, it is captured by various kinds of rent-seekers and speculators—running the gamut from "royal capitalists" (presidential families) to "crony capitalists" (private-sector businessmen who benefit from close relations with the head of a state), to "bureaucratic capitalists," "politicians-turned-capitalists," and "capitalists-turned-politicians." In other words, it is a far cry from the Japanese or the Korean style of growth, which Yoshihara claims is not a genuine form of capitalism because it places industrial policy at its core.[12] We might call this Japan-centric solipsism (as opposed to the Occidentalist solipsism of Weber and Sombart), but Yoshihara nonetheless plumbs key differences between Northeast Asia and Southeast Asia.

How does knowing the differences between the political economies of North and Southeast Asia help us understand the evolution and constraints of business enterprises in their respective areas? Comparative studies of economic development in multiethnic and homogenous societies are rare,[13] although Joseph Schumpeter did allude to the critical importance of the ethnic factor in class and business enterprise formation, in a seminal essay entitled "Social Classes in an Ethnically Homogeneous Environment."[14]

---

[12]Yoshihara, *The Rise of Ersatz Capitalism in South-East Asia.*

[13]Most studies of the relationship between ethnicity and business in Southeast Asia do not cut across regional boundaries and have not generated a useful thesis about the impact of ethnicity in economic development.

[14]Joseph A. Schumpeter, *Imperialism/Social Classes* (New York: Meridian Books, 1951). This was probably prompted by the late nineteenth-century debate on the role of the Jews in the rise of Western capitalism.

Despite the dearth of research on the subject, the ethnic dimension has significant implications for economic development and business enterprises.

In Southeast Asia, many governments have attempted to curtail the role of the Chinese through restrictive licenses, protective tariffs, ownership limitations, preferential credit allocations, and outright bans on Chinese activity in particular sectors.[15] The flip side of this coin has been massive government help to non-Chinese enterprises, including placing entire sectors under state enterprises, and giving indigenous businessmen comparatively easy access to licenses, contracts, subsidized credits, and joint ventures with foreign companies.[16] The Chinese response has run the whole creative gamut, making adaptability the highest premium in doing business. This has meant cultivating political patrons and sponsors, providing bribes and payoffs to local and central government officials to circumvent restrictions and secure protection, as well as creating so-called Ali-Baba ventures with indigenous "sleeping partners" in whose names the enterprises are registered.[17] Still, the alliance with indigenous patrons does not seem to alter the essential character of the Chinese firm. The family-oriented closed corporation, based on an individual tycoon and his family, is often thought to limit the Chinese capacity for capital mobilization and organizational expansion, but instead seems to reinforce it. In Malaysia, for instance, Malay interests participate actively in Chinese companies, but the Chinese entrepreneurs retain centralized control of the businesses by owning large blocks of shares. Lim Mah Hui's study of one hundred of the largest corporations in Malaysia reveals that the Chinese directors outnumber the Malays by two to one. Moreover, the Chinese directors tended to possess substantial ownership interests in the companies they sit

---

[15]Linda Lim and L. A. Peter Gosling, "Strengths and Weaknesses of Minority Status for Southeast Asian Chinese at a Time of Economic Growth and Liberalization," in Lim and Gosling, eds., *The Chinese in Southeast Asia*, vol. 1: Ethnicity and Economic Activity (Singapore: Maruzen Asia, 1983), p. 286.

[16]Mackie, "Changing Patterns of Chinese Big Business in Southeast Asia," p. 165.

[17]There is a large literature on this topic. For details, see Linda Lim and L. A. Peter Gosling, eds., *The Chinese in Southeast Asia*, and Ruth McVey, ed., *Southeast Asian Capitalists*.

on, whereas this was less so for Malay directors.[18] Hence, Robert Kuok can be closely associated with a vast panoply of Malay partners, including representatives from the aristocracy, the military, and the bureaucracy (but not prominent businessmen), while retaining his legendary tight control of his vast family empire.[19]

The most careful articulation to date of an "ethnic framework" of economic development is the work by James Judason, also for Malaysia. In the context of a historic pluralism deriving from ethnically based political mobilization, the goal of the national leadership is to shape development to enhance the dominant ethnic party's political base and to meet the cultural aspirations of "backward" groups. By retaining a great deal of discretionary control over the private sector and business firms, the state can facilitate expansion of its enterprises and enforce "affirmative action" in favor of the economically "backward" Malay majority.

What is the result of this "ethnic logic of accumulation" (as versus the "national logic of accumulation" that one might find in Northeast Asia)? According to Judason, it privileges the state enterprise, the surplus from which can be redistributed along ethnic lines, and also the foreign multinational corporation, which provides the state with a source of entrepreneurship that is an alternative to the Chinese (as well as providing employment in labor-intensive, export industries). To the extent that there is a business alliance, it does not unite the state and domestic enterprises and pit them against multinationals (as might be the case in more nationalist states); instead, it binds together the state and multinationals, often against the Chinese domestic enterprise. This has been called an "ethnic bypass," meaning that Malays collaborate with foreign partners to avoid dependence on the Chinese (for example, in their national car project). There are exceptions, of course; some politically influential Chinese have managed to do well in import-substitution industries such as cement, flour, sugar, and automobile

---

[18]Lim Mah Hui, The Ownership and Control of the Largest Corporations in Malaysia: The Role of Chinese Businessmen," in Lim and Gosling, ibid.

[19]Heng Pek Koon, "The Chinese Business Elite of Malaysia," in Ruth McVey, ed., *Southeast Asian Capitalists.*

assembly.[20] But the state certainly has not favored the Chinese entrepreneurs (who own most of the Malaysian manufacturing enterprises). In fact, it often harasses them for violating laws on intellectual property rights, land use, labor, and environment. The upshot is that the Chinese manufacturing entrepreneurs prefer to remain small and family-owned, engaged in a kind of "guerrilla capitalism" that limits growth, economies of scale in production, technological innovation, marketing, and international competitiveness. Thus, the consequences for regulating wages, industrial safety, occupational health, and environmental protection are disastrous. K. S. Jomo, the Malay economist, concludes that "while [the Chinese] may represent Malaysia's best chance for domestic-led industrialization, it is doubtful that they will be granted the opportunity necessary for expansion."[21] Another consequence of the harassing presence of the state, exemplified by the "New Economic Policy," has been to make the Chinese gravitate toward finance and real estate, investments that offer rapid, attractive returns and quick exit. The consequences of all this, Judason argues, are structural inefficiencies in the economy and growth rates that depend upon both commodity prices and on political priorities that emphasize employment and stable wages for purposes of the political incorporation of Malays.[22]

The historical, cultural, and institutional constraints (and opportunities) that Chinese businesses face in Southeast Asia help to explain the persistence of the family firm. But several sociologists and anthropologists who have long studied business enterprises in East Asia differ with this assessment. They have argued that Chinese business practices are the same everywhere, whether the Chinese are in the minority or the majority. Gary Hamilton and Tony Waters write:

---

[20]K. S. Jomo, "A Specific Idiom of Chinese Capitalism in Southeast Asia: Sino-Malaysian Capital Accumulation in the Face of State Hostility." In Daniel Chirot and Anthony Reid, eds., *Essential Outsiders: Chinese and Jews in the Modern Transformation of Southeast Asia and Central Europe.* (Seattle: University of Washington Press, 1997), p. 250.

[21]Ibid., p. 248.

[22]James V. Judason, *Ethnicity and the Economy: The State, Chinese Business, and Multinationals in Malaysia* (Singapore: Oxford University Press, 1989), p. 15.

A sociology of minority capitalism cannot explain Chineseeconomic success when their entrepreneurial strategies in locationssuch as Hong Kong and Taiwan are similar, if not identical, to thosethey use in Southeast Asia and other locations where they are in theminority. And if accounts are given of the entrepreneurial efforts ofthe Chinese in the People's Republic of China are correct, it appearsthat the organizational strategies of Chinese entrepreneurs in Chinaare the same as those elsewhere.[23]

In other words, capitalism is a matter of a particular cultural mentality—and we are back to a relatively straightforward reading of Weber on capitalism. (A leading expert on Chinese business enterprises, S. Gordon Redding, has titled his book, *The Spirit of Chinese Capitalism*, a parody of Weber's *The Protestant Ethic and the Spirit of Capitalism*.[24]) I maintain, however, that Chinese organizational strategy is best understood as the shadow that is attached not to some ubiquitous Chinese culture but to a minatory world where trust is low, contracts are not strictly enforced, laws may be unfair, and the politics of the ruling parties can lead to riches or ruin. Regardless of which position one takes, however, it must be acknowledged that Chinese corporate governance springs from a milieu entirely different from that of American firms. The same is true of a different form of corporate governance, the Northeast Asian variety.

---

[23]Gary Hamilton and Tony Waters, "Chinese Capitalism in Thailand: Embedded Networks and Industrial Structure." in Hamilton, Gary, ed., *Asian Business Networks* (Berlin, Germany and Hawthorne, N.Y.: Walter de Gruyter, 1996), p. 278.

[24]For work in this genre, see S. R. Clegg and S. G. Redding, eds., *Capitalism in Contrasting Cultures* (New York: Walter de Gruyter, 1990); Gary Hamilton, ed., *Asian Business Networks* (Berlin, Germany, and Hawthornd, N.Y.: Walter de Gruyter, 1996); Richard Whitley, *Business Systems in East Asia: Firms, Markets, and Societies* (New York: Sage Publications, 1992). For Korea, see Roger L. Jinelli, *Making Capitalism* (Stanford, Calif.: Stanford University Press, 1993, 1995).

CORPORATE GOVERNANCE IN KOREA

Korea is perhaps the most pristine case of nationalist mobilization for economic development, and it may be taken as the postwar exemplar of the Northeast Asian model—the original incubator of twentieth-century nationalist industrial strategies. Northeast Asia contains three capitalist countries that formed the core of the prewar Japanese empire and whose economic structures were tightly interwoven and articulated: Japan, Korea, and Taiwan. Notwithstanding the great human suffering that Japan inflicted on its former colonies, the postwar developmental trajectories of Korea and Taiwan were heavily influenced by the models and policies that Japan demonstrated for them and imposed upon them before World War II. Japan illustrated them again—by example this time—in the 1950s and 1960s, during its heyday of rapid export-led growth. Because nothing succeeds like success, Korea and Taiwan embarked on a similar trajectory of light-industrial exporting under multiyear plans, guided by strong state ministries (less strong in Taiwan than in Korea) and taking from Japan its lessons, experiences, advanced technologies, and capital. This gave all three economies a highly neomercantilist, nationalist tendency. In Japan and Korea, it meant strong state involvement with, and promotion of, big economic conglomerates (the *keiretsu* and the *chaebol*), rather than engaging in "ethnic bypassing" as in Malaysia. (Malays worried about the Chinese; but because Koreans worried about escaping dependency, they permitted much less foreign direct investment.)

The Republic of Korea has been a security state in the global system ever since its division in 1945, and it has used these security concerns to justify the logic of industrialization since the end of the Korean War in 1953. Its critical position during the Cold War enabled it to attract huge amounts of external savings—foreign aid in the 1950s and 1960s and foreign loans in the late 1970s and the 1980s. But Korea was a state born without a capitalist class of its own (and was thus bereft of the mainstay of capitalist development), so the project of independent Korea was created by a constellation of the entrepreneurial elements using a credit-based system of industrial finance.

In a nation with a dearth of accumulated capital, business had to rely on credits from banks that the state controlled and (until the 1980s) owned. Because the firms were highly leveraged, much more so than they were in Latin America or Southeast Asia, business had to maintain good relations with the state so as to avert the possibility of default (through severance of friendly credits). For its part, the state manipulated Korea's credit-based system of industrial financing so it could exert influence over the economy's investment pattern and guide sectoral mobility. The highly leveraged nature of business firms in Korea—the norm throughout Korean history—meant that even small changes in the discount rate or in concessional credit rates between sectors could dramatically affect resource allocation, because the effect of such instruments on the firms' cash-flow position was so much greater given the high debt-equity ratios. For that reason, Korean firms closely conformed to the macroeconomic policy goals of the state.[25]

We now have the skeletal outline of the different relationship of government to business in Northeast and Southeast Asia. In one fundamental way, however, there is something that these interventionist states have had in common, which brings us back to the earlier Weberian question of the absence of legal forms and social foundations for modern, legal-rational capitalist enterprise. In homogeneous Korea, as in multiethnic Southeast Asia, the state is the guarantor of property rights (albeit for different reasons), and the modal enterprise is the family firm. In other words, in Northeast Asia, too, we find a charismatic political order based on vast discretionary political power, rather than on the rule of law or norms that are legitimated over time. Both the small Chinese firm in Indonesia, which is escaping from the burdensome legal realm to the extralegal "gray economy," and the Korean manufacturing behemoth,

---

[25]For details, see Jung-en Woo (Meredith Woo-Cumings), *Race to the Swift: State and Finance in Korean Industrialization* (New York: Columbia University Press, 1992)

which believes it still needs to get even bigger, are forestalling the threat of outright confiscation.

A couple of vignettes of the politics of confiscation will illustrate how the politicization of property rights in Korea is an artifact of decades of military authoritarianism. One of the first acts of the military regime after the coup in 1961 was an anticorruption campaign that rounded up the richest men in Korea and stamped them as profiteers with "illicit fortunes," although their real crime was to engage in the political economy of the earlier Syngman Rhee regime. In the end, the situation was resolved when the businessmen were allowed to use the huge fines levied on them to establish industrial firms, donating shares in the firms back to the government. Banks, however, were confiscated, swiftly nationalized, and lined up under the direction of the ministry of finance. From this point on, big corporations could anticipate that political-regime changes would be accompanied by various kinds of shakedowns, ranging from the payment of huge bribes to so-called industrial rationalization (involving forced mergers and the like) to the outright confiscation of property.[26]

In the 1980 "industrial reorganization" that followed upon Chun Doo Hwan's coup, for instance, the three biggest *chaebol* groups were ordered to give up firms specializing in the production of power-generating and heavy-construction equipment, which were merged into Korean Heavy Industries and Construction. Saehan Autos was forced to merge with Hyundai so there would be only two makers of passenger cars; Kia and Tong-a were merged into a monopoly on trucks and buses; the heavy electric subsidiaries of Sangyong and Kolon were merged with another firm; and so on.[27] Property rights were completely insecure unless the state (often meaning the ruling dictator) approved of the firm and what it was doing, something that was mightily expedited by large political

---

[26]To see the extent of this discretionary power, see Andrew Pollack, "In California, A Distant Mirror on Korea," *The New York Times*, March 25, 1998, about how a major *chaebol* owner watched Chun Doo Hwan transfer his company and his own personal property to another business group, just because the bribes hadn't been big enough.

[27]For details, see Woo (Woo-Cumings), *Race to the Swift*, p. 178.

contributions. Business leaders could lose not only their firms but their own fortunes at the whim of the state.

A typical example was the dismantling of Kukje, Korea's sixth-largest conglomerate, in 1985. By that time, Kukje was involved in everything from manufacturing jogging shoes to construction, securities, steel-making, paper-making, shipping, resorts, tires, farm tools, and running an aluminum smelting plant. But it was also massively indebted and split by a long-standing family feud. In February 1985, the government decided to pull the plug on the firm and its preferential funding, and proceeded to dismantle it and turn its assets over to others. This involved no "due process, no bidding for assets, only a multimillion-dollar takeover operation shrouded in secrecy." The reason for this confiscation, the owner of Kukje claimed in 1988, was the paltriness of his contribution to the ruling group.[28]

This is by no means an atypical story of "corporate governance" in Korea, nor was the assault of the authoritarian regime on property rights limited to big business. During an acute financial crisis in the early 1970s, the government imposed a sudden moratorium on all payments of corporate debts owed to the private, *domestic* financial market, otherwise known as the "curb market," with market-determined—that is to say, high—interest rates. The crushing burden of interest payments on foreign loans was thus shifted overnight to small investors, who had followed their entrepreneurial instincts and put their savings in a curb market yielding much higher interest returns on financial assets than the banks.[29] In short, the problem of corporate governance cannot be resolved without addressing the problem of the continuing discretionary power of the politicians' and the bureaucrats' residual

---

[28]Mark Clifford, *Troubled Tiger* (Armonk, N.Y.: M. E. Sharpe, 1997), pp. 218–22.

[29]A total of 209,896 persons were registered as creditors through the curb market, of which 70% were small lenders with assets in the market below one million won. (At the official 1971 exchange rate of 346.1 won to US$1, this equaled $2,889). They were ordinary citizens: female factory workers saving for marriage, parents preparing for their children's college tuition, would-be homeowners, senior citizens, etc. The moratorium was to last three years, after which all curb funds had to be turned into five-year loans at the maximum annual interest rate of 18%. In reality, the rate on curb after the moratorium ended up being half of what it was before.

industrial policy, as well as a host of other problems that come under the rubric of the rule of law.

The history of the Korean *chaebol* is not old, but the roots of this form of corporate organization can be traced to Japan. Most of the big Korean firms date from the post–Korean War period, especially the mid-1960s, when the export-led "take-off" began. They were bolstered by economic liberalization that promoted export-led growth. Important measures included: financial reforms that freed, at least temporarily, financial prices from government control; massive foreign aid that continued to pour in as the result of Korea's strategic position and its substantial participation in the Vietnam War; the normalization of relations with Japan, which meant additional wherewithal for industrial financing; and the availing presence of the vast export market in the United States. In this environment of such economic munificence, the government in Korea helped create a whole constellation of can-do entrepreneurs, who became the mainstay of Korea's industrialization.

The question of the deeper origins of the Korean *chaebol* is important because the answer explains how things got to be the way they are, and may suggest possible trajectories for reform. The template for the *chaebol* was the wartime Japanese *zaibatsu*. Korea's military leaders who served in the Pacific War (like Park Chung Hee) were familiar with the model, and the extensive wartime coordination between the Japanese state and big business, with highly centralized finance as the linchpin, appealed to them. State control over finance not only made the implementation of industrial policy possible, but it also bolstered the power base of the state by creating a whole entrepreneurial class as beneficiaries of the political leadership. This was no small consideration for a postcolonial state with a military regime at the helm that was perennially struggling for legitimacy. So the idea was there to graft the *zaibatsu* into Korea; the only question was how to create the Korean *zaibatsu* in the first place, out of the ravages of colonialism and war. The answer was industrial policy that created hugely leveraged firms as the carriers of Korean capitalism (with financial repression as the core mechanism for shifting resources from savers to producers). This is not to imply that Korea's *chaebol* have functioned politically like the old *zaibatsu*, supporting aggression and huge armaments expenditures. But an examination of the similar corporate structure in Korea helps clarify the relationship between authoritarianism and its legacy on the one hand, and the type of big business on the other. It also underlines the extent and enormous complexity of contemporary reform efforts.

In the work of many Japanese historians, the term *zaibatsu* refers to family-dominated combines that developed following World War I, using holding organizations to maintain control over their industries and expanding rapidly in the heavy industrialization drives and wartime conditions of the 1930s and 1940s.[30] Keiichiro Nakagawa, a business historian at the University of Tokyo, provides a historicist definition of the *zaibatsu* as "a major economic entity established in a developing country, whose fundamental social structure is based on [an] instinctive gregarious group expressed as [a] family, to pursue an industrialization process in [the] face of international competition against industrialized countries."[31] In other words, an extraordinary family-based combination of wealth and power at home is necessary to fight more weighty and competitive foreign corporations that arrived in the world economy earlier. From Professor Nakagawa's perspective, it is not so surprising that the Korean *chaebol* of today is an atavism of the prewar *zaibatsu*.

But let's look more closely at the Japanese *zaibatsu*, in terms of their goals, market positions, size, and organization. The late economist Eleanor Hadley, who was an American staffer and later the leading chronicler of the antitrust experiment in Japan during the Occupation, said the *zaibatsu* were a "political expression referring to the estate of wealth, and by extension, to the source of this wealth, the combines." According to Hadley, the goal of the *zaibatsu* was not high-market occupancy of one, two, or a few more related markets, but an oligopolistic position running the gamut

---

[30] Eleanor Hadley, *Antitrust in Japan* (Princeton, N.J.: Princeton University Press, 1970), p. 21.

[31] Keiichiro Nakagawa, quoted in Tamio Hattori, "Japanese *Zaibatsu* and Korean *Chaebol*," in Kae H. Chung and Hank Chong Lee, eds., *Korean Managerial Dynamics* (New York: Praeger, 1989), p. 80.

of the modern sector of the economy. The largest firm, Mitsui, conducted far-flung operations in coal and metals mining, shipbuilding, ordnance, aircraft, heavy and light electrical equipment, and various other fields of manufacturing, not to mention commercial banking, insurance, and trading. A series of oligopolistic positions, often accounting for 10 to 20 percent of market output, was the fundament of this *zaibatsu*, which at the end of the war employed an estimated 1.8 million people in Japan alone, and two to three million in the whole of the Far East.[32]

In 1946, the Big Four *zaibatsu*—consisting of Mitsui, Mitsubishi, Sumitomo, and Yasuda—controlled 24.5 percent of the paid-up capital of all incorporated businesses. The next six added 10.7 percent, for a total of 35.2 percent. The same Big Four also accounted for 49.7 percent of finance, 32.4 percent of heavy industry, 10.7 percent of light industry, and 12.9 percent for "other" fields. The Big Four also accounted for 80.1 percent of foreign investment at the war's end. Additionally, the *zaibatsu* were divided into numerous subsidiaries. Of the ten firms designated by the U.S. Occupation for "dissolution," Mitsui had 294 subsidiaries; Mitsubishi, 241; Sumitomo, 166; and Yasuda, 60. The remaining six also had numerous subsidiaries: Nissan, 179; Asano, 59; Furukawa, 53; Okura, 58; Nakajima, 68; Nomura, 19.[33]

Because these firms emphasized corporate unity through family ties and coordination of the subsidiaries by the holding company and companies, they achieved tight control over the astonishing market breadth of the combines. Even when the companies were "opened," two features made the family control of the *zaibatsu* possible. One was that stock did not have to be equally paid up, meaning that the families and the holding companies could increase the "stretch" of their capital. The other was the implicit understanding that the will of the family and the holding company would prevail, regardless of their actual ownership position. Indeed, Hadley points to numerous instances in core companies at the end of the war when *zaibatsu* ownership (defined as the sum of top–holding

---

[32]Hadley, *Antitrust in Japan*, pp. 9, 23.
[33]Ibid., pp. 26, 47.

company ownership, family holdings, and cross-subsidiary ties) fell short of majority control.[34] One might think of it as a remarkable instance of the personalistic—even feudal—basis of mutual trust to corporate power. The prewar zaibatsu was an organization that represented a means of extending control far beyond the controller's corporate (or partnership) limits, thus denying independence of action to businesses within the network. The techniques to bring this about included ownership, personnel, credit, and centralized buying and selling—again with the goal of unity of purpose and action.[35] This system of enterprise worked more for market share than solely for the company's profit; indeed, companies often operated at a loss (and, of course, during the war they produced everything under government dictate).

Of particular interest in the current context of *chaebol* reform is that the power of the *zaibatsu* could not be decisively broken during the seven-year American occupation of defeated Japan, despite the full panoply of extraordinary powers vested in the U.S. commander and Pacific theater war hero General Douglas MacArthur and his Supreme Command, Allied Powers (SCAP) staff. They hunkered down and waited when they could, restructured when they had to, and transmogrified into the post-Occupation *keiretsu,* a definite improvement but by no means the thorough breakup and reform that MacArthur had planned. One great difficulty of the *zaibatsu* reform effort was to pinpoint the line where the state left off and private business began. The victorious Americans, used to drawing line in the sand of Pacific islands, could not figure out where to draw the line in Japan proper.

American staff in SCAP, many of whom were New Dealers, perceived the *zaibatsu* essentially as products of "tricks" played with holding companies: once the secrets, like the name of Rumpelstiltskin, were revealed, the whole system would come apart at the seams. Thus, the holding companies were abolished, but the system of political economy in Japan—the triumvirate of politicians (now replacing the military), bureaucrats, and business (now

---

[34]Ibid., pp. 24–25.
[35]Ibid., pp. 31–37.

called the *keiretsu*)—remained intact, favoring the producers at the expense of consumers. This experience is a strong cautionary note to those who think the reform of corporate governance in contemporary Korea will move smoothly or quickly. Because the big Korean firms formed under strong state prodding in the 1960s, it has been difficult there, as well, to delineate a meaningful line between the public and the private. In many ways, the *chaebol* have been quasi-state organizations (President Kim Dae Jung has called them "quasi-government enterprises"), and in others, they have been immense private domains, "company towns" writ large that employ, house, feed, clothe, educate, and provide credit to millions of ordinary Koreans. The *chaebol* groups are the private agency of public purpose, having been created through easy credit in the context of "financial repression" as well as labor repression—in other words, over the dead bodies of both savers and workers. The question of the *chaebol* is at the core of a whole complex of issues, involving banking, medium- and small-sized firms, land, labor, income distribution, law, and politics. It cannot be excised from the economic system of Korea and "reformed."

Let us return to Eleanor Hadley's phrase—"the estate of wealth." The *chaebols* resemble the estates maintained for decades by the DuPont Corporation in the small state of Delaware in that they meet all of their employees' needs. For example, the typical Hyundai worker drives a Hyundai car, lives in a Hyundai apartment, gets his mortgage from Hyundai credit, gets health care from a Hyundai hospital, sends his kids to school on Hyundai loans or scholarships, and eats his meals at Hyundai cafeterias. If his son graduates out of the blue-collar work force and into the ranks of well-educated technocratic professionals (which is every Korean parent's goal), he may well work for Hyundai research and development. The extreme form of this arrangement is seen in the masses of construction teams that Hyundai sends to the Middle East. Every worker departs wearing Hyundai T-shirts and caps and carrying Hyundai bags, lives and eats in Hyundai dormitories, and uses Hyundai tools and equipment to build Hyundai cities in the desert. In the same way that Kim Il Sung built a Confucian-influenced hereditary family-state in North Korea and called it

communism, the Korean *chaebol* have built large family-run hereditary corporate estates in Korea and called it capitalism.

Many also argue that corporate governance (or leadership
style) is militaristic in Korea as compared to postwar Japan—that
is, that it is more directive and authoritarian.[36] But that merely suggests another strong comparison with *prewar* Japan. Those *zaibatsu* emphasized corporate unity through family ties and the
coordination of subsidiaries, with control mechanisms that included ownership, personnel, credit, and centralized buying and selling; there was, however, a separation between ownership and
management. The families with controlling interests in Mitsui and
Sumitomo never actively participated in management, contrasting sharply with, say, Hyundai, where the founder, Chung Ju-yong,
put his sons and grandsons in charge of core Hyundai industries
and subsidiaries. It might be argued, then, that the *chaebol* are even
more autocratic than the prewar *zaibatsu*, because the former are
often the direct instruments of founding patriarchs and their
male descendants.

Here is the rub. To break up the *chaebol* is to break up Korea,
Inc. The depth of the problem can perhaps be appreciated by remembering the results of anti-trust legislation in the American experience. The dissolution of Standard Oil benefited from the
existence of forty-eight states that were often under separate or
different regulatory regimes; the results were Standard Oil of
Indiana, of California, of New York, and so on. Because Korea is
highly centralized, with no such federal structure, it has been
difficult to devise efficacious policies with regard to the *chaebol*,
despite the antipathy and resentment they engender. In fact,
some argue that the successive governments in Korea have been
at a loss to define the nature of the problems in the first place, let
alone handle them. This is startling, given the centrality of the *chaebol* in the Korean debate on economic growth, social justice, and
political power. One economist argues that, for all the crimes said
to be committed by the *chaebol*, there is still no clear articulation,
for the purpose of effective policy, of why they are so nefarious,

---

[36]Whitley, *Business Systems in East Asia*, p. 50.

either from an economic or a social-justice perspective. We need to know whether the *chaebol* problem is based on market concentration, ownership concentration, their lack of diversification, their putative lack of international competitiveness, their insistence on family ownership and control, or even their criminality in evading laws (inheritance and gift taxes, for instance).[37]

---

[37]Yu Sungmin. Nanumyonso k'oganda [Sharing, Growing] (Seoul: Mirae Media, 1996), p. 12. Also see by the same author, "Taegiop chibaekujo ui ponjil kwa chungch'aekchonmang." [Corporate Governance in Large Enterprises: Policy Prospects] (Korea Development Institute, Mimeo), and "Shinchongbu chaeboljongch'aek ui p'yongka wa daekiop ui hyokshin kwaje." [Evaluation of the New Government Chaebol Policy and the Reform Prospects for Big Business] (Korea Development Institute, Mimeo).

CONCENTRATION AND DIVERSIFICATION IN THE KOREAN *CHAEBOL*

In terms of economic concentration, the *chaebol* are strong counterparts to the prewar *zaibatsu*. Even the main organizational difference between the two—the existence of the holding company in the former but not in the latter—may well disappear in the near future.[38] Almost all the *chaebol* groups began when Korea was in a phase of export-led, light-industrial production. Lucky made toothpaste, Goldstar made radios, Samsung made clothes, and Hyundai began—with U.S. military contracts during the Korean War—to transport goods and people around in war-surplus or cobbled-together trucks and buses. Daewoo was founded just thirty years ago, in 1967. They acquired their typical large and diversified structure even more recently, during the third Five Year Plan in the early 1970s. At that time, they began to develop heavy industries, including steel, chemicals, machine tools, automobiles, shipbuilding, and power-generation. By the 1980s, electronics had also become a huge part of the *chaebol* repertoire. The expansion of these firms was stupendous: between 1970 and 1975, the three fastest-growing *chaebol* (Hyundai, Daewoo, Sangyong) grew at annual rates of 33, 35, and 34 percent, respectively. This breakneck rate of growth, combined with reliance on politically mediated debt, encouraged high risk-taking and competitive overinvestment in various industries—such as integrated petrochemicals, which more than doubled the output of ethylene at a time when world prices were declining and surplus capacity was widely anticipated. The same was often true of sectors like semiconductors, ships, steel, and cars. No wonder excess capacity bulked large as an explanation of Korea's serious economic down-

---

[38]The main feature of the antitrust action in Japan was the abolition of holding companies, and this example was followed in Korea. In recent years, however, Japan restored the legality of the holding company, and Korea may very well follow suit.

turn in 1979, leading to a loss of 6 percent of GNP in 1980. Profitability was also low in key manufacturing sectors: net profit fell to 1.8 percent in 1971, and it reached about 3 percent over the next decade.[39]

Still, there were great advantages to the state-directed "big push" of the 1970s. The experience in managing complex technologies in heavy and capital-intensive industries, requiring effective coordination and integration of separate independent components, became the basis for developing managerial skills, which could be transferred to other kinds of manufacturing. The largest, Hyundai, has carried on globe-ranging operations in automobiles, shipbuilding, construction, electronics, aircraft, machine-building, and many others. Such diversified managerial skills and market structure meant that Koreans were more likely than the Japanese to recruit senior managers from outside who possess a greater variety of managerial backgrounds and experiences than those in most large Japanese firms. Korean firms are more diversified than their postwar Japanese counterparts and incorporate more economic activities within their authority structure and, correspondingly, engage in less subcontracting.[40]

The Korean *chaebol* occupies an oligopolistic position that runs the gamut of the modern sector of the economy. For each of the seventy-eight manufacturing industries in which *chaebol* are present, there were, in 1989, an average of three groups and 3.8 group member firms operating.[41] There are many indicators of the size and the extensive market position of the big conglomerates. One indicator is to compute the value-added of the *chaebol* as a percentage of total industry, which in 1989 stood at 9.2 percent for the top five *chaebol* and 16.3 percent for the top thirty. Alternatively, one could look at sales figures as a percentage of manufacturing industries; in 1990, the top thirty *chaebol* accounted for 35 percent total sales. The same top thirty also employed some 16 percent of labor working in manufacturing. But since these numbers are liable to

---

[39]Whitley, *Business Systems in East Asia*, pp. 44-46.
[40]Ibid., pp. 43-44.
[41]Ibid., p. 44.

change as corporate governance of these firms changes and some firms become independent of the group, it is advisable to look at data for individual firms. Sales figures for the top 100 firms in 1981 accounted for 46.2 percent of manufacturing, dropping to 38.5 percent in 1987 and further to 37.7 percent in 1990; this trend is visible also for value-added: 40.6 percent of manufacturing in 1981, down to 36.5 percent in 1987, to make a small drop in 1990 at 35.1 percent. Just as the indicators for *chaebol* economic concentration can vary depending on corporate definitional boundaries, the indicators using individual firms can change drastically as a result of mergers and acquisitions.[42]

While the preceding figures indicate a formidable level of economic concentration, there is also a growing trend in the global economy of firms scrambling to survive in worldwide competition by getting bigger and more competitive. The jury is out on just how economically concentrated Korea's *chaebol* are, given the uncertainties today about the change in the corporate governance of the *chaebol* and about how to interpret economic concentration in light of the accelerating global trend toward industry mergers.

The thornier issue is probably that of diversification. Unlike the level of economic concentration, Korea's level of diversification remains high compared with advanced Western countries. In 1994, the number of affiliated firms for the top five *chaebol* averaged about forty, to a total of 210 firms, and the top thirty *chaebol* had some 616 affiliated firms.[43] This extraordinary diversification was achieved primarily by establishing new subsidiaries: the mammoth and remarkably diversified structure of the *chaebol* combined with an open call on state-mediated loans were essential to Korea's success in gaining market share around the world, because losses in one subsidiary could be made up by gains in another. This extensive diversification has been the main staple of public criticism of the *chaebol*, but perhaps that criticism should be weighed against at least three considerations.

---

[42]These figures are variously from the ROK Fair Trade Commission, and cited in Sungmin Yu, *Nanumyonso k'oganda* [*Sharing, Growing*] (Seoul: Mirae Media, 1996), p. 24.
[43]Ibid.

The first is obvious: while the *chaebol* have been criticized for failing to nurture "core competence"—thereby exploiting more fully the gains from economies of scale— diversification into many different sectors can be justified through the gains from the economy of *scope* (as versus scale) and dynamic back-and-forth synergy among firms. Furthermore, portfolio diversification reduces risk. The second and often forgotten point is that diversification went hand in hand with specialization. Out of the fifty affiliated firms for Samsung, Hyundai's forty-nine affiliated firms, LG's fifty-three, Daewoo's twenty-five, and Sunkyung's thirty-three, only a select few firms in a few sectors were responsible for the bulk of total sales figures. In the case of Samsung, only three firms were responsible for 67 percent of its sales. Even with Hyundai, which is evenly spread out in many different manufacturing sectors, five affiliated firms accounted for 70 percent of total sales. As for Daewoo, four firms accounted for 85 percent of total sales.[44] If the common complaint about *chaebol* diversification can be summed up in the remark that "even in the Olympics there aren't gold medalists who can win in both swimming and basketball,"[45] one might counter that the *chaebol* were not aspiring to win in all categories, but the incentive system pushed them in that direction. The third and last point about the merits and demerits of diversification again involves corporate governance: anytime the structure of a given *chaebol* changes as firms detach from the group, the firm is instantly "specialized." Over the years, the government has tried—and failed—to use its elaborate system of credit control to curtail the *chaebol* tendency toward diversification and to coax the groups to "specialize" in a few sectors.

The point about diversification, then, is not that it is *ipso facto* problematic, but that it results from an economic system geared

---

[44]The three Samsung firms are in electronics, trade, and life insurance; the five Hyundai firms are in general trading, automobiles, heavy industry, automobile service, and construction; the four Daewoo firms are in trading, automobiles, electronics, and heavy industry. See Yu, *Nanumyonso k'oganda* [*Sharing, Growing*] (Seoul: Mirae Media, 1996), p. 39.

[45]Remark by the Korean head of McDonald's, quoted in Mark Clifford, *The Troubled Tiger*, p. 325.

toward protecting domestic producers at the expense of consumers. The *chaebol* firm does not strive to become competitive
in all the sectors it enters because there is little incentive to do so,
given that the government protects domestic producers through
residual industrial policy, especially by limiting foreign competition. It also limits domestic competition, through the system of
"controlled competition." The important conclusion for any reform
process, then, is not to pile on more discretionary measures to force
"specialization," which the state has tried all too often (and is trying again today under Kim Dae Jung), but to liberalize the market so that open competition can take place. This liberalization would
enable the *chaebol* firms to decide for themselves whether it makes
economic sense to diversify or not.

FAMILY GOVERNANCE, TRUST, AND
RULE BY REGULATION

Family control of corporate wealth and family-dictated "corporate governance" are other practices that, over the years, the government and various critics have sought to curb. How serious is the problem of family ownership of the *chaebol*? For the top thirty *chaebol*, family ownership (defined as the share held by the family members as well as by affiliated firms) totaled 43.3 percent in 1995. The figure for the top five in 1994 was 47.5 percent, combining the family share of 12.5 percent and the 35.0 percent share for the affiliated firms. These figures, while high by comparative standards, have tended to decline over the years. In 1987, family ownership in the top thirty firms averaged 56.2 percent, while that for the top five averaged 60.3 percent. There has been a steady decrease in relative shares owned by the family and affiliated firms. But individual families still exercise too much control over corporate governance of the *chaebol*, and public stockholding remains weak, despite the quarter-century effort on the part of the Korean government to dilute family ownership of big firms, develop the equity market, and force firms to go public. For the top thirty *chaebol*, which together claimed possession of some 623 firms in 1995, the number of publicly listed firms was 172, or only 27.6 percent. This figure shows a marginal decline from 1991, when the number of listed firms was 161 out of 561 firms, or 28.7 percent.[46]

The salience of the family in Korean business has led some observers to conclude that Korean firms are really more "Chinese" than anything else, and that whether in Korea or China, family governance reflects an immature development of civil society and the rule of law. Francis Fukuyama argued in his influential book, *Trust*, that

---

[46]Yu, *Nanumyonso k'oganda* [*Sharing, Growing*] (Seoul: Mirae Media, 1996), pp. 25–26; the figures are from the ROK Fair Trade Commission. For the government effort to develop the equity market, see Jung-en Woo (Meredith Woo Cumings), *Race to the Swift*, ch. 5 and 6.

"the truth of the matter is that Korean businesses, despite their large scale, do look and behave more like Chinese businesses than like Japanese corporations." (He even titles one chapter "Korea: The Chinese Company Within.") The question of whether or not the Korean firm is more Chinese or more Japanese would not be particularly interesting (especially since the answer is neither—it is Korean), except that Fukuyama bases his argument about corporate governance on an American premise that now presents itself as the global zeitgeist. There is, according to Fukuyama, a "convergence of institutions around the model of democratic capitalism" at the "end of history," with "virtually all serious observers" agreeing that liberal political and *economic* institutions depend on a healthy and dynamic "civil society" for their vitality. In this way, Fukuyama adds an economic dimension to the argument made famous by Robert Putnam in his *Making Democracy Work*—that true democracy cannot be achieved without the presence of a thick web of civic institutions.[47] The absence of such a healthy "civil society," defined as a complex web of voluntary associations and intermediate institutions, is thought to characterize low-trust societies with Confucian and Catholic cultures where family-based firms predominate. Instead of civil society, these cultures exhibit what Edward Banfield once described as "amoral familism," meaning that people will maximize the material, short-run advantages of the nuclear family, rather than pursue individual or societal goals. The economic effects of amoral familism, Banfield famously argued, create a "very important limiting factor in the way of economic development in most of the world. Except as people can create and maintain corporate organization, they cannot have a modern economy."[48]

Amoral familism (or the absent Anglo-Saxon civil society) is synonymous with a pre-modern economy and the predominance of family firms. But there are many problems with this argument.

---

[47]Francis Fukuyama, *Trust: The Social Virtues and the Creation of Prosperity* (New York: Simon and Schuster, 1995), pp. 133–34; Robert Putnam, *Making Democracy Work* (Princeton, N.J.: Princeton University Press, 1994).

[48]Edward C. Banfield, *The Moral Basis of a Backward Society* (New York: Free Press, 1967), pp. 85, 88; quoted in Fukuyama, *Trust*, p. 99.

To the extent that one accepts this characterization of places as diverse as Korea, China, and southern Italy (Banfield's locus of specialization), one can give up any hope of corporate reform because family governance bears an indelible and ineradicable historical and cultural stamp. But the argument is wrong; it does not explain family governance of Korean corporations.

We have seen how the emergence and persistence of family-controlled firms are related to the prevalence of discretionary rule (rather than the rule of law) in Korea, growing out of institutional structures of "late" industrialization and the specific ethnic milieus that Chinese businessmen must adapt to in Southeast Asia. That is different, however, from claiming that democracy and market capitalism are not possible in the absence of Anglo-Saxon civil society and the rule of law, and that they result from high levels of trust that such societies reflect and subsequently foster. The prevalence of family firms does reflect an absence of universalistic trust and the rule of law in Korea (not to mention a country like Indonesia). However, such practices are rooted in decades of authoritarianism and the myriad discretionary rules that it has fostered to support and regulate big business, and not in some indelible (and, therefore, inescapable) cultural trait.

An interventionist state like that in Korea creates a permanent bind for itself with regard to big business, which in turn deeply prejudices the emergence of the rule of law. On the one hand, Korea is a paradise for big business, because state industrial policy favors domestic producers over consumers and foreign producers in every manner imaginable. As domestic producers become more economically and politically powerful, however, the state attempts to rein in and tame the *chaebol* through regulatory tactics, creating seemingly endless discretionary rules. These rules have been fickle, irrational, short-lived, and, quite predictably, ineffective in achieving their goals. Instead, they create the sense that the rules of the game in Korea are constantly negotiable.

The government's dilemma, or "bind," results from Korea's credit-based system for raising capital. In the 1960s, the *chaebol* relied on massive foreign aid from the United States and Japan, whose funds were vetted through the state-mediated banks. In the 1970s, big business relied heavily on cheap capital, so-called policy loans given at negative real rates (about a 6 percent loan rate in the context of 12 percent inflation, for instance) to those firms willing to conform to the dictates of government industrial strategy. Thus, the state created a structural incentive for the firms to rely on bank financing and retain entrepreneurial autonomy by staying closed to the public and inaccessible to external audits. Moreover, access to the bank-loan window required high levels of political contributions—something that cannot be entered in the books. In the mid-1990s, prosecutors determined that, during the 1980s, Chun Doo Hwan and Roh Tae Woo had amassed more than $1.5 billion in corporate political donations.

Yet the state has also been a relentless nag, trying to force firms to go public—and failing every time because of the state-created incentive structure. In the aftermath of the 1972 financial crisis and the bailout of big business through a sudden moratorium on corporate repayment of loans to the curb market, the government selected "blue chip" firms (based on profitability, equity, and asset position) and forced them to go public by threatening to slap the recalcitrants with a 40 percent corporate tax (instead of the usual 27 percent). Overnight, new public stock offerings, valued at $48 million, inundated the Seoul Stock Exchange, and the number of companies listed jumped 50 percent. The stock market received a further boost in 1974, when a special presidential decree tightened the audit and supervision of bank credit for all nonlisted (but listable, according to government standards) firms. Many more measures like these followed in the 1970s. The government also sought to control the securities market by setting low prices on new issues and determining dividends and corporate reinvestment decisions.

The *chaebol* found themselves between the proverbial rock and a hard place, between the state's punitive measures, on the one hand, and the forbidding costs of going public, on the other. They lost cheap bank credits and autonomy in business decision-making and contended with the high costs of raising undervalued equity capital, all amid continuing government intervention in corporate management. The corporate response was utterly rational. Some firms decided it was better to resist the government order, pay the tax, and bypass the palliatives that the government offered to listed firms. Others obeyed the government but without really complying: the owners themselves absorbed much of the newly issued stocks.[49] Thus, the equity market in Korea has remained relatively small.

The government made matters worse by trying to regulate *chaebol*, corporate governance and access to and monopolization of bank credit, through what surely must be one of the most arcane and intractable set of "credit controls" (*yoshin kwalli*) the world has ever known. In a system where state-mediated bank credit was extended not on the basis of economic viability but on the exigencies of industrial policy, the only way to prevent default was incessant supervision and control. This ranged from ubiquitous surveillance over the use of credit (to prevent speculation, for instance) to supervising the reform of corporate financing structures to creating a web of credit ceilings. In trying to prevent the concentration of credit in the hands of a few *chaebol*, the government came up with complex rules limiting credits to the same borrower, limiting credit per individual bank for large borrowers, and establishing credit ceilings for *chaebol*-affiliated firms. To prevent default, the government developed a series of guidelines for "early warning," procedures for "modernizing" credit evaluation, and intricate rules for default management. A special set of decrees applying only to the *chaebol* sought to improve corporate financing structures, and yet more rules sought to regulate the ratio between equity and debt in various industrial sectors. To prevent the ever-growing concentration of the *chaebol* and suppress their penchant for speculative real-estate acquisition, the state issued complicated requirements for permission to purchase land, gave various fiscal incentives for going public,

---

[49] Woo (Woo-Cumings), *Race to the Swift*, pp. 174–75.

and developed financial breaks for *chaebol* firms that "specialize" rather than continue growing into diversified fields.[50]

The price of the government's attempt to supplant the financial market was a regulatory albatross that, in the end, did not achieve its purpose—judging by the persistent reliance of Korean firms on bank credit and the continuing family control of business. One has to wonder what the state of affairs would have been had the government not intervened. Throughout the 1990s, when credit control got increasingly complicated, the borrowings by the top thirty *chaebol* as a percentage of total bank loans dropped from 19.0 percent in 1990 to 14.5 percent in 1995. Some economists have blamed government regulation for this drop.[51] The logic of Korea, Inc., put the state in the position of having to proliferate regulations to stem the worst effects of its own developmental strategy; at best, its efforts could only yield marginal successes. No regulation or special decree ever changed the essential structure of Korean corporate governance, right up to the crisis of late 1997.

---

[50]These rules are translations of the data on the purpose and methods of credit control, published by the ROK Bank Supervisory Commission, and quoted in Yu, *Nanumyonso k'oganda* [*Sharing, Growing*] (Seoul: Mirae Media, 1996), p. 102.

[51]Ibid., p. 104.

FAMILY GOVERNANCE: PART OF THE PROBLEM OR PART OF THE SOLUTION?

About 70 percent of Korea's *chaebol* groups remain in the hands of the founding family, and core responsibility for corporate governance remains situated at the top. Corporate decision-making still rests at the "commanding heights," to use a current term. To truly reform such a persistent and resilient form of corporate governance is a daunting task. Clearly, more state regulation is not the answer. The preceding section would suggest that breaking the nexus between the Korean state and the *chaebol* is a more likely avenue toward real reform. But what about the structure and governance of the firms themselves? Should they be broken up, given over to professional managers, encouraged to go public, or continue doing what they have done so well over the past three decades—keep investing, producing, and growing? All such measures presuppose an answer to this question: Is family control of big business necessarily inefficient? The answer is not as simple as one might think and depends on many things—above all, the entrepreneurial talent of the family members running the business.

Reflecting on the rise and fall of corporate families, Joseph Schumpeter remarked that capital accumulation does not happen automatically: "the captured value *does not invest itself* but must be *invested*." By this he meant that the study of capital accumulation should include behavior and motive—in other words, from the *social* "force" to the responsible individual or family. The crucial factor, he argued, is that "the social logic or objective situation does not unequivocally determine *how much* profit shall be invested, and *how* it shall be invested, *unless individual disposition is taken into account*."[52] Thus, a private corporation run by able owner-managers can be more effective than one run by professional managers; although there is no

---

[52] Schumpeter, *Imperialism/Social Classes*, p. 119.

way to insure that such will always be the case. For every advantage to owner-management of the big firm, such as speed and flexibility in corporate response, there is a disadvantage, such as a dearth of professional management skill. Likewise the owner-manager, by assuming corporate responsibility, can either create stability for the firm or generate a sense of instability by being dictatorial and arbitrary in his decision-making. Owner-managers can be more dedicated to the long-term development of the firm, utilizing their own resources, but it is also easy to imagine a nefarious collusion between corporate and private accounting.

The Korean *chaebol* shows both the advantages and disadvantages of family control. In the early days of industrialization, the can-do spirit and dedication of founding entrepreneurs, who made strategic choices and resource-allocation decisions by themselves, helped expand business by leaps and bounds. Strong central—even personal—control gave the *chaebol* much more integrated command and direction than conglomerates controlled purely through financial means. But it is also true that there was too much personal charisma and too little routinization and institutionalization. In large Korean firms, assignments are often unclear and overlapping, and the application of control systems is rarely standardized. A fluidity of roles and responsibilities characterizes top management levels; job rotation is said to be more frequent than in Japan, with senior managers often transferred between firms in the same group. Market organization is assumed to be more self-sufficient than in the Japanese *keiretsu* system, with less need to organize market connections to reduce risk and, thus, less enterprise interdependence and cooperation than in Japan.[53] But the key question is still unanswered: Are the family-run *chaebol* firms profitable or not?

The conventional wisdom is that the *chaebol* are not profitable and, in fact, are not even interested in profit. Their activity, it is said, has rarely been driven by ordinary market concerns of price or supply and demand, and instead has long pursued market share, not just operating at a loss but courting a kind of habitual

---

[53]Whitley, *Business Systems in East Asia*, pp. 46, 50.

bankruptcy—should anyone call them to account on a given day. Perhaps the most telling statistic comes from the financial crisis in 1997, when it was determined that, on the eve of the debacle, the total annual profitability across the top fifty Korean firms was less than 1 percent.

A cross-national study of corporate profitability tells a different story. Ha-Joon Chang and others have examined "post-interest-payments" profitability and found that the rate of corporate profit in Korea is indeed low, as the above data suggest. From 1973 to 1996, the post-interest-payment profitability of Korean firms was about 2.8 percent, which is low but hardly surprising—given the 333.8 percent debt to equity ratio for the time period. The same rate for the United States was 7.9 percent (1995), 5.1 percent for Taiwan (1995), and 4.3 percent for Japan (1995). Korea's corporate profitability *before* interest payments during the same 1973–96 period, however, was 7.4 percent, which is close to that of the United States at 7.7 percent and better than Taiwan's at 7.3 percent. In other words, the Korean firm is loaded with debt, but not unprofitable—a paradox in a market system but not in a system where the state mediates capital to big firms, with both having a hell-bent-for-leather growth perspective. As Chang and others have argued, low post-interest-payment profitability did not harm investment momentum in Korea because government measures ensured that the income appropriated by the financial sector would be circuited back to the manufacturing corporate sector, thus promoting continued investment.[54]

If the Korean sector as a whole is not particularly inefficient in comparison to that in the United States or Taiwan, is the same true of Korea's large *chaebol* firms when compared to smaller domestic firms? A study of profitability and productivity comparing big business with medium- and small-size firms shows that *on average* there is no big difference between the two groups. However, the record for the *chaebol* firms tended to be erratic, with some

---

[54]Ha-Joon Chang, Hong-Jae Park, and Chul Gyue Yoo, "Interpreting the Korean Crisis: Financial Liberalization, Industrial Policy, and Corporate Governance," *Cambridge Journal of Economics*, Special Issue, 22, no. 6 (November 1998).

affiliated firms showing very high profitability and productivity
and others not. Big firms tend to possess long-term advantages
because of their relentless drive to expand market shares, whether
at home or abroad. In that sense, the strength of the *chaebol*
should be measured secularly, over long swatches of time, rather
than parsed into annual measures of pure productivity. The Korean economist Yu Sungmin also argues that the *chaebol* have been
able to overcome market imperfections through internal organization and reorganization. In a context where most markets (the
labor market, financial market, technology market, the market for
corporate managers) functioned improperly, the *chaebol* compensated by creating an internal world of their own, enacting a kind
of do-it-yourself industrial reorganization.[55] In its purpose and design,
this analysis suggests, the *chaebol* constitute the more perfect
microcosm of an imperfect macrocosm, a prophylactic realm
insulated from or seeking to offset the flaws of the Korean business world.

Except for Alice Amsden's examination of the Korean ability
to absorb technology, or "learning-by-doing," this organizational
aspect of the *chaebol* has not received much scrutiny.[56] But the fact
that they kept increasing market share at home and abroad attests
to their organizational ability. The effective presence of Korean firms
in the fledgling markets of Eastern Europe, the Central Asian Republics,
and other emerging areas is testimony to the advantage that accrues
from having a vast, flexible, and well-coordinated internal organization.
This success should be considered alongside the well-known inefficiencies of the so-called convoy system, whereby even the most
inefficient unit of the *chaebol* group is kept afloat through intricate
financing agreements. In short, it is important to remember both
the good and the bad in the *chaebol*, because reform is only possible with the knowledge of what worked in the best of times, as well
as what failures brought on the worst of times.

---

[55]Yu, *Nanumyonso k'oganda* [*Sharing, Growing*] (Seoul: Mirae Media, 1996), pp. 29-32.
[56]Alice Amsden, *Asia's Next Giant: South Korea and Late Industrialization* (Oxford: Oxford
University Press, 1989).

EFFORTS AT CORPORATE REFORM IN KOREA

We have only briefly assessed the politics of the *chaebol*, but that was the overwhelming focus of Korean attention in the mid-1990s, as one *chaebol* leader after another was brought into the dock and shown to have lined the pockets of all the leading politicians as far back as the 1960s. Although the image of the flagship firms responsible for the Korean miracle was deeply tarnished, this hugely important phenomenon signaled the arrival, finally, of democratic politics in Korea. And it is only through democratic means that the deep nexus between the *chaebol* and the authoritarian state could be broken. The best news for those interested in *chaebol* reform is simply that real reform is now possible, given the election of two successive civilian presidents (Kim Young Sam in 1992 and Kim Dae Jung in 1997) and the impetus of a crisis in the economy unparalleled since the Korean War.

In the middle of an analogous crisis, U.S. President Franklin Roosevelt, in his message to Congress in 1938, called for an investigation of concentrated economic power: "The liberty of a democracy," he said, "is not safe if the people tolerate the growth of private power to a point where it becomes stronger than their democratic state itself."[57] In Korea, the problem of private power is as President Roosevelt described it, but much more so. Politicians and political parties collected huge amounts of money from the *chaebol*, offering in return loan guarantees to sustain these highly leveraged firms. No firm could avoid paying out one day lest it be declared "bankrupt" the next. The recent investigations, ultimately leading to the incarceration of two previous presidents and several big business leaders, revealed to the Korean people the operational method of patronage. Korea, Inc. proved to be far more arbitrary than Japan, Inc. Particularly in the 1980s, a racketeering

---

[57]Quoted in Hadley, *Antitrust in Japan*, p. 455.

state was the flip side of the much-touted developmental state, as the earlier, more systemic pattern of *chaebol* support for the ruling groups devolved into a kind of mad extortionism.

President Kim Dae Jung needs no tutoring in the politics or the economic liabilities of the state-*chaebol* relationship. Long a dissident who was the object of *chaebol*-provisioned political funding (he nearly won his first presidential campaign in 1971 in spite of widespread irregularities and munificent support for Park Chung Hee, whereupon there were no more elections until 1987), he wrote in his 1985 book, "The Korean economy ... has been plagued by inefficient allocation of valuable resources ... [which is] the result of government interference in almost every aspect of market functions, including pricing, credit allocation, industrial location decisions, and labor-management relations. This interference has left the Korean economy in a state of serious imbalance. The imbalances ... [include those] between large conglomerates and small or medium-sized firms."[58] The economic crisis gives him the leverage needed to pursue real reform of the Korean system, for the first time since it was established in the 1960s.

Since his election in December 1997, President Kim has reiterated his resolve to tackle "the *chaebol* problem" by instituting the rule of law and bringing transparency throughout the nexus of the state, the banks, and the *chaebol*. The establishment of effective rule of law requires, however, a particular kind of "mentality," to resort to Max Weber once again. The interventionist state in Korea has been profoundly results-oriented, privileging outcomes over established procedures and rules. This mentality is evident in the various liberalization policies that Korea has enacted over the years.

Import liberalization, for instance, has rarely meant competitive liberalization, but refers instead to ad hoc measures like the "import-diversification policy" designed to keep out Japanese products or to prevent monopolization in the domestic distribution of imports. Likewise, deregulation usually meant reducing the

---

[58]Kim Dae Jung, *Mass-Participatory Economy: A Democratic Alternative for Korea* (Lanham, MD.: University Press of America, 1986), p. 3.

number of procedural and administrative regulations and not promoting more *competition*. Even the people in charge of competition policy were often confused by what competition really meant, and whether it was actually conducive to creating competitiveness. A series of interviews with officials at the Fair Trade Commission (which was created in 1980 as an antitrust watchdog) revealed that most did not actually *believe* that more competition would increase the competitiveness of Korean firms. Privatization reforms also moved slowly, both because of opposition from vested interests and for fear that the chaebol would simply absorb any newly privatized state firms. More generally, in the last two decades, state policy toward the *chaebol* has been profoundly complex and contradictory, relying on its discretionary power more to protect and discipline the chaebol than to expose them to a transparent legal regime and a real environment of competition.

In the past, the objective of financial regulatory policy centered on the reform of the always hugely leveraged corporate finance system. In 1974, the government launched a series of elaborate ad hoc measures to curb *chaebol* reliance on the banking system and, in 1980, followed up with an effort to force big businesses to develop "core competence" and shed their large number of subsidiaries. The government closely monitored *chaebol* use of bank credit and expanded external audits. By the middle of the 1980s, it instituted a consistent policy package based on fair-trade laws. In 1992, the fair-trade law was again fortified, the use of intersubsidiary loan guarantees was restricted (if not abolished), and the loan ceiling for some *chaebol* core industries was relaxed in another effort to enforce "specialization." But all these efforts came to naught. In 1997, the *chaebols* remained as leveraged as they were in 1969 (when Korea experienced its first major debt crisis) or in the 1970s (when they were hungry recipients of the outright subsidies known as "policy loans") or after the flurry of attempted reform in the early 1980s and early 1990s. The problem of nonperforming loans has not abated either, but has remained more or less steady for the past thirty years.

The failures of past reform efforts have taught two significant lessons. One is that the most egregious *chaebol* practices, like intersubsidiary loan guarantees, should have been simply outlawed. Instead, the government issued a series of complicated regulations and deadlines to reduce the extent of these guarantees, fearing to abolish outright a practice that helped maintain the organic unity of the *chaebol* (by making it difficult for inefficient firms to "exit" without taking the whole group down). The Korean banks have long eschewed credit analysis, given decades of credit rationing, so the intersubsidiary loan guarantees (along with the demand for large collateral, usually in real estate) enabled banks to reduce their exposure. The idea was that the loan guarantee turned the entire *chaebol* group into a gigantic chunk of collateral. Because it was highly unlikely that the entire group would fail (or that the state would let it fail), this was the second-best option for the banks in the absence of thorough credit analysis (which was impossible anyway, given closely held and deceptive *chaebol* methods of accounting). For the *chaebol*, the intersubsidiary loan system was a quick way to raise a lot of capital, even if this meant that ailing firms could threaten the health of other firms. The loan-guarantee scheme also, of course, belied the pretense that all *chaebol* affiliates were legally independent entities, thus bolstering the organic unity of the group. In 1993, a newly elected government finally decided that the loan guarantees had to go, once and for all. Faced with furious opposition from the *chaebol*, however, Kim Young Sam compromised by setting a three-year deadline for reducing the guarantees to 200 percent of equity. According to the Fair Trade Commission, in March 1992, intersubsidiary loan guarantees of the top thirty *chaebol* stood at 538 percent of their equity, but steadily dropped down until they met the 1996 deadline of 200 percent.[59]

Another lesson from the past is the failure of various efforts to force the firms to specialize in core industries and not duplicate each other's efforts. Simply stated, a quarter-century of failure is testimony again to the power of the *chaebol* to resist state-of-the art discretionary policies and regulations. All told, this history attests

---

[59]Yu, *Nanumyonso k'oganda* [*Sharing, Growing*] (Seoul: Mirae Media, 1996), pp. 29–32.

to the continuing power of big business in Korea rather than to the successes of reform. No government could imagine dismantling the system until the financial crisis of 1997 forced the issue.

In the wake of the crisis, the new Korean government has instituted a number of measures to force corporate reform. The measures include ending the system of intersubsidiary loan guarantees, posting deadlines to bring the corporate debt-equity ratio down, and forcing those *chaebol* firms that cannot service their debt without support of their affiliates to go bankrupt. The new administration of Kim Dae Jung has also demanded a so-called Big Deal, meaning a swap of key subsidiaries so that each of the top *chaebol* will emerge stronger in the areas of its "core competence." This would reduce overlapping investments and allow surplus production capacity to be closed down.[60] Some of these measures, such as the decisive ending of the intersubsidiary loans (mightily helped by the demands made by the International Monetary Fund), are important departures from the past; others are not departures but are continuations of the past government policy, albeit with more "teeth."

Evidence since 1998 clearly indicates that Kim wants to break up the cozy relations of the big firms with the government and the banks. He has sought in a variety of ways to share the pain of the IMF bailout fairly, throughout society. For the first time in Korean history, he has given labor a strong voice at the bargaining table with business and government. This is certainly a major achievement and one that has generally kept labor from major strikes and disruptions, in the face of unemployment that tripled in one year (from 2 percent in mid-1997 to more than 6 percent in mid-1998). It remains to be seen if Kim intends to downsize or even dismantle the *chaebol*, which would require a systemic set of antitrust measures and competition policies that would have to be effective in the Korean context. More likely, he hopes to enact various reform measures to free the *chaebol* of state regulators and preferential lend-

---

[60]Charles S. Lee, "Give Me Your Sick: South Korea's President Kim aims to tame the mighty chaebols by cutting off credit to 55 ailing subsidiaries," *Far Eastern Economic Review* (July 2, 1998), no. 52, pp. 52–53.

ing. This would involve a kind of marketization strategy that will end the worst external problems of corporate governance and open these firms to more competitive pressures, but that will do little to reform *chaebol* governance internally.

In considering the potential of Korean reform, it might be useful to label the various efforts the Good, the Bad, and the Ugly. The ugly aspect refers to the political practices of the *chaebol*—the massive exchange of bribes and political favoritism that should be excised from the Korean system and that, under the new administration, most likely will be. The bad refers to the economic deficiencies of the *chaebol* that must be changed—the lack of competitiveness in certain industries resulting in their excessive concern to expand market share. The Kim administration is focusing on this problem more than anything, trying to get the groups to shed their many unprofitable subsidiaries and to concentrate on a few successful core businesses. Reforms in this area might move Korea closer to the structure of the postwar Japanese *keiretsu*, a highly unpopular idea from the current standpoint but one that obviously makes sense in evolutionary terms. Finally, there is the good, or the economic virtues of the *chaebol*. This good—the essential logic of the *chaebol*—needs to be maintained and even nurtured. At least that is the way all Koreans, reformers or not, will see the problem.

Much of the current reform effort is still being done through government edict rather than legislative deliberation and rule-making. Even the current democratic reformers favor the use of discretionary measures by the government because Korea, after all, has one of the oldest and finest traditions of civil service and, counting the colonial period, a century of state-directed economic growth. In times of crisis, there is a strong temptation to use this ubiquitous state structure to force industrial reorganization; the bureaucrats—who come from the best universities and constitute a respected and experienced elite—cling to the belief that the next regulation is the one that will finally achieve real reform. The history of such reform, however, should teach the Korean government that perhaps it is better to change the incentive structure and the rules of the game and stick to them—in other words, institute the rule of law—rather than try yet another round of industrial reorganization. It is time to try the path not taken: develop an abiding rule of law applicable to both corporations and the government.

At the end of the day, Max Weber's insight is still valid—that the essence of modernity is the rationalization as well as the professionalization of economic and political management, and that modernity is unthinkable apart from rational bureaucracy and the separation of the household from the corporation. In Korea, too, the predominance of the family-controlled firms must change, as routine replaces charisma, and as what began in the 1960s as the frenetic attempt to emulate Japan's success becomes more settled and institutionalized. The change will come slowly but surely, paralleling the development of the equity market and the increasing globalization of the Korean economy.

THE POLITICS OF ETHNICITY AND CORPORATE GOVERNANCE IN SOUTHEAST ASIA

The modal firms in Korea and in Southeast Asia are family businesses, big and small, that operate not within the bounds of a well-established rule of law but amid the uncertainties of many decades of authoritarian rule. But there the similarities end. Korea's economic development has been marked by ubiquitous industrial policy (now made residual), with the state creating and re-creating the business class, protecting and disciplining its members. Because Southeast Asian states are bereft of industrial policy, except where it is a device to buttress the economically disadvantaged ethnic majority, they have had a (relatively) free market, punctuated by economic affirmative action of sorts. The upshot is that family businesses in Southeast Asia rely less on the ethnically alien government and, of course, less on government-mediated capital. Thus, the business class in the heterogeneous Southeast Asia was forced into self-sufficiency and onto the market.

The differences were overdetermined, from the days of colonialism. If Japanese colonialism bequeathed to the Koreans the template of the authoritarian interventionist state and the *zaibatsu*, European colonialism bequeathed the opposite: minimal taxation, strict avoidance of deficits, and an unprotected market. Malay economist K. S. Jomo attributes the habits and practices of Chinese businesses in Southeast Asia to their historical inability to rely on the colonial government. Even when the state and the legal system became more accessible to Chinese business interests, a "Chinese business idiom" persisted that abjured close association with the government.[61] Colonial governments also left a legacy of an ethnic division of labor and a cobbled-together concept of the nation—best exemplified by Malaysia.

---

[61]Jomo, *"Chinese Capitalism in Southeast Asia,"* p. 251.

Malaysia had its origins in an explicitly negotiated "bargain" that set the stage for a peaceful transfer of power from the British in 1957. This bargain, reached between ethnic political parties representing the Malay, Chinese, and Indians, became the basis for a coalition that has ruled Malaysia since independence. Malaysia has practiced the most pronounced policy of "apartheid," Ruth McVey argues, because it was also the last to be independent from the British rule.[62] Elsewhere, ethnic compacts occurred more haphazardly, but the generalization—cobbled-together nations, ethnic divisions of labor—holds for most of Southeast Asia.

Since independence, however, Southeast Asian countries were favored by the same external environment that favored Japan, Korea, and Taiwan. They enjoyed political and economic patronage by the United States during the Cold War, which supported stable, anti-Communist regimes. They also had a close economic relationship with Japan, which soon emerged as the major industrial power and, later, the single most important external investor in the region, from Korea to Indonesia. Added to that was the exclusion of China: in the words of Benedict Anderson, the "extraordinary forty year sequestration from the global market of the greatest power in Asia—namely China."[63]

Exclusion, yes, except for the Chinese diaspora. The one glaring difference between Northeast and Southeast Asia was the critical economic role of this marginalized minority. The Chinese business presence is as old as the merchants who prospered in the ancient tribute-trade system of the region, linking Japan, Korea, and China with Central Asian and Middle Eastern trade routes. These merchants created a Chinese presence that the European colonizers found useful in their own penetration of Southeast Asia in centuries past. The modern diaspora, however, was peopled by the millions of young, mostly male, mostly illiterate people, who,

---

[62] Alasdair Bowie, *Crossing the Industrial Divide: State, Society, and the Politics of Economic Transformation in Malaysia* (New York: Columbia University Press, 1991), p. 13; Ruth McVey, "The Materialization of the *Southeast Asian Entrepreneur*," Southern Asian Capitalists (Ithaca, N.Y.: Cornell University, Southeast Asia Center, 1992) p. 25.
[63] Benedict Anderson, "From Miracle to Crash," *London Review of Books* 20, no. 8 (April 27, 1998).

between the Opium Wars in the 1840s and the onset of the Sino-Japanese War in the 1890s, left the coastal districts of Fukien and Kwangtung for the labor-hungry European colonies in Southeast Asia and independent Thailand. They spoke mutually unintelligible languages such as Hokkien, Cantonese, Hakka, Hainanese, and Teochiu, and scarcely regarded themselves as Chinese.[64] In Thailand and Malaysia, they formed the bulk of the working class, but significant numbers also worked their way up the occupational ladder to become small traders, entrepreneurs, and professionals. Particularly in the Dutch East Indies, such people came to form a middle tier between the colonial administrative apparatus and the peasant bulk of the indigenous population. The Chinese used their positions as intermediaries between Western big business and the local economy to gain knowledge of modern trade, manufacturing techniques, and the local market. They also were the interlocutors when Japanese firms sought to reestablish their presence in Southeast Asia after World War II.[65]

A variety of barriers maintained this racial division of labor. In the early stages of development, Chinese immigrants were excluded from peasant production by lack of access to land, and were concentrated in wage labor, while indigenous peasants were excluded from commercial activity by lack of access to capital and market outlets. Because they were denied access to land, the Chinese tended to keep their assets in liquid form and to invest in economic activities that generated quick returns. This racial divide quickly became a vertical division of labor as well, as upwardly mobile Chinese entered into commercial activity, often as intermediaries between indigenous peasant producers and the world market, and obtained higher returns from their investments of capital and labor. Soon the indigenous people shook loose from the land and joined wage labor at the bottom of the economic hierarchy.[66]

---

[64]Ibid.

[65]See Anderson, ibid., as well as McVey, ibid., p. 21.

[66]Linda Lim, "Chinese Economic Activity in Southeast Asia: An Introductory Review," in Linda Lim and L. A. Peter Gosling, eds., *The Chinese in Southeast Asia*, vol. 1: Ethnicity and Economic Activity (Singapore: Maruzen Asia, 1983), pp. 7, 20.

This phenomenon of the middlemen, or so-called pariah minority, is a familiar one in Europe, where the kings and magnates found them less threatening in some cases than their own population and, therefore, encouraged them to play brokering roles. "Pariah capitalism" became a subject of serious inquiry in the late nineteenth century, chiefly by German sociologists, including Werner Sombart and Max Weber. As early as 1875, analogies were being made between the Jews in Europe and the Chinese in Southeast Asia.[67] The position of the pariah minority was always precarious because of their different ethnicity and because of the activities that they engaged in, such as money lending, petty trade, and tax farming, all considered odious by the existing social morality.

Notwithstanding wide variations from country to country, the general sociological trend in Southeast Asia after independence was for upwardly mobile "natives" to claim positions in the political realm (state bureaucracies, military, and police), especially in Malaysia and Indonesia. Meanwhile, the people of Chinese ancestry were relegated to the private commercial sector. Benedict Anderson reminds us that from 1966 to 1998 not a single person of known Chinese descent became a cabinet minister, senior civil servant, general, admiral, or air marshal in Indonesia. Yet the Chinese in Indonesia have been called "the race that counts," according to Adam Schwarz, and almost all of the biggest "crony capitalists" around Suharto came from this group. This "racial" division of labor has made a marginalized minority the "real domestic motor of the 'miracle,'" has limited the growth of a vigorous "native" entrepreneurial class, and has encouraged massive profiteering on the part of state officials.[68]

---

[67]Anthony Reid, "Entrepreneurial Minorities, Nationalism, and the State," in Daniel Chirot and Anthony Reid, eds. *Essential Outsiders: Chinese and Jews in the Modern Transformation of Southeast Asia and Central Europe* (Seattle: University of Washington Press, 1997), p. 35. Sombart argued that capitalism flourished where Jews were given the greatest economic freedom because of the positive attitude toward wealth expressed in the Torah, as against the New Testament. Weber made a similar argument about the Chinese attitude toward wealth, but did not think that such was conducive to the development of modern capitalism with its many social and legal prerequisites.

[68]Benedict Anderson, "The Race that Counts," in Adam Schwartz, *A Nation in Waiting* (Boulder: Westview Press, 1995).

How is the "real domestic motor of the 'miracle'" distributed across Southeast Asia? In Malaysia, the ethnic Chinese are 29 percent of the population but account for some 69 percent of share capital by market capitalization. In the Philippines, ethnic Chinese are said to be only 2 percent of the population but control 50 to 60 percent of share capital by market capitalization. In Thailand, an estimated 10 percent of the population are ethnic Chinese, accounting for 81 percent of listed firms by market capitalization. In Indonesia, ethnic Chinese are an estimated 3.5 percent of the population, controlling 73 percent of the same. And in Chinese-dominated Singapore, they account for 77 percent of the population, representing some 81% of listed firms by market capitalization.[69]

The politics of this racial division works differently in different locations. In a culturally and racially assimilated Thailand, there is little organized opposition to the Sino-Thai business predominance. The same is true of the Philippines, where the Chinese have long intermarried with the Spanish *mestizo* elites, to the extent that today some 10 percent of the population claim partial Chinese ancestry (compared with 2 percent "pure" Chinese). In Malaysia, assimilation has been more limited, with the government committed to a race-based economic policy—known as the New Economic Policy (1970–90)—to boost Malay corporate ownership from a piddling 1.9 percent to some 30 percent by 1990. The non-Malay ownership would remain the same, according to this scheme, at about 40 percent, and foreign ownership was to fall from 60.7 percent in 1970 to about 30 percent in the 1990s. In Indonesia, the Chinese are scattered throughout the archipelago (unlike the Sino-Thais, who are concentrated in Bangkok), but the big Chinese businesses exchange state protection for economic patronage through close ties with the military and the ruling group. The Salim Group of Indonesia is reportedly the world's largest Chinese-owned conglomerate, accounting for some 8 percent of Indonesia's GNP. All this makes the reform of corporate governance a distinctly different enterprise than it is in Northeast Asia.

---

[69]Michael Vatikiotis and Prangtip Daorueng in Bangkok, "Entrepreneurs: Survival Tactics: Frugality and family values could help ethnic-Chinese businesses stay afloat in stormy economic waters," *Far Eastern Economic Review* (February 26, 1998), p. 45.

But what an enterprise it is! It thrives in highly adverse political circumstances, finds opportunities in the unlikeliest places, and turns adversities into advantages. Unlike industrial leaders in Korea or Japan who have stuck with one big idea (industrial policy), Chinese "pariah" capitalists have quickly adapted themselves to policy decisions made by the alien ethnic elites, who have but a single advantage over the Chinese in that they hold state power. Chinese businesses have thrived in all milieus, under both protectionist *and* liberal regimes. For instance, occasional nationalist restrictions on foreign-owned enterprises tended to help the Chinese by limiting competition, and when the foreign firms were localized, the Chinese often found themselves the logical partners. With import-substitution industrialization, the local-ownership requirement often helped the Chinese acquire foreign technology, and "local-content" requirements in industries such as automobiles also created new business opportunities for local Chinese enterprises. But the Chinese have also done well with structural adjustment and liberal market-oriented economic-reform programs (involving trade and investment regimes, financial reforms, deregulation, and privatization of state-owned enterprises), which frequently hurt the local private sector in the short run. These policies are more readily effected in Southeast Asia than in other developing countries because of the political weakness of the Chinese-dominated local private sector; instead of resisting the state, the Chinese just made the best of their opportunities, as usual. The Chinese were also protected against the tight monetary policies, credit rationing, and high interest rates characteristic of macroeconomic stabilization policies. This is because they have disproportionate access to alternative sources of capital abroad, from informal ethnic-based credit networks at home to internal financing in Chinese conglomerates (many of which own their own banks), and preferred-customer status among other local banks (most of which are Chinese owned).[70]

The principle of corporate governance in the Chinese firms in Southeast Asia is said to be the same as the Chinese family business else-

---

[70]Lim and Gosling, "Strengths and Weaknesses of Minority Status for Southeast Asian Chinese at a Time of Economic Growth and Liberalization," pp. 287–88.

where, as in Taiwan and Hong Kong. This does not mean that certain cultural traits are immutable but it does mean that there is a heritage of economic organization through clan lineage and *pang* (speech-group) networks, which seems conducive to economic success at earlier stages of commercial activity. The Chinese term most often used to describe business groups is not *caifa* (a translation for *zaibatsu* or *chaebol*), or *qiyejituan* (for *kigyo shudan*), but rather *quanxiqiye*, meaning "related enterprise." *Guanxi* refers to particularistic connections between persons that are based on some common or shared identification, and Ichiro Numazaki defines a *quanxiqiye* is defined as a "cluster of enterprises owned and controlled by a group of persons tied by a network of various *guanxi*."[71]

Most Chinese family businesses are small and highly specialized, and prefer informal sources of finance—family members, close friends, revolving credit associations, or the unregulated "curb," as, for example, in Taiwan. As the firms get bigger, the reliance on network tends to become attenuated, in favor of thicker ties with outsiders, which offer greater economic opportunities as well as political protection. Today, it is the small, or merely unsuccessful, businessmen who, lacking such fortuitous outside arrangements, still must resort to Chinese lineage and home-village associations. These facts form the basis of Linda Lim's argument that the peculiarities of Chinese business organization were neither necessary nor sufficient as an explanation of Chinese economic dominance or monopoly of particular lines of business in Southeast Asia.[72]

When Chinese family firms engage in "opportunistic diversification," it is with retained profits of the existing firms (unlike the Korean *chaebol*) under the management of a family member or another highly trusted close associate. Even when they grow and diversify (as, say, in Hong Kong), they tend to think in terms of their long experience in the textile industry, and their major managerial skills and commitments reflect it. Where investment requirements are too great or there are needs for political and business connections, the families enter into alliances with trusted partners

---

[71]Karl Fields, *Enterprise and the State in Korea and Taiwan* (Ithaca, N.Y.: Cornell University Press, 1995), p. 66.

[72]Lim, "Chinese Economic Activity in Southeast Asia," pp. 5, 8.

to set up new businesses, thus forming the Chinese "business groups" that operate in a variety of industries. These are not integrated through a central administrative hierarchy like the Korean *chaebol*; instead, they operate like partnerships united by common investments and mutual trust in which the critical locus of decision-making and control remains the individual family business. Large Chinese family businesses span a number of fields and are interconnected through a network of alliances and ties between family heads. Once again in contrast to the Korean *chaebol*, Chinese businesses combine managerial specialization with entrepreneurial diversification.[73] The strategic preferences of the Chinese family firm include reliance on price and cost competition, short payback periods for new investments, the intensive use of resources, and a reluctance to share control or responsibility; risks are managed largely by restricting commitments and maximizing resource flexibility.[74]

In Hong Kong, where there are many public companies, the typical Chinese-run family business invites outside equity participation by offering a minority stake in a public company within the network of family firms. Control of this public company stays within the family through direct investment in the equity by other family companies and family members, cross-holdings and cross-directorships with related companies associated with the family group, and other arrangements yielding an element of control with related parties.[75] The familism of the Chinese firm also points to the pervasiveness of the so-called Buddenbrooks phenomenon: indeed, the typical successful Chinese family business is said to go through four distinct phases—emergent, centralized, segmented, and disintegrative—in about three generations.

To some, like Francis Fukuyama, this pattern is the Chinese counterpart to the cycle that the Irish call "from shirtsleeves to shirtsleeves." It attests to the Chinese reluctance to develop and use

---

[73]For a discussion of the organizational aspect of the *chaebol*, see Whitley's chapter on Korea, and Chung and Lee, *Korean Managerial Dynamics*.

[74]Whitley, *Business Systems in East Asia*, pp. 54–55.

[75]Robert Tricker, "Corporate Governance: A Ripple on the Cultural Reflection," in *Capitalism in Contrasting Cultures*, S.R. Clegg and S.G. Redding, eds. (New York: Walter de Gruyter, 1990), p. 200.

professional management, and indicates a real problem with forward integration, especially in unfamiliar markets.[76] But to the Schumpeterian mindset, the Chinese Buddenbrooks would indicate something else—a world of perpetual destruction and creation in which the Chinese family business operates, where flexibility and innovation count as they should, and the families involved cannot rely on the state or some other political benefactor to bail them out. In any case, it is a world far apart from Northeast Asia. The reform of corporate governance in Southeast Asia toward ideal-typical Western standards seems tantamount to asking Chinese businesses to stop being—well, Chinese.

---

[76]Fukuyama, *Trust*, pp. 78–80.

CONCLUSION

The primary purpose of this essay is to suggest that the focal point of reform should be Northeast Asia, especially Korea. In addition, an eye should be cocked toward China, in order to preclude the development there of similar methods of corporate governance (given that China's leaders are increasingly attracted to the Northeast Asian model of industrial development). It was by no means only during the last year, or only under sharp IMF scrutiny, when people suddenly discovered big problems in the Korean economy. The current financial crisis gripping Korea should not have come as such a surprise, since it is the third such massive financial crisis Korea has experienced since the country "took-off" more than thirty years ago. Indeed, Korea's present crisis is not even the first to earn the epithet "the worst crisis since the Korean War" (as Kim Dae Jung called it in his inaugural address). Koreans said the same about the debt crisis of 1979–83, when Korea had difficulty servicing large outstanding foreign debts (about $40 million, third ranking in the world)—a crisis that produced modest financial liberalization in the early 1980s.

The Korean financial system has always been joined at the hip to the huge and hugely leveraged conglomerates, and it has always been vulnerable to external shocks, which threaten to bring the whole economy down like a house of cards. That this did not happen until 1997, however, was mainly because of security concerns owing to the Cold War and the conflict with North Korea. In the past, the United States and Japan promptly stepped in with large amounts of aid and credits (e.g., the $4 billion package from Tokyo in January 1983) to reactivate the economy. Even though each financial crisis pointed to the urgency of reforming the *chaebol*, prompt external support meant that nothing was really done. In spite of sharp criticism, the *chaebol* continued to grow like Topsy. Why?

The main reason is the problem we began with: Korean public good and private interest are rolled together into one large complex that is bent on rapid industrial growth. There is also considerable truth to the old adage that "nothing succeeds like success." After each of its two previous financial crises, Korea resumed pro- longed, double-digit economic growth. This probably will not occur again, however, which means the reform of Korean corporate governance has finally become a stark necessity of the new admin- istration. It is impossible to predict how this newly embarked-upon reform will develop, but we can now sum up what is likely to happen.

The first "pointer" is that Koreans are likely to think of the whole issue not in terms of legislating a new atmosphere in which the rule of law prevails, but in terms of what changes will again make the *chaebol* world-competitive firms. Korea, with or without reform, will long remain a "developmental" rather than "regula- tory" political economy. This insight is often forgotten amid much talk today about the need for new forms of regulation: the Korean crisis must have stemmed from lax regulation, *ergo*, the need to regulate anew. At the root of the Western concern for regula- tion is a doctrine of fairness, of creating level playing fields and competitive environments. This mode of regulating the corporate sector is not likely to work in the near future, because the concept of regulation carries different meaning and intent in the North- east Asian context. For all the talk about the rule of law—even if, in the final analysis, that is the most critical element in changing corporate governance and in breaking the state-bank-business nexus— regulatory reforms most likely will be pushed with an eye to hon- ing Korea's competitiveness. Koreans will have no interest in reforms that weaken their competitive firms or create level play- ing fields where the strong gobble up the weak.

The Republic of Korea has long represented the essential "developmental state," which, as I have argued, may be a paradise for big business; but in spite of the "crony capitalism" and "moral hazards" to which the IMF refers, it did succeed in making globe- ranging competitive Korean firms. Development and competition are the key; in the end, all Koreans are economic nationalists, includ- ing the new president, because they believe that, in a predatory world economy, they can afford to be nothing less. We cannot expect that the current financial crisis will bring closure to four decades of developmentalism unless we believe that history means nothing. Nor can we expect that a particular type of mentality can disappear overnight because it was proved wrong in 1997–98. The current administration in Korea has already done more than all previous administrations combined to bring about democracy in Korea, but its starting point for dealing with the *chaebol* remains the same as that of the previous regimes: tried and true discretionary measures to force industrial reorganization, something as revealing as it is predictable.

The second fact to remember in contemplating the reform of Korean corporate governance is that the *chaebol* may have emerged in the last thirty years, but the model goes back seventy years. This is another way of saying that we must be sensitive to "path dependency," to a pattern of Northeast Asian development that has characterized the whole twentieth century. Korea is not a leopard that can instantly change its spots (a point that is vividly illustrated by contemporary Japanese immobilism in the face of eight years of recession). But we do not preclude the possibility of what Barrington Moore once said—that big changes are often easier than small changes. A radical reform might, therefore, be possible. The conditions couldn't be better: a new, popular reform leadership coming to power amid palpable crisis, yielding the best opportunity since the Korean War to truly transform the system. Nonetheless, reforms, no matter how big, will be consistent with what has gone before. (It is interesting to note that the man in charge of sabre-rattling before the *chaebol* on behalf of Kim Dae Jung is none other than Pak Tae-jun, the captain of Korea's steel industry. He built up and long directed P'ohang Steel, and is known to be as familiar with the Japanese system as any Korean capitalist. So perhaps the ROK will again take cures from Japan—this time, postwar Japan.)

What *is* this postwar Japanese system to which Korea might conform? Masahiko Aoki argues that management acts as a mediator in the policymaking process, striking a balance between the interests of shareholders and those of employees. The enterprise union functions as a substructure of the firm and represents

employees in the decision-making process. [77] Given the ubiquitous presence of enterprise-union organization in Korea, the
Japanese example might also argue for Korean labor reforms
along the same lines, which would be a good counterpart to the
historically unprecedented "peak bargaining" that Kim Dae Jung
directed in January 1998 between top representatives of business,
labor, and government. If this were to be institutionalized, the ROK
would then resemble Japan's postwar pattern of political corpo-
ratism, as a political scientist would understand it.

Before this system became viable in Japan, the firm had to meet
three historical conditions. The first was the dismantling of family control of the firms, through Occupation policies in 1946 and
1947. This involved a "managerial revolution from above" through
the dispersal of share ownership as part of the dissolution
of *zaibatsu* holding companies and the replacement of previous managers by young or new ones who were less loyal to the *zaibatsu*
family. The second was a move toward Cooperative Enterprise Unions,
resulting from the defeat of various labor actions in the late 1950s.
The third was an effective insulation from hostile takeovers
through the development of mutual shareholding between companies and financial institutions, notably city banks. This was
facilitated by the stock-market crash of 1964–65, the government
purchase and freezing of stocks to stabilize the market, and later,
a concerted action by the interlocking companies to repurchase
stocks, in part to stave off foreign takeovers.[78]

Obviously, these conditions are not going to obtain in contemporary
Korea. But it is possible that the *chaebol* might, *mutatis mutandis*,
move in the direction of the *keiretsu*. The *keiretsu* is an advance-
ment on the evolutionary scale of the economic combines in
Japan, a rational/legal form of the more feudal *zaibatsu*. To the extent
that the *chaebol* was a postcolonial mutation of the *zaibatsu*, it would
be wrong not to examine the logic of historical change in Japan

---

[77]Masahiko Aoki, "The Japanese Firm in Transition," in Kozo Yamamura and Yasukichi Yasuba, eds., *The Political Economy of Japan* (Stanford: Stanford University Press,
1989), p. 265.

[78]Ibid., pp. 269–73.

with an eye to what is possible in Korea. The major problem with Korea moving toward the *keiretsu* is that the structure is predicated on domestic insularity and exclusivity, something that goes against the grain of the globalized world and against the immediate Korean necessity of attracting more foreign capital. That, and the fact that effective *keiretsu* reform took two decades in Japan.

Finally, we come back again to the "good" aspects of the *chaebol* pattern. For much of postwar Korean history, the *chaebol* were in many ways the Schumpeterian entrepreneurs of Korean development, or what he called "ephors" of capitalism. Their mammoth structure and even their inveterate reliance on state-mediated bank credit made sense, especially given the immaturity of financial markets and Korea's strategy to make an assault on the world market; that is, to wipe the floor with the advanced countries in product areas such as semiconductors, heavy and chemical industry items, petrochemicals, automobiles, and other machines. Erecting these strategies required massive investments that far exceeded retained earnings. This developmental aspect is not likely to go away, but rather will be modified or reformed to fit current circumstances. Korea's *chaebol* have had built-in advantages in economies of scale, and that is not likely to change either—nor should it. (In fact, trade statistics for Korea in early 1998 show that it was precisely the items just mentioned that have recorded an average of 30 percent growth in exports, with exports of steel products marking a 44.5 percent growth. By contrast, exports of the older-style, declining labor-intensive goods recorded a 9.9 percent growth.)

Regardless, the fact remains that there *ought* to be great change in the corporate governance of the *chaebol*, allowing more transparency, external audits, foreign participation, and more accountable management. There should be an effective institution guaranteeing minority shareholder rights and transparency in accounting. The power and function of the board of directors should be bolstered, and the role of institutional investors should grow as well, through financial deepening. Realistically, however, the Korean firm will become "more like us" only up to a point, to use James Fallows's phrase. For half a century, the United States has sought to make Korea "more like us," but the problem of reforming an economic model deeply influenced by Japan's industrial success remains.

Likewise, we should be wary of the kind of triumphalism reflected in Francis Fukuyama's "end of history," according to which the Chinese family firm is the mere reflection of low-trust societies crippled by the absence of civil society. On the contrary, the Chinese family firms that characterize Southeast Asian capitalism are perhaps the most flexible and adaptive entrepreneurial units in the world today. Sometimes, the behavior of these firms reflects a harsh world bereft of universal trust. But the reverse is also true, that the Chinese family firm is at ease with a world of trust as Fukuyama would define it. Witness, for example, the enormous success of diasporic Chinese business in highly articulated civil societies like Vancouver and Toronto. Perhaps global capitalism, with its free movement of goods and services, has made the most singularly pre-modern of corporate governance forms, the Chinese family firm, into the most highly adaptable, multicultural, postmodern firm, able to navigate in any economic waters.

This is another way of saying that no one-size corporate governance fits all, even in the globalized world of unforgiving investors and schoolmarmish IMF officials. No matter how severe the pressure for organizational convergence, it is unlikely that we will see the emergence, at the "end of history" as it were, of one superior form of corporate government to which all can adhere. It is worth remembering that it was not visionaries standing at the doorstep of the twenty-first century but culture-bound writers of the mid-nineteenth century who "looked forward to a single, more or less standardized world where all governments would acknowledge the truths of political economy and liberalism would be carried throughout the globe by impersonal missionaries more powerful than those of Christianity or Islam had ever been; a world reshaped in the image of the bourgeoisie, perhaps even one from which, eventually, national differences would disappear."[79]

---

[79] E. J. Hobsbawm, *The Age of Capital: 1848-1875* (London: Weidenfield and Nicolson, 1977), p. 83, quoted in Robert Wade, "Globalization and its Limits: Reports of the Death of the National Economy are Greatly Exaggerated," in Suzanne Berger and Ronald Dore, eds., *National Diversity and Global Capitalism.*

BIBLIOGRAPHY

Amsden, Alice. *Asia's Next Giant: South Korea and Late Industrialization.* (Oxford:Oxford University Press, 1989).

Anderson, Benedict. "From Miracle to Crash." *London Review of Books* 20, no. 8 (April 27, 1998).

Aoki, Masahiko. "The Japanese Firm in Transition." In Yamamura, Kozoand Yasukichi Yasuba, eds. *The Political Economy of Japan.* Stanford: Stanford University Press, 1989.

Banfield, Edward C. *The Moral Basis of a Backward Society.* New York: Free Press, 1967.

Berger, Suzanne and Ronald Dore, eds. *National Diversity and Global Capitalism.* Ithaca: Cornell University Press, 1966.

Bowie, Alasdair. *Crossing the Industrial Divide: State, Society, and the Politics of Economic Transformation in Malaysia.* New York: Columbia University Press, 1991.

Chew, Donald H., ed. *Studies in Corporate Finance and Governance Systems: A Comparison of the U.S., Japan, and Europe.* New York: OxfordUniversity Press, 1997.

Chirot, Daniel and Anthony Reid, eds. *Essential Outsiders: Chinese and Jews in the Modern Transformation of Southeast Asia and Central Europe.* Seattle: University of Washington Press, 1997.

Chang, Ha-Joon, Hong-Jae Park, and Chul Gyue Yoo. "Interpreting the Korean Crisis: Financial Liberalization, Industrial Policy, and Corporate Governance." *Cambridge Journal of Economics,* Special Issue,22, no. 6 (November 1998).

Chung, Kae H. and Hank Chong Lee, eds. *Korean Managerial Dynamics.* NewYork: Praeger, 1989.

Clegg, S.R. and S. G. Redding, eds. *Capitalism in Contrasting Cultures*.New York:Walter de Gruyter, 1990.

Clifford, Mark. "Family Ties: Heir Force." *Far Eastern Economic Review*.(November 17, 1994).

_____ *Troubled Tiger*. Armonk, N.Y.: M. E. Sharpe, 1997.

Doner, Richard and Daniel Unger. "The Politics of Finance in Thai Economic Development." In Haggard, Stephan, Chung H. Lee, and Sylvia Maxfield, eds. *The Politics of Finance in Developing Countries*. Ithaca: Cornell University Press, 1993.

Dore, Ronald. "Convergence in Whose Interest?" Berger, Suzanne and Ronald Dore, eds. *National Diversity and Global Capitalism*. Ithaca: Cornell University Press, 1966.

Fields, Karl J. *Enterprise and the State in Korea and Taiwan*. Ithaca: Cornell University Press, 1995.

Fukuyama, Francis. *Trust: The Social Virtues and the Creation of Prosperity*. New York: Simon and Schuster, 1995.

Gourevitch, Peter. "The Macropolitics of Micro institutional Differences in the Analysis of Comparative Capitalism." Berger, Suzanne and Ronald Dore. eds. *National Diversity and Global Capitalism*. Ithaca: Cornell University Press, 1966.

Hadley, Eleanor. *Antitrust in Japan*. Princeton: Princeton University Press, 1970.

Haggard, Stephan, Chung H. Lee, and Sylvia Maxfield. eds. *The Politics of Finance in Developing Countries*. Ithaca: Cornell University Press, 1993.

Haggard, Stephan and Robert R. Kaufman, eds. *The Politics of Economic Adjustment*. Princeton, N.J.: Princeton University Press, 1992.

Hamilton, Gary, ed. *Asian Business Networks*. Berlin, Germany, and Hawthorne, N.Y.: Walter de Gruyter, 1996.

Hamilton, Gary, and Tony Waters. "Ethnicity and Capitalist Development: The Changing Role of the Chinese in Thailand." In Hamilton, Gary, ed. *Asian Business Networks*. Berlin, Germany, and Hawthorne, N.Y.: Walterde Gruyter, 1996.

Hattori, Tamio. "Japanese Zaibatsu and Korean Chaebol." In Chung, Kae H. and Hank Chong Lee, eds. *Korean Managerial Dynamics*. New York:Praeger, 1989.

Hirschman, Albert O. *Rival Views of Market Society*. Cambridge: Harvard University Press, 1992.

Hobsbawm, E.J. *The Age of Capital: 1848-1875*. London: Weidenfeld and Nicolson, 1977.

Hutchcroft, Paul D. "Patrimonial State, Predatory Oligarchy: The Politics of Private Commercial banking in the Philippines." Ph.D.diss., Yale University, 1993.

Hutchcroft, Paul D. "Selective Squander: The Politics of Preferential Credit Allocation in the Philippines." In Haggard, Stephan, Chung H.Lee, and Sylvia Maxfield, eds. *The Politics of Finance in Developing Countries*. Ithaca: Cornell University Press, 1993.

Janelli, Roger. *Making Capitalism: The Social and Cultural Construction of a South Korean Conglomerate*. Stanford: Stanford University Press, 1993, 1995.

Jensen, Michael C. "The Modern Industrial Revolution, Exit, and the Failure of Internal Control Systems." In Chew, Donald H., ed. *Studies in Corporate Finance and Governance Systems: A Comparison of the U.S., Japan, and Europe*. New York: Oxford University Press, 1997.

Jesudason, James V. *Ethnicity and the Economy: the State, Chinese-Business, and Multinationals in Malaysia*. Singapore: Oxford University Press, 1989.

Jomo, K. S. "A Specific Idiom of Chinese Capitalism in Southeast Asia: Sino-Malaysian Capital Accumulation in the Face of State Hostility." In Daniel Chirot and Anthony Reid, eds., *Essential Outsiders: Chinese and Jews in the Modern Transformation of Southeast Asia and Central Europe.* Seattle: University of Washington Press, 1997.

Judason, James V. *Ethnicity and the Economy: The State, Chinese Business, and Multinationals in Malaysia.* Singapore: Oxford University Press, 1989.

Jwa, Sung Hee. "Property Rights and Economic Behavior: Lessons for Korea's Economic Reform." Korea Development Institute. Mimeo.

Kahler, Miles. "External Influence, Conditionality, and the Politics of Adjustment." In haggard, Stephan and Robert R. kaufman, eds. *The Politics of Economic Adjustment.* Princeton, NJ: Princeton University Press, 1992.

Kester, W. Carl. "American and Japanese Corporate Governance: Convergence to Best Practice?" In Berger, Suzanne and Ronald Dore. eds. *National Diversity and Global Capitalism.* Ithaca: Cornell University Press, 1966.

Kim, Dae Jung. *Mass-Participatory Economy: A Democratic Alternative for Korea.* Lanham, MD: University Press of America, 1986.

Koon, Heng Pek. "The Chinese Business Elite of Malaysia." In McVey, Ruth, ed. *Southeast Asian Capitalists.* Ithaca: Cornell Southeast Asian Program, 1992.

Lee, Charles S., "Give Me Your Sick: South Korea's President Kim aims to tame the mighty chaebols by cutting off credit to 55 ailing subsidiaries." *Far Eastern Economic Review.* (July 2, 2000).

Lim, Linda, "Chinese Economic Activity in Southeast Asia: An Introductory Review." In Lim, Linda and L. A. Peter Gosling, eds. *The Chinese in Southeast Asia.* Vol. 1: Ethnicity and Economic Activity. Singapore: Maruzen Asia, 1983.

Lim, Linda, and L. A. Peter Gosling, "Strengths and Weaknesses of Minority Status for Southeast Asian Chinese at a Time of Economic Growth and Liberalization." In Lim, Linda and L. A. Peter Gosling, eds. *The Chinese in Southeast Asia*. Vol. 1: Ethnicity and Economic Activity. Singapore: Maruzen Asia, 1983.

Lim, Mah Hui. "The Ownership and Control of Large Corporations in Malaysia: The Role of Chinese Businessmen." In Lim, Linda and L. A.Peter Gosling, eds. *The Chinese in Southeast Asia*. Volume 1: Ethnicity and Economic Activity. Singapore: Maruzen Asia, 1983.

MacIntyre, Andrew. "The Politics of Finance in Indonesia: Command,Confusion, and Competition." In Haggard, Stephan, Chung H. Lee, andSylvia Maxfield, eds. *The Politics of Finance in Developing Countries*. Ithaca: Cornell University Press, 1993.

McVey, Ruth, ed. *Southeast Asian Capitalists*. Ithaca: Cornell Southeast Asian Program, 1992.

Mackie, Jamie. "Changing Patterns of Chinese Big Business in Southeast Asia," In McVey, Ruth, ed. *Southeast Asian Capitalists*. Ithaca: Cornell Southeast Asian Program, 1992.

Meisner, Maurice. *The Deng Xiaoping Era: An Inquiry into the Fate of Chinese Socialism: 1978–1994*. New York: Hill & Wang, 1996.

Pollack, Andrew. "In California, A Distant Mirror on Korea." *The New York Times*, p. 2, col. 1, March 25, 1998.

Putnam, Robert. *Making Democracy Work*. Princeton: Princeton University Press, 1994.

Reid, Anthony. "Entrepreneurial Minorities, Nationalism, and the State." In Daniel Chirot and Anthony Reid, eds., *Essential Outsiders: Chinese and Jews in the Modern Transformation of Southeast Asia and Central Europe*. Seattle: University of Washington Press, 1997.

Schumpeter, Joseph. *Imperialism/ Social Classes*. New York: Meridian Books, 1951.

Schwarz, Adam. *A Nation in Waiting*. Boulder: Westview Press, 1995.

Tricker, Robert. "Corporate Governance: A Ripple on the Cultural Reflection." In S.R. Clegg and S.G. Redding, eds. *Capitalism in Contrasting Cultures*. New York: Walter de Gruyter, 1990.

Vatikiotis, Michael and P. Daorueng. "Entrepreneuers: Survival Tactics: Frugality and family values could help ethnic-Chinese businesses stay afloat in stormy economic waters." *Far Eastern Economic Review*, vol.42, February 26, 1998.

Wade, Robert. "Globalization and Its Limits: Reports of the Death of the National Economy are Greatly Exaggerated." In Berger, Suzanne and Ronald Dore. eds. *National Diversity and Global Capitalism*. Ithaca: Cornell University Press, 1966.

Weber, Max. *The Religion of China*. New York: The Free Press, 1951.

_____. *The Protestant Ethic and the Spirit of Capitalism*. New York: Charles Scribner's Sons, 1976 [1958].

Whitley, Richard. *Business Systems in East Asia: Firms, Markets, and Societies*. New York: Sage Publications, 1992.

Woo, Jung-en (Meredith Woo-Cumings). *Race to the Swift: State and Finance in Korean Industrialization*. New York: Columbia University Press, 1991.

Yi Yongki. *Hanguk kiopsoyuchibae kujo* [*Corporate Governance in Korea*].Hanguk kaebal yonkuwon [Korea Development Institute]. Seoul: KDI, 1996.

Yoshihara, Kunio. *The Rise of Ersatz Capitalism in South-East Asia*. Singapore: Oxford University Press, 1988.

Yu Sungmin. *Nanumyonso k'oganda* [*Sharing, Growing*]. Seoul: Mirae Media, 1996.

————. "Taegiop chibaekujo ui ponjil kwa chungch'aekchon-mang." [Corporate Governance in Large Enterprises: Policy Prospects]. Korea Development Institute, Mimeo.

————. "Shinchongbu chaeboljongch'aek ui p'yongka wa daekiop ui hyokshinkwaje." [Evaluation of the New Government Chaebol Policy and the Reform Prospects for Big Business]. Korea Development Institute. Mimeo.

Cultural Contradictions of Post-Communism:
Why Liberal Reforms Did Not Succeed in Russia

A Paper from the Project on Development,
Trade and International Finance

Nina L. Khrushcheva

A Council on Foreign Relations Paper

Cultural Contradictions of Post-Communism

Why Liberal Reforms Did Not Succeed in Russia

Nina L. Khrushcheva

Things that I admire elsewhere, I hate here [in Russia]... I find them too dearly paid for; order, patience, calmness, elegance, respectfulness, the natural and moral relations that ought to exist between those who think and those who do, in short all that gives worth and charm to well-organized societies, all that gives meaning and purpose to political institutions, is lost... here...

Marquis de Custine, 1839

We wanted for the better, but it still turned out as usual.

Victor Chernomyrdin, 1998

INTRODUCTION

One goal of Russia's economic reforms during the last ten years has been to establish a new class of businessmen and owners of private property—people who could form the foundation for a new model post-Soviet citizen. However, the experience of this post-communist economic "revolution" has turned out to be very different from the original expectations. For as people became disillusioned with communism due to its broken promises, the words "democracy" and "reform" quickly became equally as unbearable to large sectors of the Russian public after 1991. Such disillusion was achieved in less than ten years—a record revolutionary burnout that would be the envy of any anti-Bolshevik.

Only a few years into the reform process disappointed analysts were already posing stark questions: "Why have democratic and market reforms turned out to be such an arduous process? Why has Western-style liberalism, embraced almost everywhere in theory, proved difficult even to approximate in practice? Why has freedom not yet been established, even though the totalitarian state has been torn down?"[1] Indeed, many analysts assess the results of the past ten years as a nearly complete failure, and blame either corruption, or Western institutions such as the International Monetary Fund and the World Bank. The blame attached to the international institutions may be too simplistic, as the Bretton Woods Institutions have been around for fifty years, and many of their projects have proved successful. In addition, corruption is part of every political economy and exists to greater and lesser degrees in every country. What is significant is the consensus that Russia's political economy is corrupt on all levels. According to numerous sources[2], Russia has ranked among the ten most corrupt nations in the world for each of the past eight years. International investors complain about corruption regularly. Moreover, the 1998 financial crisis made matters much worse, inciting discussion as to whether Russia's developing economy was in fact a form of developing capitalism, or simply "oligarchism," a system where a narrow elite has "stolen the state, and everything else."[3]

---

[1]Stephen Holmes, "Cultural Legacies or State Collapse?" in Michael Mandelbaum, ed., *Post-Communism: Four Perspectives.* (New York: Council on Foreign Relations, 1996), p. 25.

[2]Transparency's International 1998 and 1999 Corruption Perceptions Index ranks Russia 76 out of 85 countries. Denmark had the top ranking as the least corrupt country, and the United States shared 17th place with Austria. On a ten-point scale, with Denmark having earned a 10, Russia scored 2.4. The United States and Austria both had 7.5, while Cameroon earned only 1.4, the lowest score; (Berlin: Transparency International, 1998 and 1999); www.transparency.de.

[3]Kenneth Murphy and Marek Hessel, "Stealing the State and Everything Else: A Survey on Corruption in the Post-Communist World," (Prague: Project Syndicate, Winter 1999); www.project-syndicate.cz.

That question has drawn attention around the world. The U.S. Senate held hearings on corruption in Russia on September 30, 1999. Public speculations about "Who Lost Russia?" triggered debates within the IMF and World Bank, inspiring a restructuring process of both institutions; Boris Yeltsin resigned; and new President Vladimir Putin has declared a "dictatorship of law and order" in his fight against Russia's lawlessness.[4]

The question of corruption only highlighted Russia's complicated transition, but its general problem with liberalism and capitalism goes beyond politics and into history and culture. According to the political scientist Stephen Holmes, corruption is not a cause but a consequence of what he calls "*cultural legacies*, those habits acquired in the past which are difficult to shake and which purportedly obstruct the successful creation and function of democratic and market institutions. Habits die hard and mentalities change slow..."[5]

A number of aspects within the Russian "national character"—the "cultural legacy"— explain the failings of liberal policies in Russia since 1991. Among these are the influence of Asian culture and the values that linger from the previous system, both of which reinforce the special role of family and friendship relationships for a Russian. The influence of these factors leaves little hope for a "faceless bureaucracy" that would operate without regard to personal preferences and sympathies, applying the law and regulations equally to all. Until now, a complete understanding of the problems posed by cultural obstacles to a properly functioning market has not been at the heart of most discussions of Russia's liberal economic reforms. However, the mixed results of the reform process, as well diverse assessments[6] by Russian actors and

---

[4]Jonas Bernstein, "Party Lines: Dictated by Law, or Nods," *Moscow Times*, March 4, 2000.

[5]Stephen Holmes, "Cultural Legacies or State Collapse," p. 26.

[6]Today only a few reformists insist that the road to capitalism that they chose by way of "shock therapy" has proven itself successful. Yegor Gaidar, Anatoly Chubais, Anders Aslund, and a few others remain confident that reforms could not have been done differently. In his book *Privatizatsiya po-rossiiski* [Privatization Russian Style], Chubais argues that the way reforms were implemented was defined by the necessity to neutralize the Soviet-style bureaucracy, because the command system never wanted to admit that

outside participants and analysts, suggest that the problems go much deeper than only the issue of bad policies, inefficient implementation, or the supposedly corrupt nature of the Russian state. "What deserves careful thought is the reform-hampering role of inherited attitudes and patterns of behavior. People do more easily what they are used to doing than what they have never done… Habits and expectations, which perversely constrict freedom of choice, can be handed down from generation to generation and survive for centuries by sheer inertia."[7] Moreover, Jeffrey Sachs, Harvard economist and early advisor to Boris Yeltsin, suggests that it is not just behavioral patterns, but also geography which, although not entirely deterministic, "conditions events" and keeps "a powerful hold even in our supposedly globalized economy… Proximity to the West induced better policies…"[8] throughout the post-communist region.

The two epigrams by de Custine and Chernomyrdin that introduce this essay suggest a simple but powerful conclusion: Russia's culture has a deep impact on any reform effort, meaning that the country is not easily susceptible to change. Why is it that the late czarist system, late communism, and post-communism all failed to generate viable alternatives other than changes that appear destructive and malfunctioning? Why is it that replacing the old regime always results in a crippled successor regime? One possible answer here is a great paradox of "tyranny," in which a "weak state" provides too much government, depriving people of the basic liberties needed to make their own decisions.[9] Such a state is ever impotent to solve the fundamental problems facing it, remaining effective only at weakening and discrediting alternative leaders. This pattern held true even after 1991, when the reform team led by the

---

a Soviet man like every other man was nothing more than 'homo economicus,' fully engrossed in the economic interests: interest in money, interest in property and profit."; see Anatoly Chubais, "Birth of the Idea," in Anatoly Chubais, ed., *Privatizatsiya po-rossiiski* (Moscow: Vagrius, 1999), p. 29.)

[7]Stephen Holmes, "Cultural Legacies or State Collapse," p. 26.

[8]Jeffrey D. Sachs, "Eastern Europe Reforms: Why the Outcomes Differed so Sharply," *Boston Globe*, September 19, 1999.

[9]See, for example, Edward Kennan, "Muscovite Political Folkways," *The Russian Review*, vol. 45, no. 2 (April 1986).

English-speaking Yegor Gaidar (deputy prime minister and later minister of economy and finance under Yeltsin) and Anatoly Chubais (deputy prime minister under Yeltsin, on and off) tolerated no alternative to themselves.[10]

This point brings to the fore another paradox: while enduring some of the worst despots in world history, the Russian people developed an almost apocalyptic fear of change, especially change of power. Change is never welcome in Russia. The end of a regime engenders not hope but a fear of cataclysm. Thus, more than in other cultures, power in Russia is subject to inertia, which creates a favorable environment to autocratic rule. The person wielding power embodies power and is followed by the population regardless of the kind of policies he implements, often even despite these policies. This attitude marked people's devotion to Stalin. It was also the secret behind the reelection of Boris Yeltsin in 1996 when, despite poll numbers that showed his popularity at its lowest point in his presidency, the Russian people nonetheless voted to reelect him, most likely reasoning, "Better the devil we know." This attitude is very often something held subconsciously rather than consciously, and is part of a centuries-old tradition, which only time and different (positive) experience could change.

The contemporary Russian scholar and cultural historian Yuri Lotman, in his final work before his death, *Culture and Explosion*,[11] offers a perspective that Russian culture, unlike the cultures of the West, embodies an underlying binary logic of opposition. With-

---

[10]Anatoly Chubais insists, "Of course our privatization was not without "minuses," however if we followed the slow A-B-C process suggested by the 'soft' reformers, we would have had much more negative outcome… Criminalization would have been *absolute*." (Anatoly Chubais, ed., *Privatizatsiya po-rossiiski*, p. 32.) It is comforting to know that the level of criminalization could have been more absolute. Now, however, there has been evidence that reforms could have taken a less radical turn if the reformers and their Western advisers had been less rigid in understanding the reforms. Traditional structures would not have been destroyed, appropriate new structures would have been built, and Russian cultural values and peculiarities of the Russian national character would have been taken into consideration. See, for example: Giulietto Chiesa, *Proshchai Rossiya* [Farewell Russia] (Moscow: Geia, 1997), pp. 35–60; Jeffrey D. Sachs, "Betrayal," *The New Republic* (January 31, 1994); Michael Ellman and Vladimir Kontorovich, eds., *The Destruction of the Soviet Economic System* (Armonk, N.Y.: M.E. Sharpe, 1998).

[11]Yury Lotman, *Kultura i Vzryv* [Culture and] (Moscow: Gnozis, 1992).

out necessarily being aware of these patterns, individuals and groups conceptualize social lives in terms of sets of absolute alternatives that admit no compromise. There is no neutral ground—either one alternative or the other must be chosen. In this choice, either one or the other must be absolutely victorious.[12] In terms of human values, Lotman gives the following sets of polar, obsolete, and stark oppositions: charity versus justice; love versus the law; personal morality (ethics) versus state law; holiness versus politics, etc. A fateful result of binary thinking, according to Lotman, is that the victor, after defeating an opponent, must always seek to annihilate the past. The past is regarded not as the foundation for organic growth, but as a source of error to be destroyed before it infects the new regime. Total destruction precedes creation; creation thus takes place in a void. Means and ends are divorced,[13] as the longed-for new world can only be constructed on the ruins of the old.

Yeltsin, Gaidar, Chubais, and their colleagues, it appears, acted in accord with this classical script of Russian history, repeating its binary logic of opposition. Reformers defined a mythological West, which was understood primarily in terms of opposition to the Soviet Union. The reason for this absolute vision followed upon Sachs's "geographical proximity" idea: it derived from the fact that, for centuries, Russia was separated from the rest of the world by physical and psychological borders, although its rulers always saw those borders as under threat. Thus the post-communist reformers, despite their liberalism, accepted the usual totalitarian formula of "we know best" when attempting to transform the old Soviet society. Communism failed because it was a bankrupt ideology. They reasoned that Russian society and economy would begin to work only by quickly adopting a viable ideology, the free-market model. Never mind that such change could only be imposed by the autocratic techniques of "ends justifying the

---

[12] This may also be the reason why many reformers keep insisting that their policies were ultimately the right ones.

[13] All Russian revolutions have operated by the rule, *tsel opravdyvaet sredstva* ["the end justifies the means"].

means." What Isaiah Berlin called "the mixture of utopian faith and brutal disregard for civilized morality"[14] when discussing the Bolshevik policies, could also be relevant when assessing the Russian liberal reform process, which ruled more often by presidential decree than democratic consent.

The essence of democracy, however, is to secure public support for government policies, which the Yeltsin government consistently failed to do. One cannot auction, privatize, or even simply redistribute the assets of a huge country among the citizens without wide citizen involvement, particularly when the populace was well aware of the high (often bloody) price paid to develop those assets.

Economic liberties, if they are to be supported by the public, can only be possible when the public and the authorities have a firm social contract with definite goals, set procedures, regulations, and codes. Although the Russian—and then Soviet—system never had such a written code, it had a strict tradition of rituals and "informal formalities" that were followed by the elite and the common people alike. When the traditionally accepted systems were formally destroyed in 1991, rituals were no longer functional either within the power elite or in between people and the government. The former unwritten set of rules was replaced by *bespredel* [limitless lawlessness], as Yeltsin's government overlooked the necessity to replace old autocratic rituals with the new modern regulation of "societal protocol." Thus, the separation between the state and society suppressed anything that Russia has even known before. Deprived of the familiar patterns and structures, people have become greatly confused about what formal functions and responsibilities mean for citizens, government officials, and businessmen in the new "capitalist environment."[15]

---

[14]Isaiah Berlin, ¡Political Ideas in the Twentieth Century,î in Isaiah Berlin, *Four Essays on Liberty* (Oxford and New York: Oxford University Press, 1969), p. 17.

[15]Some analysts call it "a crisis of morality," but I would suggest that it is rather "a crisis of modernity," in which the old paternalistic system is being forced to give way to a new, modern system of "shared responsibility."

Yeltsin's post-Communist government failed to set up a social contract between itself and the people. Russians were unaware of the price they had to pay for liberalism and were unsure of why they had to pay it. It was unclear what kind of services the government planned to offer in exchange for citizens' responsible economic behavior. People were told that they had to pay taxes, buy expensive social services and education, and not simply receive a salary but earn it. They were told to not just collect pensions but to accumulate savings throughout their lives. Before all these services had been provided for free. There was a "minor" inconvenience of the dictatorship, of course, but the trade-off was nonetheless clear. This time around, the government was asking people to support the free market economy while not giving anything in return. Witness the arbitrary officials, protection in the form of corruption, unpaid wages and pensions, etc.

To reform without clear democratic consent for the process of renewal placed the entire program at risk from the start because of the "democratic deficit" of *glasnost*.[16] That lack of support, indeed, proved to be the greatest boon to re-empowering the most reactionary—i.e., Stalinist—forces in the country. The post-Communist reformers insisted, however, that the changes to be undertaken were primarily of a technical and economic nature. Connecting these reforms, and making them comprehensible within the terms of the wider culture, was deemed unnecessary.

Indeed, far more than 50 percent of the economic reform initiatives were promulgated by presidential decree and not by any vote in the Duma (legislative assembly), where cultural and political consensus would have been necessary[17]. The reason for such neglect of the Duma is obvious. The liberal reformers led by Gaidar and Chubais reasoned that conservative deputies would block change, so it was in the interests of the country to go around them, executing decisions single-handedly. Therefore, from the start the process of economic reform consisted of a few

---

[16] *Glasnost* was widely used to make known the crimes of the past, but had no application to the processes of the present.

[17] Praim-TASS (December 21, 1998).

good men leading the way without democratic consent for their program. Later, one or two reformers sensed problems, but such insights usually arrived only after they were out of power. In his post-ministerial incarnation, for example, Sergei Kiriyenko admitted that cultural concerns should have been taken into consideration: "When the Russian people gave Yeltsin the authority to end communism, they were far away from thinking that they were supporting the end of social welfare provided by planned economy."[18]

From 1991 onward, policies imposed from the top clashed with expectations arising from the bottom, primarily because the average Russian held to long-established ideas of social justice that most people deemed more valuable that any idea of democracy or capitalism. For centuries Russians have been taught that the interests of society and the state are far more important than the interests of any individual: collectivism and solidarity should be valued more than individualism. Thus, the values of wealth, competition, and the necessity of social inequality were not accepted as inevitable by the majority of the population. Spirituality and personal ethics remained much more significant qualities.

---

[18]Transcript of Sergei Kiriyenko's lecture at New York University School of Law (November 30, 1998).

RUSSIA'S BOTTOM: THE CULTURE OF ENVY

Russian mistrust toward markets and the unconventional attitude of most Russians toward money have their roots in Russian spirituality and personal ethics. "Self-interest has no warranty in morality; material gain, a purely quantitative individual good, excludes the qualitative dimensions of life centered around service to the community,"[19] said the nineteenth-century Slavophile Alexey Khomyakov. These roots are manifested in the distinction Russians draw between 'greed' cultures and "envy" cultures.[20]

In Russian eyes, a "greed" culture tends to respect personal accumulation of money and goods, and rewards its citizens for this practice, both morally and materially. It requires working out sensible tax structures that provide for a public safety net. It also encourages philanthropy, and in general considers inequality inevitable and prosperity a sign of not just providential favor, but also a deserved result.

However, in Russia, "envy" culture is opposed by the widespread egalitarian impulse that personal economic gain is illegitimate and hurts the communal interests of the collective. The nineteenth-century revolutionary writer Alexander Herzen once exclaimed that the "Petite bourgeoisie are incompatible with the Russian character—and thank God for it!"[21] This means that instead of following the "greed" culture motto of "keeping up with the Joneses," in "envy" communities more satisfaction comes from "keeping the Ivanovs

---

[19]A.S. Khomyakov, "O starom i novom", in M.A. Maslin, ed., *Russkaya ideya*. (Moscow: Respublica, 1992), p. 58.

[20]See, for example, Johanna Hubb, *Mother Russia: The Feminine Myth in Russian Culture* (Bloomington and Indianapolis: Indiana University Press, 1993).

21 Alexander Herzen, *My Past and Thoughts* (Berkeley: University of California Press, 1982), p. 285.

down." In Russia, "equality of outcomes," a belief that material conditions in society should not vary too greatly among individual and classes, wins out over "equality of opportunities," which tends to tolerate and even encourage the open flourishing of class distinctions. There is, indeed, a signature joke that Russians like to tell about "envy" cultures: A fairy godmother approaches a poor peasant and promises him anything he desires with only one stipulation: that his neighbor get twice as much of it. The peasant thinks for a long time, and then finally says: "All right. Blind me in one eye."

"Envy" cultures aim to guarantee the survival of the group at a subsistence level, but ruin the ambitious. The very idea of profit, of tangible reward for taking an economic risk, is associated with the inequality imposed by human beings. Meanwhile, justice is identified with protecting the integrity of the helpless, disadvantaged, and weak in a given collective against the indifference and self-promotion of the strong. It is thus important to remember here that Russian culture was traditionally hostile to political democracy altogether. In the words of one of its proponents, "It is clear that the principle of majority is a principle, which does not need harmony; it is a compulsory principle, which wins only through physical superiority; those who are in the majority overwhelm those who are in the minority."[22] That Russia traditionally belongs to an "envy" culture has nourished the strong and often very attractive values of egalitarianism, compassion, inefficiency, and the dislike of consumerism.

Given such attitudes, "Homo economicus" could neither survive nor be happy in Russia's so-to-speak "Left-handed Civilization."[23] The left-hander, suggests cultural historian Alexander Panchenko, is a Russian national hero.[24] This is why, according to

---

[22]Konstantin Aksakov, *Sobranie sochinenii v trekh tomakh*, vol. 1 (Moscow, 1910), p.292.

[23]The title derived from a famous story, "The Left-handed Man," by the nineteenth-century writer Nikolai Leskov. Its hero, *Levsha*, the left-handed blacksmith, is capable of doing work that none of his Western counterparts can do, despite their technical equipment, modern appliances, and scientific knowledge. With his able left hand he shoed a flea, while his foreign visitors could not see the flea without a microscope, not to mention the flea's legs.

[24]"The Left-handed Civilization," [Tsizilizatsia Levshi] interview with Alexander Panchenko, *Nevskoe Vremya*, March 5, 1993.

Panchenko, when Russians left the countryside and the wholesome Russian soil—which in its modesty and goodness gave them the only really satisfactory life—they realized that they were "left-handed." When they moved to the city, they did not know how to reconcile their harmonious but somewhat "left-handed" qualities with the competitive, modern urban civilization, where life and business are calculating and cold and where emotions are concealed and even disdained.[25] Panchenko argues that, for Russians, little of real human value depends on the economy; all that truly matters depends on the soul and consciousness.

That sensibility, indeed, is at the root of Russia's literary tradition, from Tolstoy, Turgenev, and Chekhov to Solzehenitsyn, who loathes individualism and market values as much as any Bolshevik. To the pragmatic civilizations of the West, Russia is a developing society. Panchenko asserts that Peter the Great and Lenin tried to force on Russians the individualistic and economic values of the West. But in general Russians fear that form of civilization. Now, many Russians think that the country's spiritual strength as well as her authentic ethical civilization has been destroyed and that her great land is now so much smaller. Unable to be "Great Russians" any more, they seem to see no alternative to adopting the ways of the West. Panchenko's argument may be exaggerated and simplified, given that Russia is no longer a patriarchal culture based on agriculture, and its social and political structures bear little resembles to the old peasant society. However, the spiritual despair that this cultural deracination has inspired is real, for cultural legacies are hard to change, and only if and when society has been presented with a positive experience that it can trust, will it be able to transform.

---

[25]Mikhail Zadornov, formerly Russia's minister of finance and a current Duma member, thought the argument wrong, since, as he put it, "70 percent of the Russian population live in the cities." Another economist Alexey Makushkin responded, "*Propiska* [residency permit, stamped in Russian passports] doesn't necessarily change mentality." Even today, rural Russians treat Muscovites "with an illogical mixture of mistrust, servility and ill will. Their attitude towards foreigners is similar." See Luibov Brezhneva, *The World I Left Behind* (New York: Random House, 1995), pp. 595–96.

Russia has had no such experience. Russians—the ordinary Russians who did not get their philosophical education from Milton Friedman's books—insist that there is an almost unbridgeable gap between the entrepreneurial spirit and the Russian soul. Indeed, Russians have always considered themselves a separate civilization. Evil comes to it from "without," from the outside—from the West and from those Russian rulers who would recast Russian institutions in the West's image. Gaidar and Chubais with their "rational" policies represented just that type of figure to a majority of Russians. This point was made emphatically in an interview, entitled "Russia is not just a country, it is the whole civilization," with the contemporary Russian scholar and academic, I. Shefarevich. He explains why competition and capitalism go "against the spiritual makeup of this country..."

> The competitive situation would just come into conflict with the world-view, which has been established in the course of a thousand years. If one considers even the existing [Russian] sayings, they are all based on the idea that wealth is not an end in itself. It is not a sin, but presents at least a dangerous moral situation in which a person must be very careful in order not to harm his soul.[26]

Characteristically, when concluding the interview, Shefarevich found an even more authoritative and radical voice to support his position: "As Marina Tsvetaeva says, 'the notion of the basic falsehood of money is ineradicable from the Russian soul.' "[27]

Material possessions were understood to harm the spiritual wealth of people and thus should never be pursued and wished for.[28] Therefore, traditionally, money did not have much significance in Rus-

---

[26]V. Agafonov and V. Rokitinsky, "Rossiya - eto ne prosto strana, eto - tsivilizatsia", *Novoe Russkoe Slovo*, August 1–2, 1992, p. 5.

[27]Corruption, the scourge upon the country, skyrocketed, indeed "harming a person's soul" in the post-Soviet years because Russians discovered money. Rather than the traditional barter of privileges, goods, and services, which ultimately were limited by the actual position of a bureaucrat on the official "ladder," money has become the prime factor. Before every step of this "ladder" presented a certain set of benefits, movement up the ladder offered greater privileges, but the process was not without surveillance and some systemic control: everyone could get only as much as his position allowed him to. Money transactions now are not limited to positions and privileges, therefore the possibility of acquiring huge windfall profits has become the focus of corrupt trade. (Ibid.)

[28]G.P. Fedotov, *Sud'ba I grekhi Rossii* (St. Petersburg: Sofiia, 1991), p. 202.

sia. Culturally, Russians have been very suspicious of money
(*prezrennyj metall* or "contemptible metal," as they call it), and wealth
almost always has been considered a negative value. The old
Christian idea that a rich man has more trouble passing into
heaven than a camel does through the eye of a needle, corresponds
with the overwhelming Russian belief that concern for money somehow reflects smallness of soul and a reluctance to trust in provi-
dence. Marina Tsvetaeva, the rebellious and anti-material spirit of
Russia's intelligentsia, wrote a poem entitled "Praise to the Rich"
(1922), which nicely captures this sentiments. The more generous
toward the rich the poet pretends to appear, the more condescending
the poem means to be:

> And so, making clear in advance/I know there are miles between
> us/… I proclaim it: I *love* the rich./For their rotten, unsteady
> root/for the damage done in their cradle/… for the way their soft-
> est word is/obeyed like a shouted order; because/they will not be
> let into heaven…/I say that among all outcasts/there are no such
> orphans on earth…[29]

Whatever Russian reformers might say, wealth in Russia is far from
being perceived as a noble achievement; it is a curse, a misfortune,
something to be ashamed of and sorry for. It is also a subject of
complacent envy, because not many Russians are able to become
rich: fortunes require stability in evolutionary development, as well
as persistent efforts and consistency. "Our national characteristics:
a natural inclination to anarchy (which seen from outside, is commonly mistaken for barbarous or immature behavior), fluidity, amor-
phousness, readiness to adopt any mould ('come and rule over us'),
our gift (or vice) of thinking and living artistically, combined
with an inability to manage the very serious practical side of daily
life. 'Why bother? Who cares?' we ask. In this sense Russia offers
a most favorable soil for the experiments and fantasies of the
artist, though his lot, as of a human being is something very ter-
rible indeed…"[30]. Culturally, it is forgivable to be wealthy, but only

---

[29]Marina Tsvetaeva translated by Elaine Feinstein, *Selected Poems*. (Penguin Books, 1994),
p. 39–40.

[30]Abram Tertz (Andrei Sinyavsky). *A Voice from the Chorus* (New York: Farrar, Straus
and Giroux, 1976), p. 247.

if wealth is brought about in a "good way": by virtue, by divine miracle, by inheritance, even by gambling, as a challenge "to test one's fate."

The gambler, indeed, is the same as the fool in a fairy tale: shrewder than anyone else, more agile than anyone else. There is certain logic in fate's protection of the carefree man: after all, who else would worry about someone like him? And there is a Christian method to support the theory: the last shall be first! American folktales, on the contrary, are imbued with a rational spirit; there is not too wide a gap between dream and reality. Heroes do not just wait for help from above, they don't spend endless hours in contemplation, but constantly work and struggle. Paul Bunyan, for example, is direct, straightforward, and full of initiative. He is not miserly, but careful and precise. In Russian folklore, by contrast, work is not a constant effort, but an unpredictable burst of activity.

Therefore, working for money, a virtue so respected in the West, is not a "good way" in Russia. Russians can be great workers, as long as labor is done not for profit but for some spiritual or personal reason,[31] or is done as a heroic deed, which performs wonders, knowing no limits. For centuries the conscious, calculating accumulation of wealth has been in conflict with other Russian cultural values, such as unlimited hospitality, humility, belief in miracles (fate takes care of those who can't take care of them-

---

[31]According to cultural historian Mikhail Epstein, when a Russian "take[s] up the trade, he takes it up with all his heart as if he is marrying it." Work in Russia is becoming a mysterious dedication, "a tormenting but happy wedding ring, an unbreakable connection with the world of object, the mystery of a human being and an object becoming one's flesh... The product then carries the stamp of love, a sign that the made object is the fruit of privation..." See Mikhail Epstein, "Labor of Lust," *Common Knowledge*, vol. 1, no. 3 (Winter 1992), p. 99. This type of work, which is always connected with love, can easily produce revolutions, but hardly amounts to practical, sustainable, and considerable results in routine, everyday life. "Homo Soveticus, successor and predecessor of Homo Russicus, labored long and willingly, but his labor somehow lacked a foundation... There was no firm, lifelong tie with the object and the product of labor. His love was general, public and belonged to no one... [as] Russians are supposed to be a mystical people who find rational knowledge about the objective world alien. (Ibid., pp. 92, 102.)

selves) and in material sacrifice.[32] Therefore, Russians are capable of sending a man into space, of developing Sputnik or the best (albeit one) computer for the KGB to use in its monitoring, but are absolutely incapable of establishing consumer production of decent washing machines.

To revisit Jeffrey Sachs's "geographical" idea, perhaps it is the vastness of the Russian land that encourages such a mindset. Over the centuries Russia acquired eleven time zones, but it did not have the strength to stop, to map out a border, to build homes for many people: "We Russians still look and act like travelers. No one has a defined sphere of engagement; we have no rules for anything; we don't even have a home. Nothing that can tie us up, that can evoke everlasting sympathy and love, nothing durable, nothing permanent; everything flows by, goes by, without leaving a print either within or outside us."[33] The renowned philosopher Nikolai Berdyaev explained Russia's neglect for the discipline necessary to make the surrounding reality comfortable: "The Russian people, in accordance with its eternal idea, have no love for the ordering of this earthly city and struggle toward a city that is to come, toward the new Jerusalem."[34] Like its land, Russia's interests are sporadic and spontaneous and spread everywhere, dilettantism without methodology and any other obligation except to its fabled size, enormous spirituality, and legendary soul. Russians "raised neither to seed corn nor children. Our hero was the jack of all trades: he

---

[32]In Russia the world is not so "disenchanted" (in the famous term that Max Weber used with respect to modern Western societies). Miracles and mystery still inhere in daily life. Such beliefs provide a person with a certain kind of freedom from constraints and authorities of institutions and social structures. They are nonbinding in Russia as they are only phantoms of their true essence. People depend on their wits and their friends much more than on the fixed procedures and routines, which they find petty and boring. There is little authority in the formal authorities of the world, for Russia is a literary world where appearances seldom correspond to reality. Hence disregard for the rule of law.

[33]Pyotr Chaadaev, "Filosofskie pisma" (1831). Quoted from P.S. Taranov, *Filosofskaya aforistika*. (Moscow: Ostozh'e, 1996), p. 553.

[34]Nicolas Berdyaev, *The Russian Idea* (New York: Macmillan, 1948), p. 255.

sews, he mows, he plays the oboe. Each hand does miracles: incredible dress designs, incredible harvests, incredible melodies—while in reality we had convicts in rags, starving millions...”[35]

Western businessmen coming to Russia right after the Soviet collapse experienced a stunningly unusual way of doing business. In Western-style hotels like the Sheraton, Metropol, and the Palace, one could easily have a chance breakfast with a stranger who would offer a large oil refinery for sale. Russia has always looked with disdain at small deals. Although Moscow has always been “desperate for vegetable stands, restaurants, car washes, dry cleaners, and hardware stores... many people in business are selling oceans of natural gas, tons of gold, timber concessions the size of Michigan, or used MIG crafts.”[36]

A nation of sweeping revolutions and generalizations, where everyone is an artist who creates his or her own grandiose reality of extremes, where all artists long to write gospels instead of novels, Russians have no respect for detail. Abram Tertz, a famous dissident and contemporary Russian philosopher of culture, in his *A Voice From the Chorus*, asserted that even Russian misers do not hoard money so much as weave fancies around it. Porfiry Golovlev, Pliushkin, Pushkin’s Covetous Knight[37]—all these are very Russian characters. For the most part they merely give rein to their imagination, sitting on their coffers. They get all worked up about the idea of money, but they are not really concerned with either profit or loss.[38]

This unconventional, almost dreamy and irrational behavior only coheres into a sensible cluster if a state is rich enough economically to guarantee all citizens minimal material security at some

---

[35]Mikhail Epstein, “Labor of Lust,” p. 99.

[36]Matthew Stevenson, “Dealing in Russia,” *The American Scholar* (Autumn 1993), p. 501.

[37]The first character mentioned is the protagonist of *The Golovlev Family*, a novel by Michael Saltykov-Shchedrin. Pliushkin is one of the landowners in Nikolai Gogol’s *Dead Souls*. The Covetous Knight is a character from Alexander Pushkin’s *Little Tragedies*.

[38]Abram Tertz, *A Voice From the Chorus*, p. 106.

welfare level.[39] The enormous richness of Russia's resources has enabled the country to survive for so long through a mere redistribution of wealth without really producing much that is new. Kahka Bendukidze, president of the UralMash factories and a leading Russian businessmen, once pointed out, "Russia has the curse of a rich country, so rich with raw materials that it never had to bother to create a structure of services or a sturdy line of production."[40]

As Russian cultural historian Mikhail Epstein explains:

> At the root of word ownership is the concept of 'one's own.' And the first miracle is that ownership can be not 'one's own' but no one's, collective: an oxymoron, equivalent to a white raven or to black snow. We Russians didn't think up this most miraculous of miracles, but we worked hard to make of all humankind a collective miracle worker; and, in the meantime, as an example and a lesson to the world, we showed what can be done with our fabulous nation. Ownership was removed from the sphere of 'one's own' and became 'othership.' The peasant community of the artel, the mir of the collective farm, the landowner or the party secretary, the pre-Revolutionary bailiff or the post-revolutionary bureaucrat—all worked in concert to make it impossible for anyone to work for himself.[41]

To the Russian way of thinking, the individual was always inferior to the community because the communal way of life was so near to the ideal of brotherly love, which forms the essence of Christianity and thus represents the higher mission of the people.[42] "A commune" was seen as "a union of the people, who have renounced their egoism, their individuality, and who express their common

---

[39] Even today "Russia presents a classic example of a 'welfare state': federal, regional, and local legislation presently provides 336 various social benefits, for which 449 various categories of population are eligible..." See Tatyana Maleva, "What Sort of Russia Has the New President Inherited? Or Russia's Key Social Problems," Carnegie Endowment for International Peace Moscow Center, Briefing no. 4 (2000), quoted in *Johnson's Russia List*, no. 4307 (May 17, 2000). However, in the current neoliberal conditions "the inadequacies in the social welfare system directly follow from a social policy which [still] identifies the notion of a 'welfare state' with government paternalism..." (Ibid.) This "vicious circle" needs to be broken.

[40] *Nezavisimaya Gazeta* (August 2, 1997).

[41] Mikhail Epstein, "Labor of Lust," p. 92.

[42] See, for example, Isaiah Berlin, *Russian Thinkers* (London: The Hogarth Press, 1978).

accord; this is an act of love, a noble Christian act... A commune thus represents a moral choir, and just as in a choir a voice is not lost, but follows the general pattern and is heard in the harmony of all voices: so in the commune the individual is not lost, but renounces his exclusiveness in favor of general accord—and there arises the noble phenomenon of harmonious, joint existence of rational being (consciousness); there arises a brotherhood, a commune—a triumph of human spirit."[43] In Russia, where cultural attitudes have proven more durable and resilient than in other countries (as it has been only ten years since centuries-closed Russian borders opened for free travel and exchange), ethical values, appropriate for communal life in the village, suitable for somewhat narrow relations based on personal acquaintance, were simply transferred to the whole society. Community was seen as opposing law, abstract associations, formal organizations and personal interests. Law especially was denied any value in and of itself in comparison with the inner truth and internal ethics: "Law and custom rule the social life of people. Law, written and armed with compulsion, brings the differing private wills into conditional unity. Custom, unwritten and unarmed, is the expression of the most basic unity of society."[44]

This kind of logic, which perceives as unnecessary any social contract between the state and the people, makes sense, of course, only when a ruler embodies the symbol and the essence of Russian life. As he sees himself ruling over people united in devotion to him, he is seen as the embodiment of the faith, the highest law (religion), and the protector of the Russian way of life.

The idea of the "culture of envy" recognizes only vertical hierarchy—czar versus slave—in contrast to the "greed" culture with its horizontal hierarchy of competitive individuals. This assumes, by the state in the first instance and followed by the individual citizens in the second, that "private" benefits always come at the expense of the "public" and state. This means that if you (singu-

---

[43]Konstantin Aksakov, *Sobranie sochinenii v trekh tomakh*, vol. 1 (Moscow, 1910), pp. 291–92.

[44]Alexey Khomyakov, *Sobranie sochinenii v trekh tomakh*, vol. 3 (Moscow, 1916), p. 75.

lar) are rich and powerful, that condition comes at our expense—
we are poorer and weaker. The nineteenth-century revolutionary
poet Nikolai Ogarev looked upon the peasant community as the
equivalent of universal slavery. For him it was "the expression of
envy of all against the individual."[45] In such conditions, "for most
of Russian history, the state was for all practical purposes the property of the czar."[46] Therefore the czar, like God, has the right to
punish for sins of physical or spiritual rebellion. He is a humble
sufferer for his people (power is an evil burden and the fewer men
who had to carry it, the better), and he has to carry burdens of power,
property, decisions, responsibilities. People on the other hand
have only one responsibility—to serve their God and their czar.[47]

Unlike the Western structure of the suzerain and some free vas-
sals, Russia followed the Byzantine tradition, in which there was
only the ruler and the serfs: the ruler does not provide guarantees
or laws, but gives amnesty, mercy, and forgiveness of sins. The czar,
as God's governor, does not need explanations and proof; everyone is equal in front of him, as they are in front of God.

As Thomas Graham, former U.S. diplomat and currently
senior associate of the Carnegie Endowment, pointed out: "There
was no formal distinction between sovereignty and ownership, between
the public sphere and the private sphere. Almost by definition, public possessions were exploited for private gain."[48] Disdain for the
virtue of private property and ownership also stems in part from
the arbitrariness. The lack of definite laws for economic or human

---

[45]Valery Blagavolo, "Nikolai Ogarev. Russkie Voprosy," in *Svobodnaya Mysl*, vol. 2 (1993),
p. 110.

[46]Thomas E. Graham, Jr., "Testimony on Corruption in Russia and Future U.S. Policy Before the Senate Committee on Foreign Relations, September 30, 1999." Quoted
in *Johnson's Russia List*, no. 3538 (October 1, 1999). Graham was formerly a U.S. diplomat and currently is senior associate at the Carnegie Endowment for International
Peace.

[47]Another important part of the chain between the people and the ruler is a class of
landowners, clerks, commissars, and nomenclatura bureaucrats. In a communal structure
the excess of wealth was rejected for the sake of the village, as the land was to belong to
God, and everything else belonged to the czar, so nothing could be appropriated by any
of the intermediary classes. Owning property was ethically and spiritually illegitimate.

[48]Thomas E. Graham, Jr. "Testimony on Corruption in Russia..."

rights emerged from a world where, for many centuries the individual in charge—czar, landowner, or commissar—had sole power to determine who owned what, lived where, or even whether someone lived or died. Ideally, the perfect czar establishes a perfect rule; in reality he remains a human being and his verdicts are often far from perfect, because there are no institutional checks upon them. They are willful because they are products only of the will. Thus, the commune obeys an ideal image of the czar and mistrusts the reality of his rule. Therefore, most people still don't believe that it is worth working to acquire ownership, since it can be taken away at any moment.[49]

The case of Grigory Lopakhin in Anton Chekhov's *Cherry Orchard* is instructive here. Lopakhin's father was a *muzhik*, a slave at the Ranevskaya estate, which his entrepreneurial son, a millionaire through his own cleverness and efforts, is buying from the former owners. His plan is to cut down the cherry orchard, build small houses, and rent them out as *dachi* (vacation houses). Ranevskaya, the landowner, insists that the market value of her property is far less important than its beauty and age. According to Chekhov, Ranevskaya

---

[49]It is worth noting here that Russia is by no means a hopelessly dishonest nation. The sweeping scale of cronyism and corruption during the last ten years was first of all a consequence of traditional cultural behavior of the Russians: disregard for morality in favor of ethical relations (trust in personal ethics); disbelief in the social contract, seen as a Western invention of individuals who mistrust each other and therefore have to document their every transaction; the fact that rules and laws were established individually by the ruler in each individual case; mistrust of authorities, because rules usually depend on the leader's personal qualities rather than generally accepted, documented notion of justice. In such a society, each member of his/her commune (clan, family, circle, etc.) fends for him/herself (within the clan) as if there is no tomorrow, ever suspicious of whatever any change of power or the arbitrary mood of the one in power might bring. Secondly, when the state ceased to be either the property of the czar or the Communist Party of the Soviet Union, "various key pieces of the state remain the private preserves of specific individuals, managed primarily for private gain rather than for the public good. Moreover, unlike the Soviet period, when 'property owners' derived profit from the state's strength and control of society, today's proprietors... enrich themselves by preying on the weakness of the state, by stripping assets from property that once belonged to the state as a whole" (Thomas E. Graham, Jr., "Testimony on Corruption in Russia..."). And finally, the grandiose scale of corruption also stemmed from the routinely extreme, absolute revolutionary manner, which Russians assume in all trades they are engaged in. Thus, corruption and "oligarchism" reign supreme yet again, as did previously absolute monarchy or dictatorship of proletariat.

and her family live in a past that is vanishing. But the present, as represented by Lopakhin and his like, offer a future that is even more deadening to the soul. Although the latter deserve credit for their entrepreneurship, their coldness, calculation, and disregard for beauty are by far qualities unworthy of human life. Needless to say, this Russian ambiguity of what it really desired—beauty or rationality—contributed directly to the events of 1917, when the cherry orchard would end up belonging to neither "the past" nor "the present," but to no one. Instead, it would be owned by the state, which would waste this land, depriving it both of its beauty and of the practical use to which Lopakhin would have put it.

For all these reasons personal ownership has been considered undignified, difficult, burdensome, but also useless. In fact, for most of Russian culture the concept of "personal ownership" remains as unsettling as it was for Chekhov as it is reassuring for Americans. Abram Tertz suggests that:

> The most important quality of a Russian person is the belief that he has nothing to lose. Therefore he is disinterested and unselfish. And the straightforwardness of the people is not just hospitality but despair of a gambler. Readiness to share his last bit, because it is the last one indeed and there is nothing left, and everything is on the verge, and almost at the end… And there is lightness in thoughts, in decisions. Nothing has been saved and stored, nothing has been learnt.[50]

In a country where property and personal ownership are seen as acts of usurpation, it is no surprise that even human rights as understood in the West—i.e., political and civil rights—have always been shunned in Russia in favor of a communal idea, i.e., freedom *from* economic risks, and not freedom to invest, achieve, and retain profit. To the West, "human rights" imply freedom of individual expression against the potential tyranny of the majority: freedom of speech, press, assembly, religion, and then the intuitive sense that the right to own property guarantees all the others. In Russia, however, where profit is considered profiteering, and where even

---

[50] Abram Tertz (Andrei Sinyavsky), "Mysli vrasplokh" [Thoughts Caught Unawares], in the *Collected Works in 2 Volumes*, vol. 1 (Moscow: SP Start, 1992), p. 321.

legitimate gains are terribly vulnerable to disappearance, the "tyranny of the crowd"—being *kak vse* (like everyone else)—would be the only way to protect oneself from the tyranny of the calculating and greedy individual.

Freedom in the West means opportunity, in which a society openly embraces differences in individual talents and initiatives, understanding that there might be unequal results. Not so for Russia. There freedom meant security, not only material security but the psychological security of knowing that no one else—no one else living anywhere near you—has much more than you. For instance, under the old Soviet Constitution, Russians had the "right to rest," twenty-four-day vacations were guaranteed to everyone by his or her employer. There was also a "right to living space": a fixed number of square meters per family member. There was the right for "free education and medical care": not always of the highest quality, not always the best, but in principle it was available in equal measure for all.

Perhaps the most appreciated constitutional right was the "right to work," which meant the right "not to lose your job." The right to keep your job, no matter how shoddy your worked or how unnecessary the job itself, was the essence first of Russian communal security and then Soviet socialist security. In Chekhov's *Three Sisters* the old peasant nanny is too old to work as she once did. The sisters, however, insist that she stay in the house and help as much or as little as she can, pretending that everything remains the same. Having a job was rarely a matter of money, but rather a matter of personal belonging to a group, being *kak vse*.

This notion was driven home in 1991, the last year of Soviet rule, when a group of American businessmen of considerable wealth went on a study tour to St. Petersburg and Finland.[51] They met with high-ranking managers and officials in a various candy-production plants. During one such visit, the group was astonished to see hundreds of old women at tables wrapping little candies by hand. "This is inefficient, unsanitary, costly, unnecessary," the

---

[51]Story told in 1996 by Princeton University professor of Slavic studies Caryl Emerson in one of her lectures on Russian culture.

U.S. visitors told the manager. "In the West there are machines…"
But the manager waved his hand impatiently and took the Americans into the warehouse where a candy-wrapping machine from
East Germany was gathering dust and cobwebs. "We purchased
this machine five years ago, but no one has the heart to install it.
Those old women have a human right to a life that includes the
dignity of work," the manager said.

For the Westerners this most likely seemed to be a useless, unprofessional, even harmful practice, an obstacle on the way to progress
and prosperity. Scenes such as this also convinced Anatoly Chubais,
who in the early 1980s was just out of graduate school in St.
Petersburg (then Leningrad), to experiment with Western business methods. In the mid-eighties one of his test projects, *Payment and Reward Practices for Engineers* in St. Petersburg, proved
that change could be positive if done gradually and supported by
the majority: "We felt we were walking on air, so good the results
were. The amount of *lishnie liudi* (unnecessary, superfluous people) was reduced, production went up, people worked more effectively… Then I became absolutely convinced that regular market
mechanisms are universal. They work in the hotel business, as perfectly as they do in the turbine construction business… And one
more thing, it is absolutely useless to insert the market mechanisms
step by step…"[52] Because this microeconomics experiment worked
well when applied to a few plants in St. Petersburg, the results convinced reformers to repeat the experiment undeviatingly on the
whole country five years later. The results of that experiment
proved different, however. The dignity of work (as a cultural condition on a larger scale), so useless from the rational point of view,
is more valuable in the "left-handed civilization" than the rationale of work results, because it always comes without the indignities and difficulties of personal responsibility and personal
ownership.

There could have not been a culture more out of touch with
Adam Smith.

---

[52]Anatoly Chubais, " 'The Last Thing You Needed was Chubais!' Instead of Preface,"
in Anatoly Chubais, ed., *Privatizatsiya po-rossiiski*, pp. 9–10.

RUSSIA'S TOP: PRIVATIZATION RUSSIAN STYLE

Russia has always reveled in its uniqueness, taking pride in being separated from the rest of the world by its spiritual concepts. In 1991, however, pro-Western reformers made a decision to approach Russia's economic problems in a very rational way.

When Poland was declared a success story after applying shock therapy to its economy, it was immediately decided that what worked for Poland would also work for Russia. But Poland, as did most East European countries, remained an entirely different case. It was closer to the West, it had endured fewer years under socialism and planned economics, and private property and civil society had not been destroyed. Indeed two powerful private institutions, the Catholic Church and the Solidarity trade union movement, defied and then toppled Communist power.

Seemingly blinded by Poland's success in adopting Western economic models, Russia's liberals refused to note the difference. Pyotr Aven, who was then the minister of foreign economic relations, asserted in 1992, that "there is no such thing as a special country or a special case. From the point of view of an economist, if economics is a science with its own laws, from this point of view all countries are [*odi-na-ko-vye*] e-q-u-a-l."[53] Although Russia's policies during the last ten years were based on the preceding concept, the results suggest otherwise. The lack of context and the failure to connect methodology for change with inherited cultural values distorted the reform process from the very beginning.

Before leaving his post as chief economist of the World Bank at the end of December 1999, Joseph Stiglitz pointed out that "there was much discussion about the proper pacing and sequencing of reforms...but traditional economic theory has even less to say about the dynamics of transition than it has to say about equilibrium states; and yet it was issues of dynamics of transition that were central

---

[53]*Nezavisimaya gazeta* (February 27, 1992).

to the debate over pacing and sequencing."⁵⁴ That question of sequencing should have been paramount in the mind of Russia's reformers, but apparently it was not. According to Anatoly Chubais, Russian privatization chief from 1991 to 1996, "the aim of privatization was to build capitalism in Russia. And not just that, it was to build capitalism in just a few [*udarnykh*] shock years, meeting the norms of production which the rest of the world spent hundreds of years achieving."⁵⁵ Anders Aslund, a former Swedish diplomat and current Carnegie Endowment for International Peace associate who helped design Russian economic policy from the start, was blunt in explaining the program's haste, "In Russia privatization should be implemented as quickly as possible. Russia's peculiarity is that if property would not be redistributed quickly between people, it will simply be stolen."⁵⁶ The idea was undoubtedly correct, but for the reasons explained in the previous chapter—Russian disregard for formal laws and procedures—speed became an encouragement for theft rather than a recipe to avoid it. Inexperienced property owners were too experienced in mistrusting the regime, which used to change or alter its mind any minute, and were stealing big to protect themselves from the unexpected.

In his recent book, *Privatization Russian Style*, Chubais explains the need to rush ahead regardless of opposition, and admits that in order to destroy the old system he made a choice to accept "Leninist" methods in eliminating the old regime. "From the start of our active privatization efforts we immediately knew that we had to follow the opponent's rules of the game. Most of the bureaucrats

---

⁵⁴Joseph Stiglitz, "Whither Reforms? The Years of the Transition." Keynote Address at the Annual World Bank Conference on Development Economics. Quoted in *Johnson's Russia List*, no. 3317 (June 1, 1999).

⁵⁵Anatoly Chubais in an interview on a Russian television program "Details", June 29, 1994. Vladimir Putin, in his memoirs, which were published immediately before he was elected Russian president on March 26, 2000, suggests that Chubais is hardly aware of methodologies other than some "ephemeral ideas... He tends to get stuck, such a Bolshevik... this is the true definition of him." Quoted from the Internet version of the book at www.vagrius.com: *Ot pervogo litsa: Razgovory s Vladimirom Putinym* [First Person: Conversations with Vladimir Putin] with Natalia Gevorkyan, Natalia Timakova, Andrei Kolesnikov (Moscow: Vagrius, 2000).

⁵⁶Delovoi Mir interview, *Business World* (August 14, 1993).

that were forced to (and still have to) work had been trained in a certain [Soviet, planned economy] tradition. If we failed to find common language with them; if we didn't use familiar levers of influence, we would not have succeeded."[57] Thus "democratic dictatorship" became the means to overcome Russia's prevailing conditions, because truly democratic methods would lead only to stalemate. Most Russians were unwilling to accept the pain necessary for the birth of a new economic and political system. So, instead of methodology for explanation and education, the old administrative apparatus of communism was reused for new purposes across the expanse of Russia. Special presidential representatives were sent around the country to oversee the enforcement of presidential decrees— a policy that bore uncanny resemblance to the czar's use of personal emissaries, or to the politburo's use of commissars and representatives.

The reformers, willing to adapt the mechanisms of the state they loathed, were unwilling to seek common ground with widespread Russian cultural beliefs, no doubt for the same reason that previous Russian or Soviet power elites made decisions in the name of the people without consulting these same people. And while "common language" with the previous nomenclatura was indeed found—overriding their authority with the larger authority— the subsequent resentment among the population overrode the possibility of a positive outcome.

"Shock therapy" (macroeconomic stabilization) was considered the only way for Russia to restructure its deteriorating economy, but "shock" as some suggested came with too little "therapy."[58] In his *Notes of the President* Boris Yeltsin later explained:

> Gaidar's reforms provided the macroeconomic shift, the breakdown from the old economy. It was horribly painful, without the surgical precision but on the contrary with a somewhat rusty gnashing, when pieces and parts of the old mechanism are bloodily torn

---

[57]Anatoly Chubais, "How We Defended Privatization," in Anatoly Chubais, ed., *Privatizatsiya po-rossiiski*, p. 143.

[58]The phrase—"too much shock, not enough therapy"—was borrowed from Jeffrey D. Sachs, "Betrayal," p. 14.

away, and change finally does happen. There had been no other economic production [in Russia] except the Stalinist one; it could hardly be adapted to the contemporary environment, so this production genetically required a complete break. As this [past economy] was created in the *avral* (all hands on the pump) way back in the 1930s, we used the same method to break it.[59]

That was Yeltsin speaking in 1995, but from the start of the reform process in 1991–92 there was no transparency. There were very few attempts to explain the concepts of macroeconomics, private ownership, and privatization—as well as the necessity of "shock therapy"—to the general population. There was not even much debate about the strategies to be pursued among economists, except for those in the pro-Western liberal camp of Gaidar and Chubais.

Promises of an improved quality of life or Chubais's assurance that by the end of 1992 each Russian citizen would be able to receive his piece of state property, equal in price to at least one Volga automobile, took the form of rapidly declining living standards. For the people "shock therapy" arrived in 1993–94 as just that—the government freed prices suddenly, allowing them to increase dramatically at the same time it tried to curb growth in the money supply and increases in wages. These "reforms" were instantly felt in the following way: tens of thousands of people, including pensioners, were utterly ruined by the huge price increases. Many had to sell their personal possessions in order to survive. Equally painful, in both an economic and psychological sense, was the near collapse of the ruble. Yegor Gaidar later defended these strictly monetarist policies by claiming that if tough measures had not been taken, the monetary system might have collapsed altogether.[60] His reasoning, arriving late, was too complicated for peo-

---

[59]Boris Yeltsin, *Zapiski Prezidenta* (Moscow: Ogonek, 1994), p. 300.

[60]It did collapse nonetheless in 1998, when the financial pyramid of GKOs (short-term treasury loans) ruined the Russian market and brought the country to bankruptcy. Due to the pressures on the exchange rate, Russian foreign trade slipped into deficit in July 1997, suggesting that devaluation was overdue. Concerned over the ruble's stability, possible GKO buyers put on the brakes, leaving more than $10 billion of falling GKOs by the end of September 1998. Unable to find a solution, on August 17 the Russian government

ple to understand. An abstract explanation of the needs of the market was an insufficient counterpoint to the fear and blight in many peoples' lives.

When government policies result in such "tears and blood," they are obviously hard to accept without proper explanation, preparation, reasoning, and some trade-offs. Instead of receiving motivation, accounts, clarifications, and updates on the policies of the macroeconomic stabilization and voucher privatization, the Russian people were stunned to hear that the government felt no longer responsible for them and their welfare. Various statements from local and national government officials asserted that people must understand that they are responsible for themselves, that they should not rely on others—not the government, God, czar, not even the IMF—for their salvation.[61] Alfred Kokh, a leading privatization official in Chubais's entourage, went even further, saying that "now is the time of Social Darwinism during which a process of natural selection must take place."[62] Indeed, a number of reformers in search of a clean slate proudly compared the government's market policy with the actions of a surgeon who operates on a patient without anesthesia.[63]

As the whole process was more an experiment rather than a fully thought-through policy aimed at improving the conditions of the country and its people, the reformist spirit militantly rejected public discussion of its program, implying that professional scientists should never descend to the level of dilettantes. The "expert ethos" of the Gaidar team was well expressed in Gaidar's own book *State and Evolution*, where he explains that it was more important to select political leaders from those who regarded professional exper-

announced a 90-day moratorium on foreign dept payments and a suspension on GKO payments, and allowed the ruble to devalue from $6 to $9. The financial system was frozen, prices increased, and by September the ruble had plunged to $21. Although Sergei Kiriyenko was the prime minister who announced the 90-day moratorium, he is rarely blamed for the collapse, because Chubais (being advised by Gaidar), was said to be behind the GKO schemes. For more on the subject, see Roy Medvedev, "Obval piramidy GKO," in Roy Medvedev, *Politics and Politicians of Russia* (Moscow: Prava cheloveka, 1999), pp. 119–44.

[61]*Current Digest*, no. 12 (April 8, 1992); *Rossiiskie vesti* (September 1, 1992).

[62]*Chas Pik* (October 12, 1992).

[63]*Rossiiskaya gazeta* (September 1, 1992).

tise as being more important than political vision for the reconstruction of society. No wonder that during his administration far
more attention was devoted to economic policy than to other pressing issues facing his government, such as restoration of confidence
in the future.[64] Following this 'expert' mode, Anatoly Chubais asserted that the Soviet economy was boring because the only available
avenue was microeconomics.[65] However, he continued, small
experiments did not provide the excitement and opportunities of
the big sweeping changes.

Guided by the ultimate goal of a complete make-over and
driven by the usual Russian idea of totality, the Kremlin reformers of the 1991 generation simply could not go step by step, bit by
bit in a slow process of capitalization. Instead they had to "build
capitalism in just a few [*udarnykh*] shock years." Although this technique of "enthusiasm" was more than familiar from Soviet times,
this was also a utopian objective in regard to Russia. First because
avral [all hands on the pump] already had proved itself to be an
ultimately counterproductive policy, and second because the new
policies were perceived as Western and not authentically Russian,
while the country has always been suspicious of the West.[66]

---

[64]Yegor Gaidar, *Gosudarstvo I Evolutsia* (Moscow: Evraziia, 1995). Also see Yegor Gaidar, *Days of Defeat and Victory* (Seattle: University of Washington Press, 1999).

[65]"While I was in college, we had no serious studies in economics... Only microeconomics was available, to work with concrete factories, well, sometimes with a certain branch
of production. But what I was really interested in, was macroeconomics—dynamics of
the economic figures, and money relations, and it was really depressing that there was
no one to discuss it with." (Anatoly Chubais, "'The Last Thing You Needed was
Chubais!' Instead of Preface," in Anatoly Chubais, ed., *Privatizatsiya po-rossiiski*, p. 5.)

[66]For centuries, Russian tradition, from the Boyars, to the Slavophiles to pan-Slav-
ists and from Eurasianists to Communists, has created a nightmare vision of the West
as the kingdom of Moloch, where petty individual interests run the show. In the West
the upper classes roll in luxury while the landless workers "drink nothing but clear water
and live on insufficient bread alone." [Quoted in Paul Miliukov, *The Origins of Ideology*
(Gulf Breeze, Fla.: Academic International, 1974), p. 133]. Thus, Russia cannot follow the
West and cannot allow the West to take over Russia's spirit of equality and commune,
because the latter is the key virtue of Russian society. The Russian ethical belief that a
good society should be highly egalitarian supports the idea that in Russia "all people, by
the kindness of God, the richest as well as the poorest, eat rye bread , fish, meat and drink
kvas, even if they lack beer." (ibid.) It is precisely because of such factors as the lack of
private property or the strength of government solicitude that Russian society was seen
as being able to avoid inequalities of bourgeois society of the West.

A recent one-volume compilation entitled *The Russian Idea* gathered writings of Nikolai Gogol, Alexander Herzen, Konstantin Leontiev, Vladimir Soloviev, and other very prominent Russian philosophers and writers. Despite the diversity of approaches, there is an important unity among all opinions: the insistence that Western path can and should be avoided in the name of a harmonious and egalitarian Russian society based on a higher form of belief.[67] Anything Western in Russia was always approached with caution and mistrust; therefore, because IMF and the World Bank involvement had not been properly explained to Russian citizens, their loan policies were often perceived as imposing pain upon average people. This happened because these organizations were said to be handmaidens to corporate and political interests.[68] There was little transparency, which meant people simply were not informed that strings were routinely attached to IMF loans: the government was forced to balance the budget, establish a proper tax system, pare down official spending. All were reasonable policies and conditions, but the lack of public discussion tremendously hurt their perception in the long-suffering country.

It also did not help, of course, that foreign advisers had been let into the "holy of holies" for the Russian populace, the Kremlin—bastion of Russian power. According to Janine Wedel, a vigorous Western critic of the "Chubais clan":

> Chubais assembled a group of Western looking, energetic associates... From the start, the "young reformers" together with their Harvard helpmates chose rapid, massive privatization as their showcase reform. Harvard economist [Andrei] Shleifer became director of the Harvard Institute's Russia Project. Another Harvard player was a former World Bank consultant named Jonathan Hay. In 1991... Hay became a senior legal adviser to Russia's new privatization agency, the State Property Committee (GKI)..."[69]

---

[67]V.M. Piskunov, ed., *Russkaya ideya* [The Russian Idea] (Moscow: Isskusstvo, 1994).

[68]CNN.com transcript of the CNN NewsStand, April 17, 2000.

[69]Janine Wedel, "Rigging the U.S.-Russian Relationship: Harvard, Chubais, and the Transidentity Game," *Democratizatsiya*, vol. 7, no. 4 (Fall 1999), p. 477.

Wedel goes on as to give evidence of Chubais's nondemocratic behavior:

> Despite the fact that building democracy was a stated goal of the aid community, many aid officials embraced this [every subsequent major regulation of privatization was introduced by presidential decree rather than parliamentary action] dictatorial modus operandi... As USAID's Walter Coles, a key American official in the privatization and economic restructuring program in Russia, pointed out, 'If we needed a decree, Chubais didn't have to go through the bureaucracy.'[70]

True, in 1993 the Duma consisted of a large number of conservative forces, among them many officials who opposed market reforms. But the decision to rule by decree through chief executives and with the involvement of foreigners lacked political wisdom. By trying to gain control over all political levers of power, Yeltsin's leadership marginalized other political leaders, making them suspicious, defensive, and aggressive. As a result scandal after scandal rocked cities and regions throughout Russia; the media publicized the bribery and corruption stories in which reformers and their Western colleagues appeared in less than a moral light. In this atmosphere of a political decay the Russian population confirmed its worst suspicions of Western ideology, that "it is cut off from everything that lifts the heart above personal interests."[71]

Even more so, Western ideology started to be seen as a core of the Russian corruption problem. As Khomyakov, the Aksakov brothers, Berdyaev, and other advocates for Russia's uniqueness warned, money when taken to heart does destroy the human soul. The combination of Boris Berezovsky's shady affairs, the MMM and Chara Banks pyramid-scheme stock funds in the mid nineties,[72] the GKO schemes of 1997–98, the Bank of New York allegations

---

[70]Ibid., p. 481.

[71]Quoted in Abbott Gleason, "Republic of Humbug: The Russian Nativist Critique of the United States 1830-1930," *American Quarterly*, vol. 44 (March 1992), p. 6.

[72]MMM and Chara Banks, two of the most popular Moscow stock funds of the early 1990s, were functioning as a classic pyramid scheme: their stock prices depended only on the people who were buying shares, and each new round of investors supplied the money for previous groups.

last year, on-and-off rumors of the investigation of Yeltsin's family, especially his daughter Tatyana Dyachenko's alleged enormous accounts in Swiss banks—all this convinced the Russians even more that both Slavophiles and socialists might have indeed been right: "The Western way of life is [not only] *meshchanski*, i.e., both bourgeois, philistine and profoundly repulsive,"[73] it also represents " 'the greatest evil of all,' the vampire which sucks the blood out of the social body...—commerce".[74]

---

[73]Nicolai Berdyaev, *Sub'ektivizm i Idividualizm v obshestvennoi filosofii* (St. Petersburg: Elektricheskaya tipografiia, 1901), pp. 147–48.

[74]Alexander N. Tumanov, "Merchant, Entrepreneur and Profit in Russian Literature: The Russian Artistic Intelligentsia and Money," in Anthony Purdy, ed., *Literature and Money* (Amsterdam and Atlanta: Editions Rodopi, 1993), p. 25.

RUSSIA'S MIDDLE: VOICES OF REASON

Not all reformers, however, concentrated on just the "objective" and "scientific" laws of economics when the course for the economic reforms was being implemented in Russia. A few, like Boris Nemtsov, then deputy prime minister, started voicing their concerns about the unsavory nature of Russian capitalism even before the financial crisis of 1998: Russia has turned out to be neither socialistic nor capitalistic, but some "ugly monster" that no one could easily define.[75] Nemtsov seriously worried about how to replace the "bandit" capitalism that had been built in Russia with its "normal" version. In an interview with the *Novaya Gazeta*, he called for a new approach to reforms:

> What kind of capitalism Russia needs is now our choice to make. The first type we have already had: a nomenclatura bureaucratic capitalism, in which power, property, and money belong to the government and other officials. Second is the oligarchic type, when power, property, and money belong to a few corporations, companies, and individuals... The best one to have is when all power, property and money belong to as many people as possible. I would call this people's capitalism.[76]

Sergei Kiriyenko, in turn, explained the reason for the failure of the reforms by the fact that among other things

> Too much emphasis was placed on macroeconomic stability. Indeed, in a country with a developed market economy and a developed infrastructure, the correct distribution, or alignment, of macroeconomic factors can correctly determine the overall situation. But this was not the case in Russia, where there is no developed market infrastructure. As a result, at the macroeconomic level, companies did not try to organize their restructuring in line with macroeconomic realities. Rather, they tried, somehow, to adjust

---

[75] *Nezavisimaya gazeta* (February 25, 1998).
[76] *Novaya gazeta* (November 24, 1997).

themselves on a very small scale. As a result, we came face to face with the so-called virtual economy, where we have companies that declare losses, while all they actually do is undermine the general state of the Russian economy.[77]

Not only after 1998, with the rise of corruption scandals and overwhelming "oligarchism" and cronyism, but during the whole period of reforms, there had been voices that warned that "shock therapy" was wrong for Russia. The market economy should not have been attempted as another revolution. Even if Yeltsin standing on a tank in 1991 was enough to bring down communism, it was not enough to successfully build up the ideology of the market. For most Russians the problem with liberal reforms was that they did not go much further than just proclaiming empty slogans, which bore very little resemblance to the world they knew.

Oleg Pchelintsev, an economist from a less radical school, warned against a simplistic understanding of the market:

> We often look at the market as a simple, almost automatic transaction, 'money-product-money.' In reality the market is simple only in the minds of the propagators of neoliberalism—this Western analog of our homegrown *nauchnyi kommunizm* (scientific communism). In reality it (or better they, for there are many different types of markets) is a very complicated mechanism. There are volumes about various diversions from 'perfect competition' and one cannot simply ignore the kind of knowledge based on generations of economic experience. This is the most serious mistake of Gaidar's team.[78]

In their revolutionary zeal, the Russian "romantics of the market" forgot (or didn't want to remember) that "developed capitalism" is a system with a very complex structure of institutional and personal relations: difficult, if not impossible, to create in a *Stakhanovite* fashion by way of "shock therapy."

Economic policy throughout all years of reforms has been criticized for not paying enough attention to basic structural reforms, particularly in the privatization of industry: "70 percent

[77]*East European Constitutional Review*, vol. 8, no. 1/2 (Winter/Spring 1999), p. 56.

[78]Oleg Pchelintsev, *Russia at the New Threshold* (Moscow, 1995), p. 179.

of Russia's state-owned industry has been transformed into privately owned joint-stock companies,... [thus delivering] assets into the hands of insiders: either Soviet-era industrialists or new-era bankers."[79] The government—as have all governments in Russia during the last decade—was accused of artificially creating a huge decline in industrial production, and the failure to attend to structural reforms contributed mightily to this outcome. Vyacheslav Nikonov, president of the Moscow-based Politica Foundation, called the reform process "the most entertaining game in the human history, entitled 'Do Buy Russia,' when everything from a screw to the nuclear reactors, which formerly belonged to the state, now is being transferred to private hands."[80]

Although reformers claimed that "structure was the luxury they could not afford,"[81] Igor Yefimov, a political scientist and a Russian émigré to the United States, was warning his former compatriots as early as 1991 about the dangers of the liberal euphoria:

> Market! The market economy is said to be our only hope! Give everything to private hands, give factory managers an opportunity to compete freely, give prices the liberalization they want, don't plan, don't control, don't give orders and the country will revive immediately. And there would be no political strikes, and no hunger uprisings in Russia. But why would these things stop happening? What kind of miraculous country is Russia?
>
> In all other countries people for centuries were killing each other in the fight for private property. Is Russia, after 70 years of the most cruel economic and political restrictions, all of a sudden getting the most miraculous type of people, kind and disciplined, people who would calmly get into lines and peacefully distribute

[79]Peter Rutland and Natasha Kogan, "The Russia Mafia: Between Hype and Reality," in *Transitions*, vol. 5, no. 3 (March 1998), p. 27. Also see Svetlana Glinkina, "The Criminal Components of the Russian Economy," Working Paper no. 29, Berichte des Bundesinstituts der Wissenschaftlichen und Internationalen Studien, Koln institut für Ost Europa (1997); David Satter, "What Went Wrong In Russia?" Paper presented at The Jamestown Foundation Conference "Russia: What Went Wrong? Which Way Now?" (Washington D.C.: June 9, 1999).

[80]*Argumenty i Fakty*, no. 48 (1997), p. 5.

[81]Anatoly Chubais, "Birth of the Idea," in Anatoly Chubais, ed., *Privatizatsiya po-rossiiski*, p. 28–29.

things that each of them liked the most—one will take a wind-mill, another an airport, a third would have an electric line, fourth—the Ostankino TV tower, or a railroad, or even the atomic reactor.

And then they will all trade with each other and work together in the utmost friendly and peaceful spirit so the rest of the world will die of envy. As there, in that rest, there are still strikes, uprisings, expropriations, gangsterism, confiscation, crises, infla-tion, bankruptcies, hunger.[82]

True, the market economy has proven that it is the most effective form of economic development. But in the words of Pyotr Chaadaev, Russia's most prominent philosopher of the Western orientation, "one of the saddest features of our [Russian] peculiar civilization is that we are only now discovering universal truths, which in other places have already become truisms..."[83]: in order to enjoy the market a country needs to have durable and well-test-ed structures that will not allow the market to run wild and turn society into chaos and decay. It also required a psychological and cultural climate, in which people are prepared and ready to accept the change. Even the most hardheaded reformers recognized it at times:

> If we look at the world around us with our eyes open, we would see that socialism does not affect Sweden's prosperity, while Brazil remains unsaved by its capitalism. Because despite the fact that we were told that there is nothing in the world more important than political economy, there is something more important—the matu-rity of culture. And I am not talking here about culture which we measure by the amount of books read or poems memorized. I am talking about culture, which is concerned with the building of the environment where the individuals can live together as individu-als, not in a usual Russian commune. Creating this kind of cul-ture is a slow process. And if a society speeds up too much, it may explode like once-prosperous Lebanon, or once-industrialized Iran."[84]

---

[82] *Nezavisimaya gazeta* (October 17, 1991).

[83] Pyotr Chaadaev, *Philosophical Letters* (1831). Quoted in Alexander Panchenko, "I Don't Want to be Called Intelligentsia," *Moscovskie Novosti*, no. 50 (December 15, 1991).

[84] *Nezavisimaya gazeta* (October 17, 1991).

Political scientist Alexey Kiva, a strong Yeltsin supporter, was nevertheless warning that

> Only people who are not familiar with historical points of view might think that such hierarchy of values [communal interests, egalitarianism, hospitality, ethical responsibility versus the moral one, disregard for wealth and private property, etc.] could be built by chance because of bad czars, unfit leaders, and general confusion. Everything has its logic of development, and Russia too has had reasons to develop this way and not the other way. A political movement, any political party, would never be successful if for one reason or another it would disregard the people's spirits and beliefs. If they ignore the most sacred values of the Russian people, democrats are bound to be disappointed. Capitalism cannot be built on the basis of mere slogans, as this does not evoke good feelings among Russians and has negative associations. By using old methodology one might turn to the origins and build a new Gulag.[85]

Indeed, under the current state of the market economy, Russian citizens found themselves locked *out*, just as Soviet citizens were locked *in* under communism. In the contemporary Russian demonology, the Gulag archipelago of the 1930s labor camps has been shunted aside in favor of a "Gucci archipelago."[86]

As there was little in the old society that was of conceivable use in the construction of the new, a moral and political vacuum came into existence during the past decade, replacing the familiar structures of the old. During the current period of primitive accumulation of capital, this moral vacuum is a heavy price that the present is paying to the future in penance for the past. The Russian government might have been able to develop policies with less painful consequences had they made an attempt to maintain a more honest and perceptive, less ideological and formula-oriented, somewhat evolutionary analysis of the fundamental problems of the transition. But instead, Yeltsin reformers unwittingly reinforced the transition's most difficult qualities. Unable to step away from the traditional behavioral patterns of the elite, they failed to assure that people would constructively respond to their policies of change.

---

[85] *Rossiiskaya gazeta* (September 2, 1995).
[86] Nina L. Khrushcheva, "Where Does Russia Go?" IntellectualCapital.com, April 1, 1999.

CONCLUSION

In his introduction to the volume of articles written by the Russians after the collapse of the Soviet Union, *Remaking Russia. Voices from Within*, Richard Pipes rightly observed "that Russia's gravest problems are not economic... Economic problems appear as a consequence rather than a cause of Russia's current predicament."[87] The moral and political lessons that Lotman derived from Russia's history of tragic and ultimately self-defeating negations are reinforced by the decay caused by the painful transition from planned to market economy.

The most relevant question derived from the experience of the last ten years is whether Russia is bound to remain warped by its struggle to reconcile a market system with its inherited cultural values. Perhaps it is possible that, after the "revolutionary" mistakes of Yeltsin's regime, a new order will emerge that can achieve a pragmatic vision equally at home between Russian culture and appropriate institutions. Can ordinary Russians, and especially their political leaders, acquire an authentically evolutionary consciousness and leave behind a past based on polarization, maximalism, explosions, and outdated beliefs? True forward movement requires coming to terms with the past and not simply rejecting it, for absolute rejection leads only to endless cycles of negation and suffering.[88]

The good news is that the financial crisis of 1998—the culmination of the liberal revolution—did contribute to the beginning of this process: attitudes toward money and wealth have been slowly changing. Many now agree that the 1998 default and distress brought some positive results. Immediately following the crisis Sergei Kiriyenko suggested that devaluation and withdrawal of international investors would inspire domestic producers to work to

---

[87]Heyward Isham, ed., *Remaking Russia: Voices from Within*. With an introduction by Richard Pipes (Armonk, N.Y.: M.E. Sharpe, 1995), p. 3.

[88]A. F. Losev, *Strast' k dialektike* (Moscow: Sovetskii Pisatel', 1990), p. 68.

meet domestic consumer demand.[89] His predictions were confirmed
by Anders Aslund, who suggested that the most obvious reasons
for Russia's turnaround was indeed "devaluation, which caused an
instant halving of imports and made exports cheaper... The
industries that have grown the most, however, are not raw materials but intermediary goods, such as chemicals, pulp, paper, and
construction materials, and some manufactured goods... You see
the effect in the streets of Moscow. Suddenly, good Russian products are everywhere, while Moscow used to import 80 percent of
the goods it consumed."[90] After 1998 Russians finally realized that
the reformers were right in saying that there was no one there to
save them—neither God, nor czar, nor IMF, nor government do
care. They were then faced with having to save themselves. And
although Russia yet again found its way out of the revolution, the
price it paid has yet again been too high.

The bad news is that despite all the rationale and logic coming from the West the change is happening as a result of a revolution, with no consensus between the leaders and the people, in
truly Russian style. As Alexander Herzen has written, "disorder
saves Russia."[91] And although Russia paid a heavy price for its
reforms—socially, humanly, financially, politically—it also won't
be right to follow advocates of the Chinese model as the only possible path, now after the fact when all others failed.

China is a special case, and so has been Russia.[92] In fact, we should
stop thinking in terms of "models" altogether; otherwise we will
not come out of the vicious circle of producing lesser Americas,

---

[89]Transcript of Sergei Kiriyenko's lecture at the New York University School of Law
(November 30, 1998).

[90]Anders Aslund, "Has Financial Collapse Saved Russia?" *Project Syndicate* (January
1998); www.project-syndicate.cz.org.

[91]Quotation from Alexander Herzen in *Russkie o russkikh. Mneniia russkikhh o samikh
sebe* [Russian Opinions About Themselves] (St. Petersburg: Petro-Rif, 1992), p. 49.

[92]Comparing Russia with other transition economies, Fisher and Sahay point out that
"the case of Russia was so different from all other countries that for analytical purposes, it was considered as a group of one." Stanley Fisher and Ratna Sahay, "The Transition Economies After Ten Years," IMF Working Paper 00/30 (Washington, D.C.:
International Monetary Fund) p. 13. See also Pietro Garibaldi, Nada Mora, Ratna Sahay,
and Jeromin Zettelmeyer, "What Moves Capital to Transition Economies" (Washing-

Germanys, or Swedens. Already in 1762 Jean Jacques Rousseau warned against such a treatment of countries in general and of Russia in particular: "Peter [the Great] had a genius for imitation... He did some good things, but most of what he did was out of place. He saw his people was barbarous, but did not see it was not ripe for civilization... His first wish was to make Germans and English-men, when he ought to have been making Russians; and he pre-vented his subjects from ever becoming what they might have been by persuading them that they were what they are not."[93] This is to say that China has been more successful in its capitalist devel-opment precisely because it disregarded all models and managed to find its own way, understanding that no economic model could function properly unless it is founded upon the traditions of national development.

The lesson Russia and its liberal advisors learnt the hard way is that reform programs require synthetic and creative adaptation, that they are deeply moral and political, not just model-oriented and technical in nature. Another lesson is that "disorder," which had traditionally always "saved Russia" can and should no more be a solution to its current or future problems, for in the 21st cen-tury the country needs a new source of order appropriate to a com-plex modern society.

The most important issue that Russia faces today, in a new post-reform period, is a change in mentality. Russia's outdated psychology has to date reduced to zero all previous attempts for political and economic change. This problem has always made Russia a place where stable and predictable life is not a norm, in which the dif-ficulties have been routinely blamed on the evils of the patriarchal state, dictatorship, the West, corruption, or bad human material.

If the country is to continue with democratic and capitalist poli-cies, the next era of transition should be concentrated on reform-ing the mentality of both the elite and the people, which in turn will provide a viable environment for a new, modern, and respon-

---

[93]Jean Jacques Rousseau, *The Social Contract or Principles of Political Right* (1762). Quotation from the Internet version of the book at www.constitution.org/jjr/socon.tht, p. 19.

sible type of conduct on both sides. Future behavior can no longer be based on fear of the authorities or change but should be that of a people who are accountable for their actions and lives. Only then, an agreement for mutual benefit—a social contract—between a respected individual and the government of a law-based state will become possible.

A simple truth that has been long appreciated by other nations has yet to be welcomed by Russian society: "What man loses by the social contract is his natural liberty and an unlimited right to everything he tries to get and succeeds in getting; what he gains is civil liberty and the proprietorship of all he possesses."[94]

---

[94]Ibid., p. 8.

BIBLIOGRAPHY

Agafonov, V., and V. Rokitinsky. "Rossiya - eto ne prosto strana, eto - tsivilizatsia". *Novoe Russkoe Slovo*, August 1–2, 1992.

Aksakov, Konstantin. *Sobranie sochinenii v trekh tomakh* Vol. 1. Moscow, 1910.

Argumenty i Fakty, no. 48 (1997).

Aslund, Anders. "Has Financial Collapse Saved Russia?" Prague: Project Syndicate, January 1998; www.project-syndicate.cz.org.

Berdyaev, Nicolas. *The Russian Idea*. New York: Macmillan, 1948.

Berlin, Isaiah. "Political Ideas in the Twentieth Century," in Isaiah Berlin, *Four Essays on Liberty*. Oxford and New York: Oxford University Press, 1969.

_____. *Russian Thinkers*. London: The Hogarth Press, 1978.

Berdyaev, Nicolai. *Sub'ektivizm i Idividualizm v obshestvennoi filosofii*. St. Petersburg: Elektricheskaya tipografiia, 1901.

Bernstein, Jonas. "Party Lines: Dictated by Law, or Nods." *Moscow Times*, March 4, 2000.

Blagavolo, Valery. "Nikolai Ogarev. Russkie Voprosy". *Svobodnaya Mysl'*, vol. 2 (1993).

Brezhneva, Luibov. *The World I Left Behind*. New York: Random House, 1995.

Business World (August 14, 1993). Delovoi Mir Interview: Comments by Anders Aslund.

CNN.com transcript of the CNN NewsStand, April 17, 2000.

Chaadaev, Pyotr. "Filosofskie pisma" (1831). Quoted in P.S. Taranov, *Filosofskaya aforistika*. Moscow: Ostozh'e, 1996.

Chaadaev, Pyotr. *Philosophical Letters* (1831). Quoted in Alexander Panchenko, "I Don't Want to be Called Intelligentsia." *Moscovskie Novosti*, no. 50 (December 15, 1991).

Chas Pik (October 12, 1992).

Chiesa, Giulietto. *Proshchai Rossiya* [Farewell Russia]. Moscow, 1997.

Chubais, Anatoly. Interview on a Russian television program "Details,". June 29, 1994.

Chubais, Anatoly, ed. *Privatizatsiya po-rossiiski* [Privatization Russian Style]. Moscow: Vagrius, 1999.

Current Digest, no. 12 (April 8, 1992).

East European Constitutional Review, vol. 8, no. 1/2 (Winter/Spring 1999).

Ellman, Michael, and Vladimir Kontorovich, eds. *The Destruction of the Soviet Economic System*. Armonk, N.Y.: M.E. Sharpe, 1998.

Epstein, Mikhail. "Labor of Lust." *Common Knowledge*, vol. 1, no. 3 (Winter 1992).

Fedotov, G.P. *Sud'ba I grekhi Rossii*. St. Petersburg: Sofiia, 1991.

Fisher, Stanley, and Ratna Sahay. "The Transition Economies After Ten Years," IMF Working Paper 00/30. Washington, D.C.: International Monetary Fund.

Gaidar, Yegor. *Days of Defeat and Victory*. Seattle: University of Washington Press, 1999.

_____. *Gosudarstvo I Evolutsia*. Moscow: Evraziia, 1995.

Garibaldi, Pietro, and Nada Mora, Ratna Sahay, and Jeromin Zettelmeyer. "What Moves Capital to Transition Economies." Washington, D.C.: International Monetary Fund, 1999.

Gleason, Abbott. "Republic of Humbug: The Russian Nativist Critique of the United States 1830-1930." *American Quarterly*, vol. 44 (March 1992).

Glinkina, Svetlana. "The Criminal Components of the Russian Economy." Working Paper no. 29. Berichte des Bundesinstituts der Wissenschaftlichen und Internationalen Studien, Koln institut fur Ost Europa (1997).

Graham, Thomas E., Jr. "Testimony on Corruption in Russia and Future U.S. Policy Before the Senate Committee on Foreign Relations, September 30, 1999." Quoted in *Johnson's Russia List*, no. 3538 (October 1, 1999).

Herzen, Alexander. *My Past and Thoughts*. Berkeley: University of California Press, 1982.

Holmes, Stephen. "Cultural Legacies or State Collapse?" in Michael Mandelbaum, ed., *Post-Communism: Four Perspectives*. New York: Council on Foreign Relations, 1996.

Hubb, Johanna. Mother Russia: *The Feminine Myth in Russian Culture*. Bloomington and Indianapolis: Indiana University Press, 1993.

Isham, Heyward, ed. *Remaking Russia: Voices from Within*. With an introduction by Richard Pipes. Armonk, N.Y.: M.E. Sharpe, 1995.

Kennan, Edward. "Muscovite Political Folkways." *The Russian Review*, vol. 45, no. 2 (April 1986).

Khomyakov, A. S. "O starom i novom," in M.A. Maslin, ed., *Russkaya ideya*. Moscow: Respublica, 1992.

Khomyakov, Alexey. *Sobranie sochinenii v trekh tomakh*. Vol. 3. Moscow, 1916.

Khrushcheva, Nina L. "Where Does Russia Go?" Intellectual-Capital.com, April 1, 1999.

Kiriyenko, Sergei. Transcript of lecture at New York University School of Law. November 30, 1998.

Kiva, Alexey, in *Rossiiskaya gazeta* (September 2, 1995).

Losev, A.F. *Strast' k dialektike*. Moscow: Sovetskii Pisatel', 1990.

Lotman, Yury. *Kultura i Vzryv*. Moscow: Gnozis, 1992.

Maleva, Tatyana. "What Sort of Russia Has the New President Inherited? Or Russia's Key Social Problems." Carnegie Endowment for International Peace Moscow Center. Briefing no. 4 (2000), quoted in *Johnson's Russia List*, no. 4307 (May 17, 2000).

Medvedev, Roy. "Obval piramidy GKO," in Roy Medvedev, *Politics and Politicians of Russia*. Moscow: Prava cheloveka, 1999.

Miliukov, Paul. *The Origins of Ideology*. Gulf Breeze, Fla.: Academic International, 1974).

Murphy, Kenneth and Marek Hessel. "Stealing the State and Everything Else: A Survey on Corruption in the Post-Communist World." Prague: Project Syndicate, Winter 1999; www.project-syndicate.cz.

Nezavisimaya gazeta (October 17, 1991).

Nezavisimaya gazeta (February 27, 1992).

Nezavisimaya Gazeta (August 2, 1997).

Nezavisimaya gazeta (February 25, 1998).

Nevskoe Vremya. March 5, 1993. "The Left-handed Civilization." [Tsizilizatsia Levshi] Interview with Alexander Panchenko.

Novaya gazeta (November 24, 1997). Interview with Boris Nemtsov.

Piskunov, V. M., ed., *Russkaya ideya* [The Russian Idea]. Moscow: Isskusstvo, 1994.

Praim-TASS. (December 21, 1998).

Putin, Vladimir. *Ot pervogo litsa: Razgovory s Vladimirom Putinym* [First Person: Conversations with Vladimir Putin] with Natalia Gevorkyan, Natalia Timakova, Andrei Kolesnikov. Moscow: Vagrius, 2000; www.vagrius.com.

Rossiiskaya gazeta (September 1, 1992).

Rossiiskie vesti (September 1, 1992)

Rousseau, Jean Jacques. *The Social Contract or Principles of Political Right* (1762). Quotation from the Internet version at www.constitution.org/jjr/socon/tht.

Russia at the New Threshold. Moscow, 1995.

Russkie o russkikh. Mneniia russkikhh o samikh sebe [Russian Opinions About Themselves]. St. Petersburg: Petro-Rif, 1992.

Rutland, Peter and Natasha Kogan. "The Russia Mafia: Between Hype and Reality." *Transitions*, vol. 5, no. 3 (March 1998).

Sachs, Jeffrey D. "Betrayal." *The New Republic* (January 31, 1994).

_____. "Eastern Europe Reforms: Why the Outcomes Differed so Sharply." *Boston Globe*, September 19, 1999.

Satter, David. "What Went Wrong In Russia?" Paper presented at The Jamestown Foundation Conference "Russia: What Went Wrong? Which Way Now?" Washington D.C.: June 9, 1999.

Stevenson, Matthew. "Dealing in Russia." *The American Scholar* (Autumn 1993).

Stiglitz, Joseph. "Whither Reforms? The Years of the Transition." Keynote Address at the Annual World Bank Conference on Development Economics. Quoted in *Johnson's Russia List*, no. 3317 (June 1, 1999).

Tertz, Abram (Andrei Sinyavsky). "Mysli vrasplokh" [Thoughts Caught Unawares], in the *Collected Works in 2 Volumes*. Vol. 1. Moscow: SP Start, 1992.

_____. *A Voice from the Chorus*. New York: Farrar, Straus and Giroux, 1976.

Transparency. International 1998 Corruption Perceptions Index. Berlin: Transparency International, 1998; www.transparency.de.

_____. International 1999 Corruption Perceptions Index. Berlin: Transparency International, 1999; www.transparency.de.

Tsvetaeva, Marina translated by Elaine Feinstein. *Selected Poems*. Penguin Books, 1994.

Tumanov, Alexander N. "Merchant, Entrepreneur and Profit in Russian Literature: The Russian Artistic Intelligentsia and Money," in Anthony Purdy, ed., *Literature and Money*. Amsterdam and Atlanta: Editions Rodopi, 1993.

Wedel, Janine. "Rigging the U.S.-Russian Relationship: Harvard, Chubais, and the Transidentity Game." *Democratizatsiya*, vol. 7, no. 4 (Fall 1999).

Yeltsin, Boris. *Zapiski Prezidenta*. Moscow: Ogonek, 1994.

Korea's Comeback: The Government's Predicament

A Paper from the Project on Development,
Trade and International Finance

Hilton L. Root

A Council on Foreign Relations Paper

Korea's Comeback: The Government's Predicament

Hilton L. Root

INTRODUCTION

One year ago, Korea was in trouble. Its banking system, inadequately supervised, collapsed. Industry, lacking financial discipline, expanded unproductively with its "too big to fail" private firms crowding out smaller rivals. Labor market rigidity weakened the competitive position of Korean industry. The financial crisis that resulted gave rise to hopes that significant reform would address all three dimensions of Korea's vulnerability.

The crisis provided a window of opportunity to seek a coordinated solution, given that the overall condition of the economy was everyone's concern. However, Korea's quick recovery may have eliminated that opportunity as each interest group focused on its own well-being, resulting in social and political fragmentation. The regional focus of the 2000 parliamentary elections reflected this fragmentation. No consensus emerged on a reform agenda needed to dramatically restructure the economy.

With the government lacking support to continue comprehensive reform, new vulnerabilities began to appear. Before the crisis, the government implicitly insured depositors' bank loans to the large conglomerates. These guarantees left the banks with little incentive to develop credit analysis and loan monitoring skills necessary for prudent lending. Now, the government's increased ownership of the nation's capital assets may further weaken market discipline. Again, the insured agents, both firms and bankers, will not take proper care to manage risks.

Despite the stalled political reform process, market forces may yet change Korea precisely because the banks are unlikely to resume the central role they once played as the principal source of investment capital. Companies will have to turn to capital market alternatives—bond, equity markets, and Internet banking— for sources of new funding. As they seek new forms of financing, firms will be compelled to change management practices, concentrate on shareholder value, and adopt disclosure standards that are more rigorous than what is demanded by Korean law. The collapse of the banks will have another beneficial effect: weakening the cozy links between firms and politicians who once provided privileged access to cheap credit in exchange for contributions.

Thus, the collapse of the banking system may inadvertently accomplish what the politicians have been unable to do. Market-based financing will provide new sources of entrepreneurial capital and open the society by placing power in the hands of firms that are better adapted to a changing global market place.

Using normal accounting procedures, it would seem that the economy of South Korea is well on its way toward recovery and in record time. It often takes an average of three years after a banking crisis for an emerging market economy to return to pre-crisis economic growth (see Figure 1). Consider how favorable Korea looks using the type of data investors normally consult to forecast economic potential, illustrated in Table 1.

Korea's recovery seems exceptionally robust by these macro measurements. After three years of crisis, GDP growth in 1999 was 10.7%, reserves exceed $70 billion, inflation is in check, and the won is stable. Foreign direct investment in Korean companies was estimated at $15 billion for 1999, up from $2.6 billion in 1996. Do these strong macro indicators reflect strengthened micro institutions or do these impressive results imply that the micro foundations were never in the kind of jeopardy the pessimists suggested? Part of the recovery is due to a positive external environment led by strong U.S. growth. It is also possible that normal accounting masks the underlying weaknesses that led to the crisis. Looking back at the sources of the crisis, perhaps we can assess whether changes

Figure 1: Bank Crises: Estimated Total Losses/Costs Relative to GDP

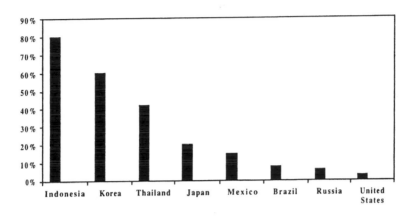

Source: James R. Barth, Daniel E. Nolle, Hilton L. Root and Glenn Yago, 2000.

Table 1: Principal National Account Indicators (Unit: %)

	1997	1998	1999
1. National Income (Nominal Term)			
GDP (Trillion Won)	453.3	444.4	483.8
GDP (U.S. $ Billions)	4,766	3,177	4,067
2. GDP Growth Rate (Real Term)	5.0	-6.7	10.7
3. Growth Rate by Type of Economic Activity			
Agriculture, Forestry and Fishery	4.6	6.6	4.7
Manufacturing	-6.6	-7.4	21.8
Construction	5.4	-8.6	-10.1
4. Growth Rate by Type of Expenditure			
Final Consumption Expenditure	3.2	-9.8	8.5
Gross Fixed Capital Formation	-2.2	-21.2	4.1
Exports	21.4	13.2	16.3
Imports	3.2	-22.4	28.9

Source: Korea, Ministry of Finance and Economy, March 2000.

underway are sufficient to reduce vulnerability to the recurrence of a crisis and improve resource allocation.

FINANCIAL SYSTEM REFORM

Problem: Existing financial institutions did not effectively match capital with profitable investment opportunities.

Causes: Before the crisis, Korean banks never acquired an adequate supervisory framework. Government supervision of banks' overseas borrowing was weak. At the same time, lenders believed the government was committed to maintaining its currency and had the means to do so. Long-standing exchange-rate pegs encouraged financial institutions to borrow abroad, convert the borrowed funds into domestic currency, and then lend domestically. International investors did not think they had to worry because their investments were brokered by local banks that were presumed to have government backing (see Table 2). Meanwhile, Korean intermediaries had little motive to develop the necessary skills in credit analysis, believing their loans were backed by the government.

Table 2: Payment Guarantees by the Government (in billions of won, as of the end of year)

	1997	1998	1999*
Total debt guarantees	13,039	71,953	83,020
(share of GDP)	(2.9%)	(16.0%)	(17.1%)
Loan guarantees	1,975	31,298	16,050
Bond guarantees	10,864	40,541	65,050
Foreign official loan guarantees	200	114	1,920

Note: * projected
Source: Joong-Ang Economist, October 26, 1999, cited in Jongryn Mo, *The Political Economy of Financial and Corporate Restructuring in Korea* (CIS Policy Analysis, February 15, 2000).

Additionally, the government insured the financing requirements of the conglomerates and implicitly underwrote their risks. Since the banks did not choose projects or make decisions about which firms should expand, they did little monitoring. They had no incentive to independently assess the plans they were financing and, as a result, did not acquire the skills necessary for effective loan assessment.

Without appropriate accounting, would-be bank regulators could not regulate the banks, which in turn could not regulate the borrowers. The government was not even able to count the number of subsidiaries belonging to each *chaebol* group (see Figure 2). Without fundamental information, credit was allocated on the basis of personal relationships or collateral. The largest borrowers got the rosiest assessments, since it was understood that they could always borrow more to pay off existing debts. So long as the economy grew, the potential of the *chaebols* was considered unlimited (see Table 3).

Figure 2: Average Number of Subsidiaries for the Top 30 Chaebols

No. of Subsidiaries

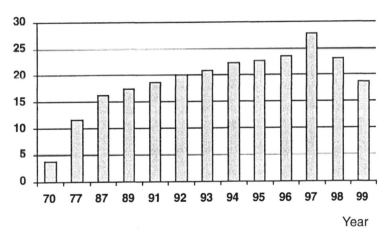

Source: Seong-min Yoo, Evolution of Government-Business Interface in Korea: Progress to Date and Reform Agenda Ahead, working paper. Seoul: Korean Development Institute, November 1997.

Table 3: Comparative Average Debt-Equity Ratios of Korean
chaebols with the Manufacturing Sector in Other
Countries (percentages)

Year	Manufacturing	Korean 30 chaebols [1]	United States	Japan	Taiwan, PRC
1991	307	403	147	209	98
1992	319	426	168	202	93
1993	295	398	175	202	88
1994	303	403	167	196	87
1995	287	388	160	196	86
1996	317	450	154	187	..

Sources: Korea Fair Trade Commission; Financial Statements Analysis, Bank of Korea;
U.S. Census Bureau; Quarterly Financial Report for Manufacturing, Mining, and Trade
Corporations; and The Quarterly Report of Enterprises; Ministry of Finance, Japan Quoted from Republic of Korea; Selected Issues, Jeanne Gobat, 1998, IMF Staff Country Report
[1]Nonfinancial subsidiaries of 30 largest chaebols

Recommended Solutions: Of course, the first matter of business is to clean up nonperforming loans. However, real reform requires
a transfer of the skills and information necessary for running the
financial system, from the government to market-based institutions. Thus, domestic banks will be forced domestic banks to
take full responsibility for the loans they authorize.

Progress in the financial sector is a prerequisite for restructuring the enterprise sector. The erosion of profit margins, low return
on equity, and low return on capital all reflect a lack of financial
discipline. Banks must be able to allocate credit on the basis of an
objective assessment of a borrower's cash flow prospects.

Korea has been chided for failing to establish accounting standards, which are considered a precondition for effective bank
regulation. Active credit analysis, however, will thrive when loans
are resold, which means that alternatives to banks must be developed. Greater independence for the central bank's inspection of
the financial sector will ensure that these alternatives are managed
according to appropriate standards.

Solving the current loan problems is only a first step; decen-
tralizing financial decisions is essential. However, during the crisis, discussions on financial reform became polarized. The

International Monetary Fund and World Bank advocated international capital and deep reform; the chaebols saw the problem simply as a liquidity issue, while President Kim Dae Jung adopted an intermediate step of moderate institutional reform (see Figure 3). The parties have not been willing to compromise, and President Kim has not had adequate political support to break the stalemate. The opponents of reform have one very powerful weapon to impede the momentum of change. They have characterized the reform process as a fire sale in which prized national assets are being sold to foreign investors at bargain prices.

Not surprisingly, the major banks in Korea have used their monopoly over information to control the loan market. An active assessment of loan performance may threaten their ability to continue controlling the loan supply. Recapitalizing the banking sector as it existed_the very organizations that have no incentive to actively monitor the performance of loans to large vested interests_would allow large financial institutions to continue to dominate the credit market.

Figure 3: Korean Financial System Reform Taking the Policy Steps in the Reform Process

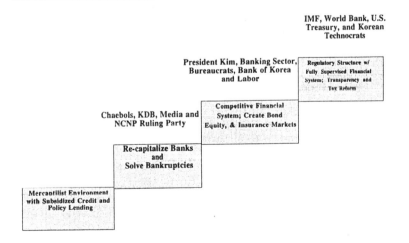

IMF, World Bank, U.S. Treasury, and Korean Technocrats

President Kim, Banking Sector, Bureaucrats, Bank of Korea and Labor

Regulatory Structure w/ Fully Supervised Financial System; Transparency and Tax Reform

Chaebols, KDB, Media and NCNP Ruling Party

Competitive Financial System; Create Bond Equity, & Insurance Markets

Re-capitalize Banks and Solve Bankruptcies

Mercantilist Environment with Subsidized Credit and Policy Lending

Post-Crisis Developments: Where is Korea now? Addressing
the financial sector, the government faced two challenges in the
aftermath of the crisis. With the initial task of cleaning up nonperforming loans, the government injected 64 trillion won to
acquire nonperforming loans, recapitalize viable financial institutions,
and support deposit insurance. In the process, a number of financial companies were closed or merged with healthier ones. However, the ratio of nonperforming to performing loans in the system
is still unhealthy. Many nonperforming banks still exist.

In 1998, the government set up a vehicle for acquiring nonperforming loans: the Korea Asset Management Corporation
(KAMCO) (see Table 4). Authorities moved relatively aggressively
to strengthen their banking systems through injections of public
funds ($23.3 billion with few conditions attached), nationalizations,
removal of bad debts, and mergers (see Table 5). The milestones
in the restructuring process included liquidation of five commercial banks whose Bank for International Settlements capital
adequacy ratio was under 8 percent. In addition, the government
merged nine banks into four and is selling two banks to foreign
investors. Banks have cut staff by 34 percent. Depositors make deposits

Table 4: Asset Resolution Strategies

Set up centralized asset management lion in company to which banking system's nonperforming loans are transferred	KAMCO has accumulated $37 bil- assets
Centralized asset management companies purchase assets at subsidized prices	Initially assets were purchased above market-clearing prices with recourse. Since February 1998 purchases have been attempted at market prices
Nature of agency: restructuring or disposition?	Not clearly defined. Mostly engaged in disposing of assets
Type of assets transferred	No particular strategy
Assets transferred	26% of nonperforming loans, equal to 10% of GDP
Assets disposed of as share of total assets transferred	4.7%

Source: Stijn Claessens, Simeon Djankov, and Daniela Klingebiel, *Financial Restructuring
in East Asia: Halfway There?* (Washington, D.C.: World Bank, September 1999).

Table 5: Financial Distress Resolutions and Bank Recapitalization Strategies

Initial government response	
Substantial liquidity support	$23.3 billion (5% of GDP)
Financial distress resolutions	
Bank shutdowns	None
Shutdowns of other financial institutions	More than 117
Mergers of financial institutions	11 of 26 absorbed by other banks
Nationalizations	4
Bank recapitalization strategies	
Public funds for recapitalization	Government injected $8 billion into 9 commercial banks; 5 out of 6 major banks now 90% controlled by the state
Majority foreign ownership of banks	Allowed, 2 completed and 1 near finalization
Weak financial institutions still in system	Many weak non-bank financial institutions remain

Note: Local currency figures converted at mid-September 1999 exchange rates.
Sources: Roy Ramos, *Financial Restructuring Scorecard* (Hong Kong: Goldman Sachs, 1999); World Bank data. Cited in Claessens, Djankov, and Klingebiel, *Financial Restructuring in East Asia: Halfway There?*

more prudently as the myth that banks cannot fail has been eliminated. They are being more selective with regard to which banks they deposit with and they are investing funds in alternative instruments. To monitor the KAMCO, the government created the Financial Supervisory Commission. This raises the question of how independent a regulatory agency that regulates a government-owned banking sector can be when no external constituency exists to demand such independence.

Korea has improved its exit framework. An independent supervisory agency now supervises different types of deposit-taking institutions on a consistent and consolidated basis. Guarantees on banking system liabilities have been phased out. A deposit insurance scheme with elements of prompt corrective action has been adopted.

Compared to other crisis countries in East Asia, capital levels appear most solid in Korea as a result of the government's injections of capital. But many challenges remain. Banks would still be undercapitalized if they were to provision adequately. Taking into account current levels of capital, loan-loss provisioning and the nonperforming loans that remain, spreads in Korea would be fairly close to historical levels. Asset management companies have not yet disposed of many assets and global experience indicates that these companies tend to be weak at corporate restructuring.

As a way of putting the issues into context, consider that when communism ended, newly private banks were saddled with significant nonperforming loans to state owned enterprises. In Hungary in the early 1990s, a large percentage of GDP was devoted to bank recapitalization; however, foreign ownership of a large portion of the banking sector was necessary to forge a competitive financial system. By contrast, in the Czech Republic, most nonperforming loans were consolidated into a state-owned institution that still has not been able to dispose of its nonperforming assets. Nonperforming loans are rolled over and real restructuring is postponed[1]. Is Korea headed for the same fate as the Czech Republic? Although the government now owns many banks that were recapitalized, no significant management changes have occurred.

As stated previously, real reform requires a transfer of authority from the government to market-based institutions, which forces banks to take full responsibility for the loans they authorize. As noted, banks had little incentive to develop the necessary credit analysis and loan monitoring skills because the government implicitly insured depositors and backed bank loans made to *chaebols*. In other words, the financial sector was a classic case of moral hazard where the insured agents did not take proper care in the managing their risks. Ultimately, it may be the adequacy or quality of monitoring and discipline intended to reduce moral hazard that matters most, not the total amount of insurance.

In theory, the extent of moral hazard can be measured by the amount of insurance extended to financial institutions. In practice, however, the problem in Korea was complicated by the presence of informal or implicit guarantees. To preserve confidence in the banking system and prevent a run on deposits, the government

---

[1]Thomas W. Hall, Economic *Policy and Financial Sector Reform in Emerging Markets: The Case of Central and Eastern Europe.* Ph.D. dissertation (Los Angeles: University of Southern California, 1999).

had to provide a blanket guarantee covering all bank deposits as well as certain other liabilities of financial institutions. In January 1998, the government also guaranteed payment of domestic bank foreign liabilities in the amount of $24 billion as part of a debt restructuring agreement with foreign creditors. Furthermore, in the summer of 1999, the government was forced to guarantee the principal of corporate securities funds issued by investment trust companies (see Table 2). During the three years of financial restructuring, the government became the largest shareholder in the financial sector, acquiring major shares in ten commercial banks, eight insurance companies, and two investment trust companies.

While foreigners now play a larger role, entry into the financial sector has been limited to two foreign banks. Considerable uncertainty about the future still exists because an overall strategy on banks, clarifying issues such as whether *chaebols* can own banks, has yet to be established. Korea's government controls assets worth more than 100 percent of GDP. In sum, three years after the onset of the crisis, financial restructuring is incomplete, much new capital is needed, and for most financial institutions, new private owners are needed. The government's increased ownership stake in banks and other financial institutions is the greatest disappointment of the reform process.

The Non-Banking Sector

The government has been less successful in addressing problems in the non-banking sector (except for closing merchant banks). Of the 2,069 non-bank financial institutions, many of which are in weak financial condition, only 242 had stopped operations as of August 1999. The top five *chaebol*-affiliated investment trust companies have continued to extend financing to their loss-making affiliates, mainly in the form of bonds with high interest rates sold to the general public as people moved out of low-yielding deposits. The small investors in these funds rarely have adequate information or protection.

More adequate provisioning for nonperforming loans may reveal further capital shortfalls. Although Korean companies have experienced large improvements in cash, data for the first half of 1999 indicate that 27 percent of Korea's publicly listed firms cannot fully cover interest payments from operational cash flows. Of the $34 billion in new funds raised by Korean corporations in 1999, more than half have gone to the top five *chaebols*. Of that capital, 7 percent was in the form of new equity, 32 percent were bank loans, and 61 percent were corporate bonds.

An undercapitalized financial sector can inspire banks to finance risky but potentially high-return projects in attempts to restore capital. Fiscal stimulus programs have already led to large deficits—more than 5 percent of GDP—and rising public debt. If all financial restructuring costs fall on the public sector, public debt levels will rise sharply from 37 percent to 48 percent. If interest rates remain at current levels, interest payments are expected to account for 6–14 percent of fiscal revenues.

Summary of Financial Sector Reform

The international community has pinned its hopes on required regulatory disclosure, but rules and regulations will not be a substitute for genuine competition among firms. Only if direct political interference and the danger of capricious taxation are eliminated will companies seeking credit want to disclose profits accurately. Then the skills of credit analysis will migrate to their higher-value users: the companies that buy and sell loans. The existence of a deep secondary market will motivate active loan assessment.

Transparency, improved corporate accountability, and governance that can facilitate proper risk pricing via the transmission of market signals will emerge—as will rating agencies and credit analysis—when institutional investors and issuers freely seek each other. Regulatory review, creditors' rights, and covenant structures are all products of economic competition that come into being as the government steps out of the direct management of credit allocation. Breaking up an oligopoly of a few large lenders will more effectively develop credit analysis than regulating disclosure into existence. Bringing foreign banks into the Korean market will be an important step in this direction.

While Korea has made significant progress during the past two years in restructuring its financial sector, corporate governance is still compromised by links between non-bank financial institutions and the corporate sector. In fact, since 1997, non-bank financial institutions have become much more important in Korea, with investment trust companies expanding considerably. Close links could reduce incentives for banks to restructure corporations and perpetuate the continued accommodation by banks of their clients' credit needs without independent monitoring and oversight.

The government needs to adjust its approach to bank and corporate restructuring, and go beyond the focus on reducing financial systems' capital shortfalls to dealing with other systemic issues. It must expand the sticks and carrots for corporate governance, for example, by linking additional fiscal resources for banks to promote corporate restructuring under a loss-sharing agreement.

But the discipline to reduce moral hazard is still wanting. No timetable exists to privatize government-held shares of financial institutions. It is even possible that in the years ahead, instead of phasing out its dominant presence in the financial market, future uncertainties may induce more government involvement.

BUSINESS REFORM

Problem: The weakness of financial-market supervision promoted unhealthy industrial development. Because the government stepped in to prevent large firms from going under, they became "too large to fail," further consolidating their grip on credit. This paved the way for their almost unlimited expansion into unrelated businesses.

Causes: First, the government conferred preferential status to industries by relieving them from competitive pressures. Then it allowed the firms to expand into areas in which they had no competitive advantage through the practice of cross-guarantees within *chaebols.* Internal cross-financing made it possible for *chaebols* to grow in seeming defiance of market forces. Although expansion started with government support of preferred sectors, firms soon moved into unrelated sectors, using finance derived from the core specialty. This risky strategy would have been unthinkable had it not been for expectations on the part of both banks and firms that the government was ultimately available to bail them out.

This ownership pattern makes it difficult for potential outside investors to assess the balance sheet risks of these entities. Transfer pricing within a conglomerate allows one subsidiary to subsidize another, thereby allowing unprofitable subsidiaries to operate. It also prevents small and medium-sized enterprises (SMEs) from operating in areas where chaebols are not efficient. In fact, many conglomerates were dragged down by their affiliates. For example, Kia Motors, despite having world-class production facilities, was dragged down by its failing sister companies: Specialty Steel, Asia Motors, and Kaisan. These shortcomings were hidden within the conglomerate structure (see Figures 2 and 4).

The balance between large and small businesses became disproportionately weighted toward the large firms to the point where they could dump their problems into the laps of smaller enterprises. Chaebols were known to force the acceptance of promissory

Figure 4: Related vs. Unrelated Subsidiary Holdings within Conglomerates

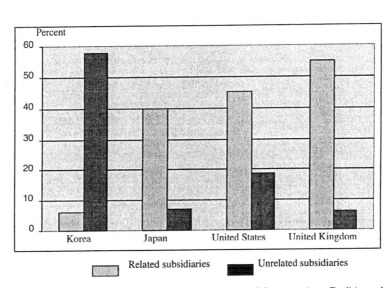

Related subsidiaries   Unrelated subsidiaries

Source: Seong-min Yoo, Korean Business Conglomerates: Misconceptions, Realities and Policies. Korea's Economy 1995. Washington: Korea Economic Institute of America, 1995.

notes with unfavorable terms on smaller firms. They could pressure those firms to cut prices on products they sold to their big brothers. Eventually, many were driven out of their specialized niches.

Solutions: *Chaebol* reform should include restricting the practice of cross-guaranteeing loans and cross-shareholding in order to trim their lines of business to core specialties. The rights of small shareholders need protection. The boards of directors and auditors should be given meaningful, independent roles. Management should be disciplined by an active market for mergers and acquisitions. Financial institutions must play an active role as investors. In the long run, the government must shed its habit of allocating resources by decree and instead set up fair competition laws to break the collusion of business and politics. Once individual Koreans own shares and demand a return on their investments, business accounting practices will fall into line with international accounting standards. However, developing efficient equity and bond markets would require diversification of *chaebol* ownership and the establishment of minority shareholder rights.

Chaebol reform addresses the very foundation of Korea's corporatist society. President Kim says that the future of Korea is tied to the development of SMEs and has attempted to reduce chaebol overcapacity through legislation. But is he ready to take the final step toward real reform, requiring *chaebol* owners to accept diversified ownership structures with management-sharing concessions, voting rights, and corporate transparency?

Figure 5: Forean Business Reform Moving on the Policy Steps of Enterprise Business Reform

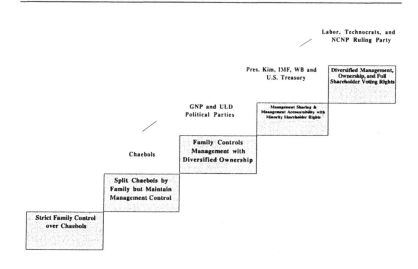

Figure 5 illustrates the compromise that would result if the *chaebols* moved up one step in the reform process while labor, Korean technocrats, and the NCNP moved down one step. However, throughout the crisis, political support for *chaebol* reform has been low and has decreased as the *chaebols* accepted only minimal reforms.

Effective equity markets will not form until *chaebols* are broken up into units whereby economic performance can be more directly observed. The pre-crisis *chaebol* components could not be assessed according to the criteria set for a normal economic rate of return and shareholder value.

The government's strategy to reform the chaebols began with what it called the "Big Deal," essentially meaning asset swaps. Koreans view the government-*chaebol* agreement on voluntary restructuring (the "Big Deal") as a significant step toward industrial consolidation. It is premised on the belief that consolidation around core competencies will eliminate the danger to otherwise healthy companies of being brought down by their nonperforming assets. However, this simply allows the conglomerates to dump the public assets that are unsalvageable and keep the jewels for themselves. In other words, *chaebols* can consolidate value for themselves at the public's expense. Moreover, the Big Deal does not replace the need for effective market discipline that comes when capital markets reward effective corporate strategies with investor capital. The Big Deal replaced the market with government. This might have made sense when the private sector was weak and lacked experience, but what sense does it make when the private sector is more knowledgeable than the government?

Post-Crisis Developments: Kim Dae Jung's government announced three principles of corporate reform in January 1998: to improve corporate governance by increasing the accountability of controlling shareholders and management; to enhance the transparency of management by eliminating cross-payment guarantees between and among *chaebol* subsidiary companies; and to improve the capital structure of firms and focus the conglomerates on core activities. In essence, he hoped to reduce debt-equity ratios to 200 percent by the year 2000 by requiring the *chaebols* to raise new equities, to sell excess assets, and to spin off unrelated affiliates, reduce lines of business and shed excess capacity (see Table 6). Three more principles were added in August 1999: limiting the chaebols' control of non-banking financial institutions; reducing insider trading and cross-subsidiary equity investments; and tightening regulations on inheritance and other types of wealth transfers among family members of *chaebol* owner-managers. Progress in corporate restructuring has been made but the outcome is decidedly mixed: the corporate restructuring program has centered on the restructuring of corporate debt. Measures to reduce corporate debt overhang are essential for the short term, but the governance structures of Korea's *chaebols* are a barrier to the company's commitment to shareholders.

The ultimate test of corporate reform is whether or not firms compete according to market principles; i.e., are they subject to market discipline? One indicator is whether the government allows insolvent firms to fail or continues to bail them out. So far, many failed entities are still operating.

Of the various components of Kim Dae Jung's economic program, the least successful has been the reform of the large *chaebols*. Although Samsung has done much to bring its debt equity ratios down, SK and LG have muddled along (see Table 6). Daewoo resisted restructuring and took on additional debt during the crisis. Hyundai increased its debt-to-equity ratio but opened the "Buy-Korea" fund that increased its equity.

The table below, based upon statistics reported by the Korean government, most likely underestimates the true relationship between debt and equity. Lower debt-equity ratios include asset re-evaluations that are questionable; actual debt ratios are not available for reasons discussed below. Combined financial statements that prevent firms from making double entries or hiding assets will not be required until 2000 and even then it is unclear whether the government will be able to enforce this requirement.

Table 6: Top 5 Chaebols: Liabilities/Equity

Group	1997	6/30/99–12/31/99
Hyundai	572%	341%–148.1%
Daewoo	470%	588%–N. A.
Samsung	366%	193%–114.7%
LG	508%	247%–169.3%
SK	466%	227%–116.4%

Source: Excludes effects of asset re-evaluations. Financial Supervisory Services (Korea)

Beyond the top five, the *chaebols* ranked from six to thirty remain in deep distress, with a negative income of 6 trillion won. Before the crisis, eighteen of the top thirty *chaebols* with assets of $86.2 billion, employing 255,000 workers, were on the verge of bankruptcy. Their debt-to-equity ratio rose from 493 percent to 784 percent during the crisis.

Many affiliates of the second-tier *chaebols* have entered into workouts under the supervision of the Korean Financial Supervisory Commission. These workouts have centered on financial restructuring, with emphasis on debt rescheduling and reductions of debt-to-equity ratios. The reductions are achieved by raising new equity, debt-to-equity swaps, and selling assets— with the proceeds being used to retire debt. Workouts are not for groups as entities but for affiliated firms within the group. These workout programs keep many nonviable *chaebols* on a life-support system of instead of letting them go bankrupt.

By September 1999, some forty-one affiliates of sixteen *chaebols* and some thirty-eight stand-alone large and medium companies (seventy-nine companies in total) negotiated memoranda of understanding (MOUs) with their creditors, rescheduling debt of 35 trillion won. Some 81 percent of debt restructuring and 34 percent of self-help measures were implemented by September 1999 (see Table 7). These workouts were done quickly amid deep concern over systemic failure. Many companies will likely have difficulty meeting their projected performance.

In the best cases to date, these workouts have produced substantial improvements in immediate financial prospects, but they have not extended to the restructuring of corporate operations. An estimated one-quarter to one-third of the restructuring would need to be renegotiated to achieve this. Many others will need to be rolled over at the end of the rescheduling period. In general, it appears that the second tier *chaebols* are having difficulty meeting their projected performance under the MOUs, while the stand-alone medium and large companies appear to be largely in compliance. Of the second-tier *chaebols* that did not enter the workout program, many are in unsatisfactory financial condition.

Table 7: Summary of Corporate Restructuring Workouts

Measure	Agreed Amounts (in billions of won)	Actual Implementation (as of 9/30/99)
Self-Help:		
Real estate sales	3,956	23%
Affiliate sales	1,047	7%
Other asset sales	995	46%
Foreign capital	1,650	58%
Rights issues	433	53%
Cost reductions/capital contributions	1,262	44%
	9,343	34%
Debt Restructuring:		
Rate reduction & deferral	23,302	96%
Deferral	4,857	93%
Conversion to equity or CBs	4,329	78%
Other*	2,412	105%
	34,900	94%
Total	43,133	81%

Note: * Includes repayment and write-offs

Source: CRCC and Financial Supervisory Services (Korea) Cited in Ira Lieberman and William P. Mako, *Korea's Structural Reform*. Korea's Economy 2000, vol. 16 . Korea Economic Institute of America, Washington, D.C., 2000.

The critical weakness of the workout process is the low number of affiliate sales. In effect, the same corporate structures still exist despite the workouts. Labor reductions and wage compressions are often the driving force behind the improvement in operational cash flows. Korea's largest corporations have shed more than a quarter of their workers.

The small business sector has stabilized after two years of widespread business failures. The economic recovery has helped small business restructuring and this sector is leading new growth and employment creation.

Future Development: As corporate restructuring continues, more nonperforming loans will arise and more capital will be needed to recapitalize the banks. Workouts have produced seventy-nine agreements—more than in any of the other crisis countries—though implementation is still far from having been accomplished. To date, three of the top five *chaebols* have implemented their capital structural improvement plans. However, new accounting and disclosure regulations are needed. Moreover, the international operations of *chaebols* remain a dark secret.

Only Samsung provides information sufficient for an independent analyst to assess the group's financial status. Even the information it provides the public falls short of U.S. Securities and Exchange Commission requirements. In general, the Korean Stock Exchange requires less information than required by the SEC, and its requirements apply to individually listed firms, not their affiliates. In the United States, the SEC provides information not only about the listed companies themselves but also their controlled affiliates. In Korea, this loophole is an important caveat since many *chaebols* consist of unlisted firms that form a substantial portion of the whole. Greater information transparency might have been a more meaningful contribution to *chaebol* reform than the "Big Deal." However, the constituency for greater *chaebol* transparency is weak. The federation of Korean industries spoke out against Kim Dae Jung when he required the major *chaebols* to provide consolidated financial statements by the year 2000.

Corporate restructuring is a complex process that will require many years. Although the financial restructuring of enterprises has progressed in a relatively successful manner, it cannot serve as a substitute for essential governance reforms: the appointment of independent directors, protection of minority shareholders' rights, and full disclosure under international guidelines.

It is still the government and not the markets that determine the ultimate fate of Korea's firms. The "Big Deal" allows the administration to act in a discretionary manner toward the *chaebols* and the government still controls the banking system. The final step toward real reform has not been made. That would require *chaebol* owners to accept diversified ownership structures with management-sharing concessions, voting rights, and corporate transparency. In fact, many observers fear that influential segments of the bureaucracy do not want to go this far toward a market based system but prefer instead to maintain administrative control.

The brightest spot in the recovery is the considerable progress made in eliminating barriers to foreign entry, though a number of restrictions remain (see Table 8).

Table 8: Changes in Foreign Direct Investment Restrictions by Sector

Finance	Manufacturing	Retail	Utilities
From 15% to 100%	From 20% to 100%	From 20% to 100%	From 0% to 49%

Source: World Bank data. Cited in Claessens, Djankov, and Klingebiel, *Financial Restructuring in East Asia: Halfway There?*

However, considerable progress needs to be made in corporate governance (see Table 9).

Table 9: Equity Rights, Creditors Rights, and Judicial Efficiency, mid-1999

Indicator	Republic of Korea
Equity Rights	
One-share, one-vote	1
Proxy by mail	0
Shares not blocked	+1
Cumulative voting	0
Equity rights score (sum)	2
Improvement over 1996	+1
Creditor Rights	
Restrictions on reorganizations	1
No automatic stay on assets	0
Secured creditors first paid	1
Management does not stay on in reorganizations	1
Creditor rights score (sum)	3
Improvement over 1996	None
Judicial Efficiency	
Timetable to render judgment	+1
Existence of a specialized bankruptcy code	1
Judicial efficiency score (sum)	2
Improvement over 1996	+1

Note: 1 denotes that equity and creditor rights laws exist, that there are time limits to render judgment, and that specialized bankruptcy courts exist.

+1 indicates an improvement over the law in place before the crisis, that is, in 1996.
Sources: Claessens, Djankov, and Klingebiel, *Financial Restructuring in East Asia: Halfway There?*; Rafael La Porta, Florencio Lopes de Silanes, and Andrei Shleifer, "Law and Finance," *Journal of Political Economy,* vol. 106 (1998), pp. 1113–55.

Since the crisis, formal minority shareholder rights have improved in Korea. As can be seen from the above table, enforcement of these rights, as reflected in measures of the efficiency of the judicial systems, remains weak. Minority rights are often violated, and valuations of firms controlled by inside shareholders are far below those of comparable firms, suggesting large-scale expropriation by the principals.[2] In Korea, large-scale financial transfers continue among firms within groups, the most recent example being the channeling of SK Telecom profits to loss-making affiliates rather than to shareholders. In two key areas_the independence of regulators and the strength of judicial systems_Korea has just begun a long process of transition to a rule-based economy. Outside directors are often unsatisfied with their roles.

[2]Stijn Claessens, Semeon Djankov, and Larry Lang, "Who Controls East Asian Corporations?" Policy Research Working Paper 2054 (Washington, D.C.: World Bank, 1999).

LABOR REFORM

Problem: Historically, labor-market rigidity has weakened the competitive position of Korean industry. Companies cannot adjust to business cycles and are forced to accept the high costs of maintaining labor during recessions, which makes economic cycles more extreme than they need to be. This labor-market rigidity makes Korean assets unattractive to foreign investors.

Causes: Directed and financed by cheap government credit, the *chaebols* subsidized social stability during economic downturns by keeping their employees and thousands of subsuppliers working. In return, the government furnished the conglomerates with a compliant labor force. This job-security arrangement, coupled with an economy that has historically had low levels of unemployment, prevented the development of a flexible labor market.

Solution: Clear and credible rules governing layoffs are crucial to bolstering foreign direct investment, particularly among bankrupt companies where redundancies are likely to be the highest. To gain support for improved labor-market flexibility, the government needs to introduce a national safety net that includes those not presently covered and extends benefits for those who are cut off after a short period.

Properly structured equity arrangements provide management with direct incentives to run companies more efficiently. Regulations allowing Korean companies to use equity ownership, particularly employee stock ownership plans (ESOPs) and stock options, offer management alternatives to cash as a means of motivating employees. Moreover, investors prefer companies with high management_ownership ratios. Increased equity incentives will also help unlock Korea's highly developed human capital.

The Korean government recently took the first policy step toward labor reform by allowing temporary layoffs of permanent employees among firms that have obtained government approval (see Figure 6). Given that Korea has no national unemployment insurance system, labor opposes unrestricted layoffs. As business and labor interests clash, most Korean political and social groups recognize the difficulty in initiating substantive labor reform. Moderate labor groups, government bureaucrats, the ministry of labor, and most political parties recognize the need for some mechanism to expand layoffs without provoking a political backlash. However, temporary or permanent layoffs are acceptable to the majority of Koreans only if the government maintains control over which employees and sectors are affected. Radical labor groups will continue to push for the old system of implicit lifetime employment. Unable to overcome labor opposition to reform, President Kim will continue to advocate government control over layoffs to retain domestic political support.

The *chaebols*, whose stake in labor reform is much greater, will continue to pursue a flexible labor market and will pressure labor to allow governmentally approved layoffs. However, most Koreans believe that a flexible labor market could expose the nation to social upheaval, which means that labor unions are able to play on their fear of the social consequences of unemployment. Consequently, when strikes and protests do occur, President Kim has made

Figure 6: Korean Labor Reform Taking the Policy Steps in the Reform Process

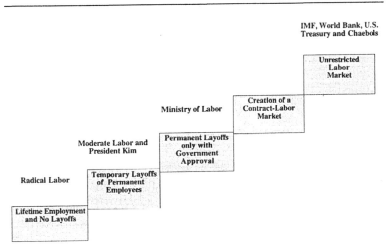

political concessions to soften radical labor demands and appease moderates. Nevertheless, Korea is unlikely to revert to the "life-time employment" of the past.

Several reform opportunities existed that were not exploited. If the conservative parties (GNP and ULD) were to politicize the labor issue in the media by claiming that the president was hostage to labor interests, they might be able to pressure labor to allow some permanent layoffs. Even so, substantive changes are not likely.

Labor is unwilling to make any significant concessions. Only temporary layoffs can occur, and these only with government approval. However, labor is willing to trade employment securi-ty for management and decision-making participation. Consequently, *chaebol* reform is closely connected to labor reform. Labor reform is potentially politically volatile. The government is thus unwill-ing to attempt it unless it can also help labor achieve some of its goals, namely opening the management system of the *chaebols* and establishing minority shareholding. Little progress has been made toward implementing such a trade-off.

Post-Crisis Developments: The criteria for labor reform can also be defined in terms of moral hazard. In the past, the government ensured employment for Korean workers through legal restrictions on layoffs and the hiring of temporary workers. Kim Dae Jung intro-duced more permissive rules on layoffs in February 1998. The flex-ibility of the labor market may be measured in terms of how responsive wages and employment are to aggregate demand. However, the issue at the company level is how easily managers can lay workers off when they are legally allowed to do so. Again the evidence is mixed. Although unemployment has risen, there have been few formal layoffs. Due to informal pressure against lay-offs, employers have reduced their work force by freezing new hires or employed informal tactics to fire workers.

The largest of Korea's *chaebols* have laid off more than 25 per cent of their workers. In publicly listed companies, payrolls have dropped 34 percent. However, these represent temporary layoffs rather than improvements in labor market flexibility as a whole. Managers depend on legal permission to lay off workers. Employ-ers have reduced their work force by freezing new hires and using informal tactics to fire workers. Dismissal conditions remain strict, requiring that employers re-hire laid off workers if they recruit within two years of the dismissal date. During the consolidation of the semiconductor industry last year, management pledged not to lay off any workers, an indication of the continuing rigidity of Korea's labor markets.

Figure 7: Unemployment Rate

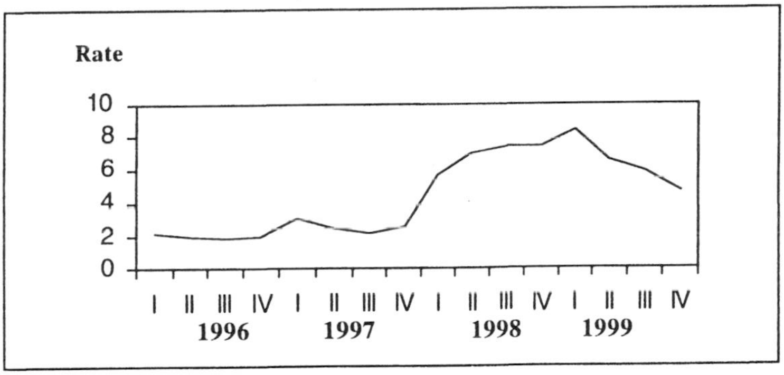

Source: International Financial Statistics, IMF; Third & Fourth Quarter of 1999 from the Ministry of Finance and Economy, Korea.

Social safety nets, such as the government-funded employment insurance system and public works programs, do exist. These were weak during the crisis however, leaving many workers without jobs or adequate benefits, and they continue to be weak.

By all measures labor has been the loser in the crisis (see Figure 7). Its organizing power has weakened and labor is divided over key issues. Reform efforts involving labor in a second tripartite committee have failed. The division of unions between large and small companies, as well as between union federations, has prevented labor from acting together. Labor's weakness has been one reason chaebols have been able to resist reform.

Will There Be a New Korea?

Compared to financial restructuring, little progress has been made on enterprise reform. While Korean banks may be able to grow out of their problems, it is doubtful that corporate restructuring has been adequate to foster financially viable corporations. Durable economic recovery depends on further progress in both areas.

Most problematic are the continuing links between non-bank financial institutions and the corporate sector. The concentration of corporate control in the hands of a few families, not to mention the strong political connections of these families, is an obstacle to deep institutional reforms.

At the outset of the crisis, significant opportunities for reform existed. When the government was on the verge of defaulting on its international payments and turned to the IMF, the crisis affected every social interest in the country. The IMF wisely saw an opportunity to draw attention to the need for fundamental institutional reform to help Korea withstand future regional downturns. However, the breathing space provided by the IMF altered the incentives of different groups to cooperate in preventing future crisis. A window of opportunity existed because the crisis cut deeply into the fabric of society and affected the ability of all groups to earn future income. The possibility of aligning all the relevant interests evaporated shortly after the bailout funds were received.

The vision of a liberal Korea came largely from international capital, with the IMF and the World Bank taking the leading role. While seeing where Korea needed to go, the IMF and World Bank were poorly equipped to overcome the political obstacles that lay in the path to reform. The interconnectedness of the issues— the importance of labor reform for gaining support for financial market liberalization—required a political, not merely a technocratic, response.

A deal brokered by international capital might have broken the stalemate between labor and banking reforms (see Figure 8). International capital might have effectively brokered structural changes had a means of trading the advantages of a more flexible labor market for concessions on financial reform by the *chaebols* been available. A trade of labor flexibility for financial market reform might have led to open markets for bond, equity, and insurance, coupled with the emergence of a contract-labor market that allows some permanent layoffs. In this scenario, the level of management sharing would be far above what was acceptable to the *chaebols.* By allowing some labor participation in management, a broad-based societal consensus might have been forged.

A grand social bargain needed to include:

• a more flexible contract labor market;

• a competitive financial system; and

• diversified *chaebol* ownership with management sharing and minority shareholder rights (Figure 8).

Figure 8: An Alternative Solution: an IMF/World Bank-Brokere Deal Linking Banking and Labor Reform

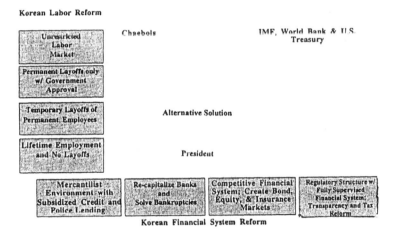

With recovery in the air, no urgency exists for the different parties to put down their differences and work to prevent future crises. Three years after the onset of the crisis, the consensus for fundamental reform seems to have evaporated and with it political cohesion to build a durable foundation for economic competitiveness. The March 2000 parliamentary elections have weakened President Kim's prospects for proceeding forward.

Improvements in the allocation of investable funds will require better-capitalized banking systems and deeper institutional reforms in financial regulation and supervision, corporate governance, and bankruptcy procedures. Loan classification and provisioning guidelines in Korea still trail international best practices. Corporate governance rules have improved but are not fully enforced. Korea has passed new bankruptcy and collateral laws, but creditor's rights have improved only marginally.

In the absence of a consensus for fundamental reform, several opportunities exist. One approach would be more fully funded pension schemes, which would operate as institutional investors that could provide independent oversight to the corporate and financial sectors. Corporate restructuring funds could be created to acquire the ownership stakes now held by banks or the state. Even if these funds remain publicly owned they can be privately managed.

One source of Korea's recovery is its relatively competent, meritocratic bureaucracy that now manages the financial system much the way it did under General Park Chung Hee.[3] Thus Korea's experience offers few lessons that can be copied by other crisis countries, most of which do not have Korea's bureaucratic capacity.

The government took a large stake in the financial sector and that stake may rise in the future. Instead of a competitive financial system, Korea finds itself with a government-directed system of finance. The ten state banks now have 58 percent of market share. The policy mechanisms of government remain opaque. A situation now exists in which government can force private actors into agreements that they are not legally obligated to perform, leaving companies with no way to protect themselves from future governments that may choose to act in an arbitrary manner.

---

[3]Hilton L. Root, *Small Countries, Big Lessons: Governance and the Rise of East Asia* (London: Oxford University Press, 1996).

Despite the augmented governmental control over the economy, many say that they cannot distinguish which way the country is going. It is difficult to distinguish between rhetoric and reality because existing institutions are inadequate for the country to undertake needed reforms. Many insiders doubt that the bureaucracy is ready for reforms that would trim its role from the levers of economic decision making. But another interpretation is that lacking legislative or judicial capacity, Korea simply has no alternative but to fall back on its traditional strength—bureaucratic capacity. Although the instruments of the developmental state are still intact, they have been considerably weakened, leaving government without the tools to articulate or implement its vision as it was able to do in the past.

If a single universal message stands out from Korea's experience of procrastination in policy reform, it is that before the bailout, the overall condition of the economy was everybody's concern. After the bailout, each separate interest could ignore the overall plight of the nation in trying to feather its own nest. Crisis can bring change when the interests of key players are at stake. The rescue of Korea from immediate disaster leaves the President weaker vis-à-vis the groups whose cooperation he depends upon. With little reason to cooperate on future reforms, from which they had little to gain and much to lose, gridlock appears to be the most likely outcome in the short-run. While these influential groups represent but a minority, civil society is still relatively undeveloped. Korea's weak political parties are organized around regions and personalities so that political authority depends upon a few well-organized groups that are in many cases stronger than they were before the crisis.

Recovery without comprehensive reform is unlikely to be politically secure or socially durable. Although partial reform has opened the country to greater foreign ownership, it also makes the country ripe for future discord and social conflict. Labor has not gained management reform; enterprises have not gained the possibility of permanent layoffs; the industrial empires still have a politically driven credit system to exploit. The few winners now own more of what is profitable, being able to foist loss-making activities onto the public. Labor has taken a beating, gaining nothing in return for what it has lost. The government now has the type of control over the financial system that it has not had since times of the developmental dictatorship. The public will be left with a huge bill for the recovery yet civil society has few ways to make its demands heard or to shape future policy. If the costs are not borne evenly, a populist backlash remains a distinct possibility; today's foreign investment may be the target for tomorrow's unrest.

Conclusion: Do Not Count on the Government

The government of Korea has not enjoyed enough support to implement the comprehensive reform program envisioned by President Kim. The voices for change have not been sufficiently strong, largely because political parties and voluntary associations are still embryonic. The parliamentary elections of 2000 further weakened Kim's ability to effect deep change. Without coordinated political reform, brokered by well-organized political parties, progress in legal reform is likely to be piecemeal and haphazard. However, where government has failed, necessity may still succeed. With the banks still years away from a full recovery and labor having suffered severe losses, the pre-crisis business environment will not return.

Certain changes seem likely despite the hesitant legislative progress. Even without the enactment of liberal labor legislation, the labor market may become more flexible. Contract labor, once instituted, may never be rescinded. Temporary layoffs may be temporary for so long that many workers will find new employment, most likely on a contract basis.

Changes in the legal and policy framework will not be the benchmark for wider changes occurring in the economy. While efforts to clean up the financial regulatory regime drag on, the search for new sources of capital will require that firms change. They will have to seek market-based financing because Korea's banks will be too weak to sustain future growth. The quest for equity finance and the rise of Internet transactions will motivate the *chaebols* to change their management practices. Attracting finance from outside the region will compel a focus on shareholder value and levels of disclosure beyond what is required by Korean law. Eventually, to woo international shareholders, a new generation of internationally trained professionals will run companies, hired and fired by independent boards. Companies will become more transparent, despite governmental gridlock, because the firms that do not adopt tougher standards will fall behind while the companies that embrace market-based financing will enjoy significant advantages.

It seems certain that firms can no longer depend on easy credit with government directing the banks where to lend. The banks will have to be more selective, which will weaken the links between *chaebols* and politicians. New forms of financial intermediation, Internet banks, bonds, equities, and venture funds will take the place of bank loans. The surviving banks will be forced to focus more on consumer services and less on high interest margins from loans of dubious quality.

Durable recovery will depend on creating strong institutional foundations upon which a new generation of financial services can be sustained. Ultimately, a legal framework that includes strong provisions for bankruptcy and the protection of minority shareholder rights will be needed to undergird effective capital markets. These changes will ensure capital-market competition, and the sooner they are institutionalized the more certain the economy will be able to resist future shocks. Competition in the financial sector is the best hope to foster a sound and prudently run banking system.

BIBLIOGRAPHY

Ábel, István, Pierre L. Siklos, and István P. Székely. *Money and Finance in the Transition to a Market Economy.* Aldershot: Edward Elgar, 1998.

Anderson, Ronald W., and Chantal Kegels. *Transition Banking: Financial Development of Central and Eastern Europe.* Oxford University Press, 1998.

Balcerowicz, Leszek, Cheryl W. Gray, and Iraj Hoshi. *Enterprise Exit Processes in Transition Economies.* Central European University Press, 1998.

Chang, Chun. *The Informational Requirement on Financial Systems at Different Stages of Economic Development: The Case of South Korea.* University of Minnesota. January 26, 2000.

Claessens, Stijn, Simeon Djankov, and Daniela Klingebiel. *Financial Restructuring in East Asia: Halfway There?* Washington, D.C.: World Bank, September 1999.

Claessens, Stijn, Semeon Djankov, and Larry Lang. "Who Controls East Asian Corporations?" Policy Research Working Paper 2054. Washington, D.C.: World Bank, 1999.

Hall, Thomas W. *Economic Policy and Financial Sector Reform in Emerging Markets: The Case of Central and Eastern Europe.* Ph.D. dissertation. Los Angeles: University of Southern California,1999.

Korea Economic Institute of America and the Korea Institute for International Economic Policy."The Korean Economy in an Era of Global Competition." Symposium. Washington, D.C.: George Washington University, September 17–18, 1999.

Korea website, http://www.fsc.go.kr

Korea website http://www.mofe.go.kr.

La Porta, Rafael , Florencio Lopes de Silanes, and Andrei Shleifer. "Law and Finance," *Journal of Political Economy*, vol. 106 (1998), pp. 1113–55.

Lieberman, Ira W., and William P. Mako. *Korea's Structural Reform. Korea's Economy 2000,* vol. 16. Korea Economic Institute of America, Washington, D.C., 2000.

Mo, Jongryn. *The Political Economy of Financial and Corporate Restructuring in Korea.* CIS Policy Analysis Series 00-1. Seoul: Yonsei University, February 15, 2000.

_____. *The Political Origins of the Asian Economic Crisis: Democracy, Gridlock, and Failed Economic Reforms in South Korea.* Seoul: Yonsei University, and Stanford, Calif.: Hoover Institution, August 24, 1998.

Ramos, Roy. *Financial Restructuring Scorecard.* Hong Kong: Goldman Sachs, 1999.

Root, Hilton L. *The New Korea: Crisis Brings Opportunity.* Milken Institute Policy Brief. Santa Monica, Calif.: Milken Institute, February 1999.

Root, Hilton L. *Small Countries, Big Lessons: Governance and the Rise of East Asia.* London: Oxford University Press, 1996.

_____, Mark Andrew Abdollahian, and Jacek Kugler. "Economic Crisis and the Future of Oligarchy", *Institutional Reform and Democratic Consolidation in Korea,* ed. Larry Diamond and Doh Chull Shin. Stanford, Calif.: Hoover Press. 1999, pp.199–232.

_____, James R. Barth, Daniel E. Nolle, and Glenn Yago. *Choosing the Right Financial System for Growth.* Milken Institute Policy Brief. Santa Monica, Calif.: Milken Institute, February 28, 2000.

_____, J. Edgardo Campos. *The Key to the East Asian Miracle: Making Shared Growth Credible.* Washington, D.C.: The Brookings Institution, 1996.

Shifting Towards the New Economy: Korea's Five-Year Economic Plan, 1993–1997. Seoul: Korea Institute for International Economic Policy, July 1993.

Yoo, Seong-min, Korean Business Conglomerates: Misconceptions, Realities and Policies. Korea's Economy 1995. Washington: Korea Economic Institute of America, 1995.

_____, Evolution of Government-Business Interface in Korea: Progress to Date and Reform Agenda Ahead, working paper. Seoul: Korean Development Institute, November 1997.

Sustainable Development and the Open Door Policy in China

A Paper from the Project on Development, Trade and International Finance

James K. Galbraith and Jiaqing Lu

A Council on Foreign Relations Paper

Sustainable Development and the Open Door Policy in China

James K. Galbraith and Jiaqing Lu

INTRODUCTION

How can one best explain China's remarkable economic growth during twenty-one years and its rise from autarky to world economic power? The exercise requires chutzpah; it demands a simplification; it cries out for the trained capacity to present a unifying theme with a weighty set of policy implications.

Fortunately the academic establishment possesses these traits in abundance. Examples range broadly from the socialist romantics[1] to the capitalist romantics[2]; the former believing that China has developed its own and specifically non-capitalist path, the latter that it is transforming itself into a free-market system. The two camps hurl paper missiles at each other in a satisfying postlude to the Cold War.[3]

But this battle is not, alas, about China. At least, it is not about China *specifically*. It is about economics, the economics

---

[1] Barry Naughton, *Growing Out of the Plan* (Cambridge: Cambridge University Press, 1995)

[2] Jeffrey D. Sachs and Wing Thye Woo, "Understanding China's Economic Performance," NBER Working Paper no. 5935 (Cambridge, Mass.: National Bureau of Economic Research, 1997).

[3] See Thomas G. Rawski, "Reforming China's Economy: What Have We Learned?" *The China Journal*, no. 41 (January 1999), pp. 139–56; and Wing Thye Woo, "The Real Reasons for China's Growth," *The China Journal*, no. 41 (January 1999), pp. 115–37.

profession, the indoctrination of students and policy analysts, and the politically and academically correct set of beliefs for those who practice development. As a result, it bears an eerie resemblance to the long history of policy discussions in China itself, which similarly are not about the actual problems of the country. Rather, they focus on the correct line and the ascendancy of adherents of one line over the adherents of another.

> *"We must stick unflinchingly to the socialist road. The road is tortuous and the struggle intense. But the future is undoubtedly bright."*

To get beyond this point, it helps to adopt an analytical framework that is rooted in the tortured history of China and of the People's Republic itself. We do not claim that what follows presents a definitive view. It is, rather, an attempt to point to the main features of the scene, and to place some of the otherwise perplexing developments since 1978, and recent choices, in their own context. Our thesis is that while political discourse in China reflects the larger intellectual conflicts familiar in the West, most decisions of policy are rooted in conditions and struggles inside China, and reflect both continuity and change in internal institutions of very long standing, rather than the import of models from the outside.

BUDGET DEFICITS AND CULTURAL REVOLUTION

First, a basic fact. Under the traditional system in China, both after the Revolution of 1949 and beforehand, fiscal process was the linchpin of the entire economy. The government collected revenue and then allocated funds to various entities and activities in China through its budget and expenditure management system. In particular, government capital spending was the dominant investment source. Therefore, the fiscal situation of China prior to economic reform almost completely reflected China's economic health. Even as late as 1994, when one of us began service as a technical adviser to the State Planning Commission, the term "macroeconomic control" meant public fiscal control almost to the exclusion of other connotations.

Thus the catastrophe of the Great Proletarian Cultural Revolution, beginning in 1966 and lasting for a decade, presented itself to the Chinese leadership as first and foremost a fiscal problem. The decade of debate, political struggle, and factional fighting, the decimation of the civil administration and the professions, and the shutdowns of schools and factories, had led the economy to the verge of collapse. All of the previous factors dramatically reduced the government's tax revenue, and the budget deficit in 1976 reached 10 billion yuan[4] for the first time in China's history[5]. The situation was further worsened by a series of events, including the 1976 earthquake in Tangshang and the death of Chairman Mao.

---

[4]The Chinese currency is the Renmimbi (RMB); the unit is the yuan. As China was isolated from the world economy at this time there is no very meaningful conversion rate between yuan and dollars for this period, especially for large budget and national accounting measures.

[5]Unless specified otherwise, all data cited in this paper are based on the *China Statistical Yearbook* 1997, and on *Key Indicators of Developing Asian and Pacific Countries*, 1992 and 1997 issues.

Aware of the peril, Party Secretary Hua Guo-Feng[6] launched a round of modernization known as the *Yang-mao-jin* (or Great Leap Forward by Imitating and Importing from the West), in the hope that China could invest its way out of trouble. But this program only worsened the situation. Overspending on capital investment and imports caused overheating, which led to a more than 52-billion-yuan deficit in the government's capital investment account. In 1979, China's current budget deficit surged to more than 17 billion yuan (more than 20 billion according to some sources), of which about 5 billion was associated with the China-Vietnam border war.[7] Overall deficits accounted for 17.7 percent of Chinese GDP in 1979. Chinese leaders had to find a way out, and this mundane fact, rather than philosophical change or ideological revelation, prompted the first wave of reforms.

---

[6]Chinese names are normally presented family name first. Here we adhere to that convention, except for references to published work, where we respect the Western order for bibliographic clarity.

[7]Tiejun Wen, "Four Cyclical Economic Crises in China". http://forum50.cei.gov.cn/. Beijing: China Economic Information Network, 1999.

BOTTLENECKS AND HEAVY INDUSTRY

The failure of *Yang-mao-jin* was rooted in the critical imbalance of China's industrial structure. By military necessity and from Soviet example, China had long targeted heavy industry as its strategic industrial sector. China's industrial strategy was reflected in the pattern of state control. In industry[8], the state had a dominant share. Sixty-six percent of State-Owned Enterprises' net fixed assets in 1978 were in industry, while agriculture accounted for only 2.8 percent of state assets. Also in 1978, SOEs accounted for 77 percent of gross industrial output and 78 percent of urban employment—74.5 million of 95 million workers. But 76.3 percent of total employment was rural, and there the state had never taken any significant share.

This heavy-industry-oriented, urban-development, state-sector policy carried an intrinsic flaw. Over time, it became obvious (as it had in Russia) that the strategy was bottlenecked by the underdevelopment of other sectors. As a result, it became a typical practice that whenever bottlenecks occurred, the government temporarily slowed down the expansion in heavy industry and allocated some resources to the bottlenecking sectors—light industry—a so-called readjustment process. Yang-mao-jin therefore put money into a sector that was already overbuilt, with the result that efficiency gains were nil while bottlenecks arose very fast.

Agriculture had of course suffered from the orientation of policy toward heavy industry. China is basically an agricultural country, and agriculture was the major income source for more than 800 million people of the one billion population in the late 1970s. Farm technology was still very primitive, and extremely labor-intensive. Output per capita in 1978 in rural China was 174 yuan, com-

---

[8]Industry was defined by China as all sectors excluding agriculture, construction, commerce, grain and foreign trade, urban public utilities, transportation, postal services, and telecommunications.

pared to a GDP per capita of 360 yuan. People were starving in many of the remote regions. To increase agricultural output was therefore not only a means of solving the imbalance problem (hence the budget deficit problem), but was also a way to increase incomes that might in turn build demand for other industrial sectors. In other words, in 1979 structural and Keynesian remedies converged at a moment of fiscal crisis.

THE AGRICULTURAL REFORM

At the same time, conditions in Chinese agriculture in the late 1970s presented major opportunities; the potential rewards to policy change were not only high, but were known to be high by the national leadership.

Much has been made, of course, of the effects of the People's Communes on agricultural productivity in China and their responsibility for the low living standards of the countryside. It is true that under the communes farm incomes were low, and investment even lower. But collective agriculture in China did not resemble that of the Soviet Union. It was not driven by a desire to realize economies of scale, and did not lead to the gigantism of the Soviet agricultural machinery industries, with their fleets of *traktorii* churning dust on the steppe.

Moreover, weak control by the state meant relatively large freedoms in the rural regions. Even after People's Communes were implemented, farmers still had their own small vegetable plots (*Zi Liu Di*, or The Land Left for Family), allocated by family size. And in many regions, families might also have a piece of mountain land that supplied their fuel for cooking and heat. Several families might also share the rights to a pond for fishing and irrigation; though the reservoirs were usually owned by either the village or the commune.

Because of these spheres of private control, so-called free-trading-markets or agriculture-trading-markets remained active in China, even through the Cultural Revolution. Launching reform first in rural areas was therefore quite a simple matter: it meant only allocating the land owned by the village to the families, and declaring that farming tools owned by villages were to be shared by farmers. These were little steps. This is important, because in the early stage any policy that radically challenged state ownership might have incurred a backlash.

Furthermore, for those leaders who launched the reform, these steps were relatively easy for another reason: they had been tried before. After the Great Leap Forward collapsed China's economy in early 1960s, Deng Xiaoping and Liu Shaoqi had launched agricultural reform, using the same prescription. Their programs dramatically increased rural income and productivity, improved agricultural supply, ended the famine of 1960–62, and to a great extent, facilitated the mini-boom in 1963–66. Mao's Cultural Revolution—with its productivity-depressing "work point" system and campaigns against market activity—was, in part, a reaction to the success of these measures, a reaction that finally ended Liu's life and sent Deng to labor camp. Fifteen years later, Deng relaunched the interrupted reform. To some extent, one may say that Deng simply fought the old enemy—the collapsing economy—using the old weapon of agricultural reform.

It is well known that China's agricultural reform was very successful. Our point is that the policy was not new to most Chinese in late 1970s, because it was simply the same policy as that of the early 1960s. According to the so-called Household Responsibility System, lands owned by villages and People's Communes were allocated to the household, as were other production resources such as mountains, small ponds, and farming tools. Work points were eliminated, and markets opened. The policy dramatically enhanced, or more precisely, restored, farmers' motivation, and also increased both output and productivity. Agricultural output increased 126 percent from 1978 to 1984, and agricultural output per rural laborer increased by 113 percent. During this period, China's growth of agricultural output outpaced GDP growth by about 28 percentage points (from 1978 to 1984, GDP increased 97.8 percent). As a result, the agricultural share in total GDP grew from 28.1 percent to 32 percent. Food poverty declined very sharply. Of great importance, the rural share in total national saving deposits increased significantly: from 26 percent in 1978 to 36 percent in 1984.[9]

---

[9]Authors' calculation, based on the data sources stated in the Footnote 4.

AUXILIARY REFORMS IN LIGHT
INDUSTRY AND COMMERCE

There were several other efforts at this stage, including the Open Door policy, industrial structure adjustment, and decentralization in domestic commerce. We will reserve the Open Door policy for a later section; the latter two issues will be discussed briefly here.

At the same time as the agricultural reforms, Chinese leaders launched efforts to redress the imbalance between light and heavy industries. In early 1979, the Chinese Communist Party decided to accelerate development in light and textile industry, planning to make the growth of these sectors match or slightly exceed that of heavy industry. Later that year, the State Planning Commission set detailed priorities to guarantee the implementation of the light industry strategy. The package of favorable policies affected energy supply, transportation, bank credit, and foreign exchange for imports. As a result, construction investment in light industry increased dramatically, from an annual average of 1.35 billion yuan during 1953–78 to 4.2 billion yuan during 1979–84.[10]

To facilitate reform in both agriculture and light industry, China also began to reform its highly centralized and rigid commercial sector. Wholesale and retail sectors were granted more autonomy. In the services sector, particular emphasis was placed on transferring state-owned food services to communities or leasing them to individuals. At the same time, the agricultural price system was reformed and prices were adjusted up significantly. The categories of goods covered by the central plan were reduced from 274 in 1978 to 115 in 1982, and then to 60 in 1984.[11] The traditional "Centralized purchase and centralized selling" system was broken up.

---

[10]Jiaqing Lu, *Inequality and Industrial Change in China and Financial Crisis in Thailand*, Ph.D. Dissertation (University of Texas at Austin, 1999).

[11]Editing Department of the Serial Books on China's Market Economy Building (EDSB), *Volume 25: Commercial Economy* (Taiyuan, China: Shanxi Publishing House, 1994).

THE SECOND PHASE: URBAN
ECONOMIC REFORM 1984–88

With rising agricultural output and productivity, nonagricultural industries also emerged in rural areas. Township and Village Enterprises (TVEs) developed quickly, because of the autonomy they enjoyed in the countryside: no plan, no control. By contrast, SOEs in urban areas were constrained by both ideology and the plan, and they still operated at a loss and without motivation to reform. After a debate in 1983 and early 1984, China decided to reform its SOEs under a modified planning economy: it would become a planned commercial economy, in which "commercial economy" was used as verbal substitute for market economy at that stage.

In October 1984, the Communist Party issued "Decisions about Economic System Reform," which outlined China's second stage of reform. This outline was very ambitious. It tried to reform virtually every aspect of the economy, including the enterprise system, plan, material supply, labor and wages, finance, commerce, prices, and fiscal and tax policy. The overarching framework was to change the type of reform pursued in China's economy from a single or isolated approach (such as reform in agriculture) to multiple and coordinated approaches (pluralistic approaches). The leadership wanted to deepen reform in rural area and allow TVE development, for instance, and at the same time reform SOEs so that there would be multiple ownership (cross-ownership) in urban areas in every aspect of the economy at once. At the micro level, enterprise reforms would go alongside such macro measures as fiscal, tax, and financial reforms.

In the event, the package proved too ambitious. Some of the new reforms, such as tax reform and further decentralization in SOEs and commerce, were successful. Others, such as financial reform and establishing a central-commercial bank system, made little progress. Thus, while fiscal reform and decentralization did give more motivation to local governments, the slow progress in banking reform led to incubation of localism and regional protection. Local officials forced banks to expand credits, even though the central government called for tightening. Local governments' purchasing increased, investment kept expanding, the economy overheated, and inflation went up. Traditional central control and adjustment instruments worked less effectively. In a long-familiar pattern, because the central government had lost control over the whole economy, fiscal conditions had worsened, and this became once again the signal for retrenchment.

THE TRANSITORY PERIOD (1988–91): ADJUSTMENT AND CRISIS

The difficulties of second-stage reform led to a second round of macroeconomic adjustment, beginning after the summer of 1988. At the same time, ideological debate heated up about the role of planning vis-à-vis the market economy. The debate centered on whether reform since 1984 had become too radical. Some Chinese leaders thought the reform itself had fueled overheating and inflation during this stage. Furthermore, the reforms involving decentralization had weakened the Communist Party leadership.

Then came the Tiananmen Square incident of early June 1989, itself brought on by widespread discontent with inflation. The June 4 crisis gave those who opposed reform more ammunition, and new initiatives in most areas came to a halt. Indeed, the adjustment was overdone; after 1990 the Chinese economy fell into a slump. When the slump became apparent, the government reacted as it had in 1976, by pouring funds into the SOEs in the hope that they might lead economic recovery. But help for the SOEs came far too late. In many cases their inefficiency was irreparable, and often the inflow of funds served only to prevent default on the SOEs' massive debts to state-owned banks. As a result, chain or triangle debt flows prevailed and the real economy showed little improvement. Clearly, yet another new round of reforms would be required.

THE THIRD ROUND OF REFORMS: 1992–97

China launched its new round of reform in 1992, on Deng Xiaoping's urging that the country create a "socialist market economy." Though still very ambitious, the new policy was much more sophisticated than the 1984 package. It covered areas such as fiscal reforms, taxation, the investment system, foreign capital policy, the foreign exchange system, and the banking system. Also, more favorable conditions were granted to foreign firms that invested in China.

Among the most significant aspects of the post-1992 reforms were the following measures:

- A goal was set to transform China's banking system into a U.S.-style central bank-commercial bank system. This goal was first enunciated in 1984, at the beginning of the second-round reforms, which were aimed at transforming the People's Bank of China into a central bank. At that time a deposit reserve system was created and reserve ratios were established. But the PBC's transformation didn't really start until three banks designed specifically for making policy loans were created in 1994 and a central bank law issued in 1995. The policy loans of China's four largest banks were transferred to the newly created policy banks, so that the big four might more easily make their transformation into commercial banks. Changing the People's Bank into a central bank meant major transfers of power from local officials, which in turn met heavy resistance from both the central bank and local governments. Overall, however, the reform proceeded as scheduled.

- On taxes, China created a system similar to that of the United States. Local and central tax collection were separated, which increased revenue for both local and central government. On the other hand, the reform also separated the obligations of central and local governments, streamlined the fiscal budget process, and made it more efficient.

• On January 1, 1994, China merged its official exchange rate with the trading market rate, and created a single exchange-rate system under a managed floating regime. At the same time, it made the Chinese renmimbi convertible under current account, a step that was believed not to be feasible before the year 2000.

• Finally, with respect to the SOEs, the new round of reforms made significant progress in establishing modern enterprise systems, especially share-holding systems. Many money-losing SOEs were either shut down, merged, or sold. Those survived were streamlined and began to operate under the new system.

With these reform policies in place, as well as a newly lowered interest rate, the economy burst to expansion. But the honeymoon did not last long. Real estate and capital investment fueled economic overheating, bottlenecks in the construction and investment sectors emerged, and double-digit inflation returned. Beginning in late 1993, economic policy was tightened again. Unfortunately for China, the difference between 1979 and 1992 is that in the latter period there were no longer large and easy gains to be had from fairly simple policy measures.

Since 1993, Chinese economic policy has in fact been comparatively tight. While growth has remained rapid by world standards, it has been far below what would have been required to absorb the massive increases in the urban labor force. Thus, while many Western observers continue to think of the Chinese experience as a success—partly because living standards continue to rise, partly because they compare it with crisis-ridden situations of Asia and Latin America, and partly because foreign investors have not suffered systemic losses in China—from a Chinese perspective the situation actually more closely resembles a crisis. The elements of this crisis include banking and debt problems, not to mention massive unemployment. To interpret the crisis, one should avoid falling into the tired argument as to whether it represents a crisis of socialism or of transformation. We believe that the problems in the 1990s fall into the classic pattern of reform-boom-overcapacity-bad debt-credit crunch-slump, already seen on numerous earlier occasions.

China experienced a real estate boom in 1992 and an investment boom in 1992 and 1993. Compared with the average growth rate of 18 to 25 percent in normal times, investment growth rates were 44 percent in 1992, rising to 62 percent in 1993, and falling back to 30 percent in 1994. Most of the new credits were extended to real estate and to the money-losing SOEs, where they fueled overcapacity in both of these sectors. Even worse, most of capacity expansion was at low levels of technology, and often highly redundant. For example, there are hundreds of automakers, most of which produce old-model and low-quality vehicles. Some of them can't sell one car a year. But still many local governments wanted to join in the race to develop the auto industry as a local "pillar industry," and so loans to the automotive sector continued.

To cool down the economy in the face of these structural problems, China has maintained a tight monetary policy since 1993. With high interest rates, demand growth became weak. At the same time, China began to reform its social-welfare system and its housing and education system, and Chinese people became more risk-averse. This deepened the structural imbalance, and consumer demand weakened further. It is true that the demand for housing loans, education loans, insurance policies, and other credit services grew. However, the financial sector had been so underdeveloped that these services barely existed beforehand. In a classic replay of the old pattern, reform and growth in one area generated a demand for linkages that could not be provided, and bottlenecks stalled the reform.

In the meantime, banking reform began. The transformation from policy banks to commercial banks reduced credit availability to the SOEs. This worsened the situations of SOEs, who have so far relied on banks for capital. Many defaulted on their loans.

In short, overcapacity, structural imbalance, weak demand due to risk-aversion (which, in turn, was due to slow progress in setting up a functional social-welfare system), and banking reform were the major factors behind the problems in China in 1990s. This is ironical and paradoxical, because risk-aversion resulted from enterprise overhaul and massive layoffs, and from the reforms in housing, education, and medical service. These reforms may yield long-term benefits. But they do have short-term adverse effects, and sometimes very fatal side effects. Can China's reform and policy and overall economy survive that long? The question is open, and we will return to it after discussing the Open Door policy.

THE OPEN DOOR POLICY—WHAT WAS IT?

The Open Door policy consists of two major types of policy change: the opening up of geographic regions to foreign investment, and the opening of specific institutions nationwide.

The geographic opening began in July 1979, when China granted the frontier provinces of Guangdong (bordering Hong Kong) and Fujian (across the strait from Taiwan) preferential policy flexibility. In May 1980, the Shengzhen, Zhuhai, Shantou, and Xiamen Special Economic Zones were created. In February 1982, the Yangtze River Delta, Zhu River Delta, and three other regions in Fujian, Liaonin, and Shandong were opened. In May 1984, fourteen additional coastal cities were opened. In 1988, Hainan Island Province—heretofore a fishing community—became the largest Special Economic Zone.

During the new round of reform in the 1990s, Pudong of Shanghai was opened first. In 1991, four border cities on the China-Russia frontier were opened. In August 1992, fifteen more hinterland cities were opened, and since that time, major cities all over China have followed suit.

Compared to the speed of geographic opening, institutional openings for foreign trade and foreign capital were slower, and have always been driven by the geographic opening.

China's sectoral opening policies have included:

With respect to trade: China has implemented a progressive decentralization of its foreign trading system and a system of export tax refunds. Moreover, it has applied the corporate system to foreign trading companies. Later, an export promotion policy was launched, which included further decentralization, introduction of the market system into foreign trade, and reform of the foreign exchange system. The Chinese currency became convertible under current account, non-tariff barriers have been cut (reducing import quotas and shortening the control list), and tariffs reduced. Most recently, of course, China has been negotiating its entry into the World Trade Organization, and further major reductions of tariffs and trade barriers are in prospect.

With respect to capital flows: In 1979, the joint venture law was issued, and foreign investment in Special Economic Zones and other coastal cities was encouraged. Later on, China improved its law and regulatory system, and began to guide foreign capital to regions or industrial sectors preferred by China. Until 1997, China's policy was to encourage foreign capital in manufacturing and other industrial sectors. By contrast, services were not a priority. Since 1997, however, various services have begun to enter China. Several foreign banks have been allowed to offer Renmimbi service. Overall China's policy was to encourage foreign direct investment (FDI), but at the same time to maintain central control of foreign borrowing and to discourage portfolio inflows. By early 1997, there was a plan to open the capital account, but the Asian crisis interrupted it.

THE ROLE OF THE OPEN DOOR POLICY

From a closed economy at the end of the 1970s, by the mid-1990s China had become the world's eleventh-largest trading country. Its openness (measured by total foreign trade as percentage of GDP) increased from 17 percent in 1978 to about 40 percent in the mid-1990s. Foreign capital investment also surged; China has become the second hottest investment destination country, second only to the United States. During the surge period of 1990 to 1996, China attracted $230 billion of foreign capital, accounting for 20 percent of total capital flows to developing countries in the period.

Chinese leaders well understand that they need capital from external sources to finance their development goals, and that they need it on terms they can afford. China's capital inflow has three characteristics under its overall open door policy package:[12]

- China has encouraged FDI. As a matter of policy and fact, external borrowing kept shrinking during this time, while FDI continued to rise. FDI is more stable than bank lending, and it can also generate industrial capacity and improve infrastructure. Finally, it is less sensitive to interest-rate fluctuations and other short-term macroeconomic factors. FDI management is also highly decentralized while foreign borrowing is relatively centralized; thus the borrower is in a relatively stronger position in dealing with FDI investors than with banks.

- China relies on developed countries for loan and debt inflow, but on Hong Kong and Taiwan for FDI. Actually, attracting capital from the large and wealthy populations of overseas Chinese was the initial motivation for China's Open Door policy, especially for its Special Economic Zones. This has, of course, proved very successful.

---

[12]Jiaqing Lu, *Capital Inflows in China: Challenges and Policies* (Taiwan: Eurasian Foundation, 1999).

The Open Door policy was also vital for meeting China's need for hard currency reserves and for paying for imports of capital equipment. From 1990 to 1996, average annual growth of exports was 16.6 percent; in 1996, manufacturing exports accounted for 85.5 percent of total exports. Mechanical and electrical goods had by that time replaced textiles as the biggest export item. In 1992, exports by foreign and joint ventures accounted for about 20 percent of total exports. But by 1996, this proportion reached 40 percent. In some coastal regions, it is as high as 50 to 60 percent.

• Finally, China's Open Door policy provides a means for importing technologies to which China would not otherwise have access. A notable example is aircraft; China has arranged with Boeing to assemble many of the passenger aircraft it purchases from that company.

In brief, China's Open Door policy is basically a mercantilist endeavor. Its goals are not a liberal trading order *per se*, but the accumulation of hard currency and technology, the encouragement of FDI, and the reduction of reliance on bank loans. In these respects, the Open Door policy has certainly contributed to relaxing supply constraints that might otherwise have derailed the reform process altogether. But it should not be mistaken for a policy of global integration and liberalization, nor has it ever been a major source of aggregate savings and investment in China. Whether this will change under the World Trade Organization agreements remains to be seen, and whether China will eventually take the risky step of capital account liberalization remains uncertain. It is difficult to see what China would gain from such a measure, and the cost of higher externally-induced instabilities would be a high one for the Chinese to pay.

THE CRISIS OF THE 1990s'

China in the 1990s faced problems not fundamentally dissimilar from those of the 1976–79 period: it had reached the limits of one type of expansion, and it needed the balancing effect of expansion in other sectors in order to move forward. However, while the path toward agricultural reform had been a familiar one in the early 1980s, the institutions of modern social, financial, and services sectors familiar in Western countries had never been properly developed in China. Slow progress in putting these institutions into place has emerged as a principal limitation on the rate of growth in China. The reaction of the authorities, which was to pursue a moderately tight policy, has led to deepening problems for the surviving state-owned enterprises, in turn leading to rising inequality of wages and earnings and massive unemployment.

In the new wave of economic reform, China began to overhaul its SOE system. The goal of the reform was to build a modern corporate system. Since then, many money-losing SOEs have been shut down, merged, or sold. This caused a sharp increase in unemployment. According to a study by Angang Hu, the government's reported registered unemployment rate was 3.1 percent in 1998.[13] But Hu's own estimate is 8 percent—a reasonable figure in our view. In 1998, new employment growth was 0.1 percent, the lowest since 1949. Overall unemployment, including layoffs and rural immigrants who lose their jobs, is higher still. Hu estimates urban unemployment at around 160 million and rural unemployment at 170 million, for a total of 330 million: a huge figure, and possibly exaggerated, but indicative nevertheless.

Living standards for those who lose their jobs are low. According to Hu, average monthly living fees a laid-off urban worker can get were 77.1 yuan in 1996, and 82.7 in 1997, about 15 percent of the

---

[13] Angang Hu, "China's Biggest Challenge in the New Millennium: High Unemployment" http://forum50.cei.gov.cn/. (Beijing: China Economic Information Network, 1999).

average monthly wage of Chinese workers in the same year. For those laid off in remote regions and provinces hosting large SOE's, particularly in northern China, the monthly living fees they can get are surprisingly low: Heilongjiang, 5 yuan per month, Qinghai, 25 yuan per month.

As a result of increasing restructuring and massive layoffs, inequality in China has jumped sharply since 1992. We have independent measures of this, which we computed from payroll and employment data by sector in the *China Statistical Yearbook*; these measures are presented in Figure 1. Our calculations—the between-groups component of Theil's T statistic—closely correspond to measures of the Gini coefficient recently prepared by Qiang Li of Qinghua University.[14] Figures 2, 3, and 4 show the regional pattern of rising inequality of wages and earnings, 1989–96. Inequality has gone up everywhere, but much more to the north and west than in the relatively prosperous southern and coastal regions, or in Beijing.

Unemployment and inequality are therefore major consequences of the 1990s reforms, even though average living standards continue to rise. In their efforts to combat these evils, the Chinese authorities face a perplexing dilemma. They have learned how to combat overheating, and to slow the economy down. But they have not developed effective means to bring it back to the high rate of growth required to absorb the newly unemployed. Indeed, price deflation has been under way since October 1997 and shows no sign of letting up. This is the legacy of incomplete sectoral development in the social sphere.

During the first months of 1998—in the wake of the Asian crisis and domestic economic slump—China began to loosen monetary policy. In addition to cutting interest rates twice, China also used both traditional and new monetary instruments to facilitate its monetary expansion. The package included removing the ceiling on commercial bank loans, encouraging commercial banks to increase loans to fixed-assets investment and to expand into con-

---

[14]Li Qiang, Presentation on Inequality in China at the Lyndon B. Johnson School of Public Affairs (University of Texas at Austin, March 2000).

sumption credits, and resuming the central bank's open-market operations. From 1998 to summer 1999, China has cut interest rates six times. Yet deflation has defeated these efforts: although nominal interest rates are low (around 5 percent to 6 percent in the summer of 1999), the real rate was still as high as about 10 percent. Therefore the squeeze on business profits remains as high as ever.

Fiscal policy has attempted to fill the gap. In 1998, China invested about 100 billion yuan in public facility and infrastructure, and in 1999, another 100 billion were expended. But fiscal policy of this kind runs into two limitations: bottlenecks in the construction sector, and the limited capacity of government to offset the massive fall of corporate investment. China's government—compared to that of the United States or Europe—is a small operation when one considers the ordinary function of government proper. Also in 1999, China began to increase living fees for laid-off workers. But a 30 percent across-the-board wage hike fell short in most Chinese regions because local governments did not have the money to fund it.

Part of the problem is the insolvency of the banking sector. Since 1994, China had made a series of reforms to strengthen its banks, but they are still loaded with bad loans from financing SOEs over the years. There are various estimates of the size of China's bad debt, but about 30 percent to 50 percent of total loans extended is a reasonable view. According to Fred Hu, restructuring the banking sector may end up costing 26 percent of GDP[15]—a very substantial sum by any standard. There are two models in restructuring the banking sector. One is the U.S. model. After the crisis in 1980s, the United States used the Resolution Trust Corporation and other instruments to liquidate the bad debts of the banking sector. After a restructuring and consolidation, the U.S. banking sector was restored to health. But in Europe, after the crisis, the region's governments supported their banking sectors in carrying the debt. They thought the debt would evaporate during the hoped-for recovery, as well as through profit. This is a slower path, and

---

[15]Fred Hu, *China's Banking Reform: A Long March*, Goldman Sachs Global Economics Paper no: 28 (1999).

it relies on a recovery actually occurring in spite of the banking problems. China is obviously following the European model, and a recovery is by no means assured.

The Asian crisis also complicated China's external trade. Devaluation in competitor countries made China face cheap competition from those countries, and also reduced demand in those countries for Chinese goods. As a result, China tried various policies to promote exports, while resisting devaluation of the renmimbi. Export tax refunds have been a major policy instrument in this regard, but China also used other policies, such as a campaign against smuggling. This campaign was aimed at curbing illegal imports, and thus at reducing the crowding-out effect of smuggling on domestic production.

THE OUTLOOK AND WHAT IS REQUIRED

The core problem is, as always: Can rapid growth be restored? Since 1994, GDP growth in China has decelerated almost continuously. While it is easy to blame either the traditional system or under-reform in the economy for the problems in the 1990s, we believe that the core of the core lies in the interplay of growth and modernization. Without major institutional innovations, high growth can not be restored. Whether the institutions can themselves be created in a climate of slow growth is a difficult and so far unresolved question.

Two important issues lie at the top of China's development agenda. One is the need to create a coordinating mechanism to overcome the cautiousness of free-market business actors in an unstable domestic and world environment. The other, closely related, is to establish a social welfare system, including a social security system and other supporting systems such as a consumption credit system, and a system for education credit and small business support. All these measures are needed in order to overcome the extreme risk aversion of household actors in an insecure world.

The traditional means of investment coordination in China has been well described by Huang[16]: it consisted of central government personnel rotating through provincial and municipal bureaucracies with the mission of assuring a unified pace of total investment. But once the bulk of investment migrated out to the business and corporate sectors, and once the provincial governments and SOEs no longer provided the bulk of investment demand, this tool is destined to lose its force. With indirect measures, such as the interest rate and credit policy, it is much easier to slow the growth of aggregate investment than to get it going again.

---

[16]Huang, Yasheng, *Inflation and Investment Controls in China : The Political Economy of Central-local Relations During the Reform Era*. Cambridge; New York: Cambridge University Press, 1996.

How is this issue handled in the West? Partly, by means of augmenting the purchasing power of consumers, through tax reductions. For this, a developed and centralized fiscal system is required; China does not yet have any such thing. And the modern history of the United States and Europe is replete with government credit initiatives—guarantees to agriculture, small business, housing, and so forth—that can be relied on to spur total effective demand. But such measures require the creation of flexible credit institutions that can extend and monitor loans to the smallest economic units in the country, including individual farms and households. Again, China does not yet have such institutions.

How did the consumption slump occur in the first place? Anti-inflation policies definitely played an important role. The boom of the early 1990s fueled rapid expansion in production capacity and economic growth. But aggregate demand was dramatically curtailed when the People's Bank adopted a tight policy in the wake of inflationary pressure in the fall of 1993. As a result, income growth slumped and so did consumption spending.

But more importantly, the current consumption slump was led by China's reform policies themselves, which have brought about structural shifts in consumption behavior, choice, and spending. In the fall of 1993, the Third Session of the Fourteenth Communist Party Congress outlined a series of key reforms. Since then, China has taken major strides in overhauling its SOEs and commercializing the housing system. This had several effects on the consumption pattern in China, and none of them were favorable.

First, the relative price or terms of trade between future consumption and current consumption has dramatically increased, because of an expected surge in the price of future consumption. Put simply, households realize that they will need to set aside current income for future use, to provide for housing and retirement. As a result, the purchasing power of the total budget for both plans decreases sharply, and current consumption declines significantly. What follows is a decline in total income, and the budget shrinks further.

While life is always full of uncertainty and insecurity, the price of bad outcomes or misfortunes was depressed to almost zero under the traditional system in China. The government offered almost everyone a job, there was no job insecurity, and while the future was uncertain no private means of insuring against it existed. The employer, or work unit, offered every family an apartment and collected only symbolic rents. Every worker had full medical coverage. Education, an investment to reduce uncertainty or get more security, was basically free. Finally, after a worker retired, he/she would receive 80 percent to100 percent of his/her last year's salary, depending on age at retirement. Moreover, workers carried over full medical coverage and other welfare packages.

But the reforms have been changing this pattern dramatically. Now, life security is becoming a private good, and very expensive to buy. As the ongoing economic restructuring continues, factories are shut down or merged, and thousands of workers are laid off or forced to retire early; those who have their jobs at the moment are paid a fraction of their official salaries. And this immediate problem is further compounded by the simultaneous reform efforts in areas such as housing, education, and the social welfare system. This means that the time of free housing, education, and medical services will be ended. Individuals will have to buy their shelter, invest in education, and pay for their health care.

In short, the early stages of reform worked in part because the *old safety net* was intact, and individuals felt at liberty to take risks. But now, the Chinese people are aware that the future is much more expensive and that life security costs dear. With a shrinking total budget, it is natural that individuals will scale down current consumption to make the future more affordable. Not surprisingly, savings increase sharply, and current consumption remains slack.

The problem is partly that Chinese people lack experience in managing risks after living in a risk-free society for decades. Dramatic changes in employment and social welfare conditions give them a huge psychological shock; and because the process is still going on, they seem not to know what will happen down the road.

Hence, they become overwhelmed by the future concern, and become extremely forward-looking. This future-overhang effect leads them to dramatically reduce current consumption in an effort to cover the worst ahead. They become more and more risk-averse, just as a very conservative person will spend most of his/her wealth in buying full insurance coverage for all he/she has. China is, in a word, in a pandemic of the Paradox of Thrift.

But there is a deeper issue as well. Not only do the Chinese people lack experience managing risks, but Chinese institutions to help them do so—in a capitalist as opposed to a communist setting— do not yet exist. Thus, the consumption slump has been worsened by lags in institutional design necessary to support the economic transition. Until a *new welfare* state comes into being, this problem will not go away. Specifically:

• There has been no consumption-enhancing mechanism such as a consumption credit market until most recently. Under the planning system, the economy was geared up for production, and consumption was a by-product. Actually, because increasing consumption would worsen the shortage and lengthen lines at outside stores and supply centers, it was rational for decision-makers in the old system to pursue a consumption-depressing policy, instead of consumption-enhancing policy. This now needs to change.

Generations of decision-makers since reform didn't feel the necessity to enhance consumption until the early 1990s, when housing reform was launched. Since there was no mortgage market in China, the sky-high price of apartments virtually scared all ordinary workers out of the housing market, and forced them to save more to afford an apartment in the future. There are similar stories in education reform, and in health care. This is in marked contrast to the Western system where consumers can use consumption-credit markets to spread the cost of housing or education over decades, and where private or public insurance similarly spreads the cost of health care.

- China didn't start to build a social welfare system for its economy until the SOE reform led to massive layoffs. As we mentioned earlier, under the traditional system, everyone had a life-time job, which also provided him or her with full medical coverage and generous retirement benefits.

While reform has been eliminating most of these benefits, the government came in only very late to build a social safety net to stabilize workers' income and share the cost of insecurity and misfortune. There is as yet no social security system, no effective unemployment insurance, no disability insurance. These systems, which so effectively maintain consumption standards among non-working populations in the West, are a critical missing element in Chinese economic reform until now. Moreover, Western advisers are enthusiastic about market systems to provide these forms of income insurance-exactly the wrong prescription for China at present. Thus, progress toward overcoming this institutional bottleneck is destined to be slow.

Because they have been so slow to build the consumption-credit system and social safety net, China's decision-makers have found that they can do very little to directly influence consumers' choices. In particular, the consumption credit market was so underdeveloped that interest-rate cuts failed to increase house sales and other demand for personal consumption credit.

In the meantime, the social safety net remains in very preliminary shape, and a three-pillar system consisting of contributions from workers, employers, and the government still looks to be a long way off. Also, the insurance industry in China is still dominated by two big state companies, and China has a long way to go before it will have an efficient and accessible insurance market. When all these factors are taken into account, it is not difficult to understand why today's future-overhang dominates Chinese society. It is also not difficult to understand why the drive to raise public spending—while it definitely did increase personal income—has so far failed to generate more consumption spending.

In sum, China's reform process has once again run into the bottleneck of an underdeveloped sector. But whereas in former times the bottlenecks occurred in agriculture or light industry, they arise today in the mechanisms of social insurance and social security that the advanced industrial democracies of the West have provided for themselves since the 1930s. China lacks sophisticated, accessible, affordable institutions of consumer, household, and agricultural credit, as well as broad-based mechanisms to support household income through tax and retirement systems. Without them, and without the pervasive security provided by the previous state system, Chinese households are unwilling to use their incomes for their own current consumption, and as a result the massively unemployed and underemployed labor force cannot be absorbed.

Is this a problem of the market, or of socialism? It is an empty and pointless question. Advanced Western market economies that fail to provide adequate assurances of social security suffer from exactly the same syndrome, and most of them have long since built institutions to overcome the difficulty. In other words, the correct way to analyze China is not as either a uniquely socialist or free-market economy. Rather, China should be analyzed as a developing country facing exactly the same range of fiscal, demand management, and sectoral-balance problems that all developing countries face, irrespective of the ideological terms they use to describe themselves. At the same time, however, analysts must recognize China's particular characteristics rooted in the evolution of its development up until now.

With this observation in mind, the way forward for China seems clear. More reform! More reform is always the solution, in China, for the deficiencies and difficulties of reform.

But this time, the reforms must truly move in a new direction for China. The new reforms must move toward the creation of market-friendly social welfare and credit systems. Moreover, such systems must be capable of creating for the Chinese people the framework of security that households, farms, and small businesses have enjoyed in the West during those periods of high prosperity and stability that have occasionally marked economic performance during the last century.

Whether such systems can, in fact, be developed under a Chinese leadership committed to a distorted free-market image of Westernization and under intense pressure to modernize by opening China to Western commercial institutions—without the benefit of the Western public institutions that accompany them in the West—remains a deep and troubling question.

* * * * * * * * * * * *

Figure 1

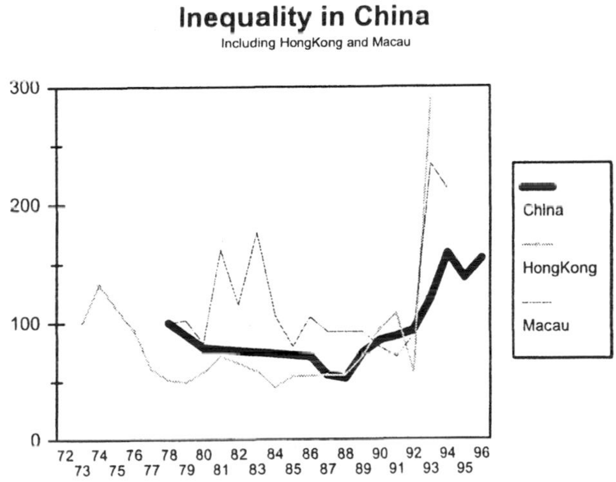

Inequality in China
Including HongKong and Macau

Data for Macau and Hong Kong are from the U.N. Industrial Development Organization (UNIDO); note that all series rise in 1993-94.

Figure 2

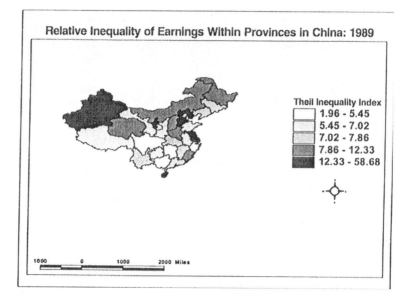

Figure 3

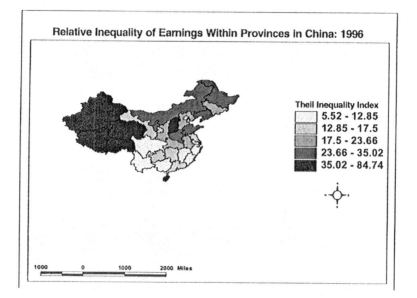

Figure 4

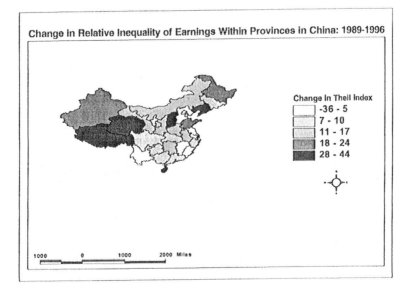

The measure is a between-groups component of Theil's T statistic computed by the authors across twelve major economic sectors for ßeach province and region in China; changes are simple differences in Theil scores. Theil methods are described in detail in working papers on the website of the University of Texas Inequality Project, at http://utip.gov.utxas.edu. ArcView ' GIS software courtesy of Environmental Systems Research, Inc.

BIBLIOGRAPHY

Asian Development Bank. *Key Indicators of Developing Asian and Pacific Countries*. Oxford: Oxford University Press, 1992.

_____. *Key Indicators of Developing Asian and Pacific Countries*. Oxford: Oxford University Press, 1997.

Editing Department of the Serial Books on China's Market Economy Building (EDSB). *Volume 25: Commercial Economy*. Taiyuan, China: Shanxi Publishing House, 1994.

Hu, Angang. China's Biggest Challenge in the New Millennium: High Unemployment. 1999. http://forum50.cei.gov.cn/. Beijing: China Economic Information Network, 1999.

Hu, Fred. *China's Banking Reform: A Long March*. Goldman Sachs Global Economics Paper no: 28, 1999.

Huang, Yasheng, *Inflation and investment controls in China : the political economy of central-local relations during the reform era*. Cambridge ; New York : Cambridge University Press, 1996.

Lu, Jiaqing. *Capital Inflows in China: Challenges and Policies*. Taiwan: Eurasian Foundation, 1999a.

_____. *Inequality and Industrial Change in China and Financial Crisis in Thailand*. Ph.D. dissertation. University of Texas at Austin, 1999b.

Li, Qiang. Presentation on inequality in China at the Lyndon B. Johnson School of Public Affairs. University of Texas at Austin, March 2000.

Naughton, Barry. *Growing Out of the Plan*. Cambridge: Cambridge University Press, 1995.

Rawski, Thomas G. "Reforming China's Economy: What Have We Learned?" *The China Journal*, vol. 41 (January 1999), pp. 139–56.

Sachs, Jeffrey D., and Wing Thye Woo. "Understanding China's Economic Performance." NBER Working Paper no. 5935. Cambridge, Mass.: National Bureau of Economic Research, 1997.

State Statistical Bureau, People's Republic of China. *China Statistical Yearbook*. Beijing: China Statistical Publishing House, 1997.

Wen, Tiejun. "Four Cyclical Economic Crises in China". http://forum50.cei.gov.cn/. Beijing: China Economic Information Network, 1999.

Woo, Wing Thye. "The Real Reasons for China's Growth." *The China Journal*, vol. 41 (January 1999), pp. 115-137.

The Paradox of Free-Market Democracy:
Indonesia and the Problems Facing Neoliberal Reform

A Paper from the Project on Development,
Trade and International Finance

Amy L. Chua

A Council on Foreign Relations Paper

The Paradox of Free Market Democracy: Indonesia and the Problems Facing Neoliberal Reform[1]

Amy L. Chua

INTRODUCTION

This paper will situate the recent problems in Indonesia in a more general framework that I will call the paradox of free-market democracy. The basic thesis I will advance is as follows. In Indonesia, as in many developing countries, class and ethnicity overlap in a distinctive and potentially explosive way: namely, in the form of a starkly economically dominant ethnic minority—here, the Sino-Indonesians. In such circumstances, contrary to conventional wisdom, markets and democracy may not be mutually reinforcing. On the contrary, the combined pursuit of marketization and democratization in Indonesia may catalyze ethnic tensions in highly determinate and predictable ways, with potentially very serious consequences, including the subversion of markets and democracy themselves. The principal challenge for neoliberal reform in Indonesia will be to find institutions capable of grappling with the problems of rapid democratization in the face of pervasive poverty, ethnic division, and an historically resented, market-dominant "outsider" minority.[2]

---

[1]This paper is based on other published articles.

[2]The recent crises in East Timor, Aceh, and the Moluccas are not the subject of this paper. Needless to say, Indonesia will also have to find ways of addressing separatist demands and ethnic conflict in its various regions as it pursues democratization and market reforms.

BACKGROUND

The Paradox of Free Market Democracy
I will begin by briefly explaining what I mean by the paradox of free-market democracy. It has to be remembered that there is a fundamental tension between the two major thrusts of international development policy: markets and democracy. Throughout the developing world, markets have characteristically produced wealth concentrated in the hands of a few. Thus, the introduction of democratic politics, which—at least theoretically—puts political power in the hands of the impoverished majority, will always be a source of tremendous potential instability. This is not a new point. Among many others, Adam Smith, David Ricardo, and James Madison all held that markets and democracy could coexist, if at all, only in fundamental tension with one another.[3] That is why these figures opposed universal suffrage, which according to Thomas Babington Macaulay, was "incompatible with private property" and thus "with civilization" itself.[4] From this point of view, free-market democracy is a paradox, a contradiction in terms.[5]

---

[3]James Madison, *Notes of Debates in the Federal Convention of 1787* (Ohio University Press, 1984), pp. 403–4; *The Works and Correspondence of David Ricardo*, vol. 7, Piero Sraffa ed. (Cambridge University Press, 1952), pp. 369–70; Adam Smith, *An Inquiry Into the Nature and Causes of The Wealth of Nations*, bk..V, ch.. I, pt. II (1776; Chicago: University of Chicago Press, 1976), p. 232

[4]Thomas Babington Macaulay, *Complete Writings*, vol. 17 (Houghton, Mifflin and Co., 1900), pp. 268.

[5]Many have discussed the "antagonistic symbiosis between democracy and market-capitalism." See Robert Dahl, *On Democracy* (New Haven, Ct.: Yale University Press, 1998), p. 161; James M. Buchanan, *The Limits of Liberty: Between Anarchy and Leviathan* (Chicago, University of Chicago Press, 1975), pp. 147–65; Jürgen Habermas, *The New Conservatism* (Shierry Weber Nicholsen, ed. & trans., MIT Press 1994) (1985), pp. 55–56; Charles E. Lindblom, *Politics and Markets* (New York: Basic Books, 1966), pp. 159, 161; Adam Przeworski, *The Neoliberal Fallacy, in Capitalism, Socialism, and Democracy Revisited*, ed. Larry Diamond and Marc F. Plattner (Baltimore: Journal of Democracy Publications, Johns Hopkins University Press, 1993).

As it turned out, of course, the paradox of free-market democracy did not prove insuperable. Far from it. In all the developed nations, this paradox has been successfully mediated by a host of institutions, substantially defusing the conflict between market-generated wealth disparities and majoritarian politics. One of most important challenges facing developing-world policymakers today is to identify these institutions and to think much more carefully and creatively about how analogous institutions might be promoted in the developing world. This is the subject of a much longer, forthcoming article I have written.[6]

The Problem of Market-Dominant Minorities and Ethnonationalism

For purposes of analyzing Indonesia, I will focus on a specific problem concerning the paradox of free-market democracy: the phenomenon of economically dominant ethnic minorities. In contrast to the Western nations and all of the East Asian Tigers, many developing countries have one or more ethnic minorities, who, for widely varying reasons, historically have dominated economically the "indigenous" majorities around them. The most prominent example is the Chinese throughout Southeast Asia. However, there are numerous other groups: Indians in East Africa and parts of the Caribbean, Lebanese in West Africa and parts of the Caribbean, Ibo in Nigeria, Kikuyu in Kenya, Bamileke in Cameroon, Tutsi in Rwanda, Russians (along with Germans, Ukrainians, and Koreans) in Central Asia, Whites in South Africa and Zimbabwe, Tamils in Sri Lanka, Bengalis in Assam-the list goes on, quite strikingly, as I have documented in detail elsewhere.[7] Moreover, in part because of historical or "path dependent" reasons, many economically dominant minorities will also tend to be *market-dominant*. In other words, their economic dominance will not dissipate but rather persist or even increase with privatization and other

---

[6]See Amy L. Chua, "The Paradox of Free Market Democracy: Rethinking Development Policy," *Harvard International Law Journal*, vol. 41 (Forthcoming Spring 2000).

[7]See Amy L. Chua, "Markets, Democracy, and Ethnicity: Toward a New Paradigm for Law and Development," *Yale Law Journal*, vol. 108, no. 1 (1998), pp. 21–26.

market-oriented reforms, at least in the near to midterm future.[8]
This certainly seems to be true of the "entrepreneurial" Chinese
minorities in Southeast Asia, who dominate the private sector and
often benefit disproportionately from foreign investment liberalization, privatization, and other market-oriented reforms.[9]

---

[8]As I discuss below in the context of the Indonesian Chinese, conventional wisdom
effectively assumes that market reforms will solve the problem of economically dominant minorities by eliminating monopolistic structures and by "leveling the playing
field." This might sometimes be the case—for example, if a particular ethnic minority
owes its economic dominance solely to political favoritism or military force. Unfortunately, the underlying causes of economic dominance are rarely so clear, and even if they
are, they will rarely prove tractable. The awkward reality is that many economically dominant minorities will also tend to be market-dominant. There are a number of reasons
for this. To begin with, "economic liberalization naturally favors private business while
reducing the role and influence of bureaucrats and the state."; see Linda Y.C. Lim and
L. A. Peter Gosling, "Strengths and Weaknesses of Minority Status for Southeast Asian
Chinese at a Time of Economic Growth and Liberalization," in Daniel Chirot and Anthony Reid, eds., *Essential Outsiders: Chinese and Jews in the Modern Transformation of Southeast Asia and Central Europe* (Seattle: University of Washington Press, 1997), pp. 285, 295.
Thus in the many developing societies in which the private sector is overwhelmingly dominated by a particular ethnic minority, economic liberalization will likely disproportionately benefit that minority, at least in the earlier years (or decades) of marketization. This
will be especially true where the economic regulations being swept away—and the state-
owned enterprises being dismantled—were originally established to curtail the economic dominance of the ethnic minority in question. Along the same lines, economically
dominant minorities frequently control (or at least are disproportionately represented in)
those sectors of the economy that are most attractive to foreign investors: for example,
finance, technology, industry, transport, and mining and other natural resources. Thus,
they often are better positioned to benefit from foreign investment liberalization (for example, in the form of lucrative joint ventures). Some of this market dominance may reflect
"superior entrepreneurialism," which itself can result from a number of factors, from culture to a history of political favoritism by colonial authorities. At the same time, more
invidiously, some economically dominant minorities may be market-dominant because,
like Whites in apartheid South Africa, they have oppressed the indigenous majorities
around them for so long that it will be decades before education levels and entrepreneurial
experience come close to being equalized. I discuss the causes of market dominance at
length elsewhere. See Chua, "Markets, Democracy, and Ethnicity," pp. 29–33.

[9]Indeed, as one source has put it (perhaps a little too vividly), the "rapid region-wide
economic growth" since the 1980s "has turned Southeast Asia into a 'South China Sea'
of ethnic Chinese capital and labor movements, greatly increasing the visibility and the
actual presence of both foreign and local Chinese in regional economies." See Lim and
Gosling, "Strengths and Weaknesses of Minority Status for Southeast Asian Chinese at
a Time of Economic Growth and Liberalization," p. 289. More recently, economic liberalization in Vietnam and Burma has led to a resurgence of Chinese commercial dominance in the country's urban areas. See Chua, "Markets, Democracy, and Ethnicity,"
pp. 22–23.

The phenomenon of market-dominant minorities has a number of sobering implications for neoliberal reform. Most crucially, the existence of market-dominant minorities, combined with other conditions prevalent throughout the developing world, converts the paradox of free-market democracy into an engine of potentially catastrophic ethnonationalism. This is because in developing countries with a market-dominant minority, *markets and democracy will tend to favor not just different people, or different classes, but different ethnic groups.* Markets will (by definition) benefit the market-dominant minority, while democracy will increase the power of the relatively impoverished majority. In these circumstances, the combined pursuit of markets and democracy will tend to produce an ethnically charged and highly unstable situation. More specifically, as I have modeled elsewhere,[10] in countries satisfying certain specified conditions, including economic underdevelopment and the presence of a market dominant minority, marketization and democratization will tend to produce highly determinate and potentially highly destructive ethnoeconomic and ethnopolitical consequences,[11] along the following lines.

First, by causing, maintaining, or exacerbating the disproportionate wealth of the market-dominant minority, marketization will cause, maintain, or exacerbate intense ethnic resentment among the impoverished, indigenous majority. Next, with democratization, this ethnoeconomic resentment will tend to be transformed into a potent ethnonationalist movement, in part because politicians will have powerful incentives to scapegoat the resented economically dominant minority and foment ethnic hatred to their advantage. The result of this process will often be the ethnicization of the paradox of free-market democracy. An aroused ethnonationalist majority will emerge. Perceiving markets as solely or principally benefiting a resented ethnic minority, that major-

---

[10] See Chua, "Markets, Democracy, and Ethnicity," pp. 33–56.

[11] To be clear, the suggestion is not that democracy is necessary (or more likely than authoritarianism) to trigger an ethnonationalist reaction. Rather, the point of the model is to explore the distinctive dynamics and problems that are likely to arise when markets and democratization are simultaneously pursued in the face of a market-dominant minority. See Chua, "Markets, Democracy, and Ethnicity."

ity will demand policies that will end the minority's economic dominance, so that the nation's wealth and identity can be reclaimed
by its "true owners." Under these circumstances, one of three
non-mutually exclusive outcomes becomes highly probable: (1) an
anti-market backlash targeting the market-dominant minority (for
example, through ethnically targeted nationalizations or economic restrictions); (2) actions aimed at eliminating the market-
dominant minority (for example, through expulsion or atrocity);
and (3) a pro-market retreat from democracy. As I have documented
in detail, each of these outcomes has occurred repeatedly throughout the developing world.[12] They are, however, perhaps most
vividly illustrated by contemporary Indonesia.

---

[12]See Chua, "Markets, Democracy, and Ethnicity."

INDONESIA

The Chinese in Pre-Colonial and Colonial Indonesia

As in all the Southeast Asian countries, the ethnic Chinese in Indonesia have long represented an economically dominant minority vis-à-vis the indigenous majority around them: in this case, the *pribumi* ("of the earth").[13] Indeed, the economic dominance of the Chinese in Indonesia predates Dutch colonialism by several centuries. According to Clifford Geertz, in pre-colonial Indonesia,

> all foreign trade in the [Tabanan] kingdom—the main export was coffee, the main import opium—was conducted by a single wealthy Chinese called a subandar, who held a royal monopoly in exchange for a suitable tribute, the remainder of the small resident Chinese population acting as his agents. Domestic trade was trifling . . .[14]

The Chinese began arriving "in large numbers in the nineteenth and early twentieth centuries, when the Dutch colonial government offered them both economic opportunity and a measure of

---

[13]This is by no means to suggest that indigenous Indonesians are homogeneous—nothing could be further from the truth. Indonesia's "nearly 200 million people are divided into hundreds of distinct cultural groups living for the most part in regional homelands, . . . from Aceh on the northern tip of Sumatra to Irian Jaya."; see R. William Liddle, "Coercion, Co-optation, and the Management of Ethnic Relations in Indonesia," in *Government Policies and Ethnic Relations in Asia and the Pacific*, ed. Michael E. Brown and Sumit Ganguly (Cambridge, Mass.: MIT Press, 1997), pp. 273, 274. "Typically, the members of each group speak their own language or dialect and have a strong sense of their distinctiveness" (ibid.). Among indigenous Indonesians, a principal "axis of conflict has been the relationship between the Javanese, who almost constitute a majority, and all the other groups, who have feared domination by the Javanese" (ibid., p. 279). Indonesians are divided along religious lines as well. Roughly 86 percent of the country is Muslim; most Balinese are Hindus, and "Protestant and Catholic adherents are heavily concentrated among specific regional ethnic groups" (ibid., p. 274).

[14]Clifford Geertz, *Peddlers and Princes: Social Change and Economic Modernization in Two Indonesian Towns* (Chicago: University of Chicago Press, 1963), pp. 25–26. Tabanan, a town in southwest Bali about twenty miles west of Den Pasar, is the former seat of a

personal security."[15] During the colonial era, wealthy Chinese
merchants, along with "Javanese aristocrats turned bureaucrats (*priyayi*),"
served as "local elite intermediaries" for the Dutch.[16] The main role
of the Chinese was to operate for the Dutch highly profitable "revenue farms and monopoly concessions for running local markets,
collecting fees, selling salt and opium, running pawnshops, and
so on. The most important of these from the 1850s to the 1880s
were the opium farms."[17] At the same time, Chinese moneylen-
ders dominated colonial Java's rural credit sector.[18] The result of
this "plural" colonial economic structure was the concentration of
economic power largely in Chinese and European hands and the
distinctly "inferior economic position of the Indonesians."[19]

The Dutch revenue farms were dismantled in the 1890s, which
caused the Chinese to seek "new investment opportunities in
kretek (clove) cigarettes, batik, and other industries hitherto dominated by the native bourgeoisie."[20] Thus, around the turn of the
century, the Chinese "came into direct conflict with a native class
for the first time in their history on the Indies."[21] As many scholars have noted, the emergence of Indonesian nationalism at the
turn of the century was inextricably bound up with "the sudden
increased impingement of aggressively competitive Chinese entrepreneurs upon the interests of the vestigial Javanese merchant class."[22]
The Sarekat Islam, Indonesia's "first popular native nationalist movement" (born in late 1911 in Central Java) was marked by "[v]iolent,
popular anti-Sinicism."[23]

---

[15]R. William Liddle, "Coercion, Co-optation, and the Management of Ethnic
Relations in Indonesia," p. 278.

[16]Takashi Shiraishi, *Anti-Sinicism in Java's New Order*, in Chirot and Reid, eds.,
Essential Outsiders, pp. 187, 195.

[17]Ibid.

[18]Ibid., p. 199.

[19]Frank H. Golay, Ralph Anspach, M. Ruth Pfanner, and Eliezer B. Ayal, *Underdevelopment and Economic Nationalism in Southeast Asia* (Ithaca, N.Y.: Cornell University Press, 1969), p. 115, see also pp. 113–18.

[20]Shiraishi, *Anti-Sinicism in Java's New Order*, pp. 187, 189.

[21]Ibid.

[22]George M. Kahin, *Nationalism and Revolution in Indonesia* (Ithaca, N.Y.: Cornell
University Press, 1952), p. 67.

[23]Shiraishi, *Anti-Sinicism in Java's New Order*, p. 187.

Post-Independence Indonesia under Sukarno and Suharto
Following independence in 1949, the relatively laissez-faire economic policies of the colonial period gave way to a period of
"professed socialist ideals." During the period of Guided Democracy (1959–65),[24] President Sukarno's nationalizations of land and
private enterprise targeted not just the British and the Dutch but
also, very explicitly, the ethnic Chinese—a concrete instance of the
first outcome noted above (ethnically-targeted anti-market backlash). Indeed, through nationalization and other measures of economic nationalism, Sukarno "indigenized" much of the
Chinese-dominated financial sector; sixty percent of Indonesia's
foreign trade; mining and most of the modern industrial sector;
and the greater part of Indonesia's importing trade, including
the lucrative, Chinese-controlled batik and rice sectors.[25] It is
important to recognize that Sukarno's nationalization programs
were far more an expression of ethnonationalism than of social
ism. Unlike in the former Soviet Union or China, Sukarno,
despite his occasionally Marxist rhetoric, never sought to eliminate the institution of private property or to level the class structure. On the contrary, Sukarno left the market system more or less
intact outside of the nationalized industries.

---

[24]"In July 1959, President Sukarno, in alliance with the central leadership of the
armed forces, decreed a return to the revolutionary constitution of 1945, under which the
president was the dominant actor in the political system. Suharto labeled his new regime
Guided Democracy (the Indonesian term is *Demokrasi Terpimpin*, which translates
more accurately as Democracy with Leadership). Although Sukarno did not have unlimited power, the system was in essence a presidential dictatorship."; see Liddle, "Coercion,
Co-optation, and the Management of Ethnic Relations in Indonesia," p. 287. Thus, Clifford Geertz has suggested that the differences between Sukarno's "old order" populism
and Suharto's "new order" paternalism "have been much exaggerated by the partisans of
both—their contrasts were mainly in style and presentation, and to some degree in dis-
ciplinary reach."; see Clifford Geertz, "Indonesia: Starting Over," *New York Review of
Books* (May 11, 2000), pp. 22, 24.

[25]See Amy L. Chua, "The Privatization-Nationalization Cycle: The Link Between
Markets and Ethnicity in Developing Countries," *Columbia Law Review*, vol. 95 (1995),
pp. 254, 269 (citations omitted). Despite his "indigenization" campaign, Sukarno was criticized by ethnic Indonesians for "his protective attitude to the Chinese minority," perhaps reflecting the gradual rapprochement under Sukarno between Indonesia and
China. See ibid., note 370, p. 269 (citation omitted).

By contrast, the thirty-year "capitalist-style" autocracy of General Suharto is a paradigmatic example of the third outcome noted above (pro-market retreat from democracy). After seizing power militarily in 1965, Suharto proceeded to quash rival political parties and to extinguish opposition of all kinds.[26] In return for the support of the World Bank and the International Monetary Fund, Suharto adopted aggressive privatization and economic liberalization policies to encourage foreign investment and rapid economic growth.[27] To that end, Suharto reached out to the Chinese business community. Throughout his rule, Suharto not only protected the Chinese politically,[28] but emphatically directed lucrative business opportunities to them.[29] These favors were returned by the Indonesian Chinese. With their "business expertise, international connections, and preexisting business links with the armed forces,"[30] they not only fueled the country's economy—Indonesia enjoyed tremendous growth during the New Order, with the economy expanding six-fold[31]—but also added enormously to the personal wealth of the Suharto family.[32]

By the end of the Suharto regime, Sino-Indonesians occupied a position of economic dominance wildly disproportionate to

---

[26]See Chua, "The Privatization-Nationalization Cycle," p. 55 (citations omitted).

[27]See ibid.; also Michael R. J. Vatikiotis, *Indonesian Politics Under Suharto* (New York and London: Routledge, 1993), pp. 39–41; Liddle, "Coercion, Co-optation, and the Management of Ethnic Relations in Indonesia," pp. 300–1.

[28]In 1971 an article appeared in the *Bangkok Post* reporting that Indonesia's *Cukongs*, consisting of about twenty ethnic Chinese, had "wide holdings ranging from airlines and banks to flour mills, import-export companies, restaurants, shipping companies, tin exporting concessions, rice milling plants, [and] timber concessions."; see Leo Surydinata, "Indonesian Policies Toward the Chinese Minority Under the New Order, "Asian Survey," vol. 16 (1976), pp. 770, 772–73. The article also stated that the *Cukongs* had a steady inside track to government contracts and investment credits and that 90 percent of project aid money ended up in the hands of *Cukongs*. The article was translated and published in *Nusantra*, a leading Jakarta daily, leading to inquiries by members of Parliament. The government denied the charges, and the editor of *Nusantra* was prosecuted and sentenced to two years in prison. See ibid.

[29]See Chua, "The Privatization-Nationalization Cycle," p. 55 (citations omitted).

[30]William Ascher, "From Oil to Timber: The Political Economy of Off-Budget Development Financing in Indonesia," *Indonesia Journal* (Cornell University), vol. 65, Spring 1998, pp. 37, 53.

[31]Geertz, "Indonesia: Starting Over," p. 22.

[32]See Chua, "The Privatization-Nationalization Cycle," p. 55 (citations omitted).

their numbers. Comprising only some 3 percent of the population,[33] the ethnic Chinese in Indonesia controlled up to 70 percent of the private economy under a number of different measures.[34] All of Indonesia's billionaires reportedly have been ethnically Chinese,[35] and, until very recently, almost all of the country's largest conglomerates were owned by Sino-Indonesian families.[36] The major exception to this rule were companies owned by the children of President Suharto, which themselves "depended for their success on state favors and links with Sino-Indonesians."[37] On a smaller scale, ethnic Chinese dominated petty trading occupations in rural areas and retail and wholesale trade in urban areas,[38] as well as the country's informal credit sector.[39] Indeed, "[p]ractically every tiny town [had] an ethnic Chinese–run general store that [was] the center of local economic life."[40]

Not surprisingly, this state of affairs provoked massive, widespread hostility among the *pribumi* majority. Suharto's

---

[33]"No reliable figures on the number of Chinese in Indonesia have been collected since the 1930 census; all later estimates . . . appear to be based on calculations that they still represent either 3 or 4 percent of the total population, although even that can be only an informed guess." See Jamie Mackie, "Economic Systems of the Southeast Asian Chinese," in Leo Surydinata, ed., *Southeast Asian Chinese and China: The Politico-Economic Dimension* (Singapore: Times Academic Press, 1995), p. 62.

[34]See, e.g., Surydinata, *Southeast Asian Chinese and China*, p. 770; "A Taxing Dilemma," *Asiaweek* (October. 20, 1993), p. 53 (reporting that, according to the Sakura Bank-Nomura Research Institute, in 1991 Indonesian Chinese comprised 3.5 percent of the population but commanded a 73 percent share of the country's listed equity); see also Lim and Gosling, "Strengths and Weaknesses of Minority Status for Southeast Asian Chinese at a Time of Economic Growth and Liberalization," p. 312 (offering similar estimates).

[35]See Joel Kotkin, *Tribes: How Race, Religion, and Identity Determine Success in the New Global Economy* (New York: Random House, 1993), p. 180.

[36]Liddle, "Coercion, Co-optation, and the Management of Ethnic Relations in Indonesia," p. 301.

[37]Ibid.

[38]Vatikiotis, *Indonesian Politics Under Suharto*, p. 101; David Lamb, "Terrorized Ethnic Chinese Still on Edge in Indonesia Southeast Asia," *Los Angeles Times*, October 3, 1998, p. A4.

[39]Following a tradition reportedly dating to the seventeenth century, ethnic Chinese ran "thousands of small factories that make everything from shoes to auto parts." These Chinese-owned "general stores" "double[d]" as credit agencies to farmers and laborers." See Michael Shari and Jonathan Moore, "The Plight of the Ethnic Chinese," Business Week (August 3, 1998), p. 48.

[40]Ibid.

resignation in May 1998 was accompanied by an eruption of vicious anti-Chinese violence, in which nearly five thousand shops and homes of ethnic Chinese were burned and looted,[41] more than two thousand people died,[42] and many ethnic Chinese women were raped.[43] Within a month, approximately 110,000 Sino-Indonesian families (including some of the wealthiest) left the country,[44] along with massive amounts of Chinese-controlled capital, estimated at $40-$100 billion.[45] The preceding events made Indonesia during this period an illustration of the second (eliminationist) outcome noted above.

Markets, Democracy, and Ethnic Conflict in Post-Suharto Indonesia
The brief, troubled government of Dr. B. J. Habibie, who took over from Suharto in May 1998, was characterized by blatant economic nationalism. As Suharto's research and technology minister, Habibie had for years advocated state-ownership of Indonesia's Chinese-dominated industrial and technological sectors.[46] After Suharto's resignation, it became clear that there was a widespread belief among the pribumi that New Order economic liberalization favored the " 'already strong' " Sino-Indonesians at the expense

---

[41]See Gregg Jones, "Fear Overwhelming Indonesia's Chinese," *Dallas Morning News,* October 4, 1998, p. 1A.

[42]See ibid. Most of those who died were "non-Chinese looters trapped in burning shopping malls."

[43]See ibid.; according to local human rights workers, " 'more than 168 women'— most of them ethnic Chinese—were gang-raped during the riots." The Habibie government denied these allegations, claiming that they were "exaggerated."

[44]See Jay Solomon, "Indonesia's Chinese Move to Increase Civil Rights After a Decades-Long Ban on Political Activities," Wall Street Journal, June 9, 1998, p. A14. While most of these families have returned to Indonesia, most have also been reluctant to reinvest in Indonesia. See Barry Porter, "Wahid Starts Drawing Home Lost Billions," *South China Morning Post,* November 2, 1999, p. 10.

[45]See Ravi Velloor, "Fix Chinese Issue, Indonesia Told," *Straits Times,* October 10, 1998, p 2; Kafil Yamin, "Economy–Indonesia: Not Too Happy With Very Strong Currency," Inter Press Service, July 2, 1999.

[46]Liddle, "Coercion, Co-optation, and the Management of Ethnic Relations in Indonesia," p. 316; Raphael Pura, "Technology Guru Stands Out in Indonesia," *Wall Street Journal,* November 21, 1994, p. B6D.

of the " 'economically weak' " indigenous Indonesians. "According to this logic, the obvious cure is a new set of regulations, a reimposition of government intervention."[47] Playing on these popular sentiments, the Habibie government (greatly influenced by Habibie's nationalistic and very popular minister for cooperatives, Adi Sasano), advanced a proposal for a "People's Economy" (*Ekonomi Rakyat*), which was based on "economic justice." The plan envisioned "the breaking up of Chinese-dominated enterprises and transferring them to the long-suffering masses, using cooperatives and small- to medium-scale industries as receivers."[48]

International pressure, together with a desire to prevent continuing flight of Chinese capital, led the Habibie administration to temper its rhetoric somewhat, assuring the Chinese at one point, for example, that "we will not nationalize assets held by the private sector and foreign companies."[49] Nevertheless, although not well known in the international community, the Habibie government expressly pursued policies of ethnically targeted market intervention (again, the first outcome discussed previously, that of an anti-market backlash targeting the market-dominant minority). Not surprisingly, the economic effects were negative. The country's recent rice shortage provides a dramatic illustration.

Until May 1998, Indonesia's rice-distribution network was dominated by ethnic Chinese traders, who operated a fairly efficient system, "despite some profiteering on their part and despite the payoffs they had to make to an increasingly venal indigenous bureaucracy."[50] After Suharto's resignation, the Habibie government—in an openly ethnonationalist move supported by majoritarian sentiment—canceled rice distribution contracts with hundreds of ethnic Chinese businesses and awarded them instead to indigenous Indonesians, some of whom had little or no

---

[47]Liddle, "Coercion, Co-optation, and the Management of Ethnic Relations in Indonesia," pp. 300–1, 316.

[48]Abdul Razak Ahmad, "People's Economy to the Rescue?" *New Straits Times* (Malaysia), December 21, 1998, p. 6.

[49]Tom McCawley Serang, "A People's Economy," *Asiaweek*, December 18, 1998, p. 62.

[50]David Jenkins, "The Business of Hatred," *Sydney Morning Herald*, October 28, 1998, p. 8.

experience in the field. The results were disastrous, part of a food
crisis in which tens of millions of Indonesians were at one time
reportedly eating only one meal a day.[51] The new state-run rice cooperatives were immediately saturated with corruption, inefficiency, and scandal. (For example, one official was accused of trying
to export illegally 1,900 tons of rice to Malaysia, while his own constituents were starving). Predictably, indigenous officials and businessmen began secretly to subcontract work out to Chinese traders
again.[52]

Indonesia's national election in 1999—protracted and vastly complicated but evidently fair and open[53]—raised great hopes in the
international community. Habibie's (and formerly Suharto's)
Golkar party lost definitively, and the proposals for a People's Economy were taken off the policy agenda (at least for the moment).
The country's new president, Abdurrahman Wahid, is widely
admired for his liberalism, tolerance, and commitment to human
rights. From the outset, President Wahid has supported both
"democratic reforms" and IMF-dictated pro-free-market policies.[54]
In other words, the combined pursuit of markets and democracy is once again the prevailing prescription.

But the point of this paper has been precisely to suggest that
the conflict in Indonesia between these two goals is likely to be
intense and combustible. With poverty pervasive, and "its banks
and largest corporations still mired in delinquent debts," Indonesia remains "in its worst economic crisis in a generation."[55] The goal
of pro-market reforms is explicitly to procure the return of foreign
investment and Chinese-controlled capital, without which experts
agree the Indonesian economy cannot be restarted.[56] (It is no

---

[51]See "Indonesia's Anguish," *New York Times*, October 16, 1998, p. A26.

[52]See "The Business of Hatred."

[53]Geertz, "Indonesia: Starting Over," p. 24.

[54]See David Lamb, "Coalition Government Likely in Indonesia," *Los Angeles Times*,
June 9, 1999, p. A11.

[55]Wayne Arnold, "New Indonesian Leadership Stirs Financiers' Skepticism," *New York
Times*, October. 27, 1999, p. C4.

[56] See ibid.; also Solomon, "Indonesia's Chinese Move to Increase Civil Rights After
a Decades-Long Ban on Political Activities," p. A14; Velloor, "Fix Chinese Issue, Indonesia Told," p. 2; Yamin, "Economy–Indonesia: Not Too Happy With Very Strong
Currency."

coincidence that President Wahid's first official visit was to China, where one of his primary goals was to secure Beijing's blessing for the return of "overseas Chinese" capital to Indonesia.[57]) But for these pro-market policies to succeed would require a degree of assurance of Chinese economic security. Such assurances may not be compatible with a genuine democratic politics in a country where, just twenty months ago, many reportedly felt that "it would be worthwhile to lose ten years of growth to "get rid of the [Chinese] problem once and for all."[58]

[57]Porter, "Wahid Starts Drawing Home Lost Billions," p. 10; "Chinese New Year to Be Publicly Celebrated," *Jakarta Post,* January 17, 2000.
[58]Velloor, , "Fix Chinese Issue, Indonesia Told," p. 2.

POLICY IMPLICATIONS

The foregoing discussion suggests a number of policy implications for the prospects of neoliberal reform in Indonesia. Consider the following:

1. Ethnoeconomic Effects of Marketization. Conventional wisdom implicitly assumes that market reforms coupled with anti-corruption initiatives will solve (or at least ameliorate) the problem of the economically dominant Chinese minority in Indonesia by "leveling the playing field." This assumption is overly simplistic—and almost certainly wrong. True, corruption and political favoritism (for example, in the form of *cukong* or patronage relationships) have clearly contributed to the enormous wealth of some Sino-Indonesians. However, treating such favoritism as the "explanation" of Chinese economic dominance begs the question of *why* those in power have chosen repeatedly to collaborate with the Chinese. The decision of so many indigenous leaders in Southeast Asia (among them, Suharto, Ferdinand Marcos in the Philippines, the Nguyen emperors in Vietnam, and a host of Thai kings) to enter into lucrative, symbiotic commercial arrangements with the Chinese is not fortuitous. Rather, it reflects, at least in large part, the longstanding success of the Chinese as a wealth-generating "middleman" minority.[59] It is important to remember that Chinese economic dominance in Indonesia predates Western "divide-and-conquer" policies. Equally important is that historically many economically successful Sino-Indonesians did *not* profit from political favoritism (and indeed suffered official economic discrimination), and that the Indonesian Chinese under Suharto were economically dominant at all levels of society. In other words, if history is any guide, Chinese Indonesians are almost certainly a market-dominant minority—one whose stark economic dominance will not necessarily dissipate, and indeed may even increase,

---

[59]See Chua, "The Privatization-Nationalization Cycle," pp. 31–32, 101–2.

with privatization, pro-competition policies, and other market-oriented neoliberal reforms.

2. <u>Ethnopolitical Effects of Democratization</u>. Indonesia faces numerous challenges as it democratizes, including the rapidity of the process,[60] the country's deep ethnic divisions, and the glaring wealth gap between the historically resented Chinese minority and the generally impoverished, indigenous *pribumi* majority. Indeed, democracy in Indonesia will raise difficulties that any sound approach to democratization will have to address. As one commentator presciently warned before Suharto's resignation, particularly because of Indonesia's limited democratic experience, excessively rapid democratization might "release a myriad of long-suppressed demands by aggrieved groups; these might destabilize the political system and lead to the reimposition of authoritarian rule."[61] Moreover, as in all ethnically divided societies, electoral campaigns can be expected to give rise to ethnic politicking and demagoguery by opportunistic, vote-seeking politicians. (During the period leading up to the 1999 election, the Islamic right "attacked Megawati as not really a Muslim but some sort of Javanese Hindu, beholden to Christians and Chinese, possibly a crypto-Communist.") In particular, anti-Chinese, ethnonationalist rhetoric can almost certainly be expected, especially if the stark ethnic wealth gap is not narrowed. It is crucial for policymakers to keep in mind that, taking universal suffrage as a given, democratization can vary along a large number of axes relevant to the paradox of free market democracy: to name a few, presidentialism versus

---

[60]As I have discussed elsewhere, the process of democratization that developing countries are being asked to embrace is *not the same as the one the Western democracies themselves went through*. In the West, universal suffrage emerged only very gradually and incrementally: All of the Western nations had massive exclusions from the suffrage, as a result of longstanding restrictions related to property ownership, payment of taxes, and other matters. By contrast, in countries like Indonesia, universal suffrage is being implemented on a massive scale and almost, by comparison, overnight. This sudden process of democratization makes the transition to free market democracy particularly volatile. See Chua, "The Paradox of Free Market Democracy: Rethinking Development Policy," pp. 311–12.

[61]Liddle, "Coercion, Co-optation, and the Management of Ethnic Relations in Indonesia," p. 319.

parliamentarism; "first-past-the-post" versus proportional representation; starting locally versus starting nationally. President
Wahid recently announced that "his Government would propose [that] the country's next president be elected directly by the
people."[62] While Wahid's promise to "respect the opinion of the
people" was received with popular euphoria, much more consideration needs to be given to the question of what kind of democracy is suitable to Indonesia in light of the tensions that will
inevitably arise between markets and majoritarian politics.

   3. <u>Creating Interethnic Stakeholding in a Market Economy</u>. The
real challenge for neoliberal reform in Indonesia will be to secure
the return of Chinese-controlled capital and to harness the economic skills and connections of the Chinese while at the same time
giving the impoverished, newly enfranchised *pribumi* majority a
genuine, sufficient stake-material, political, and psychological—
in a market economy. At some level, the Sino-Indonesians understand this. As one commentator recently put it,

> [t]he country's ethnic Chinese will be especially watching to see
> how the new government goes about narrowing the country's
> wealth gap. Both Mr. Wahid and Ms. Megawati have been opposed
> to taking from rich ethnic Chinese. Yet both acknowledge that if
> they are to eradicate anti-Chinese sentiment among the masses,
> the economic gap needs to be narrowed... How the new cabinet
> goes about addressing this sensitive issue, without scaring off
> future ethnic Chinese investment, remains one of the big unan-
> swered questions.[63]

   Along these lines, a useful counterpoint to Indonesia is provided
by neighboring Malaysia, where, since the Asian financial crisis
erupted two years ago, there has been (in striking contrast to

---

   [62]At present, Indonesia's "president and vice-president are elected for a five-year
term by the MPR, composed of 462 elected MPs, 38 military appointees, and 200
appointees representing the regions and non-political organisations. Under the country's
two-tier political system, the PDI-P won last year's parliamentary election but its leader,
Megawati Sukarnoputri, did not automatically become president." See "Wahid proposes direct poll to create 'people's president'," Agence-France Presse, March, 28, 2000.
   [63]Porter, "Wahid Starts Drawing Home Lost Billions," p. 10

Indonesia) no anti-Chinese reaction or ethnic rioting, no discriminatory ethnically-targeted market intervention,[64] and very little capital flight.[65] Part of the explanation for this is clearly Malaysia's New Economic Policy (NEP). Although the NEP has always been very controversial and problematic in a number of respects, most contemporary analysts agree that Malaysia's systematic interventions during the last thirty years have almost certainly helped "integrate and harmonize a potentially volatile population,"[66] by giving the economically disadvantaged Bumiputra majority a stake in the overall market economy and by dulling the appeal of ethnonationalist, anti-market extremism.

I have elsewhere discussed the NEP in detail.[67] Here I will only summarize.

Following the 1969 race riots in Kuala Lumpur, which were similar in many respects to the 1998 riots in Indonesia, the Malaysian government adopted the NEP, aggressively seeking to achieve " 'national unity . . . expressed as the improvement of economic balances between the races.'" Starting in 1969, the Malaysian government implemented strong preferential measures for the Bumiputra majority in sectors such as corporate ownership, education, business, employment, credit, and civil service administration. For example, after 1976, under what was effectively compulsory corporate restructuring, many Malaysian Chinese companies were required to set aside 30 percent of their equity for Malay interests (typically

---

[64]During the recent financial crisis, Prime Minister Mahathir Mohamad of Malaysia took pains to praise the Chinese community for contributing to the strength of the national economy with their "wisdom and efficiency." See Adeline Ong, "Be Disciplined to Ensure Growth," *Business Times* (Malaysia), March 8, 1999, p. 2. On the other hand, Mahathir blamed Malaysia's economic problems on foreign "'rogues,' 'morons,' 'neo-colonialists,' and an imagined conspiracy of Jewish currency traders." See Seth Mydans, "Hard Times Weaken a Malaysian Powerbroker," New York Times, October 23, 1997, p. A12.

[65]The capital controls imposed by the Malaysian government in September 1998 did "not unleash[ed] the troubles many people initially feared. No black market . . . emerged and capital flight [was not] a problem." S. Jayasankaran, "Malaysia: Return of Optimism," *Far Eastern Economic Review*, vol. 61 (March 18, 1999), p. 61.

[66]Steve Glain, "Malaysia's Grand Social Experiment May Be Next Casualty of Asian Crisis," *Wall Street Journal*, April. 23, 1998, p. A15.

[67]See Chua, "The Paradox of Free Market Democracy: Rethinking Development Policy," pp. 351–53, 355–59.

with no choice about the Malay recipient of such equity). At the
same time, the government "invest[ed] heavily in publicly owned
corporations that were operated and managed by Malays"; it also
"created a number of incentive schemes to attract private Malay
investment to these enterprises." With respect to education, the
Malaysian government implemented sweeping reforms, including preferential quotas and scholarships for Bumiputra and the establishment of elite boarding schools set up exclusively for Malays.
In addition, quotas were set for the employment of Malays in commercial and industrial firms, and non-Malay firms, including
foreign corporations, "were asked to devise plans for the training
and promotion of Malays to more skilled and upper management
positions."[68]

It is safe to say that the NEP failed to achieve some of its most
ambitious objectives. Despite inflated official claims, for example,
the NEP has not succeeded in "eradicating poverty," one of its major
goals. Moreover, even after decades of sustained governmental intervention, the Chinese minority generally remains economically dominant vis-à-vis the Bumiputra majority.[69]

Nevertheless, if the goal of the NEP is seen not as achieving
"economic parity between the races," but rather as promoting
interethnic stakeholding and thereby helping to negotiate the
paradox of free-market democracy in the face of a resented, market-dominant minority, then the NEP may well have been
extremely successful. While the NEP has not lifted the great
majority of Malays (particularly in the rural areas) out of poverty, it has helped to create a substantial Malay middle class. Between
1970 and 1992, the percentage of Malays occupying the country's
most lucrative professional positions went from 6 percent to 32 percent. Specifically, during roughly that period, "the proportion of
Bumiputra doctors rose from 4 to 28 percent, dentists from 3 to
24 percent, architects from 4 to 24 percent, engineers from 7 to 35
percent, and accountants from 7 to 11 percent." In the corporate
sector the Bumiputra ownership share of corporate stock at par

---

[68]See ibid. (citations omitted).
[69]See ibid. (citations omitted).

values jumped from 1.5 percent in 1969, to 15.6 percent in 1982, to 20.6 percent in 1995. "There is no possibility that market mechanisms could have produced such results."[70]

By creating a small but visible Malay economic elite and by bringing Malay participation into important economic sectors—for example, the construction, rubber, tin, shipping, banking, and communications sectors (all formerly dominated by foreigners or Chinese and Indian Malaysians)—the NEP has helped to promote a sense among the Bumiputra that a market economy can benefit indigenous Malays, and not merely foreign investors and entrepreneurial "outsiders." Today, in addition to the many Malay "tycoons," "[s]ome of the best medical specialists, lawyers, and architects in Malaysia today are Malay"—a fact acknowledged even among the Chinese, who in the 1960s "viewed the Malays with condescension at best, scorn at worst."[71] Mahathir Mohamad's recent reelection (which dismayed many Western observers, because of his abysmal free-speech record) is significant in a number of respects. Polls suggest that most Malays approve of Mahathir's ethnic policies. Moreover, Mahathir had the support of large numbers of Chinese Malays, including many influential members of the business community.[72]

From this point of view, it becomes much harder to conclude that Malaysia's NEP has been inefficient or "growth-retarding." On the contrary, to the extent that ethnically based market interventions help reconcile poor majorities to the inequities of a market economy, they provide a horizon of social stability for the implementation and oscillations of a market system. Thus, they arguably are a plausible way not only of reconciling democracy and markets, but also of promoting long-term investment and economic growth.

---

[70]Milton J. Esman, "Ethnic Politics and Economic Power," *Comparative Politics*, vol. 19 (1987), p. 406; see Chua, "The Paradox of Free Market Democracy: Rethinking Development Policy," pp. 351-53, 355-59 (citations omitted).

[71]See Chua, "The Paradox of Free Market Democracy: Rethinking Development Policy," pp. 356-57 (citations omitted).

[72]See ibid., p. 359 (citations omitted).

4. <u>Limits of Current Rule-of-Law, State-Building, Judicial-Reform, and Civil-Society</u> Initiatives in Indonesia. The design of all the latest reform initiatives in Indonesia (including promotion of the rule of law, state-building, independent judiciaries, and civil society) must be re-examined in light of the paradox of free-market democracy and Indonesia's particular ethnic demographics. All of these reforms are of great importance for Indonesia (as throughout the developing world). However, they are not panaceas. Indeed, if care is not taken, these initiatives could inadvertently heighten the conflict between markets and democracy. For example, the main thrust of today's rule-of-law projects in the developing world is to facilitate market activity and foreign investment, by strengthening legislative and judicial protections of property and contract. But historically foreign investors have dealt principally with Sino-Indonesians (because they represent most of the commercial class and control most of the private sector). Therefore, it is the latter who tend to benefit directly from foreign investment liberalization, while the great majority of the *pribumi* are left to wait for the trickle-down benefits of foreign investment. Thus, to the extent that today's rule-of-law initiatives succeed, they will accomplish very significant achievements, but in the process they may intensify the contest between majoritarian politics and unequal, ethnically concentrated wealth.

Similarly, it is important to recognize the limits of, and dangers inherent in, today's state-building initiatives in Indonesia. Because of Indonesia's demographics, there is a powerful tendency toward what scholars have called an "ethnocratic state," one that acts as the agent of a dominant ethnic group with respect to ideology, social policy, and resource distribution. In Indonesia's case, all the principal arms of the state—the executive, legislature, judiciary, civil service, police, armed forces, etc.—historically have been dominated by the pribumi majority (in particular the Javanese) and used to reinforce that group's monopolization of power. In these conditions, state-building becomes a more complicated, and even dangerous, proposition. All the institutions associated with state-building can serve as vehicles for ethnocratic entrenchment, exclusion, and even brutality. (Note that an independent judiciary can also be an intolerant, ethnonationalist judiciary; this was the case in Weimar Germany, as I discuss elsewhere.[73]) It is thus a grave mistake to think of ethnic conflict as a problem to be addressed *after* the process of state-building is successfully completed. Rather, the challenge is to try to structure developing-country political institutions in such a way as to avoid ethnocracy and to promote *interethnic* solutions and institutions to the extent possible. President Wahid has impressively taken steps in this direction. For example, he has included in his cabinet members of traditionally unrepresented ethnic and regional groups, including a Sino-Indonesian minister to oversee economic policy. Measures along these lines are crucial if Indonesia is to enjoy the kind of ethnic stability necessary to provide a stable horizon for neoliberal reforms to succeed.

Finally, in ethnically divided countries like Indonesia, it is entirely possible for civil society to be just as ethnocratic as the state. For example, in certain circumstances unionization or other forms of labor organization can become a vehicle for highly polarized ethnic confrontation. In Indonesia, the early 1990s saw the rapid growth of the *Serikat Buruh Sejahtera Indonesia* (SBSI), "an independent labor union that challenged the monopoly of the [Suharto] government's own corporatist union."[74] The Suharto government suppressed the SBSI "after a massive labor protest in Medan, North Sumatra, in April 1994 turned into a riot against the Sino-Indonesians."[75]

5. <u>Objectionable Practices by the Sino-Indonesian Minority</u>. It is unfortunately the case that some members of the Chinese community in Indonesia engage in practices—for example, bribery and corrupt patronage relationships—that not only are illegal or objectionable in themselves, but also reinforce invidious ethnic stereotypes and fuel bitter resentment among the indigenous majority.

---

[73]See Chua, "Markets, Democracy, and Ethnicity: Toward a New Paradigm for Law and Development."

[74]Liddle, "Coercion, Co-optation, and the Management of Ethnic Relations in Indonesia," p. 318.

[75]Ibid. Even after the SBSI was suppressed, "the number of localized wildcat strikes, particularly against companies producing for export, continue[d] to grow."

The anti-Chinese violence that erupted in Indonesia May 1998 was inseparable from the association of a few Chinese magnates with the Suharto regime's "crony capitalism."[76] As is sadly often the case, violent popular reaction unleashed itself not on the relatively few wealthy Chinese who were actually complicit (and who used their wealth to go into hiding abroad), but rather on ordinary, struggling, middle-class Chinese Indonesians, whose shops were burned and looted.

It is not, however, only the wealthiest members of economically dominant minorities who engage in illicit practices. Regrettably, the problem is more general. In Indonesia, as throughout Southeast Asia, many Chinese-controlled firms routinely violate tax laws, banking laws (including restrictions on self-lending and discriminatory lending[77]) and "laws concerning overtime regulations, workers' compensation and protection, occupational health and safety requirements, and building codes."[78] The illegal importation of cheap labor from China is a particular problem. Throughout Southeast Asia, there have been complaints about the influx of "tens if not hundreds of thousands of illegal migrant workers from the PRC, most of whom are likely to be employed in small, Chinese-owned enterprises."[79] As in the developed world, "local workers resent the competition [from illegal immigrants] and the resulting downward pressure on their wages."[80] In Indonesia, where roughly six million working age Indonesians (almost all pribumi) were unemployed in 1996, the violent protest that erupted when a Chinese conglomerate imported one thousand illegal workers from China seems understandable. The perception among an economically disadvantaged majority that a disproportionately wealthy

---

[76]Vatikiotis, *Indonesian Politics* Under Suharto, pp.14, 41, 45, 50.

[77]Ibid. pp. 41.

[78]K. S. Jomo, "A Specific Idiom of Chinese Capitalism in Southeast Asia: Sino-Malaysian Capital Accumulation in the Face of State Hostility," in Chirot and Reid, eds., *Essential Outsiders*, pp. 252.

[79]Ibid. pp. 293.

[80]Ibid.

minority disregards the country's laws and exploits the indigenous population can only exacerbate ethnic resentment.[81]

What to do about such illicit practices is less obvious. To begin with, there is often a collective-action problem. If any single firm decides to comply with workplace and other regulations and its competitors do not, that firm will likely go out of business. Thus, calling on individual businesses to take corrective measures is unlikely to have much effect. On the other hand, looking to the state is not a complete answer either. One obvious problem is that the governmental actors who would have to implement reform are often the same ones corruptly benefiting from the violations (through kickbacks or bribes). An as-yet unexploited resource here may be the surprisingly strong intra-ethnic organizations, both commercial and social, that many economically dominant minorities already have in the developing world. The success of these organizations in overcoming collective-action problems in a variety of commercial contexts—through a combination of "trust" and superior monitoring capacities—has been widely observed. If leaders of the minority communities in a given developing country can be persuaded of the importance of, and overall gains to be had from, eliminating corrupt or illicit business practices, these organizations may have the right set of incentives and capabilities to play a significant role.[82]

---

[81]See Chua, "Markets, Democracy, and Ethnicity: Toward a New Paradigm for Law and Development," pp. 373–76.

[81]See ibid, pp 374–75.